microeconomics
in context

Neva Goodwin
Global Development and Environment Institute, Tufts University

Julie A. Nelson
Global Development and Environment Institute, Tufts University

Frank Ackerman
Global Development and Environment Institute, Tufts University

Thomas Weisskopf
University of Michigan

Houghton Mifflin Company   Boston   New York

Publisher: Charles Hartford

Editor in Chief: George T. Hoffman

Sponsoring Editor: Ann West

Associate Editor: Julie Hassel

Editorial Associate: Tonya Lobato

Senior Project Editor: Carol Merrigan

Editorial Assistant: Eric Moore

Manufacturing Coordinator: Renee Ostrowski

Senior Marketing Manager: Todd Berman

Cover photo: © Tim Hall/Getty Images

Printed in the U.S.A.

ISBN: 0-618-34599-X

1 2 3 4 5 6 7 8 9-WBC-08 07 06 05 04

Brief Contents

Contents

Preface

Microeconomics in Context provides a thorough introduction to the principles of micro-economics for students taking the introductory microeconomics course. Although this text incorporates the theoretical content expected in a principles text, it delves deeper, offering a fresh understanding of the economic realities of the 21st century. Too often, introductory microeconomics textbooks have helped students learn a few useful con-cepts—and have given them plenty of practice in curve shifting—but have provided little breadth of perspective for analyzing real economic issues. These books tend to encourage students to accept models and assumptions about behavior without truly understanding or questioning what the models mean in context. *Microeconomics in Context* will, by con-trast, help students gain a deeper understanding of economic theory and its relationship to contemporary controversies of interest and importance.

This book encourages engaged and critical thinking about topics in economics. It introduces students *both* to the standard topics and tools taught in most introductory courses and to a broader and richer set of topics and tools. We have done our best to make the book readable, interesting, and relevant throughout. Whether students sim-ply take this class to gain some understanding of how economics can be useful to them or go on to study more economics or business, this comprehensive and up-to-date book will help equip them with the standard tools *and* the critical knowledge they need to succeed.

At the same time that this book introduces the many applications of economic the-ory, it provides a variety of viewpoints. Neoclassically minded instructors, and instruc-tors constrained by the requirements of the larger curriculum, can be assured that neoclassical tools are presented in full. Economics instructors who are frustrated by the lack of attention to history, institutions, gender, social divisions, ethics, ecology, or poverty in other textbooks will find much to be enthusiastic about in our treatment, because these topics are integrated throughout the book. Even some instructors who prefer the market-focused approach of other texts will appreciate this text for the way in which its exposition of the market's strengths and weaknesses encourages students to engage with the subject matter.

Content and Organization

Some of the innovative features of this text are apparent in even a quick scan of the Contents pages or the sample course outlines on pp. xxiii–xxviii. Because this textbook takes a broader and more contextual approach to economic activities, it exhibits a differ-ent overall organizational structure.

Typically, in presentations of introductory microeconomics, the demand and supply sides of markets are separated, demand being associated with households and consumption, and supply being associated with firms and production. However, this organizational structure makes it almost impossible to consider adequately many topics of real-world importance. The participation of nonhousehold economic actors in the demand side of markets (such as intra-industry trade and government demand for military products) becomes difficult to talk about. The productive activities of households, community groups, nonprofits, and governments are understated when production is limited primarily to businesses. And the role of the natural environment in sustaining production is often ignored entirely.

In order to include these broader concerns, this book diverges from other textbooks in three crucial ways:

○ First, beneath all of what are commonly thought of as economic concerns are questions about human well-being. Rather than confining "economic thinking" to questions of efficiency, this book takes on deeper issues. What do we want in life? How do we get it? What conflicts may exist between what I want and what you want? Must there always be winners and losers?

○ Second, this book reflects a more comprehensive understanding of what constitutes economic activity. Production, distribution (or exchange), and consumption are three essential economic activities, but no less important than these is a fourth: resource maintenance. If an economic system fails to maintain factories, roads, schools, and homes, or the physical and mental health of the people who make up the system, or the farmland, forests, fisheries, and other aspects of the natural environment on which these people depend, the economic activities of production and consumption become difficult or impossible. Explicit discussion of the economic activity of resource maintenance updates economics to include 21st-century concerns about environmental and social sustainability.

○ Finally, many economic activities are carried on in the "core sphere" of households and communities and in the "public purpose sphere" of governments and nonprofits. This book looks at the full spectrum of economic activities, not only at those that occur in the "business sphere."

We have organized the material in this book into five major parts in an effort to offer a more comprehensive picture of economic life than may be found in other principles texts.

○ Part I presents the themes of the book and the major actors in the economy. Students are introduced to a range of economic questions and goals and to the structure and size of the various economic spheres. Behavioral assumptions are introduced.

○ Part II introduces market institutions, basic supply and demand analysis, and elasticities. For many users, this part will contain the "meat" of the introductory course. It may be taught either before or after Part III, depending on whether the instructor wants first to discuss economic activities (Part III) or to move straight from the introductory chapters into market topics (Part II). Most of this material will look very familiar to teachers of microeconomics, although this text gives greater recognition than is typical to real-world market institutions.

○ Part III investigates the four major economic activities: resource maintenance, production, distribution, and consumption. Diverse illustrations of the roles of various economic actors in various economic activities are given—for example, household production is recognized throughout. In addition, the relatively early placement of a chapter dealing with distribution gives prominence to income inequality, poverty, and the role of transfers (as well as exchange) in creating economic well-being.

- Part IV goes more into depth on market topics by describing the idealized model of perfect competition, presenting models of market power, and analyzing various resource markets.

- Part V addresses each of the spheres (core, business, and public purpose) in turn, examining in more detail the history and growth of each and the economic theories relevant to their study.

- Part VI steps back to take an even broader view of how societies have organized economic activity by examining the strengths and weakness of markets as a mode of economic organization and briefly reviewing alternative currents in economic thought.

What Makes This Book Different from Other Texts?

This text covers the traditional topics that most microeconomics texts include but treats from a broader, more holistic perspective. The following chapter-by-chapter synopsis shows how this book manages both to be "the same enough" to fit into a standard curriculum and "different enough" to respond to commonly expressed needs and dissatisfactions.

As in other textbooks, Chapter 1 opens with a discussion of what economics is about. If you have taught with another textbook, you will find a lot of familiar topics here, including discussion of basic questions of economics (what, how, and for whom), essential economic activities (production, distribution, and consumption), positive versus normative questions, efficiency, scarcity, opportunity cost, the Production Possibilities Frontier, and the concept of an economic model. However, we immediately set these topics in the broader context of concern for well-being. We define economics as "the study of the way people organize themselves to sustain life and enhance its quality" and discuss the relationship of intermediate goals to final goals. We introduce the concepts of externalities, public goods, and transactions costs in this chapter—much earlier than in most other texts—in order to emphasize that markets, though very effective in a number of areas, are not on their own sufficient for organizing economic life in service of well-being. We introduce the "three spheres" of economic activity as well as the activity of resource maintenance.

Chapter 2 also includes material that will be familiar from other textbooks, such as the notions of choice, rationality, and self-interest and the circular flow diagram illustrating exchange between households and firms. It updates the standard treatment, however, by drawing on studies of human economic behavior by scholars such as Herbert Simon and Daniel Kahneman, and by touching on issues of organizational structure and behavior. The result is a richer picture of the complicated motivations and institutions underlying real-world economic activities.

Chapter 3 begins Part II, on basic market analysis, with material rarely found in principles textbooks. It supplements the rather abstract treatment of markets that appears in most textbooks with discussion of how markets came about and what they require in terms of legal and social supports. The chapter draws on contemporary research on institutions and the design of market mechanisms to give students insight into the complexity and variety of real-world markets.

Chapter 4 presents traditional, supply and demand analysis, including discussions of the slopes of the curves, factors that shift the curves, equilibrium and market adjustment, and the signaling and rationing functions of prices. Unlike many books that present equilibrium analysis as "the way the world works," we explicitly introduce supply and demand analysis as a *tool* whose purpose is to help a person disentangle the effects of various factors on real-world prices and quantities. We make methodological points concerning static versus dynamic models, precision versus accuracy in analysis, and market "shortage" versus human-need "inadequacy" in order to make clear both the strengths and the shortcomings of analysis in terms of supply and demand.

In Chapter 5, traditional definitions and discussions of price elasticities of demand and supply, income elasticity of demand, and the income and substitution effects of a price change are presented. Whereas many standard textbooks concentrate solely on efficiency effects when discussing markets, the contextual approach demands that power issues and distributional consequences also be addressed when touching on issues of markets and policies.

Chapter 6 begins Part III, on the four major economic activities, with a discussion of the activity of resource maintenance—that is, the vital importance of taking into consideration the effect of flows created by economic activity on the stocks of productive resources that will be available for future use. In a departure from other treatments, this book examines the crucial contributions of natural capital (that is, environmental resources), human capital, and social capital to economic activity and human well-being. It also incorporates treatments of manufactured capital (machinery and physical infrastructure) and financial capital that are often spread thinly across chapters in other books.

Chapter 7 is the first of two chapters on production. This chapter looks at production costs, including a traditional discussion of fixed and variable inputs; diminishing, constant, and increasing returns; and short-run versus long-run issues. The student learns to graph total product curves and total cost curves and is introduced to the concept of marginal cost. We put these concepts in the larger context of the overall social efficiency of production by including discussions of external costs. Examples of household, government, and non-profit production are also given. Graphs illustrating the deriving of average variable cost curves and average total cost curves are included in an appendix to the chapter. Thus instructors have the option of using the time generally spent in deriving these curves on topics that may be of greater interest and usefulness to the beginning economics student.

In Chapter 8 the discussion of production continues with a focus on decision making. We present the traditional model of the productive firm maximizing profit by applying marginal analysis, including graphs of total and marginal costs and revenues. We demonstrate how the decision about how much to produce changes with changes in the output price. We set this model in context in two important ways. First, the chapter encourages students to reflect on the idea that because of externalities, private and social net benefits from production may not be equivalent. Second, the chapter offers examples of cases where other economic actors (besides firms) make production decisions and cases where other methods of decision making are necessary. We introduce such "advanced" notions as nonconvexity, multiple equilibria, path dependence, and network externalities, using examples that students have encountered in their own lives.

Chapter 9 discusses the basic economic activity of distribution. Among the familiar topics covered are the gains-from-trade story that is now so important in discussing topical issues of global commerce, the advantages of exchange as a way of organizing the distribution of society's economic goods, and the distribution of money income. The chapter sets this discussion of exchange squarely in context by also examining several potential weaknesses of exchange as a form of distribution. In addition, it complements the discussion of exchange with a serious treatment of transfers (such as those from governments to retirees and those from parents to children) as a significant means of distribution in contemporary economies, and it discusses the strengths and weaknesses of transfers. In this way, governmental, non-profit, and intra-household distributive activities are treated as central to economic life, rather than as "interference" or as "noneconomic" flows.

Chapter 10 presents the traditional utility-theoretic model of consumer behavior. We explain the notion of consumer sovereignty, show students how to graph a budget line, and explain the rule for utility maximization derived from marginal thinking. We set this material in context by also discussing the psychological models of consumer behavior used in marketing research and the historical development of the "consumer society." Rather than equating subjective consumer satisfaction with well-being, we draw on Amartya Sen's "capabilities" approach and discuss the personal and ecological impact of high-level consumption patterns.

Part IV, "A Closer Look at Markets," begins with Chapter 11 on perfect competition. The characteristics of such a market are described, and the zero-economic-profit and efficiency outcomes are discussed. This chapter also covers the standard topics of consumer and producer surplus and deadweight loss. The discussion of this model is subtly contextualized by emphasizing that it represents an idealized, abstract case rather than a natural state of the world. Whereas other texts usually stress that policies such as rent control and taxation lead to inefficiencies (in a world of perfect competition), our treatment delves into the social and institutional context of such policies and their distributional consequences.

Chapter 12 covers traditional models of monopoly, monopolistic competition, and oligopoly. An important complement to this chapter is Chapter 16, which goes beyond these traditional analytical models to discuss contemporary issues of globalization and corporate power.

In Chapter 13 we turn our attention to markets for labor. Topics include the upward-sloping and backward-bending individual paid labor supply curves and the traditional derivation of profit-maximizing labor demand by a perfectly informed and perfectly competitive firm. We also address the traditional topics of market power, compensating wage differentials, worker motivation, and labor market discrimination. The "contextual economics approach" is evident in our treatment of household production as among the alternative uses of time and in the emphasis placed on the strength of non-market forces. Instead of focusing only on market equilibrium and efficiency, we note that in view of strong norms and the frequent lack of good information about worker productivity, historical and social factors can have persistent effects on wage and employment patterns.

Chapter 14 concludes Part IV by discussing natural resources, social capital, manufactured capital, and financial capital in a market context. Among the topics here that might be familiar from other books are the present value formula, marginal factor cost, marginal revenue product, and an overview of stock and bond markets. Unlike other texts, this book draws a distinction between "economistic" and "ecological" views of the value of natural capital, raising the question of whether valuation methods designed for relatively short-term building and equipment projects can reasonably be applied to projects with unpredictable effects over the very long term (given the complexity of natural systems). It includes a discussion of social capital, noting how this factor is sometimes traded in markets (for example, when a firm's selling price reflects its reputation and managerial expertise) and how markets can sometimes erode important aspects of social cohesion. It highlights the roles played by true uncertainty and speculation in financial markets, rather than focusing only on market equilibrium.

Chapter 15 begins Part V, on the three spheres of economic activity, by examining the economics of the core sphere, which is composed of households and community groups. Here we enumerate the many areas in which this sphere plays a crucial role in creating economic well-being (including final production, care of children, and decisions regarding consumption and human capital formation). We then discuss how the core sphere has changed from the time of the "cult of domesticity" to today and consider the problems raised by conflicts between family work and paid work.

Chapter 16 shifts the focus to the business sphere. Whereas much of beginning standard theory treats business firms as though they were individual, profit-maximizing decision makers, this chapter looks more closely at firms as real-world complex organizations. We describe the legal organization of firms and discuss the history of the growth of large vertically or horizontally integrated corporations and conglomerates. We include standard concepts such as principal–agent theory, but we also discuss ethical and organizational dilemmas in firms, contrasting "shareholder theory" with "stakeholder theory." We suggest that the growth of firms may be related to quests for personal or political power, as well as to technical economies, and that a dual structure of oligopolistic and competitive firms may serve the interests of powerful businesses. The activities of multinational corporations, the growth of global markets and global competition, and activities such as global subcontracting and offshoring are examined. The chapter concludes with a discussion of the effects of contemporary trends on human and societal well-being.

Chapter 17 takes a closer look at the public purpose sphere, which is composed of governments and non-profit organizations. This chapter includes some topics often found in other textbooks on principles of economics, such as government regulation of monopolistic trade practices, government social welfare policies, and the size of government. The attention we give to the economic activities of domestic non-profit organizations and international quasi-governmental organizations, however, is unique. Our broader approach enables us to discuss important interactions among civil society, government, and corporate groups dealing with economic issues, including the topical issue of the WTO and regulation of global trade. We show how government and non-profit organizations have historically developed to address issues of coordination, welfare, market regulation, and environmental protection.

As global economic relations have become increasingly important, it has become essential for students to understand how microeconomic relationships have developed differently, and with different results, in various countries. Chapter 18 addresses this need by looking at the larger picture of economic systems and their relationship to human well-being. We discuss capitalist and socialist systems, especially in their "corporate capitalist" and "state socialist" forms, noting that real-world economies of both capitalist and socialist types vary widely in the extent of their reliance on market and administrative modes of organization. We give a brief history of the development of modern economic systems in various parts of the world (including the effects of wars and colonization and the recent radical changes in most formerly communist countries) and provide a brief review of some comparative measures of performance in terms of living standards and sustainability.

Chapter 19 addresses what is perhaps the most salient overarching policy question of our day. In a time of welfare rollbacks and free-trade agreements justified by appeals to market efficiency, is the claim that "markets are always best" supported by rigorous economic analysis? This chapter investigates the view that free market policies are "proved" to be optimal by traditional neoclassical economic theory, including discussions of the general equilibrium model, the concept of Pareto efficiency, and the first fundamental theorem of welfare economics. We then offer an overview of the variety of contemporary economic theories, including adaptations of the neoclassical model; "new" institutionalist, "old" institutionalist, social, Marxist, post-Keynesian, and Austrian economics; and ecological and feminist approaches.

Special Features

Each chapter in this text contains many features designed to enhance student learning.

- ○ Key terms are highlighted in boldface type throughout the text, and important ideas and definitions are set off from the main text.
- ○ Discussion Questions at the end of each section encourage immediate review of what has been read and link the material to the students' own experiences. The frequent appearance of these questions throughout each chapter helps students review manageable portions of material and thus boosts comprehension. The questions can be used for participatory exercises involving the entire class or for small-group discussion.

○ End-of-chapter Review Questions are designed to encourage students to create their own summary of concepts. They also serve as helpful guidelines to the importance of various points.

○ End-of-chapter Exercises encourage students to work with and apply the material, thereby gaining increased mastery of concepts, models, and investigative techniques.

○ Throughout all the chapters, "Economics in the Real World" and "News in Context" boxes enliven the material with real-world illustrations drawn from a variety of sources.

○ In order to make the chapters as lively and accessible as possible, some formal and technical material (suitable for inclusion in some but not all course designs) is carefully and concisely explained in chapter appendices.

A glossary at the end of the book contains all key terms, their definitions, and the number of the chapter in which each was first used and defined.

Supplements

The supplements package for this book provides a complete set of teaching tools and resources for instructors using this text and a great many opportunities for student review and practice. The authors have worked closely with our associate Brian Roach to create an *Instructor's Resource Manual* and *Test Bank* to accompany *Microeconomics in Context*. For each chapter, the *Instructor's Resource Manual* includes a statement of objectives for student learning, a list of key terms, a Lecture Outline, and answers to all Review Questions and end-of-chapter Exercises. In addition, the "Notes on Text Discussion Questions" provide not only suggested answers to these questions but also ideas on how the questions might be used in the classroom. And sections entitled "Web Resources" and "Extensions" provide supplementary material and links to other passages in the book or other materials that can be used to enrich lectures and discussion.

The *Test Bank*, which is available in both print form and electronic form, includes a full complement of multiple-choice and true/false questions for each chapter, annotated to indicate the type of question (factual or applied), the difficulty level, and the correct answer. The electronic version is found in the *HMClassPrep with HMTesting CD-ROM*.

This all-in-one instructor CD contains a wealth of resources, including all the test questions and PowerPoint slides for the text. The sophisticated and user-friendly HMTesting program enables instructors to create tests quickly according to various selection criteria, among them random selection. The program prints graphs and tables as well as the text part of each question. Instructors can scramble the questions and the answer choices, edit questions, add their own questions to the pool, and customize their exams in various other ways. HMTesting provides a complete testing solution, including classroom administration and online testing features in addition to test generation. The program works for both PC and Mac-compatible computers.

The *Microeconomics in Context* website, accessible at **economics.college. hmco.com/instructors**, offers online versions of the *Instructor's Resource Manual* and *Test Bank*, PowerPoint slides with teaching tips and figures from the text, and numerous resources and updates for instructors.

For students, a printed *Study Guide* provides ample opportunity to review and practice the key concepts developed in the text. Additional self-testing and review material, including ACE self-tests for each chapter, flash cards, and links and resources, are found on the *Student Website* to accompany *Microeconomics in Context*, available at **economics. college.hmco.com/students**.

In addition, for instructors who request the Smarthinking package when adopting this text, students will have access to *Smarthinking™ Online Tutoring Service*. This live, online tutoring service provides access to trained, qualified "e-structors" from wherever students are, whenever they need help. Students may interact live online with an experienced Smarthinking "e-structor" (online tutor) between 2 and 5 p.m. and between 9 p.m. and 1 a.m., Eastern Standard Time, every Sunday through Thursday. Smarthinking provides state-of-the-art communication tools, such as chat technology and virtual whiteboards designed for easy rendering of economic formulas and graphs, to help your students practice working with key concepts.

How to Use This Text

The feedback we have received from instructors who reviewed and/or class-tested this text in its Preliminary Edition has been enthusiastic and gratifying. We've found that this book works in a variety of courses with a variety of approaches, and we'd like to share some of these instructors' suggestions on tailoring this book to meet your own course needs.

First, even if you are among those rare instructors who normally get their class all the way through a microeconomics principles text in a semester, you may find that, with a text that is quite different from those you have used before, it is harder to anticipate which chapters will require the most time. Other instructors (perhaps the majority) do not expect to cover all of the material in the textbook. In either case, it is wise to anticipate that the semester may end with some chapters not covered in class—and to plan in advance how to deal with this possibility.

On pages xxiii to xxviii you'll find several possible course plans based on different emphases (such as neoclassical, ecological, social, and public policy). We hope this will help you plan the course that will best suit your and your students' needs.

Note on Differences from the Preliminary Edition

A Preliminary Edition of this text was published by Houghton Mifflin in early 2003. If you were one of the users of that edition, you will want to note the following changes which have been made in response to feedback from class testing.

The material on market institutions and that on supply and demand have been moved to an earlier position in the book. As we have noted, however, Parts II and III can be taught in reverse order if you prefer the original ordering of topics. The order of topics in Chapters 1 and 2 has been altered, and the Production Possibilities Frontier and the concept of opportunity cost are now introduced in Chapter 1. There are now two chapters on market structure (Chapters 11 and 12) instead of one, and consumer and producer surplus analysis has been moved to Chapter 11.

In the discussion of production (Chapters 7 and 8), additional charts and graphs have been added, and the discussion of "sunk costs" has been clarified. "Thick" curves have been dropped from the chapter on supply and demand, although this material is still available in the *Instructor's Resource Manual.* The "kinked demand curve" has been dropped from the discussion of oligopoly. The detailed discussion of assets and sources of income that appeared in the chapter on distribution (Chapter 9) has been dropped. A new section on globalization has been added to the chapter on the business sphere (Chapter 16).

News boxes have been updated, and changes in wording—including the names of goods in examples—have been made in many places. The "three sectors" are now referred to as the three spheres. The "simple mechanical model" is now called the traditional model or the basic neoclassical model. "Produced capital" is now referred to as "manufactured capital," and the use of acronyms to denote various kinds of capital has been dropped. The lists of key terms have been dropped from the end of each chapter, but they are still available in the *Instructor's Resource Manual.*

A more detailed comparison of the preliminary and first editions is available on the *Microeconomics in Context* instructor website at **economics.college.hmco.com/ instructors**.

Acknowledgments

Microeconomics in Context was written under the auspices of the Global Development and Environment Institute, a research institute at Tufts University. This text has been a long time in the making, and many people have been involved along the way. An early workshop testing our "contextual approach" through a variety of interactions with students and faculty got us started. We are grateful to David Garman, of the Tufts University Economics Department, who arranged an opportunity for us to class-test a very early draft, and we appreciate the feedback we received from the undergraduates in that class.

Next, workshops held at four different universities yielded much excellent feedback about our intended approach and topic coverage, in comparison to other introductory microeconomics texts. Steven Cohn of Knox College, Illinois, was the principal organizer for these workshops, using a sabbatical and the assistance of Yahya Madra to lead the initial workshop at the University of Massachusetts at Amherst. Other workshop leaders, and important contributors to the project, included Julie Heath, chair of the Department of Economics at the University of Memphis where Professor David Ciscel participated in the workshop along with a number of graduate students; Geoffrey Schneider, who ran a faculty workshop at Bucknell University that included, as regular participants, Janet Knoedler, Tom Kinnaman, and Cathy O'Connor; and George Langelett and Michael Haupert at the University of Wisconsin.

Because more than 150 people participated in extended electronic conversations organized around the workshops, we unfortunately cannot thank them all by name for their many valuable contributions. Most of the graduate students who participated in person at the workshops were actively engaged in teaching courses in principles of economics, and we wish to acknowledge the value of their insights.

On the basis of these conversations, an early draft of the textbook was prepared in 2000. This early draft formed the basis for editions designed for transitional economies, which were translated and published in Russia (Russian State University for the Humanities, 2002) and Vietnam (Hanoi Commercial University, 2002). Economists who contributed ideas to the transitional economies texts included Oleg Ananyin (Institute of Economics and Higher School of Economics, Moscow), Pham Vu Luan and Hoang Van Kinh (Hanoi Commercial University), Peter Dorman (Evergreen College); Susan Feiner (University of Southern Maine); Drucilla Barker (Hollins College); Robert McIntyre (Smith College); Andrew Zimbalist (Smith College); Cheryl Lehman (Hofstra University); and Raymond Benton (Loyola University).

The early draft was also distributed in English to interested instructors from various colleges. We would like to thank Robert Scott Gassler (Vesalius College of the Vrije Universiteit Brussels), Julie Matthaei (Wellesley College), and Adrian Meuller (CEPE Centre for Energy Policy and Economics), who, among others, provided helpful comments on the early draft as it began to be developed for use in the introductory microeconomics course in the United States. We also are grateful for comments received from faculty and students participating in a workshop on economics education at the University of Utah, including Gokcer Ozgur.

Work on the text during the last $2\frac{1}{2}$ years, led by Julie Nelson, was greatly facilitated by feedback from Steven Cohn, as well as by careful readings and extensive commentaries on successive drafts from Jonathan Harris and Brian Roach at the Global Development and Environment Institute. Among the Tufts students who assisted in many ways with the evolving project, we especially want to thank Sucharita Kuchibhotla, Moji Terry, Samantha Diamond, and Dina Dubson for their painstaking editing and indexing work. Working toward publication of the Preliminary Edition of this textbook, we were greatly aided and encouraged by comments from Sandy Baum (Skidmore College), Jose Juan Bautista (Xavier University of Louisiana), Gary Ferrier (University of

Arkansas), Ronald L. Friesen (Bluffton College), and Abu N. M. Wahid (Tennessee State University).

With the publication of the Preliminary Edition in early 2003, the book underwent additional review and class testing. The comments we received at this stage were enormously helpful in turning the textbook into an even more effective teaching tool—and we want to thank the many instructors and students who participated in this process. Eight instructors who were exceptionally generous in giving us feedback from their classroom use of this text were Fred Curtis (Drew University), James Devine (Loyola Marymount University), Richard England (University of New Hampshire), Mehrene Larudee (Bates College), Akira Motomura (Stonehill College), Shyamala Raman (Saint Joseph College), Judith K. Robinson (Castleton State College) and Marjolein van der Veen (Shoreline Community College). We also received detailed comments from Timothy E. Burson (Queens University of Charlotte), Will Cummings (Grossmont College), Dennis Debrecht (Carroll College), Amy McCormick Diduch (Mary Baldwin College), Miren Ivankovic (Southern Wesleyan University), Eric P. Mitchell (Randolph-Macon Woman's College), Malcolm Robinson (Thomas More College), June Roux (Salem Community College), Edward K. Zajicek (Kalamazoo College), Steve Balkin (Roosevelt University), Ernest Diedrich (College of St. Benedict/St. John's University), Mark Maier (Glendale Community College), Ken Meter (Kennedy School of Government), Sigrid Stagl (University of Leeds), and Myra Strober (Stanford University). Marjolein van der Veen also reviewed text and art during the production phase, and we are very grateful for her sharp eyes!

Special thanks go to the many students who provided feedback on the text as they used it in class. We would like to acknowledge the comments of students Brian Cotroneo and Marc McDunch of Boston College; Castleton State College students Kevin Boucher, April L. Cole, Shawn Corey, Lisa Dydo, Tim Florentine, Roger Gillies, Ashley Kennedy, Nicole LaDuc, Matt Lane, Noah Bartmess, Joesph O'Reilly, Kevin Perry, James Riehl, Jessica Schoof, Josh Teresco, Jennifer Trombey, Monica Tuckerman, Craig Wetzel, and Liza Wimble; Colby College student Eric Seidel; Drew University students Sigourney Giblin, Erin Hoffman, Jennifer Marsico, Leo A. Mihalkovitz, Peter Nagy, and Sofia Novozilova; Catherine Hazzard, a student at Saint Joseph College; Stonehill College student Anthony Budri; Sarah Barthelmes, Kathryn Cash, Aris Dinitraropolous, Jen Hanley, Krista Leopold, Mary Pat Reed, E. Rose, Kaitlyn Skelley, and Ryan Tewksbury from the University of New Hampshire; Rebecca Clausen of the University of Oregon; and students from Will Cummings's class at Grossmont College.

The assistance and encouragement of Ann West, Julie Hassel, Tonya Lobato, Maria Morelli, Carol Merrigan, and others on the editorial staff of Houghton Mifflin were invaluable in the final preparation of the preliminary and first editions of the text.

All contributors of written text materials were paid through grants raised by the Global Development and Environment Institute, and all royalties from sales of the book, by agreement of the authors, support the work of the institute. We are extremely appreciative of the financial support we have received from the Spencer T. and Ann W. Olin Foundation, from the Ford, Island, Eurasia, and Barr Foundations, from the Trust for Mutual Understanding, from Abby and George O'Neill, from Houghton Mifflin, and from an anonymous donor.

Finally, we would like to thank Wassily Leontief, who initially urged us to write a book on economic principles for students in transitional economies. He provided inspiration and encouragement as we developed those texts. We also are enormously grateful to Kelvin Lancaster, who allowed us to use *Modern Economics: Principles and Policy* (a textbook that he and Ronald Dulany wrote in the 1970s) as a jumping-off point for our work on those texts.

Sample Course Outlines

The span of a term imposes severe constraints on what an instructor can teach. We believe that *Microeconomics in Context,* First Edition, can be used as the basis for a variety of approaches, depending on how much flexibility you have and how much time you would like to devote to topics and approaches that may be of particular interest to you and your students.

To help you choose the chapter assignments that make the most sense for your class needs, we have put together some ideas for course outlines. These appear below. Arranged in terms of broad "selections" and more specific "emphases," they are designed to help you choose among chapters when you find that there is not enough time to cover everything that appears in *Microeconomics in Context.*

We understand that one primary objective of the introductory course in most departments is teaching in some detail "how (neoclassical) economists think." For those instructors who either must or choose to focus exclusively on neoclassical content, the most traditional combination of the selections described below—the "base chapters," combined with some or all of the "neoclassical concepts" selection and the "neoclassical modeling" emphasis—will provide what you need. This combination of chapters does not come close to exploiting fully the richness of the *Microeconomics in Context* textbook, but the contextual discussions (a hallmark of this text) that are interwoven into the standard material will inform the students about some of the crucial assumptions and limitations of neoclassical analysis—and will broaden their understanding of economic theory.

Many instructors have somewhat more leeway and can combine coverage of traditional neoclassical ideas with other material. We expect most users of *Microeconomics in Context* (MIC) to be in this category. We suggest that you make use of the special structure of the book, which enables you to introduce neoclassical concepts in your introductory course while still reserving class time for other areas of interest. Concepts such as opportunity cost (a topic covered within the "base chapters") are important to teach, but how many beginning students have a pressing need to know about the intricacies of average variable cost curves and indifference curves? Such material will be largely irrelevant to the future lives of those who are not majoring in economics, and even economics majors often complain of boredom when this material is repeated at the intermediate level. If you are an instructor with some flexibility, you might choose the "base" selection and parts of the "neoclassical concepts" selection and combine these with one or more of the emphases described below.

Some of you may have even more flexibility, perhaps because you teach primarily nonmajors or teach outside of an economics department, such as in a public policy school, environmental sciences department, or interdisciplinary social studies department. If you are in this category, you can set the less relevant parts of the traditional neoclassical curriculum aside altogether and teach a course that is even richer in its variety of topics and intellectual scope. Such a course might include the "base" selection, some material from the "neoclassical concepts" selection, and much more material from the topical emphases.

Summary of Possible Course Options When Not All of MIC Can Be Taught

Curriculum Focus	Likely Selections
Traditional neoclassical, with emphasis on technique	Base Chapters Selection (Chapters 1, 3, and 4) Neoclassical Concepts Selection (see description below) Neoclassical Modeling Emphasis (Appendices to Chapters 7–13)
Strong focus on neoclassical concepts with other themes woven in	Base Chapters Selection (Chapters 1, 3, and 4) Neoclassical Concepts Selection (see description below) Choose from Other Emphases (see descriptions below)
Coverage of basic and traditional concepts within course tailored to instructor and student interests	Base Chapters (Chapters 1, 3, and 4) Choose from Neoclassical Concepts (see description below) Choose from Other Emphases (see descriptions below)

Suggestions for Selections That Could Be Combined to Form a Specific Course Plan

Base Chapters Selection

- **Chapter 1**, Economic Activity in Context
- **Chapter 3**, Market Institutions
- **Chapter 4**, Supply and Demand

Neoclassical Concepts Selection

Include:

- Section 4 of **Chapter 2,** Economic Actors and Organizations (rational, self-interested behavior and circular flow)
- **Chapter 5**, Working with Supply and Demand (elasticities)
- Section 1 of **Chapter 6,** Capital Stocks and Resource Maintenance (defining stocks and flows, capital)
- **Chapter 7**, Production Costs
- Sections 1, 2, and 3.1 of **Chapter 8,** Production Decisions (neoclassical producer theory: production and cost functions, marginal analysis, the decision whether to produce)
- Sections 1 and 3 of **Chapter 10**, Consumption and the Consumer Society (neoclassical consumer theory)
- **Chapter 11**, Markets Without Market Power (perfect competition)
- **Chapter 12**, Markets with Market Power ("imperfect" competition)
- Section 3.2 of **Chapter 17**, The Public Purpose Sphere: Governments and Nonprofits (regulation of monopolies and trade practices)

Consider:

- Section 2 of **Chapter 9**, Distribution: Exchange and Transfer (gains from specialization and trade)
- Sections 2, 3, 5 of **Chapter 13**, Markets for Labor (neoclassical labor markets)
- Sections 1 and 2.1 of **Chapter 14**, Markets for Other Resources (present value calculations and capital markets)
- Section 2 of **Chapter 19**, Market Systems and Normative Claims (neoclassical welfare economics)

Neoclassical Modeling Emphasis

Include:

- **Appendix to Chapter 7**, A Formal Model of Producer Costs (average total and average variable cost curves)
- **Appendix to Chapter 8**, A Formal Theory of Producer Behavior with Convexity and Perfect Competition (full neoclassical producer theory graphs)
- **Appendix to Chapter 10**, A Formal Theory of Consumer Behavior (indifference curves)
- **Appendix to Chapter 11**, A Formal Analysis of a Market with Perfect Competition
- **Appendix to Chapter 12**, A Formal Analysis of Monopoly and Monopolistic Competition

Consider:

- **Appendix to Chapter 9**, A Formal Theory of Gains from Trade
- **Appendix to Chapter 13**, A Formal Model of a Firm's Hiring Decision in Perfect Competition

Ecological Emphasis

Include:

- **Chapter 6**, Capital Stocks and Resource Maintenance (especially Sections 1, 3 and 8, natural capital and sustainability)
- **Chapter 10**, Consumption and the Consumer Society (especially Sections 2, 4, and 5, rising consumption and its ecological implications)
- **Chapter 14**, Markets for Other Resources (especially Sections 1 and 2, markets for resources)
- **Chapter 17**, The Public Purpose Sphere: Governments and Nonprofits (especially Section 3.4, environmental protection)
- **Chapter 18**, The Variety of Economic Systems (especially Section 4.3, cross-country comparisons of sustainability).

Global/International Emphasis

Emphasize:

- Sections 2 and 3 and appendix of **Chapter 9**, Distribution: Exchange and Transfer ("gains from trade" and aid issues)
- Section 5 of **Chapter 16**, The Business Sphere: For-Profit Firms (Globalization)
- Sections 2.3 and 3.2 of **Chapter 17**, The Public Purpose Sphere: Governments and Nonprofits (international regulatory institutions)
- **Chapter 18**, The Variety of Economic Systems (cross-country comparisons).

Finance/Business Emphasis

Include:

- **Chapter 6**, Capital Stocks and Resource Maintenance (especially Section 7, financial capital)

- **Chapter 8**, Production Decisions (especially Sections 3 and 4, discrete decision making and finance)
- **Chapter 10**, Consumption and the Consumer Society (especially Section 2, the marketing view of consumption)
- **Chapter 13**, Markets for Labor
- **Chapter 14**, Markets for Other Resources
- Section 3 of **Chapter 15**, The Core Sphere: Households and Communities (work/family policies)
- **Chapter 16**, The Business Sphere: For-Profit Firms
- **Chapter 17**, The Public Purpose Sphere: Governments and Nonprofits (especially Sections 3.2 and 3.3, regulation)

Public Policy Emphasis

Emphasize:

- **Chapter 17**, The Public Purpose Sphere: Governments and Nonprofits

Include:

- **Chapter 9**, Distribution: Exchange and Transfer
- Section 3 of **Chapter 11**, Markets Without Market Power (equity, efficiency, and policy)
- Section 4.5 of **Chapter 13**, Markets for Labor (discrimination)
- Section 3 of **Chapter 15**, The Core Sphere: Households and Communities (work/family policies)
- **Chapter 18**, The Variety of Economic Systems
- **Chapter 19**, Market Systems and Normative Claims

Gender Issues/Feminist Emphasis

Include:

- Section 3 of **Chapter 9**, Distribution: Exchange and Transfer (dealing with human dependency needs)
- **Chapter 13**, Markets for Labor (especially Section 4.5, discrimination)
- **Chapter 15**, The Core Sphere: Households and Communities (core sector of households and communities)

Consider:

- **Chapter 19**, Market Systems and Normative Claims

Poverty/Inequality/Social Justice Emphasis

Emphasize:

- **Chapter 9**, Distribution: Exchange and Transfer (especially Section 4, inequality)
- Section 5 of **Chapter 10**, Consumption and the Consumer Society (consumption and well-being)

Include:

- Section 5.2 of **Chapter 4**, Supply and Demand (inadequacy)
- Section 4 of **Chapter 13**, Markets for Labor (explaining variations in wages)
- Section 3.1 of **Chapter 17**, The Public Purpose Sphere: Governments and Nonprofits (social welfare policy)
- **Chapter 18**, The Variety of Economic Systems

Consider:

- **Chapter 19**, Market Systems and Normative Claims

Behavioral Economics Emphasis

Emphasize:

- **Chapter 2**, Economic Actors and Organizations (especially Section 2, motivation and behavior).
- Section 3 of **Chapter 3**, Market Institutions (behavioral aspects of market institutions)

Include:

- **Chapter 8**, Production Decisions (especially Section 3, dealing with complex and socially influenced decision making)
- **Chapter 10**, Consumption and the Consumer Society (especially Section 2, psychological and sociological aspects of consumption)
- **Chapter 13**, Markets for Labor (especially Section 4.4, worker motivation)
- **Chapter 14**, Markets for Other Resources (especially Sections 1 and 3, uncertainty and financial markets)
- **Chapter 16**, The Business Sphere: For-Profit Firms (especially Section 2 on motivations within organizations)
- **Chapter 17**, The Public Purpose Sphere (especially Section 4 on motivations within organizations)

Consider:

- **Chapter 19**, Market Systems and Normative Claims (comparison of schools of thought)

Information/Transactions Cost Economics Emphasis

Emphasize:

- Section 2.3 of **Chapter 1**, Economic Activity in Context (transactions costs and externalities)
- Section 2.4 of **Chapter 2**, Economic Actors and Organizations (information and rationality)
- Section 3 of **Chapter 3**, Market Institutions (institutional requirements of markets)

Include:

- Section 2 of **Chapter 7**, Production Costs (economic costs)
- Section 3 of **Chapter 8**, Production Decisions (sunk costs, path dependence, switching costs, network externalities)
- Section 4 of **Chapter 13**, Markets for Labor (explaining wage variation)
- **Chapter 14**, Markets for Other Resources (especially Section 1, uncertainty)
- **Chapter 16**, The Business Sphere: For-Profit Firms (explaining firm structure and size)
- **Chapter 17**, The Public Purpose Sphere: Governments and Nonprofits (especially Sections 1 and 3, the need for public institutions)

Consider:

- **Chapter 19**, Market Systems and Normative Claims

Institutionalist/Evolutionary Economics Emphasis

Emphasize:

- **Chapter 2**, Economic Actors and Organizations (especially Section 3, economic organizations)

- **Chapter 3**, Market Institutions

Include:

- Section 2 of **Chapter 6**, Capital Stocks and Resource Maintenance (evolution of capital)
- Sections 3 and 4 of **Chapter 8**, Production Decisions (path dependence and the importance of finance)
- **Chapter 15**, The Core Sphere: Households and Communities
- **Chapter 16**, The Business Sphere: For-Profit Firms
- **Chapter 17**, The Public Purpose Sphere: Governments and Nonprofits

Consider:

- **Chapter 18**, The Variety of Economic Systems
- **Chapter 19**, Market Systems and Normative Claims

Heterodox Economic Theories/Philosophy of Economics Emphasis

Emphasize:

- **Chapter 1**, Economic Activity in Context
- **Chapter 19**, Market Systems and Normative Claims

Include:

- Section 5.3 of **Chapter 4**, Supply and Demand (precision versus accuracy).

Political Economy/Marxist/Radical Economics Emphasis

Emphasize:

- **Chapter 6**, Capital Stocks and Resource Maintenance
- Section 4 of **Chapter 8**, Production Decisions (financial capital)

Include:

- **Chapter 9**, Distribution: Exchange and Transfer
- Sections 1 and 4 of **Chapter 13**, Markets for Labor (overview and variations in wages)
- **Chapter 18**, The Variety of Economic Systems
- **Chapter 19**, Market Systems and Normative Claims

Humanist/Socio-/Human Development Economics Emphasis

Emphasize:

- **Chapter 1**, Economic Activity in Context

Include:

- **Chapter 2**, Economic Actors and Organizations (especially Section 2, motivation and behavior)
- **Chapter 3**, Market Institutions (especially Section 3.2 and 4, trust and markets)
- **Chapter 6**, Capital Stocks and Resource Maintenance (especially Sections 5 and 6, human and social capital)
- **Chapter 9**, Distribution: Exchange and Transfer (especially Section 3, rationales for transfers)
- **Chapter 10**, Consumption and the Consumer Society (especially Sections 4 and 5, consumer society, well-being, and capabilities)
- **Chapter 15**, The Core Sphere: Households and Communities
- **Chapter 17**, The Public Purpose Sphere: Governments and Nonprofits

Part One

The Context for Economic Analysis

Economic Activity in Context

Why are you taking an introductory economics course? You have various goals in your life. You probably want to get a challenging and rewarding job. No doubt you also want good relationships with your friends and family. You might hope to live in a community with agreeable social interaction and good environmental quality. In some small way, taking this course is part of your effort toward reaching those goals. You may be taking economics because of personal or professional interest or because it is a requirement for your program of study. In either case, we hope that after taking this course you will be better able to progress toward your goals—and to choose them in such a way that you will be glad if you achieve them.

1 | Your Starting Point

economics: the study of the way people organize themselves to sustain life and enhance its quality

Economics is the study of the way people organize their efforts to sustain life and enhance its quality. Individuals engage in four essential economic activities: resource maintenance, production of goods and services, distribution of goods and services, and consumption of goods and services. Economists study how individuals engage in these activities and how their social coordination is achieved.[1]

Economics can be applied to help people meet personal, business, and social goals. Of course, this is not the only discipline to make such a claim. As an example, suppose you are especially concerned with the problem of AIDS, an often fatal disease afflicting millions around the world. If you wanted to develop new medicines, you would study in the sciences. If you wanted to investigate the social impact of AIDS, you might study sociology. If you wanted to work with AIDS patients, you might study nursing or social work. But how does a society determine how much time and money will be devoted to AIDS research and how much to other activities, such as AIDS prevention or the care of children orphaned by AIDS? And how much time and money go to health care, as

 The four essential economic activities are resource maintenance and the production, distribution, and consumption of goods and services.

---

[1] The terms *social organization* and *social coordination* are used here in the broad sense to mean "involving a number of people."

opposed to completely different activities, such as designing automobiles? What salary does a researcher in a university lab earn, compared to that of one who works for a pharmaceutical company or to people in other kinds of work? How are the prices of medicines determined? Are there other ways to provide medicine to people who can't pay the going price? These are the kinds of questions into which economics provides unique insight.

2 | The Goals of Economic Activity

positive questions: questions about how things are

normative questions: questions about how things should be

○ Defining poverty is both a positive and a normative task. For example, it requires us to decide whether poverty should be defined in terms of people's opportunities in life or only with respect to what they have made of those opportunities. And it requires us to decide whether a definition should look only at what people possess as private property or should also take into account access to goods and services that are provided by the society.

Social scientists often make a distinction between two kinds of questions. **Positive questions** concern issues of fact, or "what is." **Normative questions** have to do with goals and values, or "what should be." For example, "What is the level of poverty in our country?" is a positive question, requiring descriptive facts as an answer. "How much effort should be given to poverty reduction?" is a normative question, requiring analysis of what it is we value and what goals should be set. However, both of these questions require a definition of poverty; positive and normative issues are inevitably intertwined in efforts to reach such a definition. In fact, life rarely offers us neat distinctions between "is" and "ought"; more often we have to deal with a mixture of the two.

Although much of this textbook will be concerned with positive issues, in discussing goals we have obviously begun with a normative question. This is because unless we understand what economic activity is *for*, it is not clear why anyone should expend any effort to study it! Even from a strictly positive point of view, understanding normative issues is critical to understanding economic activity. That is because all economic actions are taken by human beings, whose actions are significantly affected by their goals and values.

2.1 | Intermediate and Final Goals

intermediate goal: a goal that is desirable because its achievement will bring you closer to your final goal(s)

final goal: a goal that requires no further justification; it is an end in itself

A useful way to look at goals is to rank them in a kind of hierarchy. Some are **intermediate goals**; that is, they are not ends in themselves but are important because they are expected to serve as the means to further ends. Goals that are sought for their own sake, rather than because they will lead to something else, are called **final goals**. For example, you might strive to do well in your courses as an intermediate goal, toward the final goal of getting a good job.

wealth: whatever confers the ability to produce and procure valued goods and services

Adam Smith and the Goal of Wealth. Adam Smith (1723–1790) emphasized the word *wealth* in the title of his famous book *An Inquiry into the Nature and Causes of the Wealth of Nations* (published in 1776). Wealth is often defined as the value of all the material assets owned by an individual, or, in more technical terms, as whatever confers the ability to produce and procure valued goods and services. Is **wealth** really what economics is about? Those who seek to enhance their nation's wealth generally do so because they have a notion that a wealthier country is in some way stronger, better, safer, or happier. Here the relevant final goals might be strength, virtue, safety, and/or happiness. Similarly, an individual might seek wealth as an intermediate goal leading to such final goals as security, comfort, power, status, and/or pleasure.

○ Is a good job an end in itself, or is it also a means to some other end? People may reasonably differ on such questions.

The variety of final goals held by different individuals is sometimes used as a reason for viewing the accumulation of material success as the sole purpose of economics. Implicitly or explicitly, this position rests on the argument that material wealth is a nearly universal intermediate goal because it can be used to pursue so many final goals. However, over the past two centuries, the power of human beings to achieve their material goals has increased enormously. Vast numbers of people on Earth today enjoy a material standard of living that greatly exceeds the most optimistic hopes of their ancestors of a century or two ago. We are thus in a position to know more than earlier generations did about whether material wealth has served to meet more fundamental human goals.

Very few people, we suppose, would actually prefer to live in the manner of their distant ancestors. However, we are coming to recognize that there are costs as well as benefits to the continual expansion of human control over a finite material world, and to emphasizing wealth in our human relations. Looking at the complex fallout of our achievements—including environmental degradation, stresses felt by families, and other social ills—it is clear that promotion of material wealth without concern for the ends to which wealth is used, or for the consequences of the manner in which wealth is pursued, may in fact work *against* the final goals we most desire.

Recent Trends and the Goal of Efficiency. In recent times (the past 70 years or so) many economic thinkers have focused on **efficiency** as a key goal in economic policymaking. An efficient process is one that uses the *minimum value of resources* to achieve the desired result. To put it another way, efficiency is achieved when the *maximum value of output* is produced from a given set of inputs.[2] Given this focus, economists have seen their role as advising policymakers on how to make the economy as efficient as possible.

efficiency: the use of resources in a way that does not involve any waste. Inputs are used in such a way that they yield the highest possible value of output, or a given output is produced using the lowest possible value of inputs.

An appealing aspect of the goal of efficiency is that it is apparently one that everyone can agree on. Who in their right mind would argue *for* wasting resources or for having *less* of something good when more is possible at the same cost? Because it seems so obvious that efficiency is a good thing, aiming for efficiency is often thought of as a purely technical and scientific exercise. This is not actually the case, however, because taking efficiency as a goal involves a very important normative judgment: Some standard of *value* must be adopted before the definition of efficiency can begin to be applied.

Generally, in recent times, the standard of value adopted by economists has been that of *market* value—that is, price. Using this standard, an economist would say that resources are being used most efficiently when the outputs they produce can be sold for the highest possible monetary sums. This is similar to the goal of adding to material wealth, discussed above. "More is always better," it is assumed, where the "more" is composed of things that can be sold in markets.

Other standards can be used instead, however. Many things we value are *not* bought and sold in markets; health, fairness, and ecological sustainability are examples. Policies directed toward producing the highest value of *these* outputs from given inputs may be quite different from policies designed simply to maximize the market value of production. Likewise, focusing only on minimizing the monetary costs of inputs may lead to actions with high social and environmental costs. Thinking of efficiency only in terms of market value can lead to neglect of other, perhaps more urgent considerations.

The Economics in the Real World feature "Goals Beyond Efficiency" illustrates the possibility that other values may sometimes be more important than market values—and that, therefore, other goals may sometimes outweigh the goal of maximizing the monetary value of production.

2.2 | Components of Well-Being

well-being: a shorthand term for the broad goal of promoting the sustenance and flourishing of life

How do we begin the task of describing goals? First, we introduce **well-being** as a shorthand term for the broad goal of promoting the sustenance and flourishing of life, while recognizing that this broad goal has numerous, qualitatively distinct, and sometimes changing components. We will support our understanding of well-being by noting

---

[2] Note that we refer here to the *value* of resources or of output instead of to their *quantity*. If, for example, the resources we are using are clay and human labor it would be impossible to find a quantitative measure relevant to both. If we convert both to a money value (the wages of labor and the cost of acquiring the clay), then we can seek to minimize the combined cost of the two resources. This approach assumes that cost equals value—a knotty issue which we will address below and at several other places in this book.

Goals Beyond Efficiency

The point that efficiency defined in terms of market value is rarely the only important goal is vividly illustrated in a story that a now eminent economist always tells at the first meeting of a new class.

Right after he left graduate school, this young man's first job was to advise the government of a rice-growing country on where it should put its research efforts. He was told that two modern techniques for rice milling had been developed elsewhere; either one would require a sizable (and approximately equal) investment to make it useful for the prevailing rice varieties and other conditions of this country. He was asked to calculate which of the two available technologies should be selected for development. The young economist analyzed the requirements for producing a ton of rice under each of the two competing technologies. Each of them used a mixture of labor, machinery, fuel, and raw materials. He calculated the monetary costs for these inputs, and, finding that Technology A could produce a ton of rice at slightly less cost than Technology B, he recommended that the government invest in the more "efficient" Technology A.

Returning a few years later, the economist was horrified to discover what had happened when the country implemented his suggestion. It turned out that the traditions of that country included strict norms for the division of labor: specifically, what work women were allowed to do and what was defined as men's work. Technology B would have been neutral in this regard, maintaining the same ratio of "male jobs" to "female jobs" as had existed before. Technology A, however, eliminated most of the women's work opportunities. In a society where women's earnings were a major contributor to food and education for children, the result was a perceptible decline in children's nutrition levels and school attendance.

Charged with determining which technology was best, the young economist had not asked, "Best for what?" Instead, he made an implicit assumption that the only final goal was maximizing consumption and that the only intermediate goal he had to worry about was efficiency in resource use. He has subsequently told several generations of economics students, "Nobody told me to look beyond efficiency, defined in terms of market costs—but I'll never neglect the family and employment effects again, even when my employer doesn't ask about them."

What sorts of alternative standards of value does this story suggest?

something that all living things have in common: Our nature has been shaped, to an important extent, by the process of evolution. This force has instilled in all living creatures a preference for survival and the things that are essential for survival, along with an aversion to pain, hunger, thirst, and other sensations that signal a threat to survival.

Evolution has operated not upon individuals but upon gene pools. Thus, especially in the more complicated life forms, the survival imperative works to motivate behavior that will enhance group survival. Among most animals, instinct plays an important role in motivating survival-oriented behavior. In the human species, part of this role is also played by values and built-in goals. Thus most individuals feel motivated to preserve their own lives, and they enjoy feelings of health, happiness, and comfort, which are the opposite of the pain and distress that signal threats to individual survival. At the same time, it is normal for human beings to hold values that would lead them to preserve the health of the society in which they live, as well as the health of the environment, on which, ultimately, the future survival of their species depends.

Even though the inherited preference for individual and group survival can explain quite a lot of human motivation, most people do not accept it as an adequate

The final goal of economic activity is well-being. While goals of gaining wealth or doing things efficiently may help lead to well-being, well-being itself includes many subtle and often intangible ingredients like health, happiness, good social relations and ecological balance. This family, vacationing
at Lake Wenatchee National Forest in Washington State, is evidently enjoying rest, each other's
company, and the beauty of the natural environment. Possession of a certain amount of wealth is
necessary for this family to be able to take such a vacation, but the wealth itself is not well-being.

explanation for all of our most cherished values and goals. We distinguish between the
things that make life possible (survival issues) and the things that we, as conscious
beings, feel make life worth living (quality-of-life issues). There is abundant evidence
that when the things that make life worth living are removed, many individuals go
against the dictates of survival and find some way, direct or indirect, to end their lives.
(See the Economics in the Real World feature "Goals Beyond Survival.")

In Table 1.1 we present one possible list of final goals of economic activity, summa-
rizing the careful reflection of a number of thinkers but not attempting to represent a
final consensus. The first three goals on this particular list are related to individual concerns; the last five are related to social concerns that are likely to affect individual
behavior through the medium of socially developed values. Some of the listed goals

**Goals Beyond
Survival**

A simple view of evolution might suggest that the survival imperative would always
prevail over any other motives. Yet even among animals this is not true, as illustrated
by stories of dogs that lie down and die when they have lost their master, or of birds
courting danger as they try to lure a predator away from the young in their nest. Many
famous stories of human heroism also illustrate human choices for quality of life over life
itself, or the sacrifice of present survival for the sake of future generations. A true story of
such a choice occurred during World War II, when Leningrad (now St. Petersburg) was
under siege and starvation was widespread. A researcher at the university who had been
developing improved strains of seeds locked himself in his laboratory. At the end of the
war his starved body was found there, among the containers of seed corn he had protected for coming generations.

Table 1.1 | A Sample List of Final Goals

(a) Satisfaction of basic physical needs, such as for bodily survival, growth, health, procreation, security, rest, and comfort.

(b) Happiness, including feelings of contentment, pleasure, self-respect, and peace of mind.

(c) Realization of one's potential, including opportunities for physical, intellectual, moral, social, and spiritual striving and development.

(d) Fairness in the distribution of life possibilities. Individuals and cultures differ in how they assess the "fair share" of society's resources and opportunities for each person, but the goal of fairness is universal.

(e) Freedom in economic and social relations. This means permitting individuals to make as many small and large life choices for themselves as are possible within the limits of responsible relations with others (and within the limits of their decision-making capacity, as in the case of children).

(f) Participation in social decision making. Individuals should have the opportunity to participate in the processes in which decisions are made that affect the members of society as a collectivity and thereby define and regulate the society.

(g) A sense of meaning in one's life; a reason or purpose for one's efforts.

(h) Good social relations, including satisfying and trustful relations with intimates, friends, family, business associates, and fellow citizens, along with respectful and peaceful relations among nations.

(i) Ecological balance, such that natural resources and the natural environment are sustained over the long run, for the well-being of present and future generations.

(such as the first) involve making life possible, some (such as the third) involve making life worthwhile, and yet others involve both types of concerns. You may believe that some of the elements on this list are less important than others or could even be omitted. Or you may believe that other components are important and should be added. Normative analysis is not something that is set in stone forever; rather, it develops with reflection, discussion, and changing circumstances. In any case, it is clear that any reasonable discussion of the quality of life must go beyond simple notions of wealth or efficiency.[3]

2.3 | Economics and Well-Being

Economic activity, of course, is not the only ingredient that goes into creating well-being. Economics cannot make you fall in love, for example, or prevent your being in a car accident. But economic factors may help to determine whether your job leaves you with the time and energy to date, whether your car has seat belts, and whether you have access to medical treatment. A well-functioning economy is one that operates to increase the well-being of all its members.

We have suggested for your consideration (in Table 1.1) one plausible list of final goals to be taken into account in guiding economic activity. The interrelations of these goals with each other, and with economic activity, are extensive and complex. Economic activities are often necessary to promote our final goals, but economic activities can also sometimes create "ill-being" instead of well-being, whether because of conflicts between goals or because of unintended consequences. On the other hand, some economic activities directed toward one goal have consequences that *enhance* the achievement of other goals. For example, doing work that is felt to contribute something positive in the world can add significantly to people's happiness and their ability to realize their potential, at the same time as it brings in the income that permits the satisfaction of their basic needs.

---

[3] Simplicity has sometimes been sought by inventing a single concept that is thought to cover all possible final goals. That was what the utilitarian philosophers, starting with Jeremy Bentham (1748–1832), attempted when they used the word *utility* for anything people might desire, ignoring the possibility of qualitative difference and incommensurability (that is, a lack of comparability) that might exist among various human goals. We will discuss both the uses and the drawbacks of the utility approach in this book.

Conflicts Between Goals. If the goal of immediate enjoyment is given too much emphasis, economic activity can actually decrease health and long-term happiness. A supermarket checkout counter offers a good example: Some magazines will attempt to sell you pleasure in the form of recipes for chocolate cake, and nearby is a display of health-damaging cigarettes. Temptations to easy happiness may make us unhealthy—even when we are fully informed about the consequences and are trying hard to weigh the relative importance of our goals. Other goals can also be in conflict. For example, one current public health debate concerns whether people with contagious, antibiotic-resistant tuberculosis should be *required* to accept hospital services—in locked wards, if necessary. In this case, we see that the social goal of a physically healthy population and the goal of freedom seem to demand opposite approaches. Likewise, an employer may need to decide between trying to pressure an employee to produce the largest possible quantity of some product (perhaps a product that is very important for well-being) and wanting to help employees realize their intellectual and social potential on the job.

economic actor (economic agent): an individual, group, or organization that is involved in the economic activities of resource maintenance or the production, distribution, or consumption of goods and services

○ Economic actors are not only those who are actually producing, maintaining, consuming, and/or distributing. They may also include, for example, legislators whose decisions affect the kinds of economic activity that are possible, and activists who aim to prevent certain types of economic activity.

negative externalities: harmful side effects, or unintended consequences, of economic activity that affect persons or entities (such as the environment) that are not among the economic actors directly responsible for the activity

Unintended Negative Consequences. An **economic actor**, or **economic agent**, is an individual, group, or organization engaged in one of the four essential activities listed at the beginning of this chapter—resource maintenance or the production, distribution, or consumption of goods and services. Such activity, although it is aimed at accomplishing one thing, may also produce unintended side effects that cause harm in some way, such as polluting the air or water or needlessly wasting resources. No one creates such harms intentionally, but they may result as the *unintended* consequences of the pursuit of other goals. If the harm affects mainly the economic actors who are doing the activity, it is likely that the actors will take the harm they suffer into account when deciding whether to continue the activity. But what if the action harms mainly the environment or people other than the economic actors themselves? Economists call harmful effects **negative externalities** when they mostly affect the environment or people other than those directly involved in the activity.

One example of a negative externality is a manufacturing firm's dumping of pollutants in a river, decreasing water quality downstream. Other examples of negative externalities include your "consuming" music so loudly that it disturbs your neighbors and an employer's setting up work schedules that have a negative impact on the families of the employees. If economic activities affected only the actors directly involved in decision making about them, we might be able to think about economic activity primarily in terms of individuals making decisions for their own benefit. But we live in a social and ecological world, in which actions, interactions, and consequences are generally both widespread and interknit. The idea of negative externalities reminds us of this fact.

positive externalities: beneficial side effects, or unintended consequences, of economic activity that accrue largely to persons or entities that are not among the economic actors directly involved in the activity

Unintended Positive Consequences. Externalities, however, are not always negative. **Positive externalities** are *beneficial* effects of economic activity that accrue largely to persons or entities that are not among the economic actors directly involved in the activity. Whether the effect is intended or unintended, many activities that advance one goal can also advance another.

As an example, consider families as economic actors, involved (as we shall see) in many aspects of resource maintenance, production, distribution, and consumption. Families are the location in which children first learn the basics of social relations, including communication, trust, and fairness. As mentioned earlier, good social relations and fairness are in themselves commonly held final goals. Yet families' efforts to form children in this way yield results that go far beyond family peace. For one thing, good social relations reduce **transaction costs**, which are the costs of arranging economic activities. For example, if a manufacturer wants to buy a supply of rubber hose, she needs to search for a supplier, bargain for a deal, make a contract, and see that the contract is carried out. The transaction costs will be high if information about suppliers is hard to get or if the manufacturer and the supplier do not trust each other. In the case

transaction costs: the costs of arranging economic activities of lack of trust, before money can be exchanged for rubber hose, it may be necessary to spend time and money on many meetings, lawyers, reams of contracts, and even action by the courts or police. On the other hand, if information is easily available, and if the two parties trust each other and have shared expectations, agreements are much less costly to reach and may be sealed by a simple handshake. The questions of good social relations and common standards of fairness may be particularly acute when the parties have different national and cultural backgrounds or speak different languages. These issues are critically important in relations among workers and managers. Activities that increase social understanding and foster appropriate, shared standards of fairness and honesty have "positive externalities" in that they create a better environment for other economic activities.

Other examples of positive externalities include a firm that provides education to its employees, who are then better able to carry out their roles as citizens, and a person planting for his own enjoyment a flower garden that also pleases passersby. A government might undertake actions to maintain pure water resources out of concern for citizens' health, but in the process it may also increase recreation opportunities and reduce expenditures that would otherwise have had to be made by industries for water purification. Positive externalities are the *good* side of being enmeshed in a web of economic relations.

Discussion Questions

1. You have evidently made a decision to dedicate some of your personal resources of time and money to studying college economics. Which of the goals listed in Table 1.1 was most important to you (and perhaps to your family or community, if they were involved) in making this decision? Did any of the other goals figure in this decision? If you were to write up a list of your own final goals, how would it differ from Table 1.1?

2. Certain drugs act on the nervous system to produce intense, temporary feelings of happiness. Some of these are addictive and cause people to lose all ambition except that of getting another dose of the drug. Do these drugs add to well-being? Discuss.

3 | The Issues That Define Economics

In discussing goals we have addressed the question of what economics is *for*—what its purpose is. Now we will summarize what economics is *about*: what activities it covers, and what questions it addresses.

3.1 | The Four Essential Economic Activities

We think of an activity as "economic" when it touches on one or more of four important tasks.

resource maintenance: the management of natural, manufactured, human, and social resources in such a way that their productivity is sustained

1. **Resource maintenance** means tending to, preserving, or improving the natural, manufactured, human, and social resources that form the basis for the sustenance and quality of life. Forestry projects that raise timber for future use are a commonly mentioned example of such activity, but there are many others. Child care and education prepare people for future activities, as well as directly supporting and nurturing us. Other examples of resource management include figuring out how much oil to extract from an oil field now and how much to leave for later; maintaining the transportation infrastructure (subways, roadways, etc.) of a city; and, in a factory, keeping the machinery in good repair and maintaining the necessary knowledge, skill levels, and morale of the employees.

production: the conversion of resources into goods and services

2. **Production** is the conversion of some of these resources into usable products, which may be either goods or services. Goods are tangible objects, such as bread and books; services are intangibles, such as TV broadcasting, teaching, and

Resource maintenance means taking care of natural, manufactured, human, and social resources. On August 14, 2003, an estimated 50 million residents of the northeastern United States and Canada learned—the hard way—that maintenance of the infrastructure for the delivery of electrical energy had been neglected. A fast-spreading power outage drained the skyline of New York City of its lights (in photo) and also left people stranded in Cleveland, Ohio, Detroit, Michigan, Toronto, and Ottawa. Inadequately trained operators and a lack of attention to the trimming of trees near power lines were later found to be contributing causes.

haircuts. Popular bands performing music, recording companies producing CDs, local governments building roads, and individuals cooking meals are all engaged in the economic activity of production.

distribution: the sharing of products and resources among people

exchange: the trading of one thing for another

transfer: the giving of something, with nothing specific expected in return

3. **Distribution** is the sharing of products and resources among people. In contemporary economies, distribution activities take two main forms: **exchange** and **transfer**. When you hand over money in exchange for goods and services produced by other people, you are engaging in exchange. People are generally much better off if they specialize in the production of some limited range of goods and services, and meet at least some of their other needs through exchange, than if they try to produce everything they need themselves. (We will study this in more detail in Chapter 9 of this book.) Distribution also takes place through one-way transfers, in which something is given with nothing specific expected in return. Local school boards, for example, distribute education services to child and teenage students in their districts, tuition-free. Households transfer the income and goods they receive among the various household members.

consumption: the final use of a good or service

4. **Consumption** is the process by which goods and services are, at last, put to final use by people. In some cases, such as eating a meal or burning gasoline in a car, goods are literally "consumed" in the sense that they are used up and are no longer available for other uses. In other cases, such as enjoying art in a museum, the experience may be "consumed" without excluding others or using up material resources.

Most real-world economic undertakings involve more than one of the four essential economic activities. The trucking industry, for example, can be seen both as "producing" the service of making goods more conveniently available and as playing a role in physically distributing produced goods.

In particular, the activity of resource maintenance often overlaps with the other three economic activities (production, consumption, and distribution). For example, the production of paper using recycled materials can be classified as both production, because a good is being produced, and resource maintenance, because the impact on natural resources is minimized. As another example, you may decide to distribute a memo to your co-workers via e-mail rather than regular mail to save on paper, thus engaging in resource maintenance as part of the distribution process.

Of course, not all production, consumption, and distribution activities can also be classified as resource maintenance. Consuming grossly unhealthful food does not aid in maintaining human resources. Printing out e-mail for a quick reading on single-sided paper with no recycled content would not be considered a resource-maintaining activity.

A final point on the relationship between resource maintenance and the other economic activities is that sometimes resource maintenance means *not* engaging in production, consumption, or distribution. For example, people who make voluntary decisions to minimize their unnecessary consumption are maintaining resources. Although this may look like *inactivity,* including resource maintenance as an economic activity implies that minimizing some kinds of consumption can contribute to well-being. As another example, deciding not to distribute a minor memo to your co-workers may save everyone involved valuable time resources. (One might well turn around a familiar phrase, to make it read, "Don't just do something. Stand there!")

3.2 | The Three Basic Economic Questions

The four economic activities that we have listed give rise, in turn, to the three basic economic questions:

1. *What* should be produced, and *what* should be maintained? (What kinds of products should be made, and how much of each? What resources need to be preserved?)

2. *How* should production and maintenance be accomplished? (By whom should these activities be done, and using what kinds of resources, technologies, and methods?)

3. *For whom* should economic activity be undertaken? (What are the principles and practices that will determine how the produced goods and services are distributed among different people?)

For example, the rather small social organization we call a family faces the problem of how much of its economic resources (money, credit, and so on) to use now and how much to preserve for future use. Suppose members of a family decide to spend some of their money on a dinner party. They will have to decide "what" foods to prepare. The "how" question includes who is going to cook and what recipes to use. Answering the "for whom" question means deciding who will be invited for dinner and how to take into account the food preferences and needs of the various individuals.

The complexity of decision making and the number of people involved rise steeply as we move to higher levels of economic organization, but the questions remain the same. Businesses, schools, community groups, governments, and international economic alliances all have to settle the questions of *what, how,* and *for whom.*

Discussion Questions

1. The admissions office at your college decides who will be admitted and who will not be. Is this an economic activity? Of what kind? (There may be more than one correct answer.)

2. Imagine that an engineer, an artist, and an economist are all observing the construction of a new office building. What aspects of the process might the economist notice, and what words might she use to describe what is going on? How will her description differ from that of the engineer and that of the artist?

4 | Economic Tradeoffs

As individuals and as members of organizations, people have to make choices about *what*, *how*, and *for whom*.

4.1 | Abundance and Scarcity

When you think of all the abundant natural resources in our world, all the human time and intelligence that exist, all the investments that have been made in organizing human societies, and the massive stock of machinery and other productive resources now accumulated, you realize that the world is wealthy indeed. When you are well fed, comfortably warm, engaged in interesting activities, and in touch with those you care about, you can appreciate these benefits. Although the distribution of resources is far from even, either across countries or among people within countries (a topic we will take up again in a later chapter), contemporary human society as a whole still has a rich resource base on which to build. No wonder that many world religions and ethical teachings encourage gratitude toward the sources of life's **abundance**.

It may seem odd, then, that many economists emphasize the notion of **scarcity**—that is, the notion that there is too little to go around—when discussing society's choices concerning *what*, *how*, and *for whom*. What this really means is that even with all the available resources, and even with a steady eye on the goal of well-being, not everything that is socially desirable can be accomplished, at least not all at once.[4] The current capacity of a particular hospital, for example, may allow it to increase the number of heart transplants it performs *or* increase the amount of care it can provide for the severely mentally ill, but not both. When a given resource, such as an hour of your time, is dedicated to one beneficial activity, such as studying, it will be unavailable for certain other beneficial activities, such as relaxing with your friends. Choices have to be made.

This book presents some key tools and language that can be helpful in understanding how choices can best be made about what to produce, how, and for whom, when current resources are insufficient for meeting all possible current well-being goals, and when choices need to be made between meeting well-being goals now and meeting them in the future.

abundance: resources are abundant to the extent that they exist in plentiful supply for meeting various goals

scarcity: resources are scarce to the extent that they are not sufficient to allow all goals to be accomplished at once

4.2 | Society's Production Possibilities Frontier

Economists use the notion of a societal production possibilities frontier to illustrate concepts of scarcity, tradeoffs, choice, full employment, and efficiency. To make matters very simple, let's assume that society is considering only two possible flows of output over the coming year, which can be made from a particular set of resources.[5] The classic example is to take guns as one output and butter as the other. In more general terms, the guns-and-butter tradeoff can refer to any society's more general, and real-world, choice between becoming a more militarized society ("guns") and becoming a more civilian- or consumer-oriented society ("butter").

Figure 1.1 shows a **production possibilities frontier (PPF)** for this case. In this graph, the quantity of "butter" produced over a year is measured on the horizontal axis, or *X* axis. The quantity of "guns" is measured on the vertical axis, or *Y* axis. Every point

production possibilities frontier (PPF): a curve showing the maximum amounts of two outputs that society could produce from given resources, over a given time period

---

[4] An alternative definition of scarcity, dating to the 1930s, defined resources as scarce relative to presumably unlimited human *wants*, with no consideration to whether these wants promoted well-being.

[5] The "particular set of resources" considered to be available for economic production in the coming year will be *only a portion* of a society's total resource stock. Some quantities of resources—for example, of nonrenewable mineral and energy resources—would very wisely be left idle this coming year in order to provide a base for production in years thereafter. Efficiency does *not* require that all resources be used up in a blitz of production—only that those resources deemed available for use in the coming year are managed in a nonwasteful way. The question of how to decide wisely how much should be considered to be available for production in the coming year is discussed in the following section.

Figure 1.1 Society's Production Possibilities Frontier

As you select different points along the PPF, you see that the more you get of one good, the less you can have of the other.

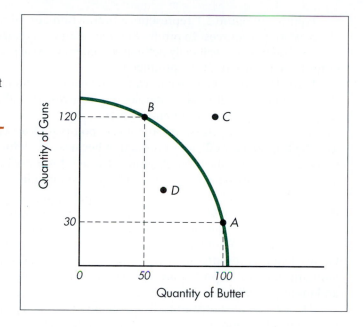

on the graph represents a pair of quantities: one quantity of guns and another of butter. The point labeled *A*, for example, illustrates production, over the year, of 100 units of butter and 30 units of guns. Point *B* illustrates production of 50 units of butter and 120 units of guns.[6]

The curve shown on the graph is the standard depiction of a PPF. The point where the curve hits the vertical axis indicates what society could produce if it devoted *all* of its resources to producing guns and *none* to producing butter. Likewise, the point where the PPF hits the horizontal axis indicates how much butter society could produce if it decided to devote itself entirely to butter production and produced no guns.

The bowed-out shape of the curve comes from the important observation that some resources are likely to be more suited for production of one good than for production of another.

We can see, for example, that we have only to give up a tiny bit of butter production to get the first 30 guns. Only a few workers, for example, need to be pulled out of butter production and set to work on plentiful supplies of the materials most suited for guns, such as easily tapped veins of iron ore and minerals for gunpowder. Gun-manufacturing plants can be built on land unsuitable for pasture. Because those resources had been left largely untapped when only butter was being produced, little is lost to butter production, whereas much is gained in guns.

On the segment between points *A* and *B*, there is a more nearly equal tradeoff, as the two processes start to compete for resources, such as land that might be used either for mining *or* for pasture, or the labor and materials that might be used either to build gun factories *or* to build plants for processing dairy products.

Movement from point *B*, into even greater gun production, comes at an increasing cost in terms of butter. The last few units of guns, from point *B* up to where the PPF hits the axis, come at a cost of nearly half the total possible production of butter! Why is this? Leaving even a few workers to tend the many cows and dairy plants would allow for a fair amount of butter production. But pulling even these last few out, and putting them to work on increasingly less accessible veins of mineral ores or on the now-crowded gun assembly lines, quickly erodes butter production while adding little to the production of guns.

---

[6] At this level of abstraction, it is not necessary to specific about what is meant by "units." You may imagine these as tons of butter and thousands of guns, if you like. Also, it is possible to imagine PPFs that include more than two products—but they would have to be graphed in three (or more) dimensions.

Point C in Figure 1.1 represents a production combination that is not attainable, given existing resources. To produce at that point would take more resources than society has. The PPF is specifically defined so that only those points on or inside it represent outputs that can actually be produced.

Point D represents a case in which society is producing less than the full amount that it could, given the particular set of resources. Usually such a point is associated with inefficiency, waste, or unemployment.

In more general terms, we can think of points such as A and B, which are on the PPF, as reflecting socially efficient production because, by definition, the production possibility frontier is a collection of points at which three socially important requirements are met. These are described in the following paragraphs.

No Involuntary Unemployment or Undesired Idle Productive Capacity. All the hours of labor effort that people desire to contribute to productive activity are actually needed, so there is no involuntary unemployment.[7] Analogously, the available stock of manufactured capital resources (such as machinery) and natural capital resources (such as land and mineral deposits) are utilized at optimal rates, so there is no unanticipated and undesired idle productive capacity.

The existence of involuntarily idle labor and/or capital resources,[8] which could be used to produce additional output, usually implies that an economy is operating at less than its potential. However, there are some circumstances under which a society may not be able to utilize all of its available resources productively. Most production requires the joint use of several types of resources; if one type is scarce, it may be technically impossible to utilize all of another, relatively abundant type. For example, a country that, in wartime, is cut off from sources of energy that it is used to importing may have idle labor and machinery that cannot operate without the imported energy. In such a case, society can reach its greatest actual productive potential even while there is still some involuntary unemployment of its more abundant resources.

More often, the existence of involuntarily idle labor and/or capital resources indicates that a society is not achieving its potential output; this has often been a major economic problem within industrialized societies. An infamous example of societies failing to realize their production possibilities was the Great Depression of the 1930s, when both output and employment fell far short of their potential in the industrialized capitalist nations of the West. Throughout their history, these countries have suffered periodic bouts of underutilization of productive capacity.

Application of Optimal Technology and Social Organization. The society is making use of the best technology and the best possible social organization of work.

Note that what is "optimal" in the use of both technology and social organization is highly dependent on context and may vary greatly from one society or one era to another. The best technique of production in any given instance will depend on the type and quantity of the available capital resources; what is best for a wealthy industrialized country will often differ from what is best for a poor or predominantly agrarian country. And the best social organization of work—in terms of motivating work effort and encouraging constructive interaction among workers—will depend on the nature and extent of the available resources, as well as on the overall culture of the society.

Efficient Resource Allocation. The resources used in the society's production processes are allocated within enterprises, and across enterprises and spheres of the economy, in such a way that each resource is deployed where it contributes most to desired production.

---

[7] Note that "full employment" of the labor force is compatible with a certain amount of unemployment attributable to voluntary job search and labor mobility, but it is not compatible with underemployment, where people involuntarily work less than full time or work at jobs that fail to make good use of their abilities.

[8] In Chapter 6 we will examine and define the variety of capital resources in more detail.

This condition is not met if reallocation of resources within enterprises, or across the whole economy, would enable society to produce increased quantities of desirable outputs. A particular enterprise may simply not use resources in accordance with the best technique. Perhaps, for example, the "gun" and "butter" activities are so badly managed that the very best pasture land is used to build the first gun factories. More of both could be produced simply by reassigning resources to more appropriate uses. Societies should obviously avoid having to make such costly changes by using the lowest-cost inputs for each process at the outset.

Different kinds of economic systems provide different kinds of incentives or commands for people to be economically efficient in the allocation of available resources, and this factor can contribute significantly to the differences in economic performance among countries. The bureaucratic socialist systems of Eastern Europe and the former Soviet Union were notorious for their inefficiency in resource allocation—both within enterprises and across the whole economy.

Whereas points inside the PPF illustrate waste or inefficiency, points along the PPF itself illustrate the important notion that scarcity creates a need for tradeoffs. Along the frontier, one can get more of one output only by "trading off" some of the other. As an old economists' saying goes, "There's no such thing as a free lunch." One interpretation of this saying is that even if someone offers you free food, you will still have to give up something—"spend" some of your valuable time, which could be used for something else—to enjoy it.

opportunity cost: the value of the next-best alternative, forgone when a choice is made

Figure 1.1 also illustrates the important concept of **opportunity cost**. Opportunity cost is the value of what one loses by not choosing the best alternative to the choice one actually makes. Looking at the PPF, we see that the cost of increasing gun production is less butter, and the cost of increasing butter production is fewer guns.

Of course, we could put on the axis many other pairs of outputs, besides guns and butter, and still illustrate these concepts. We could look at coke and pizza, cars and bicycles, or health and highways. This classic example, however, is a good one. In the real world, such guns/butter, or militarization/peacetime tradeoffs can be crucially important. (See the Economics in the Real World feature "Military Expenditure—The Opportunity Cost.")

What precise combination of outputs, such as guns and butter, or health and highways, should society choose to produce? To determine which point on the PPF would be best, we would have to have some way of figuring out which was preferable for the society. For good social decision making, this production question would have to be considered right alongside questions of resource maintenance, distribution, and consumption, because all have effects on well-being. In a society with free speech and democratic discussion, there is wide room for disagreement about what the best mix of goods might be. The PPF provides a mental image for thinking about tradeoffs but tells us little about how to choose among the possibilities it illustrates.

4.3 | Tradeoffs over Time

We have said that a PPF reflects possible production combinations given a certain set of resources. This idea deserves more investigation. Do we mean that society should look at *all* the resources it has at a point in time and then strive to employ them to produce the absolute *most* of valued outputs over the coming year?

If we consider that achieving well-being also involves questions of *how* and *for whom*, as well as activities of resource maintenance, distribution, and consumption, then the question becomes more complex—and more interesting. For example, we generally want to conserve resources so that we can produce goods not only right now but also later in our lives. And we have an obligation to future generations to include them in our considerations of *for whom*.

Some production activities are also resource maintenance activities, of course, and the flow of output from these activities adds to the stock of resources available for the

Military Expenditure— The Opportunity Cost

Even if they have never seen a gun, millions of children suffer from wars, as resources that could have been invested in development are diverted into armaments. Indeed, one of the most distressing realities of our time is that most wars have been fought in precisely those countries that could least afford them.

Despite the overall global decline in military spending from 1987 to 1994, large amounts of scarce resources continue to be devoted to armaments. Between 1960 and 1991, total annual military expenditures by developing countries rose from US$27 billion to US$121 billion. Sadly enough, some of the steepest increases occurred in the poorest countries. Angola, Ethiopia, Mozambique, Myanmar, Somalia, and Yemen have for many years spent more on their military than they have on their people's education and health. Money spent on arms could have been put to much better use. The United Nations Development Program (UNDP) has estimated that redirecting just one-quarter of developing countries' military expenditure could have provided the additional resources to implement most of the year-2000 program: primary health care for all, immunization of all children, elimination of severe malnutrition, provision of safe drinking water for all, universal primary education, reduction of illiteracy, and family planning.

The industrialized countries must share responsibility because they are the dominant arms suppliers. The top five exporters to developing countries are the five permanent members of the United Nations Security Council. With the end of the cold war, the weapons industries in the rich countries are scrambling for new markets wherever they can find them—often with the enthusiastic support of their political leaders. Although arms sales have dropped significantly in the last few years, sales to developing countries in 1994 still amounted to US$25.4 billion, all of which is money lost to development efforts. The largest single supplier has normally been the United States.

If even a fraction of the resources devoted to building military capacity could be diverted to achieving basic development goals, we would soon be living in a world with fewer social and environmental problems and far fewer and less destructive wars. ◔

Adapted from the United Nations Children's Emergency Fund (UNICEF), *The State of the World's Children* (1996).

---

technological progress: the development of new methods of converting inputs into outputs

future. Investments in plant and equipment can provide productive capacity not just for a few months but, often, for years. Production of goods and services that protect the environment, or that encourage the development of new forms of knowledge and social organization, also lead to an improved resource base. **Technological progress**, in which new methods are devised that convert resources into products, can lead to very long-run improvements in productive capacity. To the extent that production is of this sort, production can *add* to the production possibilities for the future. The PPF may expand over time, out and to the right, making previously unobtainable points obtainable, as shown in Figure 1.2.

Some productive activities contribute an ongoing flow of outputs without drawing down the stock of capital resources. Sustainable production activities, such as some agricultural and forestry processes when they are suitably planned and carried out, may not add to the resource base, but neither do they deplete it.

Many other productive activities, however, lead to resource depletion or degradation. The intensive use of fossil fuels is now depleting petroleum reserves, degrading air quality, and contributing to global climate change. Production processes that destroy important watersheds and wildlife habitats are also resource-depleting. Mind-numbing drudgery or work in dangerous circumstances can degrade human resources by leaving

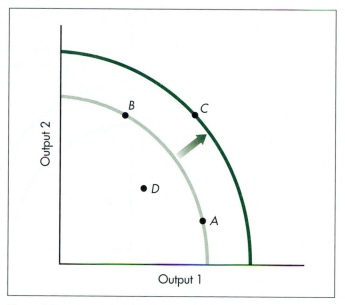

Figure 1.2 An Expanded Production Possibilities Frontier
When the PPF moves "out" (away from the origin), our choices are still constrained, but overall, it becomes possible to get more of both things than could be obtained with the "lower" PPF.

people exhausted or in bad mental or physical health. These kinds of productive activities are at odds with resource maintenance.

Taking a longer-term view, then, it is clear that getting the absolute most production, right now, out of the available resources is not an intelligent social goal. Decisions such as that involving guns versus butter need to be accompanied by another decision about now versus later. What needs to be currently produced, what needs to be maintained, and what investments are needed to increase future productivity?

Figure 1.3 shows a production/maintenance frontier, which illustrates the tradeoff between resource-depleting kinds of production and resource maintenance activities (the latter including both conservation and investment). Point *A* represents a societal decision to engage in considerable resource-depleting production in the present year, while putting little emphasis on maintenance for the future. Point *B* represents a decision to engage in a higher level of maintenance this year and in a lower level of resource-depleting production. Point *C* is, again, truly unobtainable (for now), and Point *D* represents a case of inefficiency or wasteful unemployment.

The consequences of choosing between points *A* and *B* are illustrated in Figure 1.4, where once again we portray a two-output PPF (such as that for guns versus butter). Now, however, what is depicted is conditions some time in the future and how those conditions are affected by the current choice between *A* and *B*. As Figure 1.4 shows, a decision to maintain more for the future, by choosing point *B* in Figure 1.3, leads to a larger set of production possibilities in future years. A decision to engage in considerable resource depletion, by choosing point *A* in Figure 1.3, leads to the smaller future PPF shown in Figure 1.4.

Of course, some will argue that advances in technology (which we have included as a resource-maintaining type of production) will *always* push out the PPF (as in Figure 1.2) more than resource depletion will pull it in (as in Figure 1.4). But this is no more than an assertion of belief. If this belief turns out not to be warranted, then acting on the basis of it may lead to large-scale, unfortunate, and irreversible consequences.

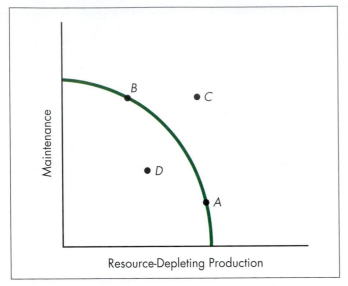

Figure 1.3 Society's Production/Maintenance Frontier
We choose not only what to produce but also how to produce it;
some production methods are more resource-depleting than others.

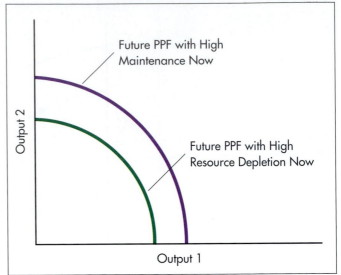

Figure 1.4 Possible Future PPFs
Present-day decisions about *how to produce* will affect the future choice-set
of what *can be produced*.

Discussion Questions

1. Suppose that your "resources" for studying can be devoted to either or both of two "outputs": knowledge of economics and/or knowledge of the subject matter of another class of yours. Would the PPF for your "production" have the shape portrayed in Figure 1.1? Discuss.

2. Consider the following possible productive activities. Which ones do you think will tend to make the PPF larger in the future? Which ones will tend to make it smaller? (There may be room for disagreement on some points.)
   a. Increasing education
   b. Manufacturing lawn mowers
   c. Building a nuclear power plant
   d. Restoring wetlands
   e. Building a new interstate highway
   f. Expanding Internet capacity

5 | The Three Spheres of Economic Activity

Economic activity takes place in three major spheres, which we designate here as the core, public purpose, and business spheres. Economists often refer to these groups as the household, government, and business spheres. In this text, however, we use the term *core* instead of *household* to emphasize the importance of communities, in addition to households, in the "core" activities described below. (Think of the maxim "It takes a village to raise a child.") We use the term *public purpose* instead of *government* to include both government organizations and the nongovernmental non-profit organizations whose activities are of growing importance in modern societies. We will explore the economic roles of the core, public purpose, and business spheres in this section.

5.1 | The Core Sphere

core sphere: households, families, and communities

Long before the invention of money, of organized markets, and of systems of government, human societies organized themselves along lines of kinship and community to undertake the economic activities essential to maintaining and improving the conditions for human life. The **core sphere** is made up of household, family, and community institutions that organize resource management, production, distribution, and consumption, usually on a small scale, and largely without the use of money. In industrialized societies the core sphere is still the primary site for raising children, preparing meals, maintaining homes, taking care of the mildly ill, and providing the sorts of informal entertainments and exchanges of support that occur among families, friends, and neighbors.

One distinguishing characteristic of the core sphere is how work activities are rewarded: Instead of yielding extrinsic monetary rewards, work tends to be rewarded directly by what it produces. For example, work in a home garden is rewarded with tomatoes, and the reward of good child care is a happy and healthy child. People may volunteer their services to their community because they recognize that living in a healthy community is important. People play cards, softball, or music together because they find these activities intrinsically enjoyable. Another distinguishing characteristic is that activities in the core sphere tend to be organized to respond to immediately perceived needs—unlike market activities, which respond to what people are able and willing to pay for.

The core sphere is obviously critical for subsistence economies, where extended families and villages may raise or make for themselves most of what they consume, with little outside trading. Although reliance on the core sphere has to some extent been reduced in the United States by the increasing use of prepared foods, child care centers, restaurants, commercial forms of entertainment, nursing homes, housecleaning services and the like, it remains significant.

Core sphere activities, however, have been—and sometimes still are—often described as noneconomic or nonproductive, because they generally do not produce goods and services for trade through a market. Consider just one activity that takes place in the core sphere: the help provided by relatives, friends, neighbors, and community

Essential economic activities take place in all three spheres of the economy: the core sphere, the public purpose sphere, and the business sphere. This family is engaged in the economic activity of production. They are cooking together in order to turn raw ingredients into a delicious meal. Because this activity is being done in the core sphere, their work will be directly rewarded by their enjoyment of dinner, and perhaps also by the companionship they share in the kitchen. Cooking is one productive activity that can be found in all three spheres of economic activity. School cafeterias and commercial restaurants provide this service as well.

that enables seniors to remain in a home setting rather than entering a nursing facility. If we were to value the actual time invested in these activities in the United States at a low wage of $8 an hour, we would find that each year about $200 billion worth of elder care is provided in the core sphere—without being recorded in gross domestic product (GDP) statistics. There are also paid home helpers, whose wages *are* recorded in the GDP. They are paid at an average national rate of $11 per hour, but their contribution to GDP is only one-sixth of the value just cited for "free" elder care in the core sphere.

Using a conservative method that values all home production time at the going (low) wage for paid housekeepers, economists have estimated that the value of household unpaid labor is about one-third of GDP. Other methods, such as valuing this time at the wages paid in the market for more specialized services (driver, child educator, home decorator, landscape designer) yield higher estimates. More important than simply calculating percent of GDP, however, is the recognition that ignoring core sphere economic functions can lead to neglect of many economic issues that are, in fact, critical to human well-being.

When the core sphere is working effectively to support the quality of life, important goods and services are provided to many, many people, even if the scale of production in each specific case is quite small. Because most core sphere activities involve face-to-face interaction, the core sphere is the primary location in which the ability to form good social relations is developed.

Of course, core spheres can also work badly or inadequately. For example, responsibilities for children or elderly and ill people may be inequitably assigned between women and men. Such responsibilities may also overwhelm the personal resources of impoverished families and communities. There are limits to what can be accomplished within small-scale, largely informal networks of personal relations. For many economic goals, more formal and larger-scale organizations are also needed. Hence the public purpose sphere.

5.2 | The Public Purpose Sphere

Kinship and community were the earliest modes of human organization, but larger organizations soon arose. Communities found advantages to banding together in larger groups for mutual protection, increased social contact, and the like.

The **public purpose sphere** includes governments and their agencies, as well as non-profit organizations such as charities, religious organizations, professional associations, and international institutions such as the World Bank and the United Nations.

public purpose sphere: governments and other local, national, and international organizations established for some public purpose beyond individual or family self-interest and not operating with the goal of making a profit

The distinguishing characteristic of these institutions is that they exist for an explicit purpose related to the public good—that is, the common good of some group larger than a household or informal community. Their definitions of the public good, however, may vary widely and may even contradict one another. They are charged with purposes such as defending a country's borders, relieving poverty, providing formal health care and education, attending to spiritual well-being, protecting the natural environment, and stabilizing global financial markets.

Organizations in the public purpose sphere tend to be larger and more formally structured than those in the core sphere, and usually they are more monetized. Work is often motivated by a mixture of pay and volunteerism. Jobs in non-profit organizations often pay less than jobs in the business sphere that require equivalent skill and entail equivalent responsibility. It is sometimes said that government employees are in public service.

Although in some instances public purpose organizations offer goods and services for sale much as businesses do, this is generally not their primary focus. Public purpose organizations usually raise much of the money they need to function by soliciting monetary contributions or, in the case of governments, requiring such contributions in the form of taxes, donations, or membership fees. Your college or university, for example, is very likely to be a non-profit or government entity. It probably relies partly on the tuition and fees you pay and partly on donations from alumni and/or government funds collected through taxation. Public purpose organizations respond to the demands of their "public," whether that public be voters, members, or other participants.

The public purpose sphere is able to provide goods and services that cannot, or would not, be well provided by core sphere institutions and businesses alone. Some of the goods and services it provides are what economists call public goods. A **public good** (or service) is one where the use of it by one person does not diminish the ability of another person to benefit from it ("nondiminishable"), and where it would be difficult to keep any individuals from enjoying its benefit ("nonexcludable").

public goods: goods for which (1) use by one person does not diminish usefulness to others, and (2) it would be difficult to exclude anyone from benefiting

For example, when a local police force helps make a neighborhood safe, all the residents benefit. Public roads (at least those that are not congested and have no tolls) are also public goods, as is national defense. Education and quality child care are in a sense public goods, because everyone benefits from living with a more skilled and socially well-adjusted population. A system of laws and courts provides the basic legal infrastructure on which all business contracting depends. Environmental protection that makes for cleaner air benefits everyone.

Because it is difficult to exclude anyone from benefiting, public goods cannot generally be sold to individual actors, as would happen if they were provided by businesses. Even if individual actors would be willing to pay, they have little incentive to pay because they can't be excluded from the benefit. Economists call people who would like to enjoy a benefit without paying for it **free riders**. Because of the problem of free riders, it often makes sense to provide public goods through government agencies, supported by taxes, so that the cost of the public benefit is borne by the public at large.

free riders: people who would like to enjoy the benefit of a public good without paying for it

In addition to public goods, some goods are provided by the public purpose sphere because, as a society, we believe that everyone should have access to them, regardless of the kind of family or community they were born in and regardless of their ability to pay. Public schooling from kindergarten through high school is a prime example. In large U.S. cities, public hospitals provide necessary emergency medical care to the poor and uninsured.[9] Non-profit organizations frequently offer services related to education, health, and welfare. Sometimes they offer these services only within a particular community (such as to members of a certain religion); at other times they work more widely and may receive subsidies from the government.

The public purpose sphere is a substantial contributor to U.S. economic activity. In the year 2000, the value of the production by non-profit organizations was about 4% of GDP, and federal, state, and local governments contributed about 11% of GDP—a total share for public purpose organizations of about 15%. In other countries, the proportion can be higher. For example, in Sweden in 1998, almost 23% of GDP was accounted for by governments and non-profit institutions.

The main strength of public purpose institutions is that (like core institutions) they provide goods and services of high intrinsic value, but (unlike core institutions) they are big enough to take on jobs that require broader social coordination. In contrast to the business sphere, the provision of goods and services itself, and not the financial results of these activities, remains the primary intended focus of public purpose organizations.

The public purpose sphere has its weaknesses, of course. Compared to the core sphere, the government, in particular, is often criticized as being cold and impersonal. Some parents prefer to home-school, for example, rather than accept what they characterize as "one-size-fits-all" public education.

---

[9] Compared to Canada and most of Europe, the United States puts less effort into these activities. For example, Canada and most European countries have more extensive public health systems, which provide widely accessible nonemergency care as well. France and the Canadian province of Quebec provide highly subsidized care and education for prekindergarten children.

Compared to the business sphere, institutions in the public purpose sphere are sometimes accused of being rigid, slow to adapt, and crippled by inefficiency through impenetrable regulations and a bloated bureaucracy. Organizations can lose sight of the intrinsic, common-good goal of providing "public service" and become more interested in increasing their own organizational budgets. Because public purpose organizations are commonly supported by taxes or donations that are often not tightly linked to the quality of their services, they may not have financial incentives to improve the quality of what they provide. Many current debates about reforms in governments and non-profits concern how efficiency and accountability can be improved without eroding the commitment of these organizations to providing goods and services of high intrinsic value.

One last problem is that because definitions of the public good vary, some people will reject the "public purpose" of some of these organizations. For example, a few non-profit organizations are thinly disguised hate groups. Trade organizations and labor unions promote the interests of (some of) their own members, while other members of society may disagree with their agendas. A continuing issue with governmental institutions is the question of *whose* interests are represented. Majority groups? Outspoken minority groups? Special interests who donate money to campaigns? Yet, because of the nature of public goods and the general interests of social welfare, the question cannot be *whether* to have a public purpose sphere but only *how* to make it function well.

5.3 | The Business Sphere

business sphere: firms that produce goods and services for profitable sale

The U.S. government defines businesses as "entities that produce goods and services for sale at a price intended at least to approximate the costs of production."[10] The **business sphere** is made up of such firms. A business firm is expected to look for opportunities to buy and manage resources in such a way that after the product is sold, the owners of the firm will earn profits.

It is sometimes thought, because the stated purpose of the firm is to buy and sell in order to make a profit, that firms act only from "self-interest" and deal only in arms-length, impersonal, voluntary exchanges. It is true that most firms that completely fail in the goal of making profits will eventually cease to exist, but the complex nature of economic actors and organizations, and of their motivations, means that profits are not the *only* thing of concern to firms.

There are two main reasons why firms may not always aim for the highest profit. First, some business managers sometimes cite being a good "corporate citizen," in regard to their workers, communities, suppliers, creditors, and environment, as motivation for some of their actions. Businesses organized on a cooperative model (including large food-marketing organizations such as Land O'Lakes for dairy products and Ocean Spray for cranberries) explicitly state their purpose in terms of providing services to their members, rather than in terms of profit. Making enough profit to stay a "going concern" is a goal of all well-run businesses: They may set a certain goal for profits while also pursuing other goals. Mindless profiteering, on the other hand—going after the last bit of profit at all costs, neglecting social and even ethical concerns—need not be how businesses are run.

Second, within a modern business corporation of any size, the activities of "the firm" are made up of the activities of many people, including its stockholders, board of directors, chief executive officer (CEO), top and mid-level managers, and employees. The interests of the various individuals and sub-organizations may be in conflict. Sometimes top officers and managers may act, for example, not in the profit-making interest of the owners but according to their *personal* self-interest. That is, they may seek to maximize their own prestige and incomes, even when this goes against the

---

[10] U.S. Bureau of Economic Analysis, "A Guide to the NIPA's," **http://www.bea.doc.gov/bea/an/nipaguid.pdf**, p. M-20, accessed February 17, 2002.

interests of everyone else involved in the firm, including those who have invested in it. Profits, and even the long-term survival of the company itself, may be sacrificed in a race for individual high salaries and lucrative bonuses.[11]

Whereas the core sphere responds to direct needs and the public purpose sphere responds to its constituents, business firms are responsive to demands for goods and services, as expressed through markets by people who can afford to buy the firms' products.

A strength of business organization is that because businesses have at least one clear goal—making profit—they may operate with superior efficiency. A profit orientation is commonly thought to drive firms to choose the most valuable outputs to produce and to produce them at the least possible cost.

The profit motivation is often thought also to encourage *innovation*: People are more motivated to come up with clever new ideas when they know they may reap financial rewards. We all benefit, in terms of our material standard of living, from business efficiency and innovations when they bring us improved products at lower prices.

The relative weakness of the business sphere comes from the fact that business interests may or may not coincide with overall social well-being. Firms *may* act to enhance social well-being—for example, by making decisions that consider all the needs of their customers and their workers and take into account externalities, including those that affect the natural environment. They may be guided in these directions by the goodwill of their owners and managers, by pressure from their customers or workers, or by government regulation.

Production for market exchange, however, has no *built-in* correction for market externalities. And sometimes "innovation" can take a perverse form. Enron Corporation, for example, in the late 1990s boosted its reported earnings primarily by inventing unusual and "innovative" accounting practices, which served to hide the extreme weakness of its financial situation from investors. In fields such as health care and education, where it can be difficult to define clear goals, businesses may increase profits by "innovatively" cutting corners on the less measurable and less-often-marketed aspects of quality of life.

The potential for social harm grows when firms gain excessive market power—that is, when they come to dominate the market in their area. They may then be able to charge socially inefficient prices (as we will discuss in Chapter 12) or to squelch socially advantageous innovations by competing firms. Good social and environmental relations are required for the business sphere to work well. But, ironically, an overemphasis on profit *alone* can tend to degrade those very same supporting relations.

5.4 | The Size of the Three Spheres

Figure 1.5 and its accompanying table give estimates of the monetary value of the annual production of goods and services in the United States by the three spheres in the year 2000, in dollar and percentage terms. The business sphere contributed 59% of production, the core sphere contributed 30%, and the public purpose sphere contributed 11%. The dollar figures add up to more than gross domestic product in that year ($9,873 billion), because an estimate of the value of unpaid household labor in the core sphere is included.[12] GDP, a statistic calculated by the government, does not currently include the value of household production.

---

[11] These issues will be addressed at more length in Chapter 16.

[12] Based on U.S. Bureau of Economic Analysis, Table 1.7, "Gross Domestic Product by Sector, 2000," **http://www.bea.gov/bea/dn/nipaweb,** published October 1, 2001, accessed October 29, 2001, with the following changes. Services of existing owner-occupied housing have been moved from "business" to "core," and unpaid household labor has been valued (conservatively) at one-third the value of GDP. In this we follow Robert Eisner, "Extended Accounts for National Income and Product," *Journal of Economic Literature* 26 (December 1988), 1611–1684.

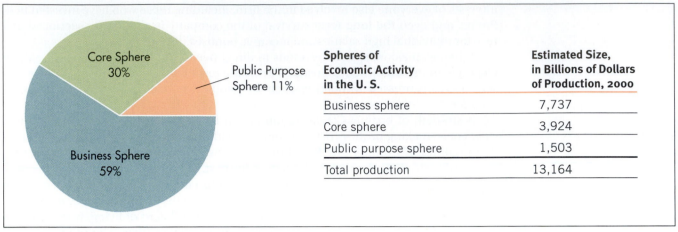

Spheres of Economic Activity in the U. S.	Estimated Size, in Billions of Dollars of Production, 2000
Business sphere	7,737
Core sphere	3,924
Public purpose sphere	1,503
Total production	13,164

Figure 1.5 Estimated Shares of the Three Spheres of Economic Activity in U.S. Production, 2000

5.5 | A Comparative Note: Less Industrialized Economies

informal sphere: businesses operating outside of government oversight and regulation. In less industrialized countries, it may constitute the majority of economic activity.

Many less industrialized economies have large **informal spheres** of small market enterprises operating outside of government oversight and regulation. Although this sphere could be classified as business because it involves private production for sale, it is also similar to the core sphere in that the activities are very small-scale and often depend on family and community connections. Like the core sphere, informal business activities are often ignored in government-compiled accounts. In the United States, street-level illegal drug trades and housecleaning services provided "off the books" by illegal immigrants are two examples of the informal sphere. In less industrialized counties, however, it is sometimes the case that *most* people are employed in small-scale agriculture, trade, and services that often go uncounted.

If this textbook were being written for use in developing countries, it would be necessary to pay a great deal more attention to the complicating reality of informal economic activity and perhaps to discuss it as a fourth sphere. However, in a text for use in industrialized countries, we can deal with this issue by simply noting, as we have just done, that informal economic activity could legitimately be classified as occurring within either the business sphere or the core sphere, leaving open the question of which of these classifications is more appropriate.

Discussion Questions

1. Education is sometimes provided within the core sphere (at-home preschool activities and home schooling), is often provided by the public purpose sphere (public and non-profit schools), and is occasionally provided by for-profit firms ("charter schools" or firms offering specific training programs). Can you think of some possible advantages and disadvantages of each of these three ways of providing education?

2. Make a list of several things that, over the last few days, you have eaten, drunk, been entertained by, been transported by, been sheltered by, or received other services from (for example, "dinner at Gina's," "my apartment," and "the health clinic"). Then, using the definitions in this section, determine which of the three spheres of economic activity provided each item.

6 | Microeconomics in Context

microeconomics: the sub-field of general economics that focuses on activities that take place within and among the major economic organizations of a society

Microeconomics is the sub-field of general economics that focuses on activities that occur within and among the major economic organizations of a society. Households and communities, governments and non-profit organizations, and for-profit businesses large and small are all involved in the essential economic activities: resource maintenance and the production, consumption, and distribution of goods and services. **Macroeconomics**, the other main sub-field of general economics, adopts more of a large-scale view, focusing on understanding national and international trends and fluctuations in economic activity taken as a whole.

macroeconomics: the sub-field of general economics that focuses on the economy as a whole

6.1 | Our Tools for Understanding

One of the important benefits of studying microeconomics is that it gives us a shared background and vocabulary, and some analytical tools, for exploring economic behavior.

Some parts of this book will deal with history, explaining how economic institutions came to be the way they are. Other parts are analytical and will, when necessary, use specialized language to help you to think clearly and communicate effectively about economic topics. It will sometimes be useful temporarily to isolate certain aspects of economic behavior from their larger historical and environmental context, in order to examine more closely the complex elements involved. Many chapters will use models to explain economic concepts. A **model** is an analytical tool that highlights some aspects of reality while ignoring others. It can take the form of a story, an image, a figure, a graph, or a set of equations, and it always involves assuming away many real-world details and complications. Models can be useful—even though they require temporarily neglecting many complications and much of the larger context—when they are understood as tools to build understanding.

model: an analytical tool that highlights some aspects of reality while ignoring others

Throughout this book, the principles being taught will be explained in terms of their relationship to the overarching goals introduced earlier in this chapter: survival and the quality of life. The economic principles presented here will not tell you everything you need to know in order to manage a business, a family, or a country, but they will provide useful ways of thinking about economic behavior. You will learn to understand and use such terms as *supply, demand, elasticity, opportunity cost, externalities,* and *public goods* to inform your own behavior as a consumer, a businessperson, a citizen, a worker, and a community member.

6.2 | The Traditional Model

traditional (or **basic neoclassical**) **microeconomic model:** a simple mechanical model that portrays the economy as a collection of profit-maximizing firms and utility-maximizing households interacting through markets

Over the last 70 years, one basic model that has been widely taught and used is what economists call the neoclassical model.[13] Because of its popularity, we will refer to this model simply as the traditional microeconomic model. The **basic neoclassical** or **traditional model** builds a simplified story about economic life by assuming that there are only two main types of economic actors and by making simplifying assumptions about how these two types of actors behave and interact.

As we will see in more detail in later chapters, the two stylized actors are *firms*, which are assumed to maximize their profits from producing and selling goods and services, and *households*, which are assumed to maximize their utility (or satisfaction) from consuming goods and services. The two kinds of agents are assumed to interact primarily through markets. Given some additional assumptions, to be explored later in this book, the model can be elegantly expressed in figures, equations, and graphs. The model is simple, and its precise results follow in a direct, mechanical fashion from its assumptions.

---

[13] For more on various schools of thought within economics, see Chapter 19.

There are some benefits to be gained from looking at economic behavior in this way. The assumptions reduce the actual (very complicated) economy to something that is much more limited—but also easier to analyze. The traditional model is particularly well suited for analyzing the determination of prices, the volume of trade, and some efficiency issues in certain cases.

We explain the neoclassical model in more detail in Chapter 2 and return to it often in subsequent chapters. There are times when its simplicity is useful. But we are dissatisfied with the ability of this model to tell the whole story, because it leaves out many features of the real world that play a critical part in economic activity. Therefore, throughout this text, we frequently discuss other factors in order to provide a more complete picture of the economy. Consider the importance of, for example, advertising, government action, processes of negotiation and administration, the multiple goals involved in well-being, struggles for economic power, and the availability of supplies of materials and energy. None of these factors is adequately accounted for in the traditional model, yet they play a significant role in our economy. Throughout this text, we address the social and physical contexts that shape—and complicate—the economy in the real world.

If you can keep in mind that models are only tools for understanding, then you will benefit from learning how to use the traditional model and the other models that are built on top of it. Even today, however, the traditional model is sometimes taken far too literally. Its very simplicity is a quality that some find appealing, whether on intellectual or political grounds. Many people claim that the traditional model "tells" us, for example, that voluntary exchange on free markets is always good and that government "intervention" (in the form of regulation or taxation) is generally bad. Or they will say that the model "proves" that self-interest, profit, and ever-increasing production of goods and services are always beneficial. Such understandings, which can be called **economistic**, confuse the assumptions of the traditional model with reality. Although it makes for comfortingly precise-looking graphs and mathematics, the traditional model on its own does not give us nearly the degree of insight that we can gain by a broader investigation, and it does not capture the full set of economic goals.

economistic thinking: thinking that confuses the assumptions of the traditional model with reality

6.3 | The Context

This book goes beyond the simple neoclassical model by offering important facts and concepts that will help you to understand the dynamic real-world economy. By providing the context in this textbook, we intend to open your eyes to the full set of economic goals and activities that exist in the real world. We titled this book *Microeconomics in Context* because, as illustrated in Figure 1.6, it discusses how economic activities, which have the goal of sustaining human life and improving its quality, take place within *physical* and *social contexts*.

The fundamental process or flow that undergirds economic activity is an ecological one: Economic activity brings natural resources into the social world and transforms them for human use. In the process, pollution and waste materials are generated, and these in turn affect the flow of natural inputs that are available.

The physical context for economic activities includes both the natural world and the built environment. The social context includes politics, culture, ethics, and other human motivations, as well as institutions and history. People are both physical and social beings; it is virtually impossible for us to take any kind of action—including economic action—outside of these contexts. At the same time, our economic actions often have important impacts on the larger physical and social contexts. A useful understanding of economics must take into account the most critical interactions between the economy and its contexts, showing how the economy is in various ways enabled and constrained by the contexts in which it is embedded, and how these social and physical influences *on* the economy are in turn affected *by* the economy. An important feature of this context has to do with the primary actors in the economy and how they are organized. We'll explore the motivations of these actors in the next chapter.

Figure 1.6 Microeconomics in Context

As described earlier in this chapter, we consider economic activity as occurring within three spheres: the core sphere, the public purpose sphere, and the business sphere. All of these are fully embedded within a social context—which, in turn, is fully embedded in the physical context of the natural and built environments.

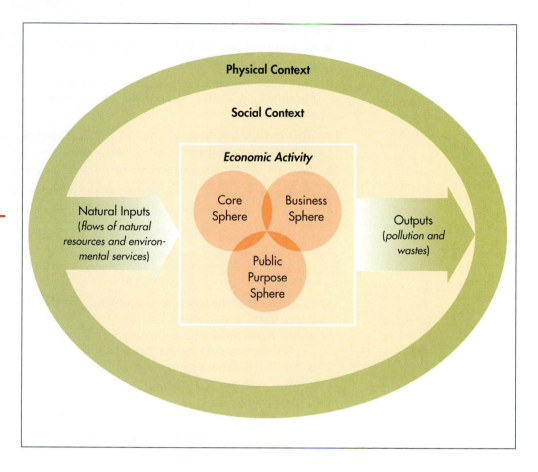

Discussion Questions

1. Describe three situations in which economic behavior could affect its physical context and three ways in which economic behavior could affect its social context. How might these influences that the economy exerts on its contexts result in changing how the contexts, in turn, affect (either support or constrain) economic activity?

2. Model building is sometimes compared to map making. If you wanted to give people directions for reaching the place where you live, what would you put on the map you drew for them? What would you put on the map you drew if someone asked you about good places to go hiking, or where the highest point is, or how close you are to your town boundary? Is it possible for a single, readable map to answer every possible question? Does the goal you have in mind for the map affect what you put on it?

Review Questions

1. Name the four essential economic activities.
2. Name the three basic economic questions.
3. What is the difference between positive and normative questions?
4. What is the difference between final and intermediate goals?
5. How is the goal of efficiency related to the goal of wealth?
6. What is an economic actor?
7. Define negative and positive externalities, and give examples of each.

8. What is a transaction cost?

9. How do abundance and scarcity create the possibility of, and the necessity for, economic decision making?

10. Draw a societal production possibilities frontier, and use it to explain the concepts of tradeoffs (opportunity cost), attainable and unattainable output combinations, and efficiency.

11. What kinds of decisions would make a PPF expand over time? What kinds of decisions would make it shrink over time?

12. What are some major characteristics of the core sphere?

13. What are some major characteristics of the public purpose sphere?

14. Why is it that businesses would find it difficult to supply "public goods"?

15. What are some major characteristics of the business sphere?

Exercises

1. In each of the following, indicate which of the four essential economic activities is taking place, and in which sphere.
   a. Ms. Katar, an executive at Acme Manufacturing, directs the cleaning up of one of the company's old industrial-waste-dumping sites.
   b. Mr. Ridge plants a garden in his yard.
   c. Ms. Fuller hands an unemployed worker a bag of groceries at a local non-profit food pantry.
   d. Private Hernandez, a recent recruit, eats lunch on the army base.

2. The notion of scarcity reflects the idea that resources cannot be stretched to meet all the goals that people desire. But what makes a particular resource "scarce"? If there seems to be more of it around than is needed (like desert sand), is it scarce? If it is freely open to the use of many people at once (like music on the radio waves), is it scarce? What about resources such as social attitudes of trust and respect? Make a list of a few resources that clearly *are* scarce in the economists' sense. Make another list of a few resources that are *not* scarce.

3. How is the concept of efficiency related to the concept of scarcity? Consider, for example, your own use of time. When do you feel time to be more, and when less, scarce? Do you think about how to use your time differently during exam week than you do when you are on vacation?

4. Match each concept in Column A with an example in Column B.

Column A	Column B
a. transaction cost	i. making money
b. negative externality	ii. the stress inflicted on a marriage by a difficult situation at work
c. an essential economic activity	iii. the airfare, time, and other expenses involved in holding a business meeting
d. normative statement	
e. economistic statement	iv. "Students should study more."
f. intermediate goal	v. "Businesses are interested only in making profits."
g. final goal	vi. production
	vii. living the best life one can

Economic Actors and Organizations

Chapter 2

In Chapter 1 we defined economic actors, or economic agents, as people or organizations engaged in one or more of the four essential economic activities: resource maintenance and the production, distribution, and consumption of goods and services. This is a fairly sweeping description; it is difficult, if not impossible, to find a person or organization that could *not* be called an economic actor, at least some of the time. In order to study economics, then, we need to have some idea about how people and organizations *behave*. Do people generally act out of self-interest, or otherwise? Is their behavior logical? Is it predictable? What happens when you put a lot of people together in a larger organization?

1 | Thinking About Economic Actors and Organizations

Economics is a *social* science—it is about people and about how we organize ourselves to provide the means for life and its flourishing. Ultimately, all economic behavior is human behavior. Sometimes institutional forces appear to take over (witness the tendency of some bureaucracies to expand over time), but if you look closely at any economic behavior, you will find that it is ultimately determined by human motivations. This fact has been widely recognized by economists, but there is a continuing debate (to which we will return at the end of the chapter) over whether it is useful to make a particular set of simplifying assumptions about human motivations and behavior—namely, that human beings can be understood as simply pursuing self-interested goals—or whether it is important to consider additional reasons advanced to explain why and how people engage in maintaining resources or producing, distributing, and consuming goods and services.

The psychologist Daniel Kahneman, a 2002 winner of the Nobel Memorial Prize in economics, believes that a more sophisticated view of human motivations is necessary in order to understand, for example, the activities that lead to stock market bubbles and other investment behavior and the different ways in which people react to good and bad economic fortune. In this chapter we will cite another psychologist and Nobel laureate in economics—Herbert Simon—who also proposed a more complex view of the motivations behind economic behavior. Of course, this is a textbook in economics, not in psychology, but, as the economics Nobel committee has recognized, our study becomes much more relevant—and therefore more interesting—when it makes use of findings from other social sciences. In fact, you may find yourself thinking about other courses you have taken as you progress through this book. Political science, history, sociology, and philosophy all connect with economics. And we attempt here to apply those connections in a way that will broaden your view of what economics means in the real world.

As a student of economics, on your next visit home you may find yourself having to explain that this course is not concerned only with business entities that interact through exchanges of money. Recent statistics suggest that about half the students who take a typical introductory economics course will probably become—or already are—business majors. If you are among this group, your further studies will teach you to think from a business perspective and to consider how business organizations can best be managed, mostly for the purpose of producing profits.

But business majors, as well as other students, are encouraged to take courses in economics in order to learn about some aspects of the broader context within which business operates. Businesses are not alone in addressing the essential economic questions: "What will be produced and maintained?" "How?" and "For whom?"

In providing this broader context, we will first discuss some basic assumptions about human motivation and behavior. Then we will consider the various ways in which people can coordinate their activities to form economic organizations. At the end of the chapter we will compare this kind of "contextual" economics with a narrower view that draws less on the other social sciences.

2 | Motivation and Behavior

What motivates people, and how do these motivations translate into economic behavior? Economists generally make an assumption of **purposeful behavior**, or **instrumental behavior**. Such behavior is motivated by particular goals, and actions are undertaken as means to those ends. Most often, we assume that these goals are conscious and—at least from a person's own perspective—are intended to advance individual and/or social well-being. Although there are situations in which people act randomly, unconsciously, or out of an intent to harm others, economic theory has been developed largely in relation to conscious, purposive behavior. With a few important exceptions, to be noted in this chapter and elsewhere, this text will retain that emphasis.

purposeful (instrumental) behavior: actions taken with the expectation that these acts will lead to desired goals

2.1 | Intrinsic and Extrinsic Motivations

A first distinction to be drawn concerning goals is to note that people act from both extrinsic and intrinsic motivations.

We say that an action is **extrinsically motivated**, or motivated by "outside" forces, to the extent that the action is taken for a reason that lies outside of a person's character and his or her relation to the activity itself. Usually these reasons have to do with either reward or punishment. Money is obviously one of the primary extrinsic motivators. You may work, run a business, make a deal, or study economics because you believe these activities will bring you financial rewards.

Besides having financial motivations, people may also undertake activities because they fear the consequences of doing otherwise or in the hope of gaining some other extrinsic reward, such as high social status or increased power. You may produce a superior economics term paper, for example, because you fear your parents' reaction if you do poorly this semester or because they have promised you a nice trip if you do well. A government official may decline a bribe out of fear of going to jail. Business leaders may seek the power and status that come with a larger firm size.

extrinsic motivation: impetus to perform an activity that arises from reasons "outside" the person and the activity, such as doing something to obtain a reward in terms of money, status, or power, or to avoid punishment

incentive: a reward or punishment that motivates action

People frequently use extrinsic motivators to try to change the behavior of others. Economists talk about the various **incentives** set up by systems of reward and punishment. Employers offer monetary bonuses or "employee of the week" certificates to encourage good work. The government offers tax rebates to encourage energy conservation and fines the worst polluters. Your university may try to discourage underage drinking by imposing monetary fines or other penalties, or it may tie scholarship money to maintenance of a certain grade point average. In all these cases, the organizations are relying on monetary or nonmonetary incentives to change behaviors by acting on extrinsic motivation.

Traditionally, economists have paid a great deal of attention to incentives, and to financial incentives in particular. Because of this emphasis, economists are often able to point out where incentives exist and may have effects on behavior, even when the incentives have been created *unintentionally* and have gone unnoticed by other analysts.

For example, suppose a civic group is concerned about teens who don't finish high school, and so it creates a center for dropouts. The center offers dropouts individualized instruction, paid child care, and a weekly monetary stipend. The civic group's intent, of course, is simply to support dropouts and help them finish their schooling. But what *incentives* does this create for those students who are still in school but are considering dropping out? These current students will have an increased *incentive to drop out* in order to qualify for the center's greater benefits. In this case, creating a program to solve a problem could cause the problem to increase! The civic group might do more good by devoting some of its resources to improving the support services provided at the school itself.

The attention that economists give to incentives can play a valuable role in efforts to evaluate the wisdom of various policies, whether in communities, businesses, or elsewhere. We need to put the focus on extrinsic motivations and financial incentives in context, however, by also considering other reasons for people's actions.

intrinsic motivation: impetus to perform an activity that arises from reasons "inside" the person, such as doing something for enjoyment or adherence to one's ethical values or sense of identity

People are **intrinsically motivated**, or motivated by "inside" forces, to the extent that the reason for action lies in the person or in the activity itself. Intrinsic motivations include direct enjoyment of the activity, as well as ethical values such as honesty and loyalty. They also involve issues of identity, such as the feeling of "who you are" or "what our organization is about." Intrinsic motivations are what make you *want* to do something, without regard to rewards or threats from the outside.

You may produce a superior economics term paper because you enjoy learning or because you feel you "owe it to yourself" always to do your best. A government employee may resist a bribe because it is the honest thing to do. A company leader may authorize an aggressive action less out of concern with profits or status than because of the personal enjoyment he or she gets from feeling smarter than the competition, or he or she may decline to market a harmful good because doing so would go against the company's core values. Most people choose their work partly on the basis of extrinsic motivations such as money and status but also partly on the basis of intrinsic motivations concerning what they like to do, what kind of person they want to be, and what kind of mark they want to leave on the world. Often both extrinsic and intrinsic motivations are at work.

To some extent, intrinsic motivations can also be used to influence the behavior of others, although this is not as straightforward as simple reward and punishment. Some employers are able to encourage superior work effort by creating an atmosphere in which employees feel that they are valued contributors to a socially important project. When employees are intrinsically motivated to want to make a social contribution, the need for external rewards and punishments declines.

At least one college claims to have found a new way to discourage student drinking—an approach based on the fact that some drinking is motivated by an intrinsic desire to identify with "the crowd." Anonymous surveys tend to show heavy or binge drinking to be much less popular than students *think* it is. Publishing the results of

Normative Interpretations of Motivations

Some people have the impression that doing something for extrinsic reasons (such as money or status) is always bad or at least not praiseworthy. If motivation by profit or the regard of others plays a part in someone's behavior, is that person selfish, materialistic, and vain? Maybe not. Money is necessary for life in a contemporary economy. People who look for higher-paying jobs or more profitable markets in order to support themselves and their loved ones need not be selfishly motivated. Likewise, people who seek some amount of status—say, by asking for a job promotion—may just be making a reasonable request based on their valuable contributions. Excessive seeking of wealth and fame can certainly cause problems, but some amount of money and social respect are necessary for living in this world.

On the other hand, are intrinsic motivations (such as enjoyment, ethics, and identity) always good? People who look down on extrinsic motivations often think so. But let's consider an example. Some racists are intrinsically motivated. They discriminate, or even engage in violence, on the basis of their belief that excluding people of another race from jobs or neighborhoods is "the right thing to do."

Some conservative economists have argued that paying *greater* attention to financial gain would improve society. In a case of such racial discrimination in housing, it is easy to see their point: A landlord interested only in the color of money won't worry about whether the hand holding the cash is black or white. (Discriminatory acts can also be motivated by financial gain, of course, so this argument should not be taken too far.)

Both intrinsic and extrinsic motivations are important in economic life, and both can serve to promote social well-being or its opposite. ◁

these surveys, and thus changing the perception of what "the crowd" is doing, has led, it is claimed, to decreases in alcohol violations at Hobart and William Smith College. Armed with better information, students apparently make more responsible choices on the basis of their own desire to "fit in," even if extrinsic rewards and punishments remain unchanged.[1]

2.2 | Self-Interest, Altruism, and the Common Good

Whose interests do people care about? In a famous statement from *The Wealth of Nations*, written in 1776, Adam Smith declared, "It is not from the benevolence of the butcher, the brewer, or the baker that we expect our dinner, *but from their regard to their own interest*."[2]

self-interested motivation: motive for action based on the goal of improving one's own well-being

Many people coming after Smith have interpreted these words in a special way. They have assumed that if people in an exchange economy just follow their own **self-interest**, acting in the way that most benefits them as individuals, the goal of societal well-being will follow automatically. Many economists read Smith's words out of context and see them as clever proof that there is no need for people to think "benevolently" about each other or about society as a whole. Smith's words have been used as an ethical justification for following unfettered economic self-interest.

Adam Smith, among others, would have disagreed with this extreme view. (His other most notable work, *The Theory of Moral Sentiments*, addressed at great length the need to take into account the welfare of others). Exchange may fail to promote social

---

[1] This program and the press coverage it has received are described at **http://academic.hws.edu/alcohol/**.

[2] *The Wealth of Nations*, 1776, Book I, Chapter 2. Emphasis in original.

well-being for a number of reasons. People may be badly informed. The situation may entail positive and negative externalities not taken into account in individual self-interested decisions. And, as pointed out by all major philosophical and religious teachings, purely self-interested decisions are often at odds with basic ethical concerns.

altruistic motivation: motive for action that reflects concern only with the well-being of others

The opposite of pure self-interest is pure **altruism**. In this case, you simply want to help other people, with no thought about yourself. A soldier who throws himself on a grenade to save his comrades, and a mother who pushes her child out of the way of an oncoming car and is crushed herself, are classic—and extreme—examples of altruism.

motivation according to interest in the common good: motive for action with the goal of improving social well-being, including one's own well-being

Perhaps more relevant to economics is the fact that much economic behavior may be motivated by a desire to advance the **common good**—the general good, of which one's own interests are a part. Striving to advance the common good means seeing your own well-being as connected to the larger well-being of society. For example, even as children we find that learning to share, rather than always grabbing or whining for the best toy, leads to more prolonged games and a much more pleasant social environment for everyone—including us. Social theorist Howard Margolis points out that, in many social situations, people act according to a rule he calls being "neither selfish nor exploited." That is, people are often willing to participate in the creation of social benefits as long as they feel that others are also contributing.

More and more, economists are realizing that a well-functioning economy cannot rely only on self-interest; it also depends on a culture that includes taking into account the common good. Without such values as honesty, for example, even the simplest transaction would require elaborate safeguards or policing.

If everyone in business cheated whenever they thought they could get away with it, business would grind to a halt. If everyone in the government took bribes, meaningful governance would disappear. In addition, people have to learn to work together to overcome problems of externalities. In regard to children or the ill, who cannot take care of themselves through market exchange, some "benevolence" is obviously in order as well. Self-interest may indeed, in some cases, serve the common good, but it cannot be the only motor for an economy that serves the well-being goals of the society. Indeed, self-interest alone cannot even be efficient. Imagine if you were afraid to put down your money before having in your hands the merchandise you wished to purchase—and the merchant was afraid that as soon as you had what you wanted you would run out of the store without paying. Such a situation would require police in every store—but what if the police themselves operated with no ethic of honesty?

Fortunately, recent experimental research on human behavior demonstrates that people really *do* pay attention to social norms, and they are willing to reward those who follow the norms and to punish people who violate them, even when this has a cost in terms of their narrow self-interest.

In the "Ultimatum Game," for example, two people are told that they will be given a sum of money, say $20, to share. One person gets to propose a way of splitting the sum. For example, this first person may offer to share $10 with the second person, or only $8 or $1, and plan to keep the rest. The second person can't offer any input to this decision but can only decide whether to accept the offer or reject it. If the second person rejects the offer, both people will walk away empty-handed. If the offer is accepted, they get the money and split it as planned.

If the two individuals act only from narrow financial self-interest, then the first person should offer the second person the smallest possible amount—say $1—in order to keep the most for himself or herself. The second person should accept this offer because, from the point of view of pure financial self-interest, $1 is better than nothing.

In fact, researchers find that deals that vary too far from a 50/50 split tend to be rejected. People would rather walk away with nothing than be treated in a way they perceive to be unfair. In the context of social relations, even the most selfish person will gain by serving the *common* good and thus walking away with somewhere around $10, rather than just looking at his or her own potential *personal* gain and quite possibly ending up with nothing.

Concern for the atmosphere we all breathe and concern about poverty that contributes to crime and violence are examples of real-world cases in which serving the common good may lead to better living for yourself and your family. In such cases, the assertion attributed to Adam Smith should be turned around: Concern for the common good may be the best way of serving your own self-interest.

2.3 | Behavior: Habit, Constraint, or Choice?

What did you eat at your last meal? *Why did you eat that, in particular?* Because economists want to explain economic behavior, we need to pay attention to why people act the way they do. Take a minute and think about your answer to the second question.

Perhaps your first thought was that you had "the usual"—you ate those particular foods because that is what you usually eat. In this case, we would say that your behavior arose largely from **habit**. Behavior that arises from habit or custom tends to change quite slowly and is often related to social roles, family, cultural institutions, and the like. For example, your eating habits are probably related to your particular age, sex, and ethnic background and to where you grew up. Habitual behavior is often performed repetitively and almost automatically, without conscious thought. You may think that the only normal breakfast in the world is cereal and milk. Or you may think that the only normal breakfast is rice and fish. In neither case have you given a lot of thought to what you eat.

Perhaps instead you explained your eating in terms of "what the cafeteria was serving" or "what I could afford." In this case, we would say that your behavior reflected the **constraints** that you faced. You may have wanted to eat something quite different, but you faced limits on your behavior. In a small way, someone else had power over you. The cafeteria manager's decisions strongly determined your behavior. Or you knew you would get into trouble if you left a restaurant or grocery store without paying. In this case, the level of your economic resources was important to your behavior. The more you have—in terms of time, money, and transportation—the more you can go where you want and eat whatever you want, freer of constraints.

Last, did you think carefully about what you were going to eat, making conscious choices between one item and another, on the basis of your personal taste preferences, your goals concerning weight, and/or what you know about nutrition? This would be an example of **choice behavior**, in which the important factors are your motivations, your knowledge, and your decision-making capabilities.

Actual behavior may arise from habit, constraint, choice, or combinations of all three factors.

2.4 | Rationality, Goals, and Information

Traditionally, economists have tended to be especially interested in choice behavior. Hence the question "How do people choose?" arises. Economists generally assume that people have the capacity to make **rational choices**.

In common speech, when we use such terms as *rational* and *reasonable* to describe an action, we mean both that the *goal* of the action is rational and that the *process* leading to the action was intelligent, appropriate, and thoughtful. It is not particularly rational, in the sense of "sane," for example, for a person to base all his actions on the goal of being a rock star if he has no talent. Nor is it rational to have a goal of committing a heinous murder. These goals would generally be considered irrational because they are not related to achievable states of personal and social well-being. There are also cases where an action is judged irrational even though the goal is reasonable. For example, it is not irrational for a person to have a goal of maintaining a healthy and attractive body

habitual behavior: repetitive behavior that involves minimal thought and is often based on social custom

constrained behavior: behavior of a person subject to limits set by others, who usually have some power over the person

choice behavior: behavior selected by a person from a range of alternatives, generally involving the person's conscious deliberation

rational choices: thoughtful choices that would normally be expected to move people toward their goals

weight. Yet a young woman suffering from the mental illness of anorexia may act on the basis of a belief that her body looks grotesquely fat, although in fact she is emaciated. The anorexic's weight loss may be based on the underlying goal of wanting to be attractive, but in fact her judgment is distorted by a neurotic perception.

Do choices that are rational, in the sense of deriving from a thoughtful and appropriate process, *always* lead toward the desired goals? Perhaps not. Because the information on which we base our choices is imperfect, and because the processes of human reasoning and group decision making are also often imperfect, we can only say that rational choices would normally *be expected to* move individuals and organizations toward their goals. Rationality means that when faced with significant decisions, people weigh the costs and benefits of alternative actions, relative to their goals—not that people always make perfect decisions.

For example, after doing the necessary research, a company may rationally decide to manufacture a new line of electronics, believing that this will improve the financial condition of the firm. However, without the managers of the company knowing it, someone else may have just invented another product that will make this firm's new product immediately obsolete. The company's decision will be unfortunate, in retrospect. But it was not *irrational* if it was based on good reasoning and on all the information that the managers could reasonably be expected to seek out and take into account. The problem was that the information the company had was incomplete.

2.5 | Optimization Versus Bounded Rationality

We have worded our discussion of rationality rather carefully so far, trying not to claim too much. But much more ambitious claims have sometimes been made, making this a rather contentious topic. In particular, the term *rational behavior* is used in the traditional model, as we will soon see, to mean behavior that *best* moves a person toward his or her goals. This kind of behavior is called **optimizing**.

optimize: to choose, out of all available options, that option which best achieves what is desired

In 1978 Herbert Simon won the Nobel Memorial Prize in economics by zeroing in on the question of information, with some surprising results. He pointed out that optimization is normally not possible for human beings, because it requires making the best decision out of the entire universe of possible choices. *Universe* here does not mean planets and stars, but rather the largest possible imaginable set of choices. Your "universe" of possible breakfasts, for example, includes everything from cereal to snake meat.

Under most circumstances it is not feasible to gather all the information that one would need in order to identify the entire range of possibilities. Could someone at least identify the optimal point at which to cease gathering additional information? Simon showed that complete knowledge is required even in order to identify that optimal point. Moreover, determining what additional information might be out there, and then gathering it, can be very costly in time, effort, and money. Accordingly, Simon maintained, people rarely optimize. Instead they do what he called **satisficing**; they choose a level of outcome that would be satisfactory and then seek an option that at least reaches that standard.

satisfice: to choose a level of outcome that would be satisfactory and then seek an option that at least reaches that standard

Satisficing can be done in a way that resembles the search for an optimal outcome. If an individual finds that the "satisfactory" level was set too low, a search for options that meet that level will result in a solution more quickly than expected, or perhaps even multiple solutions; the level may then be adjusted to a tougher standard. Conversely, if the level is set too high, a long search will yield nothing, and the satisficer may lower his or her expectations for the outcome. Even with such adjustments, however, satisficing is not the same as optimizing.

melioration: starting from the present level of achievement and continuously attempting to do better

Another explanation for behavior has been called **meliorating**, which may be defined as starting from the present level of achievement and continuously attempting to do better. A simple example is the fisherman who has found a whole school of haddock but only wants to keep one for his supper. When he catches the second fish he compares it to the first one, keeps the larger, and throws the other back. At the end of the day, the fish he takes home will be the largest of all those caught. (An attempt to perform the same exercise with choosing friends, instead of fish, may not work out so well. Why not?)

One result of using melioration as the real-world substitute for theoretical optimization is its implication that *history matters*: People view each successive choice in relation to their previous experience. It is commonly observed, for example, that people are reluctant to accept a situation they perceive as inferior to previous situations. This psychological "path dependence" (that is, the idea that where you are going depends on where you have been) is relevant to feelings about rising prices, and even more so to attitudes toward declining wages.

bounded rationality: the identification of some arbitrarily defined subset of information to consider when making decisions

Satisficing and meliorating may both be included under the term **bounded rationality**. The general idea is that, without surveying all possible options, people adopt some more-or-less arbitrarily defined subset of the universe to consider. Usually these subsets consist of the options immediately evident, along with others specifically sought out through some simple decision rule. For example, when deciding what to spend her money on, an individual may at one time confine her consideration to "major expenditures," such as a college education or an apartment; at another time she might contemplate "expenditures on food"; and at another time she might sit down to work out budget categories, pondering, for example, "How much should I spend on food each month, how much should I devote to entertainment, and how much shall I set aside for a major need like an apartment?" In your breakfast decision, you probably limited your choices to a narrow subset of possible foods.

The concept of bounded rationality thus limits the universe to which decision making is to be applied. Within this limited universe, processes such as satisficing and meliorating are rational behaviors that would normally be expected to move people toward their goals.

2.6 | Now or Later?

One last dimension of motivation and behavior is crucially important. What time frame do people consider when they have an opportunity to make significant choices about how they are going to behave?

high time discount rate: the economist's phrase for describing a strong preference for present benefits over those that might be enjoyed in the future

At one extreme, you probably know someone who has the attitude "Life is short, and tomorrow is uncertain, so let's have a good time now." Economists would tend to say that this person has a very **high time discount rate**, meaning that in his or her mind, future benefits are very much discounted or diminished when weighed against the pleasures of today. Such an individual tends to save little, spends a lot, and does not put much effort into worrying about the future.[3]

low time discount rate: the economist's phrase for describing a strong concern with future benefits, even if getting them is costly in the present

You might also know people who seem to live by the attitude "I've got to work hard and prepare now; enjoying myself will have to wait for later." Economists would say that people like this have very **low time discount rates** if by their current work they are gaining benefits for tomorrow. The later benefits loom large (that is, are *not* "discounted") in their decisions. Such individuals tend to scrimp and save and expend a lot of effort planning for the future.

Time discount rates are important in all sorts of situations. Economists usually assume that anyone who invests in a college education has a relatively low time discount rate, because present "pain" is involved in forgoing income or relaxation in order to study for some expected future gain. Company leaders with high time discount rates may concentrate on making this quarter's financial statement look good, whereas those with more concern about the future will look toward longer-term goals. In deciding on

---

[3] The technical meaning of *discount rate* will be discussed in Chapter 14.

Can Habits Be Rational?

Earlier, we contrasted acting from choice with acting largely out of habit. Can it be *rational* to have a habit? The answer is "Maybe."

Some habits work in opposition to rational choice. Your habits of eating, for example, or smoking may not be in line with what you might rationally choose if you were to compile the relevant information and then sit down and carefully weigh the costs and benefits of your decisions. Your diet might be higher in fat or more boring than serves your goals. Or you might be in the habit of studying a particular way even though, if you took the time to explore, you might find another method that would serve you much better. Your life could be improved by making such an effort at deliberate, rational evaluation.

On the other hand, very few people are going to ask for a full nutritional breakdown of every bite that goes into their mouths or spend all their time studying techniques for studying. It would, in fact, be *irrational* to go to such extremes. Why? Gathering information and then processing it by evaluating all the options is itself a time-consuming task. Habits can at times be a rational way of dealing with these costs of making conscious, deliberate decisions.

For example, you might try to maximize your progress toward your health goals by having extended consultations with a dietician and following a rigid nutrition plan. But you might rationally move in the direction of meeting your health goals—while still moving toward your other goals as well—by simply adopting a habit such as eating more fruit.

environmental regulations, people working at government agencies are forced to make decisions about how much weight to give the welfare of future generations. The lower the adopted discount rate, the more important safeguarding the well-being of future generations appears.

There is no one "right" time discount rate. An extreme disregard for the future is probably irrational in most cases. But in some circumstances—say, for a person who has been diagnosed with a fatal disease or who faces a high probability of being killed in street violence—it may be understandable.

Extreme concern for the future is also irrational if it means that an individual never, during an entire lifetime, gets around to enjoying the benefits of his or her labors. However, strong arguments can be made for taking the future very seriously when discussing actions with significant multigenerational consequences, such as environmental policies. The question of "now or later" is important in many economic decisions.

Discussion Questions

1. Suppose you are looking for a job. Compare what you might end up with if your behavior primarily reflects each of the following constellations of characteristics:
   a. Extrinsic motivations, self-interest, constraint, and a high time discount rate
   b. Intrinsic motivations, interest in the common good, choice, and a low time discount rate
2. Would you describe yourself, in general, as a person who tries to optimize, as a satisficer, or as a meliorator? Would you say that your own educational history (what schools you've gone to, what subjects you've taken, etc.) has been guided by *rational choice*? That is, has it been characterized by information gathering and deliberation? Or have you tended to rely more on habit or felt bound by constraints? Or has your behavior sometimes even been random?

3 | The Nature of Economic Organizations

Very few people live as hermits, completely providing for themselves all the food, clothing, and shelter they need. For the vast majority of us, economic life involves a great deal of coordination with other people—in our households, communities, schools, workplaces, markets, and governments. Yet such coordination of economic activity does not simply "happen." Somehow a group of people, all with their own personal needs and opinions, must coordinate their activities in order to achieve resource maintenance and the production, distribution, and consumption of goods and services.

How can we talk about "behavior" and "motivations" when we move beyond the case of an individual human person to cases of more complex organizations? What are some of the main modes by which people coordinate their activities inside economic organizations?

3.1 | Individual Economic Actors and Organizations

"Joe has decided to try for a pro baseball career."

"Worldcom Corporation acted unethically."

"The federal government decided not to regulate carbon emissions."

In these sentences, Joe, Worldcom, and "the federal government" are talked about as though each were a single, easily identifiable individual economic actor. In economics, as in common speech, we often find it convenient to talk about parts of the economic system this way. In effect, we pretend that large, complex organizations including corporations and governments are individual humans, with human-like motivations and human-like abilities to choose and act.

Does the statement about Worldcom Corporation, a company embroiled in infamous scandals at the turn of the century, mean that every employee of Worldcom acted unethically? Does the statement about the government mean that "the government" just sat down one day and made a decision about carbon regulations? Of course not. We observe outcomes (such as financial disasters or regulations) in the real world, but when we speak of these as being *actions* of individual economic *actors*, we are using mental concepts to simplify a complex situation.

Worldcom Corporation was in fact made up of numerous ownership interests, executives, managers, and employees involved in relationships with suppliers, creditors, and so on. The federal government in the United States is made up of legislative, executive, and judicial bodies involved in relationships with the electorate, lobbyists, campaign donors, contractors, foreign governments, and so on. Some individuals, such as CEOs (chief executive officers) or the U.S. president, have more power to influence action than others, but in contemporary complex organizations, any decision or action must involve the interaction and cooperation of many people.

A key to understanding the complex structures into which people organize themselves is to look for layered systems, in which some groupings are made up of smaller units but are simultaneously grouped together themselves to make a larger structure.

Consider Joe, for example, as an individual actor who belongs to the social organization of a baseball team. That team may be treated as a single unit—in economics we would call it an individual actor—in its relation to a larger organization, the league. The league, in turn, may be talked about as an individual actor in its relation to an even more comprehensive organization, the division, and so on up. An economist looking at broad patterns may lump baseball together with soccer, football, and other sports and talk about what the sports industry as a whole "thinks," "wants," or "has accomplished," as though the entire sports industry were also an individual.

These observations are reflected in two terms that are commonly used: *individual economic actor* and *organization.* In the example just given, a team or a league may be

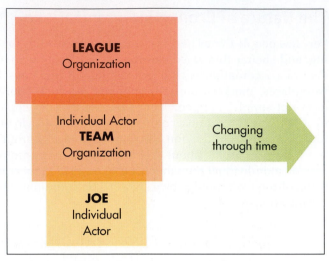

Figure 2.1 Individual Actors and Organizations
An entity can be both an individual actor and an organization.

economic organization: an entity that is made up of individual economic actors and sub-organizations, which may have common or conflicting interests

individual economic actor: an entity that is largely self-contained and acts as a unit

⊃ The individual actors and the sub-organizations within an economic organization may share common interests and/or they may have conflicting interests.

custom: body of traditions, habits, and expectations about what it is proper and necessary for people to do in given circumstances

⊃ The kinds of care given to children and the elderly may vary greatly with social and family customs. Gift giving on holidays—as evidenced by the big boom in retail sales just before Christmas in many countries where the population is predominantly Christian—is strongly governed by social customs of reciprocity.

understood as an **economic organization** to the extent that it is made up of individual economic actors and sub-organizations, which have a variety of sometimes complementary and sometimes conflicting interests. Each of these, however, is also an **individual economic actor** to the extent that it is largely self-contained and acts as a unit. Figure 2.1 shows how a team, for example, may have such a dual nature.

Systems of actors and organizations are generally not rigid and fixed. Rather, the different levels may influence each other, and the system itself may change over time, as suggested by the overlaps and the arrow in Figure 2.1. The various levels of social organization affect some aspects of Joe's life, defining what rules he plays by, how and where he practices, and how he develops as an athlete over time. Joe may, either alone or with his peers, also have some effect on the organizations. For example, he might challenge racial barriers or the existing parental leave policies of his pro team and its league, prompting changes in these organizations over time.

How do economic organizations coordinate the (perhaps conflicting) interests of their members? Social scientists have identified four major modes of organization: custom, consent, administration, and exchange.

3.2 | Economic Organization by Custom

To the extent that an organization is coordinated by **custom**, answers to economic questions of what, how, and for whom are determined by tradition and habit, perhaps passed down through generations, as well as by beliefs about obligation (what one has a duty to do) and by reciprocity (what a person owes to others). Examples include workplaces where job assignments are determined by traditional age and gender roles, and extended families in which more well-off members feel obliged to make loans to poorer relatives. Although we often think of economic organization by custom as characteristic of "primitive" societies, even in more complex societies, people often act out of beliefs about their place in the world, along with tradition and habit.

Organization by custom is good at giving people a highly defined sense of their place in the natural and social world, and it may reinforce ties of intimacy and mutuality *within* groups that share a set of norms. But it also can be rigid and constraining. It may deny individual freedom and make it difficult to form good social relations *across* groups (for example, religious or ethnic groups) that have different customs.

Organization by custom plays an important role in coordinating economic activities. This knitting cooperative in Ecuador allows women who traditionally knitted at home for their families to earn a cash income by knitting for sale. Though the knitting is now directed toward a market, it is still being done using the customary methods, patterns, and group of people—women.

3.3 | Economic Organization by Consent

organization by consent: agreement among a group of people reached through discussion or negotiation

In **organization by consent**, individuals consciously pose the economic questions and get together to agree on how to answer them. They talk, they negotiate, perhaps they bargain, and at last they come to an agreement to which, in the ideal case, all can consent. Some families operate this way—at least among the adult members. On a large scale, however, getting everyone together for consensus-based decision making is not practical. Democratic decision making, usually including some discussion and then decision making by majority vote, is often the closest a society can get to economic (and political) organization by consent. People consent not to every decision but to the general idea of going along with the majority. Decisions among corporate managers about what to produce, decisions by groups of workers on whether to organize, and decisions by legislators on how to raise and spend government funds are often made by democratic means.

⬙ Examples of a face-to-face, fully consensus-based economic system are few. They have included—at least for a time—some of the collective kibbutzim in Israel and some religious communities in the United States.

Consensual decision making allows for more flexibility and individual freedom than does organization by custom. The process of hearing and being heard during deliberation can help to create social bonds and ties of affection and reciprocity that transcend cultural boundaries. It can, however, be very time-consuming to reach decisions in this way, and it may be hard for everyone to become well enough informed to contribute intelligently to a decision. The requirements for meeting time and information gathering and assimilation may impose high transaction costs on achieving consensual decisions.

3.4 | Economic Organization by Administrative Agency

organization by administration: a means of organizing an economic unit that gives decision-making authority to some person or agency

Another way to organize an economy is to give the authority for decision making to some **administrative** agency, which then is in charge of answering the questions of what, how, and for whom. The executive branch of the U.S. government, for example, comprises many bureaucracies charged with carrying out the production and distribution plans approved by Congress. Military organizations, similar to the "command," or Communist, countries that existed prior to the breakup of the Soviet Union, organize much of their economic activity via directives from a central authority. In families organized on a patriarchal model, the father plays the role of head administrator. In many

Organization by consent means that people meet together, formally or informally, to discuss how economic activities are best coordinated. This group of doctors and nurses is meeting over lunch to discuss how work is going on their hospital unit. Some executives and managers spend their entire workday planning how to get people to agree on and support a coordinated plan of action.

▶ The size of an administrative economic organization may be limited by the amount of information it can handle. Improved bureaucratic or technological methods of information handling can increase the size to which such an organization can grow.

workplaces, administrative hierarchies mean that directives are handed down from bosses to managers and from managers to workers.

Administrative organizations with special access to information, and the ability to process it, are sometimes able to make better-informed decisions than individuals would. Decisions on pollution control, for example, may require extensive scientific study. Sometimes, however, the cost of gathering information for administrative decision making is too great. For example, in the former Soviet Union, central bureaus had to keep track of all the needs for shoes, and all the resources that go into shoes, for the entire country—an enormous task.

3.5 | Economic Organization by Exchange

Organization by voluntary exchange can answer the three economic questions in a highly decentralized manner. Economic actors make individual decisions to trade the resources under their control for the things they want to get. If you are good at braiding cornrows, for example, you might fix your roommate's hair in exchange for part of his or her pizza. You and your roommate each know your own needs and desires and engage in such a trade when you see it as in your interest to do so. No custom dictates that you must do this, and no community meeting or central directive is involved.

Sometimes goods and services are directly exchanged, as in the hairdo-for-pizza example. More commonly, in many contemporary societies, exchanges are mediated by money. Professional hairdressers exchange their services for money and in turn go exchange their money for pizza. (This saves them from having to chase around trying to find someone who both wants a hairdo and has a pizza!)

Among all the ways of answering the three economic questions, exchange allows for the greatest individual freedom in making choices, minimizes the need for time-consuming community discussions, and minimizes the amount of information that must be compiled centrally. However, like the other systems of economic organization, exchange has negative as well as positive features.

One major drawback to an exchange system is that it depends greatly on individual decision making, and there is nothing in it that necessarily requires individuals to consider the accumulated experience expressed as ethics or traditions or to engage in careful deliberation. Therefore, individual decisions may not always be the most wise, even for the person involved. Reasonable adults are usually the best judges of their own individual interests, but there are times—especially when people are tempted by addictive drugs or when they have been misinformed—when peoples' individual choices can decrease their own well-being.

Another serious drawback is that because individual voluntary exchange arrangements tend to reflect mainly the immediate interests of the economic actors involved, they may be a serious source of "negative externalities." Perhaps everyone else on your hallway becomes nauseated by the smell of the anchovy pizza you share with your roommate—an outcome that could have been avoided by a rule against bringing in smelly foods or by consensual decision making involving the larger affected group.

Finally, voluntary exchange is generally considered inappropriate for some areas of social relations for ethical reasons. Consider what would happen if *all* social organization were left to individual, voluntary exchange. Without the usual customary regard for the sanctity of human life, babies could be bought and sold. Rich people in need of organ transplants could buy hearts and livers (while poorer patients would be out of luck). Polling places could become markets for the sale of votes to the highest bidder. Professors could auction off grades. Most people would consider such a world to be lacking in important moral dimensions.

markets: social organizations set up to facilitate exchange

Markets are social organizations set up to facilitate exchange. They can be crudely defined as places where people go to buy and sell things. Economists like to classify markets into categories on the basis of what is being exchanged; hence they speak of labor markets, product markets, and financial markets. Sometimes markets take up specific, physical locations, as do a local farmer's market, the Chicago Board of Trade, and the Tokyo Stock Exchange. In the way economists talk about markets, though, the "place" is often only metaphorical. When you fill out a job application, for example, an economist would say you are "in the labor market" even if you think you are at Sal's Delicatessen. Markets, then, are more generally identified as the ways in which societies are organized by structures and customs of interaction to facilitate exchange (for example, "If you want a job, fill out an application"). Innovations such as the rise of credit card use and e-commerce are new forms of social organization designed to make voluntary exchanges even quicker and easier. We discuss markets in greater detail in Chapter 3.

market failure: when markets yield inefficient or inappropriate outcomes

Clearly, although a system of voluntary exchange has strong advantages in some areas, it cannot solve all economic problems. Economists sometimes use the term **market failure** to refer to a situation in which a market form of organization would lead to inefficient or harmful results. Traditionally, economists have considered negative externalities to be the major source of market failure. The problems of unwise individual decision-making and ethical implications, as just discussed, as well as the existence of transaction costs and public goods, as discussed in Chapter 1, can also lead to market failure. In Chapter 12, we will see how market "power" can be a source of inequity and inefficiency in exchange relations, as well.

The world we actually inhabit consists of a mixture of the four types of economic organization. The success of such a mixed system depends heavily on striking the right balance so that the different types of organization are brought to bear where they work most effectively to enhance present and future well-being.

Discussion Questions

1. As individual students, you are part of the "education sector" of the national economy. Using Figure 2.1 as a model, diagram some of the layers of economic organization that exist in between you and the education sector as a whole.

2. Sometimes economists or newspaper reporters will refer to a region as having a healthy economy, as though the economy were a person who could be ill or injured or vigorous and fit. Is the regional economy being treated as an "actor" or as an "organization" in such a case? Is it possible for an economy to be "healthy" while many people who are a part of it are not?

4 | Economic Actors in the Traditional Model

As we noted in Chapter 1, traditional economic theory focuses on a simple mechanical model of economic activity where the central economic actors are assumed to be profit-maximizing firms and utility-maximizing households. We present that model here, along with the assumptions behind it, and then show how this model differs from the broader "contextual" approach we emphasize in this textbook.

4.1 | Only Individual Actors

In the traditional neoclassical model of economic behavior, the economy is assumed to be made up *only* of individual economic actors. Firms are treated as though they simply and seamlessly absorb information, make decisions, and take action. Similarly, households are treated as though they are uncomplicated individual persons. Little attention is paid to the people and modes of organization—custom, consent, administration, or exchange—that make up these entities *as organizations*. Nor is much attention paid to any ambiguities or conflicts that might arise in coming to decisions or to how the entities might influence each other (for example, the effect of firms' advertising on households' preferences). And rather than envisioning layers of organizations mutually evolving over time, the traditional model portrays only well-defined entities interacting at arm's length.

4.2 | A Limited Set of Activities

The traditional model of the economy includes just three economic activities and makes strong and limiting assumptions about the relationships between activities and actors:

- Production, it assumes, is accomplished by firms.
- Exchange is performed in markets.
- Consumption is done by households.

circular flow diagram: a graphical representation of the traditional view that an economy consists of households and firms engaging in exchange

The **circular flow diagram** shown in Figure 2.2 illustrates the workings of the economy portrayed in this model.

As shown in Figure 2.2, the two actors (households and firms) are represented by rectangles, the activity of exchange by arrows. Flows of goods or services create the clockwise flow of the outer circle. Households are considered the ultimate owners of all assets. They supply their work effort and the services of other resources that they own (such as money and machinery) to firms via "factor markets." Firms are producers who take these inputs and produce output, which returns to the households via "product markets." Households are consumers, buying and using these products. Flows of monetary funds, exchanged for these goods and services, move in the opposite direction around the inner circle.

This diagram is useful in portraying in a very simplified way two of the major actors (households and firms) and three of the major activities (production, exchange, and consumption) involved in economic life. However, it is important to recognize that the model leaves out some key actors and activities.

For example, the natural resource base of the economy does not appear. Because of this, the circular flow diagram is a little like a "perpetual motion machine"; the economy it portrays can apparently keep on generating products forever without any inputs of materials or energy. The necessity of resource maintenance activities is ignored.

Likewise, the public purpose sphere is absent, as though an economy could function without laws, public goods, and other public services. Community groups in the core sphere are also absent. Although households appear, they are assumed not to be

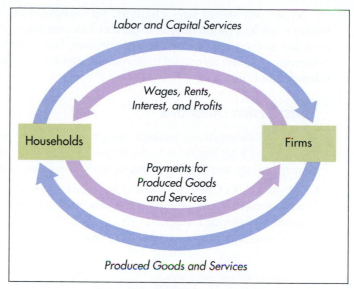

Figure 2.2 The Circular Flow Diagram
The circular flow diagram in economics represents a model in which there are only two kinds of economic actors.

involved in production activities. Transfers (a one-way form of distribution that we will study, along with two-way exchange, in Chapter 9) are not mentioned.[4]

4.3 | Restrictive Assumptions About Behavior

In the basic traditional model, actors are assumed to be extrinsically motivated. That is, people are assumed to work, produce, and engage in buying and selling purely for financial gain (unless explicitly noted otherwise). Purchases of goods and services for personal use are assumed to be made because these will bring consumers "utility," or satisfaction of their desires. Even today, the statement "He was economically motivated" is usually interpreted as meaning he was motivated by money or profit. These goals are taken for granted; in contrast to how we use the term *rationality* in common speech, economists do not question the rationality of agents' goals.

In a further simplification—which is enormously useful in facilitating mathematical modeling—it is assumed that all behavior is purely motivated by self-interest (except in rare and special cases, which are explicitly noted). The model also focuses on choice behavior and ignores behavior determined by habit or outside influence.

Finally, the model applies a rather extreme definition of rationality and an even more extreme assumption about the informational basis of choice making. Rather than construing rational processes just as something that helps actors move in the direction of their goals, the model assumes that actors behave with **perfect rationality**. Actors are assumed to choose the absolutely *best* action—the one that actually does maximize profit (the assumed goal of firms) or utility (the assumed goal of households). This idea of rationality can, in mathematical treatments, be reduced to precise statements derived from logic. The basic traditional model also assumes **perfect information**. In spite of Simon's work on satisficing in the late 1970s, it was only near the end of the 20th century that many economists began to consider more carefully the problems caused by costly and/or incomplete information.

▷ In the traditional neoclassical model, households and firms are assumed to engage in extrinsically motivated, self-interested, perfectly rational, and perfectly informed choice behavior.

perfect rationality: the assumption that actors can optimize, arriving at the decision that maximizes profit or utility

perfect information: the assumption that economic actors know with certainty everything that is important to their decision making

---

[4] In textbooks based solely on the traditional model, a rectangle representing the government would later be added to the circular flow diagram. Modifications of other limitations (such as adding consideration of imperfect information or enjoyment from work) might also be made in later chapters.

As we will see in later chapters, the assumptions of extrinsic motivation, self-interest, perfect rationality, and perfect information are simplifications that make it possible to construct many elegant theories. But in order to do justice to real-world economies, we will also need to develop analytical tools for cases where these assumptions do not hold.

Discussion Questions

1. Do you think explaining behavior using the traditional model would be easier or harder than using a broader set of tools? Do you think that using the traditional model would be more realistic and helpful, or less so, than using a broader set of tools?

2. Can you think of some instances of behavior for which the assumptions of the traditional model would fit fairly well? Can you think of other situations where the assumptions would obviously be inadequate? (Think about the activities you participate in yourself, in your home, workplace, community, religious institution, school, and so on.)

Review Questions

1. How does the study of economics differ from that of business?

2. What is the basic assumption that economists make about behavior?

3. What kind of motivation is manipulated by reward and punishment? What is the other main kind of motivation?

4. Does acting according to your own narrow self-interest always bring about the best result for you? For society? Explain.

5. There are three major factors that can be invoked to explain people's actual behavior. What are they?

6. What does it mean to say that someone chooses "rationally"?

7. How do economists describe people's preferences concerning current versus future benefits?

8. Can an entity be both an individual economic actor *and* an economic organization? How?

9. Name the four modes of economic organization.

10. Cite some advantages and disadvantages associated with each of the four modes of economic organization. When possible, specify transactions costs that may be associated with each one.

11. In what ways does the traditional model make simplifying assumptions about real-world complexities?

Exercises

1. For each of the following cases, describe the motivations for action using the terms *extrinsic* or *intrinsic*; *self-interest, altruism,* or *common good*; *habit, constraint,* or *choice*; and *high time discount rate* or *low time discount rate.* (More than one term in each group may apply.)

   a. Richard buys a lottery ticket every day because he hopes to win the jackpot and buy himself a nice car. His mother thinks he should be saving his money instead.

   b. Prashad had hoped to become an artist but had to drop out of art school for lack of funds. He is now opening a bicycle shop, hoping to earn enough money to bring a number of his relatives to the United States in the next 5 years.

    c. Olga's legal firm takes on one *pro bono* case per month (that is, a case where the client, who is usually poor, doesn't have to pay). Olga personally resents this "waste" of her firm's resources, but she is resigned to it because it is the custom of legal firms in her town. She also reasons that although she could save money right now by quietly refusing to take such cases, over time, as word got around, the reputation of her firm would become damaged and she would lose paying customers.

    d. An Le has decided to become an environmental activist, even though the pay is low and the hours long, because she can't stand being on the sidelines while, as she puts it, "future generations are in danger."

2. Describe a situation in which you made a decision you later regretted. Explain whether the decision was irrational or was rational but based on poor information.

3. Indicate whether each of the following economic activities is being organized by custom, consent, administration, or exchange.

    a. JoAnne and Jamal give each other presents on Valentine's Day.

    b. Pali rents a movie on DVD.

    c. Lynn, David, and Marika negotiate with each other about how to divide up tasks for their group history project.

    d. Frances's boss assigns her to write code for a new software product.

4. Thinking back over the last few days, give one example each of economic activities you engaged in that were organized by (a) custom, (b) consent, (c) administration, and (d) exchange. Remember that these need not involve money but must include decisions about *what, how,* and *for whom*. Think about real-life incidents where you acted from habit, came to an agreement, carried out orders, or made an exchange.

5. Suppose that two people who share a household are figuring out how to allocate between themselves the tasks of earning income, cooking, and cleaning. Think of how this economic problem might be solved using the four organizational methods. Give one example of each.

6. Chung notices that businesses are doing a bad job of restraining the amount of pollution they introduce into the water supplies. The best way to solve this, he argues, is to put the government in charge of regulating pollution levels. Discuss this issue. To what extent can "the government" be thought of as an economic actor, and to what extent is it an economic organization? What are its motivations? Whose interests will it represent?

7. Nicola notices that the government is doing a bad job of providing health education in the inner cities. The best way to solve this, she argues, is to put a business in charge of the job. Discuss this issue. To what extent can "a business" be thought of as an economic actor, and to what extent is it an economic organization? What are its motivations? Whose interests will it represent?

Part Two
Supply and Demand

Market Institutions

Chapter 3

The Internet auction site eBay, started in 1995, now has over 46 million registered users. The Grand Bazaar in Istanbul originated as a small warehouse in the 15th century, grew into a major trading hub, and is still today a mini-city of 4000 small shops. In much of sub-Saharan Africa, women are the primary merchants of agricultural products for domestic consumption, selling from stands or blankets set up in open places in villages and towns. Markets, it seems, are (nearly) everywhere.

1 | The Meaning of Markets

Markets are social organizations set up to facilitate distribution by exchange. Some forms of markets have been part of human society for millennia, but they have become an increasingly significant mode of economic organization in recent centuries. Some people say that we live nowadays in a "market society" and that the breakup of Communist rule in the former Soviet Union and Eastern Europe proves the "victory of markets."

When people talk about markets, they may be referring to a number of different meanings of the word, from very concrete to very abstract. Unfortunately (for students), academic economics has sometimes leaned too heavily on the abstractions. To remedy this, the present chapter examines markets "in context." First we will look at markets in historical context, examining how they came into being and why they increased in importance as a form of economic organization. Next, we will look at markets in their institutional context, seeing what sorts of organizations, rules, and forms of social capital are necessary for them to exist and to function well. We will also look at markets in social and environmental context, examining the extent to which emphasizing markets as a form of social organization improves or detracts from well-being. The chapter concludes with definitions of some terms that are frequently used to describe specific market structures.

In the language of economics, the word *market* is used in several different ways, and the appropriate meaning must be gleaned from the context in which it appears. We will start with the most concrete definition and move toward the more abstract.

1.1 | Markets as Places to Buy and Sell

market *(first meaning)*: a physical place where there is a reasonable expectation of finding both buyers and sellers for the same product or service

(second meaning): an institution that brings buyers and sellers into communication with each other, structuring and coordinating their actions

The most concrete and commonsense definition of a **market** is that it is a physical *location*—a place where people go to buy and sell things. This is historically appropriate: Markets such as the Grand Bazaar and the produce stands in an African village have flourished for ages as meeting places for people who wish to make exchange transactions. The same criterion applies today, even when the "market" has become a shopping center or mall, with many retail stores sharing one huge building, or a stock or commodity exchange, where brokers stand on a crowded floor and wave signals to each other. A market, as suggested by these examples, can be defined as a physical place where there is a reasonable expectation of finding both buyers and sellers for the same product or service.

1.2 | Markets as Social Institutions

The term *market* can also refer to patterns of economic behavior that are not confined to a single location. A more general definition might be that a market is an *institution* that brings together buyers and sellers.

Before we can fully understand markets, then, we have to understand what an institution is. Once again we have a word that can be understood in several ways—and again, as with markets, the most obvious association is a physical one. You may think of penal institutions (prisons), mental institutions (psychiatric hospitals), or institutions for housing parentless children (orphanages). This meaning is, in fact, incorporated into the U.S. census in a number of instances where the people being counted are specified as the "non-institutionalized population"—meaning that they are neither in prisons nor in long-term hospital care.

institutions: ways of structuring social interactions, including both formally constituted establishments and the generally recognized patterns of organization embodied in customs, habits, and laws

However an **institution** is always more than a physical structure. The term actually refers to some kind of organized behavior, by people, in a specified place—in some cases, without any physical structure. Hence we move to a more generalized definition of an institution as a formally constituted establishment that coordinates the activities of multiple individual economic actors. Institutions, so understood, may have a variety of purposes: Hospitals are primarily concerned with health care, schools are primarily concerned with education, and industrial firms are primarily concerned with production. Institutions that are primarily concerned with facilitating exchange—and that, therefore, fit into our definition of markets—include stock exchanges, shopping centers, and other establishments dedicated to buying and selling. Although such establishments often exist in physically defined markets, they may not. Internet auction sites

Markets are social organizations set up to facilitate exchange. Often markets require a specific time and location so that buyers and sellers of particular items can meet. This open-air market for grains in the village of Odumase-Krobo in Ghana takes place twice a week. The New York Stock Exchange on Wall Street is open for trading from 9:30 A.M. to 4:00 PM. every weekday. Other markets, like online auctions, may not be confined to a particular time or place.

such as eBay are market establishments, but they do not require that buyers and sellers physically meet in one place.

Even more broadly speaking, the term *institution* can also mean a generally recognized way of structuring social interactions embodied not in establishments but in customs, habits, and laws. Such institutions foster similar or coordinated behavior among people who share some cultural commonalities, even if the community sharing these institutions is large enough so that individuals in it do not know all of the other members of the community. For example, the institution of marriage is a way of organizing family relationships, and institutions of inheritance provide legal or customary methods by which people can assign their property to other owners after their death. Legal systems themselves are institutions in this more abstract sense, whereas courts, police stations, and other organizations that carry out the laws are institutions in the more concrete sense of formally established organizations.

When we understand markets as institutions, we can see that they not only bring buyers and sellers into communication with each other but also structure and coordinate their interactions. Market institutions allow buyers and sellers to exchange information and give them opportunities to complete transactions with each other, if they so desire.

For many purposes, the great advantage of market institutions over administrative, centralized planning (such as that in the former Soviet Union) is the way they make decentralized flows of information and decentralized decision making possible. No middle manager or bureaucrat needs to keep track of who wants what, what they are willing to pay, when they can deliver, etc., etc. When market institutions are working well, they enable market participants to access as much of this information as they need and to make their individual decisions based on that information.

Thinking of markets as institutions, rather than concrete places, leads to various ways of discussing *particular* markets. Many economists—some of those employed in universities and many of those employed by businesses, by consulting firms, or in government agencies—spend much of their time investigating one or more such specific institutional markets. They may track, over time, the trades made at various prices for a specific good, such as heating oil or AT&T bonds, or they may try to forecast how prices for these goods will change in the future. When such an economist speaks of a market, he or she most often means the institutional market for such a specific good.

In this sense, several different markets may operate under one roof, within the same organization. For example, in the United States the Chicago Board of Trade operates many markets for a variety of farm products, including wheat, corn, and soybeans, among many others. (Indeed, even the term *wheat* may be too general to define a market for some purposes, given the existence of such distinct varieties as "No. 2 dark winter wheat" and "No. 1 dark northern spring wheat.") Or such an institutional market might cover a number of different physical locations, such as when an economist delineates a market in regional terms. The "New England market for home heating oil," for example, may involve transactions by a number of different companies at a number of different physical locations.

1.3 | "The Market" as Pure Exchange

"the market": a phrase that people often use to mean an abstract situation of pure exchange or a global system of exchange relationships

In the most abstract terms, people sometimes say "the market" to refer to a situation of pure, unencumbered exchange. Without reference either to physical places or to social institutions, buyers and sellers are imagined to come to instantaneous, costless agreements. Very general, abstract principles are laid out to describe how "market forces" work and the effects they have on society. Sometimes the definition of "the market" is expanded to refer to the entire country-wide or global system of market relationships. Often "the market" is described as being driven by the independent, self-interested, and rational choices of perfectly informed buyers and sellers (which is how it is described in the traditional microeconomic model).

laissez-faire economy: an economy with little government regulation

This very abstract sense of "the market" underlies some of the most heated debates in economics; one side takes a "pro-market" view and the other side takes an "anti-market" view. Market advocates claim that "free" markets and a **laissez-faire economy** (one with very little government regulation) lead to economic growth and prosperity. Others believe in the importance of the market but claim that problems such as poverty, inequality, environmental degradation, and declines in social ethics can be attributed to the unchecked and unregulated "market."

Abstractions can often be helpful in understanding real-world phenomena, but it can be dangerous to reverse the process: Sometimes people start to think of real-world markets as merely "imperfect" versions of the abstract market, as though the abstract were somehow more real. What tends to get lost in such abstraction is the fact that there are actually many different kinds of markets and that market institutions—like all social institutions—tend to have both strengths and weaknesses. To examine these, we must first examine the historical rise of markets as a form of social organization. (We will revisit ideological claims about markets in Chapter 19.)

Discussion Questions

1. You attend a college or university. In what sense is it an "educational institution"? Can you identify any institutionalized patterns that structure the behavior of students and faculty at your school? (If you find this question difficult, try to imagine yourself in an educational institution in Nigeria or Tibet or in an institution at a very different level— for example, a grade school or graduate school. Using this contrast, what patterns that seem "normal" to you here and now can you identify as social institutions?)

2. In what sense is the term *market* being used in each of the following sentences? "Go to the market and get some bananas." "The market is the best invention of humankind." "The labor market for new Ph.D.s is bad this year." "The advance of the market leads to a decline in social morality." "The market performance of IBM stock weakened last month." Can you think of other examples from your own readings or experience?

2 | The Development and Expansion of Markets

Markets, as places to buy and sell, have existed for thousands of years. Yet until recently, in historical terms, they did not dominate social and economic life. In ancient societies, trading ships and overland caravans brought exotic commodities from far away, typically destined for the court or the homes of the ruling elite. Transportation was primitive, and the earliest merchants often obtained goods by barter, relying only on themselves or trusted kin to run their trading business. Some of the earliest existing examples of writing and mathematics come from records kept for purposes of commercial exchange (and taxation!) in ancient Sumeria and Egypt, around 3000 B.C. However, such limited markets had little effect on most people's daily lives. Most people relied for survival primarily on what they themselves produced within peasant households or tribal kinship groups.

Although many interesting stories can be told about the development of markets in many different parts of the world, most historians see the greatest impetus to the growth of markets as the Industrial Revolution that began in Europe in the late 18th century.

2.1 | The Industrial Revolution

In medieval Europe during the 11th and 12th centuries A.D., markets were advancing slowly beyond this ancient pattern, though markets were still far from dominating economic activity. People who lived in the towns bought food, and those who could afford to bought the limited types of goods produced by the artisans of the day. The majority of people, however, were peasants, who usually had little access to money. Most of their clothing and household goods were handmade by family members, rather than purchased in the market. Very little of the production and distribution of goods and services in the lives of medieval peasants involved market relationships.

Artisans in European medieval towns were organized into **guilds** that governed each craft, setting strict apprenticeship requirements, limiting guild membership, and

guilds: medieval European organizations of artisans or merchants regulating the sale of goods produced by the guild. Such rules, enforceable by law in most places, preserved notions of the proper, traditional, skilled way of working. Merchants were also organized into guilds that set rules about buying and selling. In the towns as in the countryside, the market had scarcely begun to affect either the sale of goods or the process of work. Only in the occasional large-scale enterprise (for example, in mining or shipping) did the conditions of work resemble modern wage labor.

The economic morality of this era in Europe, embodied in the doctrine of the Catholic Church, upheld the notion of an ethically determined **just price** for goods and defended the right of the poor to receive subsistence from others in times of need. Charging more than an item was deemed to be worth was considered immoral, as was charging interest on loans. Perhaps most important, materialism and acquisitiveness in general were condemned as sinful. On the surface, this would not appear to be an auspicious setting for the emergence of an emphasis on market exchange.

However, throughout Europe, from about the 15th century onward, market relationships gradually eroded the medieval economy. Merchants outside the guilds continually challenged the guild restrictions on trade. Landowners prospered as they moved toward more market-oriented agriculture, both in hiring labor and in selling their products—even though such actions conflicted with the traditional regulation of the grain trade and the countryside.

New attitudes toward science and technology that first appeared in Britain—such as principles of "scientific agriculture"—spread widely over the course of the 18th century, resulting in vastly increased output per agricultural worker and a corresponding decline in the proportion of the labor force needed to produce a country's food. Similarly, the engineers of England and Scotland paved the way to the modern assumption that virtually any task can be mechanized. The Industrial Revolution may be described, on the technological side, as a transformation from production processes that used hand tools in households and small enterprises to processes that used machines and power tools in factories and other large enterprises.

The expectation of material progress developed partly in response to the new powers that human beings were able to exert over the physical world with such technological innovations as steam engines, machinery for spinning and weaving textiles, and techniques of iron smelting and steel making. These innovations and many others were major causes of the pattern of sustained growth in average output per person. A critical aspect of industrialization was the increase in labor productivity, as the value of manufactured capital available to each worker increased.[1] This process continues today: A garment worker using modern, computerized equipment could accomplish enormously more than one who uses only a needle and thread. More manufactured capital per worker means that each worker can process materials and use energy (and energy-using machinery) faster. Thus, starting with the Industrial Revolution, the ratio of labor to materials and energy has continuously declined.

What happens when there is such a dramatic change in what an individual worker can produce? There were several possible results, none of which was historically inevitable. The outcome would remain uncertain until the following questions were resolved:

◐ Would people who could produce more per hour simply work fewer hours, or would they use part or all of their increased productive potential to increase their income and consumption?

◐ If there was additional income, how much of it would be received by the owners of capital and raw materials, and how much by the workers?

◐ Would the additional income be spent on increasing consumption or on investment in additional capital?

[1] We will define and discuss *manufactured capital* in Chapter 6. For now you need only to know that manufactured capital includes all physical assets that have been made by people and that can be used in further economic activities. Examples of manufactured capital include tools, machines, and infrastructure, such as buildings and roads, that enhance economic activity.

"just price" doctrine: the mandate of the medieval Catholic Church that prices charged should always be fair

These were among the questions posed by such early observers of the Industrial Revolution as Adam Smith and Karl Marx, and they continue to be relevant today. Although a leveling off of consumption would have been one solution, that road was not taken. The ability to produce vastly more was instead accompanied by the beginning of mass marketing and the birth of the view of "the worker as consumer" (see Chapter 10). Some of the profits from production were reinvested in manufactured capital, leading to increased productive capacity. Institutions evolved to deal with all this production, consumption, and investment, which was now happening on a much larger scale and affecting a larger number of people than ever before in history. More production and consumption, and more investment money seeking productive outlets, meant more exchange—and thus a need for bigger and more sophisticated market institutions. There is much that is shared among the nations of the world today. One can travel from Bangkok to Buenos Aires to Chicago to Moscow, and even to Beijing, finding in each place systems that can be described in the same few words, as a highly marketized, industrial society.

Here our overview of the history of marketization will focus on two fundamental issues. First, we will consider the connection between the spread of the market and the appearance of the Industrial Revolution in England, the earliest and most dramatic case. Second, we will describe some of the cultural and behavioral trends that have been associated with industrialization and marketization, whether as causes or as effects.

2.2 | The Case of England

Discussion of industrialization often focuses on and seems to celebrate the original experience in England, as though to suggest that the English route to the development of industry was natural, peaceful, and easily replicated in other countries. In fact, it was none of these things. Nevertheless, we too will focus on England, not to advocate its history as a model for other countries but rather to understand the process of industrialization in its first and most extensively analyzed occurrence.

The Industrial Revolution did not result from a few brilliant inventions or public policies. Rather, it was possible only because of the way in which market relations had been spreading and England's economy had been growing over the preceding centuries. A number of unique features of England's history, as well as the use of force and coercion at critical junctures, were essential to the process. By the 16th century, the challenge of the market was visible enough in England to require laws reaffirming the traditional powers of guilds and the rights of the poor to receive support from their local community in times of need. In 17th-century England, the triumph of market-oriented interests and ideas was achieved only through the long and bloody civil war of 1640–1660.

Marketization spread on many dimensions in 18th-century England. Agricultural land, labor, and products were increasingly bought and sold in markets, although there were episodic protests demanding a return to the traditional "moral economy," particularly when grain prices were high. Textile production spread throughout the countryside; spinning and weaving were often done by rural households, who bought materials from, and sold their products to, the merchants who dominated the industry. London, by far the largest city in Europe, reached a population of 500,000 by 1700, providing a huge urban marketplace for all sorts of goods and labor (in which the guilds had only fading remnants of their former power).

The gradual spread of market relationships and ideas was necessary for industrialization, but many other factors played essential roles as well. In the 18th century, British dominance of the world economy resulted from military success in numerous wars. Two aspects of this history were of particular importance for industrialization. First, the British conquest of India, formerly the world's leading textile producer, allowed the destruction of India's textile industry and opened up wider opportunities for the export of English cloth. Second, the slave trade enriched many English merchants, helping them accumulate the capital that was invested in industrialization. It also provided the

The Industrial Revolution brought about radical changes in the way people lived their lives. In the town of Witney, England, the production of woolen goods dates back to the 10th century. This 1897 photo, taken in Witney, shows women working steam-powered looms in a blanket factory. Before industrialization, the work was done in homes where women carded the wool and spun the yarn and men used hand looms to weave the yarn into cloth.

labor for cotton plantations in the Americas, which supplied the English textile industry with some of its raw materials.

Rapid industrialization began in the English textile industry in the 1780s and spread in subsequent decades to many other industries and countries. First in France, Belgium, and the United States, then in Germany and other northern European countries, and ultimately in Russia, Japan, and elsewhere, the new techniques of industrialization rapidly took hold. After World War II, the concept of "development" (and the field of development economics) appeared, reflecting the assumption that any country could and should industrialize.

2.3 | Industrial and Market Culture

What attitudes and cultural assumptions characterized the industrial era? Focusing on 18th-century Britain and the outward spread of ideas developed there, we can see important intellectual as well as economic changes. The increasingly secular (*nonspiritual*) morality and philosophy of the period moved toward justification of private property and acquisitiveness; it was now possible to suggest, for example, the formerly heretical (*sacrilegious*) idea that luxury purchases by the elite might be socially beneficial sources of employment for artisans and merchants. New religious denominations embraced visions of the good life that were entirely compatible with success in business and accumulation of wealth.

The cultural attitudes associated with the Industrial Revolution include individualism, instrumental rationality,[2] and a definition of success that is strongly tied to the acquisition of material goods. These attitudes marked significant departures from the past. For example, the idea that it is normal and morally acceptable for each person to put his or her own welfare above the welfare of others contrasted with traditional assumptions about solidarity among extended families and with religious beliefs about obligations to one's church and community. Materialism, though it can be found in some form in virtually every human culture, is discouraged in many religions.

The broad pattern of economic organization that came to be known as laissez-faire proprietary capitalism, on the other hand, is based on individual private ownership of

---

[2] *Instrumental rationality* is defined as the use of appropriate means to achieve desired ends.

Two Market Beginnings

The first reported example of a futures market, where people buy goods now for delivery later, comes from Japan in the early 17th century. A rice trader from Nagoya named Chozaemon, the story goes, was informed by a friend that the rice harvest in a particular region was going to be poor. He bought the harvest of that region from the farmers in advance, stored the rice when it came in, and then sold it after the prices had been driven up by the poor harvest. Other merchants, seeing this example, soon set up a sophisticated system of clearinghouses for futures trading in Osaka. The merchants designed the rules themselves and barred from exchange anyone who broke the rules. They communicated price data across long distances by means that included smoke signals and carrier pigeons.

In late-18th-century New York City, Wall Street was an unpaved track. People in the city who wanted to sell stocks in companies or to raise money by selling bonds had to find people to trade with through newspapers or word of mouth. In 1792, however, John Sutton opened his Stock Exchange Office at 22 Wall Street, where sellers could bring their stocks and bonds and have them auctioned off. Soon a number of competitors set up similar operations. Having trades going on at a variety of places, however, meant that no one could be sure what a price should be. A group of leading brokers got together to form a single auction, making up their own rules about how stocks and bonds should be traded and punishing people who defaulted on contracts by barring or blacklisting them. Eventually, this operation became the New York Stock Exchange. ◖

Adapted from John McMillan, *Reinventing the Bazaar: A Natural History of Markets* (New York: Norton, 2002), pp. 22–24.

capital (both physical and financial)[3], private direction of investment, and expansion of the market system of distribution. Capitalism—the new "religion" that arrived with the Industrial Revolution—contained nothing negative, and much that was positive, in its attitude toward a materialist definition of success. Adam Smith, the prophet of the new religion, provided an optimistic account of how market competition guided the force of self-interest, "as if by an invisible hand," to achieve an ideal result for society.[4]

Another fundamental result of industrialization was the accelerated pace of change: Stability and tradition characterized much of pre-industrial life, whereas continual change characterized this more recent era. The "revolutionary" nature of the modern expectation of progress can most readily be seen by comparing it to the expectations of preceding traditional societies, which are often characterized as feudal. In Russia, for example, as late as the mid–19th century, the experience of the agricultural masses was structured according to the feudal relationships of serfdom. Relative affluence was possible, but there was no basis for the establishment of what is today a common goal: that the material or other conditions of our lives will be better than those of our parents or grandparents. Most of human history has been characterized by fluctuations around a long-term constant level of material well-being. Only in the last 200 years did economic growth come to be viewed as a normal feature of human societies.

The technologies that permitted greater control over the physical world required and fostered new forms of social organization and social control. Once textiles were produced with machines rather than spinning wheels or handlooms, it became common

---

[3] *Physical capital* includes both manufactured capital—as described in Chapter 3, footnote 1—and anything that comes directly from nature, such as land, trees, metal ores, and so on. *Financial capital* is money that can be invested.

[4] Much of this book—indeed much of traditional economics—can be seen as a process of spelling out the details of that metaphor and examining when it is and when it is not applicable to reality. Different varieties of capitalism will be discussed in Chapter 18.

and profitable to concentrate production in textile factories. Steam engines were the basis of the technology that made railways possible, and railways created infrastructures of communication and permitted the transportation of people and goods at a scale and efficiency never seen before. The management required for the newly invented or newly organized industries, such as railroads and textile factories, was different from most earlier conceptions of management, in part because the new enterprises were so large.

New systems of production required more than new management and new workplaces. They also required a workforce that would be differently organized, live differently, and have, in many ways, a different identity than any workforce that had come before. The joint efforts of many human beings and machines had to be coordinated—a task that required punctuality, a high and steady level of attention, and a willingness to accept authority. These traits could be found within military, and sometimes religious, discipline but were not otherwise widespread in any society. In the early years of industrialization, there were frequent clashes between employers and workers over the unfamiliar new style of organizing work. The early textile mills, in fact, often hired women and children rather than adult men, because they would take orders more easily and would work for lower wages.

By now, there is no country that has not felt many of the effects of the Industrial Revolution. At the same time, much has been written to suggest that history is moving on to a new "post-industrial" phase. The norms of industrialism, including factory work, mass production, and mass consumption, are said to be giving way to a new era in which the central human role in production is the handling of information and knowledge. Be that as it may, the Industrial Revolution brought about tremendous changes in how people acted, thought about themselves, and organized social life.

Discussion Questions

1. As industrialization and marketization spread beyond England and beyond Europe, the sorts of institutions that were created depended both on new technologies and on existing cultural norms. For example, some Islamic societies became more industrialized, while still forbidding the charging of interest on loans. Can you think of any other examples of divergence from English patterns from your study of history or your own community?

2. The seemingly miraculous gains in productivity brought about by the mechanization of industry encouraged many leading thinkers of the 18th century to conceive of nature—and economies—as clockwork-like machines and to assume that they functioned according to "laws" similar to those being discovered in the physics of the same period. What insights might be gained by thinking about the economy as a machine? Are there limitations to this way of thinking?

3 | Institutional Requirements of Markets

Contemporary large-scale markets do an amazing thing: They allow many, many separate decision makers, acting from decentralized information, to coordinate their behavior, resulting in highly complex patterns of exchange transactions. They do not, however, operate in a vacuum. Economists have identified a number of even more basic institutions that market institutions require in order to function. We will classify these in four broad groups: individualist institutions related to property and decision making, social institutions of trust, infrastructure for the smooth flow of goods and information, and money as a medium of exchange.

▷ Markets require individualist institutions related to property and decision making, social institutions of trust, infrastructure for the smooth flow of goods and information, and money as a medium of exchange.

3.1 | Individualist Institutions of Property and Decision Making

Before people can begin to think about making an exchange, they have to be clear about what belongs to whom. Ownership is usually defined through systems of property

private property: ownership of assets by nongovernment economic actors

rights set out in law and enforced by government courts, police, and the like. For decentralized exchange to take place, people must have individually held **private property**. They also must be allowed—and sometimes encouraged—to make decisions on an individual basis (whether the "individual" here is an individual person, household, or other organization). Prices, in particular, must not be under the complete control of guilds or central bureaus but must, rather, generally be allowed to be set by the interactions of market participants themselves.

Economic organizations without such private property and decentralized decision making are not suited for markets and instead are governed by custom, consent, or administration (as discussed in Chapter 2). In the centrally planned economy of the former Soviet Union, for example, private property was limited largely to personal, consumable goods, and all productive resources were considered the property of the state. *Within* a contemporary corporation, likewise, administration—not exchange—is the prevalent form of organization. Property rights primarily reside in the owners (shareholders) of a firm and the ultimate decision-making authority resides in the board of directors and the top managers.

The institutions of private property and individualist decision making exist both formally, in codes of law, and informally, in social norms. For example, some Western economists expected markets to grow quickly in the countries of the former Soviet Union as soon as communism was dismantled and opportunities for marketization opened up. However, many people living in these countries were accustomed to being told where to work and what to do by the state. Norms of individual initiative and entrepreneurship, it turns out, do not just arise naturally. Nor did other sorts of market infrastructure appear quickly, and the Russian economy, for example, went into a severe breakdown. Many dislocated male workers turned to alcohol, and male mortality skyrocketed, reducing male life expectancy to only 58 years. According to a U.N. report issued in 1999, the transition to a market economy has been accompanied by "a demographic collapse and a rise in self-destructive behaviour, especially among men," including alcohol poisoning, alcohol-related deaths, and suicide.[5] Why were the effects less pronounced for women? The answer is unclear, but some commentators have suggested that this could be due at least in part to the fact that Soviet women had been expected to manage shopping and family consumption, as well as to work at both home production and state-assigned jobs. Because consumer markets functioned very badly, the Soviet women, more than the men, had had to develop more of the kinds of self-reliance and initiative that could help them adapt to the new market conditions.

3.2 | Social Institutions of Trust

Some degree of trust must exist between buyers and sellers. When a buyer puts down her payment, she must trust that the seller will hand over the merchandise and that it will be of good quality. A seller must be able to trust that the payment offered is valid, whether it is in the form of currency, personal check, credit card charge, or another kind of promise of future payment. Social institutions must be created to reduce the risk involved.

One way in which trust gets built up is through the establishment of direct, one-to-one relationships. This happens most readily where transactions occur among people who meet one another repeatedly. If you have dealt with some people in the past and they treated you fairly, you are likely to choose them when it comes time to trade again. Even in sophisticated contemporary economies, this kind of confidence plays an important role. Companies know which suppliers they can count on to come through on time, and consumers patronize stores where they feel comfortable.

---

[5] Michael Binyon, "Russia's Health Crisis Strikes the Weaker Sex: Suicide, Alcohol, and Accidents Are Taking Their Toll on Men," *The Times* (London), August 23, 1999, reproduced at **http://www.russia.phri.org/ tblibrary/ b82399.htm**.

Reputation also can be important in creating trust. A buyer might be fleeced by a seller in a one-on-one transaction, but if that buyer spreads the word, the seller may suffer a damaged reputation and the loss of many customers. Groups of actors on one side of the market might band together, as well, to maintain their reputation as a trade or profession. If a group of real estate agents, for example, finds that one among them is acting unethically, they may "blacklist" the agent and refuse to refer customers or pass on necessary information. Marketers try to capitalize on the tendency of buyers to depend on reputation by using advertising to link certain expectations about quality and price to a recognizable brand name and thus creating "brand loyalty" among repeat customers.

Cultural norms and ethical or religious codes can also help establish and maintain an atmosphere of trustworthiness. If enough members of a society subscribe to a common moral code and hence do not betray each others' trust, that can ease the functioning of markets.

implicit contract: an informal agreement about the terms of exchange, based on verbal discussions and on common norms, traditions, and expectations

A "contract" is a general set of terms that define an exchange agreement. An **implicit contract** is said to exist when the parties have agreed informally about the terms of their exchange. Such agreement may be based on verbal discussions and, even more, on common norms, traditions, and expectations.

explicit contract: a formal, often written agreement that states the terms of an exchange and may be enforceable through a legal system

In larger and more mobile societies, however, many market encounters take place between strangers who are unlikely ever to meet again, people often do not have easy access to information about reputation, and they may not share the same traditions and moral codes. In such cases, more formal institutions are also needed. **Explicit contracts** are formal, usually written contracts that provide a legally enforceable description of the agreed-on terms of exchange. Explicit contracts can be quite complex, including many clauses to cover a multitude of contingencies (such as "If goods are not delivered by June 1, the price paid will be reduced to . . ."). They can record agreements that cover a long period of time (for example, a sale of goods on credit or long-term leases of apartments or equipment). They may involve many parties (as in a contract between a union and an employer). For formal contracts to work, there must be laws that define contracts, state the parties' legal obligation to honor contracts, and establish penalties for those who fail to do so. There must also be systems of law enforcement to determine when someone has failed to abide by a contract and to apply appropriate remedies and penalties.

Many other institutions have evolved in highly marketized economies to deal with the issue of trust. For example, credit bureaus keep track of consumer creditworthiness, Better Business Bureaus keep track of complaints against businesses, "money-back" guarantees give consumers a chance to test the quality of a good before the purchase becomes irrevocable, and escrow accounts provide a place where money can be put until goods or services are delivered. Government agencies such as the U.S. Food and Drug Administration and local boards of health are charged with monitoring the quality and purity of many goods that are sold.

However, even in complex transactions among large groups of strangers, social norms are still essential. Detailed formal contracts are costly to write and costly to enforce. It is not practical to police every detail of every contract, and it is impossible to cover every conceivable contingency. The legal system can work smoothly only if most people willingly obey most laws and believe that it is dishonorable to cheat. In effect, relationships, social norms, and the apparatus of law are institutions that must exist side by side, reinforcing one another. None of these alone can carry the whole burden of making complex contracts work and hence making markets possible.

The laws and the social norms that are required for market economies are not solely those concerned with contract terms. An example comes from the post-communist economy that began to take shape in Russia in the early 1990s, when murders of top bankers in the new financial industry became quite frequent. Often these killings were rumored to result from disputes with other (legal or illegal) financial groups. Obviously, a stable marketized economy must ensure that competition in the marketplace remains nonviolent. This requires both strong, well-enforced, and widely accepted laws against murder and personal violence, and social norms that channel competitive feelings, anger, and jealousy of others' success into nonviolent outlets.

3.3 | Infrastructure for the Smooth Flow of Goods and Information

physical infrastructure: equipment, buildings, physical communication lines, roads, and other tangible structures that provide the foundation for economic activity

A third set of basic institutions for market functioning have to do with making possible a smooth flow of goods and information. Most obviously, there needs to be a **physical infrastructure** for transportation and storage. Such infrastructure includes roads, ports, railroads, and warehouses in which to store goods awaiting transport or sale. This sort of infrastructure can be most noticeable when it is absent, such as in economies ravaged by war.

In addition, there needs to be an infrastructure in place for the flow of information. Producers and sellers need information on what and how much their customers want to buy; in a well-functioning marketized economy, this information indicates what and how much should be produced and offered for sale. At the same time, consumers need to know what is available and how much of something else they will have to give up (that is, how much they will have to pay) to get the products that are on the market. In fact, ideally consumers should be able to compare *all* potential purchases as a basis for deciding what to acquire and what to do without.

The infrastructure for communication in industrialized economies now commonly includes a postal service, private courier services, phone lines and cell phone connections to carry voice and fax message, wire services, and the World Wide Web. Other media, such as newspapers and magazines, can also carry commercial information in the form of both reports and advertising.

3.4 | Money as a Medium of Exchange

Yet another basic institution required to facilitate the flow of exchange is a generally accepted form of money. Many different things have been used as money in the past. Early monetary systems used precious or carved stones, particular types of seashells, or other rare goods. Gold, silver, and other metal coins were the most common choice for many centuries; more recently, paper currency has become important. Today, financial instruments such as bank account balances play an even larger role; in a developed country, the amount of money that changes hands in the form of business and personal checks is several times as great as the value of transactions conducted with paper and metal currency. The use of credit cards (a form of debt, to be later paid by a bank account draft), electronic bank transfers, and payments over the Internet further facilitate the making of payments in exchange.

As with the physical transportation infrastructure, the importance of the institution of money is often most noticeable when it is absent. Interesting but relatively inadequate forms of money have sprung up when established currency and banking systems have been unavailable or unreliable. Cigarettes were a form of money in prisons and concentration camps during World War II. In countries that have experienced high rates of inflation or have other reasons for lacking trust in their own currencies, people may informally adopt U.S. dollars or other leading international currencies for local transactions—or trade may grind to a halt.

money: a medium of exchange—something that people trust has value and so will accept in exchange for goods or services. It is desirable that money also be a durable store of value and have minimal handling and storage costs.

What makes something **money**? How do you decide whether to pay for a purchase in cigarettes, pebbles, yen, or dollars? One obvious criterion is that money must be widely accepted as a medium of exchange; money is whatever everyone else thinks it is. Yet this alone is not enough. Imagine the problems that would occur if everyone agreed that heads of lettuce were money. A form of money that starts to rot within a week or two would be difficult to use! Thus a second criterion is that money must provide a durable store of value, of the same value today as at any time in the near future. If there is inflation—that is, an increase in the average price level for all goods and services—then money gradually loses a little of its value. Usually, however, inflation occurs slowly enough that people can retain confidence in the value of money from day to day.

Relatively rare episodes of "hyperinflation" (in Germany after World War I, in several Latin American countries during the second half of the 20th century, and in Russia after 1989), when prices shoot upward and money suddenly wilts like old lettuce, have led to great social stresses and inequities.

Even with durability added to wide acceptance, our definition of money is still not complete. Some durable goods would not be successful as money. Bottles of wine retain their value for many years but are too bulky and breakable to be used widely in exchanges. A final criterion, therefore, is that money must have minimal handling and storage costs. By this criterion, paper currency is better than coins, and financial records on a computer are better still.

In many cases, money is created or sanctioned by the government. However, this is not essential, as illustrated by the use of cigarettes by prisoners. Money is, ultimately, based on common agreement. Although it was once backed by precious metals in Fort Knox, the value of a U.S. dollar is now based only on the understanding that other people will take it in exchange. In this sense, money is itself a social institution of trust, as well as part of the institutional infrastructure of functioning markets.

Can communities smaller than national governments create their own money? Modern experiments with local currencies are rare but not unknown. In recent years, a number of local service exchanges have appeared in the United States, paying community members with certificates, sometimes called "time dollars," which are simply credits entered into a central computer system, when they perform valuable services for others. The "time dollars" earned by providing services can then be spent to obtain different services from other members of the local network. Participants in these networks—often retired, unemployed, or partially disabled people—are thus using new, local money to buy and sell services of value to each other. For many individuals, such a system makes the difference between isolated inactivity and productive membership in the community. The largest of these networks have mobilized substantial amounts of labor. Most remain quite small, however, and few ways have been found to exchange their "time dollars" or other "local" or "alternative" currencies for ordinary U.S. dollars or for goods produced outside the local community.

Discussion Questions

1. Have you ever signed an explicit contract for, say, a job or the lease of an apartment? What sorts of terms were explicitly spelled out? Were there other expectations that were *not* spelled out?

2. Markets require both *individualist* institutions and *social* institutions (as well as infrastructure for moving goods and information.) What do you think would happen if a society overly reinforced the individualist institutions while neglecting the social? What if it overly reinforced the social institutions while neglecting the individualist?

4 | Markets and Well-Being

Markets have some advantages as a form of social organization. They allow for a steady flow of information, in terms of prices and volumes of sales, that encourages producers to respond flexibly to consumers' desires. Profit provides feedback to owners about whether resources are being transformed from less (market-)valuable to more (market-)valuable forms. Markets also give people a certain freedom in individual decision making about which activities to engage in, and they may encourage some beneficial forms of innovation and social cooperation, as we will discuss further in our investigation of "exchange" in Chapter 9.

Markets also have some drawbacks. They make parties who trade more vulnerable to each other's actions (such as a cutting off of supplies) and to historical technological patterns (if by trading, they fail to develop key industries), as we will discuss in Chapter 9.

They have no inherent corrections for the excessive concentration of economic power and may be destructive of community. Markets do not do well, on their own, in protecting the environment, because the costs of environmental damage are generally external to market transactions. They also cannot on their own address the maldistribution of resources, the dependency needs of people with little to offer in the market, or the provision of public goods. For all these reasons, market value can easily diverge from human value.

From an historical standpoint, one result of mechanization, factory organization, marketization, and the thirsting after new ideas was the development of many new products that came to be produced in great quantities, consumed huge amounts of raw materials, and necessitated the employment of a large, newly organized workforce. On the output side, these changes were almost universally seen as progress. By the middle of the 19th century, well-to-do people in the early-industrializing countries of western Europe and America could enjoy marvels of communication, transportation, and physical comfort. The large and growing middle classes had access to running water, warmer clothes and houses, better and more varied food, and a growing choice of other consumer goods.

It is less obvious whether the associated changes in the more psychological or spiritual aspects of life have been on balance positive or negative—and whether it is possible to retain some of the positive aspects without all of the negative ones. Individualism, for example, can be a liberating force, especially when it releases less powerful groups in society from traditional relations of subservience. At the same time, individualism has caused a weakening of family ties, creating social, economic, and moral dilemmas for modern societies. It becomes necessary for formal institutions and paid labor to play many roles previously performed by families, especially such traditional roles of women within families as raising children and caring for the sick and elderly. Some countries have done much better than others in addressing these needs.

Regarding the more obviously material impacts of the Industrial Revolution, on the input side of production it is again evident that not all of the change has been for the better. Many parts of the Earth have become markedly uglier and less healthful, for humans and for the rest of nature. This is a direct result of industry's appetite for minerals and fossil fuels and of its dumping its residues of pollution into the water, air, and earth.

The requirements of industrial production, assembling large numbers of workers in factories, and efforts to realize the potential of railroads and other advances in transportation resulted in huge urban agglomerations. Especially in the early years of the Industrial Revolution, the living conditions of the masses of factory workers were marked by levels of crowding and squalor never before seen on such a large scale. The working conditions were often appallingly bad, including long hours (sometimes up to 14 hours a day, 7 days a week) for men, women, and children. Industrial accidents were common in factories where lighting and air were poor, the pace was forced, human health was little regarded, and workers were inadequately protected from dangerous machinery.

Mechanization created jobs in factories at the same time as it severely reduced the opportunity to manufacture similar items at home, and this led, in most cases, to an obvious worsening of pay and conditions. Workers' protests and attacks on machinery (most famously the Luddite movement in England, but also similar movements throughout Europe) were attempts to control both the quality and the quantity of the work to which they had access.

In the more than two centuries since the beginning of the Industrial Revolution, the lot of the workers in the early-industrializing countries has improved dramatically. Work hours have been shortened, sometimes being reduced to less than half the earlier weekly total. Vacations have been added and lengthened. Over the long haul, workers' pay and other compensation have improved while productivity has continued to grow. One of the great discoveries of the 20th century was that productivity often rose when working conditions improved. Union victories and labor-oriented legislation have not crippled capitalism and may often have made industry more productive. The lifestyle now possible for a fully employed worker in an advanced industrial country is significantly more comfortable and convenient than what the middle class regarded as luxurious in the 19th century.

These very successes, however, contained within them the seeds of further problems; indeed, such a coupling of problems with success is one of the hallmarks of modern technology. For example, public health measures and modern medicine have dramatically improved the health and lengthened the life span of people in all classes. Yet new health threats are arising from environmental degradation, and many diseases have evolved into new, drug-resistant forms that have the potential to undo much of the modern success in combating infectious illnesses.

Although the quality of work has improved for many in the 20th century, the quantity of work available has frequently been an issue. Ever since the beginnings of industrialization, fears have been voiced that machines would replace workers, leaving masses of people unable to earn a living. The steadily increasing productivity of labor in industrial societies must mean either that there is less work per person or that there is steady growth in output per person. As we have seen, both have occurred. The reduction in average working hours has not, of course, been perfectly coordinated with productivity increases so as to prevent unemployment; groups of workers are indeed thrown out of work, in some cases for painfully long periods of time. Nor has the growth of output been designed to meet any pre-existing notion of human needs or well-being.

In this chapter, we have looked at the institutions that markets require in order to function, and in Chapters 4 and 5 we will continue to study market behavior.

However, in order for markets to function *well* (that is, in the service of human well-being), more is needed. Some means must be devised to deal with excessive concentrations of market power. We will turn to this in Chapter 12, on market structures characterized by market power, and also in Chapters 16 and 17, when we discuss businesses and governments. Some means must be devised of dealing with negative externalities (the unintended consequences of economic activity), especially environmental ones. In Chapter 14 we will take up the controversial issue of whether market institutions themselves might be used to fight pollution through the creation of markets for "rights to pollute," and in Chapter 17 we will look at other possibilities for policies in this area. Nonmarket institutions, including many in the household, community, nonprofit, and government spheres (to be discussed in detail in Chapters 15 and 17), must receive resources adequate to support their important economic functions. In the final chapters of the book, we consider the many variations on market systems to be found in contemporary countries and look at ideological positions concerning markets.

Discussion Questions

1. On a sheet of paper, draw two columns. In one column, list some historical and contemporary advantages of marketized exchange, and in the other, list some disadvantages. Can you go beyond the items listed in the text?

2. "Indeed it has been said that democracy is the worst form of Government," said British prime minister Winston Churchill (1874–1965), "except all those other forms that have been tried from time to time." Some people make the same claim about more marketized forms of economic systems. What do they mean? Would you agree or disagree?

5 | Types of Markets

Markets take a wide variety of forms. They can be classified according to what is sold, how prices come to be determined, and the time period covered.

5.1 | What Is Sold?

The most obvious and well-known markets are those in which people buy and sell material things to people who will employ them for personal use. Such **retail markets** deal in food, books, clothes, household items, and so on. Some retail markets sell, instead of tangible objects, services such as banking or repairs for your car. Retail markets

retail markets: markets where goods and services are sold to consumers

wholesale markets: intermediate markets between producers and retailers

product markets: markets for newly produced goods and services

intermediate goods markets: markets for unfinished products

resale markets: markets for items that have been previously owned

factor markets: markets for labor, natural resources, and manufactured capital goods

labor markets: markets where people offer their labor services to employers

may be supplied directly by producers, but more often they are supplied by distributors and brokers who, trading in **wholesale markets**, act as intermediaries between producers and retailers.

Markets in which newly produced goods and services are sold are called **product markets**. Often economists use product markets as their primary example. For instance, the market in which new cars are sold by a car manufacturing company (usually this is via a dealership) are product markets. Other types of markets, however, are also significant. **Intermediate goods markets** sell unfinished products from one organization to another. **Resale markets** are markets for items that have been previously owned. Used-car markets are resale markets, as are markets for antique furniture. In such cases, market activity is unrelated to production, except for the production of services by agents and salespeople who facilitate the sale.

Other important types of markets include the **factor markets** in which producers purchase inputs that they will use to create new goods and services. Labor, natural resources, and manufactured capital goods are the traditional factors of production.

An especially important factor market, the **labor market** is the set of institutions through which people offer to sell their services to businesses, public agencies, nonprofit organizations, and households other than their own. The sale of labor is quite different from the sale of material goods. Unlike a physical object, labor cannot be produced first and then handed to the buyer; rather, the worker promises to do something in return for a promised payment of wages.

The employer may seek to purchase a specific service from the worker, such as cleaning the floor once a week or loading the furniture from an apartment into a truck. Or the employer may hire labor on a more general basis, to be available for so many hours a day to work on a broad category of tasks, such as the many activities involved in running an office or caring for a child. In either case there is an explicit or implicit employment contract describing the time, place, and conditions of work and the schedule of payment for that work.

Labor markets are sufficiently different from other types of markets that this topic warrants a separate chapter of its own. For now we will note that, regardless of the other terms of the employment contract, it is at times more useful to think of a labor market as an institution for *renting* the time, skill, and effort of the worker rather than as an institution for *selling* something. In spite of these peculiarities, and others that will be pointed out in Chapter 13, we can discern a market for labor in the institutions and patterns of behavior in which some people offer to rent or sell their labor, while others offer to lease or purchase it.

financial markets: markets for debt and equity finance

Financial markets provide debt and equity finance credit that enable organizations to purchase factors that they otherwise could not afford at the beginning of the production cycle.[6] Businesses anticipate that when the product is sold, they will receive enough income to cover the loan plus interest. Financial markets provide credit to consumers as well as businesses. Corporations sometimes issue new shares of their stock to increase their ability to finance from equity. (Nearly all the action on stock exchanges, however, is resale of existing stocks.)

underground markets: markets where illegal goods and services are sold or legal goods and services are sold in an illegal way

Some markets operate outside the law. **Underground markets** (also sometimes called shadow markets or black markets) are illegal markets. It might be that the good or service itself is illegal, as are heroin, smuggled antiquities, and murder for hire. Or the markets may deal in legitimate goods but in illegal ways. For example, smugglers may sell cigarettes or imported perfume at prices that do not include payment of required taxes.

5.2 | How Are Prices Determined?

At first glance, it might seem that many consumer retail markets violate one of the institutional requirements for markets that we mentioned above: that prices must generally

---

[6] Sometimes when people speak of financial markets, they mean only markets for debt.

○ Markets can be characterized by whether they have posted prices or prices determined by auction or bargaining

posted prices: prices set by a seller

markup (or cost-plus) pricing: a method of setting prices in which the seller adds a fixed percentage amount to his or her cost of supplying the item

market value: the price for an item that would be freely determined by interactions of buyers and sellers in a (perhaps hypothetical) auction-type market

auction market: a market where an item is sold to the highest bidder

open auction: an auction in which the opening price is set low and then buyers bid it up

Dutch auction: an auction in which the opening price is set high and then drops until someone buys

sealed-bid auction: an auction in which bids are given privately to the auctioneer

double auction: an auction in which both the buyers and sellers state prices at which they are willing to make transactions

be allowed to be set by the interactions of market participants themselves. In an old-fashioned open-air bazaar or flea market, such interaction is obvious. Buyers and sellers haggle about prices. In a typical retail market in an industrialized society, however, you don't "interact" so directly with the retailer to determine the price of bread or a shirt. The price is listed on the shelf or a tag. Either you pay the **posted price** set by the seller, or you don't buy the item.

Such fixed, posted prices are most often used when an appropriate price for a good can be at least approximately known. Very often, retailers are in the habit of using **markup** (or **cost-plus) pricing**. They look at the prices they themselves paid to buy the items from their distributors or wholesalers (who, in turn, had probably used mark-up pricing in buying from the goods' producers). Then they mark up the prices by fixed percentages. Markups can vary from as little as 10 to 15% for some goods to 200 to 300% (the standard at some high-end retail specialty jewelry shops and art galleries). They try to make the markups high enough so that they will generally make a profit on their sales to customers, but low enough so that customers won't be overly discouraged from buying. Then they sell to all customers at that posted price.

Even though you don't haggle with the cashier at The Gap or Lucky Supermarket, the fact that you *can* decide whether to buy or not to buy is itself a form of interaction. Over time, retailers will take note of what moves off the shelf most quickly and will then order more of it and/or raise its price. They will also take note of what doesn't sell so quickly and will then reduce their order from wholesalers or mark the items down. The retailers' purchases from the wholesalers, and the wholesalers' purchases from the producers, in turn give these suppliers information that they can use in deciding how much to order or produce and how to set *their* prices.

You may not be able to bargain directly, but your actions, in combination with the actions of other customers, ultimately affect the prices and quantities offered in the market. These adjustments should tend, at least in theory, to lead posted prices toward reflecting what economists call the market-determined value, or **market value**, of the item.[7] Market value, to be discussed in detail in the next chapter, is the price that would be freely determined by interactions of buyers and sellers in a (perhaps hypothetical) auction-type market.

Auction markets are markets in which an item is sold to the highest bidder. Auction markets are used when the appropriate price for an item is relatively unknown and there are many possible buyers and/or sellers. Auctions are typically used to sell items such as antique furnishings, valuable artwork, and corporate stock. Auctions can take many different forms, and some economists study the variety of incentives and behaviors that accompany the different institutional structures. Real-world auctions offer interesting opportunities to observe how market value comes to be determined.

In an **open auction**, an opening price is set low, and then potential buyers top each other's bids until only one bidder remains. This is what many people first think of when they think of an auction, and it is the main type of auction used on eBay. In a **Dutch auction**, an opening price is set high and then drops until a buyer offers to purchase the item. The name comes from its use in the Dutch wholesale cut-flower market. **Sealed-bid auctions** get their name from the fact that the bids are given privately to the auctioneer, who then selects the winning bidder. In contrast to an open auction, the bidders are not supposed to know how much others value the item. Sealed-bid auctions are often used to sell commercial real estate (where the high-price buyer wins) and to allocate construction contracts (where the low-price seller of construction services wins). In a **double auction**, both buyers and sellers state prices at which they are willing to make transactions. The New York Stock Exchange is a double auction.

---

[7] The fixed price is most likely to move toward "market value" if markets are competitive, the flow of information is good, the adjustment process is given enough time, and no big changes in market conditions occur in the meantime.

Within these major forms of auctions, there are further nuances. Should there be a time limit on bidding? Should the winner pay the price he or she bid or the price offered by the second-highest bidder? Should items be sold separately or in bundles? Perhaps surprisingly, economists have discovered that the exact structure and nuances of an auction market can have substantial effects on the market price that results.

bargaining: an activity in which a single buyer and a single seller negotiate the terms of their exchange

In markets with **bargaining**, a *single* buyer and a *single* seller negotiate the price of an item, for which no definitive market value has been established. Residential real estate, for example, is generally sold by way of such negotiated agreements, as are used cars. (Sometimes there is also a posted price, but both parties understand that it is merely a starting point for negotiation.) Salaries of high-level managers, professionals, and unionized employees—and, notably, of sports and entertainment stars—are commonly set by bargaining. The presence of *potential* other buyers and sellers, however, is obviously important in determining the relative bargaining strength of the two parties. A seller who knows he can easily find other eager buyers, for example, will quickly walk away from an unfavorable deal. A seller with fewer options will have less ability to hold out for good terms.

5.3 | What Time Period Is Covered?

spot markets: markets for immediate delivery

In **spot markets**, buyers and sellers contract for immediate delivery of a specified amount of a good or service. In the Dutch fresh-flower market, buyers and sellers from many countries make spot market trades in these perishable goods. Many large cities have "day labor" offices, where employers and laborers make 1-day agreements for work. Spot markets can respond quickly to changes in conditions of demand and supply.

futures market: a market in which it is possible to negotiate in the present for the purchase of something that will be delivered in the future

In **futures markets**, buyers and sellers contract for later delivery of a good. Futures markets are very important in the trading of raw materials, including agricultural commodities, and for foreign exchange. Many companies, for example, want some assurance that they will be able to get the supplies they need at the time they need them and at a reasonable price. They would rather negotiate for a specific price and quantity well ahead of time than trust that they will be able to get what they need on spot markets when the time comes.

long-term contracts: contracts whose terms extend over a long period of time

Many market transactions are governed by **long-term contracts**. Businesses often sign long-term contracts with their suppliers of energy or raw material, rather than using spot or futures markets. Contracts generally bind both buyer and seller to a specific price (or range of prices) for every transaction over a span of time. If, during this time, the spot market price should happen to rise above the contracted-for price, the seller will still be obligated to sell at the price stated in the contract. Similarly, if the spot market price falls, the buyer is still obligated to pay the higher contractual price. The price can change only if the contract is renegotiated, perhaps after several months or a year or more. Long-term employment agreements are another example of contractual exchange. Individuals often sign long-term rental agreements or enter into long-term mortgages.

5.4 | Markets in the Traditional Microeconomic Model

In the *traditional microeconomic* model, the featured market is a double-auction, spot, product market, in which firms/producers sell directly to households/consumers. We introduced the assumptions of this model briefly in Chapters 1 and 2, and we will elaborate on its analysis of producer and consumer behavior in Part III. The assumptions of this model allow for very clean and elegant mathematical/graphical expositions of market behavior in a world of such producers and consumers. These will also be described in Part III.

In the next two chapters, you will learn about analysis of supply and demand—the most basic tool in the economist's toolbox when it comes to analyzing markets. Although the theory of supply and demand is at its most elegant when viewed through the lens of the traditional model, this does *not* mean that supply and demand analysis applies only within that model. On the contrary, we can often gain insight into many real-world markets—markets in which governments and nonprofits participate, in which firms buy from each other, and/or in which imperfect rationality and imperfect information are the norm—by thinking in terms of supply and demand.

Discussion Questions

1. Reviewing the different types of markets outlined in this section, think about whether you have ever directly participated in a market of each type. If so, describe specific instances.

2. The Internet has opened up a whole new set of markets for everything from antiques to airplane tickets. Pool your knowledge with that of others in the class, and, for the types of markets listed in this section, think of as many examples as possible that are *online*.

Review Questions

1. Give three different meanings of the term *market.*
2. Briefly describe how patterns of agriculture, industry, and trade changed during the Industrial Revolution.
3. Briefly describe some important changes in cultural attitudes that accompanied the Industrial Revolution.
4. Describe four main categories of institutional requirements for markets.
5. Give several examples of ways in which trustworthiness can be established.
6. Give several examples of the infrastructure necessary for market functioning.
7. Describe several ways in which the Industrial Revolution and marketization have improved human life.
8. Describe several ways in which the Industrial Revolution and marketization have created problems.
9. List nine different types of markets in terms of what is sold.
10. List three major types of markets in terms of how prices are set.
11. List three types of markets in terms of the time period covered.

Exercises

1. Give an example of each of the following:
   a. An institution, in the sense of social custom, that governs how you behave when you enter a clothing store
   b. A market, in the sense of establishment, where you might go to buy music
   c. A cultural attitude that changed during the Industrial Revolution
   d. A formal social institution that builds trust
   e. A physical infrastructure for the flow of goods
   f. An infrastructure for the flow of information
   g. An early form of money

2. Give an example of each of the following:
   a. A retail market
   b. A product market
   c. A resale market
   d. A factor market
   e. An underground market
   f. An auction market
   g. A market with bargaining

3. Match each concept in Column A with an example in Column B.

   Column A

   1. explicit contract
   2. markup pricing
   3. implicit contract
   4. an ill effect of the early Industrial Revolution
   5. an informal institution that builds trust
   6. a strength of markets
   7. a drawback of markets

   Column B

   i. failure to account for environmental externalities
   ii. a signed lease for an apartment
   iii. concern for your reputation
   iv. the expectation that an employee will be polite to customers
   v. have helped raise the material standard of living of many people
   vi. use of child labor
   vii. setting price equal to cost plus 20%

4. Imagine trying to run a contemporary market economy without each of the following. What problems do you think would arise? What might people have to do to get around the lack of each one?
   a. Money
   b. The expectation that most people won't cheat
   c. An organized way of keeping people from adulterating foods or selling medicines that don't work
   d. A system of roads, canals, or railways
   e. Phone and computer connections
   f. An expectation that individuals will take the initiative in decision making

5. To some economists, the medieval "just price" doctrine seems quaint, if not ignorant. "Prices should be whatever market forces dictate!" they say. On the other hand, experiments with the "Ultimatum Game" (discussed in Chapter 2) seem to indicate that people can have very strong beliefs about what is fair and may act on these beliefs. Do you think the two views of prices can be reconciled? What might be some of the issues involved?

Supply and Demand

Suppose you want to buy a new computer. What price will you have to pay to get what you want? Suppose you make your living by braiding leather belts. Can you expect to sell more belts this year than last? For anyone interested in buying or selling, it is important to know the prices and quantities that characterize market transactions. From the viewpoint of economic analysis, not only do we want to know what is going on right now in markets, but we would also like to be able to explain how the current prices and quantities came to be what they are—and maybe even to predict where they are going in the future.

1 | Explaining Prices and Quantities

Economists, government agencies, and private market research firms all gather data on the quantities of goods and services that change hands, and the prevailing prices, in a variety of markets. For example, the U.S. Department of Energy records that the prices of crude oil bought by U.S. refiners fluctuated during the period 1969–2002 as shown in Figure 4.1. The same agency also reports that, for the same period, the quantity of crude oil sold to U.S. refiners followed the pattern shown in Figure 4.2.

 Three main modes of investigation are empirical, theoretical, and historical.

Many economists and statisticians are employed gathering and working with such data. But what sense can we make of them?

Explaining variation in prices and quantities, we will see, involves using three main modes of investigation: empirical, theoretical, and historical. **Empirical investigation** is the observation and recording of specific happenings in the world. It is especially convenient when the happenings of interest can be adequately described in terms of numerical data. However, useful empirical investigation of a specific item of interest may also be represented in words or images. When the observations take the form of showing how a numerical economic variable changes over time, as in Figures 4.1 and 4.2, we call them **time series data**.

empirical investigation: the observation and recording of the specific phenomena of concern

time series data: observations of how a numerical variable changes over time

theoretical investigation: analysis based in abstract thought

The adjective *empirical* is usually contrasted with *theoretical*, where the latter refers to statements that are made on the basis of mental constructs and processes, such as assumptions and logical deductions. This chapter describes, in some detail, economists' **theories** of supply, demand, and market adjustment. As you will see, the models we

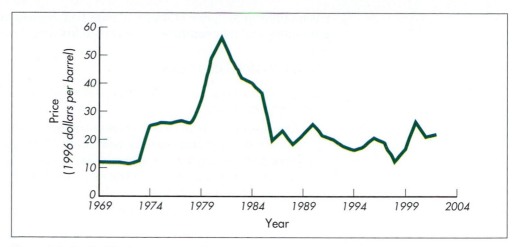

Figure 4.1   Crude Oil Prices to U.S. Refiners, 1969–2002
Empirical data from the U.S. Department of Energy show how oil prices in the United States (measured in inflation-adjusted dollars per barrel) fluctuated during recent decades.

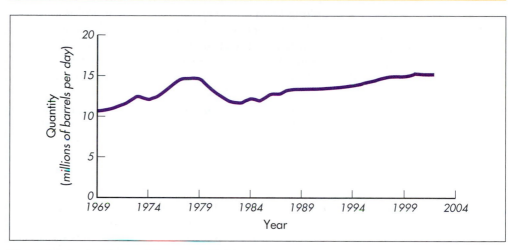

Figure 4.2   Crude Oil Quantities to U.S. Refiners, 1969–2002
Empirical data on the quantity of oil processed by U.S. refiners (measured in millions of barrels per day) show how this quantity varied over recent decades.

Data sources: U.S. Department of Energy, *Annual Energy Review* and *Monthly Energy Review.*

introduce are based on thought experiments. Rarely having recourse to controlled laboratory experiments, as in the physical sciences, economists create theories based on assumptions about the motivations of economic agents. Then they build on those theories by carefully reasoning out their implications for economic behavior.

All this takes place in our heads—hence the term *thought experiment.* "Is the resulting theory true?" you may rightly wonder. Generally, that question cannot be strictly answered "yes" or "no." Better questions to ask about economic theories include "Does the theory offer insight?" "Does it focus on things that we consider important?"

In the last section of this chapter, we will explore a crucial third mode, knowledge of **historical** events—that is, observations of happenings in the near or distant past, within the context of what went before and what came after, that are broader than the more narrowly focused empirical investigation. Using the example of the market for crude oil, we will see how empirical observation, theories of supply and demand, and a knowledge of history can combine to help us understand real-world markets. We choose the U.S. national market for oil as our historical example because energy is a crucial resource.

historical investigation: study of past events

Fluctuations in the price of crude oil have had dramatic effects on the U.S. and global economies, and they continue to concern industries, citizens, and policymakers.

Discussion Questions

1. Verbally describe, in a short paragraph, what happened to crude oil prices during the period 1969–2002.

2. Astronomers throughout recorded human history have observed the relative locations of particular stars and constellations. Generations of sky-watchers have kept records about dramatic phenomena such as solar and lunar eclipses. Some have used mathematical formulas to try to express these relationships and their changes over time. Describe how the three modes of investigation just described were involved in the discovery that the planet Earth revolves around the sun.

2 | The Theory of Supply

We will start with the following thought experiment. Suppose there is a condominium apartment building where all the apartments are identical, and each apartment has a different owner. We will assume that ten of the owners might be interested in selling their apartments. For the purposes of this thought experiment, we will assume that they are intelligent, well-informed people who will weigh the costs and benefits of their actions. We also assume that the owners will make choices that are in their own, private and—for this analysis—monetary interests. As we noted in Chapter 2, economists often like to make this assumption of self-interested rational behavior, because if it were true, it would make human behavior much simpler and more predictable (and economics more like an "exact" science). For the purposes of this thought experiment, then, we will ignore many real-world complications. We will not allow, for example, that any owner might be poorly informed about the market for apartments, that any might be unwilling to sell to people of some ages and ethnic backgrounds, or that any might be tempted to act in ways not in their own financial interest out of motivations such as friendship, compassion, or avoidance of hassle.

Our hypothetical owners are assumed to be interested only in price. Although all ten owners desire to sell if they can find a buyer who will pay them what they want, each one has a slightly different idea of what would be an acceptable price. All ten sellers would be willing to sell their apartment if they were offered $100,000, but there is one who would hold out for that price and sell for nothing less, whereas the other nine sellers would also be willing to sell at $99,000. Similarly, there is another seller whose lowest acceptable selling price would be $98,000 and another who would go only as low as $97,000. In fact, it turns out that each time the price drops by $1000, there is one fewer person willing to sell an apartment. None would be willing to sell at $90,000.

2.1 | The Supply Schedule and Curve

The result of this pattern is shown in Table 4.1, which we call a supply schedule. A supply schedule shows us, in the form of a table, the quantity of a good or service that would be offered by the sellers at each possible price.

supply curve: a curve indicating the quantities that sellers are willing to supply at various prices

From the supply schedule, we can graph a **supply curve**, as shown in Figure 4.3, which shows the same information in a different form. If we ask how many apartments will be offered for sale at a price of $96,000, for example, we can look across from

Table 4.1	A Supply Schedule for Apartments										
Price ($1000s)	100	99	98	97	96	95	94	93	92	91	90
Quantity of Apartments Supplied	10	9	8	7	6	5	4	3	2	1	0

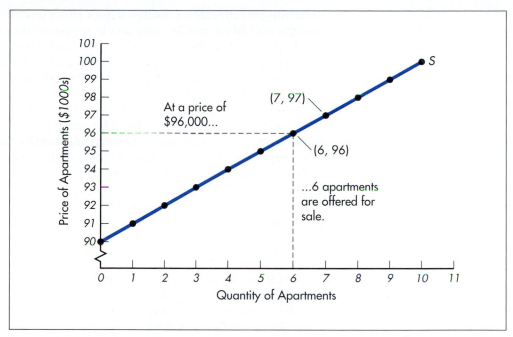

Figure 4.3 The Supply Curve for Apartments
The supply curve shows the same information as the supply schedule. At higher prices, more apartments are offered on the market by people who are in a position to sell.

$96,000 on the vertical (price) axis over to the supply curve, and then drop down to the horizontal (quantity) axis to find that the answer is 6. We conventionally draw the supply curve as a continuous line, even though we know that it is not normally possible to buy fractional pieces of apartments.[1] (Remember, this is just a thought experiment.) Also for ease in presentation, we have started the vertical axis in Figure 4.3 at a number other than zero.

Note that the supply curve in Figure 4.3 slopes upward. This seems reasonable; it is consistent with an expectation that suppliers of a good or service will tend to offer more for sale, the higher the price they receive.[2] If someone offered you $500 for this textbook right now, you would probably sell it, whereas at $20 you would hang on to it (we hope). If a new electronic device commands a high price, we expect more businesses to jump into producing it. Price and quantity have a "direct," or "positive," relationship along the supply curve. That is, they move in the same direction. When the price rises, the quantity supplied rises as well.

In our example of the apartment market, each owner has only the option to supply either 1 or 0 apartments. The curve we have drawn thus represents the entire **market supply** from all the owners. In other cases, however, we can think of individual people or enterprises as having their own individual upward-sloping supply curves. A local noodle shop, for example, might be willing to expand its activities if it could charge more per meal. The relation between price and quantity supplied for this one business would be its **individual supply** schedule or curve. In such a case, you could derive the

market supply: the supply from all sellers in the market

individual supply: the supply from one individual seller

---

[1] The alert math student may notice that Figure 4.3—and most other graphs used in this book—violate common mathematical conventions about functions. Here we are thinking of quantity as a function of price. A mathematician would therefore put price on the horizontal axis and quantity on the vertical. It is an unfortunate accident in the history of economics that supply and demand analysis has consistently reversed this mathematicians' convention!

[2] Sometimes this tendency is referred to as the law of supply. Such a choice of words may reflect a somewhat misguided attempt to make economics sound more "scientific." As we will see in later chapters, especially the one about labor, this "law" does not hold everywhere.

market supply schedule for noodles in your entire town by adding up the quantities that all of the individual noodle shops would supply, at the various prices. For example, if one shop offered 50 meals at a price of $5 each, another shop 25 meals, and a third 20 meals, then the market supply curve would show a quantity of 95 meals at a price of $5. To find the entire market supply curve for noodles, you would repeat this exercise for other possible prices as well.

We see movement *along* a supply curve when we note, for example, that the quantity of apartments that will be offered for sale rises from 6 to 7 as the price rises from $96,000 to $97,000. This is a case of **change in quantity supplied**. It is important to refer to movement along a supply curve as change in the *quantity* supplied in order to avoid confusion with the topic of the next section.

change in quantity supplied: movement along a supply curve in response to a price change

Check yourself by answering this question with reference to Table 4.1 or Figure 4.3: By how much does the *quantity supplied* change when the price changes from $97,000 to $100,000?[3]

2.2 | Changes in Supply

change in supply: a shift of the supply curve in response to some determinant other than price

In contrast to *changes in quantity supplied*, we say that there has been a **change in supply** when the *whole* supply curve shifts.

Why might the whole curve shift? In our apartment example, suppose that our group of 10 owners is expanded by 2 more owners in the same building, who decide they want to move away to live closer to their families. Suppose these owners would both be willing to sell for $90,000 or more. The numbers in the Quantity of Apartments Supplied line in the supply schedule would increase by 2, all the way along. The supply curve would shift from S_1 to S_2 as illustrated in Figure 4.4. Now, at a price of $96,000, for example, 8 owners are willing to sell. We can describe this increase in supply by saying either that "supply has risen" or that "the supply curve has shifted out." (Some students may find it confusing that a supply *increase* shifts the supply curve *down*. Remember to start the "story" by reading across horizontally from the price axis. Then you will notice that the shift goes out toward *higher* numbers on the quantity axis.)

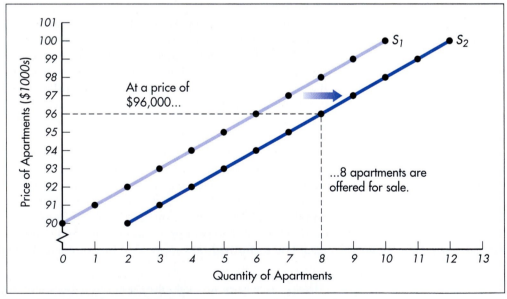

Figure 4.4 An Increase in Supply
The supply curve shifts outward (to the right) when sellers decide either to supply a larger quantity to the market at a given price or to charge less for a given quantity.

---

[3] Answer: The quantity supplied rises by 3 apartments, from 7 apartments up to 10.

We would see the same result if, instead of new sellers entering the market, for some reason each of the existing sellers became willing to accept $2000 less. In this case, as well, 8 owners would now be willing to sell at a price of $96,000, whereas before it took a price of $98,000 to get 8 owners to want to sell. This would also be termed an "increase in supply," and again the supply curve would shift as illustrated in Figure 4.4.

We cannot really say, then, that there is simply one supply curve representing a market. Anything that changes the quantity supplied at a given price moves us to a new curve. (Recall that if price alone changes, that is a movement *along* a curve.) When we represent what we think reasonable supplier behavior might be by drawing a single supply curve, we are assuming that we can hold "all else constant." If we were to try to derive a supply curve *empirically*, we would need to run the kind of experiment that can be done in some of the physical sciences. We would want to hold everything else in the market constant while varying just the price, and watch to see what different quantities are supplied at the different prices. Some exercises like this have been done in laboratory settings by experimental economists, but empirical attempts to discover supply curves in real-world markets are complicated by the fact that rarely is "all else constant." The affection of working economists for supply and demand analysis is not really based on such empirical results—or lack of them. We simply find that it is often useful to run a thought experiment in which we assume that suppliers act "as if" they knew what they would offer for sale at all prices.

In the real world, sellers might be individuals, families, businesses, community organizations, or government agencies. They may sell things that already exist (such as apartments), or produce new goods and services for sale, or sell bonds or corporate shares. Any of the factors that might cause them to change the amount they offer for sale at a given price will cause a change in supply. The possible factors are too many to list in a generalized statement about supply.

2.3 | Supply by Businesses as Producers

In the traditional microeconomic model introduced in earlier chapters, the model of the economy is simplified to the case where, except for the supply of labor and capital services by "households," the only supplier of goods and services is "the firm." The circular flow diagram (discussed in Chapter 2) invites us to concentrate on the sale of newly produced goods and services by firms (also called producers) to households (also referred to as consumers).

nonprice determinants of supply: everything affecting the quantity supplied, except the price for which the product can be sold

In this simple case, some major **nonprice determinants of supply** can be identified. They include

1. The available technology of production
2. Resource prices
3. The number of producers
4. Producer expectations about future prices and technology
5. The prices of related goods and services

Consider, for example, a firm that produces leather belts. A recent innovation in leather-tooling machines may allow belts to be produced at lower cost. This improvement in technology (nonprice determinant 1 in the foregoing list) would allow each belt to be sold at a lower price.[4] Thus the supply curve would shift downward at every point. Note that such a downward shift is graphically equivalent to a shift *outward*, as shown in Figure 4.4; supply curve S_2 is both below and to the right of curve S_1. We say that "supply has increased."

Resource prices (nonprice determinant 2 in our list) would include the price of leather, wages for labor, and the interest charge on bank loans. If resource prices rise, producers will usually need to raise the price they charge for each unit of their output. The

---

[4] Might it be possible for the firm's owner to keep the prices high and keep the benefits of lower costs to himself or herself, in the form of higher profits? We will discuss this more when we talk about market power in Chapter 12. Right now, we assume that some of the cost savings are passed along to consumers.

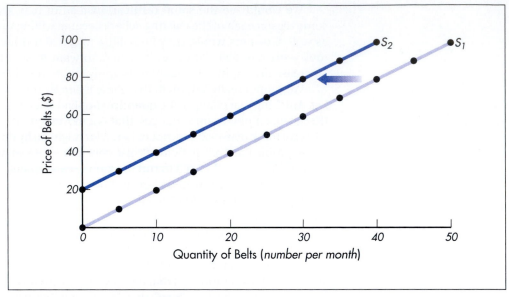

Figure 4.5 A Decrease in Supply
The supply curve shifts backward (to the left) when sellers decide either to supply a smaller quantity to the market at a given price or to charge more for a given quantity.

result is likely to be a decrease in supply, such as is shown in Figure 4.5. We describe this by saying either that "supply has decreased" or that "the supply curve has shifted back."

Clearly, if more firms start producing belts, the market supply will increase (nonprice determinant 3). The effect of expectations (nonprice determinant 4) can be tricky. If a belt producer expects that the prices for leather products will increase soon (perhaps he or she has been following farm news that affects leather supply), he or she might hold back some output for now, to sell later when such products will command a higher price. On the other hand, if he or she hears that an even newer, more productive technology has been adopted by other firms in the industry, he or she might be eager to supply as much as possible now, before the price is driven down.

Finally, suppose that a belt producer discovers that people will pay a great deal more for handmade leather cell phone pouches than for belts, so the firm completely switches over to this new line of production. In this case, the price of a related good (nonprice determinant 5) has induced the firm to reduce its output of belts, causing the supply of belts to decrease, as shown in Figure 4.5.

Discussion Questions

1. Verbally explain the difference between a change in *quantity supplied* and a change in *supply*. Considering the supply side of the market for lawn-mowing services, what kind of change (*increase* or *decrease*, in *quantity supplied* or *supply*) would each of the following events cause?
   a. There is a rise in the price of gasoline used to run power mowers.
   b. There is a rise in the going price for lawn-mowing services.
   c. More people decide to offer to mow lawns.
   d. A new lawn mower is invented that is cheap and makes it possible to mow lawns in half the usual time.

2. Sketch a supply curve graph illustrating a student's willingness to sell his textbooks from all his classes, right now. Assume the student will receive offers of this sort: "I'll give you [a fixed number of dollars] apiece for all the books you want to sell."

Carefully label the vertical and horizontal axes. Suppose that at an original offer of $30 per book, the student will be willing to sell three books, because he knows he can replace these three for less than $30 each at a local bookstore. Mark this point on your first graph. Assume further that at $40 he would be willing to sell four books, at $50 he would supply five books, and so on. Now, on separate graphs labeled (a),(b), and (c), show this line and his offer at $30 and the precise new *point* or an approximate new *curve* that illustrates each of the following changes in conditions. Consider them separately, returning to the condition of no Internet resources in part (c).

a. He is offered $70 per book instead of $30.

b. He discovers that the textbook materials for many of his classes are available free on the Internet.

c. The local bookstore raises its prices substantially.

3 | The Theory of Demand

Now let us return to our thought experiment about the imagined small market for condominium apartments. We will assume that there are only ten potential buyers and that they, like the ten potential sellers, are well informed and make their decisions on the basis of rational self-interest. However, they have a different point of view. They regard $100,000 as too high, and none of them will purchase an apartment at that price. However, one of them (who may have either a lot of money or an especially strong need for an apartment) is willing to buy for $99,000; that individual and another potential buyer are both willing to buy if the price drops to $98,000; and so on.

> ◯ "A very poor man may be said in some sense to have a demand for a coach and six [horses]; he might like to have it; but his demand is not an *effectual demand*." (Adam Smith, *Wealth of Nations,* pt. 1, chap. 7.)

3.1 | The Demand Schedule and Curve

Table 4.2 is the demand schedule that reflects this case. A demand schedule shows us, in the form of a table, the quantity of a good or service that buyers are willing to purchase at each possible price.

From the demand schedule we can graph a **demand curve**, as shown in Figure 4.6. If we ask how many apartments potential buyers will be willing to buy at price of $96,000, for example, we see, by reading horizontally across the graph and dropping down to the quantity axis, that the answer is 4.

Sometimes, to clarify that this demand schedule and curve represent offers by people who are willing *and able* to pay the given prices, economists refer to them as representing **effective demand**.[5] As you will see in the quotation in the sidebar, the term used by Adam Smith, more than 200 years ago, was *effectual demand*. The level of effective demand depends on, among other things, the distribution of income in the population. Many more people may *want* to live in these apartments than are listed in the table—they may even be homeless and desperate for housing. But because they cannot afford these prices, their "demand" is not *effective* demand. Markets do not, by their nature, take into account wants or needs that are not backed up by the ability to pay.

> **demand curve:** a curve indicating the quantities that buyers are ready to purchase at various prices

> **effective demand:** the *desire* for a product that can be translated into *purchasing behavior* because it is backed up by *enough money* to pay the going price

Table 4.2	A Demand Schedule for Apartments										
Price ($1000s)	100	99	98	97	96	95	94	93	92	91	90
Quantity of Apartments Demanded	0	1	2	3	4	5	6	7	8	9	10

[5] The term *effective demand* was first used by the famous economist John Maynard Keynes (1883–1946). His use of the term—and the way it is employed by modern Keynesians who are pursuing his specific macroeconomic interests—is quite different from the way it is used in this and other microeconomics texts. You do not need, now, to know about the more specialized Keynesian use. Just be warned that if you go on to study advanced economics, you may someday encounter the term with quite a different meaning.

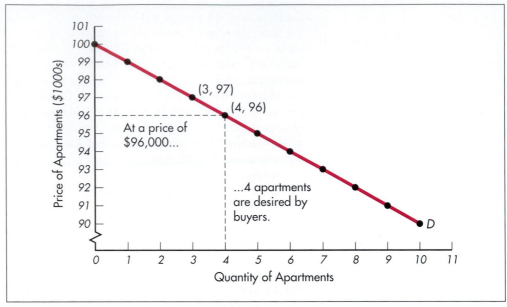

Figure 4.6 The Demand Curve for Apartments
The demand curve shows the same information as the demand schedule. At higher prices, fewer apartments are desired by people looking to buy.

Note that the demand curve in Figure 4.6 slopes downward. It seems reasonable to expect that, generally, the higher the price of a good, the fewer people will want to buy.[6] If a book is very expensive, you might look for it in the library rather than buying it. A business may think about hiring its own accountant if the accounting firm it has used raises its rates. Price and quantity have an inverse, or "negative," relationship along the demand curve. That is, when price rises, quantity demanded falls.

market demand: the demand from all buyers in the market

individual demand: the demand from one individual buyer

The curve we have drawn is the entire **market demand** curve for our small market for apartments. As was the case with supply, you can also imagine cases where it is reasonable to think of individual people or enterprises as having their own **individual demand** schedules. For example, the number of books you buy as an individual probably varies with price. The individual schedules can be summed to determine the market demand schedule.

Movement *along* a demand curve—for example, if we note that the quantity of apartments that will be purchased falls from 4 to 3 as the price rises from $96,000 to $97,000—must always be referred to as a **change in quantity demanded**.

change in quantity demanded: movement along a demand curve in response to a price change

Check yourself by answering this question with reference to Table 4.2 or Figure 4.6: By how much does the *quantity demanded* change when the price changes from $97,000 to $100,000?[7]

3.2 | Changes in Demand

change in demand: a shift of the demand curve in response to some determinant other than price

As with supply, we distinguish between a *change in quantity demanded* and a **change in demand**. When there is a change in demand, the whole curve shifts.

---

[6] This is sometimes called the "law of demand." Like the "law of supply," it does not always hold. Sometimes, for example, a smart marketer will find that buyers will want more of a good if it is sold as a "prestige" good at a high price.

[7] Answer: The quantity demanded drops by 3 apartments, from 3 apartments down to 0.

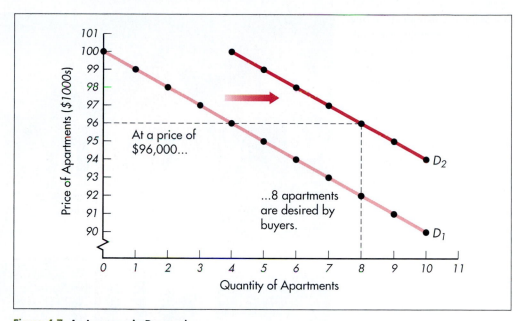

Figure 4.7 An Increase in Demand
The demand curve shifts outward (to the right) when more buyers want to buy at a given price or when buyers are willing to pay a higher price for a given quantity.

Why might the whole curve shift? Suppose there is a large movement of population into the area around our hypothetical apartment building. Many more people need housing. Specifically, suppose that at every price there are now 4 more willing buyers. At a price of $90,000 there will now be 14 buyers instead of 10, at $96,000 there will now be 8 buyers instead of 4, and 4 people are even willing to pay $100,000. Such a change is illustrated by the shift from D_1 to D_2 in Figure 4.7. We say that "demand has risen" or that "the demand curve has shifted out." (Because of the curve's negative slope, in this case shifting out also means shifting up.)

We would see the same result if, instead of new buyers entering the market, for some reason each of the existing buyers became willing to pay $4000 more for an apartment. In this case, as well, 8 buyers would now be willing to buy at a price of $96,000, whereas before these 8 buyers were willing to buy only when the price was no higher than $92,000. This would also be termed an "increase in demand," and again the demand curve would shift as illustrated in Figure 4.7.

Just as with the supply curve, we cannot count on demand curves being well defined unless we make the strong assumption of "all else constant." Demand curves are best seen as a theoretical tool.

In the real world, buyers might be families, businesses, governments, or anyone. They may buy existing goods or newly produced goods and services. The case of business demand for inputs is an interesting one. A bakery does not buy flour just because the baker likes flour, nor does it hire workers just because the baker wants company. It demands flour and labor services because it wants to be able to make and sell bread. When an enterprise wants an input because it expects that there will be a demand for its output, we call this **derived demand**.

derived demand: demand for an input that is based on demand for the output it will help to produce

nonprice determinants of demand: everything affecting the quantity for which there is effective demand, except the price for which the product is being sold

3.3 | Demand by Households as Consumers

In the traditional model, consumers of produced goods and services are identified with households. Accepting this simplifying assumption for the moment, we can more explicitly detail some of the important **nonprice determinants of demand**. These include

Households use markets to buy many things recently produced by business firms, such as new furniture or haircuts. Yet consumers also buy from other households and from government and nonprofit organizations; and they buy other items that do not represent current production, such as land and used cars. These historic apartments in Austria, for example, have undoubtedly passed from one homeowner to another many times. Preferences, income, the availability of substitutes and complements, expectations, and the number of consumers influence the level of demand by households, regardless of the seller and good or service bought.

1. Tastes and preferences
2. Incomes and/or available assets
3. Availability and prices of related goods and services
4. Consumer expectations about future prices and incomes
5. The number of consumers

To illustrate these nonprice determinants of demand, imagine that you are in a store where you see an item of potential interest to you. Let's say that you have been needing a small table for your room, and you spot one in a department store. Perhaps your first question will be related to determinant 1 in the foregoing list: Does the table look acceptable to you, given your preferences regarding color, style, and the like?

Next you are likely to look at the price tag, and you will immediately relate the price of the table to determinant 2 in our list: the money you have available to spend on anything. The higher your income, the more able you are to buy this good.

You will also consider nonprice determinant 3: other ways in which you might spend your money. Perhaps it makes more sense to save up and buy a whole new desk. Economists call goods like this table and desk **substitute goods**, because one can be used instead of the other. The price of substitute goods can be important in explaining demand. If the price of the desk falls, for example, you become more likely to buy it. Then, because you are more likely to purchase the desk, you become less likely to purchase the small table. A *de*crease in the price of a substitute good tends to *de*crease the demand for the good in question. Figure 4.8 illustrates how a drop in the price of desks would decrease the market demand for tables.

On the other hand, perhaps you have seen a nifty sliding tray that could attach to the underside of the small table. This may make the small table more appealing (if you can afford to buy both), and you are more likely to buy it. Economists call goods such as these, which are used together, **complementary goods**. The price of the complement would thus be a relevant "determinant of demand" (determinant 3 again). Demand for the good in question tends to *de*crease with an *in*crease in the price of a complementary good. If hot dogs got tremendously expensive, for example, demand for mustard would fall.

substitute good: a good that can be used in place of another good

complementary good: a good that is used along with another good

Table 4.4 | Supply and Demand Schedules After an Increase in Supply (Only)											
Price ($1000s)	100	99	98	97	96	95	94	93	92	91	90
Quantity of Apartments Supplied	12	11	10	9	8	7	6	5	4	3	2
Quantity of Apartments Demanded	0	1	2	3	4	5	6	7	8	9	10

associated with Third World malnutrition (the protest against Nestlé's aggressive promotion of infant formula in places where consumers lacked clean water to mix with it or enough money to prepare the formula at full strength) or with large numbers of dolphin deaths (the successful campaign to reduce demand for tuna products obtained without consideration of dolphin by-catch). As consumers and other people who are affected by the actions of corporations increasingly find ways to make known their feelings about negative externalities, we can expect to see more and more nonmarket pressures affecting supply and demand conditions.

It is best to think of the model of market adjustment toward equilibrium as offering one sort of explanation of human social behavior among many others, rather than as exactly characterizing price and quantity variations in the real world. Equilibrium analysis is limited by the reality of constant change in the world, and nonmarket forces may also effectively combat the equilibrating tendency of market forces. Market adjustment analysis can tell us what to expect from normal market forces: Most generally, disequilibrium situations create forces that will tend to push prices toward an equilibrium level.

4.3 | Shifts in Supply and Demand

With the two curves now combined, we can investigate how market forces will tend to respond to changes in the underlying nonprice determinants of supply and demand.

Back in our condo market, let's consider what would happen if 2 more sellers (willing to sell for $90,000 or more) were to join the original group of 10 sellers before the action

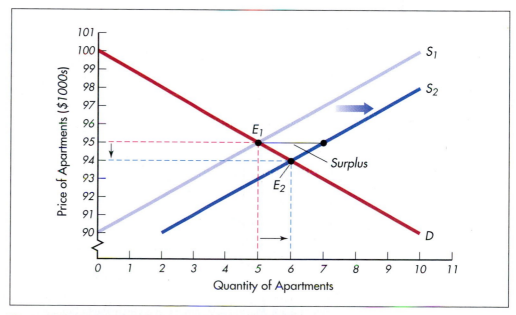

Figure 4.11 Market Adjustment to an Increase in Supply
With an increase in the supply of apartments, there now would be a surplus at the original equilibrium price of $95,000. Market adjustment forces should cause the price to fall until a new equilibrium is established at a price of $94,000. Six apartments will sell at this new equilibrium price. The equilibrium price has fallen, and the equilibrium quantity has risen.

Table 4.5 | Supply and Demand Schedules After an Increase in Demand (Only)										
Price ($1000s)	100	99	98	97	96	95	94	93	92	91	90
Quantity of Apartments Supplied	10	9	8	7	6	5	4	3	2	1	0
Quantity of Apartments Demanded	4	5	6	7	8	9	10	11	12	13	14

happened. How would the auction's result differ from the result we found with just the 10 sellers? Table 4.4 shows the combined schedules with the two additional sellers. Recall that the additional sellers shift the supply curve out to the right. Figure 4.11 shows that a surplus results at the original equilibrium price of $95,000, with 7 potential sellers chasing only 5 potential buyers. The market-clearing price will have to be lower after the increase in supply. At $94,000, 6 sellers can close deals with 6 buyers, and the market clears. As Figure 4.11 illustrates, *an increase in supply will tend to* decrease *price and* increase *quantity*.

On the other hand, suppose that we have only the original 10 sellers, but the population of willing buyers rises, as shown in Table 4.5. With the demand curve shift shown in Figure 4.12, we see that at the original equilibrium price of $95,000, a shortage results, with 5 potential sellers and 9 willing buyers. The price will be bid up to $97,000, where 7 transactions will be made. As Figure 4.12 illustrates, *an increase in demand will tend to* increase *price and* increase *quantity*.

Note that both increases in supply and increases in demand tend to increase the quantity transacted. Their price effects, however, go in opposite directions. Increases in supply make the good more plentiful, driving its price down. Increases in demand mean that more buyers are in the market, driving up the price. Likewise, decreases in supply and decreases in demand both tend to decrease the quantity transacted. A decrease in supply will tend to raise the price, because the good is harder to get. A decrease in demand will tend to decrease the price, as fewer buyers attempt to obtain the good. These effects are summarized in Table 4.6.

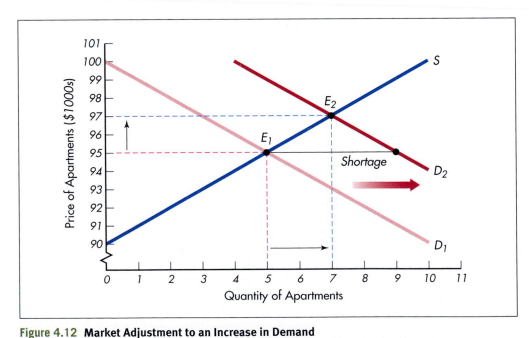

Figure 4.12 Market Adjustment to an Increase in Demand
With an increase in demand, there would be a shortage of apartments at the original equilibrium price of $95,000. Market adjustment forces should cause the price to rise until a new equilibrium is established at $97,000. Seven apartments will sell at this new equilibrium price. The equilibrium price has risen, and the equilibrium quantity has risen too.

Table 4.6	Summary of the Effects of Shifts in Supply and Demand	
	Effect on Equilibrium Price	**Effect on Equilibrium Quantity**
Increase in Supply	fall	rise
Decrease in Supply	rise	fall
Increase in Demand	rise	rise
Decrease in Demand	fall	fall

In our thought experiment, a new equilibrium is reached. In real-world markets, we will expect market forces to exert pressure in the direction of equilibrium, whether or not a new equilibrium is reached.

Discussion Questions

1. Think about the market for high-quality basketballs. In each of the following cases, determine which curve will shift, and in which direction. Also draw a graph and describe, in words, the changes in price and quantity. (Treat each case separately.)
   a. A rise in consumers' incomes
   b. An increase in wages paid to the workers who make the basketballs
   c. A decrease in the price of basketball hoops and other basketball gear
   d. The nation becoming obsessed with soccer
2. Have you ever found yourself shut out of a class you wanted to take because it was already full? Or has this happened to a friend of yours? Analyze this situation in terms of surplus or shortage. Are classes supplied "on a market"? Do you think it would be good if they were?

5 | Topics in Market Analysis

Before moving on to explaining real-world prices and quantities, we should stand back and ask a few framing questions. What functions do markets perform? Can we ever say that a quantity is "too little"? How much confidence should we place in the precision apparently offered by our theoretical graphs?

5.1 | Signaling and Rationing

signaling function of markets and prices: to carry information throughout the economy

rationing function of markets and prices: to determine who gets what

Markets and market prices perform two important functions. In performing their **signaling function**, they carry information from one part of an economy to another. In performing their **rationing function**, they determine who gets what quantity of any given resource.

In market systems, decisions tend to be made in a decentralized way, with everyone involved looking to markets for important pieces of information. Producers who see the price of their output rising will have an incentive to produce more. Buyers who see the price of a desired good rising will have an incentive to try to economize on its use, perhaps searching for other resources that can be substituted in production (if the buyer is a producer) or in consumption (if the buyer is a final user). It is considered to be a strength of market systems that they give people **incentives** to produce the most valuable goods while using the cheapest ones. For example, as the Japanese market for washing machines shrinks, some producers are likely to switch to making other products.

market incentives: market signals that motivate economic actors to change their behavior (perhaps in the direction of greater economic efficiency)

On the other hand, because market signaling can only tend to create this helpful economizing to the extent that the goods in question are valued *in the market*, this method of signaling has drawbacks. Clean air is not marketed, for example, so it might become polluted by a production process even if, in terms of well-being, it is more important than the goods being produced. The washing machine story was interesting in that it implied that consumers may force some degree of internalization of environmental externalities by buying "green" products, thus penalizing the producers that are relatively more polluting. However, externalities are generally perceived by economists as defects in the system, which make it impossible to assume that markets will automatically give the right signals.

The other function of the market is rationing—that is, the market system has a distributional role, determining who gets what amount of any given resource. Usually, people think of rationing in terms of government action in times of shortage. For example, during World War II people were issued ration cards indicating how much they would be allowed to buy of gasoline and certain foods. Some cities with high property values try to ensure that at least some "affordable housing" stays available, by subsidizing the construction of a set of houses and then offering them for sale at a low price. This tends to result in shortage, with more eager buyers than available houses. Because allowing the prices to be bid up would defeat the purpose of keeping the homes "affordable," cities commonly ration out the housing by using a lottery and criteria of need. Some people will get houses, and others will not.

Freedom of choice is often emphasized as an outstanding characteristic of markets, so it may seem surprising to say that at the heart of a market is a device for rationing. But rationing can be performed by the impersonal market as much as by government decision makers. For example, rationing occurs in the market for condos we have been examining. In the original scenario, 5 potential buyers get houses, and 5 do not. In the case of city governments, need and luck determine who gets the property; in the market, the rationing is based on people's ability and willingness to meet the going price.

5.2 | Shortage, Scarcity, and Inadequacy

It is important to distinguish between the conditions of "shortage," "scarcity" and "inadequacy." They all in some sense indicate an insufficiency in supply, but the terms have distinct meanings in economic analysis.

We have seen that a *shortage* is a situation in which willing and able buyers are unable to find goods to buy at the going price. We usually think of this as being the result of disequilibrium, but it may also be deliberately created. Sometimes producers intentionally choose a production and pricing strategy that will create shortages—whether of certain luxury cars, for which there is a long waiting list, or of heavily advertised toys, whose popularity is increased by the fact that kids can't get them right away. The shortage could be eliminated, and equilibrium achieved, if the producers raised the price enough. However, they have calculated that their long-run profitability will be higher if they permit a shortage to create a mystique around their product. For example, a temporary shortage of a new vehicle, such as the Chrysler PT Cruiser when it first came out, might have increased sales in the long run by generating a media "buzz."

Economists think of *scarcity* as a more general condition. As we discussed in Chapter 1, a fundamental scarcity of resources relative to everything people might need or want is what requires individuals and societies to make choices. It might be that hundreds of people would be delighted if they could move into the condos we have been discussing, because these condos are nicer than their current apartments. Nice condos are scarce—as are diamonds, Rolls-Royces, and a million other things—and prices are irrelevant in the determination of scarcity. Whereas scarcity is about an imbalance between what is available and what people would *like* to have, regardless of what they can afford, shortage is about an imbalance between the *effective* quantity demanded and the quantity supplied, at a given price. Looking at Figure 4.12, we see that if the price of apartments is set at $95,000, there is both a scarcity and a shortage. At a price of $97,000 we still have a scarcity relative to human needs and desires, but because everyone who is willing *and able* to pay gets a condo, there is no shortage. Perhaps rather unhelpfully, this means that even if hundreds of poor people are homeless and living on the streets, an economist may be able to say that there is, strictly speaking, no "shortage" of housing.

Not all kinds of scarcity are alike. We tend to feel differently about the scarcity of expensive cars (in situations when transportation needs can be met by cheaper forms of transportation) and the scarcity of affordable housing. When something that is necessary for minimal human well-being is not getting to everyone who needs it, we may use

inadequacy: a situation in which there is not enough of a good or service, provided at prices people can afford, to meet minimal requirements for human well-being

the term **inadequacy** to refer to this more important kind of scarcity. Food, shelter, and basic health care, for example, can be in inadequate supply relative to needs. Table 4.7 summarizes the characteristics of the three forms of insufficiency in supply.

Why all this attention to insufficiency? Besides shortage, surplus in markets is also possible. As we also noted in Chapter 1, abundance can be seen as a fundamental characteristic of the world (relative to the basic support of life), right alongside scarcity. And if we reject the idea that "more is better"—a topic we will take up in Chapter 10 on consumption—then not only is inadequacy a problem, but so also is *too much* (as when overeating destroys basic health). Indeed there is a symmetry between notions of excess and lack, on all counts.

5.3 | Precision Versus Accuracy

In our thought experiment about condo sellers and buyers, we visualized everyone meeting in one big room to make their deals. We assumed that all actors had firm beliefs about the prices they were willing to accept or pay, and that all had the same access to information. We assumed that the nonprice determinants of supply and demand changed slowly enough that we could meaningfully think about there being well-defined supply and demand schedules, which could be (conveniently) represented by straight lines on a graph. We assumed that there was smooth adjustment to precise new equilibrium levels of quantity and price after each change—for example, to an equilibrium where 6 condos change hands at a price of exactly $94,000 each.

In the real world, many of these assumptions are commonly violated. The numbers of buyers and sellers of condos, for example, may shift from week to week, and the deals are likely to be individually negotiated, with people not necessarily knowing what their neighbors have paid. You may have noticed that gas prices can vary within a city or even a single block. If you have ever compared notes on the fare you paid for an airplane flight with the people sitting around you, you know that a variety of prices may be possible even within the same market. In an actual market for condos, a savvy real estate agent will probably express his expectation of the price a condo will bring as a *range* of prices—for example, "in the $90,000 to $95,000 range."

This illustrates an important point about the relationship of analysis using supply-and-demand graphs to the real world. When an economist draws distinct lines and finds specific numbers for the equilibrium price and quantity, she is being **precise**—that is, exact—but she is not being particularly realistic. When the smart real estate agent specifies a range of possible prices, he is aiming to be **accurate**—that is, correct—but he is not being very precise.

precise: describes something that is exact (though it may be unrealistic)

accurate: describes something that is correct (even if only in a general way)

Often there is a tradeoff between accuracy and precision. The same issue arises in many areas of science: accurate description of complex phenomena often seems to be at odds with precise quantitative formulation of a problem. One of the most interesting recent responses to this dilemma is the development of engineering models based on "fuzzy logic." This approach rejects the assumption that all statements are either entirely true or entirely false; for example, the statement "The temperature in this room is comfortable" becomes gradually less true as the temperature deviates from the optimum. Mathematical modeling based on this perspective has led to advances in process control and other areas of engineering. Fuzzy logic is equally applicable in fields outside engineering. The statement "He is middle-aged" is untrue of a 20-year-old and a 70-year-old, and perhaps clearly true of a 45-year-old. But middle age does not begin abruptly at 40 or 43, nor does it end abruptly

Table 4.7	Distinguishing Three Forms of Insufficiency in Supply		
	Considered a Fundamental Characteristic of the World?	Always Disappears at Market Equilibrium?	Related to Basic Human Needs?
Scarcity	yes	no	no
Shortage	no	yes	no
Inadequacy	no	no	yes

some years later. Rather, it is a more or less appropriate description of people at varying ages. "He is middle-aged" may be perfectly accurate, without being precise.

Ideally we would like our economic analyses to be characterized by both accuracy and precision—but sometimes we have to choose between these qualities. How should we decide which to choose?

Precision often has the virtue of simplicity. For example, it is easier to contemplate a single point than it is to deal with ranges of various possibilities. Precision and simplicity together are qualities that are often helpful—sometimes essential—if one is to translate elements of reality into readily understood mathematical representations and graphs. For work that is purely abstract and conceptual—in which, for example, the buyers' side of a market is envisioned in the form of a demand curve—the simplicity attendant upon precise expression is very appealing.

In contrast, accuracy, with its attendant imprecision, is especially important when we are attempting to understand the real world in concrete, contextual terms. We keep the theory "in our head" to help us understand economic life, but what we actually observe is often—as in the case of widely varying condo prices or airline fares—more messy and complicated than a simple graph could represent.

If we mistakenly confuse precision with accuracy, then we might be misled into thinking that an explanation expressed in precise mathematical or graphical terms is somehow more rigorous or useful than one that takes into account particulars of history, institutions, or business strategy. This is not the case. Therefore, it is important not to put too much confidence in the apparent precision of supply and demand graphs. Supply and demand analysis is a useful, precisely formulated, conceptual tool that clever people have devised to help us gain an abstract understanding of a complex world. It does not—nor should it be expected to—give us in addition an accurate and complete description of any particular real-world market.

Discussion Questions

1. In Chapter 1 we discussed the three basic economic questions: *What* should be produced, and *what* should be maintained? *How* should production and maintenance be accomplished? *For whom* should economic activity be undertaken? Discuss how market signaling and market rationing provide some answers to these questions.

2. Explain which of the three kinds of insufficiency in supply is illustrated by each of the following, and why.
   a. You go to a store to buy a certain computer game and find that it is sold out.
   b. Jasmine can't afford to go to a doctor.
   c. Rafe can think of dozens of music CDs he'd like to buy, but he also would like to buy lots of new clothes.

6 | Explaining Real-World Prices and Quantities

How do the theories of supply, demand, and market adjustment help us to understand the real world? Generally, it would be a mistake to think that supply and demand curves actually exist as they appear in the graphs in this book; the theories are best understood as extended thought experiments. For the most part, what the theories offer is a useful vocabulary and a mental image for helping us make sense of real-world markets. We are equipped to make better sense of variations in prices and quantities when we can identify a particular market, can identify its buyers and sellers, can keep track of which factors affect sellers and which affect buyers, and can have a sense of the direction in which various events should "shift the curves."[8]

---

[8] Sometimes economists find it useful not only to imagine the curves as being upward- or downward-sloping and as shifting left or right, but also to think of them as having particular slopes or shapes. This topic will be addressed in the next chapter.

6.1 | The Case of Market Data on Crude Oil

Take, for example, the data on U.S. crude oil prices and quantities with which we began this chapter. Unlike our simple hypothetical model of a handful of condominium apartments transactors, the crude oil market is real, complicated, and of far-reaching importance. Crude oil is the resource from which are derived gasoline for transportation, heating fuels for homes and offices, and inputs to the production of materials such as plastics. The events that have occurred in the last few decades in the global and national petroleum markets have received considerable attention, because fluctuations in prices and quantities have had tremendous impact across economies at national and international levels.

We will focus on the market in which U.S. oil refineries buy crude oil. Sellers include both U.S. petroleum-extracting companies and foreign producers. Among foreign producers, some are in countries that belong to the Organization of Petroleum Exporting Countries (OPEC), and others are not. All these producers together are the "suppliers" of crude oil in the market we will examine, and the "demanders" are the U.S. refineries. U.S. refineries' demand for crude oil is a derived demand. That is, how much they want to buy as an input to their production processes depends, ultimately, on how much of their outputs, such as gasoline, are demanded by their customers, which include U.S. businesses, households, and public enterprises.

Figure 4.13 presents the same time series data as shown in Figures 4.1 and 4.2, but in a single graph, where both prices and quantities are measured along the vertical axis.[9] Some of the price points are labeled with the year they occurred, for ease of reference. For example, in the year 2000, the price that was paid by refineries averaged about $26 per barrel, and the quantity bought by refiners averaged about 15 million barrels per day.

Note the big patterns: Over some periods in the early years, the price was relatively flat before it rose sharply, fell, and then fluctuated within a narrower band. The quantity of crude oil bought by U.S. refineries rose somewhat, then fell off somewhat, and then gradually rose again. This sort of behavior, in which prices show large fluctuations in proportional terms, while quantities fluctuate much less in proportional terms, is fairly typical in markets for many raw material commodities. To the extent that prices are set in auction-type spot markets (which is often the case for at least some portion of the marketed raw materials), prices can change rapidly in response to changes in market conditions. The physical quantity, however, is harder to change. On the supply side, once the oil is loaded on the boat it cannot be put back into the ground, nor can new pumping derricks be built in a day. On the demand side, once embodied technologies that make

Figure 4.13 Crude Oil to U.S. Refiners, Price, and Quantity, 1969–2002

The actual prices and quantities recorded in the market for crude oil are both measured on the vertical axes of this graph. For example, in the year 2000 the price that was paid by refineries averaged about $26 per barrel, and the quantity bought by refiners averaged about 15 million barrels per day.

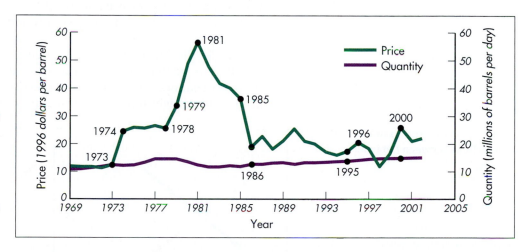

---

[9] The graph expresses prices in "real" dollars in order to express the price of oil relative to other goods. That is, the prices shown have been adjusted to eliminate changes that are due to inflation in the economy at large. In microeconomics, it is the price of one good relative to another that is most relevant. But sometimes the whole price level can change—as with the inflation that occurred in the United States in 1973–1974 largely because of these increases in oil prices. This is a topic for macroeconomics.

Figure 4.14 Crude Oil to U.S. Refiners: Relationship Between Price and Quantity
Price and quantity data are plotted against each other on this graph. Again we can see that in the year 2000, the price that was paid by refineries averaged about $26 per barrel, and the quantity bought by refiners averaged about 15 million barrels per day.

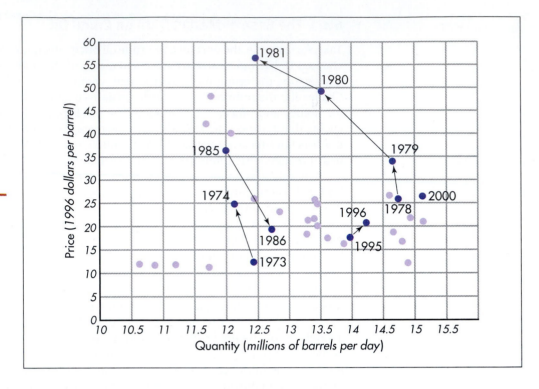

use of cheap oil are in place (such as large cars and home fuel oil furnaces), it can take time to find ways to cut back. Thus price tends to be more flexible than quantity.

6.2 | Making the Transition from Fact to Theory

The data in Figure 4.13 are displayed again in Figure 4.14, but in a different format. As in the theoretical diagrams just developed, quantity is now on the horizontal axis and price is on the vertical axis. Some of the points are labeled by year in order to remind us that the graphs really are portraying the same information. For example, in Figure 4.14, we see the same information that we just examined for 2000: a price of about $26 and a quantity of about 15 million barrels a day. This graph helps us make the transition from data alone to the combined use of empirical data and theory. We have drawn arrows between some sets of points that we will refer to later.

It might be tempting to think of drawing supply and demand curves through any point to make it appear that each data point represents a market equilibrium, as shown, for example, for the data point for the year 2000 in Figure 4.15(a). But we need to recall, in fact, that the market adjustment theory tells us only about the probable *direction* of market dynamics, not about their speed or whether an equilibrium is reached. The same point might represent a disequilibrium, where, for example, pro-

Figure 4.15 Various Possible Connections Between Data and Theory
(a) Can the empirical data from the year 2000 be represented as an equilibrium in the oil market?
(b) Or do they correspond to a disequilibrium in the oil market?

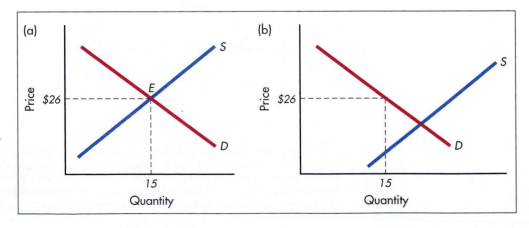

ducers would like to supply more but, because of physical or political constraints, cannot do so, as illustrated in Figure 4.15(b).

Finally, we need to remember that there may be considerable variation in prices and quantities. In fact, "the market" for crude oil bought by U.S. refineries consists of a number of markets. Refiners buy Alaskan oil of one particular grade on one market, while another market may deal in OPEC oil of a different type. Prices on all these markets may change by the day or hour. The "price" we have given for the year 2000 is an index, or composite, of all the different prices that occurred in all such markets over all the days of the year.[10] During 2000 the average number of barrels per day varied, month to month, from 13.7 million to 15.8 million, and the real price similarly varied from $24 to $30 per barrel. Sometimes the simplicity and precision of the "supply and demand theory" diagrams tempts analysts to forget the real-world complications that would be involved in a truly *accurate* representation of a market.

The day-to-day movements in particular parts of the oil market can be so complex, viewed in detail, that many economists spend their entire careers trying to make sense of them. How can we make sense of all this? Without getting into full detail, the theory can still help us to analyze some of the major swings. Recall two important conclusions of the theory:

> When the *supply* curve shifts, price and quantity tend to adjust in *opposite* directions.

> When the *demand* curve shifts, price and quantity tend to adjust in *the same* direction.

Looking at Figure 4.14, we can see that in the period from 1979 to 1981, prices were rising while quantities were falling. From our theory, we have a hunch that *supply* shifts were the main factor behind these movements. Looking at the smaller change from 1995 to 1996, we see that price and quantity both rose. Our theory indicates that we will want to pay special attention to *demand* changes that might have occurred.

6.3 | Adding History

Having examined empirical and theoretical considerations, we need information from history to complete our story.

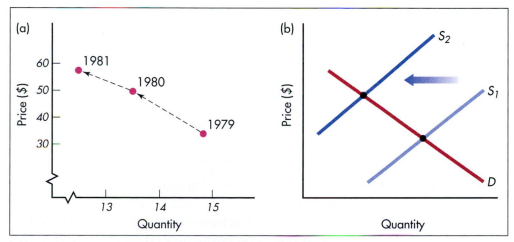

Figure 4.16 The Oil Market: 1979–1981 Middle East Disruptions
(a) The empirical data show the price of oil rising and the quantity bought and sold falling over these two years.
(b) Theoretically, we can interpret the historical events of these two years, which explain the changes we see in the empirical data, as a leftward shift of the supply curve for oil.

---

[10] For example, if one-third of the oil sold at $30 and the other two-thirds at $24, then a simple index, or composite, price might be calculated as $(1/3)30 + (2/3)24 = 26.

A Supply Story. In 1979 Iran experienced a revolution. The Shah was deposed, and tensions between the United States and the new government led to President Carter's banning all U.S. imports of Iranian oil. These events, and the war between Iran and Iraq that began in 1978, created disruptions in supply that partly explain changes in the market over the period 1979–1981. Figure 4.16(a) shows the real-world data for this period. Figure 4.16(b) shows how we can visualize the effect of these historical events on the oil market in terms of a leftward shift in the supply curve.

As supply declined, the price of crude oil shot up. Quantities demanded were, however, slower to adjust, because many final users of petroleum products found themselves, in the short run, stuck with technologies designed for cheap oil. Over a period of time, the quantity fell, thanks to reduced fuel use by households, increased fuel efficiency in home heating and industrial uses, and more fuel-efficient cars.[11]

A Demand Story. Turning to a later period, one of the factors contributing to the rise in both prices and quantities from 1995 to 1996 was the fact that the United States experienced a very cold winter. The rise in demand for refined heating fuels thus contributed to a rise in derived demand for crude oil. Figure 4.17(a) shows the data for the period 1995–1996. Figure 4.17(b) shows how we can visualize the effect of this historical event on the oil market in terms of a shift to the right in the demand curve.

Supply and demand analysis, and the theory of market adjustment, thus help us understand some of the factors underlying this real-world market. Similar stories can be told for other historical changes in market conditions for oil.

A Warning. Some caution is in order. In the real world, supply and demand sometimes shift at the same time, and for a number of different reasons, so that our stories are not always so clear. Sometimes we have to take into account that we start from a disequilibrium position, as a new historical event charges onto the scene before the economy has had a chance to "catch up" with the last one. The fact that a variety of prices and quantities may be possible in the same market also complicates the picture. In the oil market,

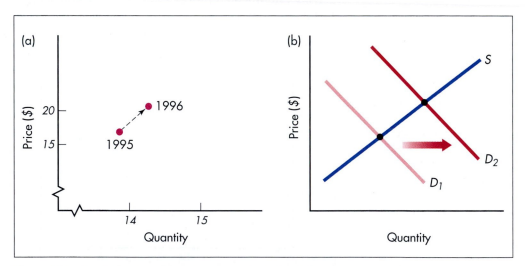

Figure 4.17 The Oil Market: The Cold Winter of 1995–1996
(a) The empirical data show the price of oil rising and the quantity bought and sold rising over this time period.
(b) Theoretically, we can interpret the historical events of this winter, which explain the changes we see in the empirical data, as a rightward shift of the demand curve for oil.

---

[11] This economizing was short-lived, however. Looking at the longer time series graph, you can see that once oil prices fell again, oil consumption resumed its upward path. As shown in Figure 4.14, oil consumption in 2000 was higher than it had ever been.

for example, factors such as the size of inventories held by producers and the demand for commodities that arises from financial speculation can lead to complicated adjustments. At times, the directions of actual changes in price or quantity may not confirm our predictions from theory. Although the theory of supply and demand is an important tool, economists need to know much more about their markets than theory alone.

6.4 | Price Floors and Price Ceilings

price floor: a law or agreement that puts a lower limit on prices

price ceiling: a law or agreement that puts an upper limit on prices

Crude oil markets also give us prime real-world examples of the ways in which economic actors sometimes deliberately *prevent* market adjustment processes from occurring. **Price floors** are laws or agreements that state that prices will not be allowed to fall below a certain level. **Price ceilings** are laws or agreements that state that prices will not be allowed to rise above a certain level. In the case of oil, history saw market forces subordinated to both, through revenue-maximizing and political forces.

Price Floors and Producer Cartels. You no doubt noticed in the time series graph that, in addition to the time of the Iranian disruptions, prices also rose sharply during 1973–1974 and 1978–1979. These rises, and part of the rise from 1979 to 1981 as well, can be largely attributed to the price floors set by the OPEC oil-producing countries. The OPEC countries had figured out that they would gain more revenue from their oil sales by selling less but charging a lot more for it.[12] Consider Figure 4.18, however. The price floor can be illustrated in a supply and demand diagram as a line that cuts horizontally above the equilibrium point. Left on its own, the market would (eventually) settle at price P_E. But the price floor says that all transactions must take place at price P_{floor} or above. At this price, sellers would like to supply a quantity such as Q_S, whereas buyers are willing to purchase only quantity Q_D. (If the price floor cut below the equilibrium point, it would have no effect. Why?)

cartel: a group of producers who mutually agree to limit their production in order to sustain a price floor

The producers obviously cannot just declare a high price and sell all they want. In order to maintain the high price, they have to form a **cartel**. A cartel is a group of producers who mutually agree to limit their production to something like Q_D, in order to keep prices high at a price like P_{floor}. (We will discuss cartels in more detail in Chapter 12 where we deal with market power.)

A cartel, however, is not a particularly stable form of economic and social organization. Each member has an incentive to try to sell a little more than its allotted

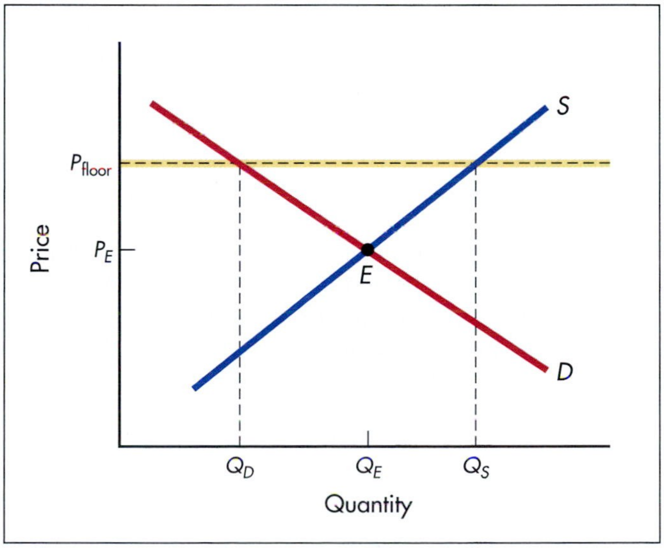

Figure 4.18 A Price Floor
When a law or agreement puts a floor on prices that is above the equilibrium price level, sellers will be able to sell only the quantity that buyers are willing to buy—that is, the quantity Q_D. The price will generally be higher, and the quantity bought and sold lower, than they would be if market forces were allowed to work.

---

[12] We will discuss how they knew this would raise revenues when we examine the "price elasticity of demand" in the following chapter. The actual effects of a price floor also depend on the elasticity of the supply curve, an issue we will illustrate in Chapter 11 with the example of rent control.

Figure 4.19 A Price Ceiling
When a law or agreement puts a ceiling on prices that is below the equilibrium price level, buyers will be able to buy only the quantity that sellers are willing to sell—that is, the quantity Q_S. The price will generally be lower, and the quantity bought and sold lower, than they would be if market forces were allowed to work.

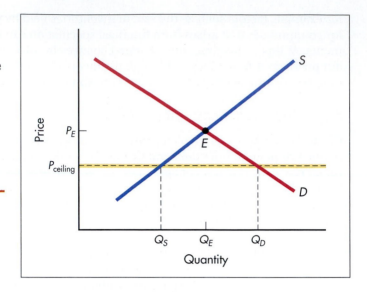

amount or offer just a little discount to its buyers in order to increase its share in the total offerings. But if all the members keep on doing this, the cartel—and the above-equilibrium price—will collapse over time. OPEC, in this way, was no different from other cartels. Up until 1981 the spectacular run-up in prices included many price increases declared by OPEC. But after 1981 the cartel found the price floors harder and harder to maintain. Some OPEC countries started offering discounts. Non-OPEC suppliers, meanwhile, reacting to high world prices, increased their production. The sudden drop in prices to U.S. refiners from 1985 to 1986 that we see in the time series data was largely due to Saudi Arabia's giving up on trying to maintain the OPEC price.

As the theoretical graph indicates, such a price drop is the predicted result of removing the price floor and allowing market forces to reassert themselves. You might say that market forces finally won out—for a while—but in the meantime, oil prices took a wild ride for over a decade.

Price Ceilings and Government Rationing. Look back at the flat area of the price line in Figure 4.13 from 1974 to 1978. After the first supply cutbacks, in 1973 and 1974, the U.S. government was fearful of the inflationary and distributional effects of letting the economy react to the full impact of the world price increases. It was under a lot of political pressure by consumers, manufacturers, and transportation companies for protection from the price rise. Because of these worries and pressures, the U.S. government enacted controls on the prices that could be charged by domestic oil producers. Refiners still had to pay the world price for imported oil, but this price ceiling meant that they could purchase U.S.-produced crude oil at lower, regulated prices.

A price ceiling is illustrated in Figure 4.19 as a line that cuts below market equilibrium. The price is allowed to go no higher than $P_{ceiling}$. Of course, at $P_{ceiling}$ the quantity demanded exceeds the quantity supplied. Because the market for oil could no longer perform the rationing function through price adjustments, the government had to step in and directly ration the limited quantity supplied among the competing demands.[13] The Department of Energy decided which activities and regions would have the highest priority for getting oil and directed the limited quantities there. Many people remember

---

[13] Recall that the market rations by price and ability to pay: If market forces had been left in charge, the poor, elderly apartment dweller in Minnesota would have gotten no heating fuel, while rich owners of recreational vehicles in Florida could still have filled up their tanks.

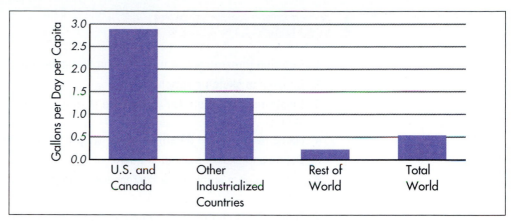

Figure 4.20 Global Consumption of Oil per Capita, 1998
Residents of the United States and Canada use, directly or indirectly, more petroleum per person than residents of other industrialized countries, and far more than residents of the rest of the world.

Graph source: U.S. Department of Energy, http://www.eia.doe.gov/pub/oil_gas/petroleum/analysis_publications/ oil_market_basics.

waiting in their cars in long lines for gas or being able to buy only on certain days of the week, according to their license plate number.

In 1979 the price controls began to be lifted. What was the effect on prices? Look back at the time series data.

6.5 | A Last Thought

The United States is a major user of petroleum, because of both the size of the U.S. population and the high per capita consumption that characterizes the United States and Canada. As illustrated in Figure 4.20, this use is very high even when compared to other industrialized countries. Although U.S. producers and consumers were distressed about many of the adjustments they were forced to make during the times of high oil prices, one might wonder whether a high price is really such a bad thing. In spite of spikes in prices, throughout recent decades U.S. consumers have been buying more cars and driving them more miles. Many European countries, which levy extremely high gasoline taxes, seem to achieve a standard of living as high as, or higher than, that of the United States without such intensive oil consumption. Given the pollution, and particularly the global warming effects, caused by burning fossil fuels, many believe that the price of oil paid by U.S. consumers is currently too low.

Discussion Questions

1. Observers of Mount Simon University have noted that over the last few years, both the tuition charged and the number of students attending the university have risen. What sorts of things could explain this behavior? Explain using supply and demand analysis where tuition is the "price" and number of students is the "quantity." Carefully distinguish between movements *along* curves and shifts *of* curves.

2. Sometimes when price ceilings are imposed, illegal markets (historically called black markets) spring up, where willing buyers and sellers trade, in secret, at prices other than the regulated one. Suppose that, in our original example of condominium apartment sales (Table 4.3), a legal price ceiling had been set at $92,000. Explain, using a graph illustrating a price ceiling, why some buyers and sellers might be tempted to go outside the law.

Review Questions

1. Describe three modes of investigation that economists use.
2. Define and sketch a supply curve.
3. Illustrate on a graph: (a) a decrease in quantity supplied and (b) a decrease in supply.
4. Name five nonprice determinants of supply for a product sold by firms.
5. Define and sketch a demand curve.
6. Illustrate on a graph: (a) a decrease in quantity demanded and (b) a decrease in demand.
7. Name five nonprice determinants of demand for a product purchased by households.
8. Draw a graph illustrating surplus, shortage, and equilibrium.
9. Name two types of models, in terms of their treatment of time.
10. Name two functions of markets.
11. Name three ways in which supply can be insufficient.
12. Describe two ways in which laws or agreements can put limits on market adjustment.

Exercises

1. Explain in words why the supply curve slopes upward.
2. At a price of $5 per bag, William is willing to supply 3 bags of oranges, Margarite 2 bags, and Felipe 5 bags. At a price of $7 per bag, William is willing to supply 5 bags, Margarite 4 bags, and Felipe 7 bags. Graph and carefully label the individual supply curves, and then graph the market supply curve for oranges (at these two prices).
3. At a price of $8 per ticket, Shalimar goes to 2 movies per month, Wen goes to 1 movie per month, and Adam goes to 3 movies per month. At a price of $10 per ticket, Shalimar goes to 1 movie, Wen goes to 0 movies, and Adam goes to 2 movies. Graph and carefully label the individual demand curves, and then graph the market demand curve for movie tickets (at these two prices).
4. Between January 1999 and September 2000, crude oil prices to U.S. refiners tripled. Which of the following could be possible explanations? (There may be more than one.) Illustrate *one* of the cases you chose with a supply and demand graph.
   a. OPEC cut back its sales to the United States.
   b. The northeastern United States suffered cold weather.
   c. Winter was mild in Europe.
   d. Concern about global warming caused U.S. drivers to drive less.
5. Suppose a newspaper report indicates that the price of wheat has fallen. Which of the following events (all fictional) could be possible explanations? (There may be more than one.) Illustrate *one* of the cases you chose with a supply and demand graph.
   a. A drought has hit wheat-growing areas.
   b. A new science report indicates that rice is bad for one's health.
   c. As a consequence of increasing health concerns, tobacco farmers have begun growing other crops.
   d. The government has increased its price floor for wheat.

6. Match each concept in Column A with an example in Column B.

Column A	Column B
a. substitute goods	**i.** self-interested rational behavior
b. a nonprice determinant of demand	**ii.** tea and coffee
c. a nonprice determinant of supply	**iii.** the price of resources
d. rationing	**iv.** hunger
e. economists' frequent assumption	**v.** tea and milk
f. derived demand	**vi.** consumer income
g. inadequacy	**vii.** wheat purchased by a bread manufacturer
h. complementary goods	**viii.** "Purchase a ticket to enter."

7. For exercise 4, illustrate in a *single* graph *all* of the cases you chose. (This challenging exercise will give you an opportunity to go beyond anything shown in the text.)

Working with Supply and Demand

Chapter 5

To most people, elasticity is something they trust will keep their underwear in place. To economists, on the other hand, *elasticity* is a technical term, referring to how responsive buyers and sellers are to changes in prices and other factors. Economic actors on both the buying and selling sides of a market often need to know more about supply and demand than just the general factors discussed in the last chapter.

1 | How Much Money Will Sales Bring In?

For example, how did the OPEC countries know that when they raised the prices they charged for crude oil, as we saw in Chapter 4, their revenue would go *up*? A seller's revenue is the flow of total proceeds from sales, over some time period, found by taking the number of units sold during that time and multiplying this by the price(s) at which they sold. In equation form (and assuming that all units sell at the same price),

$$\text{Revenue} = \text{Price} \times \text{Quantity} = P \times Q$$

For example, if the price is $30 per barrel and a producer sells 100 barrels in a month, the producer receives revenue of $3000 for that month.

If sellers have no market power, they must sell at the market-dictated price. The only thing they get to decide about is quantity. Many sellers, though, do have some discretion in pricing, and the most powerful sellers have considerable leeway in how they set their price. Revenue depends on price in two ways:

1. Most obviously, a higher price will bring higher revenue if the quantity sold remains unchanged. We can see this from the foregoing equation. If the oil producer can sell 100 barrels at $40, instead of at $30, the producer will clearly make more money.

2. But less obviously, what happens to revenue also depends on *how responsive the buyers are to the price change.* Higher prices tend to reduce Q, the quantity demanded. (We counted on this tendency when we drew demand curves as downward-sloping in Chapter 4.)

When the OPEC countries raised their prices, they no doubt were conscious of the fact that higher prices tend to make buyers want to buy less. They were betting, however, that the decrease in quantity demanded would not be so great as to counteract completely their increase in price. In terms of the equation, they expected that the net effect of the rise in price and the fall in quantity would be higher revenue. Let's illustrate this graphically.

OPEC raises its price:

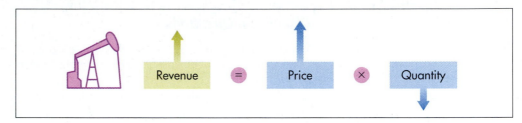

The arrows in the diagram indicate the direction and the strength of changes. To keep the equation "in balance" across the equals sign, the rise in price, with little negative effect on quantity, must lead to a rise in revenue.

However, a rise in price does not always bring a rise in revenue. When sellers raise their prices, it is also possible for their revenue to go down, if the price increase drives away many buyers. For example, suppose your community Midnight Basketball program decides, as a fund raiser, to sell hot dogs at a stand at a local street fair. You charge $4.00 per hot dog, and so does another stand a few feet away from yours. You (and the people at the other stand) can dash out at any time to buy more raw hot dogs at a local store, and your staff can easily handle customers without their having to stand in long lines, so meeting whatever quantity is demanded by customers is not a problem. What will happen if you raise your price to $5.00? If the other stand keeps its price at $4.00, you might still sell a few hot dogs—perhaps some people will fail to check the other seller's price. But overall, the quantity you sell will probably fall considerably as everyone goes to the other stand, and your revenue will drop. Again, we can illustrate this graphically.

Midnight Basketball raises its price:

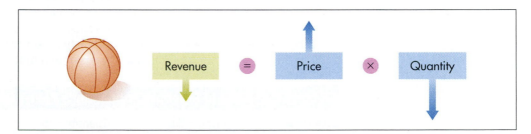

As you can see, when they are thinking about changing their prices, it is important for sellers to consider the possible *responsiveness of buyer behavior* to the price change. Economists characterize economics actors' responsiveness to changes in conditions using a measure called **elasticity**. OPEC members knew that their revenues would go up (if they could hold their cartel together) because they had figured out that the demand they faced was *price inelastic*, or not very responsive to price changes. On the other hand, the community program selling hot dogs had better not raise prices, because it

elasticity: a measure of the responsiveness of economic actors to changes in conditions

faces buyers whose decisive responses indicate a demand that is markedly *price elastic,* or very responsive to price changes.[1]

The same concept can also be applied to other kinds of responsiveness. This chapter examines the price elasticity of demand, the price elasticity of supply, and the income elasticity of demand. The concept of elasticity is important not only to sellers of goods and services who want to predict the effect of price changes on revenues. It is also important to buyers who want to understand their expenditures and (as we will see in later chapters) to policymakers in their decision making about taxes, tariffs, and regulations.

Discussion Questions

1. You sometimes hear of instances of "price gouging," where someone will sell an item for far more than the usual price. For example, scalpers at sold-out concerts or sporting events may try to resell a ticket with a face value of $30 for $100 or more. In economists' terms, are scalpers counting on demand being price inelastic (like the demand for crude oil) or price elastic (like the demand for Midnight Basketball's hot dogs)?

2. Suppose you are making the pricing decision for the Midnight Basketball program. If you know that the other stand will keep its price at $4.00, do you think your revenues would be higher or lower if you *dropped* your price to $3.75? Illustrate using the revenue equation and arrows, as in the examples given in the text. (For further discussion, consider whether expecting the other stand to maintain its price is a reasonable assumption.)

2 | The Price Elasticity of Demand

Executives at Braeburn Publishing are trying to decide what price to charge for a new book of poetry. Although the firm competes with many other firms in the market for books in general, it has sole rights to sell this particular book, so it has some power over the price it sets. In order to see how responsive demand for the new poetry book is to variations in price, Braeburn Publishing decides to test-market it in two locations that are very similar in terms of consumer preferences and incomes but are far enough apart so that the company can set a different price in each location.[2] Table 5.1 and Figure 5.1 show the data the marketing department has collected on prices, quantity sold during the month of the test, and the resulting revenue. In Location A, 5 copies sold at a price of $5, whereas in Location B, 4 copies sold at $8. Just as in this example, real empirical data on prices and quantities are generally limited to specific *points.*

It is often helpful, however, to think of elasticities first in terms of theoretical supply and demand curves, and we will take this approach first. When we look at the respon-

Table 5.1	Sales of Braeburn Publishing's Poetry Book		
Location A	Price = $5	Quantity = 5	Revenue = $5 × 5 = $25
Location B	Price = $8	Quantity = 4	Revenue = $8 × 4 = $32

---

[1] So far, we have talked about only the revenue side of a seller's decisions. To make a fully informed and rational decision, people who want to sell a good or service will also have to take into account how much it cost them to produce it.

[2] The two locations should have similar consumers so that the company can infer that any difference in quantity demanded is due to the difference in price, rather than to different consumer characteristics. In the real world, such test marketing would probably include more than two locations and be more sophisticated in other ways as well. We present a simplified case.

Figure 5.1 Sales of Braeburn Publishing's Poetry Book

Braeburn Publishing would like to figure out how best to set the price for its poetry book. It might undertake test marketing in two locations to see how variations in price affect the quantity demanded.

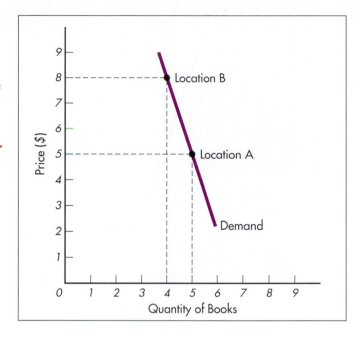

siveness of quantity demanded to price, we can think of it as a movement along a demand curve that encompasses the points we observe. Later, we will introduce a mathematical approach.

2.1 | Price-Inelastic Demand

price-inelastic demand: a relationship between price and quantity characterized by relatively weak responses of buyers to price changes. In this case, revenues to the seller change directly with the price.

Demand for a good is **price inelastic** if the effect of a price change on the quantity demanded is fairly *small*. In this case, revenues move *in the same direction* as the price. A rise in the price for an inelastically demanded good will tend to increase revenue, whereas a fall in the price will tend to decrease revenue.

There are three main reasons why demand might be inelastic:

- ⊙ There are very few good, close substitutes for the good or service.
- ⊙ The good or service is something that people feel they *need*, rather than just *want*.
- ⊙ The good or service is a very small part of a buyer's budget.

For example, there are no good, close substitutes for petroleum products in the operation of standard motor vehicles or fuel-oil furnaces. When OPEC suddenly increased oil prices, some final buyers were able to switch to using substitute forms of energy, but for many this was not technologically possible. Of course, people's lives would have been severely disrupted if they could not get to work or warm their homes, so oil was also a *needed* good. Both these factors made the demand for oil relatively inelastic. The last reason—the good or service being a small part of the buyer's budget—was not the case for oil. But there are cases where this reason applies. You can guess that few people will change their driving habits just because the toll on a bridge rises from 50¢ to 60¢, for example.

The effect of a price change for an inelastically demanded good is shown in Figure 5.2, which illustrates the data derived from Braeburn Publishing's test markets. Recall that to find the area of a rectangle, you multiply its height times its width. Hence the area of the large, olive and dark green rectangle A in Figure 5.2 is its height (price of $5) times its width (quantity of 5 books), or $25. This is just price × quantity, which means that the rectangular area A measures revenue in Location A. Look at how revenue differs in Location B, where the price was set at $8. The revenue indicated by the large, blue and dark green rectangle B is $8 times 4 books, or $32. On the

Figure 5.2 Sales and Revenues for Braeburn Publishing's Poetry Book: Price-Inelastic Demand

Braeburn Publishing's revenues in the two locations are represented by the rectangles A and B, whose areas are equal to price × quantity. Because the dark green area belongs in both rectangles, we can compare the "left over" parts and see that revenue in Location B is greater than revenue in Location A. Raising the price of the poetry book *raises* revenue, because the quantity demanded is not very responsive to price.

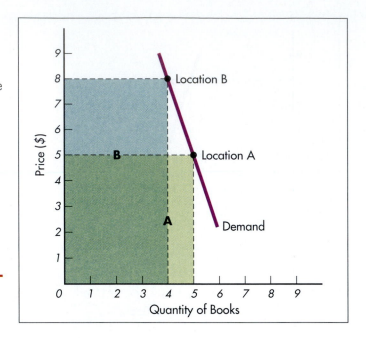

graph, because both rectangles share the dark green area, you can just compare the parts "left over"—either just blue or just olive green—to see which revenue is greater. Clearly, revenue is greater with the higher price, in Location B.

2.2 | Price-Elastic Demand

price-elastic demand: a relationship between price and quantity characterized by relatively strong responses of buyers to price changes. In this case, revenues to the seller change inversely with the price.

Conversely, of course, demand for a good is **price elastic** if the effect of a price change on the quantity demanded is fairly *large*. In this case, revenues move *inversely* with price. A rise in the price for an elastically demanded good will tend to decrease revenue, whereas a fall in the price will tend to increase revenue.

There are three main reasons why demand may be elastic:

⊃ There are a number of good, close substitutes for the good.

⊃ The good is merely wanted, rather than needed.

⊃ The good makes up a large part of the budget of the buyer.

For example, in the case of the hot dogs sold at the fair by the Midnight Basketball program, there were a number of good, close substitutes. Buyers could just go to a neighboring hot dog stand. To the extent a good is merely wanted (as is ice cream), rather than needed (as are basic foodstuffs and medicine), demand for it will tend to be more elastic. Studies typically find that demand for airline travel is more elastic for people going on vacation than for business travelers. Demand also tends to be more price elastic when the good makes up a large part of the budget of the buyer, because then the buyer will be more motivated to seek out substitutes.

Braeburn Publishing also test-markets a new mystery novel, but it turns out that many similar mysteries are being marketed at the same time. As shown in Table 5.2 and

Table 5.2	Sales of Braeburn Publishing's Mystery Novel		
Location A	Price = $5	Quantity = 5	Revenue = $5 × 5 = $25
Location B	Price = $8	Quantity = 2	Revenue = $8 × 2 = $16

Figure 5.3 Sales and Revenues for Braeburn Publishing's Mystery Novel: Price-Elastic Demand
Unlike in the case of its poetry book, Braeburn Publishing faces an *elastic* demand for its mystery novel. Raising the price of the mystery reduces the quantity demanded by so much that revenue *decreases*.

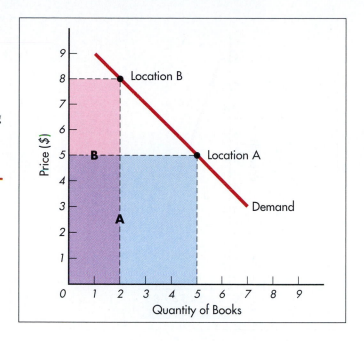

Figure 5.3, demand for this mystery novel is price elastic. At a price in Location A of $5 and quantity demanded of 5, revenue is $25 (just as it was for the poetry book). But for the mystery, a higher price of $8 in Location B is associated with a much smaller quantity sold, only 2 units. Revenue is only $8 × 2 units = $16 in Location B. Rectangle B in Figure 5.3 is smaller than rectangle A. With a higher price, revenue is lower.

2.3 | Elasticity and Slope

You will notice that the elastic demand in Figure 5.3 involves a noticeably flatter curve than the inelastic demand in Figure 5.2. It is true that *when you compare movements along demand curves that go through a specific point on graphs with the same scale,* as in Figure 5.4, the flatter demand curve will represent the more elastic demand and the

Figure 5.4 Comparing Elasticities on Curves That Pass Through a Common Point
You can't always tell which of two demand curves represents the more elastic demand just by noting which is flatter, but if the curves you are comparing *are on the same scale and go through the same point*, the demand represented by the flatter one is more elastic.

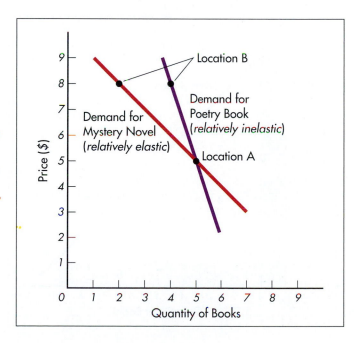

Figure 5.5 Sales of Braeburn Publishing's Mystery Novel: Another Scale

A relatively elastic demand curve can be made to look "steep" just by changing the scale of the graph. (This is the same demand curve for the mystery novel as shown in Figure 5.4.)

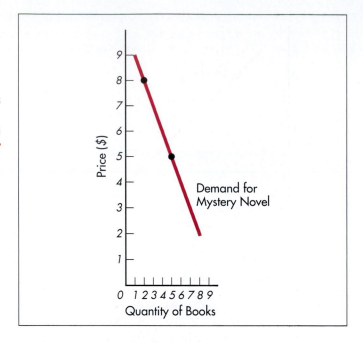

steeper one the less elastic demand. Noting that both the poetry book and the mystery novel had the same price and quantity combination in Location A, we can show both implied demand curves in Figure 5.4, and we note that the demand curve for the more elastically demanded good (the mystery) is also flatter.

Elasticity is *not* just the same thing as slope, however. For one thing, we could make any curve seem "flat" or "steep" by changing the scale of the axis. Figure 5.5 shows the same demand curve for the mystery novel as before, but with a different horizontal scale. This curve looked "flat" in earlier graphs; now it looks "steep."

For another thing, elasticity varies at different points along a straight-line curve. Figure 5.6 shows a simple, straight-line demand curve with a moderate slope. An

Figure 5.6 Elasticity Varies Along a Straight-Line Demand Curve

Moving from point *A* to point *B*, demand is inelastic. Moving from point *B* to point *C*, demand is elastic.

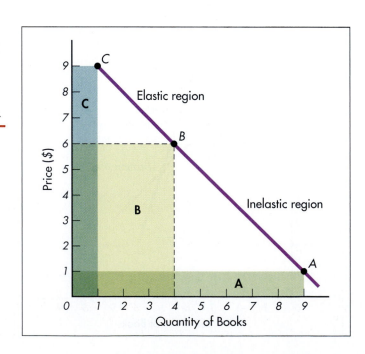

increase in price such that sales move from point *A* to point *B* clearly increases the revenue rectangle. The rather thin rectangle A clearly has a smaller area than the new, more "squarish" rectangle B. Demand is *inelastic* for this shift from a low to a medium price. However, *further* increasing the price such that sales are represented by point *C* leads to a drop in revenue: Demand is *elastic* when prices are in this high range. There is no way around actually checking what happens for any *specific* price change. Elasticity, then, is not, in general, a concept that applies to demand curves throughout the full possible range of prices, so it is not identical to slope.[3]

In two extreme cases, however, we can identify elasticity from the slope. This is possible when the demand curve is perfectly vertical, or **perfectly inelastic**, and when it is perfectly horizontal, or **perfectly elastic** (where *elasticity* is understood to mean price elasticity). Both cases are shown in Figure 5.7. Although these are largely just economists' thought experiments, we can think of some cases where real-world demand might come close to these extremes.

Perfectly Inelastic Demand.   Perfectly inelastic demand means that quantity demanded does not respond at all to price. Suppose you are on medication, and you must take exactly three pills a day to survive. Would a 10% increase in the price of the medication change the quantity you demand? Chances are your demand would be perfectly inelastic in the range of that price change, because you unquestionably need the medicine.

Think about what happens to revenue if the price increases and demand is perfectly inelastic. With quantity demanded fixed, the revenues collected by the seller go up dollar for dollar with the price increase. In the case of much-needed goods with very inelastic demand, such as lifesaving drugs and basic foodstuffs, private financial incentives may be at odds with social well-being. Powerful sellers interested only in extracting the greatest possible revenue could raise the price to the absolute highest that people could pay.

For this reason, in markets for certain kinds of health care commodities or basic foodstuffs, governments sometimes step in to set a regulated price that gives the seller a fair return but not an excessive one, while ensuring that many people will get what they need. Controversy has arisen over whether that practice is appropriate for the pricing of AIDS medication and also erupted, in the wake of September 11, 2001, over drugs to treat anthrax.

perfectly inelastic demand curve: a demand curve that is vertical, which means that quantity demanded does not respond at all to price

perfectly elastic demand curve: a demand curve that is horizontal, which means that quantity demanded is extremely sensitive to price

Figure 5.7 Perfect Inelasticity and Perfect Elasticity
When quantities are completely unresponsive to price, the curve is vertical, reflecting perfectly inelastic demand. When any change in price would bring about an "infinite" change in quantity, the curve is horizontal and demand perfectly elastic.

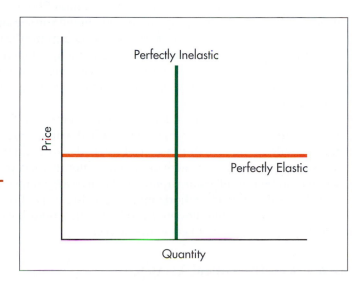

---

[3] You can test this statement mathematically later on, if you wish. There is, in fact, a "constant-elasticity" shape for a demand curve. Instead of being a straight line with a constant slope, a constant-elasticity demand curve is a curved line bowed in toward the origin.

Deal Paves Way for Generic HIV Drugs

NEWS in context

PRETORIA—AIDS activists and two major pharmaceutical companies reached milestone agreements that allow generic drug makers in South Africa to produce life-extending medication for those infected with the deadly virus, officials announced yesterday.

. . . The agreements . . . are expected to result in another major drop in price for the antiretroviral drugs. . . . Currently, the lowest price for antiretroviral medicine in the developing world is slightly less than $300 annually; the cost can be more than $10,000

in the United States and other wealthy countries, where the drugs are protected under patent laws.

. . . [South Africa's] Competition Commission [ruled] in October that GlaxoSmithKline and Boehringer had violated the country's Competition Act by excessive pricing and refusing to license their patents to generic manufacturers in return for a reasonable royalty.

. . . Over time, advocates and complainants hope, the price for the . . . therapy will fall to about $150 annually. ○

Adapted from an article by John Donnelly, *Boston Globe*, December 11, 2003.

How is it that a 1-year supply of the same good can be priced at $300 in one place and at $10,000 in another? What is it about this good that allows the producers to charge $10,000 in wealthy countries?

Sometimes sellers themselves are guided by notions of what is a "fair" price. Economists have noticed that few stores, for example, raise the price of umbrellas during rainstorms. The stores could almost certainly get away with charging higher prices to people whose only alternative is to get soaking wet. However, the sellers also know that if they want repeat business from their customers, they should not ruin their reputation for fair dealing by engaging in such price gouging.

Perfectly Elastic Demand. Perfectly elastic demand, on the other hand, means that any price change, no matter how small, leads to an "infinite" change in quantity demanded. For example, suppose your Midnight Basketball hot dog stand shares a location with another community group selling the exactly same brand of hot dog. If you price your hot dogs even 5¢ or 10¢ above your competition, why should you sell any at all? Would any customer ever come up and say, "Give me a hot dog, and charge me the higher price?" The horizontal demand curve represents a case where you can sell "as much as you want to" at the "going price," but nothing at all if you raise your price. A seller that has to take the going price as given is called a **price taker.** (This corresponds to a market structure of "perfect competition," to be discussed in Chapter 11.)

price taker: a seller that faces perfectly elastic demand for its good

One case where demand tends to be very elastic in the real world is in the market for general-skilled labor, when general-skilled workers are plentiful. Employers are the buyers or demanders in this case. If all you had to offer on the labor market were general skills, such as flipping burgers or sweeping floors, then you and all workers similar to you would be the sellers or suppliers. Chances are you would face a demand curve for your labor that would be horizontal at a going wage. Competing against many other sellers, with an undifferentiated product, you would have very little or no ability to affect the wage you would get in the market.

2.4 | A Mathematical Approach

Mathematically, an elasticity is the ratio between the percentage changes in two economic variables, such as between quantity and price (or, as we will see later, between quantity and income). The price elasticity of demand, when approached mathematically, measures the responsiveness of quantity demanded to a change in price, with both expressed in percentage terms. It is defined as

$$\text{Price elasticity of demand} = \left| \frac{\text{\% change in quantity demanded}}{\text{\% change in price}} \right|$$

where the vertical bars indicate absolute value. The number inside the absolute value sign is usually a negative number, because our basic insight about demand is that a rise in price (a positive sign in the denominator of the fraction) will lead to a decrease in quantity demanded (a negative sign in the numerator of the fraction), and vice versa. Taking the absolute value turns the negative number into a positive number. When we talk about a "big" responsiveness to price, then, we can represent this by an elasticity with a higher positive value on the number line. (Without taking the absolute value, we would have to talk about -2 being "bigger" than -1, which would be confusing.)

For example, if a 10% increase in price leads to a 5% reduction in quantity demanded, then the price elasticity of demand would be calculated as

$$0.5 = \left| \frac{-5\%}{+10\%} \right|$$

The numerical values taken by these calculated elasticities can be related to the changes in revenues discussed earlier, because it is also true that[4]

$$\text{\% change in revenue} = \text{\% change in quantity demanded} + \text{\% change in price}$$

For example, for the case just described, where a 10% increase in price leads to a 5% reduction in quantity demanded,

$$+5\% = +10\% + -5\%$$

In this case, the price elasticity is 0.5, and the increase in price raises revenue by 5%.

We know from our earlier discussion that when the revenue changes in the same direction as price—as it does here—demand is price *in*elastic. It turns out that whenever the price elasticity is between 0 and 1, this is the case. The relationships between calculated values and the implied responsiveness are summarized in Table 5.3. When demand is "unit elastic," revenue is unaffected by a price change. For example, if a 10% increase in price makes quantity demanded fall by 10%, the price elasticity is equal to 1 ($= |-10\%/+10\%|$) and the percent change in revenue is 0 ($= -10\% + 10\%$).

Table 5.3 | Relationships of Price Elasticity to Quantity and Revenue Change		
If Price Elasticity of Demand Is:	**Then Quantity Response to Price Is:**	**And Revenue Response to Price Change Is:**
0	perfectly inelastic (no change)	very big, in same direction
greater than 0, less than 1	inelastic (little change)	in same direction
1	unit elastic (same percentage change)	no change
greater than 1	elastic (big change)	in opposite direction

---

[4] A mathematician can derive this from the formula for revenue by taking the natural logarithm of each side and then taking the derivative, which yields a percentage change formula for infinitesimal changes. For non-mathematicians, you can prove to yourself that this holds by calculating percentage changes for one of our examples (using the log-difference method described in the accompanying Math Review) and plugging them in. It holds only approximately for the midpoint formula described in the Math Review and often doesn't hold well at all for the conventional method.

Calculating Percentage Changes

Three methods of calculating percentage changes are often used, but only for one of them do the equations discussed in the text hold exactly.

1. Conventional formula. The most common method, which is good enough for many cases in which percentages are needed and is generally used in everyday life, divides the difference between two numbers by one of the numbers, considered to be the base, and multiplies by 100.

Percentage change = [(new number − base)/ base] × 100
(conventional formula)

For example, suppose we take the case of Braeburn Publishing's poetry book (described in Table 5.1), letting the Location A price of $5 be the "base" and the Location B price of $8 be the "new number." Thus

% change in price = [(8 − 5)/5] × 100
= [3/5] × 100 = 60%

We say that the $8 price is 60% greater than the $5 price.

The problem with this method is that if we shift the assignments of "new number" and "base," we get a different number. Treating $8 now as the base, can we say that $5 is, likewise, 60% less than $8? No, we cannot. Recalculating yields

% change in price = [(new number − base)/ base] × 100
= [(5 − 8)/8] × 100
= [−3/8] × 100 = −37.5%

We say that $5 is 37.5% less than $8. Is the percentage difference in price between Location A and Location B 60% or 37.5%? This can be confusing.

2. Midpoint formula. One way to solve this problem is to divide, within the brackets in the above formula, by the *average* of the two numbers. The modified formula is

Percentage change = [(new number − base)/ ((new number + base)/2)] × 100
(midpoint formula)

Using the same numbers, treating 5 as the "base" and rounding to three significant digits at each stage, we get

% change in price = [(8 − 5)/((8 + 5)/2)] × 100
= [3/6.5] × 100 ≈ 46.2%

A similar calculation, using 8 as the "base," yields the same number but with a negative sign. Note that 46% is somewhere between the two numbers given by the conventional formula, as it should be. (You can check your mastery of this formula by solving for the percentage change in quantity when sales of the poetry book drop from 5 books to 4 books. You should find this comes out to be about −22.2%. The calculated price elasticity, therefore, will be |−22.2%/46.2%| = 0.481.) The midpoint formula is an approximation, but a useful one.

3. Log-difference formula. Now that scientific calculators are generally available, it is not so hard for students to use the method actually employed by most practicing economists who study market behavior. The "ln" key on your calculator or the LN() function in most computer spreadsheets gives the natural logarithm of a number. We'll leave the explanation of why this works for your math class, but another way to compute percentage changes is to take the difference between the natural logs of two numbers:

$$\text{Percentage change} = [\ln(\text{new number}) - \ln(\text{base})] \times 100$$
(log-difference formula)

$$\% \text{ change in price} = [\ln(8) - \ln(5)] \times 100$$
$$\approx [2.08 - 1.61] \times 100 = 47.0\%$$

On many calculators, you would enter this by pressing the keys in the following order: 8, "ln," minus sign, open parenthesis, 5 , "ln," close parenthesis, equals sign, multiplication sign, 100, equals sign. Note that the result of 47.0% is close to the result for the midpoint formula. (You can check your mastery of this formula by solving for the percentage change in quantity when sales of the poetry book drop from 5 books to 4 books. You should find this comes out to be about −22.0%. The calculated price elasticity, therefore, will be $|-22.0\%/47.0\%| = 0.468$.) The only errors in the log-difference procedure come from rounding.

Table 5.4 shows some price elasticities that economists have estimated for a few common consumer goods and services.

Table 5.4 | A Few Estimated Price Elasticities

Good or Service	Estimated Price Elasticity
Cigarettes	0.20
Day care center services	0.28
Beef	0.61
Clothing	1.1
Ford Escort automobile	2.8

Discussion Questions

1. Consider the goods and services for which estimated elasticities are given in Table 5.4. Can you think of some reasons why cigarettes, day care center services, and beef are inelastically demanded? Can you think of some reasons why clothing has near unit elasticity, and why Ford Escorts are elastically demanded?

2. Suppose that when Winged Demons Athletic Shoes offers a 15% discount on its latest model of shoe, it finds it sells 20% more of them. Calculate the price elasticity for these shoes. Describe whether demand is price elastic or price inelastic, and describe what happens to the company's revenues when it offers the discount.

3. (If the box on calculating percentage changes is assigned.) Calculate the price elasticity of demand for the case of Braeburn Publishing's mystery novel; see the data given in Table 5.2. You may use either the midpoint or the log-difference formula (unless your instructor says otherwise). Also calculate the percentage change in revenue.

3 | The Price Elasticity of Supply

price elasticity of supply: a measure of the responsiveness of quantity supplied to changes in price

Just as movements along a demand curve can be described by elasticities, so can movements along a supply curve, which reflect the **price elasticity of supply**.

Suppose, for example, that a manufacturing company is having trouble getting adequate supplies of a needed component that is an input to its production process. Only a limited number of companies have the equipment to make this particular component, and those companies are not willing to produce more of it at the going price. The company's buyer might consider offering the suppliers a higher price. By how much will the buyer need to sweeten its offer to induce suppliers to supply the quantity of components that the company needs? What the company's buyer needs to know is the responsiveness of quantity supplied to price.

Once again, one can look at this in graphical terms. The manufacturing company faces an upward-sloping supply curve for the component: It cannot buy all it wants at the current offered price, but it may be able to motivate some component makers to increase their capacity (or motivate additional firms to enter the business of making these components) if it offers more money.

Figure 5.8 shows the current price and quantity situation at P_0 and Q_0 and illustrates two different scenarios for what could happen as the buyer raises the price offered. Just as for demand curves, relatively flatter supply curves mean more responsiveness of quantity to price, and hence greater elasticity, *assuming that comparisons are being made from the same point, on graphs with the same scale.* Relatively steeper curves (through the same point, on a graph with the same scale) are less elastic (or more inelastic), which means that quantity supplied is less responsive to changes in price. If the supply curve is relatively flat, like supply curve S_A, then the buyer only has to raise the offer he or she makes a little, from P_0 to P_A, to meet the quantity goal.

If, on the other hand, the supply curve is relatively steep, like curve S_B, then the buyer will have to raise the offer considerably, up to P_B, to meet the quantity goal. In the case of supply, rectangular areas on the graph representing $P \times Q$, reflect the total amount the buyer will end up *paying*. As we can see from Figure 5.8, the buyer will hope that supply is relatively elastic (more like S_A) if he or she is to avoid the additional cost represented by the shaded area.[5]

A perfectly inelastic supply curve is vertical and indicates that supply is completely fixed. The supply of authentic 1940 Chevrolets, for example, can no longer be adjusted, no matter what the price. A perfectly elastic supply curve is horizontal, indicating that buyers can buy all they want at the going price. As individual consumers, for example, each of us makes up such a small part of the total market for things like supermarket groceries and mass-produced clothing that such a horizontal curve is a reasonable representation of what we face. We generally pay the same price, no matter how many units we buy of a good. These extreme cases are illustrated in Figure 5.7, where the lines are now interpreted as supply curves.

The price elasticity of supply can be formulated mathematically as follows:

$$\text{Price elasticity of supply} = \frac{\%\text{ change in quantity supplied}}{\%\text{ change in price}}$$

Because the price elasticity of supply is generally expected to be positive (or, at a minimum, zero), the formula does not require taking the absolute value.

---

[5] If the cost of getting the parts is judged to be too high, of course, the manufacturing company may need to consider switching to a substitute input or even suspending production of the output that requires this part.

Figure 5.8 The Price Elasticity of Supply

If a buyer faces an upward-sloping supply curve, she will need to raise the price she offers if she wants to increase the quantity she can purchase. The more inelastic the supply curve is, the more she will have to push up the price to make suppliers respond, and the more she will end up paying.

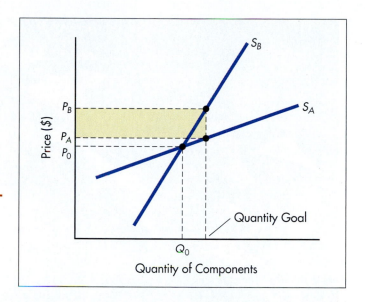

Discussion Questions

1. Suppose that a government alternative-energy program is having difficulty hiring enough engineers to work on a project and so raises the wage it offers to pay by 15%. Who are the buyers in this case? Who are the sellers? What does the wage represent, in terms of the present topic of discussion? If the project finds that employment applications then increase by 30%, what can you conclude about the price elasticity of supply of engineering labor?

2. Economists draw supply curves as upward-sloping. But sometimes, as consumers, we notice that the price per unit goes *down* if we buy more of something, not up. For example, a liter bottle of Pepsi costs less per ounce than a can of Pepsi, warehouse stores sell breakfast cereal in "jumbo size" for a low per-unit price, and clothing stores offer "buy one, get one free." Can you think of some reasons why sellers might offer such prices?

4 | Income, Price, and Buyer Behavior

In Chapter 4 we noted that demand curves shift when there are changes in nonprice determinants of demand, including consumer income. The effect of income changes can be explored more fully and can also be generalized to the cases where buyers might be businesses, governments, nonprofits, or community groups. Price changes, meanwhile, are said to have both "income effects" and "substitution effects."

4.1 | Income Elasticity of Demand

normal goods: goods for which demand rises when ability to pay rises, and falls when ability to pay falls

inferior goods: goods for which demand falls when ability to pay rises, and rises when ability to pay falls

Goods for which demand rises when a household's income rises are called **normal goods**. As people can afford more, they tend to buy more. However, demand for some goods may fall, and these goods are called **inferior goods**. Individuals and families tend to buy less of poor-quality goods or goods associated with living in poor neighborhoods (such as rat poison) as incomes rise.

A "normal good" is one which people buy more of as their ability to spend increases. This purchase of flowers is taking place in a street market in Danang, Vietnam, a country where average incomes have been growing in recent years. While very poor people are unlikely to buy flowers, the more affluent can afford to spend money on items that may not directly sustain life but make it more pleasant. Flowers, along with quality foods and stylish clothing, are examples of normal goods.

Households, however, are not the only economic actors that have to work within a budget. Divisions of businesses, branches of government, and other organizations also find that the administratively set budgets for their operations may be more generous or less so. Businesses that make high profits can often be found spending more on holiday parties and other on-the-job perks that can also be characterized as normal goods. Offices operating under tight budgets may spend more on low-grade copier paper, an inferior good. As discussed in the previous chapter, income changes—or, more generally, changes in any overall ability to pay—shift the demand curve, changing the quantity demanded at any price.

Drawing on a concept analogous to the price elasticity of demand, economists often summarize responsiveness of demand to income in terms of the **income elasticity of demand**:

income elasticity of demand: a measure of the responsiveness of quantity demanded to changes in income

$$\text{Income elasticity of demand} = \frac{\% \text{ change in quantity demanded}}{\% \text{ change in income}}$$

Unlike the price elasticity of demand or supply, which we generally expect to take particular signs (negative within the absolute value signs for demand, positive for supply), the income elasticity of demand can be either positive or negative.

The income elasticity of demand is negative for inferior goods and positive for normal goods. When it is positive but less than 1, demand is called income inelastic. Spending rises with income, but less than proportionately. For example, when income rises by 10%, spending on a particular good may rise by only 5%. When the income elasticity is positive and greater than 1, a good not only is bought more as ability to pay rises, but also takes up a greater *share* of total spending by the buyer. For example, income may rise by 10%, but spending on the good rises by 20%. When the income elasticity is greater than 1, demand is called income elastic. (You may note that if some goods are income elastic, other goods *must* be income inelastic—or a buyer would end up exceeding his or her budget!)[6]

Because buyers in many markets may be business or government divisions constrained by administratively determined budgets, rather than households constrained by their income-determined budgets, one could more inclusively think about naming the measure of the responsiveness of demand to changes in ability to pay the "budget elasticity of demand." However, the term *income elasticity* is in more common use.

Income elasticity is represented graphically as in Figure 5.9. Recall that whereas changes in prices lead to movements *along* the buyers' demand curve, changes in ability to pay *shift* the curve. To get a clear idea of the income elasticity, we would compare purchases between cases where income changes but price is kept constant. The shift from curve D to curve D_A represents income-inelastic demand, because a 100% increase in income leads to an increase in quantity demanded of less than 100%, at a given price. The shift from D to D_B represents income-elastic demand, because the same 100% rise in income leads to quantity demanded rising more than 100%.

4.2 | Income and Substitution Effects of a Price Change

income effect of a price change: the tendency of a price increase to reduce the quantity demanded of normal goods (and to increase the quantity demanded of any inferior goods)

Price changes, represented by movements *along* a demand curve, also have what economists call an **income effect** component. This is because, for any buyer, an increase in the price of any *one* good that this buyer purchases reduces her or his *overall* purchasing power (given a set income or budget). If you could buy 12 apples and 5 oranges at a given set of prices, and then the price of oranges rises, you can no

Figure 5.9 The Income Elasticity of Demand

A change in income *shifts* the demand curve. If demand is *income inelastic*, the demand curve does not shift far (only to D_A), and there is a only a small increase in quantity demanded at a given price. If demand is *income elastic*, the shift is more dramatic (to D_B), and the percentage increase in quantity demanded (as shown by the shift from Q_0 to Q_B) is larger than the percentage increase in income.

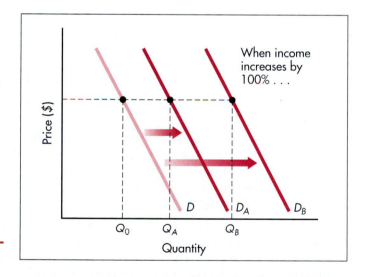

---

[6] You may sometimes see income-elastic goods referred to as luxuries, because the rich spend proportionately more on them than the poor. By the same token, inelastically demanded goods are sometimes called necessities. These designations, however, are only economists' shorthand for specifying ranges of the income elasticity and have nothing to do with human well-being. For example, studies of consumer demand usually find cigarettes to be, by this definition, "necessities" because poorer people (who are more likely to smoke) spend a greater proportion of their income on them, whereas clothing is a "luxury" on which the rich spend proportionately more! Obviously, for sustaining life, the reverse is true, and it may be best to avoid these misleading terms when discussing elasticities.

longer achieve your previous bundle of purchases—a result similar to the case where your income falls. Any price rise for a good you usually purchase makes you, in a sense, poorer. Because you are now poorer, your response to the price rise will depend, in part, on which goods are normal and which (if any) are inferior, in the special sense we are using here.

If both apples and oranges are normal, you, now being poorer, will tend to buy less of each. If, on the other hand, apples are inferior goods to you, which you buy only because you can't afford more oranges, you will tend to buy even more apples (but fewer oranges) when you are made poorer by a rise in price. (What if oranges were, instead, the inferior good?)

substitution effect of a price change: the tendency of a price increase for a particular good to reduce the quantity demanded of that good, as buyers turn to cheaper substitutes

Economists distinguish between the income effect of a price change, which results from the change in the overall ability to pay, and the **substitution effect** of a price change, which has entirely to do with *relative* prices. For example, suppose the prices of apples and oranges start out at $1 and $1.50 per pound, respectively, and then both rise, to $2 and $3 per pound. Both are now more expensive, but the prices *relative to each other* remain the same: oranges are still one-and-a-half times as expensive as apples (1.5/1 = 3/2 = 1.5).

However, if the price of the oranges rises to $2 per pound while the price of the apples remains at $1, the oranges are now twice as expensive as apples (2/1 = 2). Oranges have become *relatively* more expensive (and apples *relatively* cheaper).

When one good gets more expensive relative to others, people will look for ways to substitute toward the cheaper goods (assuming that the good is desired for its usefulness rather than for status). If you think that apples and oranges are good substitutes for each other, then the rise in the relative price of oranges will tend to make you buy fewer oranges and more apples. If the price of natural gas water heating rises relative to the price of solar water heating, one can expect any household or organization that uses hot water to lean more toward solar than before, when the time comes to replace its system. To gauge the direction of the substitution effect, you don't need to know whether the good is normal or inferior.

Both these effects act together whenever there is a price change.

- ◑ If the good is normal and its price rises, both the income effect and the substitution effect will tend to lead to a reduction in the quantity demanded of the good. The quantity demanded falls with a price rise, both because the buyer is poorer and because other goods now look relatively more attractive.

- ◑ If the good is inferior and its price rises, the income effect will encourage *greater* expenditures, at the same time as the substitution effect pushes toward *lower* expenditures. In general, though, we expect that the substitution effect will be stronger than the income effect in the case of inferior goods, so the demand curve will still be downward-sloping.

The exception, where a price rise for an inferior good leads to such a large income effect that demand *increases,* is called the case of a "Giffen good." It is rare in practice, especially in the industrialized countries. In very poor countries, however, it is sometimes the case that the poorest of the poor spend a large proportion of their income on a basic foodstuff, such as low-quality rice or starchy roots, and tiny amounts of income on more expensive vegetables and protein-rich foods. If the price of the basic foodstuff rises, survival may demand that they stop purchasing the more expensive foods entirely and make up for these lost calories by buying *more* of the basic foodstuff. In terms of market analysis, the demand curve for the basic foodstuff will be seen to slope *upward* (and the price elasticity will be positive, even *before* taking the absolute value). In terms of well-being, of course, the situation represents a human disaster; the starchy food will not supply the vitamins or protein needed for healthy functioning and development.

5 | Short-Run Versus Long-Run Elasticities

So far our analysis has been static. That is, we have been assuming that adjustment from one equilibrium point shown in our graphs to another equilibrium point happens without any lapse of time. In the real world, the time taken for adjustments is important. For example, we noted how the price elasticity of demand for a good depends on the availability of substitute goods. If substitutes are readily available, demand for the good in question will tend to be more price elastic than it would be if substitutes were hard to get. But what if substitutes are hard to get *right away* but easier to get *over time*? It is possible for a good to be very price inelastic in the short run but more price elastic as people can make adjustments over time. We can distinguish **short-run elasticity**, which measures relatively immediate responses to a price change, from **long-run elasticity**, which measures how much quantity responds after economic actors have had some time to adjust.

For example, in Chapter 4 we discussed how after the oil price shocks of the mid- and late 1970s, U.S. consumers of oil products initially paid very high prices for them, with little initial drop in quantity demanded. Another way to characterize this situation is as one of relatively inelastic demand, as illustrated by the short-run demand curve in Figure 5.10. Estimated short-run elasticities of demand for gasoline, for example, tend to be in the range of 0.1 to 0.4. Over time, however, the quantity of oil

short-run elasticity: a measure of the relatively immediate responsiveness to a price change

long-run elasticity: a measure of the response to a price change after economic actors have had time to make adjustments

Figure 5.10 Short-Run and Long-Run Demand

The amount of time over which responsiveness to a price change is observed can make a difference. Because people will seek out substitutes for a good whose price has risen, demand may be more price elastic in the long run than in the short run.

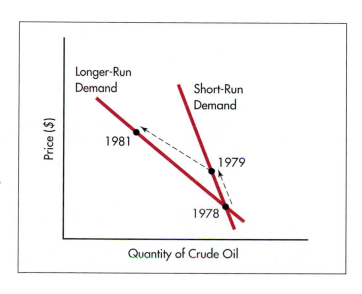

demanded dropped a bit more, as people were able to adopt more oil-conserving strategies and technologies and find substitutes for OPEC oil. Estimates of the long-run demand for gasoline, for example, tend to be between 0.6 and 1.1. We can think of this drop in quantity demanded due to adjustments over time in terms of a somewhat more elastic demand curve; it is labeled longer-run demand in Figure 5.10. Of course, if the price of oil had stayed very high, we might have seen even more elasticity over an even longer run, instead of the return to rising quantity demanded that actually occurred.

In Chapter 4 we had introduced another way of approaching the time required for adjustments: thinking about some price and quantity combinations as reflecting points of *dis*equilibrium (though tending, over time, toward equilibrium—if no further changes were to occur—because of the market adjustment process). Both kinds of explanations can be valid. Remember that the curves we draw are only thought experiments we use to try to organize our understanding of the world.

Discussion Questions

1. Maria rents on a month-to-month basis an apartment that she can barely afford, in a market where apartments are hard to find. Her landlord announces that she is doubling the rent, effective immediately. What is likely to be Maria's short-run response (say, over the next few days or weeks)? What might be her likely long-run response (over the next few months)?

2. Suppose that new technological breakthroughs make solar water heaters extremely cheap to run, compared with water heaters that use fossil fuels, and only moderately expensive to install. Illustrate on a graph what you might expect the short-run and long-run demand adjustments to this price drop to be. What sorts of factors affect how long, in real time, it might take for the "long-run" situation to occur?

Review Questions

1. When a seller changes the price charged for a good or service, what can happen to the quantity sold? How does buyer responsiveness to price affect the seller's revenue?

2. Sketch a graph showing how a seller's revenue changes as the price it charges, and the quantity purchased, change along a demand curve.

3. List three reasons why demand for a good or service may be elastic. List three reasons why demand for a good may be inelastic.

4. Sketch, on a single graph, a relatively price-elastic demand curve and a relatively price-inelastic demand curve. (Make sure they go through the same point.)

5. Sketch, on a single graph, a perfectly price-elastic demand curve and a perfectly inelastic demand curve.

6. In which case does the seller have more power: when it faces a perfectly inelastic demand curve or when it faces a perfectly elastic demand curve?

7. Write out the equation for calculating the price elasticity of demand.

8. Write out the equation for calculating the percentage change in revenue, given the percentage changes in quantity demanded and in price.

9. Describe quantity and revenue responses to price changes when the price elasticity of demand takes on the following values: (a) 0, (b) between 0 and 1, (c) 1, (d) greater than 1.

10. (If the box on calculating percentage change is assigned.) Write out the equations for calculating percentage change, according to the conventional, midpoint, and log-difference methods.

11. Sketch, on a single graph, a relatively price-elastic supply curve and a relatively price-inelastic supply curve. (Make sure they go through the same point.)

12. Write out the equation for calculating the price elasticity of supply.

13. Give one example of a normal good and one example of an inferior good.

14. Write out the equation for calculating the income elasticity of demand.

15. Can you illustrate the income elasticity of demand using a single demand curve? Why or why not?

16. Explain how a price change has both "income effects" and "substitution effects" on buyer behavior.

17. Explain why the long-run elasticity of demand for a good may differ from the short-run elasticity.

Exercises

1. For each of the following items put on the market, discuss whether you think the demand the seller faces will be price inelastic or price elastic, and explain why.
   a. A new CD by an extremely popular recording artist
   b. One share of stock, when there are millions of shares for that company outstanding
   c. Bottled drinking water, at a town in the desert
   d. Your used textbooks, at the end of the term

2. Match each concept in Column A with the corresponding fact or example in Column B.

   Column A

   a. price-inelastic demand
   b. inferior good
   c. income effect of a price change
   d. perfectly price-elastic supply
   e. unit price elasticity of demand
   f. perfectly inelastic supply
   g. normal good
   h. perfectly elastic demand
   i. substitution effect
   j. income-elastic demand

   Column B

   i. an income elasticity of +1.4
   ii. a 12% rise in price is associated with a 12% fall in quantity demanded
   iii. dining out more often because your landlord reduced your rent
   iv. expenditures on a good rise when ability to pay rises
   v. any rise in price will cause quantity demanded to drop to 0
   vi. buying fewer muffins (and more donuts) because the relative price of muffins has risen
   vii. revenues rise as the seller raises the price
   viii. what you face when buying milk at the grocery store
   ix. the acres of land in downtown Chicago
   x. people spend less on this as they get richer

3. Calculate the price elasticity of demand for the following cases:
   a. When price rises by 5%, quantity demanded drops by 10%.
   b. When price rises by 10%, quantity demanded drops by 2%.

    c. When price rises by 0.05%, quantity demanded drops by 99%. (Which extreme case is this approaching? Note that the price rise is a *fraction of 1%*, not 5%.)

    d. When price rises by 99%, quantity demanded drops by 0.05 %. (Which extreme case is this approaching?)

    e. When price falls by 10%, quantity demanded rises by 2%.

4. Calculate the percentage change in revenue that would result from each of the actions in exercise 3.

5. Braeburn Publishing decides to try to cut its costs of printing books by cutting the price it offers to companies that supply it with paper.

    a. Suppose the supply is perfectly price inelastic (at least in the short run), because Braeburn buys the entire output of the Morales Paper Company. With no other customers (for now), Morales has no choice but to sell to Braeburn. Illustrate on a graph what will happen to the quantity Braeburn buys, the price it pays, and the amount it will spend on paper.

    b. Suppose, instead, that the supply of paper is very (but not perfectly) price elastic, because all the companies that sell paper to Braeburn can easily sell their paper elsewhere. Illustrate on a graph what will happen to the quantity Braeburn will be able to buy, the price it will pay, and the amount it will spend on paper, if it follows through with its plan to offer a lower price. (*Hint:* Refer to Figure 5.8, but this time illustrate a price *drop,* rather than a price rise.)

6. Use the formulas for elasticities to answer the following questions.

    a. When Mariba's income rises by 10%, her expenditures on carrots rise 12%. What is Mariba's income elasticity of demand for carrots? Are carrots, for her, a normal or an inferior good?

    b. Suppose the price elasticity of demand for milk is 0.6. If the grocer raises the price of milk by 15%, by what percentage will milk sales decrease as a result of the price increase? Will the grocer's revenue from milk sales go up or down?

    c. Suppose that the price elasticity of supply for paper is 1.5. You notice that the quantity of paper supplied decreases by 6% as the result of a change in the price of paper. Determine by what percentage the price of paper must have declined.

7. Clark Marketing Services has found, through market tests, that the demand for Sonya's Peanuts has a price elasticity of 0.5 and an income elasticity of 1.8. You, an economist employed by Sonya's Peanuts, have been asked by the executives of the company to explain what this means for their pricing policy and choice of sales outlets. They have been thinking of lowering their prices and concentrating on selling to discount stores. What do you advise? Explain in a paragraph.

8. Many environmentalists think that a rise in the price of petroleum products to consumers would be a good thing. Many policymakers believe that a rise in the price of higher education (say, through increased tuitions), on the other hand, would be a bad thing. Discuss why these beliefs might be held, using the concepts of "externalities" and "substitution effects of a price change."

9. Look at the estimated price elasticity of demand for cigarettes in Table 5.4. If the government raises taxes on cigarettes, this raises the price to the consumer. The extra revenue collected from the higher price goes to the government. Describe in a few sentences the effectiveness of taxing cigarettes as (a) part of a campaign to stop people from smoking and (b) a way of raising revenue.

Part Three

Resource Maintenance, Production, Distribution, and Consumption

Capital Stocks and Resource Maintenance

Chapter 6

You wouldn't think of going into a bookstore to buy textbooks unless you had money in your checking account, a wad of bills in your pocket, or a credit line on your credit card. You would feel pretty silly if you had to put books back because you discovered at the checkout that you had insufficient resources. You would feel even more uncomfortable if you went hungry for the next week because, although you could pay for the books at the checkout, your bookstore purchase left you with no way to pay for food. In checking your account balances before you go to the store, and being sure you don't do anything unwise, you are engaging in a simple "resource maintenance" activity. Economists would say you were paying attention to your personal stock of financial capital. However, economists' definitions of the terms *stock* and *capital*, as well as *investment*, may be different from what you expect.

1 | The Nature of Capital Stocks

capital stock: a quantity of any resource that is valued for its potential economic contributions

In common usage, *capital* often means only *financial* capital. We hear this in everyday references to "capital markets," "undercapitalized businesses," and "venture capital." Likewise, when laypeople use the term *stock,* they mean primarily ownership shares in enterprises, traded on the "stock market." *Investment* to many people means simply buying a stock or bond. A *capitalist* is a person whose financial resources are invested in productive enterprises. To an economist, however, a **capital stock** is a quantity of any resource that is valued for its potential economic contributions.

More fundamentally, you are aware that farmers cannot grow the food you eat without seeds to plant, land to plant them in, and plows to till the soil. This would be true even in subsistence economies that do not use financial capital. Seeds, land, and plows are examples of what economists call physical capital—tangible objects that make it possible for people to sustain their lives and well-being. Like you in the bookstore, a society would be unwise if it did not pay attention to the quantity and quality of all its productive resources before beginning an activity, and if it did not also plan ahead, considering the impact its activities will have on resources available in the future.

Capital stocks may increase or decrease as a consequence of natural forces, as in the case of a natural forest, or they may be deliberately managed by humans to provide needed inputs for the production of desired goods and services. When the quantity or quality of a resource is increased now in order to make benefits possible in the future, humans are undertaking **investment**. The employee who puts funds into her individual retirement account (IRA) is investing in her future—and so is the business that trains its workers, the subsistence farmer who sets aside seeds for his next planting season, and the community that works to clean up its air and water. The activity of resource maintenance—one of the four essential economic activities defined in Chapter 1—consists of carefully attending to natural and human-directed changes in the quantity and quality of all capital stocks.

1.1 | Stocks Versus Flows

It is important, for understanding capital stocks and resource maintenance, to distinguish stocks from flows.

Stocks are measured *at a particular point in time*. For example, the water-holding capacity of the pool at the base of a waterfall can be measured, and the water in the pool at any instant in time would be considered a stock. The balance in your checking account on January 1 of last year is a stock, as is the inventory of tools at Precision Product's warehouse as of this Tuesday. The quantity of hair on your head is a stock.

On the other hand, **flows** are measured *over a period of time*. For example, the water that goes off a cliff in a waterfall is a flow; it can be measured as a quantity per minute or per hour. The deposits and withdrawals you make to your checking account are flows; your bank statement will tell you what the various flows were during a month. The flow of newly produced tools into the warehouse, and the flow of tools out of the warehouse as they are sold, can be measured over the day or week. The number of haircuts you had in the last year is a flow of services. (It is impossible to keep a stock of haircuts in a warehouse; whereas flows can be either goods or services, stocks can be only goods.)

Flows are like a movie; stocks are like a still photograph. Flows can either add to stocks or decrease them. Figure 6.1 is a generalized **stock-flow diagram**, which shows how flows change the level of a stock, over time, by either adding to it or taking away from it. Figure 6.2 illustrates the specific example of a non-interest-bearing checking account. Starting with an initial balance, flows of deposits add to the stock, and withdrawals subtract from it.

investment: actions taken to increase the quantity or quality of a resource now, in order to make benefits possible in the future

stock: something whose quantity can be measured at a point in time

flow: something whose quantity can be measured only over a period of time

stock-flow diagram: a diagram that illustrates how stocks can be changed, over time, by flows

Figure 6.1 The General Stock-Flow Diagram
Starting from an initial quantity of a stock, flows into and out of the stock determine how great the quantity is the next time the stock is measured.

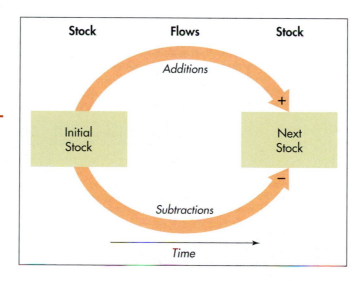

Figure 6.2 Stocks and Flows for a Checking Account

Starting from an initial stock of funds in a checking account on January 1, flows of deposits over the month add to the stock in the checking account, and flows of withdrawals subtract from it. The balance drawn on February 1 reflects the effects of deposits and withdrawals during January.

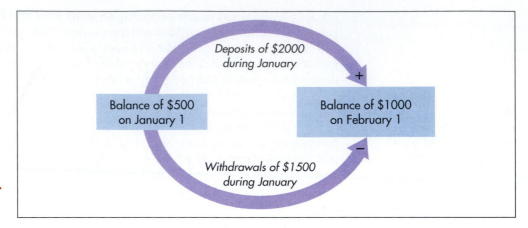

Figure 6.3 gives an alternative representation of the relationship between stocks and flows, this time showing a stock at only *one* point in time. Like water running through the tap (additions) and the drain (subtractions) of a bathtub, flows raise or lower the level of the water in the tub (stock).

1.2 | The Five Forms of Capital

natural capital: physical assets provided by nature

manufactured capital: all physical assets that have been made by people

financial capital: funds of purchasing power available to facilitate economic activity

human capital: people's capacity for labor and their individual knowledge and skills

social capital: the stock of trust, mutual understanding, shared values, and socially held knowledge that facilitates the social coordination of economic activity

Capital can be classified as natural, manufactured, human, social, or financial capital. **Natural capital** consists of physical assets provided by nature, such as land that is suitable for agriculture or other human uses, sources of fresh water, and stocks of minerals and crude oil that are still in the ground. **Manufactured capital** is physical assets that are generated by applying human productive activities to natural capital. These include such things as buildings, machinery, stocks of refined oil, and inventories of produced goods that are waiting to be sold or to be used in further production.

We mentioned financial capital first, at the beginning of this chapter, not because it is the most important (in fact, it is the one type of capital that an economy could conceivably do without) but because it may be the most familiar to you. **Financial capital** consists of the funds of purchasing power (commonly referred to simply as money) available to an economic actor at a point in time. **Human capital** is made up of individual people's capacity for labor, particularly the knowledge and skills that each can personally bring to his or her work. **Social capital** is the stock of trust, mutual understanding, shared values, and socially held knowledge that facilitates the social coordination of economic activity.

Figure 6.3 A "Bathtub"-Style Diagram

Like water flowing into a bathtub, flows that add to a stock will tend to raise its level over time. Like water flowing out of a bathtub, flows that subtract from a stock will tend to lower its level over time.

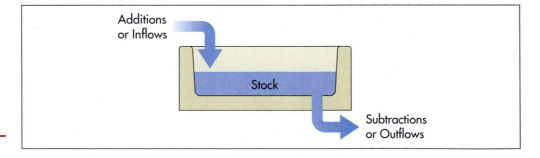

In this photograph of volunteers building a Habitat for Humanity house for a homeless family, we see some of the many kinds of capital stocks that are necessary for economic activities. The wood has come from the world's stock of forests. The hand tools in use here are examples of manufactured capital. Human capital provides the ability to do physical and mental labor. The values that bring the workers together and the sharing of carpentry knowledge are examples of social capital. The financial capital necessary to buy the land and materials for this project, in advance of any payments by future occupants, comes from donations.

physical capital: assets that are tangible (that is, can be seen and touched)

Capital can be in physical form, intangible form, or both. Capital takes the form of **physical capital** when it can be touched or seen. Natural capital is primarily physical in form. Anything we make use of in the physical world either comes directly from a natural capital stock—as with a fruit picked from a wild tree—or has been transformed from its original, natural form. Even such human inventions as plastics, microchips, and advanced medicines are all made out of something physical that was at one time a part of a stock of natural capital.

intangible capital: sources of productivity and well-being that cannot be seen or touched

Intangible capital is less visible but no less important. A machine, for example is not only a hunk of physical metal but also the embodiment of intangible individual and social knowledge. Paper money is more than just physical paper; only because it also represents intangible, socially created trust can it be used in payment. Manufactured and human capital generally include a mix of physical and intangible elements, whereas for financial and social capital, the intangible aspects may be the more pronounced. Books and technology, for example, embody social capital in the form of knowledge, but social capital also includes the intangible realms of culture, ideas, ethics, and norms.

Not all capital can be assigned to only one form. When people deliberately create stocks of new hybrid seeds through selective breeding, for example, such seeds may be seen as partly natural and partly produced—and also as embodying human and social knowledge. Most actual cases, however, can be more clearly classified.

Discussion Questions

1. Linda thinks a rich person is someone who earns a lot of money. Meng thinks a rich person is someone who has a big house and owns lots of stocks and bonds. How would the distinction between stocks and flows lend clarity to their discussion?

2. Think of some common activity you enjoy. For example, perhaps you like to get together with friends and listen to CDs while popping popcorn in the microwave. List the stocks of natural, manufactured, human, and social capital you draw on when engaging in this activity.

2 | The Evolution of Capital

In order to create some reference points and to illustrate how an economic analysis of resource maintenance can be related to the real world, we will imagine a voyage through time, in which we will observe the economic activities of a succession of farming families. As you read through these scenarios, ask yourself what forms of capital are being employed in each case.

Family 1 lives in the late Neolithic era (3000–4000 B.C.) in a place where there is plenty of fertile land and no population pressure. When one patch of land loses its fertility, this family can easily find a new area to plant. The activity of farming consists of collecting seeds from wild plants, using a digging stick (a branch with one end hardened by the heat of a fire) to scratch holes in the ground, dropping the seeds in the holes, covering them over, and praying for rain. The family subsists on what it produces for itself.

Two thousand years later, their remote descendants in Family 2 inhabit a far more complex world. Population density is much increased, and this family has a clear idea of the boundaries between its fields and its neighbors'. The rituals in which much knowledge about farming has been codified include ceremonies for selecting the best grains from each harvest, both as religious offerings and as seeds for the next planting. Other precepts decree that the same crop should not be planted in one place for more than two years in a row. Insect pests are recognized and squashed; birds and other insects that prey on these pests are protected by custom and folklore. Furrows are prepared for the seeds by dragging a wooden plow through the ground. One neighboring family, considered very wealthy, has a pair of oxen that pulls its plow and contributes manure as fertilizer. Our less wealthy family returns crop residues to the soil to maintain its fertility.[1] If our poor family has a very bad year, it must ask the wealthy family for a loan of seeds to start the next year's crops.

Many more centuries pass; we have come nearly to the present. When we reach Family 3, the first thing we notice is how much the noises of farm life have changed. The rumble and whir of heavy machinery seems to be everywhere. Tractors, combines, and other machines have replaced much human and animal labor. Now there are far fewer people on each acre of land, and each farming family produces much more food than it needs to eat. The excess is collected in huge trucks that carry it to nearby processing factories, in preparation for the trips that will take the processed foodstuffs to distant cities. The seeds for planting also come from far away, as do the chemicals that are liberally applied to the fields to rid them of weeds and pests. The rules of farming are now usually learned from books and formal schooling, rather than being passed down in the form of tradition. Because the seeds and fertilizers are so expensive, the family mem-

---

[1] The agricultural system described here is often given the name *traditional*. For a very long time (from about 2000 B.C. to about 1500 A.D.) traditional agriculture prevailed over much of the earth. It is still found in some places today.

bers start each planting season with a large bank loan, which they then pay off after the harvest. They finance their equipment purchases with longer-term loans.

One more very short jump in time, and we overshoot the present, landing a decade or two into a possible future. Family 4 farms with a "low-input" agricultural system. Much is the same as it was with their grandparents (Family 3), but there are some significant differences. The same area of land shows a few more people, and the generally less massive machinery is used somewhat differently. For example, there is less use of machine-sprayed pesticides; instead, as was the case long ago with Family 2, there are people in the fields scouting for insect pests. Some other important concepts from Family 2 have also returned, including the use of crop rotation. Computer-driven processes monitor moisture very finely, field by field, and apply only the precise amount of water that is needed. The need for fertilizer is also analyzed by computer and is met partly with chemicals, partly with animal and plant wastes. Seeds and knowledge still come from off the farm, but the knowledge is not applied in blanket form; instead, the off-farm learning includes education on how to adapt general knowledge to specific conditions of soil, micro-climate, and mini-ecosystem.

Discussion Questions

1. List, as best you can, the examples of natural, manufactured, human, social, and financial capital exhibited in the stories of these four farming families.

2. Draw a simple chart (like Figure 6.1) illustrating how the stock of one type of capital used in the farming stories would change from the beginning of one season to the next.

3 | Natural Capital

In the stories about farming given above we can recognize at least land and wild seeds as important forms of natural capital. Besides seeds and land, natural capital includes supplies of energy and raw materials (raw in the sense that they have not been processed by human activity), clean air, clean water, and the variety of animal and plant species. In the early farming stories, manure used as fertilizer may be regarded as a flow that comes from a stock of natural capital (the farm animals).

3.1 | Renewable and Nonrenewable Natural Capital

renewable resource: a resource that regenerates itself through short-term processes

Forms of natural capital can be distinguished in terms of whether they are renewable. A **renewable resource** regenerates itself through biological or other short-term processes, which may be helped out by human activity. The quantity and quality of its stock depend simultaneously on the rate at which the stock maintains its productivity and grows and on the rate at which it is harvested or polluted. A healthy forest will go on indefinitely producing trees that may be harvested, yielding a flow of lumber that will be used up in production processes such as papermaking.

nonrenewable resource: a resource that can only diminish over time

Other kinds of natural capital are **nonrenewable resources**. Their supply is fixed, although new discoveries can increase the stock that is known to be available. For example, there is a finite amount of fossil fuel reserves, and a finite amount of each kind of mineral, available on the earth.[2] For nonrenewable resources, there are no self-regenerating flows, and the stock can only diminish over time as a result of human use and/or natural deterioration, as illustrated in Figure 6.4(a).

---

[2] The length of the time period considered is important here. Oil reserves could be "renewed" from today's organic matter—but only over millions of years, far beyond the span of many human generations. Similarly, if the species diversity that has been lost in the last century is ever replenished, this process will require thousands or even millions of years.

A renewable natural resource can regenerate itself under suitable conditions. Stocks of fish, like these sardines being loaded on a fishing boat near Quiberon, France, will replace themselves through natural reproduction if they are not overharvested. The Food and Agriculture Organization of the United Nations estimates, however, that 24 percent of all major marine fisheries suffer from overfishing, and another 50 percent are fully exploited. For this reason, national and international bodies have attempted to regulate ocean fisheries in order to maintain their productivity.

How much of its stock of natural resources a society chooses to turn into inputs to current production processes, rather than to preserve for the future, is clearly a very important economic question. Even those natural inputs that are renewable—such as lumber from forests and fish from the seas—may be extinguished if so much of them is destroyed or extracted that they can no longer renew themselves, as illustrated in Figure 6.4(b). In addition, there are limits to the ability of nature to absorb polluting

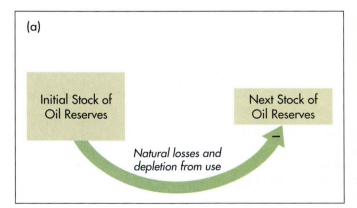
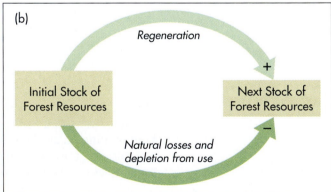

Figure 6.4 Depletion of Natural Capital
(a) A Nonrenewable Resource. A nonrenewable resource cannot be replaced. It can only be used up.
(b) A Renewable Resource Being Depleted. A renewable resource may be replaceable, but if it is used up too quickly, it may become depleted.

by-products of production processes. There are also tipping points past which degraded natural capital may dramatically alter in some essential respect. For example, in the case of climate change, rising global temperature due to human-made emissions from the burning of fossil fuels and the use of other chemicals may bring dramatic changes within this century. Ocean levels could rise by up to a meter because of melting of the Antarctic ice cap and other factors. This could cause the flooding of many low-lying areas, including New Orleans, south Florida, and Bangladesh. Some island nations are already losing significant land mass. Resource maintenance for natural capital means tracking the size, quality, and changes in natural resources and making wise decisions about their management.

3.2 | Technology and Natural Capital

substitutability: the possibility of using one resource instead of another

Sometimes, when it is pointed out that processes of production and consumption in the industrialized nations are currently depleting many important natural capital stocks much more rapidly than they can be replenished, the issue of **substitutability** is raised. That is, the depletion of any one resource (such as fossil fuels) is a less serious problem for future well-being if other resources (such as nuclear or solar energy) can be cheaply and safely substituted for it in production and consumption. The extent of substitutability that can be achieved depends both on the characteristics of the resources and on the speed of technological advance.

During the late 19th century and the first half of the 20th century, there was a widely shared confidence that human beings could find adequate and timely solutions to any problems they created. In the late 20th century, however, this faith began to fade in light of increasing ecological damage. Ecologists emphasize the complexity of natural systems and our relative ignorance about long-term, irreversible, or potentially catastrophic effects of economic behavior on the natural systems that support us. They suggest that, instead of placing blind faith in technological progress and economic substitutability, society should adopt a **precautionary principle**. In other words, we should err on the side of caution, preferring to cooperate with natural systems rather than assuming we can safely replace them. Or, as stated by one group of experts, "When an

precautionary principle: the principle that we should err on the side of caution when dealing with natural systems

---

Panel Tells Bush Global Warming Is Getting Worse

NEWS in context

A panel of top American scientists declared today that global warming is a real problem and is getting worse. . . . In a much-anticipated report from the National Academy of Sciences, 11 leading atmospheric scientists, including previous skeptics about global warming, reaffirmed the mainstream scientific view that the earth's atmosphere is getting warmer and that human activity is largely responsible.

. . . [T]he journal *Science*, published by an American scientific organization, recently carried an open letter signed by 16 prestigious scientific panels in countries around the world calling for "prompt action" to reduce emission of the gases,

such as carbon dioxide, that trap heat as in a greenhouse. The increase in temperatures, the editorial said, "will be accompanied by rising sea levels, more intense precipitation events in some countries and increased risk of drought in others and adverse effects on agriculture, health and water balance." It continued, "We urge everyone— individuals, businesses and governments—to take prompt action to reduce emissions of greenhouse gases."

Many international business executives have been pressuring the administration to move more aggressively on the issue. . . . ◑

Adapted from Katharine Q. Seelye with Andrew C. Revkin, *New York Times*, June 7, 2001. Copyright © (2001) by The New York Times Co. Reprinted with permission.

How serious do you believe the issue of change in global climate is? On what do you base your beliefs?

activity raises threats of harm to the environment or human health, precautionary measures should be taken even if some cause and effect relationships are not fully established scientifically."[3]

sustainable socioeconomic system: a system in which the overall quality and quantity of the resource base required for sustaining life and well-being do not erode

A **sustainable socioeconomic system** creates a flow of whatever is needed (in an economic system, this is goods and services) by using its renewable capital stocks without depleting them. Although some portion of some (especially nonrenewable) capital stocks may be used up in the process of production, the overall quality and quantity of the resource base for sustaining life and well-being are preserved.

Discussion Questions

1. Give three examples of renewable natural capital. Give three examples of nonrenewable natural capital. (Do not duplicate examples given in the text.)

2. Do you think that a cheap and safe substitute for the use of fossil fuels in cars will ever be found? What about a substitute for the ozone layer, an atmospheric layer that protects the earth from damaging radiation from the sun? Discuss.

4 | Manufactured Capital

In our illustrative stories about farming, you probably recognized the primitive digging stick, the early plow, and the heavy modern farm equipment as examples of manufactured capital. The stock of manufactured capital is the stock of physical things produced by human beings, which in turn are used to produce other goods. In a modern context, manufactured capital includes such things as roads, factories, communication systems, buildings, machinery, computers, equipment, and inventories. The major form of manufactured capital is fixed manufactured capital. Inventories are another form of manufactured capital.

4.1 | Fixed Manufactured Capital

fixed manufactured capital: manufactured goods that yield a flow of productive services over an extended period of time

Most of what we consider to be manufactured capital is in the form of **fixed manufactured capital**, which is designed to supply a flow of productive services over an extended period of time. When economists speak of "capital" as an input to production, they usually mean that *stocks of manufactured capital*, such as tools, machines, buildings, and infrastructure, yield *flows of* capital *services*, such as making it possible to dig or drill more rapidly, expediting communications and transportation, or giving shelter. The fixed manufactured capital stocks themselves are not used up during the production process (aside from normal wear and tear), nor do they become part of the product itself.[4]

If you find the distinction between stocks and flows confusing, consider the example of a tax accountant renting an office from a real estate firm. The stock of manufactured capital here—the physical office itself—belongs to the real estate firm, but the service arising from the use of the office space is an input flow into the production of services to the tax account's clients. Similarly, when truckers drive along a highway, they

---

[3] This well-known formulation of the precautionary principle, sometimes called "the Wingspread statement," was spelled out in a January 1998 meeting of scientists, lawyers, policymakers, and environmentalists at Wingspread, the headquarters of the Johnson Foundation in Racine, Wisconsin.

[4] Manufactured goods that *are* used up during the production process (such as refined fuel) or that become *part* of the final product (such as electrical components that go into a radio) are *not* fixed manufactured capital. They are called "intermediate goods" (discussed in Chapter 7) when considered as part of a flow of production over time, and are part of "inventories" when measured at a point in time (see the next section).

are using the services of the government-provided physical road. The actual physical office and the road are not in themselves inputs into production—they do not get used up or converted into something else on the way to creating new goods and services. Only the *flow of services* yielded by these capital goods can properly be referred to as inputs.

The stock of fixed manufactured capital is increased when people decide to make physical investments—that is, to build or improve productive assets. Although fixed manufactured capital is not directly used up in the process of production, physical assets commonly lose their usefulness over time, as computers become obsolete, roads develop potholes, and equipment breaks. Commonly, these losses are referred to as **depreciation** of the manufactured capital stock. Resource maintenance activities for fixed manufactured capital include all the checking, cleaning, protection, and repair activities needed to keep buildings, machines, and other manufactured capital in good working order.

depreciation: decreases in the value of a stock of capital due to wear-and-tear or obsolescence

4.2 | Inventories

inventories: stocks of raw materials or manufactured goods being held until they can be used

A smaller amount of manufactured capital exists in the form of **inventories**. Inventories are stocks of raw materials or produced goods that are not currently being used but are expected to be used in the foreseeable future.

Like other forms of capital, inventories contribute to production. For example, you cannot start baking bread until you have accumulated a stock of flour, nor can you provide retail services selling shoes until you have an inventory of shoes. Also like other forms of capital, inventories are valuable assets. If you were to sell your shoe store, the value of your stock of salable shoes would be figured into the price of the business. But unlike fixed manufactured capital, inventories are generally meant to be used up relatively quickly or to become part of another product, rather than to provide a flow of services over an extended period of time.

Recall the definition of a stock as something measured at a point in time. Imagine that at one single moment we could freeze all useful manufactured goods where they are—including those in warehouses and on shelves—and make a long list. Everything on the list that is not fixed manufactured capital would be counted, *at that moment*, as inventory manufactured capital. (If we start the economy rolling again, however, we will see that inventories are constantly being added to and drawn down, as stocks of materials are used up and goods are sold.)

4.3 | Manufactured Capital in Core and Public Purpose Spheres

When we think of manufactured capital as the stock of physical assets that provide inputs to productive activities, it is important to remember that productive activities take place in all spheres. Sometimes economists discuss manufactured capital largely in terms of business investment, ignoring the manufactured capital stocks that have accumulated in the core and public purpose spheres. This approach can be traced back to reliance on the traditional model of economic behavior that we introduced in Chapter 1. Remember that this model views only firms as "producers" who make usable goods and services, whereas households are viewed only as "consumers" (and suppliers of labor) who use up the goods and services. This model downplays the productive activities of households and governments; neighborhoods and nonprofits—other important parts of the core and public purpose spheres, respectively—are rarely mentioned at all.

In terms of the traditional model, a stove bought by a restaurant represents an investment in manufactured capital, but exactly the same stove bought by a household would be classified as mere consumption and not thought to be productive at all. Obviously, to account fully for the productive capacity of an economy, manufactured

Manufactured and Natural Capital Compared

As a general rule, substitution tends to be easier for manufactured capital than for natural capital. When it wears out or is destroyed, manufactured capital can often be replaced with something as good or better. The importance of this characteristic may be seen by comparing the decline of the classical Greek and Roman civilizations with the post–World War II recovery of European countries.

The growth of cities in classical civilizations required intensive use of agricultural land to support the growing nonagricultural population. Significant quantities of the soil upon which Greek and Roman agriculture depended were lost to erosion; additional areas of the Roman Empire suffered salt build-up in the soils (a common result of irrigation). Eroded soils can be renewed, but only (in the normal course of events) very slowly. Salty soils are even harder to repair. The loss of agricultural productivity is believed to be one of the reasons for the decline of these ancient civilizations. In this case, destruction of natural capital meant the loss of a civilization.

The recovery of Europe in the middle of the 20th century, after World War II, offers a dramatically different example. Vast amounts of infrastructure, equipment, and other types of manufactured capital were destroyed in the war. However, in those parts of Europe that were already well along the path to industrialization, and that had a well-educated, highly motivated workforce and a solid social infrastructure, recovery was rapid. They were able to rebuild and to reestablish a higher level of productivity than had existed before the war.

The field of economic studies has existed for about two and a half centuries. For the first 200 years of this time, it was taken as obvious that manufactured capital

capital should be accounted for in similar ways, no matter who holds it.[5] Production by households, neighborhoods, nonprofits, and governments depends on stocks of manufactured capital, just as much as production by businesses does.

> ### Discussion Questions
>
> 1. Come up with one new example of each of the following: fixed manufactured capital, inventory, investment, depreciation.
> 2. In the early 20th century, photos or drawings of big factories with tall stacks belching smoke were popularly used to represent the productivity of the contemporary economy. What images come to mind now, when you think of economic activity in the early 21st century?

5 | Human Capital

In our farming examples, the people working the farms had the health and energy they needed to labor on their land, and they demonstrated various kinds of knowledge and skills. They also needed to know which seeds to plant and how to manage the available planting technology, be it digging sticks, ploughs, or more complex machines. These

---

[5] A similar issue arises in distinguishing "intermediate goods" (see the previous footnote) from "final goods" (see Chapter 7). Some economists, assuming that households can only "consume," would classify bags of flour (and anything else) sold to a household as final goods. Flour, however, requires further processing (cooking or baking) before it can be used (that is, eaten)—whether that processing occurs at a baking company or in a home kitchen.

made the difference between more productive and less productive systems. Natural capital was, for the most part, simply taken for granted. This point of view evolved because the discipline of economics grew up with the Industrial Revolution. By 1950 a dozen or so human generations had been exposed to experiences that taught lessons similar to that of the postwar reconstruction of Europe—namely, that each new generation of manufactured capital tends to be more productive than what has gone before.

However, that was not the only lesson about the characteristics of different kinds of capital that emerged in the half century after World War II. The astonishingly rapid rebirth of war-devastated Europe showed that human and social resources (the human capital and social capital we will shortly discuss) are essential complements to manufactured capital. At the same time, critical natural capital constraints were once again becoming prominent. The importance of building and maintaining factories, machinery, and communications systems has not diminished, but it has become increasingly evident that we can no longer take for granted an adequate quantity and quality of water, air, soil, and the other species that live on planet Earth. Indeed, it is becoming apparent that productivity is based on a much more complex set of factors. Not only is it necessary to extract productive flows from the variety of kinds of capital resources; attention must also be paid to ensuring that these flows can be sustained. It is in this context that the distinctions between stocks and flows, and the importance of natural, human, and social capital, have come to the fore. ◔

characteristics—an individual's health, energy, knowledge, and skill—are all included in the term *human capital*. Such individual productive capabilities must be created and enhanced through nurturance, education, training, and other aspects of life experience.

The raw quantity of human capital in an economy might be crudely measured in terms of the number of adults in its population who are of normal working age. To attempt to measure its quality, measures of health status and/or of years of schooling achieved might also be considered. As with the various kinds of physical capital, we can think of human capital as a stock of capabilities, which can yield a flow of services. **Labor** is the name that economists use to refer to the flow of effort, skill, and knowledge that humans directly provide as inputs into productive activities. Because it is a flow, labor is usually measured over a period of time, such as by the number of person-hours of work of a particular skill that has been used in the course of a week or month.

Human capital has physical aspects, which are material and can be seen and touched, and it has intangible aspects as well.

5.1 | Physical Human Capital

To the extent that we consider humans as one of the many species in the natural world, our physical survival, our energy, and our genetic diversity can be thought of as physical capital in a human shape. Manual labor, for example, taps human physical energy, just as another productive process might tap a stock of fossil fuel. Thus the term *human capital* is based on an analogy between a human being and a passive resource or machine. Although some people find this analogy offensive, others find it to be a useful way of analyzing an important input to production—as long as it does not lead to treating human beings as though they really were machines!

Health, strength, fitness, and innate intelligence are important forms of physical human capital. In circumstances of deprivation, where some workers perform below

labor: the flow of time, effort, skill, and knowledge that humans directly provide as inputs into productive activities

their potential because they are weakened or distracted by hunger or illness, basic nutrition and medical care can be seen as important ways of investing in human capital, as well as direct contributions to well-being. This is particularly true in the case of growing children, whose future capabilities can be permanently stunted by deprivation at critical times.

5.2 | Intangible Human Capital

The historical uniqueness of the two and a half centuries since the start of the Industrial Revolution, in which standards of living have risen many-fold for large parts of an expanding human population, rests more than anything else upon the dramatic rise in output of the average worker. As we have noted, this rise in output per worker—often referred to as **labor productivity**—was once associated almost exclusively with the accumulation of manufactured capital. It was evident that the countless generations of workers who cultivated fields with hoes and digging sticks were able to produce less, per worker, than later generations who had access to draft animals and plows; the productivity of the latter was in turn outstripped by their successors who had tractors.

labor productivity: the level of output that can be produced per worker

However, as the computer revolution and related events have rapidly expanded the category of "knowledge workers" (people whose jobs consist largely of processing and applying, and sometimes creating, knowledge about the social and physical world), it has become evident that the continuing rise in productivity does not depend only on physical capital and sheer human effort. It also depends on intangible kinds of capital, including the knowledge, skills, and habits embodied in individuals.

Formal education, as well as less formal ways of acquiring skills (such as early childhood education in homes and preschools, reading, and training acquired on the job) are important contributors to human capital. As you read this paragraph, you are investing in your own human capital, in the form of an economics education. Clearly, human capital has a way of building on itself over time. Consider the labor inputs to your homework, for example. Presumably, your intelligence and your fund of prior knowledge are not used up when you do one set of problems; they are still available to be drawn on for the next set. These things, along with your general level of energy and alertness and your study habits, are the human capital stock from which you derive the flow of services that allow you to do your homework. Studying, in turn, is an investment in human capital. After you finish your homework, your stock of knowledge has increased.

Discussion Questions

1. In what ways is it useful to think of human bodies and brains as though they were like productive machinery? What might be some drawbacks of this way of thinking?
2. When, in the life of a particular human being, does the process of acquiring human capital begin?

6 | Social Capital

In our farming stories, the families drew on important stocks of social capital in addition to the human capital of the individual farmers and the manufactured and natural capital. Social capital consists of the cultural transmission of knowledge, ideas, and values, along with the social organization and workplace relationships that shape production, forming the social context of economic activity. We will discuss here two important types of social capital: technology and social organization.

6.1 | Technology

technology: methods for combining resources to produce outputs

Imagine that Gail is a farmer from the third family we described earlier. On one field she grows beets, on another alfalfa. We can use the word **technology** to summarize how Gail applies inputs to produce these crops. The technology for producing anything is very much like the recipe for producing, for example, a beef stew. The recipe, or the technology, comprises a list of needed inputs as well as a prescription for the way to combine these inputs and what actions need to be taken to transform them into outputs. Different technologies—and different recipes—will use inputs more or less efficiently to produce results that can differ very widely.

In Gail's situation, if both the inputs and the technology stay constant, and if the weather is unchanged every year, she might expect the output of each field to be the same each year. But there is considerable risk that such an expectation would be wrong, because it ignores the feedback effect of economic activity on the physical resource base—in this case, the effect of farming on the fertility of the soil. If farmers repeatedly plant the same crops in the same soil without replenishing the nutrients the plants take up, the soil fertility will gradually diminish, and similar inputs will yield less output in each succeeding year.

If our Family 1 faced declining yields, it could just move to another location. That option is available to almost no 21st-century farmers. Facing declining yields, Gail must look for other ways of doing something different. The first thing she needs is knowledge of what has gone wrong and how to correct it. She might seek this knowledge in books, by taking a course at some educational institution, by asking a neighbor, or by contacting a specialist. That is, she may make an effort to improve her own knowledge by tapping into forms of socially held knowledge.

Much knowledge is socially held. For example, some farming communities possess traditions that tell all farmers, in general terms, what to do to prevent soil exhaustion. One such tradition may be the knowledge that it is beneficial to apply various fertilizers to the soil: These may be manure from animals or humans, or crop residues, or even seaweed. Another tradition found in both ancient and modern farming communities is the idea of crop rotation. Appropriate crop rotation schedules can boost output without any change being made in any of the other inputs, such as the physical capital or the hours of labor applied to production.

The discovery that some crops are especially good at preparing land for other crops has been made repeatedly throughout history.[6] Whenever this discovery emerges— (whether from the shifting agriculture patterns of Family 1 or from the chemical- and machinery-intensive patterns of Family 3), it can be called a change in technology—a special kind in which the physical inputs have not changed but are simply applied in a different way. The technology available to a society is the collection of known recipes for using resource inputs to produce outputs. In modern times, technology has progressed via advances in basic and applied sciences, leading to inventions of new products and new techniques of production. Improvements in technology also result from the efforts of workers, managers, and engineers at the site of production to adapt and improve their techniques and their products.

embodied technology: technology incorporated into forms of manufactured capital

How does technology enter the production process? There are two major alternatives. On the one hand, it can be **embodied** in manufactured capital; for example, a new car or truck may embody specific recent advances in fuel combustion and transportation technology. In this case, the new fuel combustion technology is used in production

---

[6] This knowledge was not available to all users of "traditional agriculture" but, rather, emerged from time to time in various localities with reference to specific crops. The difference between such traditional knowledge and modern, scientific knowledge is that the latter includes an understanding of the general principles (such as soil chemistry) that explain when crop rotation will be more, and when less, effective.

disembodied technology: technology in the form of shared understandings and procedures

if and only if the new vehicles are used. Social capital in this case is a form of physical capital. On the other hand, technology can be **disembodied**, potentially enhancing the productivity of many different inputs used in production. Such intangible technologies may consist of shared understandings and procedures; for instance, people who are familiar with motor vehicles may share a general knowledge of such principles as "When the engine starts to make a terrible grinding noise, stop and add oil." (Several tragic stories from developing countries demonstrate that in the absence of this particular knowledge, new machinery can quickly be destroyed.) This technology is not embodied in any one type of engine or vehicle, yet it makes the use of many types of vehicles more productive. Technological social capital may be owned by the community at large, or its use may be restricted to smaller groups. Patents and copyrights allow certain kinds of embodied and disembodied social capital to be controlled by a limited group of people.

The technology that is embodied in equipment or other material things clearly overlaps with our concept of manufactured capital. If either output per acre or output per hour of labor input increases because wooden plows are replaced by metal ones, we can describe the change in terms of an increase in manufactured capital (here manufactured capital has increased in quality and perhaps in quantity as well). However, crop rotation is an interesting example because it can be achieved with no additional input except the immaterial input of knowledge. Why, then, was the practice widely ignored during the early period of modern intensive agriculture, and why is it being rediscovered today? The answer is found not so much in the knowledge held by specific individuals as in the belief system of a culture.

6.2 | Social Organization

social organization: structured ways of coordinating human activities

In our farm family examples, people not only had the knowledge and physical resources to farm but also had forms of **social organization** that coordinated their activities within their families, villages, and communities in a way that promoted production and resource maintenance. These processes involve interconnected networks of human labor, so they pose not just engineering problems but also human problems of motivation and social relations.

Strong counterexamples of the absence of social organization will make the presence of social organization more clear. Suppose that our Family 2 had no way of protecting the boundaries of its fields from those of its neighbors, so at harvest time its neighbor could reap what this family had sowed. What incentive would our family have to invest in planting its fields? Or suppose that warring bands roamed the land, frequently setting fire to the crops in invaded territories. How productive could our farm family be? Social organization encompasses the broad social and organizational capacities (including laws and ways of enforcing them) that enable people to trust and cooperate with one another, thereby reducing the costs of economic interactions and transactions. Thus social capital includes such cultural aspects of people's behavior as the prevailing standards and expectations of nonviolence, honesty, respect, reliability, initiative, and originality.

Social capital also includes the cultural beliefs and fashions of thought that determine what knowledge is applied, which scientific questions are researched, and which technological possibilities are explored. A growing public awareness of the hazards posed by global warming, for example, could be considered a form of social capital, because it increases the ability of society to respond to a significant threat to its future well-being.

In contemporary industrialized economies, the term *social capital* is most often used to refer to characteristics of a society that encourage cooperation among groups of people (such as workers and managers) whose joint, interdependent efforts are needed to achieve a common goal (such as efficient production). This kind of capital is built up

The Ties That Lead to Prosperity: The Economic Value of Social Bonds

NEWS in context

In small cities scattered across Lombardy and the Veneto, family-owned manufacturers making everything from textiles to brass fittings generate the highest per capita incomes in Italy. In certain villages in Tanzania, people with strong social ties have developed strong commercial ties, too, making their villages wealthier than neighboring towns with fewer social groupings. In the Chicago area, families that moved out of segregated Chicago housing projects to the suburbs are flourishing, whereas their counterparts who left the projects but stayed in the city are still floundering economically.

What do these far-flung places and people have in common? They are all examples of a powerful, newly recognized economic force at work—social capital. In communities and neighborhoods across America and around the world, social ties have long been a subject of study for sociologists, psychologists, and political scientists. Now economists are assessing how the social fabric affects individual choice and economic growth. . . . Hard to measure

and difficult to define, social capital comprises an intricate web of relationships, norms of behavior, values, obligations, and information channels.

. . . Stephen Knack of American University and Philip Keefer of the World Bank found, in a recent study of 29 countries, that high levels of trust in the Netherlands, Norway, and Switzerland were associated with strong economic performance from 1980 to 1992, after adjusting for differences in other variables, such as education levels. More significantly, incentives to innovate and accumulate capital are stronger in countries that exhibit high trust, because business can operate with a high degree of confidence about the future. Japan, Norway, and Switzerland are high-trust nations with a high level of investment as a share of gross domestic product. . . .

The ties that bind families and communities do more than make people feel good—they make the economy go 'round. Gradually, a factor of growth that no one can measure in dollars is being seen to have great value. ◔

Adapted from Karen Pennar, *Business Week,* December 15, 1997.

Why might incentives to innovate and invest be low in societies with low levels of trust?

to the extent that a society is characterized by strong norms of reciprocity, which lead people to trust and help one another, and dense networks of civic participation, which encourage people to engage in mutually beneficial efforts rather than seeking only to gain individual advantage at the possible expense of others. Business accountants have led the way in recognizing one kind of social capital—goodwill—which they view as a significant business asset that makes a firm more valuable than one might think from looking at its physical assets alone. Goodwill includes a number of intangible factors, such as a firm's good reputation among its customers and creditors, good management, and good labor relations. It has become common practice to list goodwill among the assets of a firm that is up for sale.

Social capital resembles other forms of capital in that it generates a service that enhances the output obtainable from other inputs, without itself being used up in the process of production. Recognition of this concept by economists is fairly recent and has been strengthened by the observation that variation in social capital across communities and societies can help to explain some of the differences in their economic development.

It is obvious that social capital as a whole cannot easily be measured quantitatively; however, there are some questions that cannot be answered in any way except by referring to social capital. Earlier we asked a question of that sort: "If knowledge about crop rotation has existed over many centuries, why was it applied at some times and not at others?" Social capital, including cultural beliefs, is the best answer.

7 | Financial Capital

When it had a bad year, our farm Family 2 had to borrow seeds for planting from its wealthier neighbor. By contrast, Family 3, living in a society with sophisticated financial institutions, borrows money from a bank. These monetary funds are an example of financial capital.

It is in the nature of most production processes that you have to pay for inputs before you can profit from outputs. Before it can make its first sale, a start-up business needs to buy or rent a building and equipment, hire staff, and amass inventories of materials and supplies. You, as a student, need to pay for textbooks well in advance of receiving any increase in salary that your education might eventually earn you. Local governments often build a major bridge before collecting the tolls that will pay for it. Financial capital is what allows all these productive activities to get going, in a money economy, in advance of the returns that will flow from them.

Financial capital is a largely intangible form of capital: Its importance in the economy relies on the social beliefs that sustain the financial system, much more than on the physical paper or the electronic documents that record its existence. Economists distinguish between two different forms of financial capital: equity finance and debt finance.

7.1 | Equity Finance

Suppose that one year Gail, the farmer in our third family, has such a good harvest that she can lay aside enough money to buy the seeds and fertilizer she will need for the next year. Any business that finances investments for its future production out of its own funds (that is, wealth) is said to be using **equity finance**. *Equity* means having an ownership right.[7] People may be able to finance production processes out of assets that they themselves own.

equity finance: an economic actor's use of its own funds to finance investments that will support future production

Like other capital stocks, financial capital can be thought of in terms of stocks that increase or decrease over time and that provide a flow of services into production. Gail increases her financial capital stock by laying aside the proceeds from her last harvest. She will use (and, in fact, use up) her equity financial capital as she spends it on supplies for the next productive season.

What are the commonest sources of equity finance? Individuals may finance their productive activities out of money they have inherited or saved from their wages. Governments finance some programs out of accumulated past taxes. Businesses may accumulate funds by retaining some of their profits. People add to their stock of equity financial capital by saving, and they diminish their stock of equity financial capital by spending.

---

[7] This use of the term *equity* should not be confused with another meaning of the same word, "justice or fairness."

Large businesses may also use markets to increase their access to equity finance. We will discuss the stock market, in which claims to shares of ownership in a corporation are sold, in Chapter 14.

7.2 | Debt Finance

As we originally told the story, Gail's family takes out annual loans from a bank for seeds and fertilizer and longer-term loans for land and equipment. Not having enough equity capital of their own, they use **debt finance** to gain access, temporarily, to the purchasing power of *other* actors' wealth.

debt finance: money obtained by borrowing and used to cover some costs of an enterprise

One can think of taking out a **loan** as "renting" financial capital—renting the use of money. Just as an office can be rented and *used* productively by one enterprise while it is *owned* by another, the services of the financial capital in this case are *used* by the farm family, even though the financial capital itself is *owned* by the bank's depositors. Of course, just as in the case of an office, the "renter" will pay a fee. Borrowers agree not only to repay the **principal** (the original amount) of the loan but also to give the lender **interest**, usually calculated as a percentage of the principal. (If the family should default—not be able to pay back the loans—the bank can usually take over ownership of the farm in exchange for its lost funds.)

loan: money borrowed for temporary use, on the condition that it be repaid with interest

principal: the original amount of money borrowed

interest: the charge for borrowing money

Banks and similar institutions, such as credit unions, are not the only providers of debt finance. Governments and large companies often raise financial capital directly by

---

ECONOMICS in the Real World

Another Example of Opportunity Cost

At first blush, it may seem that equity finance should be a much cheaper way of financing productive endeavors than borrowing; it avoids the cost of paying interest to the bank. Economists point out, however, that equity finance is not, in fact, free.

Farmer Gail actually has various choices about what to do with any equity financial capital that she may accumulate. Plowing it back into her own farming business, over the next season, is only one possibility. She might also leave it deposited at a bank and earn interest on it for the entire next year. Or perhaps her cousin is starting an exciting new business, and she could invest in that and reap a share of its eventual profits. Opportunity cost is (as we discussed in Chapter 1) what economists call the value of what one loses by not choosing the *best* alternative to the choice one actually makes.

Suppose that Gail is confident that if she invests in her cousin's business she will get at least a 25% return on her investment. Suppose, with crop prices expected to be low in the coming year, she can anticipate only a 10% return on her next farm season. She has to decide what to do with her money. From a financial perspective, she would be better off investing in her cousin's enterprise and letting her fields lie fallow. Rather than thinking of her own money as coming "free" to her farming enterprise, she should realize that it will "cost" her a 25% return—the lost proceeds from her forgone best alternative. Because her financial benefit from investing in farming (a 10% return) is more than canceled by the cost of investing in farming (a lost 25% return), she should not farm.

Of course, uncertainty about returns from the two enterprises, and nonfinancial concerns about the effects of not farming, might lead Gail to a different decision. From a financial perspective, however, it is important to realize that equity finance carries the cost of "the road not taken."

If relatives, friends, or organizations are helping you pay for your college education through gifts or grants, is this financing "free"?

selling bonds, which are financial instruments that promise repayment of funds with interest. Bond markets will be discussed in Chapter 14.

7.3 | A Note on Terminology

Whereas land and seeds, tools and machinery, and able-bodied, adequately trained and trustworthy workers are essential for production, much production could go on without financial capital. However, in modern economies, financial capital is such an important facilitator of economic processes that the term *capital*, as noted at the beginning of this chapter, has often been used to refer to financial capital only. *Investment* is commonly taken to refer to buying stocks and bonds, and *stocks* is taken to mean ownership shares in enterprises.

In contrast, we will use *capital* in this book to refer to natural, manufactured, human, and social capital as well as to financial capital, although the more general terms *resources* and *assets* could also be used. We will use *investments* to mean actions taken to increase the quantity or quality of any productive resources, and *stock* will denote the level of a resource at a given time.

Creating added confusion, when economists trained in traditional economics talk about capital, they are most often referring to *manufactured* capital. They tend to neglect discussion of natural, human, and social capital. What they most often mean when they refer to investment is the acquisition of new manufactured capital. However, sometimes their discussions move back and forth without warning between manufactured capital and financial capital—that is, between physical means of production and financial instruments. In order to minimize confusion, we will try to be quite specific in our use of all these terms.

Discussion Questions

1. Financial capital is important not only within the business and government spheres but also in the core sphere. What major assets do families often borrow to buy?

2. Explain how the concept of opportunity cost can influence the way you think about your use of financial capital.

---

8 | Sustaining Capital Stocks

It is only recently that the field of economics has formally recognized that natural capital, human capital, and social capital are at least as critical to production as manufactured and financial capital—and sometimes more so. Along with this realization has come a recognition that all of these forms of capital are subject to erosion as well as growth. Because all production begins with, and depends on, the availability of the necessary capital stocks—including, in most cases, all five kinds that we have discussed—it is important to consider how these capital stocks are produced and maintained and what circumstances might endanger their quantity or quality. The necessity of attending to the basic economic activity of resource maintenance has become more pronounced.

For example, what happens if stocks of manufactured capital are not maintained? If our stocks of housing, roads, communication systems, factories, and equipment are wearing out without being replaced, the standard of living, as normally measured, will decline. What about social and human capital? If formal education systems, norms of childrearing, or socially accepted patterns of behavior change in ways that cause a deterioration in the level of education and health of a population, or in such cultural and ethical aspects of behavior as the prevailing standards and expectations of honesty, reliability, initiative, and originality, then it is likely, again, that standards of living will decline in the future.

New developments in technology may help in maintaining important capital stocks. This zero-emission fuel cell bus in London is part of a nine-city European trial. Its electrical engine is fueled with liquid nitrogen, and emits only water vapor. The participating pilot cities will study the environmental, technical, and financial performance of the busses over 2 years to ascertain their contribution to preserving the stock of clean air.

These are issues that must always be taken seriously, but at this moment in history the deterioration of natural capital stocks is a more widely recognized problem. Only in recent decades have we encountered global limits on the capacity of nature to absorb the intended and unintended effects of our economic activity.[8] Increasingly, humans have gone beyond harvesting the annual produce of seas and soils and have begun to deplete the sources of renewal and growth—such as stocks of fish and plankton, soil fertility, and entire biosystems—on which natural output depends. It is possible for economic activity continually to augment stocks of manufactured capital and human capital, more than offsetting any decline associated with the depreciation of manufactured capital and the retirement or death of people with enhanced labor skills. In contrast, the impact of economic activity on the stock of natural capital is most often negative; either the existing stock is drawn down (when natural resource inputs are used), or the quality of the stock is diminished (as by the introduction of waste products).

The stock of renewable natural capital can be maintained or augmented by wise resource management, and the (apparent) stock of nonrenewable resources can be increased by new discoveries. Moreover, the problem of a deteriorating natural resource stock can be allayed or postponed by technological and organizational changes that reduce the amount of natural resource depletion or waste product generation associated with a given amount of production. Yet the fact that the global biosphere is finite

---

[8] On a somewhat more local scale, such limits have frequently been encountered before, and they have indeed resulted in the downfall of both large and small civilizations in the past. From 3000 to 2400 B.C., for example, the ancient culture of Mesopotamia thrived between the Tigris and Euphrates rivers. But irrigation led to salinization and erosion of the soil, decreasing crop yields and eventually bringing about the collapse of the culture. Today the area is desert. The major difference today is that many human activities have global implications, and the natural limits that are being tested are often global ones.

suggests that sooner or later, there will be a limit to the size of the physical flow of production that can be maintained over time.

Many types of decline can be reversed, so these observations should not be taken as cause for despair. They do, however, point to the fact that economic policy and analysis are not simple matters. The economic health of a contemporary society depends as much on schools and family support systems as on factories and roads; it depends on workplace morale as well as on protection of air, soil, water, and biota. And whether we are thinking about the long-term or the short-term health of the economy and the individuals in it, we must judge economic activities not only in relation to their intended effects but also in terms of their unplanned effects on the physical and social environments.

Review Questions

1. What distinguishes a stock from a flow?
2. What are the five major types of capital?
3. What are the two main types of natural capital?
4. What are the two main types of manufactured capital?
5. What are the two main types of human capital?
6. What are the two main types of social capital?
7. What are the two main types of financial capital?
8. What distinguishes physical from intangible capital?

Exercises

1. Which of the following are flows? Which are stocks? If a flow, which of the five major kind(s) of capital does it increase or decrease? If a stock, what kind of capital is it?
   a. The fish in a lake
   b. The output of a factory during a year
   c. The income you receive in a month
   d. The reputation of a business among its customers
   e. The assets of a bank
   f. The equipment in a factory
   g. A process of diplomatic negotiations
   h. The discussion in an economics class

2. Draw and label five stock-flow diagrams, one new example for each of the five kinds of capital.

3. Consider the case of a new computer anti-virus software package.
   a. In a paragraph, briefly describe the capital stocks that provided the resource base for its creation.
   b. Which of the four economic activities is anti-virus software designed to enhance?

4. A forest originally has 10,000 trees. Suppose the forest naturally replenishes itself by 10% per year. That is, at the end of 1 year, if nothing else happened, it would have $10,000 + (0.10 \times 10,000) = 11,000$ trees. (This assumption is not biologically accurate, but it keeps the math simple.) Suppose that 1500 trees are harvested at the end of each year.
   a. How many trees will the forest have at the end of 1 year, when you account for both natural replenishment and the effects of harvesting?
   b. How many trees will there be at the end of 2 years? (*Note:* Base the 10% replenishment amount on the number of trees that exist at the beginning of the second year.)

    c. How many trees will there be at the end of 3 years?

    d. For the harvest of trees to be sustainable, what is the largest number of trees that could be harvested each year (starting with the original stock of 10,000 trees)?

5. Jeremy owns his own house free and clear, with no mortgage, in an area where there is no property tax. He says that therefore, except for utilities, it doesn't cost him anything to live there. Is Jeremy correct? How would an economist apply the concept of opportunity cost to determine how much Jeremy's housing really costs him?

6. Match each concept in Column A with an example in Column B.

Column A	Column B
a. equity finance	**i.** fish in the ocean
b. social capital	**ii.** starting a business by using money you have saved up for that purpose
c. a renewable natural resource	**iii.** iron ore
d. fixed manufactured capital	**iv.** spare parts at an auto repair shop
e. human capital	**v.** a factory building
f. inventories	**vi.** a shared language within a community
g. a nonrenewable natural resource	**vii.** your own health

Production Costs

Chapter 7

Think about something that is produced in a pretty obvious way—corn, for instance. You know that to grow corn you would need—at a minimum—access to good soil, water, sunshine, seeds, and labor for sowing and harvesting. On a modern farm, you would also use fertilizer, financing, and equipment. If you wanted your farming enterprise to be financially successful, you would need to keep careful track of the costs of all the things that go into the production process, and you would need to make good choices about how much of each to use. As a society, we need also to take into account costs that the individual farmer might ignore, such as the damage to waterways done by fertilizer run-off from the fields.

1 | The Production Process

inputs: resources that go into production

outputs: the results of production

waste products: outputs that are not used either for consumption or in a further production process

The second of the four basic economic activities is *production*. The economic activity of production converts some resources, which we call **inputs**, into new goods and services, which we refer to as **outputs**, as a flow over some period of time. The way in which this production occurs depends on available technologies. Production processes can also lead to undesirable outputs, such as **waste products**. We consider only *useful* outputs to be economic goods and services.

In ordinary usage, the term *production* usually refers to the processes during which some material thing is physically converted into something more useful. Cotton fiber goes into a textile mill and comes out as cotton fabric. This fabric is then shipped to another location, printed with small red hearts, cut into pieces, sewn into boxer shorts, distributed through wholesalers, and eventually marketed by retailers. Or households may purchase the cotton fabric and use it to produce homemade nursery curtains or Halloween costumes. To most people, the various stages of manufacturing per se would be regarded as production, but the transport, distribution, and sale that are involved would not.

As we might suspect, economists also regard manufacturing, along with such kindred enterprises as mining and farming, as production, but they do not restrict the term to these activities alone. Rather, they view production more generally as the transformation of resources or commodities into things that will ultimately be useful to consumers. To a resident of Chicago, a Toyota sedan in a downtown showroom is most assuredly different from the same vehicle at the factory in Japan. The transport of an automobile over an ocean and across half a continent thus constitutes production in the broad economic sense. After all, Texas oil "producers" don't actually make oil; they merely transport it from its natural state under the ground to the nearest refinery. Similarly, such activities as storage, packaging, and retailing all can be interpreted as forms of production.

Nor is production confined to processes that involve tangible goods. Production also includes providing services. Accordingly, from an economist's point of view, physicians, child care givers, mechanics, musicians, park rangers, lawyers, professors, housecleaners, tax auditors, and massage therapists all are engaged in production.

In production processes, the quantity of output that is produced is related to the quantity of resources used and to the effectiveness with which those resources are combined. Were we to ask a chef how to prepare one of his specialties—say, ginger chicken—we would be given an answer in terms of inputs (ingredients) and technology or techniques of production (the proportions and order in which the ingredients must be combined, as well as the appropriate preparation times and temperatures). Because a chef is clearly engaged in processes whose outputs are fundamentally different from their inputs, it might seem that the chef's response to our question would provide a key to the theory of production in economics.

The chef's recipe is an instance of technology. As we noted in Chapter 6, the available technology—the methods available for converting inputs to outputs—can be thought of as a form of accumulated social capital. But the chef's description would be incomplete from the economist's point of view. The services of human capital will also be needed to bring the ingredients together, in the form of a certain number of hours worked by the chef, with a certain amount of skill and expertise, and perhaps the services of some assistants as well. Services of manufactured capital will also be drawn on, if only in the form of a number of hours of service from a stove and cooking pot.

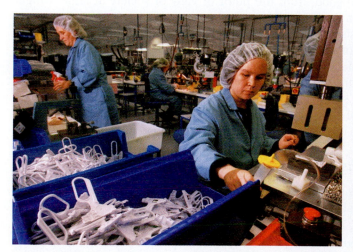 

The manufacturing assembly line is an image often associated with "production." These workers at ConMed Corporation in Utica, New York, are manufacturing disposable laproscopic scissors for use in surgeries. The production of services is also important in contemporary economies. The French-Canadian circus troupe, Cirque Du Soleil (shown here performing in London), produces entertainment services. The inputs include rehearsal time, costuming, and choreography, while the output is a performance. In both examples cooperation and coordination among the workers are important to their productivity.

Production Inputs and Outputs

The simplest production of a carved toy would require, as inputs, a piece of wood, a knife, and the time, skill, and effort of the person doing the carving; these three requirements are examples of natural, manufactured, and human capital, respectively. The most obvious output is the finished toy. What other output might there be? Consider the shavings that fell from the knife. Perhaps in this simple production process they are of very little importance; the shavings will just be swept up and put in a trash can. However, the shavings might have some potential uses that are being overlooked. If it is not just one carved toy that is being produced, but hundreds—and not just a few shavings, but barrels full—then they might be regarded as a resource for producing heat rather than as a waste product. And if they continue to be treated as waste, their disposal is potentially a cost to someone. If that cost is not borne by the producer, it becomes a negative externality. Examples of social capital in this story might include a broad understanding, in the society at large, of the concept of negative externalities, as well as a generally accepted business norm for turning waste into resources. ◗

Although it is not embodied in the physical output being produced, financial capital facilitates the gathering of the necessary resources, in advance of receipt of payment for the output. In this chapter, we are more concerned with the "real," or nonfinancial, aspect of production, so we leave the question of the use of financial capital until the next chapter. Note that, as we saw in Chapter 6, the actual inputs into production from manufactured, social, or human capital often consist of a flow of services, rather than actual depletion of the resource itself. The production process is also not instantaneous; it clearly requires some time to complete.

intermediate goods: goods that will undergo further processing

final goods: goods that are ready for use by people

Some productive processes turn out **intermediate goods**—goods that will undergo further processing before they are ready for use. When a good is ready for use, it is a **final good**. Raw chicken that has been produced by ranchers and slaughterhouses is an example of an intermediate good, from the point of view of society at large. Ginger chicken, ready for eating, is a final good.[1]

The economist's analysis of production starts with a statement of what specific quantities of inputs—flows of materials and services arising from the existing stocks of natural, manufactured, human, and social capital—are required to produce a specified flow of output over a given time period.

This chapter describes some conceptual tools that can be helpful in discussing technology and the costs of production. In the chapter that follows, we will discuss production-related decision making and the benefits that follow from production.

Discussion Questions

1. What distinguishes the economic activity of production from the activity of resource maintenance? Of consumption? Of distribution?

2. Think about the processes involved in producing this textbook. Describe these processes, making use of the following terms: *input, output, waste products, intermediate good, final good.*

[1] This definition varies somewhat from that used in creating the National Income and Product Accounts (NIPA) from which gross domestic product figures are calculated. The NIPA define all goods sold to households as "final goods," even if more processing (such as cooking) will be needed to make them usable by people. As noted in Chapter 1, GDP does not include productive activities that go on within households.

2 | Economic Costs

Sometimes, in common speech, the term *economic costs* is used to mean strictly financial or monetary costs—just whatever a farmer, for example, pays to a supplier for fertilizer. But economists themselves give the term quite a different meaning when they discuss social decision making about production. Rational decision making should ideally include consideration of *all* relevant costs and benefits, whether or not they are easily summarized in monetary terms.[2]

As we will show below, important divergences between the obvious monetary costs of production and the *true* costs of production can occur when opportunity costs are different from accounting costs, when transaction costs are significant, or when there are external costs.

2.1 | Accounting Costs Versus Economic Costs

At the end of the last chapter, we saw an example of the importance of opportunity costs in the case of Gail's farm. Gail's accounting system for her farm business will list the cost of seeds, fertilizer, fuel, and so on as costs of producing a crop this season. If she takes out a loan to finance the business, the interest she pays on the loan will also be entered as a cost. The wear and tear on her farm equipment might be entered as a depreciation cost—which can be thought of as funds set aside toward replacing the equipment when it wears out. Some business accounting systems, however, include as costs *only* items that correspond to such actual money outflows. Gail's **accounting costs**, totaling $48,000, are listed in the top section of Table 7.1.

accounting costs: the costs of a project, figured in terms of monetary outflows alone

Suppose that, in addition to taking out a bank loan, Gail also uses her own equity capital (retained earnings from the previous season) to finance some of the costs of farming. There will be no interest payments to record on this use of her own funds. The use of equity capital will appear to be "free" in accounting terms. But we know that this money does not really come free: By investing in her own farm, Gail loses the financial return that she could have gained elsewhere.

Table 7.1	Gail's Costs of Farming	
Accounting Costs		
Seeds	$20,000	
Fertilizer	3,000	
Fuel and transportation	5,000	
Interest on bank loan	15,000	
Depreciation of equipment	5,000	
Total Accounting Costs		$48,000
Opportunity Costs		
Forgone return on equity capital	$12,000	
Forgone salary	30,000	
Total Additional Costs		$42,000
Total Economic Costs		$90,000

---

[2] This is the ideal. In practice, unfortunately, "economistic" thinking sometimes leads people not to count anything that cannot easily be measured in dollar values.

economic costs: the costs of a project, including opportunity costs

In general, to calculate the true **economic costs** of a productive activity, we want to figure out how much value had to be *taken out of* other productive activities in order to do the activity in question. The accounting cost figures given for seeds, fertilizer, and so on should be included in economic costs, because the use of these inputs by Gail's farm *takes them away* from use elsewhere.[3] But we also need to add in some nonaccounting costs, such as the opportunity cost of Gail's use of her own equity capital for the season. In Gail's case, this would be the return of $12,000 that she would have gotten if she had invested her equity capital in her cousin's business instead of in her own farm. Similarly, although Gail does not pay herself a salary for the time she spends on farming, an economic consideration of costs would include the cost of her time, figured in terms of its value in its next-best use. Perhaps the next-best use of her time would have been to take a job in town at $30,000. This lost salary should also be added as a cost.

If Gail looks at the full economic costs of farming over this season—rather than just at the accounting costs—she will find that farming is more costly than she may have initially thought. Whereas her account books show costs of $48,000, it is really costing her $90,000 to farm for the season.

The same concept applies to consideration of the costs of production in any realm. To take another example—with a quite different result—think about the government of an economically depressed county, which is considering whether to invest in repairing a roadway. The project will hire people who would otherwise be unemployed and will pay them a legal minimum wage or a union-negotiated wage. The *accounting* costs for this labor, included in the project's budget, will be the actual wage paid. To figure the *economic* costs of this labor, however, from the perspective of society's production possibilities, you have to think about how much this road project pulls out of other productive activities that would otherwise have been undertaken. If the workers would otherwise have been unemployed, neither working for a wage nor productively engaged at home or in their communities, the answer might be that not very much is lost elsewhere. The economic costs, in this case, will be *below* the accounting or budgetary costs. The project is pulling otherwise unused resources into valuable activity. In terms of the societal production possibilities frontier (Chapter 1), the project moves the economy *toward* the full-employment frontier, not *along* the frontier. The project is therefore cheaper, in terms of its drain on real societal productive capacity, than an accounting analysis would suggest.

Comparisons of accounting cost and opportunity cost, then, may find either one of these to be greater than the other, depending on the potential value of productive inputs in their next-best use. Opportunity costs give the better guideline for economic decision making about what projects should be undertaken, because they take into account the real value of what is given up.

2.2 | Transaction Costs

Recall (from Chapter 1) that transaction costs are the costs of arranging economic activities. These also need to be taken into account in making production decisions.

For example, considerable research indicates that teenagers tend to be groggy in the early morning and would tend to be more alert in their high school classes if high schools started at mid-morning, instead of at the early-morning hour favored in many school districts. Yet few school districts have changed their hours to a more productivity-enhancing schedule. Why? One reason may be transaction costs. Changing the school schedule in response to this research might mean altering bus schedules, renegotiating union contracts with teachers and other staff, and, no doubt, holding many meetings of

---

[3] From a societal point of view, we are assuming that the amount Gail pays for these inputs represents their value in alternative production. That is, the monetary amounts she pays for them reflect their value if the physical resources had been used elsewhere in the economy. We can also think of these monetary costs as representing an opportunity cost from the point of view of Gail, as an individual economic actor. The money she spends on seeds, fertilizer, and so on is money she *forgoes* spending on a barn roof or a Florida vacation.

the school board and parent groups. The school district needs to take into account not only the benefits of a proposed change but also the transactions costs of getting the change implemented.

Similarly, suppose Patrick's Cards and Games, a retail firm, realizes that having a new store location in operation would increase its economic profits. But gathering information about possible new locations, paying executives to make the needed decisions, hiring lawyers to close the lease on the space, and advertising for and hiring a manager and employees would all be costly. A project that looks beneficial or profitable in the absence of such transaction costs may not look so attractive—and may not seem wise to undertake at all—when the transaction costs necessary to make it happen are considered.

In a world with no transaction costs, more beneficial projects could be undertaken. It is worthwhile considering whether projects to reduce transaction costs might themselves be production-enhancing. For example, projects that enhance community feeling within a high school district might make important negotiations go much more smoothly, or streamlining local laws might reduce the costs of opening new stores. However, transaction costs remain a fact of life and cannot be overlooked when one is making decisions.

2.3 | Internal and External Costs

In the case of Gail's farm, Gail needs to take into account the opportunity costs of her money and time to come to a wise economic decision concerning her own personal decision to farm. We consider such costs "internal" to the decision making of the economic actors directly involved in this activity. In this case, they are **internal costs** for Gail. But there may be larger costs to be taken into account as well—costs that Gail, as an individual, may be less concerned with but that affect others around her or society at large. As we noted in Chapter 1, negative externalities are harmful side effects of economic activities that affect actors who are not directly involved. When considering the costs of production, we call these **external costs**.

For example, the manure Gail spreads on her fields may make life unpleasant for residents of a suburb located downwind, or the chemical pesticides she applies may harm the local insect and bird life.

Social consideration of the goal of well-being demands that both internal and external costs be taken into account when one assesses the true value of each productive activity or of each production technique.

For example, zoning laws, which regulate whether a plot of land can be used for farming, residential, commercial, or industrial purposes, are designed to minimize the sort of conflict over the externalities associated with land use that can arise between suburbanites and manure-spreading farmers. Similarly, the United States outlawed the use of the pesticide DDT in farming after it was found to have long-lasting effects on bird and human health. Some companies now consider fuel efficiency when buying fleets of cars or trucks, not only because of the effect it will have on their own bottom line but also because they are concerned about carbon dioxide emissions and global warming. These examples illustrate how consideration of external costs can lead to more socially beneficial outcomes.

2.4 | Costs and Productive Efficiency

At any given time there is some limited number of known production processes. Taken collectively, these processes constitute a society's available technology. For a modern society, the available technology clearly comprises a vast array of productive processes. The question arises, however, whether all these processes actually constitute relevant production alternatives. Some may be so costly that they should not even be considered.

As discussed in Chapter 1, an efficient use of resources produces the maximum possible value of output for a given set of inputs, without unnecessary waste or expense.

internal costs: the costs of a project, from the perspective of the economic actor(s) making the decisions

external costs: the costs of a project that are borne by persons, or entities such as the environment, that are not among the economic actors directly responsible for the activity

technically efficient: the quality of a production process if no other process exists that can produce the same output with smaller quantities of some input(s) and no more of other inputs

Inefficient processes waste resources. Suppose that only two processes exist to produce a given output. If Process A can produce exactly the same level of an identical output as Process B, but with less of some inputs and no more of others (or, equivalently, if A can produce more output than B with the same level of inputs), then Process A is said to be **technically efficient**. Process B is, by comparison, technically inefficient.

In a world where everyone had perfect information about the relationship of inputs to outputs, was rational, and was able to choose a production technique with no limits based on what had gone on before, no one would choose to produce in a technically inefficient manner. Perfect information, you should recall from Chapter 2, means that economic actors know with certainty everything important to their decision making. Rationality means that people intelligently weigh the costs and benefits of their actions. But the real world is not always characterized by perfect information and rationality.

For example, suppose you need to study for an exam. You think you can get 95 points on it (the output) with 4 hours of studying (the inputs), but because you don't know in advance how hard the exam is going to be, you might rationally choose to study an extra hour "just to be sure." This is an example of uncertainty and imperfect information. Or perhaps you are a compulsive and nervous type and, even with good information, tend to keep on studying even when you know it would be more rational to take a break. After the fact, you might realize that this was a technically inefficient choice. For another example, a manufacturing company might continue to use a technically inefficient process because it has not heard about an innovation that has arisen elsewhere in the economy or because its management is slack. Or it may be that having limited access to financing prevents the firm from adopting a new innovation quickly.

For much of the present discussion of production, however, we will assume perfect information, rationality, and ease of adjustment. Although they are not entirely realistic, these assumptions enable us to highlight certain simple aspects of production. With these assumptions, we can say that no one would choose to produce in a wasteful, technically inefficient manner. In a later section of this chapter, we will "add back" some real-world complications.

A process that is technically inefficient today may not have been so a hundred years ago because its inefficiency may be relative only to processes discovered during the intervening century. Over time, new processes are invented that render old processes technically inefficient and thereby obsolete.

The picture becomes much more complicated when processes are compared that use a variety of inputs in varying combinations. Suppose, for example, that ginger chicken can be produced using either Process A, which involves 1.5 hours of the chef's time along with 1 hour of the time of a less-skilled assistant, or Process B, which uses 1 hour of the chef's time and 2 hours of the assistant's time. The first process uses more of the chef's time, whereas the second uses more of the assistant's time. Because the chef and assistant have different skills, we cannot simply add up their hours. We cannot say that one process is more *technically* efficient than the other, because neither uses "less of some inputs *and no more of others.*" Assuming that the output is exactly the same and that all other inputs stay the same, which process should be chosen?

To answer this question, we have to go back to the broader notion of *economic* efficiency, which says that an efficient process involves no unnecessary waste *or expense.* In the case of the ginger chicken, to make a decision about efficiency we would need to know the *expenses* entailed by the two different processes. This brings us back to the question of how to measure costs.

2.5 | Social Costs and Efficiency

social costs of production: the costs of a project, both those borne by the economic actors involved and those borne by others, figured in terms of opportunity costs

The full **social costs of production** take into account all affected parties. Full social costs, like the economic costs discussed above, should be figured on an opportunity-

Table 7.2	Calculating Costs of Production for Two Processes		
Process	**Cost of Chef's Time**	**Cost of Assistant's Time**	**Total Cost for Labor**
A	1.5 hr × $30/hr = $45	1 hr × $10/hr = $10	$45 + $10 = $55
B	1 hr × $30/hr = $30	2 hr × $10/hr = $20	$30 + $20 = $50

cost basis. In addition, they take into account external costs that might be missed by an individual decision maker. True social and economic efficiency, then, means that a production process should involve no unnecessary waste or expense when these expenses include the full social costs.

Returning to our case of ginger chicken production, we can illustrate both simple and more complicated cases. Recall that we were comparing Process A and Process B, neither of which is more *technically* efficient than the other. If the social opportunity cost of the workers' hours is simply equal to their wages, then the social decision is easy and is equivalent to what a restaurant boss would choose on strictly financial grounds. If the chef's wage is $30 an hour and the assistant's wage is $10 an hour, then, as shown in Table 7.2, Process B is the least-cost alternative. Process B is *economically* efficient, given this pattern of wages, and thus of expenses.

Suppose, however, to make things more complicated, that the assistant needs to leave work 1 hour early today to take a culinary school class that will greatly improve his or her skills. The opportunity cost of his or her additional hour, should Process B be chosen, may then be far higher than the wage. The worker, the boss, and society may all gain more from the added skills derived from the class than from the assistant's contribution to immediate ginger chicken production.

For example, suppose that the opportunity cost of the assistant's first hour is simply $10. That is, the assistant would add $10 worth of production in his or her next-best employment. But suppose the opportunity cost of the second hour devoted to ginger chicken production—which, if engaged in, would cause the assistant to miss the culinary class—is an improvement in human capital worth $50 (supposing, somewhat unrealistically, that we could easily place a monetary value on it). Process A would still cost $55, but Process B would now cost $90, as shown in Table 7.3. Process A is actually less costly in a full social sense. It is economically efficient and should be chosen.[4] Looking only at the immediate financial aspect of a decision may lead to **false economies**—actions that appear to be cost-saving but turn out to be more costly over the longer run.

Looking at internal accounting costs is often a good first approximation, but for good social decision making, we need the more comprehensive view that considering opportunity costs and external costs provides.

false economies: cost savings that are illusory because long-term and/or social costs have not been taken into account

Table 7.3	Calculating Costs of Production for Two Processes, with Additional Opportunity Cost		
Process	**Cost of Chef's Time**	**Cost of Assistant's Time**	**Total Cost for Labor**
A	1.5 hr × $30/hr = $45	1 hr × $10/hr = $10	$45 + $10 = $55
B	1 hr × $30/hr = $30	(1 hr × $10/hr) + (1 hr × $50/hr) = $60	$30 + $60 = $90

---

[4] In this case, the restaurant boss will bear a personal, immediate financial cost of $5 by choosing the process that lets the assistant go to the class. Is this fair? In our present concentration strictly on the efficiency aspects of production, we leave most questions about the distribution of costs until later. Designing methods of assigning costs in such a way as to give incentives for private economic actors to act in socially beneficial ways is currently a topic of interest to many economists.

3 | The Production Function

Although actual production decisions are often a matter of trial and error, economists often make the mathematically convenient assumption that we have perfect information about the effect on output of variations in the quantities of inputs. This enables us to define a **production function**, an equation or graph that represents the relationship between a set of inputs and the amount of output that they can produce over a given time period. Production functions typically do not exist "out there" in the real-world economy, but this mental construct can help us think about certain aspects of production in a very simple, and sometimes useful, way. We will use the notion of a production function to introduce the important concepts of diminishing returns, returns to scale, and technology choice.

production function: an equation or graph that represents a mathematical relationship between types and quantities of inputs and the quantity of output

3.1 | Thinking About Inputs and Outputs

Many, many inputs go into real-world production processes. One way to list them might be to categorize them according to the resource base from which they arise. For example, the land on which a factory is built comes from natural capital. (The land itself is not used up in production. It is the services of land that are an "input" to production.) The factory building, although it was built from materials that were originally part of natural capital, is transformed into manufactured capital. Likewise, the inventories of materials and energy resources that must be on hand to begin production come both from nature and from previous human activity.

Assembly line workers, supervisors, office workers, and executives, who will add flows of the services from their human capital, are also needed. Social capital in the form of technology and norms of workplace relations will shape the production process. Natural capital may also be used as a depository for the waste products from the production process. Whether the production location is a factory, a hospital, a school, a home, a military base, or a simple newsstand, some variety of inputs is needed.

In a very general sense, any production function could be mathematically expressed as follows:

$$Y = f(\text{natural capital, manufactured capital, human capital, social capital})$$

where Y represents a quantity of output, $f()$ is read "is a function of," and the inputs include the services of sustainable capital stocks—natural, produced, human, and social—discussed in Chapter 6, as well as their direct depletion.[5] Ultimately everything,

---

[5] Crucially, in a modern society, financial capital is required in order to get the production process moving, in advance of sales of output. Financial capital is not in the equation, however, because the function—and the present chapter—focus on production in a real, material sense. The role of financial capital will be discussed at the end of Chapter 8.

even materials and intermediate goods, arises from that resource base. Alternatively, we could be more specific. For example,

$Y = f$(natural gas, raw cotton, produced dyes, services of loom attendants, . . .)

where the output in question is cotton fabric.

But both of these production functions are too complicated to be useful in helping us grasp some basic principles of production. Instead, economists often employ a simplification, imagining a process that requires only two inputs, fixed and variable. **Fixed inputs** by definition are those for which the quantities do not change, no matter what the level of production. An example of a fixed input would be a building lease or employment contract. If you have already signed a year's lease on a building or a year's contract with a professional employee, you are not very free *right now* to reduce your use of these services. You may find it hard to expand your use of such inputs as well, because buildings take time to be built and professionals take time to train and develop. By contrast, **variable inputs** are those for which the quantities can be changed very quickly. For example, if you lease computers by the week or hire contract workers by the day, the computers and workers would be considered variable inputs to your production process. The production function can then be written

$Y = f$(fixed input, variable input)

This allows for simple two-dimensional graphing and for a relatively easy way of keeping track of costs. Obviously, few products come from only two inputs! If it helps, you may think of each input as a composite of a number of specific goods or services.

To economists, the **short run** is a time period in which at least one input to production is fixed in quantity. A farmer, for example, may be temporarily constrained by the size of his or her land holdings, and by the amount of equipment he or she owns, but can vary many other inputs, such as seeds, fertilizers, and labor. In other production processes, an organization may be constrained by a lack of space, a shortage of materials, a dearth of suitably talented workers, or any other input to production. The key aspect is that some **limiting factor** creates a **capacity constraint**. Even with access to unlimited amounts of all the *variable* inputs, production can go only so far.

In the **long run**, on the other hand, the quantities of all inputs may be varied.

3.2 | Graphing the Relationship Between an Input and an Output

A graph is a convenient way to visualize the relationship between quantitative items of interest.

Suppose, for example, we are interested in how the amount of fertilizer that has been applied to a field over the course of a growing season is related to the amount of corn that can be harvested at the end of the season. Because such relatively simple relationships between agricultural inputs and outputs have been studied for years—informally by farmers and in modern times by agronomists and agricultural economists—we actually know a good deal about them. Historically, economists' basic idea of a graphical "production function" arose from such informal and formal knowledge about agricultural production.

Table 7.4 and Figure 7.1 show the results of an actual study of the effect of applying various amounts of nitrogen fertilizer on corn yields over a season. The study was performed in Missouri in the late 1990s.[6]

Selecting a sample of fields that were similar to each other, and then averaging over the results (to abstract from variability among the fields in such things as weather and

fixed input: an input to production that is fixed in quantity, no matter what the level of production

variable input: an input to production the quantity of which can be quickly changed, resulting in changes in the level of production

short run: (in terms of production processes) a time period in which at least one input to production cannot be varied in quantity

limiting factor: the fixed input that creates a capacity constraint

capacity constraint: a case in which some fixed input (or inputs) limits the amount that can be produced in a given period of time

long run: (in terms of production processes) a time period in which all inputs to production can be varied in quantity

---

[6] Figures and numbers are based on a figure in Peter Scharf and Bill Wiebold, "Nitrogen Prices—How Do They Affect Optimum N Management?" *Integrated Pest & Crop Management Newsletter* 11(2) (February 2001), **http://ipm.missouri.edu/ipcm/archives/v11n2/ipmltr1.htm**, accessed March 14, 2002. Nitrogen can be obtained from renewable, organic sources such as manure or alfalfa, or from chemical fertilizer produced using nonrenewable natural gas. This study looked at nitrogen from chemical sources.

Table 7.4	Results of Corn Production Study								
Nitrogen Application (lb/acre)	0	20	40	60	80	100	120	140	160
Corn Yield (bu/acre)	100	115	127	137	145	150	154	157	159

positive or **direct relationship:** the relationship between two variables when an increase in one is associated with an increase in the other

ceteris paribus: a Latin phrase meaning "other things equal" or "all else constant"

soil type), the study shows that increased nitrogen application is associated with increased corn yields. A relationship in which a rise in one variable is accompanied by a rise in the other is called a **positive** or **direct relationship**. When two variables have a positive relationship, the line representing their paired quantities slopes *upward*, reading from left to right.

To interpret this as a production function, we can think of nitrogen fertilizer as being the variable input, while all other factors that might affect the yield—such as seed, water, insect control, soil salinity, and cultivation—are kept (intentionally and artificially) *fixed* across fields, as much as possible. In economics, when we want to isolate the effect of one particular variable on another, we hope to study the particular relationship **ceteris paribus**, or "with all else constant." This is a basic research technique used in other analytical studies as well. For example, health researchers try to determine the effect of diet *alone* on a disease, sometimes by choosing as research subjects people whose sex, age, and level of exercise ("all else") are pretty much identical ("constant").

You should recall that the horizontal axis on graphs is often referred to as the *X* axis and that the vertical axis is called the *Y* axis. Each point represents a pair of observed data values: one for *X*, which in this case is a quantity of nitrogen fertilizer, and another for *Y*, which in this case is a quantity of corn yield. Conventionally, when describing a particular point, we mention the *X* value first and then the *Y* value. The point labeled in Figure 7.1, for example, indicates that applying nitrogen at a rate of 40 pounds per acre is associated with a corn yield of 127 bushels per acre. Usually, graphs start at the "origin" point (0, 0). However, note that in Figure 7.1, for graphical convenience, we have started the *Y* axis at 90 bu/acre. Application of extra nitrogen is not strictly required for corn to grow: With zero application, an acre will still yield 100 bushels.

In Figure 7.2 we take a closer look at the slope of the curve at various points. Curves that are straight lines have constant slopes. It is well known, however, that in the case of the fertilizer–yield relationship, the effectiveness of fertilizer tapers off as more is used.

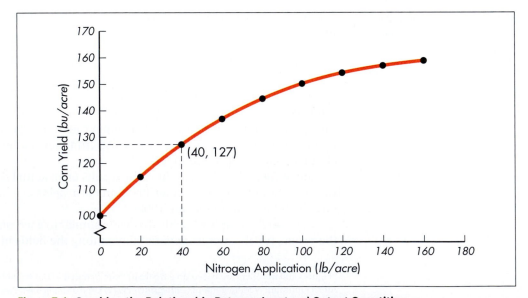

Figure 7.1 Graphing the Relationship Between Input and Output Quantities
A study of the effects of the application of nitrogen fertilizer shows that nitrogen input and corn output are positively (or directly) related over a growing season.

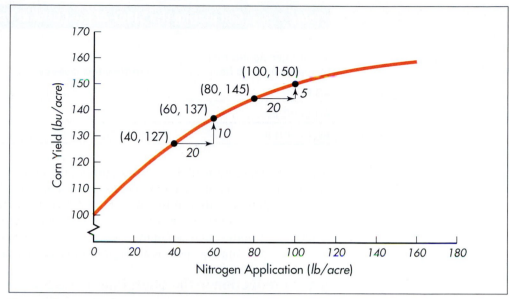

Figure 7.2 Examining the Slope of the Curve
Moving to the right and comparing each marked point on the curve to the one before, we find that each point on the curve indicates an additional 20 lb of nitrogen application and varying amounts of additional corn yield. The slope of the curve flattens out as we move to the right, as each additional 20 lb of nitrogen results in a lesser quantity of additional corn.

Look carefully at Figure 7.2, finding again the point that represents 40 lb/acre of nitrogen and 127 bu/acre of corn. What happens when application goes from 40 to 60 lb/acre, which is a 20-unit increase? According to the graph, yield rises from 127 to 137 bu/acre, which is a 10-unit increase. In case your algebra is rusty, let us remind you that the slope is defined as the vertical "rise" divided by the horizontal "run." In this case, the "run" is the 20-unit increase in nitrogen, and the "rise" is the 10-unit increase in corn, as labeled on the graph. Thus the slope of the line connecting these two points is 10 ÷ 20, or 0.5. In words, an additional 20 pounds of fertilizer is associated with an additional 10 bushels of corn, so each additional *1* pound of fertilizer is associated with a *1/2*-bushel rise in corn yield.[7] Table 7.5 shows this calculation and the calculated slope of another segment as well.

Check your skills by calculating the slope of the line as nitrogen application goes from 60 to 80 lb/acre. The run is again 20 units. What is the rise? What is the slope?

The opposite of a positive relationship is a **negative** or **inverse, relationship**, in which an increase in one variable is associated with a fall in the other one. A well-known negative relationship in agriculture, for example, is that between the salinity (or salt content) of the soil and crop yield. To study the relationship between salinity and yield, we would again want to hold "all else constant," and this time the "all else" would include fertilizer application. Figure 7.3 shows the much-studied relation between soil salinity and corn yield for a situation (fertilizer, cultivation, etc.) in which the maximum yield, at very low salinity, would be 150 bu/acre.[8] A curve indicating a negative, or inverse, relation slopes *downward*, reading from left to right.

As you can see in Figure 7.3, as salinity rises (that is, as we move out along the line, in the direction of increasing numbers on the horizontal axis), yield falls (the points on the line correspond to *lower* numbers on the vertical axis). At a salinity level of 16, corn

negative or **inverse relationship:** the relationship between two variables if an increase in one is associated with a decrease in the other

---

[7] We abstract here from curvature in the line connecting the points, because the treatment of slopes in the case of a smoothly curving line would require calculus.

[8] The graph is derived from the aforementioned corn yield study, as well as from Robert Hill and Richard T. Koenig, "Water Salinity and Crop Yield," *Utah Water Quality*, May 1999, AG—425.3, **http://extension.usu.edu/publica/agpubs/ag425-3.pdf**, accessed March 14, 2002. The measure of salinity is electrical conductivity in decisiemens per meter.

Table 7.5 | Calculating the Slope of the Curve at Various Points

As Nitrogen Application Increases by 20 lb from . . .	Corn Yield Increases by . . .	So the Additional Yield per Pound of Nitrogen (the slope of the curve) Is . . .
40 to 60 lb	137 − 127 = 10 bu	10 bu ÷ 20 lb = 0.5 bu/lb
60 to 80 lb	?	?
80 to 100 lb	150 − 145 = 5 bu	5 bu ÷ 20 lb = 0.25 bu/lb

can no longer grow at all. The slope of this straight line is a constant, *negative* number.[9] We include this case for completeness in discussion of graphical relationships, not because salt is an "input" into production of corn. Quite the opposite is the case. Rising salinity of soil is currently a serious problem in some areas, especially areas of intense irrigation. A figure such as Figure 7.3 should remind us that attention to resource—in this case, soil—management is an important economic activity.

3.3 | Production in the Short Run

All the facts about graphing reviewed in the previous section may have been familiar to you from math classes, but economists also have another name for the slope of a production function at any point. We call it the **marginal return** to the variable input.[10] It is the amount that the *last unit* of the variable input adds to production of the output, given an existing capacity constraint.

Economists have observed that for many sorts of processes, production will exhibit **diminishing marginal returns** in the short run after some point. That is, after some point, applying more of the variable input to a fixed quantity of other input(s) simply does not yield so much. Often, economists leave out the word *marginal,* taking it to be understood, and simply say *diminishing returns* or, sometimes, *decreasing returns.*

Think about the corn example: If there were *not* diminishing marginal returns, you could feed the whole world from one farmer's field just by adding more and more nitrogen fertilizer forever. In fact, however, as more and more nitrogen is added to the same amount of land, eventually the corn plants become unable to make use of the extra amounts. Yields will tend to taper off, as we saw in Figure 7.2 and Table 7.5. We calculated that adding one more pound of nitrogen from a starting point of 40 lb/acre would lead to

marginal return: the additional quantity of output gained by using an additional unit of a variable input (with all other inputs held fixed)

diminishing marginal returns: the case where the use of an additional unit of a variable input produces a lesser quantity of output than did the previous unit of the input

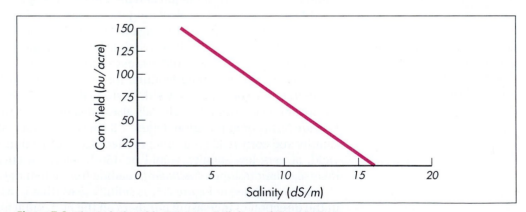

Figure 7.3 The Relationship Between Salinity and Corn Output
A study of the effects of accumulated salt in soil shows that salinity and corn output are negatively (or inversely) related.

---

[9] The topmost point in the graph is (3, 150) and the lowermost is (16, 0), giving a *negative* "rise" of −150 for a "run" of 13. The slope is thus approximately −11.5.

[10] Sometimes this is referred to as the *marginal product* or the *marginal physical product.* In common conversation, however, economists tend to use *marginal return.*

a half-bushel (0.5 bu) of additional corn yield and that starting from 60 lb/acre, another pound of nitrogen would lead to 0.4 bushel of additional corn yield. Starting from an even higher level—80 lb/acre—an additional pound of nitrogen would boost the yield even less—only a *quarter*-bushel (0.25 bu). (Eventually, the graph would turn *downward*, with a negative slope, as additional fertilizer "burned" the crop.) These successive drops in additional yields illustrate "diminishing returns" to the application of nitrogen.

total product curve: a curve showing the total amount of output that can be produced when the quantity of one input is varied (other inputs held fixed).

Economists call curves such as those in Figures 7.1 and 7.2, which illustrate the amount of output that can be produced when the quantity of one input is varied, **total product curves**. The total product curve in the case of diminishing returns, as we have seen for corn production, gets flatter as you move out to the right. We reproduce this shape in Figure 7.4a.

To be complete, however, we also need to consider that some production processes, in some ranges of output, can exhibit **constant marginal returns**. The total product curve in the case of constant returns is a straight line, as illustrated in Figure 7.4b. Each additional unit of the variable input adds the same amount to production.

constant marginal returns: the case where the use of an additional unit of a variable input produces the same quantity of output as did the previous unit of the input

increasing marginal returns: the case where the use of an additional unit of a variable input produces a greater quantity of output than did the previous unit of the input

Some processes even exhibit **increasing marginal returns**, at least over some range of production. In this case, each additional unit of the variable input adds *more* to output than the last unit did. The total product curve gets steeper as you move out to the right, as illustrated in Figure 7.4c.

Increasing returns may arise from factors such as learning, specialization in the use of an input, or other synergies. You might find, for example, that practicing the guitar 30 minutes a day adds virtually nothing to your skills but that by practicing an hour a day, you can really "take off" as a musician. The marginal return to the second half hour is greater than that to the first. As another example, a very small restaurant may experience increasing marginal returns as it expands its labor force. The owner may find that hiring a second employee to attend to customers and dishes, thus enabling the cook to specialize in cooking instead of running back and forth, more than doubles the meals the restaurant can serve. Parents and other child care providers often find that preschool-age children are happier and develop some skills more rapidly when there are at least two of them, rather than one alone, because of the "inputs" of stimulation that they provide for each other.

Although economists historically paid far more attention to diminishing returns than to increasing returns, the changing economy may require changes in emphasis. The agricultural and industrial sectors of the U.S. economy and similar economies, upon

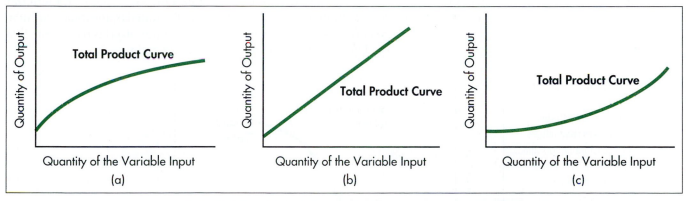

Figure 7.4 Total Product Curves with Diminishing, Constant, and Increasing Returns
(a) For a total product curve with diminishing returns, each additional unit of the input results in a lesser increase in output than did the previous unit of the input. The curve gets flatter—that is, the slope of the curve gets smaller—as we move from left to right.
(b) With constant returns, each additional unit of the input results in the same increase in output. The slope of the curve is constant.
(c) With increasing returns, each additional unit of the input results in a greater increase in output than did the previous unit. The curve gets steeper—that is, the slope of the curve gets larger—as we move from left to right.

which models of diminishing returns were built, are now a smaller proportion of national productive activity than they used to be. Meanwhile, in the fast-growing service sector, which includes activities that involve information and learning, increasing returns play a larger role.

It is also possible for a production process to exhibit *all* of these patterns. Figure 7.5 shows increasing marginal returns at very low levels of production, such as for the restaurant expanding inputs from one to two employees, or the child care provider increasing output from the care of one to the care of two children. This span may be followed by nearly constant returns for some levels of production and then by diminishing returns at high levels of production. To envision why diminishing returns eventually take hold in these cases, think about employees starting to crowd and bump into each other within the fixed confines of the restaurant, or a single adult trying to care for too many children.

3.4 | Costs in the Short Run

Once we understand the technology of production, it is interesting to see what this implies about costs. We can divide costs into two types. **Fixed cost** is the cost of the factors that are fixed in supply. A farmer, for example, may have to make payments on land and equipment even if she sows no crop at all. In contrast, **variable cost** consists of expenditures on the variable inputs. In the farmer's case, variable costs will include the costs of fertilizer, seeds, and labor.

Returning to the corn and nitrogen example, in which the researcher holds all inputs except fertilizer "constant" or "fixed," the only variable cost will be for nitrogen. Suppose that fixed cost per acre is $500 and that nitrogen can be purchased in 20-lb increments, for $6 per 20 lb.

Total cost is the sum of the fixed and variable costs that are incurred for each bushel of corn yield. Table 7.6 and Figure 7.6 illustrate the costs of producing various quantities of corn per acre. Even if the researcher applies *no* nitrogen fertilizer, $500 of expenses will be incurred for each acre for the season. Recall that with no fertilizer, the yield is 100 bu/acre. Note that the leftmost column in Table 7.6 is identical to the bottom row in Table 7.4: What is happening—though it is not explicit in the new table—is that fertilizer use is growing in increments of 20 lb as we move from row to row down the table. The total cost per acre goes up by $6, from $500 to $506, as the first 20 lb of fertilizer is applied. Then the total cost rises an additional $6 to $512 as fertilizer application rises to 40 lb, and so on.

In Figure 7.6, we now put the quantity of corn yield on the horizontal axis and put total cost on the vertical axis. For graphical convenience, we start the axes near the no-fertilizer point (100, 500) instead of at (0, 0). The fixed cost of $500 is illustrated by the total cost curve starting at $500, where none of the variable input in question (fertilizer) is used. Note that the slope of the curve in Figure 7.6 increases as we move to the right.

fixed cost: the cost associated with using fixed inputs, which is the same no matter what quantity of output is produced

variable cost: the cost associated with using variable inputs, which rises with the quantity of output

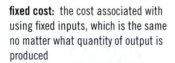

Figure 7.5 A Possible Pattern of Returns

The production process illustrated here shows initial increasing returns, followed first by constant returns and then by diminishing returns, as the quantity of the input increases.

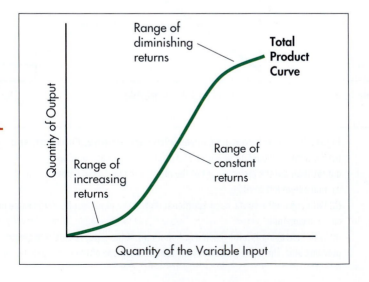

Table 7.6 | Costs of Corn Production per Acre

Corn Yield (bu)	Fixed Cost ($)	Variable Cost ($)	Total Cost ($)
100	500	0	500
115	500	6	506
127	500	12	512
137	500	18	518
145	500	24	524
150	500	30	530
154	500	36	536
157	500	42	542
159	500	48	548

marginal cost: the cost associated with producing the last unit of output

Marginal cost is the cost of producing the *last* unit of output. Because production of corn in the short run is considered to be characterized by *diminishing* marginal *returns*, it will also be characterized by *increasing* marginal *costs*. This is because, although the cost for a given increment of fertilizer stays the same, successive increments of fertilizer add less to yield. Once again, the economists' "marginal" concept is the same as the mathematicians' "slope."

What is the marginal cost of pushing the corn yield per acre from 127 to 137 bu? According to Table 7.6 and Figure 7.6, it costs $512 to produce 127 bu and $518 to produce 137 bu. Thus it costs $6 to produce these additional 10 bu. We would say that the cost of an additional bushel, along the segment of the curve between these two points, is $6 ÷ 10 or $.60 per bushel. This calculation is shown in Table 7.7.

What is the marginal cost of going from 137 to 145 bu? It costs another $6—for another dose of fertilizer—to produce this additional 8 bu. The cost of an additional bushel, along the segment of the curve between these two points, is $6 ÷ 8 or $.75 per bushel. Check yourself by calculating the marginal cost of corn increasing production from 145 to 150 bu.

The marginal cost, which is the same as the slope of the curve, is doubled when we compare the segment at the 145- to 150-bu output level with the segment at the 127- to

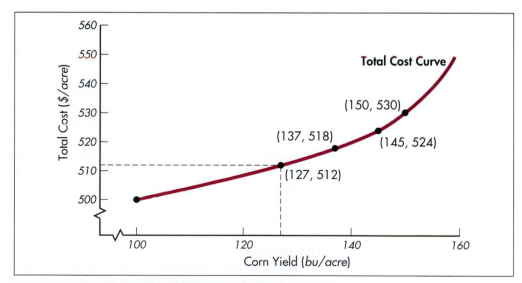

Figure 7.6 The Total Cost Curve for Corn
If no nitrogen (the variable input) is applied, the production process incurs $500 of fixed costs and no variable costs, and 100 bu/acre is produced. As nitrogen is purchased and applied, more corn can be grown on each acre. The total cost of producing corn rises because of the addition of variable costs.

Table 7.7 | Marginal Cost of Corn Production Per Acre

As Corn Yield Increases from ...	The Yield Rises by ...	While the Total Cost ... of Production Rises	Therefore, the Cost for the Additional Bushels (the marginal cost) Is ...
127 to 137 bu	10 bu	$6	$6 ÷ 10 bu = $.60/bu
137 to 145 bu	8 bu	$6	$6 ÷ 8 bu = $.75/bu
145 to 150 bu	?	?	?

increasing marginal costs: the case where the cost of producing an additional unit of output rises as more output is produced

total cost curve: a curve showing the total cost associated with producing various levels of output

137-bu output level. Diminishing marginal returns to fertilizer application have led to **increasing marginal costs** for corn production.

The **total cost curve** in Figure 7.6 is characterized by a slope that gets *steeper* as you move to the right, precisely because the total product curve in Figure 7.1 (and Figure 7.2) gets *flatter* as you move to the right.

In computing the marginal cost, we ignored the fixed costs. This is correct, because we assumed that fixed costs would be paid whether or not any nitrogen fertilizer was used, and we were interested only in the cost of the "last," "additional," or "marginal" bushel of harvest. A fuller discussion of costs appears in the appendix to this chapter.

The important part of this discussion of diminishing marginal returns and increasing marginal costs is not so much the algebra involved, or even the graphs, though both can be helpful. The significant implication for producer behavior is that diminishing marginal returns and increasing marginal costs mean that in the short run, the quantity of production will tend to be naturally limited.

Diminishing returns mean that it doesn't make sense for the farmer to try to feed the whole world from one plot. Increasing costs mean that at some point, production will become too expensive relative to benefits received (e.g., revenue from sales of the harvest) to be worthwhile. In the next chapter, diminishing returns are assumed in the case of the profit-maximizing competitive firm. Because marginal costs are increasing, whereas the price the firm receives for its output is constant, the traditional microeconomic model gives a neat diagrammatic explanation of how a firm will choose a unique, profit-maximizing level of output.

constant marginal costs: the case where the cost of producing an additional unit of output stays the same as more output is produced

decreasing marginal costs: the case where the cost of producing an additional unit of output falls as more output is produced

What if marginal returns are constant, as illustrated in Figure 7.4b? Then we will have **constant marginal costs**. In this case, each unit of the variable input (which has a constant price) adds exactly the same amount to output, so the cost for each additional unit is the same. The total cost curve will be a straight line.

What if marginal returns are increasing, as illustrated in Figure 7.4c? Then we will have **decreasing marginal costs**. To portray a total cost curve with increasing marginal returns, you would draw a line that rises but also *flattens out* or curves toward the horizontal axis as you move to the right. Increasing marginal returns mean decreasing marginal costs, because additional production is getting *cheaper* as output increases.

Sometimes, all of these possibilities are combined in a graph such as Figure 7.7. Figure 7.7 shows the pattern of costs that corresponds to the pattern of returns that we saw in Figure 7.5: decreasing marginal costs, followed by constant and then increasing marginal costs, as the quantity of output increases. In the lower part of the graph, the pattern of marginal costs is graphed explicitly.

For certain production processes, such as the application of fertilizer to corn, curves like these can actually be quite accurately graphed on the basis of real-world studies done by research institutes. In most cases, however, these curves are only hypothetical. Rarely would lone producers, concerned with providing for a family or staying in business, have the luxury of being able to conduct such a study. While they were holding some inputs constant, and varying others from zero up to high amounts in order to find out what exactly their total product curve and total cost curve were, they could starve or go out of business!

Figure 7.7 A Possible Pattern of Costs

If the production function is like that shown in Figure 7.5, then the total cost curve will look like the top curve in this diagram. A range of decreasing marginal costs (shown by a slope that gets progressively flatter) will be followed by constant and then increasing marginal costs (illustrated by a slope that gets progressively steeper). This pattern of marginal costs is shown explicitly in the lower diagram here: Marginal costs first fall, then are constant, and later rise.

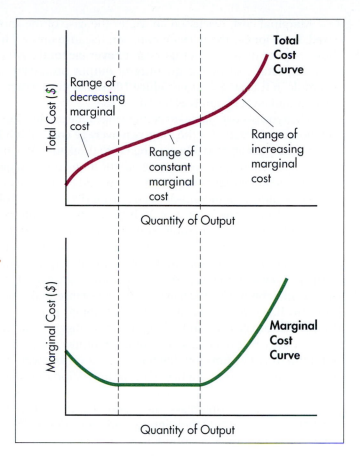

These graphs do, however, give us a visual image that can help us think about the many ways in which production and cost may be related, for many producers. We will see that the concepts of diminishing returns and increasing returns, in particular, are important throughout the study of microeconomics.

3.5 | Production and Costs in the Long Run

In the long run, as we noted earlier, all inputs are variable. A farmer can buy or rent more land or equipment. A factory owner can build a new factory. More engineers can be trained in software development, if skilled engineers are the short-run fixed input. A manager/owner may be able to expand by hiring an assistant, if his or her own time for decision making is the limiting factor. A child care enterprise can expand from a private home to a larger center, if space is the capacity constraint.

Given sufficient time to acquire the needed machines or other resources, or to make other necessary adjustments, a producer should be able to remove all obstacles to getting the highest net benefits from production, which means producing the most valued output at the lowest cost. Although in the short run there is a capacity constraint of space, equipment, skills, or time, in the long run these constraints can be loosened up. Then a question arises: "How big should an enterprise get?"

Why do we observe, for example, small neighborhood child care centers and single-worker locksmith businesses, but not small neighborhood steel foundries or hospitals? Many factors can contribute to the explanation of enterprise size, and some of these (related to history, culture, and the level of demand for a producer's output) will be explored in later chapters about businesses, households, and governments. Here we will examine technological and cost-related reasons why one size, or scale, may be more advantageous than another.

average cost (or **average total cost**): cost per unit of output, computed as total cost divided by the quantity of output produced

Marginal cost, discussed above for the case of the short run in which one input is fixed, is no longer the relevant concept, because now *all* inputs can be varied. We can, however, calculate the **average cost** (or **average total cost**) per unit of production just by dividing total cost by the quantity of output produced, at any production level. For example, if it costs $500 to produce 100 units, the average cost per unit at the 100-unit production level is simply $500/100 = $5.[11]

long-run average cost: the cost of production, per unit of output when all inputs can be varied in quantity

The type of cost that takes center stage for examination when the entire scale of production can be varied is the **long-run average cost**, which is the cost per unit of output when all inputs are variable. It is logical to think that, to whatever extent possible, enterprises will tend to grow to a size where the long-run average costs are lowest. Enterprises bigger or smaller than this optimal size would be unnecessarily expensive to run.

For example, a locksmith needs primarily a set of tools and a van to go into business. To double the output of a single-locksmith enterprise would require a second locksmith, another set of tools, and another van. Except for perhaps some small savings in costs, such as advertising or billing, there is no reason to believe that the new, larger firm would be any cheaper to run, per unit of output, than the old, smaller one. In fact, if the new locksmith has to service customers a longer driving distance from headquarters, it may be more expensive. It may therefore make more sense for each neighborhood to have its own local locksmith (though perhaps a group of locksmiths might jointly hire advertising and billing services). Bigger is not necessarily better.

economies of scale: these occur when the long-run average cost of production falls as the size of the enterprise increases

On the other hand, a steel foundry requires a very sizable investment in plant and equipment, and a hospital that has only a few beds would be either exceedingly expensive to run (as a consequence of underutilization of skilled labor and laboratory facilities) or exceedingly limited in its services. Enterprises in such industries tend to get big because of what economists call **economies of scale**. Some processes tend to drop in cost as they expand *all* their inputs and their output. You could build a single foundry furnace to turn out a few pounds of iron a year—but it might cost its weight in gold to produce. A foundry reaches a stage of low costs per unit only when it is putting out steel in much larger quantities.

constant returns to scale: these occur when the long-run average cost of production stays the same as the size of the enterprise increases

diseconomies of scale: these occur when the long-run average cost of production rises as the size of the enterprise increases

A process exhibits economies of scale when, in the long run, average cost declines as output capacity increases. It exhibits **constant returns to scale** over the range where the long-run average cost is constant. Finally, it exhibits **diseconomies of scale** if the long-run average cost rises with output. These conditions are illustrated as a U-shaped long-run average cost curve in Figure 7.8.

What might cause diseconomies of scale? It is generally thought that no matter how many technical economies of scale there may be, for most enterprises there is a point where they just get too big for all the human beings and all the functions involved to be managed effectively. Some of the big business mergers of recent decades were inspired

Figure 7.8 A Possible Pattern of Long-Run Average Costs
In the long run, producers can alter the scale of their production process. They will want to find a size that gives them low per-unit costs. If their operation is too big or too small, their per-unit costs can be unnecessarily high.

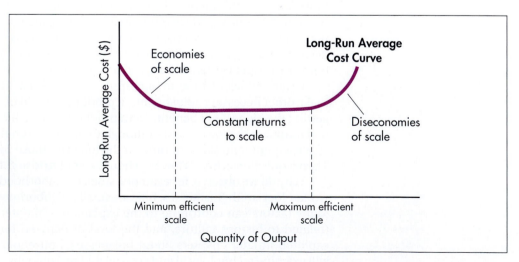

---

[11] Calculation of average costs in the short run is addressed in the appendix to this chapter.

by hopes of reaping economies of scale (as well as market power, or simply because it was believed that bigger would be better). Such hopes were sometimes disappointed, as shown in the News in Context feature "Hospital Network Could Be Split Up."

minimum efficient scale: the smallest size an enterprise can be and still benefit from low long-run average costs

For many production processes there appears to be a **minimum efficient scale**. This is the point where the long-run average cost curve begins to bottom out, as shown in Figure 7.8. For locksmiths, the minimum efficient scale might be the output level corresponding to a one-person shop; for a home child care center, it might be three preschoolers. (Levels of output *less* than these may leave some resources underemployed, thus creating the downward-sloping portion of the long-run average cost curve.) On the other hand, the minimum efficient scale for a foundry or hospital might be output corresponding to millions of dollars of investment and scores of employees. Given the problems of managing very large organizations, one can also posit the existence of a **maximum efficient scale**.

maximum efficient scale: the largest size an enterprise can be and still benefit from low long-run average costs

3.6 | Technology Choice

Another important issue in the economics of production is that of technology choice. If two or more processes exist that can make the same output, which should be chosen? Producers, to be economically efficient, will need to choose the process that entails the least cost.

input substitution: increasing the use of some inputs, and decreasing that of others, while producing the same good or service

With various technologies available, producers can engage in **input substitution**, using less of one input and more of another, as costs and availability change. In the case of the chef cooking ginger chicken, for example, we saw that Process A would be chosen under some circumstances and Process B under others. In the case of corn farming, nitrogen can be obtained from renewable, organic sources such as manure and alfalfa, or from chemical fertilizer produced using nonrenewable natural gas. Generally, whenever prices change, producers will want to substitute cheaper inputs for inputs that have become more expensive. From a social perspective, input substitution will enhance well-being when the choices made take into account external as well as internal costs.

Of particular importance, historically, has been the process of substituting the services of machinery for hours of human labor. This is dramatically exemplified in the American folk hero John Henry, the railway worker who pitted himself against the new

Hospital Network Could Be Split Up

NEWS in Context

The trustees of CareGroup Healthcare System, [Massachusetts] second-largest hospital and physician system, are considering breaking up the network, one of dozens formed during the 1990s as a better way to provide health care. . . .

During the 1990s, more than 1000 U.S. hospitals merged to gain clout in negotiating with managed-care insurance companies and to become more efficient at a time when employers were demanding lower insurance premiums. But the mass consolidation of the health care industry has had mixed results. At least 90 mergers have broken up, and many more are troubled.

"This is a trend all over the country," said John McDonough, a former state legislator and now an associate professor at the Heller School at Brandeis University. "There was frenzy in the 1990s; hospitals wanted to get as big as possible so they would have as much market share and [as many] referring physicians as possible. The rush to get their chairs together before the music stopped led people to make deals that didn't look so good in terms of business fundamentals. There were a lot of good ideas that went sour."

From an article by Liz Kowalczyk in the *Boston Globe*, January 16, 2002, p. E1.

Is bigger always better? What term might an economist use to describe a business that has become too big to effectively manage?

steam drill that threatened to take jobs away from him and his fellows. In his heroic effort, John Henry fulfilled his promise to "die with a hammer in my hand."

However, as production has expanded—and, with globalization, the possibility of moving production to any part of the world—there have been some interesting counter-examples. There is a complex story to be told about swings in the garment industry between high-tech, machinery-intensive U.S. production systems and cheap-labor-based "off-shore" production. Successive waves of technology have made it possible to replace workers with machines that could do increasingly intricate pattern cutting, sewing, and the like. Such new technologies have tended to move the locus of production back to the United States where machinery is cheap relative to labor.

But these moves have repeatedly been countered by the discovery (sometimes by different, competing firms) of yet another source of even-lower-wage (but adequately educated) workers, most often in Asia or the Caribbean. Production has then shifted toward those places where labor is cheap relative to machinery. Several times it seemed clear that this story would end like John Henry's, with the triumph of machinery. However, the latest chapter, about niche marketing and nearly instant gratification of specific (computer-transmitted) consumer tastes, has created a new opportunity for worker versatility and intelligence to compete with the tireless speed of machines. Take a look at the tags in your clothes the next time you rearrange your drawers and closet. What countries seem currently to be most involved in garment manufacture? What do these countries have in common?

Discussion Questions

1. Ethan likes to hike up mountains, but he prefers hikes where the steepest part of the climb comes first, followed by a gentler climb (once he's a little tired) and then an easy return downhill. He hates going on hikes that start out going into valleys (because then he has to hike back uphill after he is tired), and he is bored by uphill hikes that don't vary in their steepness. Characterizing the shape of terrain using terms that we have used to describe economics graphs, decide which of the following hikes Ethan would prefer (starting on the left and hiking toward the right) and what he would dislike about each of the others.
   a. "inverse relationship," followed by "direct relationship" with "increasing returns"
   b. "positive relationship" with "constant returns," followed by "negative relationship"
   c. "direct relationship with "increasing returns," followed by "direct relationship" with "diminishing returns," followed by "inverse relationship"
   d. "positive relationship" with "decreasing marginal cost," followed by "positive relationship" with "increasing marginal cost," followed by "negative relationship"

2. Back in 1898, the writer and social analyst Charlotte Perkins Gilman argued that the small-scale production of meals by individual women in individual kitchens was inefficient. Although people might want to keep their own kitchens so that they might occasionally engage in cooking as a hobby, she argued, "food would be better, and would cost less" if it were prepared in communal dining rooms or eating houses. How does her assertion fit with the economist's notion of economies of scale? Have we seen any evidence of movement in the direction she suggested?[12]

Review Questions

1. What is "production?"
2. What is the difference between accounting costs and economic costs?
3. Explain how transactions costs and external costs can affect economic decision making.

---

[12] Charlotte Perkins Gilman, *Women and Economics* (New York: Harper Torchbooks, 1966). The quotation is from p. 243.

4. Distinguish between technical and economic efficiency.

5. List all the factors that can make the social cost of production differ from the internal accounting cost of production.

6. What is a production function?

7. What distinguishes the short run from the long run?

8. Describe the meaning of diminishing returns, constant returns, and increasing marginal returns, and explain how each might come about.

9. Sketch a total product curve illustrating increasing returns, constant returns, and diminishing returns.

10. Distinguish among fixed cost, variable cost, total cost, and marginal cost.

11. Sketch a total cost curve illustrating fixed cost and decreasing, constant, and increasing marginal costs.

12. Sketch a long-run average cost curve illustrating economies of scale, constant returns to scale, and diseconomies of scale.

Exercises

1. Kai's records show that last month he spent $5000 on rent for his shop, $3000 on materials, $3000 on wages and benefits for an employee, and $500 in interest on the loan he used to start the business. He quit a job that had paid him $3000 a month to devote himself full-time to this business. Suppose that he has to pay the lease on his shop and the interest on the loan whether he produces or not. However, suppose that at any time he can change the amount of materials he buys and the hours he gives his employee and that he can also go back to his old job (perhaps part-time).
   a. What are the accounting costs of operating his shop for the month?
   b. What are the economic costs?
   c. Which types of costs of running his business for a month are fixed? Which are variable?

2. For each of the following pairs of production processes, determine which process is more technically efficient, or indicate that it is impossible to tell. (Assume that the outputs are identical and that the other inputs are held constant.)
   a. Process A uses 6 gizmos; Process B uses 7 gizmos.
   b. Process A uses 6 gizmos and 5 gadgets; Process B uses 6 gizmos and 4 gadgets.
   c. Process A uses 6 gizmos and 5 gadgets; Process B uses 7 gizmos and 4 gadgets.

3. What would be the economically efficient production technique, in the ginger chicken example given in Table 7.2 and Table 7.3, if the opportunity costs of the workers' time were equal to $14/hr for the chef and $10/hr for the assistant?

4. A non-profit organization dedicated to health care wants to open a new hospital near a residential neighborhood. A group of residents of that neighborhood protests this decision, claiming that traffic caused by the hospital will increase noise and auto emissions. The hospital rejects the idea of building a wall to contain the noise and fumes, claiming that this would be too expensive. Describe in a few sentences, using at least two terms introduced in this chapter, how an economist might describe this situation.

5. The production relationship between the number of chapters that Tiffany studies in her history book (the variable input) and the number of points she will earn on a history exam (the output) is as follows:

Chapters Studied	0	1	2	3
Test Score	15	35	60	95

a. Graph the total product curve for exam points. Label clearly.
b. What is the marginal return of the first chapter Tiffany reads? And what is the marginal return of the third chapter she reads?
c. How would you describe, in words, this pattern of returns?

6. Suppose you have started a small business doing computer consulting. Match each concept in Column A with an example in Column B.

Column A	Column B
a. transaction cost	i. the more months you work at consulting, the better you are at it
b. fixed input	ii. the way you irritate your roommate by working late at night
c. variable input	iii. the lost salary you could have had as an employee elsewhere
d. opportunity cost	iv. the more hours at a stretch that you work without a break, the less effective your consulting time becomes
e. external cost	v. the time you spend consulting
f. increasing returns	vi. the computer you initially purchase as you start the business
g. diminishing returns	vii. the time you spend working on contracts, billing, and such activities necessary to set up agreements with your clients

7. Suppose that in a first hour of work, Lynn can hand-knit four pairs of mittens. In a second consecutive hour, Lynn can hand-knit three pairs of mittens, and in her third hour of work, as a consequence of fatigue, she can hand-knit only one pair. Suppose she works for up to 3 hours and makes a wage of $15 per hour.
a. Make a table relating the number of hours worked to the number of pairs of mittens produced, and graph the total product curve for the production of total pairs of mittens. Label clearly.
b. Looking at labor costs only (ignoring, for the purposes of this exercise, the cost of the yarn she uses and any fixed costs), make a table relating costs to the number of pairs of mittens produced. Graph the total (labor) cost curve for the production of mittens. Label clearly.
c. How would you describe in words the pattern of marginal returns? The pattern of marginal costs?
d. What is the marginal return, in pairs of mittens per hour, of her second hour of work? Of her third hour of work?
e. What is the marginal cost, in dollars per pairs of mittens, as she goes from an output of four pairs of mittens to an output of seven pairs of mittens? What is the marginal cost of the eighth pair of mittens?

Appendix to Chapter 7

A Formal Model of Producer Costs

A1 | The Assumptions

In this model, the only producer considered is "the firm." We will assume that the firm produces only one good, hair dryers. We suppose that the firm has already decided on a scale of production and made its choice of technologies, so we can focus only on its cost structure over a short-run period, such as a month. It is also assumed that there are no nonmonetary opportunity costs or external costs that need to be taken into account. We assume we have perfect information about the cost structure of the firm regarding its production over some given period. In this model, we assume that the firm's production technology is primarily characterized by diminishing returns to its variable inputs.

A2 | The Firm's Short-Run Costs in Detail

The costs of hair dryer production over a month are described in Table 7.8. The first column gives the quantity of hair dryers; the second column gives the marginal cost of each additional hair dryer. The firm has fixed costs of $20, which it must pay even if it produces no hair dryers. Thus the total cost of producing 1 hair dryer is $20 plus the marginal cost of going from producing no hair dryers to producing 1 hair dryer ($20 + $12 = $32), the total cost of producing 2 hair dryers is the total cost of producing 1 hair dryer plus the marginal cost to produce the second ($32 + $8 = $40), and so on. The Total Cost column is the basis for the total cost curve shown in Figure 7.9. Note that Table 7.8 and Figure 7.9 indicate a brief span of decreasing marginal costs at very low levels of production, followed by increasing marginal costs. (Compare Figure 7.9 with Figure 7.7.)

Table 7.8 | Costs of Hair Dryer Production ($)

Quantity of Hair Dryers	Marginal Cost	Total Cost	Average Total Cost	Variable Cost	Average Variable Cost
0		20		0	0.00
1	12	32	32.00	12	12.00
2	8	40	20.00	20	10.00
3	8	48	16.00	28	9.33
4	9	57	14.25	37	9.25
5	10	67	13.40	47	9.40
6	14	81	13.50	61	10.17
7	20	101	14.43	81	11.57
8	35	136	17.00	116	14.50
9	55	191	21.22	171	19.00

Average total cost is the cost per unit, or

Average Total Cost (*ATC*) = Total Cost/Quantity

For example, the total cost of producing 3 hair dryers is $48, so *ATC* = $48/3 = $16. Remembering that

Total Cost = Fixed Cost + Variable Cost

we know that

Variable Cost = Total Cost − Fixed Cost

Because fixed cost in this case is $20, the Variable Cost column is $20 less than the Total Cost column at every level of output.

Average variable cost is the variable cost per unit, or

Average Variable Cost (*AVC*) = Variable Cost/Quantity

For example, the variable cost of producing 2 hair dryers is $20, so *AVC* = $20/2 = $10.

These short-run cost figures are graphed in Figure 7.10. The *MC* and *AVC* curves initially slope downward, because the hair dryer production technology was initially characterized by a span of increasing returns. But for most production levels, these curves slope upward, as diminishing returns (increasing costs) come into play. The *ATC* curve starts out very high at low quantities of production and then gets closer and closer to the *AVC* curve as the quantity produced increases. This is because at low levels of production, the fixed cost of $20 is "spread out" over only 1 or 2 hair dryers. With more and more hair dryers being produced, the initial fixed cost is "spread out" over more and more units.

The *MC* curve cuts the *AVC* and *ATC* curves at their lowest points. This makes sense. To use an analogy, suppose your average grade in this economics class is very high, and then a low grade is added to it. This will bring your average down. On the other hand, if your new grade is higher than your past average, your average will rise. We see on the graph, likewise, that when the marginal cost is below the average, the average is falling. When the marginal cost is above the average, the average is rising.

A3 | Total Cost and Total Variable Cost as Areas

To determine the area that represents total cost, recall that if *ATC* = total cost/quantity, then it must be the case that total cost = *ATC* × quantity. Locating the point on the *ATC*

Figure 7.9 The Total Cost Curve for Hair Dryers

This graph shows a numerical example of a total cost curve.

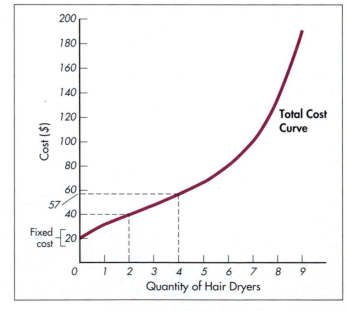

Figure 7.10   Marginal and Average Cost Curves

The *MC* curve shows the cost of producing the last unit. The *AVC* curve shows per-unit variable costs. The *ATC* curve shows per-unit total costs (variable costs + fixed costs).

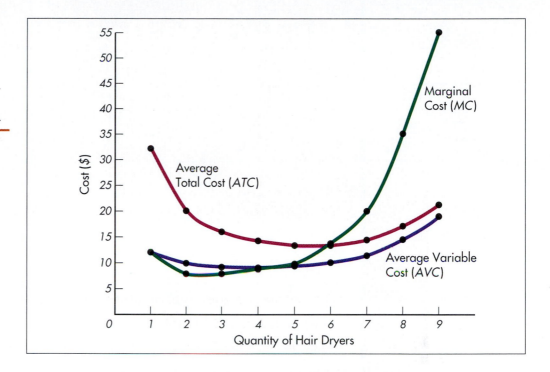

curve that corresponds to 7 units of output, we can draw a rectangle from there back to the origin. The shaded area in Figure 7.11 has an area equal to *ATC* × 7, which is just the total cost of producing 7 units. (You can check this in Table 7.8. There 7 × 14.43 ≈ 101, where the wavy "equals" sign means "is approximately equal to.")

On the graph, total variable cost would be represented by a rectangle whose upper right corner rests on the *AVC* curve.

Figure 7.11   Total Cost as an Area

Total cost can be computed as the quantity of output times the per-unit cost of producing that quantity of output. Graphically, this is a rectangle with width equal to the quantity of output and height equal to the average total cost of producing that quantity of output.

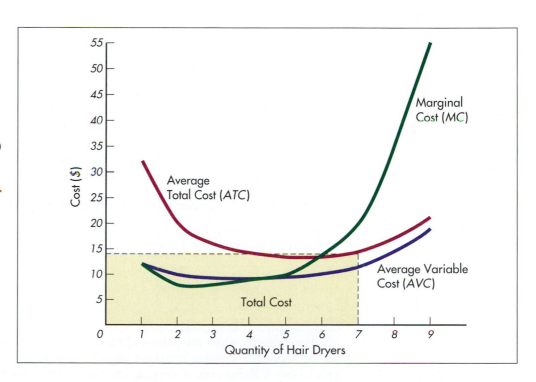

Production Decisions

In just one week in 2002, U.S. motor vehicle manufacturers produced nearly 41,000 cars, over 45,000 light trucks, and over 3000 medium and heavy trucks. Meanwhile, governments at all levels in the United States produced and maintained a great deal of transportation-related goods and services, such as interstate highway expansions, local roads and bridges, enforcement of traffic laws, and local bus services. According to U.S. census data, 75% of U.S. workers commute by car alone to their jobs. Only 4.7% use public transportation. Is this mix of private and public production of transportation goods and services the best for meeting society's goals?

1 | Goals and Decision Making

Even in such a relatively simple case as growing corn (which we examined in the last chapter), learning about the costs of production of a good or service takes you only part way to making an intelligent production decision. For good economic decision making, you also need to know what the *benefits* are from producing, from both an individual and a societal perspective. And you need to approach your production decisions with solid, reasonable *ways of thinking* that are suited to your particular situation.

1.1 | Goals and Economic Benefits from Production

Production is always directed toward some goal. Such goals may include immediate well-being for particular people, financial gain, future productive capacity, and/or resource maintenance. In the real world, of course, individuals, businesses, families, communities, and governments all engage in production. A thorough treatment of the goals and benefits of production must allow for economic actors to be motivated by both extrinsic and intrinsic goals (as discussed in Chapter 2) and must take into account external benefits from production.

For example, when you paint a table simply for pay or because you need a table, you are extrinsically motivated. Other extrinsically motivated activities include cooking a meal only to satisfy hunger and starting up a business only in the hope of generating profits. On the other hand, you might paint a table because you enjoy painting or might cook a meal because you consider being a good cook an important part of who you are. A couple might open a newspaper stand in part because they like the social contact they get working in it and have always dreamed of having their own small business. These are intrinsic benefits.

Some productive activities are motivated in both ways, of course. Lynn may enjoy playing baseball and also get paid as part of a professional team. Meng, who enjoys caring for people, may also support family members by becoming a professional nurse. Gail, the farmer in our earlier example, may farm partly because she needs to support her family and partly because she feels loyal to farming as a "way of life."

Financial considerations, including considerations of profit, are only one part—though an important one—of the reason why production takes place. The extrinsic and intrinsic goals held by individuals and organizations give a much more complicated picture.

internal benefits: the benefits of a project from the perspective of the economic actor making the decisions

Such benefits, considered from the point of view of the individual economic actor, are **internal benefits** from production. They accrue to the actor who does the productive activity.

From the point of view of society as a whole, the goals of individuals and organizations may be seen to lead sometimes toward, and sometimes away from, individual and social well-being. Mindless profiteering by businesses, for example, may lead to narrow decision making that creates terrible working conditions for employees and neglects important social costs. Public management directed toward promoting the interests of only a select group may also detract from social well-being. Social capital, in the form of social norms that encourage responsible behavior, is important in keeping productive activities oriented toward the goal of well-being.

external benefits: the benefits of a project that accrue to persons, or entities such as the environment, that are not among the economic actors directly responsible for the activity

For a full social accounting of the benefits of a productive activity, we need to account not only for how the activity affects the actors involved but also for the **external benefits** that might be created. For example, when a corporation undertakes a program of watershed restoration, that program not only pays off in terms of enhancing the firm's corporate self-image as a "good citizen" but also aids the wildlife of the area. Gail's

Both external benefits (positive externalities) and external costs (negative externalities) need to be considered when calculating the society-wide effects of production. People buy the vehicles produced by the global auto industry because of the transportation services they provide. But as this photo of a smog-obscured Los Angeles skyline makes evident, private benefits need to be weighed against social costs such as air pollution. Governments have sought to reduce this negative externality in part by using regulations, such as emissions standards, to change the way producers design their vehicles.

farm may provide an expanse of open space that benefits the citizens of a crowded city and may preserve prime topsoil for future generations.

Does it seem that economics is asking you to consider too many factors in deciding about any simple productive activity? The problem is that if you consider only accounting costs, internal costs and benefits, and extrinsic motivations for production, you can come up with an analysis that both fails to describe real-world behavior and gives misleading signals about social decision making. Consideration of opportunity costs, external costs and benefits, and intrinsic motivations is indispensable both for good description and for good guidance for household, community, business, or government policy.

1.2 | Weighing Costs and Benefits

Now that we have discussed costs and benefits of production, we need to address the question of which production processes should be undertaken, and to what extent. We want the benefits that flow from production. But we also know that getting the benefits entails costs: Doing any particular production activity uses resources of time and physical goods (often acquired by purchase) that could have been used elsewhere.

In general, full social efficiency and economic efficiency are achieved when production processes are chosen that maximize **net benefits**. Net benefits are the difference between the total benefits from production and the total cost, where both are measured in terms of a complete social evaluation. To the extent that you try to think about whether any productive activity is worthwhile to society as a whole, you need to think in terms of all possible benefits, as well as full social costs. Analysis according to net benefits makes for good decision making, whether in the core, public purpose, or business spheres of the economy.

You do this in a casual way, for example, when you decide how much to study for an exam. Your main personal benefit will be in terms of learning and grades, and perhaps you also intend to put your learning to use in ways that benefit society. Because studying takes time, you will incur opportunity costs in terms of time lost for other activities—and perhaps you will impose external costs on your friends, who were counting on you to join them in a basketball game. If you are a rational decision maker, you will take into account the benefits and costs of the various activities you might engage in, in order to reach a good decision. If you believe the net benefits of studying will be the highest, you will study.

Many governments try to formalize this sort of decision making by using **cost/benefit analysis**, which seeks, in principle, to evaluate thoroughly the relevant costs and benefits of projects, from highway building, to workplace safety, to environmental protection. The positive side of using such analysis is that it requires government regulators and contractors to take into account, explicitly, both the cost side and the benefit side of the issue that must be decided.

One problem with implementing such an analysis, however, arises from the fact that some costs and benefits are easier to measure than others. It is relatively easy, for example, to determine how many jobs will be lost if a section of rainforest is preserved. It may even be relatively easy to convert the number of jobs lost into a cost that can be expressed in dollars. It is harder to quantify the benefit to social well-being that accrues from preserving natural diversity and endangered species. If an analyst thinks "economistically," taking into account only the costs and benefits that are easy to measure in market-determined monetary terms, important benefits and costs may not be taken into account. It is often better to think of the cost/benefit approach as providing a framework for talking about forgone opportunities and goals as one part of a public discussion, not to think of it as a rigid procedure that will automatically yield a "correct" answer.

For businesses, a critical benefit in any calculation is the receipt of **revenue** from sales of their products. Businesses have, as an important goal, the making of **economic profit**, which is the difference between their revenue and their economic costs. Economic profit is a broader concept than accounting profit but a narrower concept than net benefits. It is broader than accounting profit because it is calculated on the basis of economic costs (including opportunity costs) rather than just accounting costs.

Sidebar notes:

◯ A general guideline for socially beneficial production is to choose productive activities that maximize net benefits.

net benefits = total benefits − total cost

cost/benefit analysis: a procedure, often used by governments, for attempting to determine the net benefits of proposed projects

revenue: the amount received from sales of produced goods and services

economic profit = revenue − economic costs

It is narrower than net benefits because it does not include benefits or costs that are external to the firm.

To the extent that firms have goals beyond maximizing their economic profit, and take into account externalities and thus social costs, they make decisions that would also be in accord with a net benefit evaluation. But to the extent that firms look only at their own revenue and economic costs, decisions by individual firms may not be socially optimal.

Social efficiency in production decisions requires that all economic actors—whether individuals, governments, businesses, or other—try to get the greatest possible social value of output at the least possible social cost. If a producer produces less of value than the amount it was possible to create from the resources, or if it incurs more cost than necessary in producing an output, the producer is acting inefficiently.

To understand more about production decision making, we will examine some further concepts related to production and its costs.

Discussion Questions

1. What are the main internal benefits (both extrinsic and intrinsic, if any) that you expect to gain from taking this economics course? Do you think there may be any external benefits to those around you from your getting an education in economics?

2. "No expense should be spared in ensuring workplace safety!" Discuss this slogan. Would following this advice lead to increased social well-being? (*Hint:* Think about a production possibilities frontier—as discussed in Chapter 1—with "worker safety" on one axis.)

2 | Marginal Thinking

Marginal thinking in economics means evaluating incremental (small) changes in production (or input use) levels in order to find an optimum. We began studying marginal thinking in the last chapter when we investigated marginal returns to variable inputs, and marginal costs. In some cases, marginal thinking leads to better economic decision making than what our immediate intuition or common sense would suggest.

2.1 | Comparing Marginal Benefits and Costs

marginal benefit: the benefit that accrues from producing the last unit of output

An important insight that arises from marginal thinking is the following: To the extent that the actions of a producer up to a point in time can be taken as "given," the producer's decision about what to do *next* depends only on marginal cost and marginal benefit. **Marginal benefit** is, of course, the benefit from the incremental unit.

For example, airlines sometimes offer very low fares. Although it might cost an average of $300 per seat to fly a full plane on a particular route, they might sell tickets for some seats for only $150. Obviously, if they offered these low fares to everyone, they would not be able to meet their costs and would go out of business.

How can they offer low fares, and why would they? Common sense would seem to indicate that they should charge each passenger a fare that covers the *average* cost of producing the service. If the plane holds 10 people, for example, and it costs roughly $3000 to fly the route, it would seem that the airline would need to charge each passenger at least $300.

But suppose an airline already has decided to fly a particular flight as scheduled and has filled 6 of the seats on the plane with business travelers who have paid a substantial fare for their tickets. Now the airline is facing the choice of flying the flight with the last 4 seats empty or trying to entice on some additional passengers. The *extra* cost involved in taking on more passengers, after the flight is already scheduled, fueled, and staffed, is minimal—perhaps a snack, a little extra fuel in the plane, and a bit of ticket-processing effort. If the airline can fill the remaining seats at fares that exceed this small *marginal* cost, the airline will come out ahead.

Common sense is correct in telling us that the airline can't sell to *everyone* at less than the average cost. But once it has decided to fly the flight as scheduled, the airline has nothing to lose by selling the *marginal* seats at something closer to *marginal* cost. Economics encourages us to remember to consider the marginal effects.

Under certain assumptions about the nature of the production function, costs, and benefits, the general rule that societal production choices should attempt to maximize net benefits can be stated differently. We stated the rule earlier in terms of total benefit and total (social) cost, but we can sometimes express it in *marginal* terms. The rule is that net benefits are maximized when producers engage in an activity *up to the point where the marginal benefit equals the marginal cost.*

▶ Marginal thinking, when applied to production decisions, compares the cost of the last unit of production (the marginal cost) with the benefit of the last unit of production (the marginal benefit).

2.2 | Marginal Thinking: The Example of Profit Maximization

We will demonstrate how marginal thinking can be used to identify the highest possible level of net benefits for one stylized case, that of a price-taking firm within the traditional model.

Suppose we look at the decisions of a business firm that produces one output, hair dryers. Suppose the firm has already decided on a scale of production and made its choice of technologies, so we can focus on its decision about how many hair dryers to produce over some short period of time—say, a month. Suppose there are no externalities in either costs or benefits; the benefit from production is simply the revenue from sales of hair dryers produced in a month, and the social cost is simply the firm's economic cost over that month. Then, in this simple case, the firm will maximize net benefits by maximizing economic profit—that is, the difference between revenue and economic costs over the month.

▶ Given certain assumptions, net benefits can be maximized when the marginal benefit is set equal to the marginal cost.

If you read the appendix to the previous chapter, you have already encountered this firm and its cost structure. We repeat the most relevant facts about its cost structure in regard to marginal thinking here, in columns (a) through (c) of Table 8.1. The firm has fixed costs of $20, which it must pay this month even if it produces no hair dryers. Hence the total cost of producing 1 hair dryer is $20 plus the marginal cost of going from producing no hair dryers to producing 1 hair dryer ($20 + $12 = $32), the total cost of producing 2 hair dryers is the total cost of producing 1 hair dryer plus the marginal cost to produce the second ($32 + $8 = $40), and so on.

The Total Cost column, column (c), is the basis for the total cost curve shown in Figure 8.1. Figure 8.1 tracks dollar values on the vertical axis and the quantity of hair dryers on the horizontal axis. For example, 2 hair dryers can be produced at a total cost of $40. Note that column (b) in Table 8.1 and the shape of the total cost curve in Figure 8.1 indicate a brief span of decreasing marginal costs at very low levels of production, followed by increasing marginal costs.

Table 8.1 | Costs and Revenues in the Production of Hair Dryers ($)

Quantity of Hair Dryers (a)	Marginal Cost (b)	Total Cost (c)	Marginal Revenue (d)	Total Revenue (e)	Total Profit (f)
0		20		0	−20
1	12	32	20	20	−12
2	8	40	20	40	0
3	8	48	20	60	12
4	9	57	20	80	23
5	10	67	20	100	33
6	14	81	20	120	39
7	*20*	101	*20*	140	*39*
8	35	136	20	160	24
9	55	191	20	?	?

Figure 8.1 The Total Cost Curve for Hair Dryers

The total cost curve, like those derived in the previous chapter, shows how much it costs to produce the quantity of hair dryers indicated on the horizontal axis.

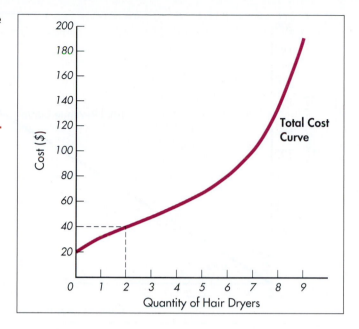

marginal revenue: the revenue received from the last unit sold

We will further assume that the firm faces a constant price for its output.[1] We will assume that hair dryers sell for $20 each, so the firm's **marginal revenue**—the revenue from each additional unit sold—is constant at $20, as shown in column (d) of Table 8.1. Total revenue is computed in column (e) and graphed in Figure 8.2. For example, if the firm produces no hair dryers, it makes revenues of zero, whereas if it produces 4 hair dryers, it makes revenues of $80. The total revenue curve is a straight line with a slope of +20 (that is, each unit sold—the "run"—brings in another $20—the "rise").

The firm will want to get the most (total) economic profit and will do this by trying to find the level of production flow for the month that maximizes the difference between (total) revenue and (total) cost.

As we see in column (f) of Table 8.1, the firm would lose money at very low levels of output. If it produced 0 hair dryers, it would still have to pay its fixed costs of $20, so it

Figure 8.2 The Total Revenue Curve for Hair Dryers

The total revenue curve shows how much revenue can be collected from the sale of hair dryers. Because we have assumed that each hair dryer sold goes for the same price (here shown as $20), the total revenue curve is a straight, upward-sloping line.

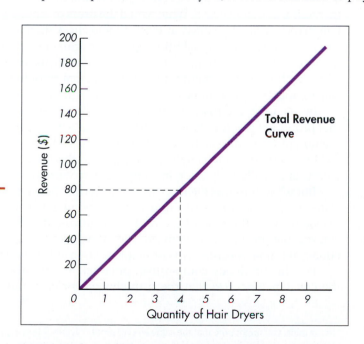

[1] As we will see in Chapter 11, the assumption of constant price is related to the assumption that the firm is in a "perfectly competitive" market.

Figure 8.3 Profit and Loss
The vertical distance between total revenue curve and the total cost curve represents the profit or loss to the firm at each level of production. At quantities (levels of production) where the total cost curve is *above* the total revenue curve, the firm makes losses. The firm makes positive profits at quantities where the total cost curve is *below* the total revenue curve.

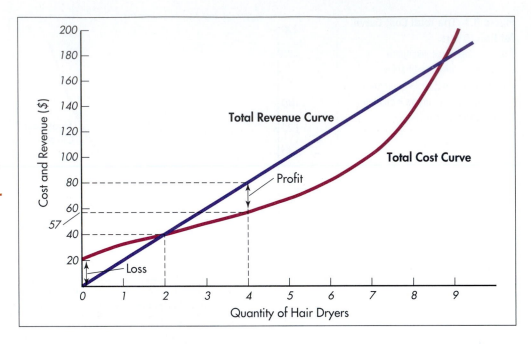

would have a loss (that is, a negative profit) of $20. This is illustrated in Figure 8.3, where at 0 units of product, the total cost curve is $20 higher than the total revenue curve. Producing 2 units, it would make just enough ($40) in revenues to cover its costs of production ($40). Economic profits are 0 where the two curves cross. We can see that if the firm produced 4 units, its revenues would be $80, its costs would be $57, and it would make $23 in profit. Profits are indicated by the vertical distance between the total revenue curve and the total cost curve. But is a profit of $23 the best the firm can do?

Continuing to the right in Figure 8.3, we see that the vertical distance between the two curves is at its widest somewhere between 4 and 9 hair dryers. Table 8.1 shows that profits are higher at a quantity of 7 hair dryers.[2] At 7 hair dryers, revenues are $140, costs are $101, and the firm makes a profit of $39. We can also see that if the firm produces additional units after the seventh, profits will start to shrink again (because of the increasing marginal costs). What would the firm's revenues and profits be if it produced 9 hair dryers? (Calculate these in Table 8.1 and check them on the graph, to test yourself.)

One aspect of marginal thinking is to imagine the firm doing this exercise of slowly increasing its production, while paying attention to what happens to costs and revenues with each incremental unit. But marginal thinking also leads to a new, simpler rule for maximizing profits.

In the upper graph in Figure 8.4, we've noted that it is at production of 7 hair dryers that profits are greatest. It is also the case that the total cost curve has, at the level of production of 7 hair dryers, the exact same slope as the total revenue curve. Note that the total cost curve is relatively flat compared to the total revenue curve off to the left of 7 units and is relatively steep in comparison to it off to the right of 7 units.

⊙ Given certain assumptions, profits are maximized when marginal cost equals marginal revenue (the revenue from the last unit sold). This principle is abbreviated as "set *MC* = *MR*."

But what does this mean in economic terms? Recall that earlier we showed how the *slope* of revenue and cost curves at any point reflects *marginal* revenue and cost, respectively. In the case of the profit-maximizing firm with no externalities, then, we can see that profits are maximized when the quantity is chosen such that marginal cost equals marginal revenue. This principle is often abbreviated as "set *MC* = *MR*."

For this (perfectly competitive) price-taking firm, the marginal revenue is simply the constant price (*P*) that the firm charges for each hair dryer sold, so we can also

---

[2] In the table, you might note that the same level of profit is achievable at a quantity of 6 hair dryers. The mathematical reasoning behind "marginal thinking" applies most elegantly when you can *continuously* vary the number of units—for example, if you could think of producing 6.5 or 7.2 units. In order to approximate this in the integer-unit examples used in this book, always look to the *highest* quantity level at which profit is maximized.

Figure 8.4 Profit Maximization
Profits are at their greatest at the level of production where the distance between the total revenue curve and the total cost curve is the largest. Because at this point the two lines have the same slope, we can also say that profits are maximized by choosing the level of production where marginal cost equals marginal revenue.

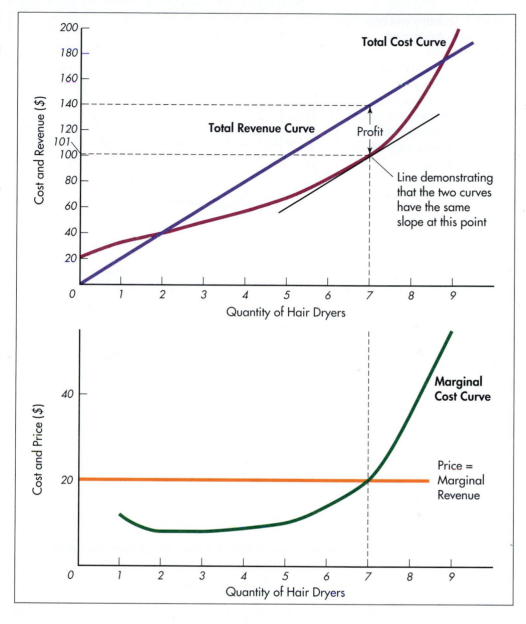

○ For price-taking firms, the profit-maximization principle can be abbreviated as "set *MC = P*."

express this as *MC = P*, where *P* stands for "price." The lower portion of Figure 8.4 shows that the profit-maximizing production level can also be derived by examining the marginal cost curve directly. This curve can be plotted from the data in Table 8.1—for example, at a production level of 7 hair dryers, the marginal cost is 20. Setting *MC = P* is graphically portrayed by looking for the point where the marginal cost curve intersects a horizontal line representing (the constant) price.

Marginal thinking can also be applied, under certain assumptions, to producers' decisions about their use of inputs. In later chapters on factor markets, for example, we will see that under certain assumptions, additional hours of labor should be hired until the value of the output produced by the last hour of labor is equal to the hourly wage paid. Marginal thinking is helpful for examining how producers can make optimal decisions when they have a well-defined objective, knowledge about costs, and cost structures of certain well-defined forms.

2.3 | Profit Maximization When the Price of Output Changes

For reference in later chapters, it is useful to point out here what happens to the hair dryer producer's decision as the *price of output varies*. Figure 8.5 reveals that at a price

Figure 8.5 Quantity and Price for the Profit-Maximizing Price-Taking Firm
As the price of output rises from $20 to $35, the profit-maximizing producer will change the amount produced in order to keep price equal to marginal cost. The higher the price, the more the hair dryer producer will supply to the market.

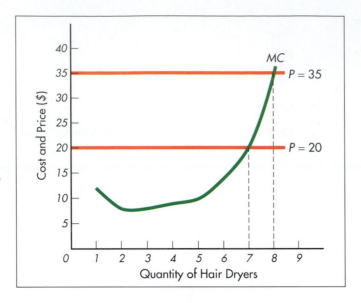

of $20 per hair dryer, the "set $MC = P$" rule indicates that this price-taking producer should supply 7 hair dryers to the market. If the price were to instead be $35 per hair dryer, what should the producer do?

Table 8.2 shows the new problem for the firm for selected levels of output. The cost structure is unchanged from Table 8.1. Only the revenue and profit numbers need updating to take the new output price into account. In Table 8.2 we can see that the $MC = P$ rule dictates that 8 units should be produced when the price is $35, because the marginal cost of production is $35 at that quantity. At this price and level of production, the firm makes a profit of $144. This new decision is also illustrated in Figure 8.5.

We can see that—at least over this range of prices—an increase in price leads the profit-maximizing firm to supply a larger quantity to the market. This provides one elegant justification for the upward-sloping supply curve discussed in Chapter 4.

The idea that sellers are usually willing to supply larger quantities to the market at higher prices is more general than the traditional model example, however. Higher prices are usually also associated with larger quantities offered for sale in industries characterized by market power (as well as competition), in resale and asset markets (as well as product markets), when the seller is a government or an individual (as well as when it is a firm), and so on.

2.4 | The Assumption Underlying Reliance on Marginal Thinking: Convexity

In order for marginal analysis and the "set $MC = MR$" rule to be the sole relevant guideline for business decisions about the level of output to produce, it is necessary that production technology, costs, and benefits all follow certain prescriptions. Economists have elaborated these limitations in detail, using a number of terms derived from mathematics, but the main idea is that the situation must be one that can be graphically illustrated as a smooth path up to the point of maximum net benefits (or, in the special case, profits).

You can think about the search for the point of highest net benefits as analogous to the search for the highest point of an island, on whose beach you have landed after a

Table 8.2 | Cost and Revenue ($) When the Price of Hair Dryers is $35

Quantity of Hair Dryers	Marginal Cost	Total Cost	Total Revenue	Total Profit
6	14	81	210	129
7	20	101	245	144
8	*35*	136	280	*144*
9	55	191	315	124

Figure 8.6 Profit (Convex Case)
Under the assumptions of convexity, the firm's profit problem has only one "hill," and marginal thinking will guide the firm to the profit-maximizing output level.

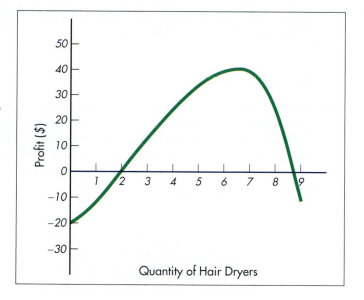

Quantity of Hair Dryers

shipwreck. One way to reach the highest point would be to do a thorough survey of the whole island, use appropriate instruments to determine where the highest point is, and then hire a helicopter to fly you up to that point. But if your resources are limited and you can get around only on foot, a reasonable strategy is to start walking and be sure always to head upward (or at least never to head downward).

It is easy to see that this strategy will be successful if you happen to start out in the vicinity of the highest peak; upward movements will take you directly to the summit of that peak. For the strategy to be fail-safe, however, it must be the case that the surface of the island is completely devoid of any smaller peaks, so that no matter where you start on the perimeter, you never have to go down in order to climb back up to the highest point. In mathematical language, such an island would be completely "convex."

In the case of hair dryers, we saw that at an output price of $20, profit would start out negative, then become positive and grow, and then shrink and became negative again, if the firm produced more and more hair dryers. This pattern of profits is illustrated in Figure 8.6. Like our imaginary island, the hair dryer profit curve has a single "hill." No matter at what level of production of hair dryers our firm begins, it will arrive at the top of the hill by following the strategy of increasing or decreasing production by 1 unit at a time ("start walking") in the direction of higher profit ("always head uphill").

convexity: a mathematical term used to describe the special assumptions necessary for marginal thinking to lead to maximization of net benefits. With convexity, net benefits can be maximized by taking incremental steps along a smooth path.

Problems characterized by convexity lend themselves easily to mathematical analysis.[3] Economists now often use the word **convexity** to describe the characteristics of economic problems that can be addressed by marginal thinking alone.[4]

---

[3] In particular, they lend themselves readily to calculus. The mathematically minded student may have noticed that the economist's concept of "marginal" would, when the changes considered are very small, be identical to the mathematician's concept of "derivative." The hair dryer production problem is to find the level of production (y) that maximizes profits (usually denoted π); that is,

$$\text{Max } \pi = R(y) - C(y)$$
$$y$$

where $R(y)$ is the total revenue function and $C(y)$ is the total cost function. (In the simple case in the text, $R(y) = p \times y$, where p is the output price.) This is a standard calculus problem of optimization, and the solution is easily described (under certain assumptions about the shapes of these functions, including those referred to in the text under the name of "convexity") as occurring where $R'(y) = C'(y)$—that is, where marginal revenue equals marginal cost.

[4] In mathematics, a convex set in three-dimensional space is one in which you can draw a straight line between any two points, and the line will also be in the set. In the case of an island with one smooth hill, for example, a mole could burrow directly from any point on the hill to any other point, staying in dirt the whole time. A *nonconvex* set is one in which some such straight courses lie partly outside the set. Imagine two hills, with a valley in between them. To go in a straight line from a point on one hill to a point on the other, the mole would have to jump out of the dirt and pass through the air. The two-hill island is therefore *nonconvex.*

Many real-world economic problems, however, display various "nonconvexities." In these cases, marginal thinking cannot guarantee that either net benefits or profits will be maximized.

Discussion Questions

1. Explain, in terms of returns to production (discussed in the previous chapter), why hair dryers become increasingly profitable to make over some levels of output and then become less profitable to make after some level of output is exceeded. That is, why does the total cost curve in Figure 8.4, to the right of the output level of 2 hair dryers, have its distinctive shape?

2. Suppose that hair dryer production has a fixed cost of $32 (instead of $20) but has the same variable costs as shown in Table 8.1. Recalculate Table 8.1, adding $12 to each total cost number to reflect this, and sketch the new total cost curve on a graph. Revenue per unit is unchanged at $20. Sketch the total revenue curve on the same graph. What is the firm's break-even level of production now? Where is the firm's profit-maximizing level of output? Is this the same as or different from that for the case in the text? Looking back at the $MR = MC$ rule, should it surprise you that the answer to the question of profit maximization (has/has not) changed?

3 | Discrete Decision Making

discrete decisions: decisions that involve "jumps" between different distinct choices

Sometimes incremental decision making—looking only at marginal effects—is insufficient for wise economic decision making. Some decisions require **discrete decisions**—jumps between choices that are distinct and separate from each other. Discrete decision making is necessary when an economic problem is characterized by **nonconvexity**.

nonconvexity: a mathematical term used to describe a number of situations in which marginal thinking is an inadequate guide to maximization of net benefits

Of course, from the point of view of real-world decision makers, large or "either/or" decisions are perhaps more the norm than the exception. To build a bridge or not? To enter a market or not? To start this new product line or that one? What about developing a revolutionary new technology? These sorts of leaps form the exciting edge of production decisions for project managers, entrepreneurs, innovators, and productive workers in all parts of the economy.

Marginal analysis can help in comparing alternative projects and in "fine-tuning" a production project once it is started, but the big question of whether to engage in the project at all—determining whether net benefits are likely even to be positive, to say nothing of their being at their maximum—is another example of a discrete choice. Building a little bit of a bridge is often not a useful approach. Even small-scale production decisions often involve a discrete decision, such as whether to base household meal production on a gas stove or an electric one. In the real world, such decisions are made in the context of past decisions, and with imperfect information and much uncertainty about what the future will bring. Decisions made now also have effects on the future, which may be unpredictable.

Some sources of nonconvexity in economics problems can be examined even if we continue to think of production decisions in terms of decisions of a single producer, without regard to history and the passage of time. A discussion that ignores the passage of time, focusing on optimal decisions without paying any attention to how they might be achieved over time, is called **static**.

static analysis: analysis that does not take into account the passage of time

To explore other causes of nonconvexity, we will need to be more explicit about the fact that real-world production takes place in real-world historical time. At any period of time, society and individual producers start not with a blank slate but with a stock of natural, manufactured, human, social, and financial capital and under the constraint of institutional arrangements and contracts that may not be easy to change. Discussions that take into account the starting point of a process and its development over time are said to attend to **dynamic** issues. Of particular importance to the discussion of production are cases in which dynamic processes are irreversible: The past sets limits on the present, which no current action can reverse.

dynamic analysis: analysis that takes into account the passage of time

3.1 | The Discrete Decision Whether to Produce or Not to Produce

In discussing our hair dryer producer earlier in this chapter, we presented only cases in which the prices of hair dryers ($20 and $35) were such that the producer could make a positive profit. The only question was how to choose the production level that would yield the *greatest* profit, given each price. Over some range of variation in prices for its product, the firm will make smooth decisions, increasing production a little if prices go up a little, and decreasing production a little if prices go down a little, following the *MC = MR* rule.

But at some crucial point, if prices go down too far, it would be better for the producer to make a "jump"—a discrete choice—to producing nothing at all. The producer would be better off closing up shop. But there are two perhaps surprising aspects to the question of how this decision should most logically be made.

First of all, the decision to shut down does *not* simply come at the point where the producer starts to make losses, in the short run. Recall that in the short run the firm will have to pay fixed costs (for example, the lease on a factory or other long-term obligations) whether it produces or not this month. It may be less costly to continue to operate, and lose some amount of money, than to shut down and have to pay the fixed costs with no revenues coming in at all. Specifically, if the firm can make enough to cover its variable costs (for example, costs for materials or wages for employees hired by the day) and at least a bit of its fixed costs, it should keep operating this month—at least it can pay some of the fixed costs out of revenues. If, on the other hand, the firm cannot even cover its variable costs, then it should shut down.

As a numerical example, consider the hair dryer producer's decision if the price of hair dryers were $10 (instead of, as in the previous examples, $20 or $35). The cost structure is unchanged by the change in output price, so only the revenue and profit numbers in Table 8.1 need changing. In Table 8.3 we can see that the *MC = P* rule dictates that 5 units should be produced when the price is $10, because the marginal cost of production is $10 at that quantity. At this price and level of production, revenues are $50 and costs are $67, so the firm *loses* $17 by producing. Would it be better to shut down? No. If the firm produced 0 units, it would still have to pay its fixed costs of $20. (See the top row of the table.) Losing only $17 is better than losing $20. The firm should continue to produce—at least until it can get out of its factory lease.

But what if the price dropped by another dollar, to $9? Now, looking at Table 8.4, we see that the *MC = P* principle would dictate that the firm should produce 4 hair dryers. Is this really best? The firm loses $21 by producing 4 units, but it would lose only $20 if it shut down. With this additional dollar drop in price, the firm, instead of following the *MC = P* rule, should make a decision based on its *discrete* options: to produce or not to produce. It should shut down.[5]

The second perhaps surprising thing about this decision whether to produce or not is that *it doesn't matter how big the fixed costs are.* As long as there is something left over,

> In the presence of unavoidable short-run fixed costs, a firm should produce, even if it makes losses, as long as its revenues at least cover its variable costs. But it should shut down if its revenues do not even cover its variable costs.

Table 8.3 | Cost and Revenue ($) When the Price of Hair Dryers Is $10

Quantity of Hair Dryers	Marginal Cost	Total Cost	Total Revenue	Total Profit
0		20	0	−20
1	12	32	10	−22
2	8	40	20	−20
3	8	48	30	−18
4	9	57	40	−17
5	**10**	67	50	−17

[5] These points are illustrated graphically in the appendix to this chapter.

Table 8.4 | Cost and Revenue ($) When the Price of Hair Dryers Is $9

Quantity of Hair Dryers	Marginal Cost	Total Cost	Total Revenue	Total Profit
0		20	0	−20
1	12	32	9	−23
2	8	40	18	−22
3	8	48	27	−21
4	**9**	57	36	−21
5	10	67	45	−22

after variable costs are paid, to go toward paying the fixed costs—*whatever they may be*—the firm should continue to produce. Whether the fixed costs are $20 or $2 million doesn't matter. The rational decisions of the hair dryer producer—to produce at a price of $10 and quit if the price fell to $9—would be utterly unchanged by any different level of fixed costs. (You can prove this to yourself by adding some amount—say, $100—to each of the total cost figures in the last two tables and seeing whether doing so changes the decision.)

This is a specific example of a more general economic principle concerning dynamic decision making: *Sunk costs shouldn't matter to present decision making.* A **sunk cost** is a cost that, from the point of view of the present time, is the proverbial "water over the dam." The expense has already been incurred (or committed to) and cannot be reversed.

sunk cost: an expenditure that was made in the past and is now irreversible

This principle often seems to contradict "common sense." Humans seem to have an illogical but psychologically strong tendency to want to make substantial past investments "pay off." People sometimes run very unprofitable (but costly) factories, stay in bad (but lengthy) careers, or wear bad (but expensive) haircuts far too long, because they have trouble letting their earlier investments be "water over the dam." The more expensive the factory or the haircut is, or the longer our training for the career, the stronger our tendency is to want to "stick with it." Logically, however, the size of our past investment is irrelevant. The logically correct question to ask is which choice (producing or not, this career or another, etc.) makes things better *now*. The past is the past.

Another real-world human complication, however, arises when stopping production means closing factories or other businesses. This can be very painful when these enterprises have been the lifeblood of a local community economy. A full accounting of the costs and benefits of a change takes into account the social well-being costs of such transitions, in addition to the strictly financial concerns.

3.2 | Multiple Equilibria

An equilibrium, in mathematical terms, is a resting point, where forces balance out and no further change occurs. Following marginal thinking, once a firm finds a level of production where $MC = MR$ (which is where a profit "hill" is at its highest point), it has solved its problem and need search no longer. When there are multiple equilibria (*equilibria* is the plural form of *equilibrium*), more than one resting point exists. Although the single-equilibrium case is convenient for its mathematical tractability, there is no reason to believe that it is more common in real life than multiple equilibria. Many economists have devoted attention to this issue in recent decades.

For example, suppose Iris's Place, a café, serves lunches to local office workers and evening snacks to students from the local university. It is currently open from 11 a.m. until 10 p.m. It could be that if Iris experimented with different hours of operation, she would find that her profits would rise somewhat if she stayed open longer. Perhaps student demand for snacks is high from 10 p.m. until midnight, and her revenues would exceed her costs during these additional 2 nighttime hours.

Figure 8.7 Profit (nonconvex case)
In this case, there are *two* top-of-the-hill "resting places" (or *equilibria*). Marginal thinking alone may not get a decision maker to the highest profit level.

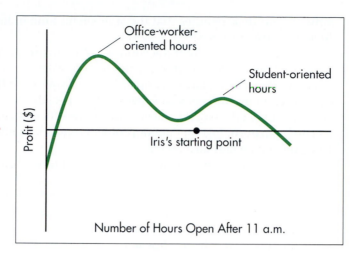

However, she might also find that her profits would rise *even higher* if she drastically *reduced* her hours. Perhaps by opening only from 11 a.m. until 2 p.m., she could still earn substantial revenues from selling full lunches to office workers, while being able to save considerably on expenses. She would reduce her need for staffing from 11 hours a day to just 3 hours a day. If hired labor is expensive, this could be a very profitable move.

In this case, Iris's profit maximization problem would have two "hills," as shown in Figure 8.7. A "local maximum," or small hill, exists at the hours of operation that cater to the students, and a "global maximum," or highest hill, exists under a quite different strategy, implying even fewer hours of operation, with a valley in between.

If Iris starts at the point indicated in the figure and uses marginal thinking, she will climb to the top of the small hill. To find whether the higher hilltop actually exists, she would need to go beyond marginal thinking. Iris's decision problem is characterized by nonconvexity. *Discrete* decision making is necessary.

3.3 | Lumpiness and Increasing Returns

Two other factors that can bring about a need for discrete decisions in a static context are lumpiness and increasing returns.

Lumpiness. In the real world, it may be that some inputs can be obtained, or outputs can be sold, only in discrete, or "lumpy," quantities. Even in our example of hair dryer production, the company is assumed to be able to produce only integer numbers (1, 2, 3, . . .) of hair dryers. If profits are maximized at some fractional level of production (say, 6.5 hair dryers), the firm will have to decide between producing 6 and producing 7. In the real world, producers have to decide whether to add another taxi to a fleet, another retail store to a chain, or another regional office to a social service bureau—not half a taxi, $\frac{3}{4}$ of a store, or 90% of an office.

Increasing Returns. In the societal "production possibilities frontier" discussed in Chapter 1, it was assumed that some resources were more suitable for one kind of production than for another. Therefore, both gun production and butter production would yield diminishing returns as more and more of the resources that could be transferred from production of butter to production of guns, for example, were combined with limited quantities of the resources that were most appropriate for guns. This gave the production possibilities frontier its bowed-out shape.

What if, instead, two goods require very, very similar inputs in order to be produced, and each good has an *increasing* returns production function? This might be the case, for example, for an accounting office, where the question is whether to produce a large quantity of monthly spreadsheets as Microsoft Excel products or as Lotus 1-2-3 products. Each production process includes the purchase of the relevant software and then requires that the staff spend time in learning to use it and in producing the spreadsheets.

Does it make sense for the accounting office to produce a little bit of each of the two outputs? Probably not. Learning is one reason. Workers tend to get better and better at using a particular software program, the more experienced they are with it. The value of synergies among workers also suggests that specialization in one or the other output would be more efficient. When everyone in the office is using the same software, workers can brainstorm together about problems and solutions and can avoid having to do time-consuming file conversions.

The accounting office's production possibilities frontier in this case will probably look more like Figure 8.8, with a *bowed-in* shape. Attainable output is highest when the office specializes in one kind of output or the other and is lower when it tries for a mix of outputs. Rather than trading off a little bit of Excel production for a little bit of Lotus production in a marginal fashion, the office is likely to make an either/or choice. It is likely choose to produce either at point *A* with all Excel output or at point *B* with all Lotus output. Point *C*, reflecting a mix of products, is an inferior choice.

Sometimes this sort of case is also referred to as having a "corner solution," because the preferred point is at an extreme "corner" of the graph.

3.4 | Bringing in History: Path Dependence and Switching Costs

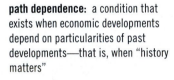

path dependence: a condition that exists when economic developments depend on particularities of past developments—that is, when "history matters"

Path dependence is a term borrowed from the mathematics of dynamic systems; it summarizes in a general way the idea that "history matters" in determining how production technologies—and entire economies—develop. When a process is path dependent, the way it develops may depend crucially on the "initial conditions" of the problem. The present state of manufactured capital or human capital, for example, can be thought of as making up part of the initial conditions for current production decisions.

We have already seen a simple case of path dependence in our image of Iris "climbing" the rightmost profit hill in Figure 8.7. With no way to know the shape of the overall profit function for her café, she may be acting reasonably by applying marginal thinking, starting at the level of hours her café is already open. This starting point, in terms of hours, can be called the "initial condition" of the problem and is indicated by the dot on the horizontal axis. Using marginal thinking starting from the hours indicated by the dot in the figure will cause Iris to climb the small hill and to end up keeping her café open for longer hours.

But what if the initial condition had been different. What if she had started at a point of being open, say, only until 5 p.m. instead of until 10 p.m.? She then would be starting from a spot a little farther to the left in the graph, on the slope of the taller hill. If she *then* experimented with her hours, her marginal thinking would tell her to reduce her hours. It may be only a small, chance event that caused her initially to open her café

Figure 8.8 A Production Possibilities Frontier with Increasing Returns
Sometimes production becomes more efficient the *more you specialize* in one type of output or the other. Producing a little of each (point *C*) is then inefficient.

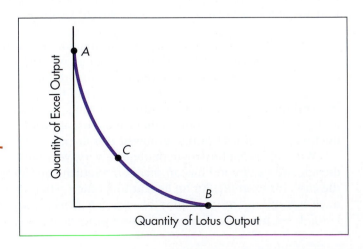

switching costs: the transaction costs associated with a change in production technology

for one set of hours, rather than for another—perhaps a random suggestion from a friend—yet that small chance event may have large effects on the entire future development of her café.[6]

Switching costs are the transaction costs associated with a change. If the accounting office decided to change from all Excel production to all Lotus production, for example, switching costs would include the costs of ordering and installing new software. Switching costs would also include the costs of training all employees how to use the alternative software, as well as some lower productivity during the period when employees are still getting accustomed to the new technology.

High switching costs can lead to actions not being taken at all or to relatively large, discrete changes as producers forgo making small, marginal adjustments. Decision makers will wait to make a change until they foresee the kinds of substantial benefits that will make up for the costs and hassle of transitioning to the new process.

The question of switching costs has come to the fore in the last 30 years, because technological advances and increases in global trade have resulted in large structural changes in economies. Some goods can now be produced more efficiently abroad, but ceasing to produce them here requires shutting down U.S. factories and laying off U.S. workers. It is easy to say that (most) unemployed workers and empty factories will eventually find new jobs and new uses—but what about the switching costs of *getting* there? In the United States, the Trade Act of 1974 attempted to ease some of the costs associated with the closing of plants and factories as a consequence of increased foreign competition. The act created programs of "adjustment assistance" to industries, workers, and communities adversely affected by changing patterns of international trade. In order to help workers who lose their jobs, for example, the programs have sometimes offered government-funded training in new skills, allowances to help workers relocate to a new area, and/or unemployment compensation to tide workers over until they get new jobs.

Some forms of economic analysis have tended to neglect the importance of history, concentrating only on static efficiency. When we bring in dynamics with switching costs and path dependence, we see that even if people are always making the best possible, most rational choices given the information they have in hand at the time, questions of how to maximize net benefits become much more complicated.

3.5 | Bringing in Social Context: Network Externalities

Besides taking place over time, production decisions also take place within a rich social context. Many technologies, such as standards in computers and telecommunications, are widely shared. A production technology is characterized by a **network eternality** if people find it more useful to adopt, the more *other* people have adopted it.

network externality: (in production) a property that a particular technology exhibits when it is advantageous to adopt that technology because other economic actors have adopted it

We discussed a small-scale network externality when we noted that an accounting office is more likely to choose just one software package, instead of allowing its workers to use either Excel or Lotus, because then workers can share their problem-solving discussions. On a larger scale, the presence of network externalities has been used to explain such things as the domination of VHS videotaping technology (over Betamax, an early rival) and the domination of the personal computing market by PC and Macintosh standards. Such technologies exhibit not just increasing returns at the scale of a single firm but also increasing returns, or "positive feedback," over the economy as a whole.

As more people adopted PC technology, for example, more software was written for it and research went into improving it. Likewise for Mac. You might invent a superior

---

[6]Although the two may seem contradictory, the idea (discussed earlier) that the size of sunk costs *shouldn't* matter is consistent with the notion that history *does* matter (in the sense described in our discussion of path dependence). For example, suppose that yesterday you got a bad—but expensive—haircut. You really would be happier today getting your hair cut again (by somebody else). You go have it cut again, considering yesterday's expense to be like money thrown down the gutter. This is an example of wisely ignoring sunk costs. On the other hand, the path of history constrains you. Your new hair style cannot, physically, involve *longer* hair than yesterday's, only *shorter*.

computer platform tomorrow—and many people claim that inventions technically superior to many products in common use do exist—but chances are it will not be marketable. This is partly because of path dependence (the fact that people have already invested in PC and Mac equipment and related knowledge) and individual-level switching costs (the fact that individuals would have to spend time learning your system).

More important, most computer users are already "locked in" to PC or Mac products through the network externalities created by the technical interrelatedness of software development and hardware upgrades. They won't adopt your technology until they can be assured that a lot of software will be written for it, that upgrades will be available in the future, and that they will be able to communicate easily with others—which is most readily assured if others are using the same software. But none of this can be assured until your invention has been widely adopted across a whole network of users. Your problem is that in order to *get* widespread adoption, you must already *have* it! Unless you are in a position to create a widespread network out of nothing—perhaps, for example, by blanketing the country with free computers and training—your technically superior invention won't get off the ground.

A similar problem exists for a city that is trying to increase the use of public transportation in order to decrease road congestion and pollution. If most of the people in the city use the public transportation system—as in New York City and some European cities—it will seem like a normal thing to do, residential and workplace location patterns will reflect the availability of public transport, the buses and subways will run frequently, and service may be so good that people freely choose it over using a private car. On the other hand, if few people use public transportation, it may be stigmatized, routes and services will (in the absence of massive subsidies) tend to be very limited and inconvenient, residences and workplaces will tend to sprawl, and thus ridership will be further discouraged. We could also use vocabulary previously introduced and call this a case of multiple equilibria. One equilibrium (or resting point) exists at low ridership levels, where network externalities have not been developed, and another equilibrium exists at high ridership levels, where they have. Even though the high ridership level might be superior from a number of points of view, the city may be stuck, by path dependence, on the "small hill" of low ridership.

Network externalities create another way in which individually rational decision making can lead to complications in the discussion of production processes. (See the Economics in the Real World feature "QWERTY.") What seems rational in a static, individualistic context may not seem so rational, or may not be achievable, when economic behavior is placed in its historical and social context.

Discussion Questions

1. Which of the following could be characterized as largely marginal decisions? Which more clearly need to be addressed by discrete decision making?
   a. Deciding whether a factory should increase its production level by 1%
   b. Deciding between a career in finance and a career in architecture
   c. Deciding whether to build a new wing on a hospital
   d. Deciding how many staff hours should be assigned to a particular work project

2. Columnist Marilyn vos Savant received the following letter: "My husband and I have sat through some truly awful films! I think we should leave during the first part if we don't like the film. My husband thinks we'd be wasting money and hopes it will improve with time. What would you do?"[7] What would be your reply? What economic concept does this illustrate?

---

[7] "Ask Marilyn," *Parade Magazine*, March 31, 2002, p. 10.

QWERTY

A minor but classic example of path dependence and network externalities is the choice of layout for typewriter (and computer) keyboards. The conventional QWERTY layout (named for the letters in the top left row) was developed in the 19th century and rapidly became the norm throughout the English-speaking world. It was actually designed to *slow down* typing in order to avoid the problem of keys jamming on old-fashioned typewriters!

Studies with modern typewriters and computer keyboards have shown that the QWERTY layout is far from the most efficient; alternative designs—such as the Dvorak keyboard, introduced in the 1930's—could save time by enabling letters that commonly appear together to be typed more rapidly in sequence with different fingers. Yet efforts to market the more efficient keyboards have consistently failed.

The major reason for the failure of alternatives to the QWERTY layout is that it has historically been built into a whole interlinked, economy-wide structure of equipment and training in writing and printing activities. Office equipment manufacturers are all set up to produce it. Keyboarding classes all teach it. A shift to a more efficient layout would entail substantial switching costs before the efficiency gains could be realized.

In sum, you type on a QWERTY keyboard not because it is the most technically efficient but because everybody else uses it. ○

Based on "Clio and the Economics of QWERTY" by Paul A. David, *American Economic Review* 75 (May 1985).

4 | Financial Capital as an Input to Production

For most of the foregoing discussion, we have concentrated on the nonfinancial inputs to production derived from natural, manufactured, human, and social capital. We've considered financial capital only to a small extent, in noting that the cost of borrowing or the opportunity cost of using equity capital must be counted as part of economic costs.

If benefits or revenues from a project could always immediately cover the financial costs of production, then we could be assured that any project that maximizes net benefits could, in fact, be implemented. But in the real world this is rarely the case, so we must explore in more detail how projects actually come to be undertaken.

For a firm, because production normally precedes sales, inputs must be purchased before revenues are obtained from the sale of output. Hence the firm must be able to pay wages and other costs in the present, in order to produce something that will be sold in the future (next week, next month, or even next year). The firm must therefore have access to financial capital, either through its own equity capital or through borrowing, to start a production process. Later on, it can use revenues to pay off any debts.

Governments face the same problems as firms, along with additional ones, for their production processes. In many cases the financial benefits arising from public projects do not accrue automatically to the government. For example, a government agency may build a bridge and then let everyone use it free. In other cases, the benefits do not take financial form. For example, an agency may restore wetlands in order to maintain ecological diversity for future generations. Financial capital for such projects must be raised through means such as taxation and borrowing, and it may not be appropriate to expect these projects ever to "pay back" in entirely financial terms.

Households, as well, require financial capital to undertake production. One of the forms of household production recognized in national accounts is the production of "services of owner-occupied housing." In order to purchase a house, most homeowners have to take out a loan in the form of a mortgage. People also often spend from savings or borrow to finance other sorts of home production. For example, they may borrow to invest in a stove or use savings to allow a parent to cut back on work hours to care for an infant.

In the traditional model of the economy, the importance of financial capital for production is often neglected. This would be justified if there were **perfect capital markets**, where any project that is profitable were able to find financing. Logically, it is true by definition that a project that makes an economic profit will be able to pay a going return on the capital it uses—because we include the cost of capital in calculating economic costs. In theory, then, an investor or lender should be willing to invest in or lend to such a project. Therefore, it seems that raising capital should not be a problem.

In the real world, however, financial markets are far from perfect. Because no one knows the future, there is always an element of risk in committing funds now to a project whose profits won't be realized until some future time. Lenders and investors will thus tend to be less willing to back enterprises that are just starting out and therefore have no track record or credit history. Lenders are less willing to lend to people or firms who cannot put up collateral (something of value that will be forfeited if the loan is not paid) for the loan.

For reasons that are less (or not at all) economically rational, some lenders also discriminate against members of minority groups and/or women. In some cities, banks have been found to "red-line" certain districts, usually poor and populated by racial and ethnic minority groups, making home mortgages there hard or impossible to get.

Because financial markets don't perfectly reflect what will be desired in the future, a political climate that is opposed to tax increases or new bond issues may prevent local governments from carrying out crucial projects.

The problems of finding financing on private markets are even more severe in cases where the benefits do not take primarily financial form. Economic actors are said to face a **capital constraint** when they cannot find financing for their project.

Clearly, because such capital constraints affect some economic actors more than others, there is no "even playing field" in financial markets. A large, established business, with considerable opportunity to retain earnings, sell shares, or borrow, has a definite advantage over smaller and newer potential producers when it comes to obtaining financing. Similarly, an individual who can tap into family wealth or connections has greater access to capital than someone who is poorer. The old saying that "them as has, gets" is often true when it comes to private financial capital.

To some extent, government programs such as, in the United States, mortgage guarantees and Small Business Administration loans attempt to address the financing problems of less-advantaged producers. In Canada and many European countries, paid maternity and paternity leaves (and/or subsidized nonparental care) ease the problem of financing the home (or out-of-home) production of care for young children. In some poor countries, programs of micro-lending (such as the Grameen Bank) seek to extend credit to some of the least-well-off small entrepreneurs, many of whom are women. Social programs that direct financial capital toward socially beneficial but quite unprofitable projects, such as taking care of the homeless mentally ill, facilitate production that otherwise would not be done. In the absence of such conscious efforts to provide financing assistance, however, many production projects with high net social benefits will likely fail to be undertaken.

Because of the prevalence of capital constraints in the real world, it is also the case that economic actors often have to pay more attention to accounting or budgetary costs, and less to real economic opportunity costs, than would be ideal. For example, the repair of a roadway in an economically depressed county, as discussed in Chapter 7, may indeed be a socially beneficial project, drawing unemployed workers into highly valued production. However, it may not be undertaken when the government has to pay attention to the accounting costs of the project, relative to a fixed budget that is not under its control. In reality, the county government will face its own "opportunity cost" question related not to the societal production possibilities frontier but, rather, to its own constrained choices as

perfect capital markets: idealized markets for loans or equity shares, in which all profitable ventures can find funding

capital constraint: (in production) a situation in which an inability to obtain financing imposes limits on production decisions

an economic actor. Perhaps both the roadway project and a local bridge project would yield high social net benefits in the absence of capital constraints. With limited access to financial capital, however, repairing the roadway would mean *not* building the bridge. If the bridge is judged to be the more important use of the limited budgetary funds, the roadway will not be repaired.

Discussion Questions

1. Money obviously doesn't physically build cars or tend to patients—these processes require materials, machinery, social knowledge, and labor. What does it mean, then, to say that financial capital is an "input" to production?

2. Suppose the hair dryer producer whose costs of production are listed in Table 8.1 must pay its costs of production today (both fixed and variable) and will not be able to collect its revenues until next month. Suppose the hair dryer producer can raise only $57 with which to start production. What is the producer likely to do? Will net benefits be as high as they can be?

Review Questions

1. Is profit making the only goal of production? What are some other goals?
2. What is the difference between an internal benefit and an external benefit?
3. What is the general guideline for making socially beneficial production decisions?
4. What are some advantages and disadvantages of using cost/benefit analysis to analyze public projects?
5. What are some factors that can make profit-maximizing decisions diverge from decisions that would maximize social net benefits?
6. Why can it sometimes be profitable to sell a good or service at less than the average cost of producing it?
7. Sketch a total cost curve and a total revenue curve for a (traditional model) price-taking firm facing circumstances that can be described as "convex," indicating the profit-maximizing level of output.
8. Using a graph, describe how a (traditional model) price-taking firm that follows the "set $MC = P$" rule responds to price changes.
9. Explain why a firm might decide to continue producing even though it is losing money.
10. List seven reasons why economic decision making may require discrete decision making. Give an example of each.
11. Describe several causes of capital constraints.

Exercises

1. A non-profit organization dedicated to health care is opening a new hospital near a residential neighborhood. For each of the following, indicate whether the item would be considered an internal benefit or an external benefit. Are the internal benefits related to intrinsic or extrinsic motivations?
   a. Helping people recover from illness
   b. Neighbors feeling more secure, with a hospital close at hand in case of emergency
   c. Revenues collected from health insurance companies
2. The TKTS booth in Times Square in New York City offers cheap theater tickets. To buy there, you must be willing to stand in a long line during the afternoon to get tickets for that same evening.

a. If it costs a theater an average of $80 per patron to put on a play, why would the theater ever offer to sell tickets for only $50?

b. If the producers of this play offer $50 tickets at the TKTS booth, why don't they also offer them in advance or on the Web?

3. Suppose a firm that manufactures stereos has the following cost structure:

Quantity of Stereos	Total Cost ($)
0	50
1	100
2	200
3	400
4	800

a. How much does this firm have in fixed cost?

b. Graph the total cost curve for this firm.

c. Suppose that stereos sell for $200 each. Following the example of Table 8.1, create a table showing the total revenue, total cost, and total profit (= revenue − cost) at each level of production.

d. Add to your graph columns showing the marginal revenue (or price) and marginal cost of each level of production.

e. Add a total revenue curve to the graph you created in part (b). Indicate with arrows the approximate quantity at which the vertical distance between the two curves is the greatest.

f. Would the firm make a profit by producing and selling only 1 stereo? Would 1 stereo be the best output level for the firm? What is the output level that maximizes profits?

4. Continuing with the stereo firm described in the previous problem, consider how the firm's decision-making problem will change as the selling price of stereos changes. For each of the following, make a new table.

a. If the price per stereo were $100, what would the profit-maximizing level of output be? How much profit would the firm make?

b. If the price per stereo were $20, what would the profit-maximizing level of output be? How much profit would the firm make?

5. Match each concept in Column A with an example, drawn from your "production" of yourself as an educated person, in Column B.

Column A

a. path dependence
b. sunk cost
c. switching cost
d. discrete choice
e. network externality
f. multiple equilibria
g. marginal thinking

Column B

i. the fact that people in your chosen career do well with either a B.A. or a Ph.D. degree, but an M.A. degree adds no value

ii. getting on Instant Messenger, because your study group friends are on it

iii. the fact that the majors now available to you depend on the college you chose

iv. the tuition you paid for this semester

v. comparing the costs and benefits of taking one additional class

vi. deciding on a major

vii. starting work on one major, and then deciding to change and consequently having to take extra classes

Appendix to Chapter 8

A Formal Theory of Producer Behavior with Convexity and Perfect Competition

A1 | The Assumptions

In the appendix to Chapter 7 and in the text of the present chapter, we have discussed a firm producing hair dryers. In the traditional model, the "theory of producer behavior" is built around the image of such idealized firms, assumed to be concerned only with profit maximization, that make their static decisions on the basis of solving convex problems. In this appendix, as in the chapter text, we assume that the firm must take the price of its output as a fixed number, completely outside its control. As will be further discussed in Chapter 11, this reflects an assumption that the firm has absolutely no market power, or, in other words, is in a situation of "perfect competition." In this appendix, we will give a graphical exposition of decisions of this hair dryer producer in more detail.

Table 8.1 gave a comprehensive view of the hair dryer firm's revenues, costs, and profits over the course of a month, on the basis of cost information derived from the appendix to Chapter 7 and, to start with, a constant selling price per hair dryer of $20.

A2 | Profit Maximization

Recall that when the firm's economic problem is characterized by convexity, as is the case here, the firm will maximize profits when it sets marginal revenue (MR) equal to marginal cost ($MR = MC$). Marginal revenue, in this case, is just the market-dictated sales price of hair dryers, so we can restate the guideline as $P = MC$, where P is the output price.

Figure 8.9 takes the cost curves derived in the appendix to Chapter 7 and adds a price curve. This curve, which we have labeled P, is just a horizontal line indicating that

Figure 8.9 Profit Maximization (including average cost curves)
Adding the average cost curves derived in the appendix to Chapter 7 gives more detail to the problem facing the hair dryer producer.

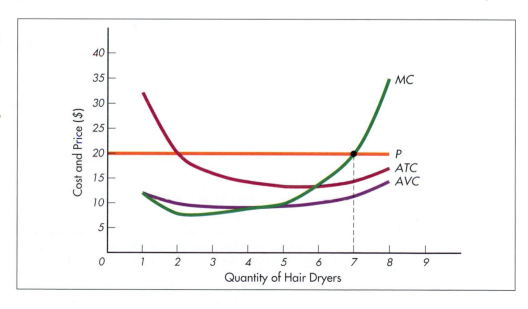

Figure 8.10 The Total Revenue Rectangle

Total revenue, which is equal to price times quantity, is represented in the graph by the area of the rectangle that has a width equal to the quantity produced and a height equal to the market price.

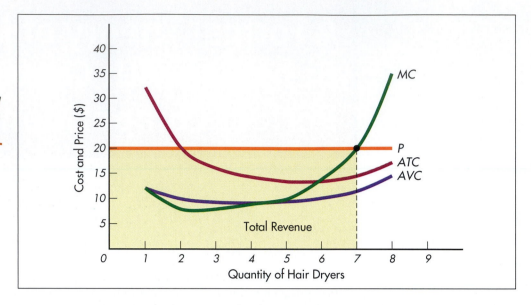

the firm receives $20 for each unit it produces. We can see on the graph that the P curve and the MC curve cross at about 7 units. Approximately 7 hair dryers is therefore the profit-maximizing level of output when the price is $20, as we saw in the chapter.[8]

A3 | Total Revenue, Cost, and Profit as Areas

We can identify areas in these figures that represent total revenue and economic profit. The area of the shaded rectangle in Figure 8.10 represents total revenue. Recall that the area of a rectangle is its length times its width, and note that the length of this rectangle is 7 units and the width is $20. The area represents $140, the total revenue from selling the 7 units. We draw this rectangle by finding the point where the price line intersects the MC curve and then drawing, from that point, a line perpendicular to each axis.

Recall that the area that represents total cost is determined by finding the point on the ATC curve that corresponds to 7 units of output and drawing a rectangle by the same means just described. The blue area in Figure 8.11 has an area equal to $ATC \times 7$, which is just the total cost of producing 7 units. (From Table 7.8, this is $14.43 \times 7 = 101$.)

Economic profit is the area that is left over after we subtract total cost from total revenue. This is represented in Figure 8.11 as the narrow, yellowish rectangle lying above the total cost rectangle. At 7 units of output, the hair dryer firm makes positive economic profit of $39 (as also indicated in Table 8.1).

A4 | Response to Variations in Output Price

We can now also examine how the firm would respond to changes in price for its output. Suppose the cost structure of the firm remained unchanged but the selling price of hair dryers rose to $35 each. The price line would now be horizontal at $35, as shown by P_{high} in Figure 8.12. As discussed in the text, the profit-maximizing level of output at this price is 8 hair dryers.

We can identify two particularly important price levels. The first is the one at which, even following the guidelines for profit maximization, the firm will still just break even. This would be when the total cost and total revenue rectangles exactly overlap, which will happen if

---

[8] As we discussed in footnote 2 above, we say "approximately 7 hair dryers" because marginal analysis is exactly correct only when applied to completely continuous and "smooth" problems. As we can see in Table 8.1, profits are also $39 at 6 units of production. If the slope of the marginal cost curve was allowed to continously change, there might be a level of production *between* 6 and 7 that would take profits even a little higher. In advanced economics courses, the analysis is applied to such "smooth" problems using calculus.

Figure 8.11 Total Revenue, Total Cost, and Profit

The total cost of producing a given number of hair dryers can be found by taking the number of hair dryers times their per-unit cost. In the graph, this is represented by a rectangle with the width of 7 (the number of hair dryers) and the height of the *ATC* curve at a quantity of 7 (the per-unit cost). The difference between the total revenue rectangle and the total cost rectangle represents economic profit.

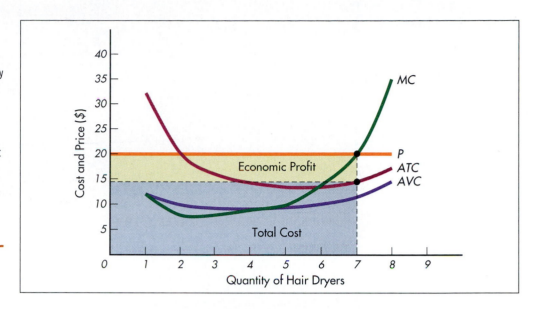

break-even price: the price at which a profit-maximizing firm makes zero economic profits

the price line intersects the *MC* curve just as it crosses the *ATC* curve. This is illustrated in Figure 8.12, by the price line P_B. The firm would produce about 5 or 6 units and would just break even. We can call this the **break-even price** for a profit-maximizing firm.

A second interesting price is the one below which it would be better for the firm to shut down. Recall the guideline that, in the presence of fixed cost, a firm should keep producing as long as its total revenues exceed its total *variable* cost. On the graph, total variable cost would be represented by a rectangle whose upper right corner rests on the *AVC* curve. The line P_S, which intersects *MC* just at the minimum point of the *AVC* curve, represents the shut-down price. The firm would produce 4 units at this price, but at any lower price, it would shut down and produce none.

At prices above P_B, the hair dryer producer will make positive economic profits. At prices between P_S and P_B, the producer will make economic losses but should stay in business because it can cover its variable costs and put some revenue toward paying its fixed costs (such as its factory lease). At prices below P_S, the firm should shut down—the revenue it gets selling each hair dryer wouldn't even cover the variable cost (e.g., materials and labor) of producing that hair dryer. Thus, in the traditional model, the short-run individual supply curve (see Chapter 4) for the profit-maximizing, price-taking firm is the part of the *MC* curve that lies above the *AVC* curve.

▷ The short-run supply curve of the individual price-taking, profit-maximizing firm is the part of the *MC* curve that lies above the *AVC* curve.

Figure 8.12 Quantity Response to Variations in Price

At prices above the point where the *AVC* curve crosses the *MC* curve, the firm should produce. In this range, higher prices induce the firm to supply a greater quantity of output. At prices above the point where the *ATC* curve crosses the *MC* curve, the firm makes positive economic profits. At prices below the point where the *AVC* curve crosses the *MC* curve, the firm should shut down.

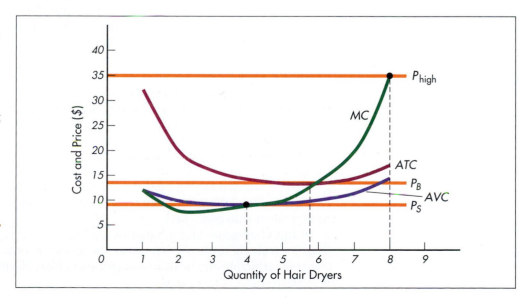

Distribution: Exchange and Transfer

Chapter 9

The top-earning chief executive officer of a U.S. corporation in 2000 was John S. Reed, who was paid $293 million by Citigroup. The richest person on the planet, at the time of this writing, is Bill Gates, founder of Microsoft, who has a net worth of $52.8 billion. The average benefit paid by the U.S. social security program in 2000 was $767 per month, or $9204 per year. In the United States, manufacturing firms pay an average of $19.86 in average hourly compensation to production workers. In Korea such firms pay an average of $8.33 per hour, and in Mexico the figure is $2.46 per hour.

1 | Who Gets What, and How?

In previous chapters, we discussed economic goals, economic actors, and the economic activities concerned with resource maintenance and production. The third essential economic activity is distribution, the sharing of products among people. In this chapter, we will consider the processes by which resources and produced goods and services come ultimately to be owned and/or used by various individuals and groups within local economies and around the world.

At first glance, the answer to questions about distribution may seem obvious: "Most people get what they can buy with what they earn." It is true that, for many adults, purchasing from wage income, and perhaps interest or other earnings on financial assets, is the primary way of acquiring things. How did you get what you needed, however, when you were 5 years old? How will you get what you need if you become critically ill, or when you are 80 years old? What happens to the part of your paycheck taken out by the government? What happens to the accumulated wealth of rich people when they die? How does a non-profit organization survive if it doesn't sell any products? What determines distribution across countries? How do power and conflict affect who gets what?

In this chapter we take a broad sweep, from the sorts of distribution systems that affect individuals to those that affect the global economy. We will see that certain economic principles are helpful in thinking intelligently about distribution activities at all levels of social organization.

Figure 9.1 Examples of Exchange Relations
In exchange relations, flows move in both directions.

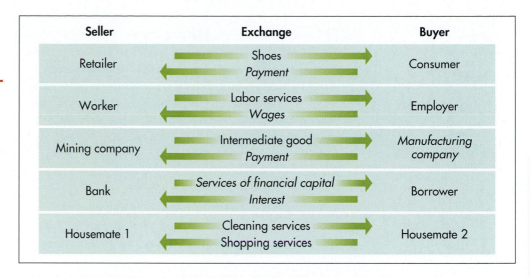

1.1 | Exchange and Transfer

Exchange in markets is one form of distribution—and one that we examine at great length in parts of this text. In exchange transactions, two actors come to an agreement to trade with each other on mutually agreed-upon terms. Something is delivered, and something is expected in return, in a *quid pro quo* ("something for something") relation.

In markets, exchanges typically involve a flow of goods or services, or of ownership rights to assets, from seller to buyer, in return for a monetary payment. The seller might be a shoe retailer, for example, and the buyer a consumer, as illustrated in Figure 9.1. Or the "seller" might be a worker, and the "buyer" of the worker's services an employer. Figure 9.1 lists other examples of market exchange, including relations between businesses and relations that involve financial institutions. In this list, monetary flows are printed in italics.

Presumably, when people *voluntarily* enter into an exchange, they believe that the value of what they are getting is at least as great as the value of what they are giving. Exchanges can also take place outside of markets. For example, within households people often make implicit trades, as when one person agrees to do the cleaning *if* the other person shops. The last example in Figure 9.1 shows an exchange that might be negotiated by someone who wants to "buy" cleaning services through **barter** (nonmonetary exchange).

Distribution by means of one-way transfer, however, also has a very significant role to play in explaining distribution in contemporary economies. Transfers are flows of money, assets, goods, or services for which nothing specific is expected in return—or at least nothing specific at the current time. Examples of transfers are listed in Figure 9.2

barter: exchange of goods, services, or assets directly for other goods, services, or assets, without the use of money

Figure 9.2 Examples of Transfer Relations
In transfer relations, flows move in only one direction.

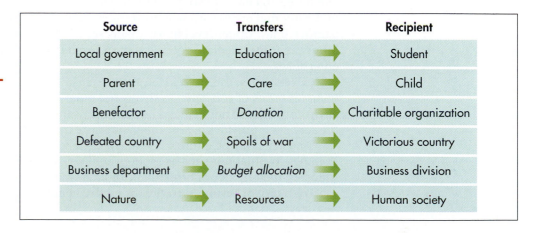

ECONOMICS in the Real World

Are Taxes "Exchange" or "Transfer"?

The case of taxation offers an interesting case for thinking about exchange and transfer. When you pay income taxes to a government, are you "paying" for services you receive or just "giving" over some of your resources? In a sense, you are doing both.

As a member of society, you benefit from roads, police and fire protection, national security, environmental protection, social insurance, educational services, and many other programs run by governments. In this sense, the taxes you pay are in exchange for the services you receive.

On the other hand, your choice about what services you will get is rather limited, and the amount of taxes you pay may not be in proportion to the services you receive. In a democracy, compromises mean that virtually everyone will be more pleased with some government priorities than with others. Your taxes will help pay for roads and schools, even if you have no car and no children, and for the military, even if you disagree with how it is run. In this sense, your taxes also share something of the nature of a one-way transfer.

Government general taxes, such as income taxes, are distinct from government-imposed *user fees,* such as tolls collected at bridges and the landing fees charged to airlines by municipal airports. User fees are clearly part of a *quid pro quo* exchange, where users pay for specific services that governments produce. Certain specific taxes also have something of the nature of user fees. Revenues from gasoline taxes, for example, are often used specifically to fund road maintenance, and revenues from cigarette taxes have at times been designated to fund health care, on the principle that those who buy these products tend also to be users of the corresponding services. You might think of government revenues as lying along a continuum, with user fees at the "exchange" end, general taxes farther toward "transfer," and specific taxes in between.

Sometimes economists use the term *transfers* in a more specific sense, to mean government payments to households, such as social security benefits and welfare. We are using the term in a more general sense, to include all one-way relations.

(monetary flows are in italics). Public education, for example, is provided to all U.S. students through high school. Although there is a general expectation that students should therefore study and become good citizens, there is no clear *quid pro quo*. Students do not have to pay fees or perform specific tasks to qualify for public education.

The goods, services, and hands-on care that children receive from their parents are other examples of transfer, as are bequests that people leave to their descendants. Donations to charitable organizations are also transfers. Transfers are an integral part of the internal organization of businesses and governments that are run along administrative lines. Upper-level departments set the budgets for lower-level divisions, and inputs and intermediate goods are transferred from place to place within productive enterprises.

In a general sense, we also rely on the transfers we receive from the natural environment, in terms of sunshine, fresh air, and other resources. These too are transfers; the environment does not demand anything of us in return. Nor does nature charge us for the services it provides in absorbing our waste materials.

Transfers may be entirely voluntary, or they can involve elements of coercion. For example, in situations such as robbery and war, weaker parties are forced to hand over (transfer) their money or property involuntarily, with nothing given in return.

Voluntary or involuntary, the distinctive characteristic of transfers is that they are one-way.

Some economic transactions may have characteristics of both exchange and transfer. For example, if Maria chooses to work for a struggling social advocacy organization, she may make half the pay she would receive doing the same work for an established business. Thus she is engaging in exchange (working for pay) but also, in part, transferring, or donating, her time to the organization.

The categories of exchange and transfer are useful in thinking about distribution, even if real-world cases don't always fall easily into just one category or the other.

1.2 | Ownership and Distribution in Social and Historical Context

Basic social understandings guide distribution. Understandings about *what* can be owned, *who* can own these things, and the *legal rights* concerning exchange or transfer that come with ownership vary across time and across cultures.

What Can Be Owned? At the most fundamental level, social understandings define what can and what cannot be owned. In the days of slavery, for example, it was considered legitimate for one human being to own another. Slaves themselves had no claims over any property, or even over their own bodies, much less over the goods they helped to produce. Slaveholders had complete ownership rights: They could benefit from the services that the slave's labor provided and could buy, sell, or bequeath slaves and the slaves' children.

We no longer, of course, believe that it is morally acceptable for people to own other people. However, controversies about what can and what cannot be owned continue. Some of the most heated debates about property rights today involve "intellectual property": knowledge, technology, and creative works. Legal systems of patents, copyrights, and trademarks have traditionally been used to allow creators of intellectual property to gain some private economic return from their creations by having the exclusive right to sell them, at least for specified periods of time.

Should information about human genes be subject to private ownership? Should advances in life-saving medicines be private property, even if the patent holder's desire to sell them at high prices means that human lives will be lost? On the one hand, private ownership of intellectual products may encourage innovation. On the other hand, private ownership may overly limit the public's access to the innovation, boosting the profits of a company but detracting from the common good. Economic analysis does not offer clear answers to these questions, but it reminds us to examine and weigh both the advantages and the disadvantages of proposed rules concerning property.

Who Can Own? Social understandings also define *who* is allowed to own things. Until the Married Women's Property Acts of the late 1800s, for example, women in most states in the United States had to give all control of any money they brought into a marriage, whether by inheritance or earnings, to their husband. They were legally entitled to support from their husbands, but whether a husband gave his wife anything above what was necessary for her bare subsistence was entirely up to him. Women could not sign contracts or take out loans on their own account.

Although legal advances in the United States now allow more categories of individuals (including African Americans and women) to own things, the idea of "individual ownership" is less emphasized in other cultures. In some Native American cultures, for example, people "own" important natural resources only cooperatively as clans and as part of an ongoing partnership with nature.

What Rights Come with Ownership? Variations in social understandings about what can be owned, and by whom, have led to complicated legal definitions concerning ownership. For example, an economic actor who has only what is called, in legal terms, a **use right** to a property can use and control the property, but cannot necessarily sell it or give it away.

use right: the right of an owner to use or control a designated property, but not necessarily the right to sell it or give it away

Restrictions on ownership rights are common in cases of intellectual property. When you purchase recordings of songs or movies on physical media, for example, you have purchased the right to enjoy them personally, but not the right to duplicate or distribute them. Restrictions may apply to other kinds of property as well. For example, ownership rights in contemporary China reflect a continuing belief that resources such as land should not be privately owned but should, rather, be held communally. Currently, therefore, foreign investors in China can "buy" land on a use-right basis only, for terms of up to 70 years.

As another example, consider that in the United States, you certainly have "use rights" to your own kidneys. You are also, in the case of kidneys, allowed to donate one to a family member, a friend, or even a total stranger, if you wish. However, because of social beliefs about the proper limits of markets, you are not allowed to *sell* one of your kidneys.

An important function of governments in the public purpose sphere, in all countries and communities, is to define and enforce rights to ownership and to the set of rights that go along with ownership of specific kinds of property. Social understandings about ownership, exchange, and transfer—often expressed in a community's legal codes—set the context for an economy's distribution activities.

Discussion Questions

1. In your own life so far, how big a role has exchange played in giving you what you need to live (that is, to what extent have you received assets, goods, or services *because of something specific you have traded in return*)? How big a role has transfer played? Do you expect this to change in coming years?

2. Should you be allowed to sell one of your kidneys if you want to? Some people argue that this would make more organs available and thus save the lives of people who die while on long waiting lists for transplants. Others believe that making organs salable would lead to poor people being pressured into making decisions that are at odds with basic human dignity. What do you think?

---

2 | Principles of Exchange

In Chapter 1, you learned about the production possibilities frontier, which illustrates how a society might make tradeoffs between the production of two different goods, reaching higher output levels if it efficiently uses its resources. We showed how some points, representing combinations of the two outputs (guns and butter), would be unattainable. But to take our analysis only that far, it turns out, would be misleading.

Points outside a societal production possibilities frontier represent unattainable levels of *production*, for the society on its own. However, they may not reflect unattainable levels of *consumption*. The key to this apparent magic trick is in the benefits that can arise from a system of exchange. Economists like to call these benefits the "gains from trade."

In addition to the economist's picture of the "gains from trade," people often point to other important advantages from a system of exchange, as well as to important disadvantages.

2.1 | Gains from Trade

David Ricardo, in *On the Principles of Political Economy and Taxation* (1817), presented a highly influential explanation of the gains from trade. He used the example of two goods—wine and cloth—and two countries—Portugal and England. Although here we give a simple numerical version of his story, using production possibilities frontiers, the point is more general. The principles might be applied to any pair of economic actors that might both produce and exchange goods or services—two housemates, two companies, or two states, for example.

Figure 9.3 Portugal's Production Possibilities Frontier

Portugal can produce 200 bottles of wine if it specializes in wine, or 100 bolts of cloth if it specializes in cloth. Or it can produce any combination on the line between these two points. It would like to *consume*, however, a larger bundle—represented by point *A*.

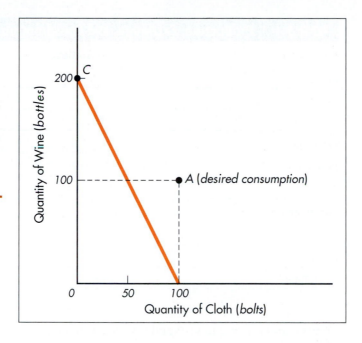

Returning to Ricardo's story, suppose that, given its resources, Portugal can produce a maximum of 200 bottles of wine, if it devotes all its resources to wine, or 100 bolts of cloth, if it devotes all of its resources to cloth. In Figure 9.3, we have, for mathematical simplicity, assumed constant returns, so the production possibilities frontier is just a straight line. Meanwhile, England can produce a maximum of 200 bottles of wine or 400 bolts of cloth, as illustrated in Figure 9.4.

Suppose that the Portuguese would like to be able to consume 100 bottles of wine and 100 bolts of cloth, as represented by point *A*, and the English would like to be able to consume 100 bottles of wine and 300 bolts of cloth, represented by point *B*. As we can see, if each relies only on its own production possibilities, points *A* and *B* are unachievable.

But suppose that Portugal produced only wine and England produced only cloth. This production combination is illustrated in the Production section of Table 9.1 and by

Figure 9.4 England's Production Possibilities Frontier

England can produce 200 bottles of wine if it specializes in wine, or 400 bolts of cloth if it specializes in cloth. Or it can produce any combination on the line between these two points. It would like to *consume*, however, a larger bundle—represented by point *B*.

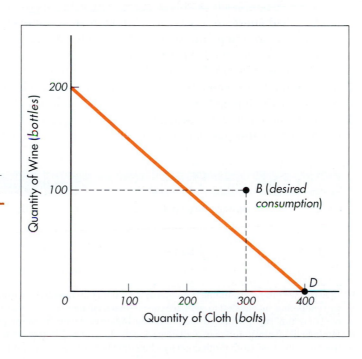

Table 9.1 | Production, Exchange, and Consumption of Wine and Cloth

Production	Wine (bottles)	Cloth (bolts)
Portugal	200	0
England	0	400
Total	**200**	**400**
Exchange		
Portugal	sell 100	buy 100
England	buy 100	sell 100
Consumption		
Portugal	100	100
England	100	300
Total	**200**	**400**

points *C* and *D* in Figures 9.3 and 9.4. Total production would be 200 bottles of wine and 400 bolts of cloth.

Further, suppose that Portugal and England were to agree to *exchange* 100 bottles of Portuguese wine for 100 bolts of English cloth, as listed in the Exchange section of Table 9.1. Now Portugal and England could each *consume* the quantities listed in the Consumption section of Table 9.1. Note that their total consumption does *not* exceed the total amount produced of each good. Yet Portugal would consume at point *A* and England at point *B*—the desired points that they could not each reach on their own!

The "magic" behind this result is that Portugal and England differ in their opportunity costs of production. For every bolt of cloth that Portugal produces, it forgoes production of 2 bottles of wine.[1] For every bolt of cloth England produces, it forgoes production of only half a bottle of wine. We say that England has a **comparative advantage** in cloth production, because cloth costs less in terms of the other good (wine) in England than in Portugal.

comparative advantage: the ability to produce some good or service at a lower opportunity cost than other producers

These examples probably occurred to David Ricardo himself, because in his time, England had energy resources (coal) that made it relatively good at industrial production such as spinning and weaving. Meanwhile, it had a relatively cool and cloudy climate that was not suitable for growing grapes.

Portugal, likewise, has a comparative advantage in production of wine. An additional bottle of wine comes at the cost of half a bolt of cloth when produced in Portugal but requires giving up 2 bolts of cloth when produced in England, as noted in Table 9.2. Portugal has a relatively warm and sunny climate, good for grapes, but in Ricardo's time it did not have the energy resources for industrial production possessed by England.

Table 9.2 | Comparative Advantage

Country	Opportunity Cost of **1** Bolt of Cloth	Opportunity Cost of **1** Bottle of Wine
Portugal	2 bottles of wine	$\frac{1}{2}$ **bolt of cloth**
England	$\frac{1}{2}$ **bottle of wine**	2 bolts of cloth

[1] You can see this by examining the slope of the production possibilities frontier in Figure 9.3. Comparing the two endpoints, moving left to right, we can see that a fall (or negative "rise") of 200 bottles of wine is accompanied by a "run" of +100 bolts of cloth. Because the curve is straight, the slope is therefore −200/100 = −2 throughout. At any point, then, reducing wine production by 2 bottles (that is, a fall or "negative rise" of 2) is needed to increase cloth production by 1 bolt (that is, to create a "run" of 1 unit to the right).

principle of comparative advantage: gains from trade occur when producers specialize in making goods for which their opportunity costs are relatively low

The appendix to this chapter gives a more comprehensive explanation of comparative advantage, but, simply speaking, the **principle of comparative advantage** says that you should *specialize* in what you do (relatively) best. Even if it turns out that one of the countries is more efficient at producing *both* goods, it will still pay that country to specialize. The country with low production costs in all goods should still buy the good that it is *relatively* less efficient at producing from the higher-cost country (see appendix). Only if both countries have the same opportunity costs will there be no possible gains from trade. In Table 9.2 we have used boldface type for the cells that reflect the *low* opportunity costs.

David Ricardo's example was of trade between countries, but the principle of comparative advantage has also been used to show how other economic actors can reap gains from trade. Organizations seek gains from trade when they specialize in some particular area—say, production of training workshops—while contracting with other companies to provide supporting services—say, transportation or advertising design. You may reap gains from trade in your household if, instead of splitting all chores 50/50, you put the person who is relatively more efficient at shopping in charge of shopping and the person who is relatively efficient at cleaning in charge of cleaning.

The mere fact that some companies, or some people, *could* be self-sufficient in producing everything they need doesn't mean that they *should* provide everything for themselves. The story of specialization and gains from trade is a powerful one.

2.2 | Other Advantages of Exchange

Specialization and trade can lead to improvements in economic efficiency, as the "gains from trade" story points out. Trade allowed Portugal and England, in this story, to organize more efficiently their use of resources for producing wine and cloth. The result was a more highly valued level and combination of outputs than the countries could have achieved through self-sufficiency. Many commentators also point to additional advantages of systems based on exchange.

Incentives. Exchange relations give economic actors clear incentives to be productive: Because these relations are *quid pro quo*, in order to get something, you must have something to give! Unless you happen to be sitting on a pile of wealth, this means that you have to do or make something that other people value before you can participate in exchange. If you see something you want, and exchange is the only way to get it, exchange relations provide a strong extrinsic motivation to participate in productive activities.

In particular, *decentralized* exchange through markets is thought to have advantages, in terms of incentives, that lead to efficiency even in the case of changing conditions. In decentralized market exchange, individual actors make agreements to trade at a particular moment in time or for some span of time specified by a contract. When that particular trade is completed, each partner can choose to try to continue this trading relationship or can look for new ones.

Suppose that after trading with England for some time, Portugal discovered that it could get more cloth (or other valuable goods) by growing table grapes for Germany than by producing wine for England. In a system of decentralized, or "free market," unregulated exchange, it could freely move resources into producing the more highly valued product.

A system of market exchange gives producers incentives to produce those goods that command the highest market value.

Noncoercion. In addition to its offering "gains from trade" and efficiency-enhancing incentives, many economists also feel that exchange is a morally praiseworthy form of distribution because of its *noncoercive* nature. People enter into exchanges *voluntarily*. As we noted in Chapter 1, freedom is among the final goals you might hope for in an economic system. Presumably, if what you are offered in exchange does not meet your idea of what you think your item is worth, you can refuse to make the trade.

The noncoercive nature of exchange is often contrasted with forms of transfer that include elements of coercion backed up by force. Robbery is a blatant form of coercive

Some argue that the principle of comparative advantage accounts for why certain kinds of labor-intensive manual work, such as clothing and semiconductor assembly, now rarely take place in high-income nations. Lower-income countries with relatively large pools of people willing to work at low wages, it is argued, have a comparative advantage in such work. Around 2003 this story took a new spin, as high-speed telecommunications connections allowed firms in the United States to also tap into India's pool of educated, English-speaking young people. Indian computer programmers as well as these employees of a call center in Bangalore work for lower wages than their U.S. counterparts.

▷ The potential advantages of exchange as a form of distribution include efficiency, efficiency-enhancing incentives, noncoercion, and the creation of common interests.

transfer, but even the mandatory payment of taxes is implicitly enforced by threats of fines or jail. The noncoercive nature of exchange is most often highly praised by economists with a conservative or libertarian political bent.

Creation of Common Interests. Finally, some economists argue that exchange relations encourage economic actors to think in terms of their common interests. Rather than each actor watching out for just himself or herself or close kin, exchange relations bind actors together in a sort of cooperative venture. Classical economists, such as David Ricardo and Adam Smith, often argued along these lines. Indeed, writers of that era often waxed eloquent on the moral and community-building advantages they saw in a system of exchange. A 17th-century business textbook, for example, claimed that

> [Divine Providence] has not willed for everything that is needed for life to be found in the same spot. It has dispersed its gifts so that men [*sic*] would trade together and so that the mutual need which they have to help one another would establish ties of friendship among them. This continuous exchange of all the comforts of life constitutes commerce and this commerce makes for all the gentleness of life. . . ."[2]

If England and Portugal came to rely on each other for trade, such thinking goes, they might think twice about engaging in a war with each other. Citizens of any city, such writers argued, would likewise be motivated to act more respectfully to each other when they shared commercial interests.

---

[2] Jacques Savary, *Le Parfait Négociant* (Paris, 1675), quoted in Albert O. Hirschman, *The Passions and the Interests* (Princeton, NJ: Princeton University Press), pp. 59–60.

You can find real-world cases where this appears to be true. The United States, after World War II, for example, acted beneficently toward the decimated countries of Europe. It gave them significant aid for rebuilding their industries and infrastructure though a program called the Marshall Plan. Why? The actual name of the act that created the Marshall Plan was "The Economic Cooperation Act of 1948." U.S. policymakers realized that the U.S. economy would not prosper unless the economies of its major trading partners prospered as well.

In contemporary times, as well, some theorists invoke the image of a market-based "global village," in which countries, linked by economic interdependence, also enter into harmonious mutual understanding and cultural exchange. Advocates of **free trade** argue that increased globalization of economic activity, free of barriers set up by governments, will lead to greater good for all.

free trade: exchange in international markets not regulated or restricted by government actions

2.3 | Problems with Exchange

David Ricardo's simple example of two countries and two goods, however, neglects issues of political, social, and environmental context that can sometimes offset "gains from trade" or eliminate them altogether. Because rational thinking about the role that societies should give to exchange as a mode of distribution requires weighing both benefits and costs, we must also examine the drawbacks of organizing distribution by exchange.

Vulnerability. One obvious potential problem with specialization and exchange is that each party becomes more vulnerable to the actions of its trading partners. Supplies of the things you need, and markets for what you sell, could deteriorate or be cut off at any time. This is as true for individuals and businesses as for nations. If you let your housemate specialize in shopping and cooking, for example, you may find yourself hungry if the exchange relationship suddenly breaks down. Businesses may find themselves unable to obtain needed inputs when the source of the inputs is not under their direct control. If Portugal and England were to go to war, to continue the earlier example, or if Portugal were to find a better buyer, England might find itself temporarily with an excess of cloth and no wine to drink. This may, of course, be a relatively trivial issue for nonessential, and readily replaceable, goods and services.

It is, however, a far more serious issue at the national or international level when the goods in question are resources such as oil, minerals, food, or water, the lack of which would seriously weaken an economy or nation. In the United States, for example, some of the same people who argue for "free trade" in most goods also argue for increased development of domestic petroleum resources, on the grounds that excessive reliance on imports decreases economic self-sufficiency and military preparedness.

It is also a serious issue for countries who rely strongly on sales of one or a very few export goods for much of their national income. In Ethiopia, for example, producing coffee for export is currently the sole, or vastly dominant, source of cash income for about one-quarter of the population. When the price of the export commodity is high in international markets, such national economies do well. When prices weaken—or plummet, as coffee prices did in 1989—economies dependent on single exports are subjected to major crises that are beyond their control. Besides making an economy vulnerable to the whims of its trading partners, widespread monoculture (growing of a single kind of crop) has other risks as well. It can make agricultural economies more susceptible to crises arising from events such as drought or an agricultural pest or disease. In a more diversified economy, some sectors and crops may do well while others are hard hit; in a very specialized agricultural economy, the entire economy may spin into crisis from one adverse event.

▷ The potential disadvantages of exchange as a form of distribution, and of the specialization that often accompanies exchange, include increased vulnerability, locking into disadvantageous production patterns, abuse of power, and the destruction of community.

Thus, although the "gains from trade" diagram is correct as far as it goes, the benefits of specialization and trade must be weighed against their costs. When *diversification* increases national security, economic stability, or ecological diversity, then a decision *not* to rely on trade for certain things may be better than pure specialization.

Lock-in. We discussed problems of increasing returns, lock-in, and network externalities when discussing production decisions in Chapter 8. As we saw, some production processes are characterized by increasing returns: The more you do, the more efficient you get. In dynamic economic systems, patterns of comparative advantage can change over time as a consequence of learning by doing.

To draw a personal analogy, it may have seemed more efficient for you, back in your early schooling when you were first doing simple arithmetic problems, to use a calculator. Chances are your teachers told you that you couldn't use a calculator, however. They demanded that you not take the easy (and, in the short run, more efficient) way out of struggling with problems and, instead, build up a base of cognitive skills (for greater long-run efficiency). They didn't want you to become locked into an arithmetic "production technology" that was dependent on the presence of a calculator.

Similarly, an important question for a company deciding which lines of business to enter, or for a country trying to build a healthy national economy, is whether it should engage in some kinds of production that look pretty inefficient now but have the potential to improve with time and growth. Should a country, for example, stay locked into its current pattern of comparative advantage—for example, by importing cars and not even thinking of building a domestic auto industry? Or should it, at least temporarily, restrict automobile imports, while developing its own auto industry past the start-up stage?

The **infant industry** argument claims that sometimes governments should protect domestic industries from foreign competition until they become able to compete on world markets. Usually the government subsidizes the industry, or puts very high taxes (called **tariffs**) on imports of the good, or limits the quantity of the good that can be imported by imposing **quotas**. These policies, which seek to shelter domestic industries from foreign competition by reducing or eliminating opportunities for international exchange relations, are called **protectionist**. Many industrializing countries have engaged in such **import substitution** policies in attempts to diversify their (earlier, often agriculture- or mining-based) economies.

The down side is that current potential "gains from trade" are sacrificed. The up side is that, over the long run, the country might be able to increase its national productivity and competitiveness and thus avoid getting locked into a disadvantageous pattern of production and trade.

Whether the gains from protectionist policies outweigh their costs is a matter of dispute. Many analysts point to long-term government protection of persistently high-cost production in India and some countries in Latin America as evidence that, once started, infant-industry policies tend to serve political special interests, rather than the interests of rational economic development.

On the other hand, many economic historians point out that, into the early 20th century, industries in France, Germany, the United Kingdom, and the United States all developed behind stiff tariff protection. These early industrializing countries bought raw materials from colonized or previously colonized areas, while refusing to open their markets to imports of many manufactured goods. Japan, Taiwan, and South Korea are more recent examples of countries in which some varieties of protectionist policies were important in the history of their industrial development.

Coercion and Power Differentials. Our simple story of England and Portugal ignored the real-world political context of exchange relations. Some element of voluntariness is always present in exchange, but real-world exchange relations are also heavily influenced by the relative power of the parties involved.

For example, we described England and Portugal as exchanging 100 bottles of wine for 100 bolts of cloth—a 1:1 ratio. But what if England were more powerful and could demand different terms, more in its own favor? England might have such a power advantage if it were the only seller of cloth or the only buyer of wine (we will discuss such "market power" in Chapter 12), or through its military might, or through controlling important financial institutions or access to technology. Whatever the source of its power, suppose

---

infant industry: an industry that is relatively new to its region or country

tariffs: taxes put on imports

quotas: restrictions put on the quantities of good that can be imported

protectionist policies: the use of tariffs and quotas to protect domestic industries from foreign competition

import substitution policies: policies undertaken by governments seeking to reduce reliance on imports and encourage domestic industry. These often include the use of industry subsidies as well as protectionist policies.

England were to demand that Portugal give it 100 bottles of wine in exchange for *only 60* bolts of cloth, or the deal was off. Production, exchange, and consumption under this deal would be as described in Table 9.3. England would end up consuming more, and Portugal consuming less, than in the consumption outcome described earlier.

Would Portugal *voluntarily* accept such an exchange? Looking back at Figure 9.3, you can see that a consumption pattern of 100 bottles of wine and 60 bolts of cloth is still outside of Portugal's own production possibilities frontier. Thus Portugal might, indeed, still find it advantageous to trade rather than go it alone. (Note that if England offered only 50 bolts of cloth or less, Portugal would not trade, because it could do at least as well on its own.)

England does not need to coerce Portugal directly into trading: Portugal's trade is still voluntary. But if England has more power than Portugal, it can force Portugal to accept terms of trade that favor England. Similarly, if Portugal were the country with more power, it might be able to enforce terms of trade in *its* favor (say, 100 bottles of wine for 150, rather than 100, bolts of cloth). Similarly, if you and your housemate engage in specialization and exchange of your services, a variety of equitable and inequitable distributions of tasks are possible, based on your relative bargaining power. (This will be discussed further in Chapter 15.) Just because an exchange is *voluntary* doesn't mean that it is fair or that differences in power are irrelevant.

Similar struggles for power go on *within* countries that are considering engaging in world trade. Countries in the real world are not simple, unitary decision makers but rather are made up of diverse citizens, workers, companies, and so on. Although importing wine may be to the advantage of England as a whole, in the sense shown in our graphs and charts, it would probably be disastrous for *part* of England—namely England's (few) previous wine producers, who would lose their livelihood.

A concern for human well-being, rather than just for efficiency per se, demands that such distributional considerations be taken into account. When a major industry is threatened by increased trade, the ill effects on certain people and regions can be deep and prolonged. For example, Detroit, formerly a bustling industrial city, became depressed—part of the U.S. "rust belt"—as auto manufacturing moved increasingly overseas. In parts of Africa during the late 20th century, increases in export agriculture, run largely by men, caused hardships for those engaged in subsistence agriculture, primarily women and children. It may be that efficiency gains for the country as a whole outweigh local losses. But the local losses, and the costs of redistribution policies designed to alleviate hardship and move people to new occupations, must be properly weighed when the benefits and costs of entering exchange relationships are considered.

Table 9.3	A Different Outcome of Exchange and Consumption	
Production	**Wine (bottles)**	**Cloth (bolts)**
Portugal	200	0
England	0	400
Total	**200**	**400**
Exchange		
Portugal	sell 100	*buy 60*
England	buy 100	*sell 60*
Consumption		
Portugal	100	*60*
England	100	*340*
Total	**200**	**400**

Destruction of Community. Exchange relations do not invariably increase social respect and cohesion, or prevent war, or aid in the recovery from war. Examples of the opposite effects can also be found.

Although the notion of citizenship in a nation-state long played a fundamental part in defining community identity for much of the world, current tensions between government and corporate interests are causing much controversy. In Ricardo's time it was natural to think about global trade in terms of the actions and policies of countries such as England and Portugal, but in the 21st century, discussing trade in terms of Microsoft and DaimlerChrysler might be at least as appropriate and meaningful. Business companies have grown ever larger and have become able to move their financial capital and their physical production facilities across international boundaries with increasing ease.

This leads to a dilemma for governments. Traditionally, democratic governments have been able to enact policies perceived to be in the public good, even though they are not always in the perceived self-interest of business actors. Minimum standards for pay and safety on the job, for example, as well as environmental standards and taxation to support public projects, are widely considered necessary for a healthy, just society. Yet such policies are often opposed by some in the business sphere, because they may increase costs and decrease profits.

With capital increasingly mobile, businesses exclusively concerned with profits are able to move their operations to countries with lower labor and environmental standards and taxes. Countries that want to hold onto their business base may therefore find themselves drawn into a "race to the bottom," in which they compete to attract businesses on the basis of their national *lack* of attention to social and environmental concerns. Powerful corporations can also attempt to influence international organizations and agreements directly. These issues began receiving more public attention in the United States after the 1999 "anti-globalization" demonstrations at the Seattle meetings of the World Trade Organization. The ability of peoples to make democratic decisions about the direction of their societies is threatened when the power of democratic governments is overshadowed by the power of nondemocratic economic interests.

Neither does commerce necessarily add to world peace. To give some dramatic recent examples, it is unlikely that the Gulf War of 1990–1991 would have occurred if the countries of the Persian Gulf had not been important suppliers of petroleum to the United States. While the U.S.-led attack on Iraq in 2003 was explicitly justified by security concerns (that is, by the search for "weapons of mass destruction"), the administration also cited the special "national interest" that the United States has in this oil-exporting region in justifying intervention. The relations created by trade in oil have not always been peaceable ones.

Possible negative effects of exchange on social life are also reflected in the fact that, as we have noted, most societies have decided that certain items, such as kidneys, votes, and babies, should never be a part of exchange relations. "Commodifying" such things, by treating them as though they were on a par with shoelaces or cars, is thought to destroy the bonds of respect necessary for social life. Exchange relations also do not take appropriate account of social and environmental externalities, as discussed in Chapter 1.

2.4 | Summing Up

When is exchange a good way to organize distribution, and when is it harmful? We have seen that exchange relations carry the potential for increasing human well-being, when compared to states of individual self-sufficiency, through incentives toward creating the highest (market) value of production and the encouragement of relatively peaceful economic relationships. However, they also carry the potential for decreasing human well-being, by reducing local self-control and creating incentives for the abuse of economic and coercive power. An economic analysis, then, cannot proclaim any system of distribution to be "good" or "bad" without carefully considering the context. A solid economic way of thinking reminds us to take both benefits and costs into account, in every case.

Discussion Questions

1. Think of a recent situation in which you bought something that you could, if you had wanted to, have produced for yourself (a restaurant meal you could have cooked, a bus ride when you could have walked, or the like). Do any of the advantages of exchange discussed above apply to your case? What about the disadvantages?

2. Debates between advocates of "free trade" and advocates of "protectionism" have gone on for hundreds of years. What is your own level of awareness about current debates, which are now often framed in terms of pro- and anti-"globalization"? Do you feel more sympathy for one side than for the other? Are there some things you believe you would need to know more about—in terms of theories and/or real-world facts—to be able to decide with confidence whether increased world trade, in a specific situation, would be a good idea?

3 | Principles of Transfer

▶ The potential advantages of transfer as a form of distribution include efficiency gains in some areas, satisfaction of needs and fairness, and the creation of social bonds.

Exchange plays a large and crucial role in economic life, but transfers are likewise important. Consider that, in order for exchange to happen, each party to a trade has to have something to give. However, because humans mature quite slowly compared to other animals, we go through extended periods of infancy and childhood during which our individual capacities for economic production are minimal.

In addition to having something to give, each party also has to be able to receive. When someone who owns assets dies, however, it is obvious that nothing can be given to him or her in return for those assets (at least in this world). Yet distribution of the assets left behind must be accomplished somehow.

One-way transfers, then, are also a necessary and vital part of economic life. Just like exchange, organizing distribution by relations of transfer has several noteworthy advantages and disadvantages.

3.1 | Gains from Transfer

We have seen that not all distribution can be, or should be, organized by relations of exchange. What are some advantages of using transfers?

Efficiency. In some cases, systems of transfer lead to increases in efficiency over what could be achieved using only exchange. Transfers can be employed to promote the best use of economic resources without waste or unnecessary expense.

In Chapter 1, for example, we discussed public goods. Public goods, such as national defense and environmental protection, cannot be provided through exchange transactions because of the problem of "free riders." Many individuals would like to be able to *get* the good (recall that individuals cannot be excluded from enjoying a public good), without having to *give up* anything in exchange. Public goods *can* be provided, however, as general transfers to the population as a whole, financed by general taxes. When public goods furnish the necessary support and infrastructure for a well-functioning economy, efficiency at the societal level is increased by the use of non–*quid pro quo* relations.

Sometimes, even if a good is not strictly a public good, transaction costs or problems in capital markets make a transfer system more efficient than a system of exchange. For example, it might conceivably be possible for governments (or private companies) to provide residential streets on a strict fee-for-service basis. They could set up toll booths at every street corner, so that only the people who actually used a particular block of a particular street on a particular day would have to pay for its construction and maintenance. However, the costs of gathering such tolls would, at least with present technology, be prohibitive. Levying taxes—general ones, or perhaps specific ones on residential property or gasoline—are a more efficient solution.

One of the reasons why education is commonly financed in part by transfers, including scholarships, grants, and subsidized or guaranteed loans, is imperfections

Urban public parks and playgrounds allow people to enjoy open space and recreational activities without paying a *quid pro quo* fee. These children in Vancouver, British Columbia, are thus the beneficiaries of a transfer from the city government. Such playgrounds are not "public goods" in a strict sense, insofar as they could conceivably be fenced in with access limited to those willing to pay a fee. However, since the late 1800s urban playgrounds have commonly been publicly provided in cities of North America. Reformers initiated this practice, believing that easy access to safe recreational facilities was important for the health and development of poor children who would otherwise lack places to play other than the streets.

in capital markets. As discussed in Chapter 8, if capital markets were "perfect," then all profitable ventures—including investing in an education—could be financed privately. Knowing that you would make plenty of money in the future as a brain surgeon, you could, if markets were "perfect," find private banks willing to finance your full college and medical school education, no matter how poor you were when you entered college. Such private, unsubsidized loans are a form of exchange: The bank would give you the money now, in exchange for your promise to pay it back in the future, with interest. In the real world, no bank will take on this risk. Transfers—from taxpayers, alumni, and other groups, in the form of grants and loan guarantees—are necessary to enable many students to invest in such productivity- and efficiency-enhancing educational activities.

General taxes have something of the nature of a mandatory transfer, because the authority that enforces the payment of taxes (with the threat of fines or jail) has power over the actor who has to give something up. On the other hand, voluntary transfers tend to give the *donor* a certain degree of power over the *recipient*, because the donor can decide what form a transfer should take and whether it will be given at all. This power relation can have efficiency-enhancing effects, at least from the point of view of the donor. Transfers can be used to support, and/or create incentives for, certain kinds of behavior on the part of recipients.

Your spouse or parents, for example, probably feel they are enhancing your long-term productivity and well-being if they are helping pay for your education. They may be much less willing to give you cash to use however you want, if they think you will use it for a party or a fast car. Economists call transfers of specific goods or services **in-kind transfers**, as contrasted to cash transfers, which simply deliver money.

in-kind transfers: transfers of goods or services

Donors use transfers to try to increase efficiency in other contexts, as well. Social service agencies in the government and non-profit sphere often supply their clients with in-kind benefits, such as apartments and medical care, rather than cash transfers. Especially if their clients have impaired judgment as a consequence of substance abuse or mental incapacity, in-kind transfers are thought to be more efficient than cash (which may be misspent) in promoting actual client welfare.

International agencies often attach "strings" to their transfers to impoverished or indebted countries, trying to give their nation clients incentives to change their behavior. The International Monetary Fund (IMF) and the World Bank, for example, are international organizations that make loans and give other aid to countries in economic distress. The economic theories used by these agencies have tended to stress small governments and "free trade" as necessary conditions for economic growth. Hence the organizations have required that many countries adopt structural adjustment policies (SAPs) as a condition of receiving loans or other aid. The SAPs instruct governments to take steps such as reducing social welfare spending and abandoning import-substitution policies. Decision makers at these organizations believe these policies will lead to more efficient national economies, though a number of other economists disagree.

Satisfaction of Needs; Fairness.

Satisfaction of Needs; Fairness. The list of possible final goals presented in Chapter 1 included the satisfaction of basic physical needs, and fairness.

Our individual basic needs during some spans of our lifetimes—as infants and children, or when incapacitated by age or illness—cannot be satisfied through exchange, because we have little or nothing to give at those times. During childhood, we have no choice but to rely on others—grown-ups in our families and communities—to transfer to us the care, shelter, and food that we need to survive and flourish. Economists at the U.S. Department of Agriculture estimate that parents in a middle-income, two-parent household will spend $160,140 (or $237,000 when adjust for expected inflation) to raise a child born in 1999 to age 18. We may rely on such transfers again later in life if we become incapacitated by injury, ill health, or old age. Simply by being human, people inevitably have **dependency needs**. Historically, it was primarily women who were put in charge of providing the direct, hands-on components of transfers to children, the sick, and the elderly.

Individuals might be able to avoid relying on cash transfers late in life, of course, if they have put away enough of their own income for retirement or a "rainy day." Given uncertainty about the future, however, few people actually tend to save enough entirely on their own. Dealing with problems of dependency later in life can be aided by public or private systems of insurance or pensions. In such programs, people agree to contribute to these systems while working, in order to have the right to draw transfers from the systems if, later on, they meet with an accident, fall on hard times, or live longer than they expected.

Similarly, people in cities that have suffered earthquakes, or in countries languishing in drought-induced famine or ravaged by war, often find that their survival depends on transfers from elsewhere. Whether accomplished within families, communities, or nations or on an international scale, freely given transfers, with no thought of specific returns from the recipient, are often indispensable for the support of human life.

Transfer systems can be designed to enhance fairness. Often, when it comes time to fund a public project, decisions are based at least partly on the **ability to pay** of various actors in the economy, rather than entirely on exactly what each receives. For example, both poorer and richer children might benefit equally from a public school in a town. If schooling were provided purely on an exchange basis, the students would all be required to pay the same tuition. More often, however, such expenditures are financed by a percentage tax on property or income so that richer households, who have more ability to pay, shoulder more of the cost.

Transfers can also go farther and be used to even out perceived inequities that result from distribution by exchange. Although people have different ideas about what

dependency needs: the needs to have others provide one with care, shelter, food, and the like when one is unable to provide these for oneself

ability-to-pay principle: the idea that the more resources you have, the more you should be required to contribute to public projects is fair or equitable, as will be discussed below, transfers can be used to redistribute money or goods from those who have a lot to those who are believed to have unfairly gotten too little. Government systems of income taxation and income support may (or may not) be designed to be redistributive. The countries of Scandinavia lead the world in redistributive policies, combining high tax rates on affluent households with generous income support and social programs for the less affluent.

Creation of Social Bonds. Harmony in social life arises not just because people need the goods or services supplied by others but also because people develop direct ties of trust, respect, and gratitude. Transfers can play a very important role in creating social capital.

Gift giving can help deepen good relations in families and friendships, as well as on larger and even international scales. Many corporations are aware of the goodwill they can generate by donating to local philanthropies. Many of the older residents of the German city of Berlin think of Americans with gratitude to this day because of the vital supplies airlifted in by the United States when the city was blockaded by the Soviet Union during 1948–1949. Knowing that people in your family or community will support you in rough times, as you support them in their time of need, creates feelings of security and satisfaction that can't be bought on any market.

3.2 | Problems with Transfer

Systems of transfer, of course, also have drawbacks.

Inefficiency. Relations of transfer can create inefficiency as well as efficiency. Transfers, just like payments in a market, create systems of incentives. Faced with incentives, economic actors may adjust their behavior.

One of the primary problems noted with systems of transfer is that people may become less hard-working, less careful, or less responsible when they know there is a familial or social "safety net" ready to catch them if they fall. Economists use the term **moral hazard** to describe situations in which people have an incentive to change their behavior in undesirable ways to take advantage of an agreement or a policy.

moral hazard: a situation that encourages actors to change their behavior in undesirable ways in order to take advantage of a policy

For example, high payments for welfare or disability programs may encourage people to claim they are unable to do paid work, even when they could. Poor countries may become dependent on food aid for too long after a famine, neglecting the development of their own agricultural sector. Insurance for theft may make people more careless about locking their car doors. The expectation of financial aid from colleges may cause parents to save less for their children's education.

Transfer policies may be intended to *help* or *protect* the poor or unlucky, but their very existence may tend to *increase* behavior associated with some kinds of poverty and bad "luck." Because the transfer system reduces the costs to an actor associated with situations such as poverty, injury, or theft, the actor may, upon rational calculation, decide to take fewer steps to avoid these situations. Support for valid dependency needs may, perversely, also encourage unnecessary dependency.

Sometimes moral-hazard effects may be unavoidable, and good decision making just requires balancing this disadvantage against the advantages of a particular transfer system. At other times, transfer policies might be designed with an eye to reducing possible moral-hazard effects. For example, policies could require that a disability be documented by a panel of physicians, international aid could be switched from food to seeds and supplies, and insurance companies could give discounts for the installation of car security systems.

Mandatory transfers, such as income taxes, also change incentives in ways that can decrease overall social efficiency. High tax rates on wages, for example, may cause people to reduce their work effort. In Chapter 11 we will discuss in more detail how, and when, taxation may entail some amount of welfare loss.

▷ The potential disadvantages of transfer as a form of distribution include inefficiency and moral hazard, perpetuation of inequality, and resentment due to coercion.

Perpetuation of Inequality. We often like to believe that success in our society is based on individual merit, but in fact the sort of family situation we start out in tends to matter a lot. In the United States, far more than in a number of other industrialized countries, we have put the primarily responsibility for providing for children on individual parents, and have protected parents' rights to bequeath assets to their offspring.

The kind of family you come from is important, because families in our society are the primary sources of goods and services for children's development. Children in middle-class and richer families tend to receive gifts of care, goods, and services that give them a better chance for a safer life, better health, and better education. Poor families may care just as much about their children, but resources in poor families must necessarily be spread more thinly, requiring hard choices.

Social programs such as Head Start, which provides high-quality early childhood care and education to a limited number of poor children, attempt to alleviate some of the inequality in family transfers. Social patterns such as residential segregation by income, on the other hand, tend to intensify the problem. Economists have studied "neighborhood effects," by which they mean the effect that the sort of environment a child grows up in has on his or her future earnings. Even if a child from a middle-class family and a child from a poor family are equally hard-working later on, the middle-class child has started out with the considerable advantage of higher family transfers and a different set of community resources and social capital.

Transfers in the form of inheritance of monetary wealth or the ownership of assets also tend to increase inequality and decrease the extent to which differences in wealth are based on differences in merit. Even transfers given to philanthropic, non-profit organizations can help to perpetuate inequality. Elite art museums, funded by charitable contributions, for example, may sometimes provide a good that is a "public good" for only a small—and generally wealthy—segment of the population.

Thus, even though we often think of market outcomes as reflecting individual effort, family and community transfers are critically important in creating the "starting line" for the market "race." In a similar way, countries start at very different places in terms of the "transfers" they can receive from the natural environment, and the history of their development. Some countries start out rich in natural resources; others are in resource-poor areas of the world or have had their resources depleted through, for example, intensive mining during their history as colonies.

Resentment. Not all transfers lead to good feelings and community building. Especially when linked to elements of coercion, transfers can create feelings of resentment that can fracture a society.

Resentments may arise on the donors' side. Taxpayers, for example, may resent the fact that some of their money is going to pay for welfare for people whom they perceive to be lazy and unworthy. (In fact, nearly three-quarters of recipients of Temporary Assistance for Needy Families, the main U.S. "welfare" program, are children.)

Resentments may also arise on the recipients' side. You might resent it if your family "treats you like a child," carefully watching how you spend what they give you. Recipients of in-kind aid, or governments forced to implement SAPs, may similarly feel that donors are abusing their power in a controlling and domineering way. Instead of building relationships of harmony and gratitude, such transfer systems may, in the long term, contribute to the breakdown of economic and political relations, and perhaps even to violence.

3.3 | Summing Up

When is transfer a good way to organize distribution, and when is it harmful? We have seen that transfer relations are necessary for cases where people are not, in fact, self-sufficient, or have nothing to offer in exchange, or cannot receive anything in return for their assets. Transfers carry the potential for increasing human well-being by allowing for the efficient provision of certain kinds of goods, providing for basic needs and promoting fairness, and creating community feeling. However, they can also decrease human well-being by changing incentives for the worse, perpetuating inequality, and creating resentment due to coercive use.

A solid economic way of thinking reminds us to take both benefits and costs into account in every context. One of the important activities that professional economists engage in is seeking to quantify the actual, real-world, relative size and importance of the different advantages and disadvantages of transfer that we have identified in theory.

Discussion Questions

1. First, think about how your college education is being financed. How much of the financing are you doing entirely on your own? How much is being contributed by family, college, government, or other sources of transfers? (Recall that most state schools are at least in part subsidized by taxpayers and that most private schools are at least in part subsidized by alumni or other groups.) Second, review the lists of advantages and disadvantages of transfers. Do any of them apply to your case?

2. Think about your own childhood or that of a friend. How were your (or your friend's) dependency needs taken care of? Do you think that "neighborhood effects" influenced your (or your friend's) ambition for education or a career?

4 | Distribution Outcomes in the United States

Where do you stand, in terms of outcomes of the distributional process? Is your family relatively rich? Relatively poor? When we are concerned with human well-being, we need to be concerned with how people get goods and services or the income with which to buy them. This question is more complex than it may first appear, because of the variety of ways in which people come by their means to well-being.

For example, many goods and services are distributed through exchange and transfer, as just discussed. Sometimes, however, people get important goods and services through production for their own use. If you grow your own food in a garden, for example, you are essentially both producing and "distributing" food—to yourself. In economies based on subsistence agriculture, such production for one's own use is an immensely important way of "distributing" economic goods. Even in industrialized countries, many families prefer to produce at least some services (such as child care, cooking, and recreation) for themselves. As we saw in Chapter 1, activities in the core sphere, most of which do not involve money, account for about 30% of total national production.

Although we cannot neglect goods that are self-produced or distributed in-kind, economists have traditionally tended to spend most of their time analyzing the distribution of *money income* and, to a lesser degree, *monetary wealth*. This may be largely because money income is most easily measured. For most of the rest of this chapter, we will discuss the distribution of these within the U.S. economy. Comparisons among national economies will be taken up in the next chapter and in Chapter 18.

4.1 | The Distribution of Money Income

The most commonly used measure of household money income simply adds up a household's pre-tax incomes, from sources including wages and salaries, rent, interest, and profits, and cash transfer payments received from government agencies (such as social security and welfare payments), over the course of a year. Using this definition, the U.S. Bureau of the Census has calculated the household income distribution shown in Table 9.4 for the year 2000.

The table includes data on the share of aggregate income received by each fifth of the population, from poorest to richest, and by the richest 5%. It also includes actual income levels at the upper limits of each fifth (except the last).

Table 9.4	Distribution of U.S. Household Income in 2000	
Group of Households	Share of Aggregate Income (%)	Upper Limit of Each Fifth ($)
Poorest fifth	3.6	17,950
Second fifth	8.9	33,005
Middle fifth	14.8	52,272
Fourth fifth	23.0	81,960
Richest fifth	49.6	not available[3]
Richest 5%	21.9	not available[4]

Source: U.S. Bureau of the Census, *Current Population Reports, Money Income in the United States: 2000*, P60–213, September 2001, appendix table, **http://www.census.gov/prod/2001pubs/p60 – 213.pdf**.

To see what this table means, imagine dividing up U.S. households into five equal-sized groups, with the poorest households all in one group, and the next-poorest in the next group, and so on. The last group to be formed contains the richest one-fifth (or 20%) of households. The highest-income household in the poorest group would, according to Table 9.4, have an income of $17,950. This group, the poorest fifth, received 3.6% of all the household income in the country. The richest fifth, those with incomes above $81,960, received 49.6%—very close to half—of all the income received in the United States.

Suppose we further separate the richest group into two groups: those that have incomes less than $145,526 and those that have incomes higher than this. The group with household income above $145,526 constitutes the richest 5%, or one-twentieth, of the population.

Sometimes the discussion of income groups proceeds in terms of *percentiles* instead of fifths. (Fifths are also called quintiles.) The bottom fifth corresponds to the 20th percentile, because one-fifth equals 20%. The bottom two groups together lead up to the 40th percentile. For example, we could say that the income share "at the 40th percentile" is 3.6% + 8.9%, or 12.5%. The bottom three groups lead up to the 60th percentile, and the bottom four lead up to the 80th percentile. (With the last group, we arrive at 100%.)

The same Bureau of the Census publication also reports data on incomes by race and ethnicity. Instead of giving these figures in terms of fifths of the population, however, it reports the percentages of households in various income classes. For example, overall, 13.4% of U.S. households have incomes of at least $100,000. Looking at households classified as "Asian and Pacific Islander," however, we see that 22.7% of households in this group have incomes in this range. For white non-Hispanic households the figure is 15.2%, whereas 6.1% of black households and 5.8% of Hispanic-origin households have incomes above $100,000.[5]

4.2 | Measuring Inequality

Once the data on households or individuals are arranged in order of income, as in Table 9.4, many different measures of inequality can be constructed. For instance, we could calculate the ratio of the income share of the richest to that of the poorest fifth of the population; in this case we would get 49.0/3.7 = 13.2. That is, the richest fifth has about 13 times the income of the poorest fifth. Or we could calculate the ratio of the level of income at the 80th percentile of the distribution to the level of income at the 20th percentile, or any one of many similar ratios.

---

[3] The upper limit of both the richest fifth and the richest 5%, by definition, is the income of the richest household in the country; data shown here are based on a statistical sample, which does not allow a precise estimate of the country's highest incomes.

[4] The lower limit of the top 5% is $145,526.

[5] P60-213, Table A-1.

Lorenz curve: a line used to portray an income distribution, drawn on a graph with percentiles of households on the horizontal axis and the cumulative percentage of income on the vertical axis

However, each simple ratio is somewhat arbitrary, focusing on some parts of the income distribution while ignoring others. Economists frequently prefer to use a more comprehensive measure that reflects the shape of the entire income distribution. This measure involves one graph and one ratio based on that graph.

The graph used to describe inequality is the **Lorenz curve**—named after the statistician who first developed the technique. A Lorenz curve for household income in the United States, based on the data in Table 9.4, is shown in Figure 9.5. To construct this curve, you first draw the axes, as shown in the figure. The horizontal axis represents households, lined up from left to right in order of increasing income. The vertical axis measures the cumulative percentage of total income received by households up to a given income level.

In our example, the data shown in Table 9.4 are entered into the Lorenz curve in Figure 9.5 as follows. First, point A represents the fact that the lowest 20% of households received 3.6% of total income. Point B indicates that the lowest 40% of households received 3.6% + 8.9% = 12.5% of total income, point C indicates that the lowest 60% of households received 3.6% + 8.9% + 14.8% = 27.3% of total income, point D similarly shows the income of the lowest 80%, and point E shows the income of the lowest 95%. The Lorenz curve must start at the origin, at the lower left corner of the graph (because 0% of households have 0% of the total income) and must end at point F in the upper right corner (because 100% of households have 100% of the total income).

If income were distributed equally among all households, the Lorenz curve would be a straight line connecting the origin and point F (the diagonal line in Figure 9.5). This line thus represents a situation of maximum equality. At the other extreme, if one household received all the income, the Lorenz curve would hug the horizontal axis until all but the very last household was accounted for and then shoot up to point F, creating a vertical line at the right-hand side. Such a line would represent a situation of maximum inequality.

In all real situations, Lorenz curves for distributions of income will fall between these extremes. Graphically, the curve will sag downward to some extent below the diagonal, as in Figure 9.5. The more the curve sags, the greater is the extent of inequality in the income distribution. This observation led a statistician by the name of Corrado Gini to introduce a numerical measure of inequality known as the **Gini ratio**, which is defined as the ratio of the area between the Lorenz curve and the diagonal to the total area under the diagonal line.[6] Referring to areas A and B in Figure 9.6, the Gini ratio is

Gini ratio: a measure of inequality, based on the Lorenz curve, that goes from 0 (perfect equality) up to 1 (complete inequality)

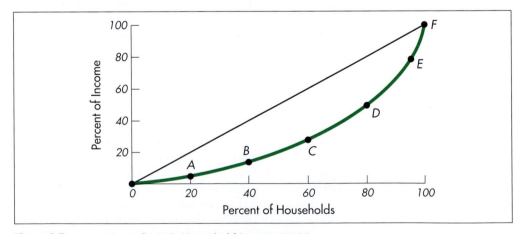

Figure 9.5 Lorenz Curve for U.S. Household Income, 2000
A Lorenz curve is a way of graphically portraying an income distribution. For example, point C indicates that the poorest 60% of households received about 27% of total household income. If income were perfectly equally distributed, the Lorenz curve would be a straight line from point A to point F.

---

[6] Sometimes this is called the Gini coefficient.

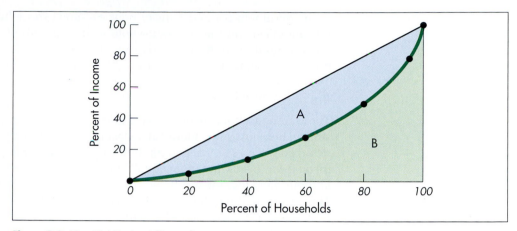

Figure 9.6 The Gini Ratio, $A/(A + B)$
The Gini ratio (or Gini coefficient) sums up the income distribution in a single number: the ratio of the area A to the sum of the areas A and B. If income were perfectly equally distributed, the Gini ratio would be equal to 0.

$A/(A + B)$. Clearly, the Gini ratio can vary from 0 for perfect equality to 1 for complete inequality. The Gini ratio for U.S. household income in 2000 was 0.460.

The Gini ratio for the United States is higher than that of all other industrialized countries, signifying that the United States has a greater degree of income inequality. The Gini for Canada, for example, is about 0.32, while the United Kingdom has a Gini of 0.36, Germany of about 0.30, and Japan and Sweden each of about 0.25. Countries with more unequal distributions of income than the United States tend to be less industrialized countries, such as Brazil (0.59) and Nigeria (0.51).[7]

4.3 | Varying the Definition of Income

Perhaps, you might object, something is wrong with the measure of income we are using. Higher-income people, after all, pay more taxes, so they really don't have control over all the money income they have been counted as receiving. Meanwhile, poor people may qualify for noncash programs such as food stamps, or for subsidized housing and medical care, and arguably the value of these should be included.

On the basis of considerations such as these, the U.S. Bureau of the Census has experimented with at least 15 different definitions of personal income. One definition, for example, is meant to approximate more closely what the distribution of income would be, if—hypothetically—it depended only on the activities of businesses and non-profits (and excluded governments). For this definition, the Census Bureau starts with the measure of pre-tax money income we have been working with up to now and subtracts government cash transfers. Then it adds the value of health insurance fringe benefits paid by businesses for their (often middle-class or higher) employees and the value of net capital gains (usually earned by the relatively wealthy). Under this definition, the Gini ratio, not surprisingly, rises to 0.506, showing greater inequality. The share of the bottom fifth drops to 1.1% of income, and the share of the top fifth rises to 55.1%.

Adjusting that measure of income for the effects of the tax system causes some change at the top, but little at the bottom. After taxes, the share of the top fifth falls to 51.2%, while the share of the lowest fifth rises only to 1.4%. When the Census Bureau further adds in the effects of both cash government transfer programs *and noncash* programs (such as food stamps, Medicare, and Medicaid), the distribution becomes somewhat less unequal. According to this last definition, the share of the lowest fifth is 4.6%, the share of the top fifth 46.7%, and the Gini ratio is 0.411.

---

[7] The World Bank, *World Development Indicators*. Data are generally from the 1990s. Because of differences in methods of calculation, the Gini coefficient for the United States in the World Bank data is 0.41.

Government tax and transfer policies—and especially the transfer side—have significant effects on the U.S. household income distribution. Even with the most thorough accounting for transfer aid to low-income households, however, the income of the top fifth of the population is still roughly ten times that of the bottom fifth.

4.4 | Income Inequality over Time

The U.S. household income distribution has been recorded every year since 1967. A similar but not quite identical measure, the family income distribution, has been recorded since 1947. These data show that inequality was gradually decreasing—that is, income was becoming more equally distributed—until 1968. In that year, the Gini ratio for household income was 0.388, the lowest (most equal) on record in the United States The income of the richest fifth of households was 10.7 times the income of the poorest fifth. Since 1968 the Gini ratio—like virtually all other measures of inequality—has increased in nearly every year.

Why has inequality been increasing in the United States for the last 35 years? One point that economists agree on is that some of the increase in inequality has been due to changing demographic characteristics of the U.S. population.

Increases in the proportion of the population that is aged and in the number of single parents have tended to drive down incomes at the low end. Of the households in the lowest income group shown in Table 9.4, about 40% had a householder age 65 or over, and only about 20% contained a married couple. People too old to work and people in single-parent households (where paid work and caring activities compete for a limited resource—the adult's time) often lack economic resources. Although children are only 26% of the U.S. population as a whole, they make up 37% of the U.S. poor. A household is defined as poor if its income falls below a poverty threshold based on its family size. In 2000, the poverty threshold for a family of four was $17,603.

Meanwhile, the entry of women into the labor force in increasing numbers has helped boost the incomes of married-couple households at the top. About 80% of the households in the top fifth include married couples, and about an equal percentage include two or more earners. (Only about 7% of households in the bottom fifth contain two earners.)

Demographic change, however, is only part of the story and cannot explain the whole pattern of increasing inequality. Economists continue to debate the relative importance of at least three other explanations. (Note that all three of these explanations propose reasons why the poor have become poorer or more numerous and that the third one also addresses why the rich have gotten richer.)

First, international trade has been increasing. Competition from imports has eliminated many industrial jobs that formerly fell in the middle of the U.S. income distribution. If middle-income industrial jobs are replaced by lower-income service and retail jobs, inequality will increase.

Second, new technologies such as computers and biotechnology have become more important, increasing the incomes of skilled workers who understand and use the new techniques and equipment, while leaving behind the less-skilled workers who remain in low-technology occupations.

Finally, unions have grown weaker and government policy has become markedly less supportive of unions and low-wage workers, whereas the compensation given to top executives and board members of large corporations has skyrocketed. According to studies done by *Business Week*, in 1980 chief executive officers (CEOs) of large U.S. corporations earned an average of 42 times the amount earned by the average hourly worker. In 1990 they earned 85 times as much, and in 2000 they earned 531 times as much.[8]

---

[8] See Business Week Online, "We're Back to Serfs and Royalty," by Jennifer Gill, April 9, 2001. **http://www.businessweek.com/careers/content/apr2001/ca2001049_100.htm**. In 2000 the average salary of the CEOs at the 365 largest U.S. companies was $13.1 million; the average hourly worker was paid $24,649.

In short, along with demographic change, either trade, technology, or changes in government and business policies—or some combination of these factors—might account for the rise in inequality within the United States.

4.5 | Wealth Inequality

The distribution of wealth—what people own in assets—tends to be much more unequal than the distribution of income—what people receive in the course of a year. Most people own relatively little wealth, relying mainly on labor income and/or government, non-profit, or family transfers to support their expenditures. Those who do own substantial wealth are generally in a position to put much of it into assets that increase in value over time and/or yield a flow of income and dividends—which can in turn be invested in the acquisition of still more assets.

The distribution of wealth is, however, less frequently and less systematically recorded than the distribution of income. One study estimates that the Gini ratio for the distribution of wealth in the United States was 0.83 in 1995—indicating much more inequality than is found in the distribution of income.[9] The same researcher concludes that in 1998, the top 1% of U.S. households owned about 38% of all household assets and the top 10% owned about 71%, whereas the bottom 40% owned only 0.2%.[10]

Ownership of some wealth is usually a very good thing, because it can help households maintain their accustomed consumption patterns, should income temporarily be low. What a number of analysts find most troubling about large disparities in wealth, however, is that great wealth confers both economic and political power on its owners. When the ownership of wealth is highly uneven, the power to direct the operations of businesses and to influence government policy through campaign contributions and the like may become concentrated in the hands of relatively few.

4.6 | Equity as a Goal

Unlike the goal of efficiency, which has a specific technical meaning that we have discussed in earlier chapters, there is no single standard of equity or fairness. Yet to many people there is something disturbing about the current degree of income and wealth inequality in the United States. What are some standards that can be used to judge whether a society has reached a goal of equitable treatment of its citizens?

At least five different standards of equity have been suggested; several of them have strong but indirect implications for the allowable differences in incomes and wealth.

Equality of outcomes is an easily stated—but rarely adopted—standard of equity. We could say that the most equitable society is the one in which the satisfaction that people derive from economic activity is equalized. The idea of everyone being equally happy has a certain appeal, but no country has ever tried to translate this into practice by exactly equalizing wealth or incomes. In all existing economies, at least some degree of inequality of outcomes is thought to serve as an important incentive for people to develop skills, to work, and to innovate. Moving toward strict equality of outcomes might squash these motivations and, to use an old saying, kill the goose that lays the golden egg.

Equality of opportunity is another popular standard. According to this principle, all individuals should have the same opportunity to acquire the things they value. Once given the same opportunities, people who are ambitious and want to work hard to acquire wealth should be able to do so. People who choose not to take as much advantage of these opportunities can accept a lesser economic standing. This standard has the appeal of rewarding effort, while putting everyone on a presumed "level playing field."

---

[9] Edward N. Wolff, "Recent Trends in the Size Distribution of Household Wealth," *Journal of Economic Perspectives* 12 (Summer 1998), 131–150.

[10] Edward N. Wolff, "Recent Trends in Wealth Ownership, 1983–1998," (Working Paper 300, Jerome Levy Economics Institute).

Dozens of Rich Americans Join in Fight to Retain the Estate Tax: Buffett, Soros, and Gates's Father Call It Only Fair

SEATTLE, Feb. 13—Some 120 wealthy Americans, including Warren E. Buffett, George Soros, and the father of William H. Gates, are urging Congress not to repeal taxes on estates and gifts.

President Bush has proposed phasing out those taxes by 2009. But a petition drive being organized here by Mr. Gates's father, William H. Gates Sr., argues that "repealing the estate tax would enrich the heirs of America's millionaires and billionaires while hurting families who struggle to make ends meet."

The billions of dollars in government revenue lost "will inevitably be made up either by increasing taxes on those less able to pay or by cutting Social Security, Medicare, environmental protection and many other government programs so important to our nation's continued well-being," the petition says.

In addition to the loss of government revenue, the petition says, repeal would harm charities, to which many of the affluent make contributions as a way of reducing the size of their estates. . . .

Mr. Buffett, the Omaha investor who ranks fourth on the *Forbes* magazine list of the richest Americans, said in an interview that he had not signed the petition itself because he thought it did not go far enough in defending "the critical role" that he said the estate tax played in promoting economic growth, by helping create a society in which success is based on merit rather than inheritance.

Mr. Buffett said repealing the estate tax "would be a terrible mistake," the equivalent of "choosing the 2020 Olympic team by picking the eldest sons of the gold-medal winners in the 2000 Olympics."

. . . Among those signing [the petition] are Mr. Soros, the billionaire financier; the philanthropist David Rockefeller Jr., former chairman of Rockefeller & Company; Steven C. Rockefeller, chairman of the Rockefeller Brothers Foundation; Agnes Gund, a philanthropist whose family owns stakes in many companies; and Ben Cohen, a founder of Ben & Jerry's.

. . . Estate taxes are assessed on the net worth of an individual at death. There is no tax on the first $675,000, and under current law that exemption is to rise to $1 million by 2006. (Farms and family businesses already enjoy the $1 million exemption.)

But amounts above that threshold are taxed at rates that begin at 37 percent and rise to 55 percent, the rate that applies to anything greater than $3 million. The estates of fewer than 48,000 Americans a year—2 percent of annual deaths—pay the tax. Nearly half the total is paid by the estates of the 4000 people who die each year leaving $5 million or more.

. . . Mr. Bush and congressional Republicans who support the plan say that estate and gift taxes discourage savings and investment. Repeal, they assert, would increase economic growth by rewarding those who build great fortunes and creating incentives for them to invest more. Mr. Bush says his plan would save those now subject to gift and estate taxes $236 billion over the next decade.

(After this article appeared. Congress passed a bill that would phase out and temporarily repeal the estate tax.)

By David Cay Johnston, published on Wednesday, February 14, 2001, in the *New York Times*. Copyright © (2001) by The New York Times Co. Reprinted with permission.

Although a society can try to approach this standard through programs like public education and anti-discrimination law, it is a hard standard to apply in any strict sense. If opportunity is to be equal in each generation, then no material wealth should be passed along by inheritance. Neither should some children be able to start out in safe neighborhoods with parents who encourage them, while others grow up surrounded by crime or indifference. We see that creating equal opportunity for the next generation would mean great changes in this one.

And what does it mean to create "equality of opportunity" if some people are naturally endowed with greater intelligence or talents than others? Should society try to even out the opportunities for everyone to be rewarded for their work? Or should it allow those endowed with more talent to get more economic gain for less work

Dying for a Tax Cut

NEWS in context

What taxpayers got last year was a very s-l-o-w drop in death-tax rates and an increase in exemptions until, in the year 2010, rates abruptly plunge to zero. Then, like Mr. [Freddy] Krueger, the tax will leap from its grave, fully restored to its original voracious rate of 55%. This happens to be one of the highest rates in the world, outdone only by the likes of slow-growth Japan. . . .

The arguments against the death tax are economic but especially moral. It is an unjust double tax on income already taxed, when it was earned. It is a tax that falls especially hard on the families of those who die young—since the passing of each generation means a fresh round of confiscatory levies. It is a tax that during a time of deep private grief empowers the government to muscle in and fill its pockets. The death tax also warps incentives, penalizing those who work hard and save, and diverting energy from genuinely productive uses to tedious, expensive games of tax strategizing.

By the time these perverse incentives play out, and the tax lawyers collect their fees, the death tax doesn't even raise much revenue. It dragged only some $28 billion from taxpayers in 2000, or less than 2% of total federal revenue.

Editorial in the *Wall Street Journal*, April 16, 2002, Eastern Edition.

Debate about how much inheritances should be taxed has gone on for centuries. Some argue that rich people should be able to bequeath their assets to their children tax-free. Others argue that there should be a steep tax on inheritances. What are some of the arguments on both sides? For example, how might the ability to leave a big bequest affect the donor's incentives to work? How might the receipt of a big bequest affect the recipient's incentives to work? What are other advantages and disadvantages of allowing (or limiting) bequests?

effort? What does "equality of opportunity" mean, if we compare our current generation with generations of people who will live in the future? (Should we take conservation of natural resources more seriously, to give them an equal shot? Or should we trust that future technological improvements will make them better off than we are now?)

Equal rewards for equal contributions is a more exchange-based standard. According to this principle, those who contribute the most to an economy should be entitled to receive the most in return. Discrimination should not be allowed among individuals who do the same work, some say, but nondiscriminatory market outcomes, even fairly unequal ones, are acceptable, whether they are due to differences in work effort or innate talents. In support of this view, there is a long-standing belief that people are entitled both to the products of their labor and to the fruits of their property (where property is viewed as the product of past labor).

It is often difficult to determine just how much each individual has contributed to the general welfare, however. Sometimes market rewards seem to go in the opposite direction from productive contributions. On the basis of the *Business Week* survey mentioned earlier, for example, a writer for the magazine concluded, "Overall, the link between CEO pay and company performance remained fuzzy." The examples given included the CEO of Walt Disney Co., who in 2000 received a salary increase, stock options valued at $37.7 million, and a bonus of $11.5 million, even though over the previous three years the net income of the company he led had fallen by more than half.[11]

---

[11] Louis Lavelle, "Executive Pay," *BusinessWeek*, April 16, 2001, **http://www.businessweek.com/magazine/content/01_16/b3728013.htm**, accessed May 5, 2002.

Other contributions, such as those that parents—and, traditionally, most often mothers—make by raising the next generation of workers and citizens, are not rewarded with market incomes at all. Market evaluation cannot be the only means of measuring the value of a contribution. But it is difficult to specify just how contributions *should* be valued and rewarded.

Equal rights are sometimes emphasized as an alternative to focusing on income or wealth. Societies often specify certain goods, services, and constitutional liberties to which each individual should have an equal claim. Modern democracy, for example, usually assumes the principle of "one person, one vote." This means that all eligible citizens must have an equal right to cast a ballot and be represented in the electoral system. Nobel laureate economist Amartya Sen has suggested a rather direct link between democracy and economic outcomes. Famines, where thousands or millions of people in a country die of hunger, Sen points out, tend to occur in dictatorial states (even, sometimes, in the face of plentiful food supplies) and have not arisen in democratic ones, where those in power are accountable to the people.

A rights-based interpretation of equality assumes that equal rights are more fundamental to well-being than a particular level of material goods. There is no agreement, however, on just what these rights should include or on how they should be related to economic issues. Among the things that have been thought to belong to everyone by right, in some (but not all) countries, are free education, free health care, and easy access to information and technology for family planning.

A counterargument to a rights-based approach might point out that rights given in law could sometimes be empty in the presence of other inequities. For example, the right to vote could become nearly meaningless if extreme concentrations of wealth undermined the ability of common people to have any real influence on politics and policy.

Attention to the least fortunate presents a different interpretation of equity. Most recently proposed by the philosopher John Rawls, it also echoes positions traditionally taken by many religions. According to this principle, the success of a society depends not on its members' average, or total, well-being (if such a thing could be calculated) but rather on its treatment of those who are worst off. In this view, it isn't so important what the ratio of incomes of the top and bottom groups is, so long as the dignity and living standards of the people at the bottom—who may be very young, very old, disabled, or mentally ill—are as high as they can be.

This standard suggests a special concern with poverty, which we will take up again in the next chapter when we discuss consumption, living standards, and "capabilities." As a standard of equity, some people find this interpretation flawed, because it says nothing about the fairness of a distribution over the middle and upper ranges.

Which definition of equity should an economist use? There is no simple answer; different people have strongly held political and ethical preferences for one or another concept of equity. It should be clear from our description that in particular situations, the different concepts may have conflicting implications.

Discussion Questions

1. What do you think is the minimal amount of annual income that an individual, or a small family, would need to live in *your* community? (Think about the rent or mortgage on a one- or two-bedroom residence, etc.) What does this probably mean about where the average level of income in your community fits into the U.S. income distribution shown in Table 9.4?

2. What standard(s) of equity appeal to you most? Why? Can you given any reasons, beyond those in the text, why your chosen standard is particularly good? Can you think of any weaknesses beyond those mentioned in the text?

Review Questions

1. What distinguishes the two major forms of distribution from each other?
2. What are three major questions that must be answered by a societal definition of ownership rights?
3. What do economists mean by "gains from trade"?
4. How can a society consume outside its production possibilities frontier?
5. What are four advantages of exchange relations?
6. What are four drawbacks of exchange relations?
7. What are three advantages of transfer relations?
8. What are three drawbacks of transfer relations?
9. State two statistical facts about the distribution of U.S. household income.
10. How is a Lorenz curve constructed?
11. What effect do taxes and transfers have on the distribution of U.S. household income?
12. What has happened to U.S. income inequality over time? What are some reasons for this?
13. How does the distribution of wealth compare with the distribution of income?
14. What are five possible standards for judging the equity of a distribution?

Exercises

1. Which of the following are examples of exchange? Of transfer?
   a. De Beers mining company sells diamonds to wholesalers.
   b. De Beers mining company takes diamonds from the mines.
   c. You pay interest on credit card balances.
   d. Your bank donates posters for a local community fair.

2. Jolly Universal (JU) and Buttercup Paramount (BP) are two companies in different locations; each produces both movies and popcorn. If JU puts all its resources toward movies, it can produce 2 movies, whereas if it puts all its resources toward popcorn production, it can produce 8 tons. BP can produce either 2 movies or 2 tons of popcorn. (Both can also produce any combination on a straight line in between.)
   a. Draw production possibilities frontiers for JU and BP, carefully labeling them.
   b. Suppose customers in JU's market would like 1 movie and 6 tons of popcorn. Can JU produce this?
   c. Suppose customers in BP's market would like 1 movie and 2 tons of popcorn. Can BP produce this?
   d. What is the slope of JU's production possibilities frontier? Fill in the blank: "For each movie that JU makes, it must give up making ____ tons of popcorn."
   e. What is the slope of BP's production possibilities frontier? Fill in the blank: "For each movie that BP makes, it must give up making ____ tons of popcorn."
   f. Which company has a comparative advantage in producing movies?
   g. Create a table like Table 9.1, showing how JU and BP could enter into an exchange relationship in order to meet their customers' desires.
   h. Suppose you are an analyst working for JU. Write a few sentences to the CEO of the company describing what business arrangement JU should make with BP, and why.
   i. Would your advice change if BP insists that 1 movie is worth exactly 4 tons of popcorn?

3. Match each concept in Column A with an example in Column B.

Column A	Column B
a. a benefit of exchange	**i.** creates extrinsic motivations for market production
b. comparative advantage	**ii.** a gift of food
c. diversification	**iii.** meets needs of those with nothing to exchange
d. specialization	**iv.** cattle ranching in Wyoming uses up little farmland, whereas cattle ranching in Minnesota would come at the expense of crops
e. a problem with free trade	
f. a protectionist policy	
g. a problem with protectionism	
h. a benefit of transfer	**v.** some children get much less from their families than others do
i. an in-kind transfer	**vi.** basing an economy on both agriculture and industry
j. a dependency need	**vii.** a tariff on imports
k. moral hazard	**viii.** the need to be cared for when you are sick
l. a problem with transfer	**ix.** taking "sick days" off work, when you aren't sick
	x. may serve political special interests
	xi. creates vulnerability to loss of important imports
	xii. basing an economy on agriculture only

4. Statistics from the government of Thailand describe the household income distribution in that country, for 2000, as follows:

Group of Households	Share of Aggregate Income (%)
Poorest fifth	5.5
Second fifth	8.8
Middle fifth	13.2
Fourth fifth	21.5
Richest fifth	51.0

Source: National Statistics Office Thailand, "Household Socio-Economic Survey," Table 9, http://www.nso.go.th/eng/stat/socio/soctab6.htm.

a. Create a carefully labeled Lorenz curve describing this distribution. (Be precise about the labels on the vertical axis.)

b. Compare this distribution to the distribution in the United States. Would you expect the Gini ratio for Thailand to be much higher or lower or about the same? Why?

Here we explore in more detail the "gains from trade" example given in the text. There, for simplicity, we showed a case where both countries completely specialize, because their level of desired total consumption just happens to match each country's total production level with complete specialization. Graphing a *joint* production possibilities frontier for the two countries enables us to relax this assumption, while also exploring more fully the concepts of opportunity costs and comparative advantage.

Recall that in this example, Portugal can produce a maximum of either 200 bottles of wine or 100 bolts of cloth. Portugal's production possibilities frontier was shown in Figure 9.3. Examining its slope more closely reveals that, moving left to right starting at the (0, 200) point, a fall (or negative "rise") of 200 bottles of wine is accompanied by a "run" of +100 bolts of cloth. Because the curve is straight, the slope is therefore −2 throughout. At any point, then, reducing wine production by 2 bottles (that is, a negative "rise" of 2) is needed to increase cloth production by 1 bolt (that is, to create a "run" of 1 unit to the right).

England can produce a maximum of 200 bottles of wine or 400 bolts of cloth, as was shown in Figure 9.4. The slope of its production possibilities frontier is $-\frac{1}{2}$ (= −200/400). For each additional bolt of cloth, England gives up producing half a bottle of wine.

In Figure 9.7, we create a *joint* production possibilities frontier for the two countries. Suppose they both start out producing only wine. Adding Portugal's 200 bottles to England's 200 bottles, we find that jointly they can produce 400 bottles if they produce no cloth, as shown at the point (0, 400). Now suppose that they would like to consume *some* cloth, and they make a joint decision about where it should be produced. They see that if Portugal produces the first bolt of cloth, it will cost them 2 bottles of wine. If they have England produce the first bolt of cloth, it will cost them only half a bottle of wine. Clearly, they should have England produce it. This kind of reasoning will tell them to have England produce not only the first bolt of cloth but also every succeeding bolt of cloth, as long as possible. Portugal will keep producing only wine, at its maximum level of 200 bottles.

The possibility of exploiting England's relatively low-cost cloth production runs out when these two countries reach point *A*. At point *A*, England produces the maximum amount of cloth it can—400 bolts—and Portugal still produces only wine (200 bottles). This was the point used as an example in the text, for simplicity. Now if they want to continue to have even more cloth (and less wine), they will have to have Portugal produce it. Each extra bolt of cloth will now cost 2 bottles of wine, up to the point (500, 0), where they both produce only cloth.

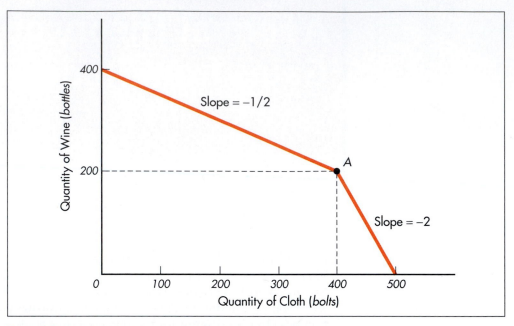

Figure 9.7 A Joint Production Possibilities Frontier

By specializing efficiently, England and Portugal together can produce these combinations of wine and cloth. To the left of point *A*, Portugal produces only wine while England produces wine and some cloth (at an opportunity cost of $\frac{1}{2}$ bottle of wine for each bolt of cloth). At point *A*, England produces only cloth and Portugal only wine. To the right of point *A*, Portugal produces some cloth (at an opportunity cost of 2 bottles of wine for each bolt of cloth).

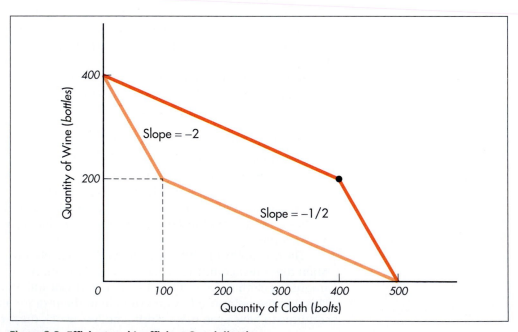

Figure 9.8 Efficient and Inefficient Specialization

If England and Portugal specialized in an inefficient way, the joint production possibilities frontier would bow *in* rather than *out*.

What if, instead, the countries were to follow their comparative *dis*advantages, having Portugal change to cloth production first, and England only after Portugal was producing at capacity? Figure 9.8 contrasts the efficient production possibilities frontier with this case. With inefficient full specialization represented by the kink point where Portugal produces 100 bolts of cloth and England produces 200 bottles of wine, the production possibilities frontier bends *inward*. The bold line is the efficient production possibilities frontier, and the lighter line reflects the most inefficient production choices. As you can see, following the rule of comparative *advantage* leads to a much larger production possibilities frontier than doing the reverse! A similarly inefficient result would follow if you were better at cleaning, and your housemate at shopping, but you tended to shop and your housemate tended to clean.

absolute advantage: the ability to produce some good or service at a lower absolute cost than other producers

Along with the concept of comparative advantage, economists also discuss the concept of absolute advantage. A producer has an **absolute advantage** when, using the same amount of some resource as another producer, it can yet produce more. Usually labor hours are the resource considered. For example, suppose that in a 1-hr time period you can buy enough groceries for 6 days *or* clean 3 rooms. Your housemate, on the other hand, moves more slowly and can buy enough groceries for only 3 days, or clean only 1 room, in an hour. You clearly have an absolute advantage in production of both these services. Does this mean you should do all the work? (See whether you can figure out the answer before looking at the footnote.)[12]

---

[12] No. Comparative, not absolute, advantage should guide the assignment of tasks. Although you have an absolute advantage over your housemate in both activities, your housemate has a *comparative* advantage in shopping. That is, to get enough groceries for 6 days would "cost" only 2 rooms' worth of cleaning if your housemate does it (taking 2 hours). On the other hand, if you shop for 6 days' worth of food, the opportunity cost is more—the 3 rooms you could have cleaned. Therefore, on efficiency grounds at least, your housemate should shop and you should clean. (You can also come to the same result by examining your own comparative advantage—in cleaning.)

Consumption and the Consumer Society

The average U.S. resident, in a year, eats 269 pounds of meat, uses 605 pounds of paper, and consumes energy equivalent to 8 metric tons of oil. Forty years ago, the average American ate 197 pounds of meat, used 366 pounds of paper, and consumed energy equivalent to 5.5 metric tons of oil. In the United States, there is about 1 passenger car for every 2 people. Europeans have about 1 passenger car for every 3.5 people. Developing countries have, on average, about 1 passenger car for every 68 people.[1] What does economics have to tell us about these differences in consumption?

1 | Consumption: Final Use

Consumption is the process by which goods and services are, at last, put to final use by people. Consumption is at the end of the line of economic activities that starts with an evaluation of available resources and proceeds through production of goods and services and distribution of goods and services (or the means to acquire them) among people and groups. At last, the goods and services themselves come to be used. The effect of this consumption, including depletion of resources and generation of waste as well as enhancement of human survival and flourishing, determines the resource base for the next round of economic activity.

1.1 | The "Sovereign" Consumer?

Much of economic discourse, from Adam Smith onward, has assumed that everything we value about the functioning of an economy is to be found in the final demand for goods and services. As Smith said, "Consumption is the sole end and purpose of all production and the welfare of the producer ought to be attended to, only so far as it may be necessary for promoting that of the consumer" (*The Wealth of Nations*, 1937 Modern Library edition, p. 625).

The belief that consumer satisfaction is the ultimate economic goal and that the economy is fundamentally ruled by consumer desires is called **consumer sovereignty**.

consumer sovereignty: the idea that consumers' needs and wants determine the shape of all economic activities

---

[1] Statistics are from the World Resource Institute database, 2001. Figures are for 1996, 1998, and 1961.

226

Is this belief valid? That is, are the final goals of economic activity all to be found in the act of consumption?

Arguments in Favor of Consumer Sovereignty. There are, indeed, two quite different answers to the question of why consumers are important in economics. One is the traditional assumption, as stated by Smith, that final consumption is the ultimate purpose of all economic activity; production, distribution, and resource maintenance exist solely to increase the well-being of consumers. In this view, consumers are the *justification* for economic activity and therefore for economic theory as well.

The other answer is that consumers keep the economy going by generating demand for goods and services. Without this demand, the supply side of the economy would expire: How long can producers keep producing if no one buys their goods? From this perspective, consumers as a source of demand are central to the *mechanism* that makes the economic system run.

Arguments Against Consumer Sovereignty. Regarding the "justification" argument for consumer sovereignty, it is important to remember that although the end products of production derive their value solely from their contribution to the well-being of society and of individual consumers, the *process* of production is valuable for other reasons as well. People are more than just consumers. Consumption activities most directly address **living standard** (or **lifestyle**) **goals**, which have to do with satisfying basic needs and getting pleasure through the use of goods and services.

But people are also often interested in goals such as self-realization, fairness, freedom, participation, social relations, and ecological balance. These goals may be either served by, or in conflict with, their goals as consumers. People also often get intrinsic satisfaction from working and producing. For many people, work defines a significant part of their role in society. Work can create and maintain relationships. It may be a basis for self-respect and a significant part of what gives life interest and meaning.

If the economy is to promote well-being, all these goals must be taken into account. An economy that made people moderately happy as consumers but absolutely miserable as workers or community members could hardly be considered a rousing success.

Regarding the view that consumer sovereignty is the fundamental mechanism that guides economies, we need to recall that consumers—as members of complex larger organizations including families, communities, corporations, and nations—are subject to many influences from social institutions. The idea of a "sovereign consumer" implies someone who independently makes decisions. But what if, instead of being independent, those decisions are heavily influenced by community norms and aggressive marketing by businesses? Who "rules" then? When we look at an economy from this perspective, we can see that consumer behavior is often cultivated as a means to the ends of producers, rather than the other way around.

1.2 | Who Are the Consumers?

We generally think of consumption as something that benefits individuals. When one person eats an apple, no other individual person can benefit from that apple. We also tend to think of consumption decisions as being made by individuals and families, and not so much by businesses, governments, or other organizations. In contemporary economies, however, consumption decisions and consumption benefits are more complicated than this individualistic picture implies.

The fact that individuals (except for hermits) always live in society complicates the discussion of consumption. In Chapter 1, for example, we talked about public goods. Consumption of a public good, such as a pleasant city park, can be experienced by many people at the same time. Decision making about whether to build a park is done at a community level, not by an individual.

Even within a household, both decision making and enjoyment of consumption may involve more than one individual. Adults may negotiate about what to produce or

---

living standard (or **lifestyle**) **goals:** goals related to satisfying basic needs and getting pleasure through the use of goods and services

purchase. (This will be discussed more in Chapter 15.) The heat from a home furnace is a small-scale "public good," because everyone in the household benefits from it.

Many goods and services are also consumed by people while performing their roles in business or other organizations. For example, some employees are given opportunities to satisfy their individual needs for food and entertainment through business lunches and employer-sponsored sports outings.

In practice, however, economic analysis concerning consumption tends to focus on "the consumer" as the unit of analysis. The individual decision maker is assumed to be making consumption choices for himself or herself or on behalf of his or her entire household.[2] By imagining the consumer to be an individual economic actor, such analysis ignores both the larger issues of social consumption and the complications of decision making and enjoyment within households.

Limiting analysis to the individual level is a useful simplification for some purposes. In the rest of this chapter, we will look at two major theories about how individuals make consumption decisions: the marketing view and the utility theory view. Then we will examine consumption from a society-wide perspective and address the effect of consumption on human well-being.

Discussion Questions

1. How important to you are your lifestyle goals, relative to your other goals? A recent survey asked respondents to indicate whether each of the following was absolutely necessary, very important, somewhat important, not very important, or not at all important "for you to consider your life as a success." How would you answer?

   Earning a lot of money

   Seeing a lot of the world

   Becoming well educated

   Having an interesting job

   Helping other people who are in need

   Living a long time

   Having a good marriage

   Having a good relationship with your children

   Having good friends

   Having strong religious faith

2. Who makes the important consumption decisions that affect your life, right now? Who decides where you will live, what you will eat, what you will wear, how you will get around, and so on? To what extent are these individual decisions, and to what extent are they family or societal decisions?

---

2 | Consumer Behavior: The Marketing View

Marketing professionals have a job to do: They want to persuade consumers to purchase their organization's product. To do their jobs, they have to have a good understanding of what makes people want to buy and consume. Most often, their focus is on why a consumer would choose a particular brand of a product, at a particular time and place. Social science research, primarily from psychology and sociology, forms the basis for the standard marketing view of consumer behavior.[3]

---

[2] Data, however, are usually collected only for households, and this leads to some problems in using theoretical intuitions about individuals to explain observed consumption patterns by family groups.

[3] Standard marketing textbooks usually include a similarly extensive discussion about marketing to organizations such as businesses and governments. Although that is highly relevant to our discussion of markets in general (Chapters 3–5 and 11–14), our focus here is on consumers envisioned as individuals or households.

2.1 | The Decision-Making Process

The marketing view portrays consumers as going through a five-step decision-making process:

1. *Problem recognition.* In this stage, the consumer perceives that he has a want or need. The consumer compares his situation to some situation he would consider to be better, and his desire to move to the better situation is aroused. For example, the consumer might feel hungry or feel unsatisfied with her current athletic shoes, which are shabby compared to those in advertisements.

2. *Information search.* In this stage, the person seeks information about how this want might be met. She may search her own experience, looking for ways in which she has satisfied it in the past. Or she might consult external sources of information, such as friends, family, newspapers, advertising, and packaging. For example, he might be attracted by the photos on the packages of frozen dinners in the supermarket. The packages give him information about the product inside. Because humans have a limited availability to absorb information and can assess only a limited number of options, this process is likely to be very fragmentary—the consumer will generally move on to the next stage knowing only *some* things about *some* alternatives.

3. *Evaluation of alternatives.* After gathering information, the consumer compares the various alternatives about which he or she has gathered information. Goods and services are said to have **attributes** (or **characteristics**) that are the real items of interest to the consumer. The consumer will lean toward the alternative that has the bundle of attributes that best meets his or her desires. For example, a consumer might be interested in how a dinner tastes, in its nutritional value in terms of calories and fat content, and in whether it will satisfy his desire to try new things (or stick to old ones). He will compare brands and decide which one fits his priorities best. If he is deciding on athletic shoes, the fashionableness of various brands may weigh heavily—or even be the overwhelming factor—in his choice.

4. *Purchase decision.* Having developed an intention to buy something, the consumer will (barring interference or unforeseen events) follow through and make the purchase.

5. *Postpurchase behavior.* After the purchase, the consumer will decide whether he or she is satisfied or dissatisfied with the good or service. Consumption, in the marketing view, is seen as something of a trial-and-error process.

> **attributes (or characteristics):** the specific qualities of a good or service that are of interest to the consumer

Marketing professionals are interested in all aspects of this process, because each step gives them opportunities to try to sway consumer choices toward their organization's products. They may try to create new desires, for example, or try to inform the public in greater detail about the value of their product. They may design improved websites to make sure customers aren't frustrated in making their intended purchases. Or they may inform their own organization of changes in design that could improve customer satisfaction (and thus bring more repeat business).

2.2 | Consumer Motivation and Behavior

Why do consumers want what they want? Why do they buy what they buy? In an effort to answer these questions, the standard marketing view draws on a wide variety of research about individual motivations and social influences.

Psychological theories of motivation can shed light on why people come to desire certain things. One frequently used categorization breaks down human perceived needs into five categories:

1. Physiological needs, such as hunger and thirst
2. Safety needs, for security and protection

3. Social needs, for a sense of belonging and love

4. Esteem needs, for self-esteem, recognition, and status

5. Self-actualization needs, for self-development and realization[4]

A consumer's recognition of a need—step 1 of the decision process—can include one or many of these categories.

Psychological theories can also shed light on why people sometimes consume in unpredictable, even seemingly irrational, ways. It is no secret that sex is used to sell everything from cars to magazines, or that soft drink ads appeal more to a desire for a sense of belonging and self-esteem than to a desire to relieve thirst. People know, at a conscious level, that the tie between such advertising campaigns and what they actually will get by buying the product is tenuous at best. But that doesn't stop such campaigns from being successful!

Psychologists have noted that the degree to which we perceive a need is clearly related to two important factors: our own past experience and the experience of groups to which we compare ourselves. These create reference points and reference groups, in light of which people evaluate their own well-being and state of need.

We humans seem to be more tuned in to *changes* in our perceived satisfaction than to the absolute level of satisfaction we experience. We take as our **reference point**, in judging what we want and need, any situation to which we have become accustomed. If we are used to eating out once a week, that seems normal to us. We may not feel any particular joy in eating out once a week. If we change, and start eating out three times a week, we will feel a surge of pleasure. But once we have adapted to the new situation, the pleasure tapers off and we come to think of the new situation as normal. (We will

reference point: a situation to which we have adapted. We have a tendency to notice changes in satisfaction relative to this point, rather than our absolute level of satisfaction.

Advertising seeks to create or accentuate dissatisfaction by calling to consumers' attention a problem, real or imagined, that can presumably only be solved with the purchase of a particular good or service. This Indian man pedals a rickshaw past a billboard advertising new vehicles in advance of New Delhi's Auto-Expo 2004. The advertisement of luxury goods obtainable only by the rich may accentuate poor people's sense of relative deprivation and social exclusion.

---

[4] This is the well-known "Maslow's hierarchy of needs" based on Abraham H. Maslow's *Motivation and Personality* (New York: Harper & Row, 1970).

even feel deprived if we must cut back to "only" twice a week.) For this reason, as marketers well know, to the extent that we seek jolts of happiness, we can be continually attracted by stimuli that promise us something more, new, or different.

The picture of consumer behavior that emerges from the marketing synthesis of social science research portrays consumption as very much a *social* behavior, in far-reaching ways. **Reference groups** are particular groups of people who influence the behavior of a consumer because the consumer compares himself or herself with them. **Membership groups** are groups to which the person belongs, such as families, student communities, and groups of co-workers. Membership groups are important sources of information and also sources of pressure to conform to group practices and norms. Another kind of reference group, an **aspirational group**, is a group to which a consumer *wishes* he or she could belong. People often buy, dress, and behave like the group—management personnel, rock stars, sports teams, or whoever—with whom they would like to identify.

reference group: a group to which we compare ourselves

membership group: a group to which we belong

aspirational group: a group to which we would like to belong

> ### Discussion Questions
>
> 1. What advertisement, either in print or on TV, have you seen recently that sticks in your mind? What product is it trying to sell? At which of the stages of your decision process do you think the ad is aimed? Which human need is it targeting? Which human need do you think, rationally, the product itself would most *logically* satisfy? Is the advertisement directed to that need?
>
> 2. How important do you think reference groups are in explaining your own consumer choices? How important are they in explaining the choices of people you see around you?

3 | Consumer Behavior: The Utility Theory View

In contrast to the marketing view, the utility theory view (favored by economists in the 20th century and earlier) portrays consumer behavior as relatively simple, rational, and untouched by social influences. Rather than focusing on choices made by people who live in a social context—and sometimes have unruly emotions and incorrect perceptions—the utility theory view focuses on behavior that individual consumers would *logically* pursue, given certain assumptions. The effect of these assumptions is to emphasize the traditional, money-measured economic variables of incomes and prices.

This view emphasizes that consumers are constrained in their spending by the amount of their total budget. It asks the question of how consumers should, rationally, allocate that limited budget over the various goods and services that they may want. How should consumers make tradeoffs between one desired thing and another?

3.1 | The Budget Line

budget line: a line showing the possible combinations of two goods that a consumer can purchase

The first important concept in the utility theory view is that of the **budget line**. This shows the combinations of two goods that the consumer can purchase, given his or her monetary resources and the prices of the two goods.

An example of a budget line, for chocolate bars and bags of nuts, is shown in Figure 10.1. Suppose Quong has $8 to spend. To be brief, we will call this his income. Suppose that chocolate bars cost $1 each and bags of nuts sell for $2 apiece. (We will let P_C indicate the price of chocolate per bar and P_N the price of nuts per bag.) If Quong spends his $8 on chocolate alone, he can buy 8 bars, as indicated by the point where the budget line touches the vertical axis. If he buys only nuts, he can buy 4 bags, as indicated by the (4, 0) point on the horizontal axis. He can also buy any combination in between. For

Figure 10.1 The Budget Line
The budget line shows the combinations of goods that the consumer can buy with a given income.

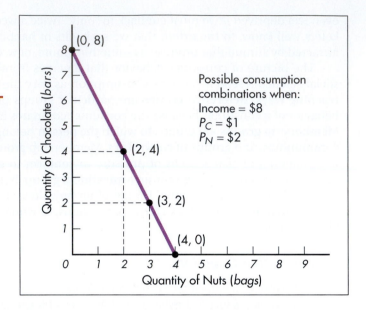

example, the point (2, 4), indicating 2 bags of nuts and 4 chocolate bars, is also achievable.[5] This is because $(2 \times \$2) + (4 \times \$1) = \$8$.

Assuming that Quong likes chocolate and nuts and that he will spend his whole budget of $8 on them, the budget line defines the choices that are *possible* for him. Points above and to the right of the budget line are not affordable. Points below and to the left of the budget line are affordable but do not use up the total budget. In this kind of model, economists assume that people always want *more* of at least one of the goods in question. Consuming below the budget line would hence be inefficient; funds that

Figure 10.2 Effect of an Increase in Income
With an increase in income, the budget line shifts out in a parallel manner. The consumer can now buy more of either good or of both.

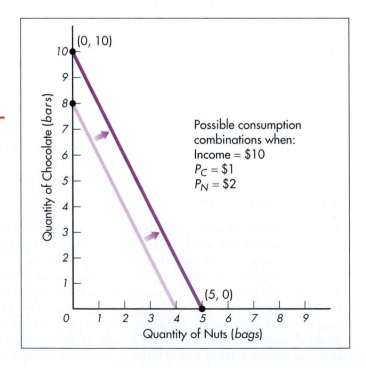

[5] We draw the line as continuous for the sake of simplicity, although we assume that Quong buys only whole bars and whole bags, not fractions of them.

Figure 10.3 Effect of a Fall in a Price
With a fall in the price of one good, the budget line rotates out.

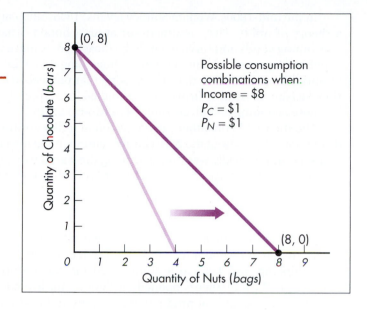

Possible consumption combinations when:
Income = $8
$P_C = \$1$
$P_N = \$1$

could be used to satisfy Quong's desires are being left unused. Therefore, economists assume that the consumer will choose to consume at some point *on* the budget line. (Note the similarities to the production possibilities frontier introduced in Chapter 1, illustrating choices facing a society.)

The position of the budget line depends on the size of the total budget (income) and on the prices of the two goods. For example, if Quong had $10 to spend, instead of $8, the line would shift out in a parallel manner, as shown in Figure 10.2. He could now consume more nuts, or more chocolate, or a more generous combination of both.

If (starting at the original income of $8) the price of nuts were to drop to $1 per bag, the budget line would rotate out, as shown in Figure 10.3. Now, if Quong bought only nuts, he could buy 8 bags instead of 4. With the price of chocolate unchanged, however, he still couldn't buy more than 8 chocolate bars.

What would happen if *both* prices fell? Suppose that Quong's income was $8, the price of a chocolate bar fell from $1 to $.80, and the price of a bag of nuts fell from $2 to $1.60. If he bought only chocolate, he could buy 10 bars. If he bought only nuts, he could buy 5 bags (= $8/$1.60). But this is just the budget line given in Figure 10.2! We see that if both prices change by the same proportion, the effect on the budget line is the same as though there had been a change in income, with no change in prices. This demonstrates that what is important to the consumer is not just his monetary income but his **real income**—that is, the purchasing power of his income—which also depends on prices.

The budget lines tells us what combinations of purchases are possible, but it doesn't tell us how the consumer will decide *which* combination to consume. To get to this, we must add the theory of utility.

real income: the purchasing power of income, with prices taken into account

3.2 | Utility

Jeremy Bentham (1748–1832), the British moral philosopher, conceived the idea that human conduct is guided by a calculation of pain versus pleasure; an action is taken only if the pleasure it brings outweighs the pain it causes. From this idea it was an obvious next step to associate some actual quantity of pleasure (or pain) with each action: It is this quantity that came to be known as **utility**.[6]

utility: the pleasure or satisfaction from goods, services, or events

---

[6] One meaning of the word *utility* is "usefulness." The meaning intended here is broader than that; it refers to a common fund of human well-being that (in Bentham's utilitarian philosophy) was conceived of as deriving from the sum of all realized human values.

In the mid-1800s, William Stanley Jevons (1835–1882) and others further developed a theory of utility. They assumed—or at least hoped—that the utility obtained from consuming goods and services could be measured numerically, much as weight is measured in kilograms or length in meters. Imagining this to be so, they developed a theory of optimal consumption decision making that parallels the theory of optimal production decision making by firms that we studied in Chapter 8. Just as firms maximize profits, these economists said, consumers maximize *utility*.

The theory of consumer maximization of utility continued to dominate economic discussions throughout the 20th century, although the idea that utility could actually be measured numerically was dropped along the way. It was replaced with the notion that it is convenient to assume that people act "as if" they maximized such an entity.

3.3 | Marginal Thinking in Consumer Decision Making

Marginal thinking led to the *MC* = *MR* rule (profits are maximized when marginal cost equals marginal revenue) for production (under a number of assumptions). Can marginal thinking also lead to a simple rule for consumption decisions? Under what assumptions? Utility theory opened the door to this investigation.

Just as the shapes of production functions and cost curves are considered important in discussing a marginal thinking approach to production, the shape of the **utility function** (or **total utility curve**) is important in discussing the utility theory view. The utility function measures, in imaginary units called **utils**, the amount of satisfaction or utility derived from different levels of consumption of a good.

An example of a utility function, with its assumed characteristic shape, is shown in Figure 10.4. Consumers are assumed to experience **diminishing marginal utility** as they increase consumption of any one good. Marginal utility is simply the utility gained from the last unit of a good or service that is consumed.

As we see in Figure 10.4, the first chocolate bar that Quong consumes gives him 9 utils. He's hungry, and it tastes really good. The second bar raises his total utility to 14 utils. Note, however, that the *additional* (or marginal) utility from eating the second bar is only 5 utils, as indicated by the arrows on the graph. Both the total and the marginal utility received from each additional bar are tracked in Table 10.1. Quong enjoys the second chocolate bar, but his desire for it is less acute than the desire he had for the first bar, so the marginal utility is less.

The third chocolate bar only gives him 3 additional utils; Quong is starting to get full. The fourth gives him no extra utils, because Quong is getting bored with the taste of chocolate. The fifth actually lowers his utility (gives him marginal utility equal to −1), because he starts to feel ill. The total utility curve rises steeply, then flattens out, and potentially turns down. Each successive unit gives a smaller and smaller addition to

utility function (or **total utility curve**): a curve showing the relation of utility levels to consumption levels

utils: imaginary units in which utility is measured

diminishing marginal utility: the tendency of additional units of consumption to add less to utility than did previous units of consumption

Figure 10.4 Utility from Chocolate
Utility rises steeply with the first few chocolate bars and then more slowly as the consumer gets sated. It may even turn downward as *over*consumption decreases the consumer's satisfaction.

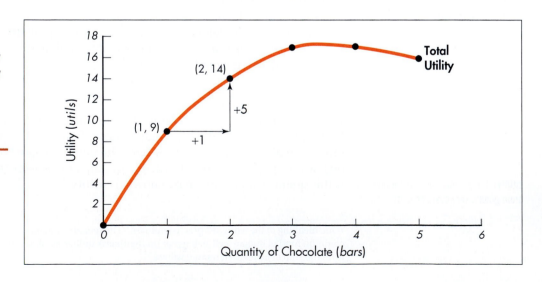

Table 10.1 | Utility from Chocolate Bars

Number	Total Utility	Marginal Utility (MU_C)
0	0	—
1	9	+9
2	14	+5
3	17	+3
4	17	+0
5	16	−1

utility. It seems intuitively likely that, for many goods, diminishing marginal utility will set in as desires are satisfied.[7]

3.4 | Deriving the Rule for Utility Maximization

Now a question arises: How can Quong maximize his utility derived from chocolate and nuts when constrained by a money income of $8? How many chocolate bars should he buy, and how many bags of nuts? The answer lies in the following procedure: *Consider how to spend one dollar after another, allocating each dollar in such a way as to maximize the utility derived from it.* To use a hill-climbing analogy, Quong should start spending, always making sure that his next step (expenditure) takes him up the hill as far as possible.

Table 10.2 will help us see how Quong can logically best solve this problem. The table reproduces the numbers for the marginal utility of chocolate (MU_C) from Table 10.1. We can suppose that Quong has a similarly shaped utility function for bags of nuts—a function that also exhibits diminishing marginal utility. Figures for his MU_N are also listed in Table 10.2. Each time Quong decides how to spend his next dollar, he is interested in the value he will get *per dollar*. Therefore, we also calculate in this table *MU/P*, or the *utility value of additional consumption per dollar* that pertains to each good.

Quong's first dollar should be spent on chocolate, to obtain 9 utils, because this is the biggest increment to utility obtainable. What to buy next? If he buys more chocolate next, he will only get 5 utils for his dollar, whereas if he buys nuts, he will get 7 utils per dollar (for his next $2). His next $2 should therefore be spent on nuts. He now has 1 chocolate bar, 1 bag of nuts, and $5 left to spend ($8 − $1 − $2). His satisfaction level is 23 utils (= 9 + 14).

Looking at his third expenditure, we see that switching back to chocolate would get Quong 5 utils/dollar but staying with nuts would get him 6 utils/dollar. So, he should continue to buy nuts. After this purchase, he will have 1 bar of chocolate, 2 bags of nuts, and $3 left to spend. He has accumulated utility of 35 utils (= 9 + 14 + 12).

Table 10.2 | Maximizing Utility from Chocolate and Nuts

Number of Bars or Bags	Chocolate (P_C = $1 per bar)		Nuts (P_N = $2 per bag)	
	MU_C	MU_C/P_C	MU_N	MU_N/P_N
0	—		—	
1	+9	9	+14	7
2	+5	5	+12	6
3	+3	3	+10	5
4	+0	0	+4	4
5	−1	−1	+2	1

---

[7] Addictive goods, such as tobacco, are an exception to this rule. For addictive goods, consuming a little bit can *increase* the individual's desire for more of the same.

With his remaining $3, he will do best to buy one more bag of nuts and one more bar of chocolate. *Both his last bag of nuts and his last chocolate bar give him the same marginal utility per dollar: 5 utils.* In the end, he will purchase 2 chocolate bars and 3 bags of nuts, spending $8 to get 50 utils (= 9 + 14 + 12 + 10 + 5).[8]

This result—to maximize utility, the last dollar spent on each good should produce the same marginal utility—is true in general, not just in this example. If it were not true, and the last dollar spent on good *X* produced more utility than the last dollar spent on *Y*, then the consumer could increase her utility by switching a dollar from *Y* to *X*. She can continue increasing her utility in this manner until the marginal utility of her last dollar spent on each good is equal. If we add a third good, *Z*, or as many as we want, the rule remains the same.

This rule can be stated in mathematical terms: To maximize utility, the consumer should equate the marginal utility per dollar derived from each good:

$$\frac{MU_x}{P_x} = \frac{MU_y}{P_y} = \cdots = \frac{MU_z}{P_z}$$

where MU_x is the marginal utility per unit of good *X*, P_x is the price per unit of good *X*, and similarly for *Y*, . . . , *Z*, which represent all other goods purchased by the consumer.

▷ Given certain assumptions, utility
is maximized when a consumer
equates the marginal utility per dollar
over all purchases. This is summarized mathematically as
$$\frac{MU_x}{P_x} = \frac{MU_y}{P_y} = \cdots = \frac{MU_z}{P_z}$$

3.5 | Further Developments and Complications

By now, you've probably noted a number of similarities between the mathematical, marginal analysis of consumer behavior and the model of the profit-maximizing firm (with convexity) presented in Chapter 8. The utility function looks a bit like a total product curve; the rule of equating *MU/P* ratios looks a bit like the rule for setting *MR* = *MC*. This is not just coincidental. The approach—setting up the analysis in terms of a smooth, convex problem of optimization—is the same in both the production and consumption cases.[9]

In the production case, we also showed how the optimal decision could be demonstrated using tangencies on a graph (Figure 8.4). The same is true for consumption. You will find that demonstration in the appendix to this chapter.

The utility theory view has often been extended to include a wide range of individual choices beyond the purchase of consumer goods. Instead of looking at just money resources, for example, economists have made budget lines that include *time* resources and have then asked how people can choose the combination of income and leisure that will maximize their overall utility. (This will be elaborated on in Chapter 13, on labor markets.) Economists have also extended utility theory to looking at individual choices about whether to have children, join social groups, commit crimes, or vote.

The theory has also been extended to examine consumer choice in terms of desires for various characteristics of goods, and services from them, rather than desires for specific goods themselves. For example, when we buy a car, we are seeking the characteristics of style, efficiency, reliability, capacity, and so on. We will not actually consume the car but will consume the services contributed by its characteristics: the feelings we receive from driving a stylish car; the transportation it provides; its efficiency, reliability, and safety; its ability to carry passengers or material things according to its capacity;

---

[8] You can check to see that this procedure and consumption combination give Quong more utility than other combinations that cost $8. For example, if he spent all of his $8 on nuts, he would be able to buy 4 bags and get 40 (= 14 + 12 + 10 + 4) utils. Or if, after buying 2 bags of nuts and 2 chocolate bars, he spent the rest of his income on chocolate, he would get 43 utils (= 9 + 14 + 12 + 5 + 3 + 0).

[9] In the case of utility theory, the optimization problem can be written (for the case of two goods, *X* and *Y*), as

$$\text{Max } U(x, y) \qquad \text{subject to } P_x x + P_y y = \text{Income}$$
$$x, y$$

where $U(x, y)$ is a function that gives the utility derived from various combinations of quantities of goods. This is a standard calculus problem of constrained optimization. Derivation of what are called the first-order conditions gives the "equate the marginal utility per dollar" guideline for utility optimization that is described in the text and shown graphically in the appendix.

and so forth. Utility theory has been applied, for example, to analyzing how a consumer may make tradeoffs between characteristics such as better gas mileage and better safety.

As with the case of production, marginal thinking about consumption also breaks down if the underlying assumptions are violated. The utility theory approach to consumer behavior assumes that people are rational, autonomous decision makers. It assumes that all benefits from consumption choices can be compared and summed up, so that only one measure—utility—needs to be considered. It assumes that consumers' preferences (what they like and what they don't like) can be taken as given and that consumers have perfect information. It assumes that there are no externalities in consumption, and no multiple equilibria or other nonconvexities, that could complicate the maximization problem.

Some economists have recently relaxed some of these assumptions, while still subscribing to the utility theory view. For example, the treatment of the nonconvexities that follow from "network externalities" (as discussed in Chapter 8, on production decisions) was first formulated primarily in terms of consumption. You may find it advantageous to read certain books or go to certain movies if your friends make the same choices too, because then you can discuss the books or movies with them. Such extensions of utility theory move it somewhat in the direction of taking into account the social context of consumption.

Other economists, although they may appreciate the insights that utility theory can give into matters of prices and income in limited cases, are less confident that utility theory is useful in explaining much of consumer behavior. With advertising expenditures in the United States now equal to 2% of GDP (General Motors alone spends $4 billion per year on ads), the idea that consumer preferences are independently determined and rationally followed may be hard to swallow. What a rational, well-informed consumer would *logically* do and what real-world consumers *actually* do may not always be related closely enough for utility theory to be useful.[10]

The idea that all benefits from choices can be summed up into one factor, "utility," has also come under fire. It seems reasonable to think that the satisfactions from chocolate and nuts can be compared, and perhaps even summed, but it is harder to believe that people can make such simple comparisons in *all* their choices. Can we compare the utility from eating chocolate to the "utility" from having open-heart surgery, and both of these to the "utility" of a college education—or of voting or of having children? Although some economists freely make such comparisons, others believe that such comparisons, over realms in which people may have qualitatively different beliefs, values, and goals, stretch the model too far.

> ### Discussion Questions
>
> 1. Budget lines can be used to analyze other kinds of tradeoffs. Suppose you have a total "time budget" for recreation of 2 hours. Think of two activities you might like to do for recreation, and draw a budget line diagram illustrating the recreational possibilities open to you. What if you had 3 hours, instead?
>
> 2. Explain each of the following in words.
>   a. Why the total utility curve is drawn with a particular shape
>   b. The reasoning behind the rule that to maximize utility, marginal utilities per dollar spent should be equated

4 | The Consumer Society

Having explored how social context may (or may not) be included in the marketing and utility theory views of *individual* consumer behavior, we now switch gears and look more directly at long-term historical and social factors that influence consumption.

---

[10] A thoroughgoing believer in "consumer sovereignty" will reply that if advertising exists, it must be because consumers *desire* that it exist.

The modern consumer is not an isolated individual making purchases in a vacuum. Rather, we are all participants in a contemporary phenomenon that has been variously called a consumerist culture and a consumer society. To say that some people have **consumerist values** or attitudes means that they always want to consume more and that they find meaning and satisfaction in life, to a large extent, through the purchase of new consumer goods. Consumerism has emerged as part of a historical process that has created mass markets, industrialization, and cultural attitudes that ensure that rising incomes are used to purchase an ever-growing output.

consumerist values: the belief that meaning and satisfaction in life are to be found through the purchase and use of consumer goods

4.1 | The Birth of the Consumer Society

Look back into history and you will find patterns of consumption very different from those that exist today. Turn the clock back just a few centuries, and almost no one in any country spent a significant amount of time or resources on shopping for goods produced far from home. As we saw in Chapter 3, before the Industrial Revolution—that is, before the late 18th century in England or before the middle of the 19th century in the rest of Western Europe and North America—the vast majority of each country's population lived in rural areas and worked in agriculture. Their clothing and household possessions were extremely limited by today's standards and were typically made by household members or by artisans from the same village. Fashions, technological change, and social pressure did not drive people constantly to make new purchases; rather, individual material goods were used, with repairs if needed, for decades. Major items such as winter coats were expected to last a lifetime or more; they were often passed from one generation to the next.

A small elite, of course, had long enjoyed higher consumption standards and habitually bought luxury goods and services. Elite consumption created employment for small numbers of artisans and merchants, often clustered around the courts and trading centers of each country. However, purchases by the elite were not large enough to transform a predominantly agrarian economy. Rather, elite consumption depended on the existence of agriculture, because upper-class incomes were directly or indirectly derived from rents, taxes, or other payments extracted from rural areas.

The Industrial Revolution clearly transformed production. It is less obvious, but equally true, that it transformed consumption. Large-scale industrialization began in the British textile industry; the amount of cotton used in that industry rose from less than 3 million pounds in 1760 to more than 360 million pounds annually in the 1830s. Thus within one lifetime, the production of textiles in Britain was multiplied more than 100-fold. Luxury consumption by the English upper class did not grow nearly that rapidly. Who, then, bought and used the vast outpouring of cloth?

In the early 19th century, roughly two-thirds of the increased output was sold to other countries around the world. Much of it went to less developed areas such as India, which was rapidly becoming a British colony (and where the British conquest was followed by the destruction of India's formerly thriving textile industry) and to the newly independent states of Latin America, where British merchants displaced the earlier commercial connections to Spain and Portugal.

There were limits, however, to the possibility of growth through expansion into foreign markets. As other industries followed textiles, and other countries followed Britain's example of industrialization, much of the growing output was inevitably sold at home or to other relatively developed countries. Thus mass production required mass consumption. (Even when two-thirds of England's burgeoning textile output was sold abroad, the domestic absorption of the remaining one-third involved sweeping changes in English patterns of consumption.) Over the course of the 19th century, both the growing middle class and the working class became consuming classes as well.

4.2 | Workers Become Consumers

At the dawn of industrialization, it was not at all clear that workers could or would become consumers. Early British industrialists complained that their employees would work only until they had earned their traditional weekly income and then stop until the next week. Leisure, it appeared, was more valuable to the workers than increased income. This attitude, widespread in pre-industrial, pre-consumerist societies, was incompatible with mass production and mass consumption. It could be changed in either of two ways.

At first, employers responded by lowering wages and imposing strict discipline on workers to force them to work longer hours. Early textile mills frequently employed women, teenagers, and even children, because they were easier to control, and could be paid less, than adult male workers. As a consequence of such draconian strategies of labor discipline, living and working conditions for the first few generations of factory workers were worse than in the generations before industrialization.

Over time, however, agitation by trade unions, political reformers, and civic and humanitarian groups created pressure for better wages, hours, and working conditions, while rising productivity and profits made it possible for business to respond to this pressure. A second response to the pre-industrial work ethic gradually evolved: as workers came to see themselves as consumers, they would no longer choose to stop work early and enjoy more leisure; rather, they would prefer to work full-time, or even overtime, in order to earn and spend more.

In the United States, the "worker as consumer" worldview was fully entrenched by the 1920s, when the labor movement stopped advocating a shorter workweek and instead focused on better wages and working conditions. The old philosophy was never entirely displaced by the new; both repressive and consumerist approaches to motivating workers continue to exist today, the former being particularly prevalent in low-skill, low-wage industries. But mass consumption, and the consumerist attitudes that support it, became increasingly important to the economic system.

Note that if workers are also important as consumers, the attitude of employers toward wages may become more complex. Under the old model, where workers had to be strictly controlled and most products were sold to elite or foreign customers, business owners had an unambiguous interest in keeping wages as low as possible, in order to stay profitable and competitive. Under the new model, where the same people are workers and consumers, should business owners favor low wages to limit production costs, or high wages to create more consumer demand? The answer is both: If an individual business could arrange the whole world solely to maximize its own profits, it would pay its own employees as little as possible—while everyone else would be paid, and would spend, as much as possible.

This change in the economic interests of businesses was only occasionally recognized in explicit terms by business leaders themselves. Henry Ford, the founder of Ford Motor Company and developer of the assembly line, made a point of keeping wages high enough, and the price of his cars low enough, that his employees could afford to buy cars. The owners and managers of beer and liquor companies have sometimes backed liberal, pro-union politicians, perhaps reflecting an awareness that higher wages are good for their line of business. But for the most part, businesses continued well into the era of the consumer society to struggle against wage gains for their own and for other workers, not realizing how ironically essential it was for them periodically to lose some ground in that battle.

The bifurcation in the business view of people as workers and as consumers is mirrored throughout society. Work is associated with an ascetic, prudent, saving, and rational ideology—what the sociologist Max Weber referred to as "the Puritan ethos." At the same time, the ethos of consumerism includes a focus on pleasure and a conviction that it is right to seek the satisfaction of selfish desires. In the modern economy, the same person is often expected to embrace both roles.

4.3 | Institutions of the Consumer Society

Many of the institutions that sustain and promote mass consumption first took shape near the end of the 19th century—in the same period, it turns out, when economic theory

Has Advertising Gotten Out of Hand?

Advertising in the United States is big business. Advertising Age, a company that analyzes the advertising industry, estimates that spending on TV, radio, and print advertisements in 2000 was around $99 billion, or about $350 per American. When spending on other forms, including direct mail, phone marketing, and Internet ads, was included, total spending on all forms of advertising was estimated to be over $222 billion in 1999. This amount exceeds the entire annual GDP of many countries, including Denmark and Saudi Arabia.

By the mid-1990s, the average American adult was exposed to about 3000 ads every day. Advertising is evident in an increasing number of private and public places, including school textbooks, hospital emergency rooms, and even fortune cookies. Some analysts claim that advertising increases the availability of information and allows consumers to make better choices, but an increasing number of social advocates are calling for limits on commercialism. For example, some groups are especially concerned about the effect of media advertising on the health of young women and children.

Media advertising contributes to eating disorders among young women, some public health analysts claim. Mediascope, a non-profit research and policy organization, reports that

> . . . today's fashion models weigh 23% less than the average female, and a young woman between the ages of 18 [and] 34 has a . . . 1% chance of being as thin as a supermodel. However, 69% of girls in one study said that magazine models influence their idea of the perfect body shape . . . "the media markets desire. And by reproducing ideals that are absurdly out of line with what real bodies really do look like . . . the media perpetuates a market for frustration and disappointment. Its customers will never disappear," writes Paul Hamburg, an assistant professor of Psychiatry at Harvard Medical School.[11]

first gave consumers a central role to play. Department stores appeared in the big cities of England, France, and the United States, creating comfortable semipublic spaces in which consumers could contemplate many different purchases. New packaging technologies were developed, allowing the distribution of goods in bags, cans, and bottles. This technological advance made it possible for the first time to create nationally and internationally known "brand names" in the marketing of foods, beverages, cosmetics, and other goods.

Advertising. Above all, advertising emerged as an essential component of the marketing and distribution of goods. Although advertising has existed as a specialized profession for only about a century, it has become a force that rivals education and religion in shaping public values and aspirations. In the United States today, the amount of money spent annually on advertising exceeds total U.S. public expenditures (by federal, state, and local governments) on police protection, natural resources, and higher education combined (see the Economics in the Real World feature "Has Advertising Gotten Out of Hand?").

Advertising is often justified by economists as a source of information about products and services available in the marketplace. But although it certainly plays that role, it does much more as well. Advertising appeals to many different values, to emotional as well as practical needs, and to a range of desires and fantasies. The multitude of advertisements that we encounter carry their own separate messages; yet on a deeper level, they all share a common message—they are selling the joys of buying, promoting the idea that purchasing things is, in itself, a pleasurable activity.

The presentation of consumption as pleasurable and ever-expandable helped to address the nagging question of a growing industrial economy: What would happen to

---

[11] Mediascope, "Body Image and Advertising," **http://www.mediascope.org/pubs/ibriefs/bia.htm**, accessed May 17, 2002.

Such advertising keeps the diet industry going strong, but perhaps at a substantial cost in terms of the mental and physical health of many young women.

Advertising targeted at young children is particularly worrisome because children lack the ability to resist commercial messages. Research reported in a recent volume of the *Journal of Developmental and Behavioral Pediatrics* illustrates the effects of TV ads on children's requests for products. The study found that a school-based effort to reduce TV viewing by third- and fourth-graders significantly reduced their requests for toy purchases. The cigarette manufacturer Philip Morris was recently criticized for dispensing 28 million book covers to American schools for free distribution to students. Although the book covers carried apparently anti-smoking messages, one editorial noted that "What you've got is a book cover that looks alarmingly like a colorful pack of cigarettes."[12]

Some countries have passed laws designed to limit or regulate advertising aimed at children. For example, TV ads selling toys to children are banned in Greece between 7:00 a.m. and 10:00 p.m., and Sweden and Norway ban all advertising aimed at children under the age of 12. In the United States, some legislators have proposed increasing the regulation of ads targeted at children and banning ads in schools, but no serious attempt has been mounted to reduce the onslaught of ads directed at children. For now, this work seems to be left to non-profit groups, such as Mediascope and Commercial Alert, an organization that seeks to prevent commercial culture from exploiting children and "subverting the higher values of family, community, environmental integrity, and democracy."

Do you think advertising has gotten out of hand? Do you enjoy ads? Do you think the present volume of advertising is socially beneficial?

the producers, with their continuously growing production capacity, if people were to decide that they had enough? This was considered a serious question in the first half of the 20th century, particularly during and after the Great Depression of the 1930s. It became possible to foresee a situation in which all the basic needs of an entire population could be met—and to forecast a disastrous end to economic activity as we know it, if people therefore stopped buying more stuff. For example, an American retailing analyst named Victor Lebow proclaimed,

> Our enormously productive economy . . . demands that we make consumption our way of life, that we convert the buying and use of goods into rituals, that we seek our spiritual satisfaction, our ego satisfaction, in consumption. . . . We need things consumed, burned up, worn out, replaced, and discarded at an ever increasing rate (quoted in William Witt, "The Overconsumptive Society," op-ed, *Chicago Tribune*, February 18, 1982, sec. 1, p. 17).

John Kenneth Galbraith, a prominent U.S. economist and social critic, argued that advertising by producers is increasingly needed to make affluent consumers keep buying their products—and that therefore it is no longer socially important to satisfy consumer desires, because they do not originate within the consumer:

> If production creates the wants it seeks to satisfy, or if the wants emerge *pari passu* [at an equal pace or rate] with the production, then the urgency of the wants can no longer be used to defend the urgency of the production. Production only fills a void that it has itself created (*The Affluent Society* [Boston: Houghton Mifflin, 1958], chap. 11).

[12] "Judging a Book Cover," *Star Tribune* (Minneapolis, MN), January 17, 2001.

Consumer Credit. Another institution created to support the consumer society was expanded consumer credit. Up through the early 1900s, cultural values about spending in the United States emphasized thrift, prudence, and living within one's income. Poorer households were forgiven for using installment purchasing (payments over time) and small loan agencies only if they needed the funds to purchase the necessities of life. Middle-class households borrowed for buying homes and furniture, but other spending for immediate pleasure was frowned upon.

With mass production of automobiles and household appliances, however, came a large expansion of institutions of consumer credit. By the 1920s department stores were issuing charge cards, and automobile financing was common. Economist E. R. A. Seligman was a key figure in convincing the public that consumer credit was a sound idea. In a study funded by the head of General Motors, he argued that credit purchases were vital to stimulating economic growth and that condemning luxury purchases was not possible because the definition of a luxury varied from individual to individual. In the 1950s the first general-purpose credit cards were issued by banks.

By 1998 about three-fourths of U.S. households had at least one credit card. Although some cardholders use them only for convenience, paying off their balances in full each month, other cardholders use them as a form of borrowing by carrying unpaid balances, on which they pay interest. In 1998 about 40% of families carried unpaid credit card balances. The average amount of credit card debt among households with at least one credit card was $8,367 by the end of 2001. In that year, total outstanding consumer credit in the United States topped $1.5 trillion.

4.4 | Changes in Other Institutions

Besides creating new institutions of mass advertising and consumer credit, the consumer society also changed how people thought about households and about the infrastructure for public consumption.

Households as Consumers. In primarily agricultural societies, when everyone in a family pulled together for survival, households were often recognized as important locations of production. With the rise of consumerism, however, the work of women in households came to be portrayed as managing the "consumption" behavior of their families. Many of the new goods and services being marketed were substitutes for goods formerly produced using household labor, generally the labor of adult women, perhaps aided by children. Factory-manufactured clothing replaced home-sewn, for example, and bakery bread replaced home-baked. Other new goods, such as gas and electric stoves replacing coal and wood for cooking, made home production more efficient.

You might think that such innovations would reduce the hours of labor spent on housework, but economic historians have found otherwise. The average number of hours devoted to homemaking by full-time homemakers stayed constant, at over 50 per week, from 1900 into the 1960s. The new goods were accompanied by pressure to raise household consumption standards. With access to a refrigerator, stove, and supermarket, women were expected to prepare more elaborate and varied meals; with access to washing machines, standards of clothing cleanliness rose. Labor effort in household production remained high, even though such work was commonly referred to as "consumption."

Displacement of Public Consumption. The growth of consumerism has altered the balance between private and public consumption. Public infrastructure has been shaped by the drives to sell and consume new products, and the availability of public and private options in turn shapes individual consumer choices.

In the early 1930s, for example, many major U.S. cities—including Los Angeles—had extensive, relatively efficient, and nonpolluting electric streetcar systems. Then, in 1936, a group of companies involved in bus and diesel gasoline production, led by General Motors, formed a group called the National City Lines (NCL). They bought up electric streetcar systems in 45 cities, dismantled them, and replaced them with bus systems. U.S. government support for highway construction in the 1950s further hastened the decline of rail transportation, made possible the spread of suburbs far removed from workplaces, and encouraged the purchase of automobiles.

Many of the choices you have, as an individual, depend on decisions made for you by businesses and governments. In some cases, such as public transportation, consumption possibilities display the phenomenon of "path dependence" discussed in Chapter 8: Los Angeles would look much different today—more like the older sections of many East Coast and European cities—if it had been built up around streetcar lines rather than cars and buses. Even today one can see tradeoffs between public (or publicly accessible) infrastructure and private consumption. As more people carry cell phones and bottles of spring water, pay telephones and drinking fountains come to be less well maintained in some cities, leading to more people needing to carry cell phones and bottles of spring water.

Discussion Questions

1. How much do you know about how your grandparents or great-grandparents lived? Would you describe them as living in a "consumer society"? What consumer institutions affected their lives?

2. Would it be possible for the United States to have an economy that does *not* rely on ever-increasing sales of consumer goods? What might such an economy look like? What values might be promoted in place of consumerism? What problems might arise in moving toward, or living in, such a society?

5 | Consumption and Well-Being

As we noted earlier, consumption activities most directly address people's living standard (or lifestyle) goals. People generally have other goals as well, goals involving self-realization through work, fairness, freedom, ecological balance, and the like, which may be either supported or undermined by their actions as consumers.

Looking at the contribution of consumption to individual and social well-being requires taking a broader view than that of marketers, who are primarily interested in selling their products. It also means taking a broader view than that taken by utility theorists, who are primarily interested in modeling consumer choice under specialized assumptions about rational individual behavior.

5.1 | Old Utility Theory, New Utility Theory, and Capabilities

What is the relationship then, between consumption and well-being? Can social well-being be increased by any particular policies or practices related to consumption?

Old Utility Theory. In the old-fashioned utility theory view, individual well-being was simply equated with pleasure. However, because some of the early theorists thought that utility could be measured and summed not only within a person, but also across persons, the theory was sometimes used to draw conclusions about social well-being.

Some of these economists assumed that everyone has similar utility functions, characterized by diminishing marginal utility. If so, then taking away $1 that a rich person would have spent on a luxury good such as caviar would cause little decrease in utility (because she is on the flattened-out part of the total utility curve). Giving that same $1 to a hungry poor person who has high marginal utility (that is, who is on the steep part of the same curve) to spend on a necessity such as bread would cause an increase in overall utility that more than outweighed the loss to the rich person. This is a fancy way of saying that satisfaction of **wants**—what people simply desire—

wants: what people simply desire

needs: what people require for a healthy, flourishing life

should take a back seat to satisfaction of **needs**—what people require for a healthy, flourishing life.

Thus such economists, when comparing two societies with the same overall level of consumption (or income), felt safe in concluding that the society with a more nearly equal distribution would have higher social well-being (that is, a higher sum of utilities) than the less egalitarian society. This principle was used to justify redistributive policies and a concern with poverty.

New Utility Theory. The new utility view, well established by the mid– to late 20th century, shared the same basic normative ideal as the old utility view: The satisfaction of consumer desires was the goal of economic activity.

However, by this time the notion of utility as a measurable entity had been dropped, and economists had come to believe that utility could *not* be compared across individuals. Consumer sovereignty held sway, but now in a very individualistic form. Because people were assumed to act rationally in their own self-interest, their actions were taken to reveal their true preferences and were assumed therefore to serve their own well-being, however they might individually define it.

These assumptions had two significant implications for discussions of well-being. First, through the emphasis on choice and the abandonment of interpersonal comparisons, discussion of wealth and poverty faded away. It was argued that distinguishing wants from needs was impossible. How could food be considered a necessity, it was argued, if some people choose to fast (even to death) for religious or political reasons? How could good dental care be "needed" in the United States if people in poor countries often survive without it? Given that "needs" could not be clearly and rigorously distinguished from "wants," or necessities from luxuries, discussions of poverty were considered less scientific than discussions of rational consumer choice. Issues of minimal necessary consumption levels, basic needs, poverty, and redistribution were rarely addressed in the economics of this period, except by specialists.

The second implication was that any suggestion that consumers were acting unwisely—that consumer behavior perhaps did *not* serve to advance their standard of living or more general goals—was generally dismissed as paternalistic. No one except the individual should be able to say what is good for him or her, the argument went. The choices and preferences of the sovereign consumer were sacred.

If someone ate a high-fat diet and developed heart disease, for example, it might be assumed that the person had calculated that the pleasure she derived from eating the high-fat diet outweighed the drawbacks of ill health. To encourage her to eat a better diet—or to campaign to keep advertisements for junk food out of schools—would be paternalistic interference. Exceptions to this belief were occasionally granted if it could be shown that one of the assumptions of the view had been violated. (Usually this was the assumption that consumers possessed "perfect information." For example, it might be that the consumer was not well informed about the relationship between diet and disease.)

capability approach: The economic approach that assesses institutions and policies in terms of the opportunities they create for people to live valuable lives

Capabilities. Nobel laureate economist Amartya Sen, in the late 20th century, proposed a different approach. He argued that social evaluations of peoples' advantage and disadvantage should be done on the basis of "capabilities," rather than satisfaction of their desires. The **capability approach** evaluates institutions, policies, and actions in terms of the opportunities they give people for valuable ways of living.

It is widely assumed, for example, that being adequately nourished, being in good health, being well sheltered, and avoiding premature death are good things. People might add to the list certain more complicated valuable ways of living, such as having self-respect, being able to participate in community life, being happy, being able to form intimate relationships, and being able to live in harmony with nature.[13]

---

[13] Some of these valuable ways of living were suggested by Sen, others by philosopher Martha Nussbaum.

The capabilities view allows for more complex goals than either version of the utility theory view. It changes the focus to objective criteria such as opportunities for health and participation, and away from subjective feelings of pleasure or satisfaction. It resurrects the concern with poverty and deprivation that was lost in the new utility theory view. However, with its emphasis on *opportunities* rather than outcomes, it also preserves some of the respect for individual choice that characterizes the new utility view. We don't worry about people who are hungry because they choose to fast, according to this view, as long as they have the capability of eating well (if they should choose to).

Sen's capability approach was influential in bringing discussions of well-being back into economics. Instead of looking just at whether people get pleasure from their consumption choices, it directs us to look at whether societies, and societal consumption patterns, permit people to live healthy lives, in harmony with each other and nature.

5.2 | Inadequate Consumption: Poverty

The division of the world's human population into portions defined by their consumption characteristics was pioneered in 1992 by ecologist Alan Durning.[14] He described the high-consuming fifth of the world as those who travel by car and air, eat meat-based diets, live in spacious, single-family residences, and discard much of what they purchase as packaging or post-consumption waste.

The next three-fifths of the global population may look deprived, when compared to the high-consumers—and, to the extent that that is their reference group, they may feel deprived—but they are well-off indeed when compared to any but the richest individuals of 200 years ago. Their ancestors would have envied them their healthy diet

Absolute deprivation occurs when people are not able to reach even minimal standards of nutrition, shelter, clothing, and sanitation. This young girl in Cambodia spends her days scouring a garbage dump in search of recyclable materials. The few cents she earns helps her family buy food. Worldwide, 1.2 billion people suffer from absolute poverty.

---

[14] Alan Durning, *How Much is Enough?* (New York: Norton, 1992).

(grain and vegetable based, with some meat); the convenience of bicycles and public transportation; work that is made productive through the assistance of mechanized tools; light, heat, and running water in homes and workplaces; much improved and convenient sanitation; and a level of schooling that was available to only a very few in, say, the year 1800.

absolute deprivation: the lack of the minimal necessities for sustaining life

The bottom one-fifth of the global population suffers from **absolute deprivation**. What constitutes absolute deprivation? If a household is unable to obtain minimal nutrition, shelter, clothing, and sanitation for its members, most people would agree that it is deprived of the necessities of life. Some people would add other services, such as elementary education and basic health care, to the list of necessities. The United Nations defines absolute poverty as subsistence on less than U.S.$1 per day. Worldwide, 1.2 billion people suffer from absolute poverty, and 826 million people suffer from undernourishment.

The poorest of developing countries, particularly in sub-Saharan Africa and South-central Asia, are simply too poor to lift their entire populations out of absolute deprivation. Increasingly, however, the more economically successful developing countries in Asia and Latin America have sufficient resources to provide basic necessities to all; the fact that absolute deprivation still exists for the poor in these countries reflects inequality in the distribution of income. Absolute deprivation may also vary with factors such as race and ethnicity, and even within households by age and gender.

Because inadequate consumption is not simply a matter of having a low household income, however, even in regions that could be generally characterized as middle- or high-consuming, examples of absolute deprivation can still be found. As the capability approach points out, well-being depends on resources relative to needs. Some people—particularly young children and the ill and handicapped—have dependency needs for care, as well as needs for special goods and services (such as education or medicines) that healthy adults in the prime of life do not require. Even people with fairly high household incomes may sometimes, then, find themselves lacking basic necessities. Advocates for the elderly, the sick, and children, for example, often claim that the United States has an inadequate system of care. A recent nationwide study of child care centers rated only 8% of infant care centers as good to excellent; 40% of infant centers were judged to be so inadequate that children's safety was potentially jeopardized. According to a *Consumer Reports* study in 1996, about 40% of nursing homes repeatedly fail to pass the most basic health and safety inspections. In such situations, people's fundamental needs for care and safety are not being met.

Absolute deprivation is only one type of inadequacy, however. As we noted earlier, psychological research also tells us that people's perception of their own well-being depends on the consumption patterns they see in the people around them—their reference groups. Modern information technology has created a new source of discontent: The predominant images shown to all the world are of the affluent one-fifth—or, indeed, of even more elite subgroups. The result is the creation of widespread feelings of

relative deprivation: the feeling of lack that comes from comparing oneself with someone who has more

relative deprivation, the sense that one's own condition is inadequate because it is inferior to someone else's circumstances. The richest man in a small village can be quite content with traditional clothing and diet, an outdoor latrine, and water drawn from a communal well, so long as that way of life is consistent with honor and self-respect. However, if his reference group changes—for example, if he begins to compare his circumstances with what he hears of life in the city—all that he has will begin to seem poor, mean, and disgraceful.

The government-defined poverty level in the United States is $18,400 for a family of four in 2003–2004. This income would be at or above the national average in many countries; in most developing countries a family income of $18,400 would put that family well above the poverty level. It may be possible to buy the bare physical necessities of life for this sum, even in the United States—at least in areas of the country with low housing costs.

Yet it is likely that most of the Americans who fell below the poverty level (12.1% in 2002) do not feel able to enjoy a "normal" American lifestyle. They clearly do not have the resources to buy the kinds of homes, cars, clothes, and other consumer goods shown on American television. They may need to rely on inadequate public transportation and wait in long lines for health care. People with sufficient physical means of survival may still feel ashamed, belittled, and socially unacceptable if they have much less than everyone around them. It is unlikely that the 16.7% of U.S. children who live in poverty start out on an "even playing field" with nonpoor children, in terms of nutrition, health care, and other requirements.

The fact that people who cannot afford to consume at "normal" societal consumption levels feel relative deprivation suggests that poverty, even relative poverty, is not conducive to promoting capability goals such as self-respect and the ability to participate in community life.

Would it be good, then, for everyone to aspire to the "normal" level of consumption enjoyed by middle-income (or upper-income) Americans? This question brings us back to the issues of capabilities, from another angle. When does consumption serve to provide people with healthier, more fulfilled lives? Are there times when it does not?

5.3 | Excessive and Misdirected Consumption: "Affluenza"?

Increasing consumption is unquestionably a goal of great importance in situations where people have insufficient goods and services. However, as the human race grows richer, it becomes increasingly important to recognize that more consumption is not always better. Increasing consumption can be worse for individuals who suffer ill health from overeating, psychological disturbances from certain kinds of overstimulation, and (some say) spiritual malaise from exclusive or excessive attention to material things. In short, there can be such a thing as too much consumption.

At some point, the drive for pleasure can begin to cut into other goals and can even undermine health. For example, diets high in sugars and fats can lead to people becoming overweight. Obesity, in turn, is a risk factor for all four leading causes of death in the industrialized world—stroke, heart disease, cancer, and diabetes. In the United States, about 300,000 people a year die from health problems related to obesity. Obesity is a growing problem among the more affluent classes in developing countries as well, even as consuming too few calories remains a serious problem for the very poor.

As we have seen, psychological research indicates that people's feelings of well-being adapt over time to their situation (or reference point). To the extent that a society emphasizes the consumption of material goods, this means that subjective feelings of happiness and satisfaction can be maintained only by continually "ratcheting up" the pleasures to be had by consuming them.

A long line of distinguished economists has pointed out this ratcheting-up effect and the great degree to which consumption in affluent societies tends to be less about staying alive and healthy than about achieving status or "keeping up with the Joneses." Thorstein Veblen (1857–1929) wrote about "conspicuous consumption." John Kenneth Galbraith's *The Affluent Society* (1958), Tibor Scitovsky's *The Joyless Economy* (1976), Juliet Schor's *The Overspent American* (1998), and Robert Frank's *Luxury Fever* (1999) took up this theme. A recent special on public television focused on the "disease" of "affluenza." The use of reference groups creates a paradox in consumption: We can apparently never have enough to be satisfied, because (unless we are Bill Gates) there is always someone with more than we have.

Does more consumption make people happier? In surveys of people *at any point in time,* people with more to spend generally report themselves as somewhat more satisfied with their lives than do people with less to spend. This makes sense, given both the stresses of being poor and the way people lower down tend to compare themselves, negatively, with people higher up. Even so, factors less directly related to consumption, such as good health and good relationships, often contribute more strongly to people's self-reported sense of satisfaction.

Over time, however, more consumption does *not* seem to be related to more happiness in affluent societies. In 1957, for example, 35% of respondents to a U.S. survey indicated that they were "very happy." Between 1957 and 1998, the purchasing power of the average U.S. citizen roughly doubled. In 1998, the proportion saying they were "very happy" was a little lower, at 32%.

Even people with abundant purchasing power seem to find their situation only "normal," or even lacking, once they have gotten used to it. Juliet Schor reports that in a 1995 survey, over a third of respondents in households with income between $75,000 and $100,000 agreed with the statements "I cannot afford to buy everything I really need" and "I spend nearly all of my money on the basic necessities of life." Even 27% of those with incomes above $100,000 agreed that they "cannot afford to buy everything I really need."

The situation of rising consumption levels has been compared to one in which one row of a crowd of spectators stands up in order to see better. Everyone behind them then has to stands on tiptoe, just to see as well as before. All are more uncomfortable, and only a few have achieved a better view.

5.4 | The Ecological Impact of Consumption

More consumption of goods that use up resources in their production and generate waste materials also means more degradation of the natural environment. A U.S. standard of living for everyone on the globe is simply impossible. Analysts have estimated that giving everyone in the world U.S.-style diets and other consumption patterns would require an extra two to four planets to supply resources and absorb waste.

High-consuming countries have an impact on the natural environment that is out of proportion to their populations. As mentioned at the start of this chapter, for example, the average American consumes 269 pounds of meat each year. Per capita meat consumption in industrialized countries is about three times that in the developing world. Although some livestock are fed from land unsuitable for crops, livestock currently also consume about 37% of the world's grain harvest. Because livestock are relatively inefficient converters of the calories in grain to calories for human consumption, high-meat diets mean less food is available for direct human consumption. Growing pressure on the world's available cropland, along with environmental damage from fertilizer run-off, pesticides, depletion of aquifers, and soil salinization make U.S.-style diets an unsustainable proposition.

As we also noted at the start of this chapter, there is about 1 passenger car for every 2 people in the United States, 1 for about every 3.5 people in Europe, and 1 for every 68 people in developing countries. Carbon dioxide emissions arising from the burning of fossil fuels (such as gasoline in cars) have been conclusively linked to problems of

Figure 10.5 World Population by Region, 2001

Although the vast majority of the world's population lives in countries of the global South . . .

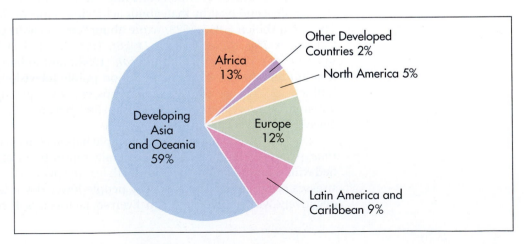

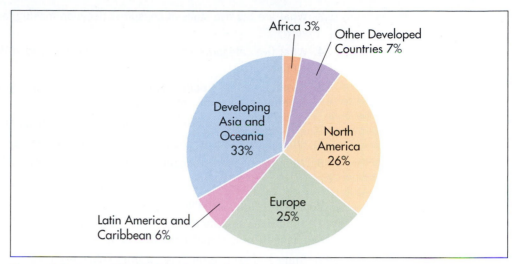

Figure 10.6 Carbon Dioxide Emissions by Region, 1997

. . . the countries of the global North generate more than half of the emissions linked to global warming.

(Source: United Nations Population Division, "Population, Environment and Development 2001," http://www.un.org/
esa/population/publications/ pdewallchart/popenvdev.pdf.)

global warming. According to United Nations figures, for example, North America has
about 5% of the world's population, as shown in Figure 10.5. However, as illustrated in
Figure 10.6, North America generates over one-quarter of the world's carbon dioxide
emissions.

Increased use of private cars also competes with food production for the use of
land, because car travel requires paved roads and parking lots. For example, it has been
estimated that if China were to increase its car ownership to the U.S. level (1 car for
every 2 people), it would need to pave over an area for parking lots and roads equivalent
to more than half of its current rice-producing land!

As public awareness of environmental damage increases, some beneficial changes
in consumption patterns have been accomplished. Reduced use of chlorofluoro-
carbons (formerly used in refrigeration and air conditioning) has slowed depletion of
the Earth's ozone layer, and use of unleaded fuels has reduced the release into the
atmosphere of toxic lead. More remains to be done, however, to encourage healthy and
sustainable patterns of consumption.

Discussion Questions

1. Tiffany is very happy with her fifth brand-new sports car. Jonelle is unhappy, because her
   computer is slower than all her friends'. Marcus is worried because he can't afford his
   prescribed high-blood-pressure medication. Describe the well-being of Tiffany, Jonelle,
   and Marcus from the old utility, new utility, and capability views.

2. Do you think the society we live in suffers from "affluenza"? If so, do you think there is
   a cure?

Review Questions

1. Which goals does consumption address?
2. At what levels of social organization (individual, household, work group, society) does
   consumption take place?

3. What are the five steps of consumer decision making, according to the marketing view?

4. What five categories of needs have psychologists identified as sources of consumer motivation?

5. How do reference points and reference groups play a role in consumer behavior, according to the marketing view?

6. What question does the utility theory view of consumer behavior seek to answer?

7. What does a budget line represent? Draw an example.

8. What happens to a budget line when income changes? When one price changes?

9. Why is real income, not just monetary income, important for consumer decisions?

10. When was utility theory first developed?

11. What does a utility function represent? What important concept is illustrated by changes in its slope? Draw an example.

12. State and explain the rule for utility maximization.

13. In what ways has utility theory been extended? In what ways has it been criticized?

14. How did the consumer society come about historically?

15. What are two major institutions that were invented to support the consumer society?

16. What are two major institutions in society that were modified by the turn to consumerism?

17. Describe the relationship between utility and well-being in the "old utility theory" view.

18. Describe the relationship between utility and well-being in the "new utility theory" view.

19. Describe the criteria for good policies and actions advocated in the "capability" approach.

20. What is the difference between absolute and relative deprivation?

21. What fraction of the world's population suffers from absolute deprivation?

22. Does increasing consumption always increase people's well-being? Explain.

23. How are people's consumption levels related to their reported happiness at any point in time? Over time?

24. Could the world sustain its population if everyone had a typical U.S. level of consumption? Explain.

Exercises

1. Both the marketing view and the utility theory view make assumptions about consumers. How do they compare? Make a list of similarities and contrasts. (For example, the utility view assumes that consumers have perfect information. Does the marketing view assume that?)

2. Monifa plans to spend her income on concert tickets and movie tickets. Suppose she has an income of $100, the price of a concert ticket (P_C) is $20, and the price of a movie ticket (P_M) is $10.
   a. Draw, and carefully label, a budget line diagram illustrating the consumption combinations that she can afford.
   b. Can she afford 6 movie tickets and 1 concert ticket? Label this point on your graph.
   c. Can she afford 2 movie tickets and 6 concert tickets? Label this point on your graph.

    d. Can she afford 4 movie tickets and 3 concert tickets? Label this point on your graph.

    e. Which of the combinations mentioned just uses up all her income?

3. Continuing from the previous exercise, suppose that Monifa's income rises to $120. Add her new budget line to the previous graph.

4. Next, suppose that Monifa's income stays at $100, but the price of concert tickets drops from $20 to $12.50 each.

    a. Draw and carefully label both her original and her new budget lines.

    b. Can she afford 2 movie tickets and 6 concert tickets after the price drop?

5. Finally, suppose that Monifa's income rises to $120, the price of movie tickets rises to $12, and the price of concert tickets rises to $24.

    a. Draw and carefully label her budget line.

    b. How does this compare to her budget line in exercise 2?

    c. What economic principle does this illustrate?

6. Suppose that the price of a concert ticket is $20, the price of a movie ticket is $10, and, at her chosen utility-maximizing consumption level, Monifa's marginal utility from concert tickets is 60 utils. What must her marginal utility from movie tickets be?

7. Match each concept in Column A with an example in Column B.

Column A	Column B
a. problem recognition	**i.** "The one who dies with the most stuff wins."
b. attribute of a good	**ii.** the standard of living you are used to
c. social needs	**iii.** getting bored with the third TV show in a row
d. reference point	
e. reference group	**iv.** not being able to afford to eat like people around you
f. diminishing marginal utility	
g. consumerist values	**v.** buying a gun, rather than relying on a police force for protection
h. displacement of public consumption	
i. absolute deprivation	**vi.** the number of speeds of a bicycle
j. relative deprivation	**vii.** "I'm not as cool as I'd like to be."
	viii. models in magazine advertisements (for some people)
	ix. lacking adequate food
	x. the need to be loved

8. Various U.S. government agencies, among them the Food and Drug Administration (FDA) and the Environmental Protection Agency (EPA), include "consumer protection" as one of their goals. The FDA, for example, decides whether drugs that pharmaceutical companies want to sell are safe and effective, and the EPA decides whether particular pesticides are safe for consumer use. Some people feel that such government oversight unnecessarily interferes with companies' freedom to sell their goods and with consumers' freedom to buy what they want. Indicate how you think each of the following individuals would evaluate consumer protection policies, in general.

    a. One who believes strongly in consumer sovereignty

    b. One who believes strongly that consumers make rational choices

    c. One who believes that consumers sometimes have less than perfect information about what they are buying

    d. One who believes that consumers can be overly influenced by marketing campaigns

    e. One who believes that policies should focus on human capabilities

A Formal Theory of Consumer Behavior

A1 | The Assumptions

In the traditional model, the only consumer is "the household," as described in Chapters 1 and 2. The household/consumer is assumed to have clearly defined preferences over all the goods it might consume and to want the consumption bundle that maximizes "utility," the sum of its satisfactions. The household/consumer is assumed to be well informed, autonomous, and rational and to consider only its own preferences, budget, and prices in coming to a consumption decision. For simplicity, we will continue to look at the case of only two goods, which we will call X and Y.

In this appendix, we will derive the graphical interpretation of the utility maximization rule given in the text.

A2 | The Budget Line and Its Slope

The combinations of X and Y that are available to the household are shown by a budget line, like that in Figure 10.7.

The budget line arises because the sum of the consumer's expenditures must add up to—not exceed—the consumer's income. Mathematically,

$$P_x x + P_y y = \text{Income}$$

Figure 10.7 The Budget Line and Its Slope

Geometrically, the slope of the budget line is $-P_x/P_y$

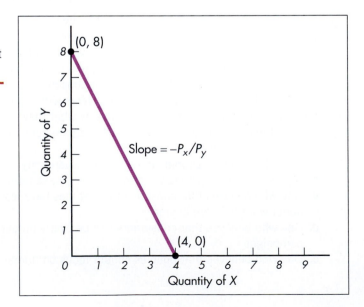

where x and y now denote the quantities purchased of each good. This equation can be rearranged, algebraically, into slope-intercept form (that is, $y = a + bx$, where the a intercept gives the value of y when x is equal to zero, and b is the slope of the line). This yields

$$y = \frac{\text{Income}}{P_y} - \frac{P_x}{P_y}\,x$$

For example, in Figure 10.7, income could be $40, the price of X could be $10, and the price of Y could be $5. The budget line crosses the y axis at $40/5 = 8$ units of Y and has a slope of $-10/5 = -2$. (Note that the line happens to be identical in its position to that in Figure 10.1 in the text—another example of the importance of real, not just monetary, income.)

In general, we note that the budget line has a slope equal to $-P_x/P_y$.

A3 | Indifference Curves

indifference curve: a curve consisting of points representing combinations of various quantities of two goods, such that every such combination gives the consumer the same level of utility

The consumer's preferences concerning the two goods can be illustrated on the same graph by using the thought device of **indifference curves** pioneered by Nobel laureate economist Paul Samuelson. Indifference curves show combinations of the two goods with which the consumer would be equally satisfied.

Indifference curves are thought to have the characteristic, bowed-in-toward-the-origin shape shown in Figure 10.8. This shape arises because we assume that the consumer experiences diminishing marginal utility for both X and Y.

Suppose the consumer starts out at point A, with a large amount of Y (6 units) but relatively little X (only 1 unit). At point A, the consumer has a fairly low marginal utility of Y, because she is already consuming a lot of it, and a fairly high marginal utility of X, because she has only a little of it. (Refer to the shape of Figure 10.4 if necessary. Utility flattens out if you have a lot of a good and rises steeply if you have little.) She will be willing to give up some of the Y—marginal units from which she is getting relatively little utility, anyway—to get more of X, a good that still has fairly high marginal utility. If she is just willing to give up 2 units of good Y to get 1 additional unit of good X, then she is indifferent between point A and point B. The slope of the indifference curve can be mathematically shown to be equal to $-MU_x/MU_y$. As we see on the graph, the slope of the indifference curve between point A and point B is approximately -2 ($= $ rise/run on a straight line between the points $= 2/1$). The ratio of marginal utilities, MU_x/MU_y is

Figure 10.8 An Indifference Curve

An indifference curve shows all combinations of goods that give the consumer the same level of utility. Its slope is $-MU_x/MU_y$.

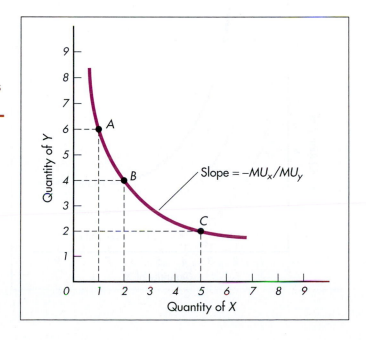

marginal rate of substitution: how much of one good the consumer is willing to give up to get more of another

called the **marginal rate of substitution**. It tells how much of one good the consumer is willing to give up to get more of the other.

However, at point *B*, the consumer's marginal utility from good *Y* will have risen from what it was at point *A*, because she is consuming less of it. Meanwhile, her marginal utility from *X* will have fallen, because she is consuming more of it. She will be more reluctant to give up more units of *Y* in exchange for further units of *X*. Likewise, because she is now consuming more *X*, she is less eager to get more of it than she was before. This means that if she is presented with further opportunities to trade, she will demand *more X* to compensate her for giving up any more *Y*. If forced to give up 2 more units of Y, Figure 10.8 shows that she will now require *3* more units of *X* to keep her just as happy. The approximate slope of the indifference curve between point *B* and point *C* is −2/3, and the marginal rate of substitution is now approximately 2/3. Indifference curves tend to be steep at low levels of consumption of *X* and then flatten out as you move to the right, as a consequence of diminishing marginal utility. Thus we have a falling marginal rate of substitution.

A4 | Utility Maximization

Different levels of utility are represented by different indifference curves. Because the utility theory view assumes that consumers always want more of at least one good (and usually of both goods), this "more is better" assumption means that utility rises as you move upward and to the right on the graph. Figure 10.9 shows three examples of indifference curves, corresponding to three different levels of utility.

The consumer's problem, then, is to get to the highest level of utility possible, given his budget. This problem and its solution are illustrated in Figure 10.10. The consumer can afford many points on the lowest indifference curve—much of the curve lies below and to the left of the budget line. If he chose to consume at point *C*, he would use up all his budget. But this is not the best he can do. Points *A* and *B* both would give him more utility than point *C*, and point *D* would give him even more. Points *B* and *D* are unobtainable, however, because they are above the budget line.

Figure 10.9 Different Levels of Utility

At points upwards and to the right, the consumer gets more of one or both goods. Under the "more is better" assumption, his or her utility is thus judged to be higher.

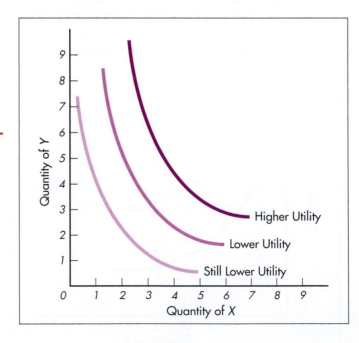

Figure 10.10 Utility Maximization

The consumer maximizes utility by getting on the highest achievable indifference curve, given his or her budget. This happens at point A.

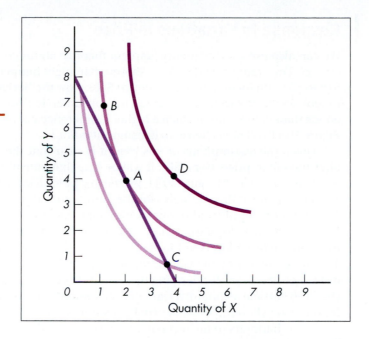

The best the consumer can do is get onto the indifference curve that just touches his budget line, at point A. At point A, the two curves just touch and have the same slope. That is,

$$\frac{-MU_x}{MU_y} = \frac{-P_x}{P_y}$$

which can be algebraically rearranged into

$$\frac{MU_x}{P_x} = \frac{MU_y}{P_y}$$

This is the rule that was discussed in the text.

Figure 10.11 Response to a Price Change

If the price of good X falls, the consumer will be able to reach a higher utility level.

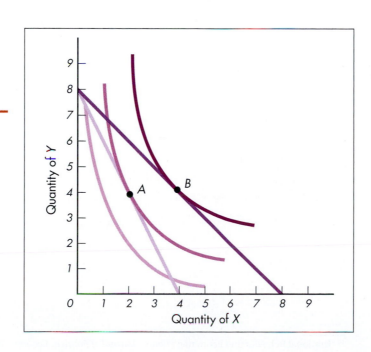

A5 | Response to Variations in Price

We can also use a utility theory graph to theorize about consumer responses to a price change. For example, Figure 10.11 shows what might happen if the price of X drops from $10 to $5 (with income held constant at $40). Now the budget line is higher at all points, except where it meets the Y axis. The consumer is thus able to afford more of the goods than before and to reach a higher indifference curve. The consumer portrayed in Figure 10.11 will now choose to consume at point B.

Given the assumptions of this view, it is clear that the consumer has higher utility after the fall in price. Generally, it will be true that consumers will buy more of a good when its price falls. In Figure 10.11, we see that point B is farther to the right than point A.

This is one of the rationales for the downward-sloping demand curve discussed in Chapter 4 on supply and demand. By no means, however, is it the only explanation. First, downward-sloping demand curves may be a useful tool for analyzing the behavior of many other kinds of buyers, such as businesses, nonprofits, and governments. The foregoing is not an explanation for their behavior. Second, the tool of utility theory is not necessary for deriving the demand curves, even for household/consumers. (In a 1962 article, economist Gary Becker showed that market purchases of a good will tend to rise when prices fall, even if consumers act only impulsively or out of habit.)[15]

What happens to the level of purchases of good Y when the price of good X falls? This is hard to predict without knowing more about the particular goods. This question was discussed under the topics of "substitutes" and "complements" in Chapter 4. Effects of income changes on consumer behavior, and the way in which price changes can include "income and substitution effects," were discussed in Chapters 4 and 5.

---

[15] "Irrational Behavior and Economic Theory," *Journal of Political Economy* 70,1–13

Part Four

A Closer Look at Markets

257

Markets Without Market Power

Chapter 11

Chances are you have heard politicians or media commentators expound on the benefits of "free markets." One of the benefits claimed for "free markets" is that they result in economic efficiency—in resources being used to get the highest possible value of output. Behind this political argument is an economic model—a model of markets in which no one individual, company, or institution has power over the market, or, to put it in terms favored by economists, markets in which "perfect competition" reigns. This chapter discusses economists' idea of perfect competition and explains how, under the assumptions of perfect competition and the traditional model, questions of equity and efficiency are addressed.

1 | Understanding Market Power and Competition

market power: the ability to control, or at least affect, the terms and conditions of the exchanges in which one participates

Having power means having the ability to influence something. **Market power** is the ability to control, or at least affect, the terms and conditions of the exchanges in which you participate. One of the characteristics of the market structure called perfect competition is that individual economic actors have *no market power*. (We used this assumption in Chapter 5 when we discussed the idea that some sellers are "price takers.")

People often have a very hard time understanding the traditional neoclassical view of market power and competition. However, because they are important in political and ethical discussions about the merits of markets as a form of social organization, it is important to understand the arguments correctly. The traditional neoclassical view that evolved in economics during the 20th century is distinct from the views that might be taken by many noneconomists, including, for example, "corporate climbers" and "concerned citizens."

⊳ In the hypothetical situation called perfect competition, economic actors have *no market power.*

The Corporate Climber View. From the point of view of an individual business company (or a non-profit or state-owned firm that also sells goods or services), market power usually seems like a *good* thing. You want to be able to influence people to buy what you are selling. You want to be able to command a high price for what you sell. You want to have the power to bargain for low prices for the resources that you buy. You want your organization to grow, increasing its size and command over resources. Your goal may be to get a large share of the market (or markets) in which you sell. You would like to become recognized as a leader in your industry (or maybe in many industries).

The existence of competition, on the other hand, is usually seen as a bad thing from the perspective of the corporate climber. You actively strategize in order to "beat" competing companies. You try to buy them out or, even better, come out with a new innovation that puts you in a class of your own! The dream of the individual corporate climber is to become a corner-office executive with a powerful firm, secure from competition—to be a Bill Gates!

The Concerned Citizen View. Many people, on the other hand, thinking of market power primarily in terms of the size and financial clout of organizations, find it undesirable and even scary. They believe that "big business" or "big government"—or even worse, the two in league with each other—threatens the freedoms of the "little person." They cite examples of big businesses and/or corrupt agencies acting callously or unethically, jacking up prices on goods that people need, forcing workers to accept low wages, or pushing around the little person with lawsuits or excessive regulation. They may fear that the government might just become an extension of wealthy interests and become oblivious to the state of the average citizen.

At the same time, "competition" may also be viewed negatively by concerned citizens. Businesses often cite the "need to stay competitive" as their reason for slashing jobs, taking over smaller companies, refusing to implement voluntary pollution controls, or moving their production overseas, all of which are perceived as harmful. From the point of view of a concerned citizen, neither market power nor tooth-and-nail competition serves the interests of a peaceful and humane society. The dream of the concerned citizen is decentralized power, along with ethical and cooperative behavior that serves the common good.

The Traditional Neoclassical View. Like the concerned citizen view, this view considers market power to be generally *bad*. Why is this? As a social science, economics tends to make normative judgments from the point of view of society as a whole, not just from the perspective of one particular actor. The traditional neoclassical view, focused entirely on efficiency goals, notes that market power can create inefficiency. (We will demonstrate this in the next chapter.) Hence it considers market power to be largely harmful (except for certain unavoidable cases).

Unlike both the corporate climber and concerned citizen views, however, the traditional neoclassical view considers competition *good*. How can this be so? The term *competitive market* does not imply the use of cutthroat policies. Instead, it is shorthand for the case in which so many buyers and sellers interact in a market that no one of them is able to develop much in the way of market power. The fact that some other economic actor is always competing with you—trying to take away your customers or your workers, or poised to buy from your suppliers—is what keeps you on your toes and makes you run your organization efficiently. Competition, to an economist, *means* decentralized power. The image of a self-regulating, harmonious, "free" competitive market is at the core of traditional neoclassical economics.

Consider an analogy to sports. The corporate climber is like the individual team, which would like to prove itself the best and win the gold trophy, perhaps at any cost. The concerned citizen is like a fan, who wants to see all the teams have a chance to play the sport and is disgusted when excessive emphasis on winning leads teams to cheat and otherwise act badly. The traditional neoclassical economist is like the manager of the league, who sees the manager's task as ensuring that there are sufficient teams of roughly equal quality, that the season will be interesting, and that the athletes will be challenged into improving their performance. Can a sports industry—or an economy—promote a stimulating but not excessive emphasis on "winning," with appropriate consideration for all the interests involved?

2 | Perfect Competition

2.1 | The Conditions of Perfect Competition

The model of perfect competition starts with the assumptions of the traditional neoclassical model and then adds some further conditions:

1. There are *numerous small sellers and buyers*, so small that no individual seller or buyer can affect the market price.

2. Within any particular market, *only one kind of good or service* is traded. All units of that kind of good or service *are identical;* hence, buyers won't care which firm they buy from.

3. Producers of the good or service can *freely enter or exit* the industry. There are no barriers preventing a new firm from joining the market or preventing an existing one from leaving it.

4. Buyers and sellers all have *perfect information*. They all know where the good is available, at what prices it is offered, and whether profits are being made.

Implicit in this ideal are the traditional model's assumptions about the production and cost structures of the competitive firms. Firms' production functions are assumed to display the smooth pattern of short-run diminishing returns over relevant production levels that we discussed under the topic of "convexity" in Chapter 8. Firms are assumed to rely on marginal thinking to make profit-maximizing decisions.

Another assumption is that the (long-run) minimum efficient scale of a producer in this industry is fairly small, relative to the level of demand for the output of the industry. In other words, production is characterized by constant returns to scale, not by economies of scale. This is important because, if it were *not* the case, the market might not be large enough for the many efficient firms assumed by the theory.

In addition, exchange is envisioned as taking place in big double-auction spot markets. Like the hypothetical apartment sellers and buyers in Chapter 4, everyone (hypothetically) gathers together. Someone compiles all the offers to buy and to sell and determines what the market-clearing price will be. The price is announced, and everyone who wants to exchange at that price does so. The theory of perfect competition does not concern itself with market institutions, the identity of the hypothetical auctioneer, or transaction costs. "The market determines the price," it is said.

With these assumptions, every individual seller is a price taker, as discussed in Chapter 5. *Market* supply and market demand curves can have various slopes, but the *individual* seller always faces a perfectly elastic demand curve. She can sell as many units as she wants—as long as she charges the market price. If she raises her price, all the business will go to lower-priced competitors, and she will sell nothing.

2.2 | Examples of Perfect Competition?

Examples of perfectly competitive markets in the real world are hard to come by. In older textbooks, agricultural commodities such as wheat were often given as examples of commodities traded in perfectly competitive product markets. It was argued that one

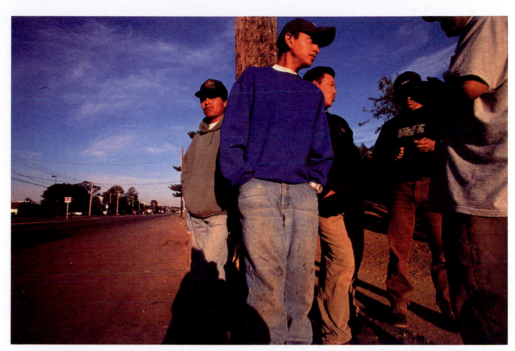

Markets for relatively unskilled labor sometimes approximate the assumptions for perfectly competitive markets. These Mexican immigrant day laborers are waiting for agricultural work by a street corner in New York State. Farmers or labor contractors will come by and hire the number they need for the day. There are numerous buyers and sellers, and the work is pretty much the same from man to man and from job to job. Therefore, the workers tend to be "price-takers," who will work at the "going wage" or not at all.

farmer's wheat (of a given type) was pretty much identical to the wheat (of the same type) sold by other farmers, and that no individual farmer had any perceptible influence on the market price. In fact, in contemporary industrialized countries, agricultural markets tend to be highly organized and regulated, with farmer-supported marketing boards, government-guaranteed minimum prices, long-term contracts, and the like deliberately influencing the terms and conditions of the market.

Perhaps the markets that most closely approach perfect competition today are not product markets at all, but certain financial resale markets. For example, the conditions that prevail in the spot market for buying and selling a few shares of a very large, publicly held corporation approximate the most important conditions. The shares are all identical. Because this is a financial resale market, the cost of "production" is irrelevant. Well-defined stock exchanges set up a structure under which the going price becomes common knowledge. When there are very many outstanding shares of stock, the trading of a few shares does not affect the price (or other conditions of trade). If you own a few shares of stock and think of selling them, your broker will quote you a price—take it or leave it. The demand curve you face, as an individual seller, is horizontal.

In some labor markets, as well, conditions may approximate perfect competition. Workers with only the most general of skills (such as flipping burgers or sweeping floors) may provide, from an employer's point of view, fairly identical services. When there are many such "sellers," they may find they have a choice of a job at "the going wage" or no job at all.

2.3 | Profit Maximization Under Perfect Competition

Returning to the hypothetical example of a perfectly competitive firm, the amount this producer will want to sell will depend on demand for the product and on the firm's cost structure.

The individual price-taking firm faces a perfectly elastic demand curve, as shown in Figure 11.1(a). As we saw in Chapter 8, a firm facing a "convex" profit-maximization problem will maximize profit by setting marginal revenue equal to marginal cost ($MR = MC$). In perfect competition, the marginal revenue is constant and equal to the market-determined price, so the competitive firm produces where $P = MC$. The individual firm's supply curve—showing how much it would produce at each price—is just a portion of its MC curve (as derived in Chapter 8).[1] In Figure 11.1(a), with a price of P_E, the profit-maximizing individual firm with the given MC curve (that is, individual supply curve) will produce 100 units.

The market supply curve in Figure 11.1(b) is simply the horizontal sum of the supply curves of the individual firms. By assumption, the 100 units of output supplied by this one firm represent only a small portion of the *market* quantity demanded of this good, 10,000 units. The market demand curve has the usual slope, and we have assumed that all individual buyers are also, similarly, price takers. The price facing each individual firm is the price determined at the **competitive equilibrium** point E.

How much economic profit will the profit-maximizing competitive firm make, then, over the long haul? Perhaps surprisingly, the answer is "zero"!

Recall (from Chapters 7 and 8) that the costs of capital and the opportunity cost of the entrepreneur's time are considered *economic* costs, which need to be subtracted from revenues to find *economic* profits (even if such costs are sometimes neglected in the calculation of *accounting* profits). A firm is said to make **zero economic profit** when revenues are just sufficient to compensate for the use of labor, materials, and other physical inputs; financial and physical capital; and the time inputs of the entrepreneur—all at the opportunity costs of their supply. Sometimes this is also called **normal profit**, to reflect the fact that *accounting* profits are just high enough to compensate the entrepreneur for his or her time input.

What would happen in a competitive market if a firm were to make **positive economic profit** (or **above-normal profit**)? This would mean that the firm is receiving

> ○ The profit-maximizing perfectly competitive firm sets price equal to marginal cost ($P = MC$).

competitive equilibrium: the equilibrium in a market where all buyers and sellers are price takers, unable individually to influence the price they pay or charge

zero economic profit (or normal profit): the amount (zero) that is left over when revenues just meet the opportunity costs of supplying all resources, including an entrepreneur's capital and time

positive economic profit (or above-normal profit): the amount by which revenues exceed opportunity costs

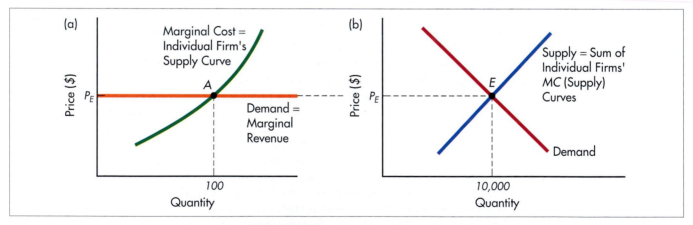

Figure 11.1 Demand and Supply
(a) For a Perfectly Competitive Individual Firm
(b) In a Perfectly Competitive Market
In a perfectly competitive market, each individual firm faces the price for its output that is determined in the market. Supply in the market is determined by the sum of the individual firms' marginal cost (or individual supply) curves.

---

[1] It is only a *portion* of the MC curve because at very low prices, the firm will not be able to cover even its variable costs. It will prefer to go out of business, rather than sell at those prices. A full graphical explanation is given in the appendices to Chapter 7, Chapter 8, and the present chapter.

revenues above and beyond the opportunity costs of its resources. For example, suppose you are an entrepreneur running your own firm, selling your output of Q_1 units at the market-determined price P_1, as shown in Figure 11.2(a), corresponding to the market equilibrium E_1 in Figure 11.2(b). After paying for all resources *other than your time*, you have $70,000 left over. Your next best opportunity for use of your time is a job that would have paid $40,000 for the same amount of your time. Hence $40,000 of your income from your business is an economic cost, and the $30,000 over and above that is pure *positive economic profit*.

Remember that in perfectly competitive markets, everyone has perfect information, and new sellers can enter at any time. Wouldn't other people like to make an extra $30,000, too? New producers will come into your market. As they do, the supply curve (which depends on the number of producers) will shift to the right, as shown by curve S_2 in Figure 11.2(b). It will continue to shift as long as positive economic profits attract new entrants to the market.

Of course, this will cause the market price to fall. In Figure 11.2, the price is shown as dropping to P_2. The price drop will reduce revenues (from the large rectangle with point A at one corner to the smaller rectangle with point B at one corner in Figure 11.2a) and reduce profits. The market supply curve will stop shifting only when all firms in the market are making zero economic profit.

Conversely, if for some reason the selling price in the market were too low, so that firms were making economic losses, some firms would *exit*. The exit of some firms would cause the supply curve to shift to the left and the market price to rise. The process would again stop when all firms were just making zero economic profit.

In theory, all these adjustments happen instantaneously, and every resource is always used in exact accordance with its opportunity cost. In applying this model to relatively competitive markets in the real world, economists say that "in the long run, competitive pressures should drive economic profits toward zero."

Competition, in the traditional neoclassical economist's view, is hence rather passive—especially compared to the corporate climber's more active and aggressive understanding of the term. The perfectly competitive firm simply takes the market price as given, sets $P = MC$, and smoothly enters or exits as need be.

▷ Entry and exit of firms is what drives economic profits to zero in perfectly competitive markets.

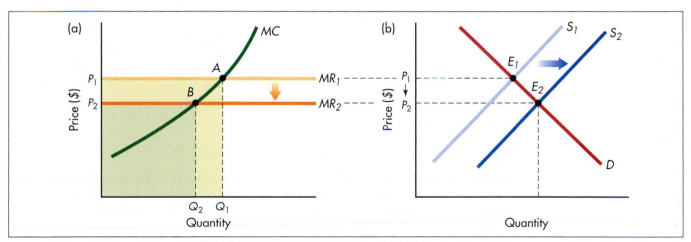

Figure 11.2   The Effects of the Entrance of New Firms into a Competitive Market
(a) On the Individual Firm
(b) On the Market
When new firms enter a perfectly competitive market they increase supply, driving down the competitive market price. This in turn decreases the revenues received by the individual firms (and their profits).

Discussion Questions

1. "Why would anyone *run* a business if they couldn't make a profit?" This is a frequent response to economists' idea that a market could be characterized by "zero economic profits" for all firms.
    a. In words, explain what economists mean by zero economic profits and why an entrepreneur would choose to continue running a perfectly competitive business.
    b. Explain why perfectly competitive firms are assumed to earn zero economic profits in the long run.
2. Look back at the conditions for perfect competition. Do you think any of the following industries are likely to be characterized by something approaching perfect competition? Why or why not?
    a. Manufacture of automobiles
    b. Manufacture of pharmaceuticals protected by patents
    c. Retail sales of state lottery tickets

3 | Efficiency and Equity in the Case of Perfect Competition

Suppose that all markets operate under the assumptions of the traditional model and the additional conditions specified by perfect competition (including the implicit assumptions about scale and transaction costs). Suppose that buyers as well as sellers are price takers. The traditional model also makes the following assumptions:

○ Production and consumption generate no externalities, either positive or negative.

○ There are no public goods.

○ All costs and benefits are captured in this static model—there are no effects spread out over time.

○ Society is not concerned about distribution—the current distribution of ability to pay is considered acceptable.

Under these assumptions, perfectly competitive markets are efficient and lead to the best possible social outcomes.

Under these assumptions, any market supply curve can be taken to reflect the *social* marginal cost of production, and any market demand curve can be taken to reflect the *social* marginal benefit of consumption. At the hypothetical competitive equilibrium at the intersection of the supply and demand curves, the price that people are willing to pay for the last unit produced is exactly equal to the marginal cost of producing it. This result is sometimes called **allocative efficiency** to emphasize that resources are allocated to various production processes on the basis of the exact marginal value of the goods and services to buyers.

allocative efficiency: the allocation of resources to their most (market-)valued uses

3.1 | Perfect Competition and Long-Run Efficiency

Recall that in the "long run," firms not only enter and exit but also can adjust the scale of their operation, growing larger to take advantage of economies of scale or smaller to minimize diseconomies of scale. Figure 11.3 reproduces the long-run average cost curve from Chapter 7. As long as market demand is sufficient to keep many firms in business, no competitive firm will operate on the downward- or upward-sloping parts of this curve.

Why? The sloping sections of the curve indicate operation at high levels of per-unit costs. Any firm incurring such high operating costs would be put out of business by the entry of firms that operate at more efficient, low-unit-cost levels. If even the most efficient firms make zero profits, then any firm that is less than fully efficient must make

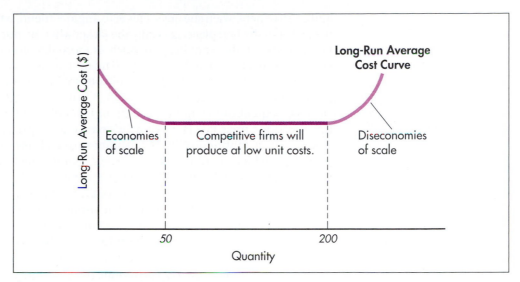

Figure 11.3 Long-Run Efficiency in Production
Perfectly competitive firms will operate at the scale that gives them the lowest possible unit costs, because otherwise they would make negative profit.

losses. Competition will drive firms to seek the lowest-cost scale of operations, choosing a size of operations between the minimum efficient scale (shown as an output level of 50 units in Figure 11.3) and the maximum efficient scale (shown as an output level of 200 units).

The story of perfect competition has often been extended to incorporate some notions of dynamics and innovation. Suppose many firms are operating at minimum average costs, all making zero economic profits, and then one firm invents a new technology or tries a new management practice that reduces its costs even further. Such a firm may temporarily make positive economic profits—which is, presumably, the reason why it would attempt such innovations. But with free entry and perfect information, all other firms will soon follow suit. Any firm that doesn't will end up with a higher-than-minimum cost structure and will make economic losses. Competition, it is said, drives firms to innovate and to adopt efficient practices rapidly.

The idea of an economy characterized everywhere by perfect competition (with no externalities, no concerns about inequality, and so on) represented a sort of "best of all possible worlds" for traditional neoclassical economics. In such an idealized economy, all goods would be produced exactly according to buyers' willingness (and ability) to pay, all resources would be compensated exactly according to their opportunity costs, and all production would be accomplished at minimum costs to society. A more detailed graphical analysis of perfectly competitive firms is provided in the appendix to this chapter. The normative weight given to the idea of a perfectly competitive economy in neoclassical analysis will be further discussed in Chapter 19.

3.2 | Consumer and Producer Surplus

Under the assumptions listed at the beginning of this section, we can use supply and demand graphs to analyze the effects of some types of policies on well-being.

How much is a jacket you buy for $60 worth to you in well-being terms? The answer is not necessarily $60. Suppose you are willing and able to pay up to $80 for a particular jacket but find that you can actually buy it for only $60. You've made a gain, above and beyond just getting the jacket, when you purchase it. It is as though you bought the jacket *and* received $20! Perhaps a friend of yours is willing and able to pay $70 for the jacket: She gets the jacket

consumer surplus: the excess (summed over all the buyers in a market) of the amounts that buyers would be willing to pay for a good or service, over the amounts that they actually pay

and a $10 benefit when she buys it for $60. Another friend, who is willing to pay only $60 for the jacket in the first place, gets only the jacket when he purchases it and no extra benefit. Economists call the extra benefits, such as those that you and your first friend received, **consumer surplus** when they are added up over all the buyers in the market.

If you and your friends are the only buyers in the market for this particular type of jacket, consumer surplus would be $20 + $10 + $0 = $30. More generally, Figure 11.4 shows an equilibrium supply and demand model for a competitive market in which all the buyers are price takers (paying the going market price, P_E), and demand can be represented by a continuous line. Consumer surplus is given by the green area above the price line (which represents what buyers *actually* pay) and below the demand curve (which represents what buyers are *willing to* pay).

Similarly, suppose a perfectly competitive firm has a marginal cost of producing a jacket of $50 but can sell it for $60. The producer makes a gain of $10 on that jacket, above the minimum that would induce it to offer the good on the market. Economists call these extra benefits **producer surplus** when they are added up over all the sellers in the market. The existence of producer surplus is consistent with the idea that firms in perfect competition make zero economic profits: In this situation the value of producer surplus is exactly what firms need to pay their *fixed* costs of production.

producer surplus: the excess (summed over all the sellers in a market) of the amounts sellers actually receive, over the amounts that would make them just willing to supply the good or service

Figure 11.5 shows producer surplus in a competitive market. In such a market, all sellers are price takers, so they all sell at price P_E. Producer surplus is the purple area below the price line and above the market supply curve (because the latter reflects the minimum prices that competitive producers will accept to supply their good or service).

3.3 | Deadweight Loss

Recall that an *efficient* situation is one in which resources produce the maximum possible value of output, without unnecessary waste or expense. Consumer and producer surplus are measures of how much—in addition to the actual price paid—a given market outcome is valued, in monetary terms, by the individual actors who take part in it.

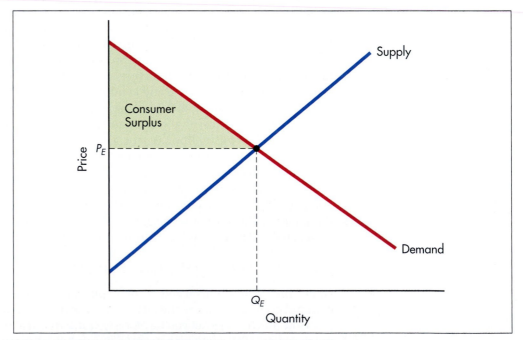

Figure 11.4 Extra Benefits to Buyers
Consumer surplus is the difference between what consumers are willing to pay (represented by the demand curve) and what they actually pay for each unit of the good (represented by the market price).

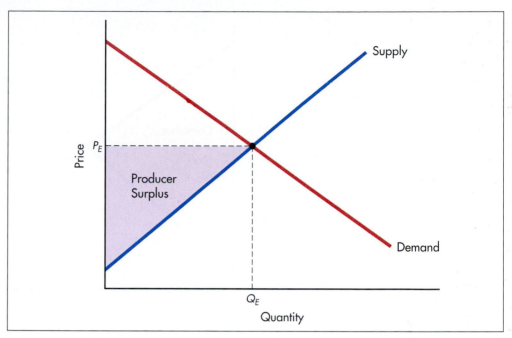

Figure 11.5 Extra Benefits to Sellers
Producer surplus is the difference between the minimum price that would induce producers to supply a good (represented by the supply curve) and what they actually receive for each unit of the good (represented by the market price).

Hence, under the assumption that only individual monetary valuations matter, if either consumer or producer surplus is reduced below the maximum possible given existing resources, the resulting situation is considered to be *inefficient*.

Examining Figures 11.4 and 11.5, you can see that consumer and producer surplus are maximized when price and quantity are at their competitive equilibrium levels. At competitive equilibrium, producer and consumer surplus would be triangles reaching all the way out to Q_E. But suppose that for some reason people were allowed to trade only a quantity of Q_1 instead of Q_E, as shown in Figure 11.6. (We will discuss the prevailing prices as we get into specific cases a little later.) The dark yellow area of surplus would be lost, and surplus would be reduced to the light yellow area. The dark yellow area graphically represents the inefficiency that would arise if people were not allowed to make mutually beneficial trades. This kind of inefficiency carries the special name **deadweight loss**.

deadweight loss: the loss in efficiency (measured in terms of producer and consumer surplus) that is said to arise if market transactions take place at other than the competitive market equilibrium level

3.4 | Policy Analysis: Taxation

Deadweight loss can happen for an number of reasons, one of which is government taxation. Governments need to raise funds to pay for, at a minimum, the provision of security, roads, and other public goods.

Taxation can drive a "wedge" between what a buyer pays and what a seller gets. An excise tax, for example, adds a set dollar amount to the price paid for any unit of a good. Gasoline and cigarettes often carry excise taxes. Letting the dollar tax amount be t, we have $P_{buyer} = P_{seller} + t$. (For example, we have \$5.05 = \$5.00 + \$.05 if the tax is a nickel per unit.)

Figure 11.7 shows how this can create deadweight loss. Sellers of the good get the price represented by supply curve S. But buyers of any quantity of the good have to pay not only the price indicated by curve S for a particular quantity but the tax on that quantity as well. The price paid by the buyers for any quantity can thus be indicated by the curve $S_{plus\ tax}$—a curve that lies t units vertically above S.

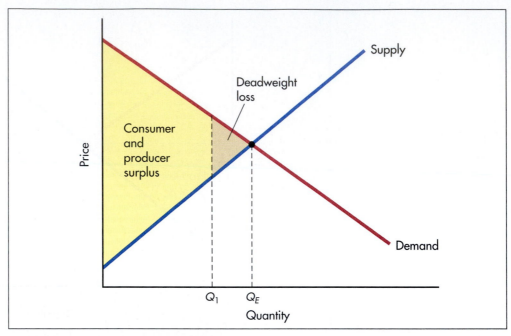

Figure 11.6 Lost Surplus and Inefficiency
If for some reason people are not allowed to trade at the price and quantity determined by equilibrium in a perfectly competitive market, some benefits to society will be lost. This loss is called deadweight loss.

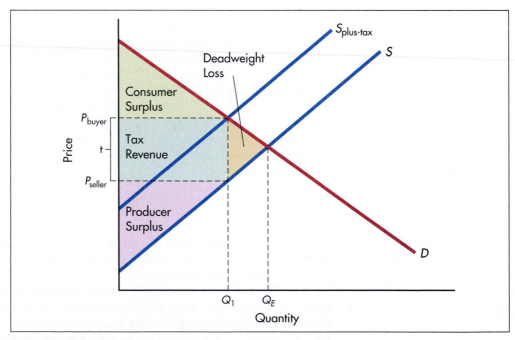

Figure 11.7 Effect of a Tax
An excise tax means that the price paid by the buyer is higher than the price received by the seller. Because the plus-tax price causes consumers to buy less than the competitive equilibrium quantity, deadweight loss occurs. Tax revenue goes to the government to fund its projects.

We draw this graph by drawing these two supply curves. Then we read off, from the intersection of the plus-tax supply curve and the demand curve, how much buyers will buy at this plus-tax price. Dropping down to the quantity axis from this point on the demand curve, we see that quantity demanded will fall to Q_1. For selling this quantity, the sellers receive P_{seller}, so producer surplus is the area below the P_{seller} line (and above the regular supply curve). Buyers pay P_{buyer} and have consumer surplus above this price line (and below the demand curve).

The rectangle in the middle is tax revenue, $t \times Q_1$, collected by the government. Deadweight loss, represented by the dark yellow triangle, is created.

What has happened to producer and consumer surplus in Figure 11.7? Producers get only P_{seller}, so producer surplus is reduced, relative to the competitive equilibrium. Consumers have to pay P_{buyer}, so consumer surplus is likewise reduced. All the areas to the left of Q_1 represent redistribution among the various economic actors—in this case, from buyers and sellers to the government. The lost area to the right of Q_1 represents a loss to society as a whole. Trades are not being made at the most efficient level.

Does the existence of this deadweight loss mean that governments should never engage in taxation? Of course not. If the value of what the government does with the taxes (creating infrastructure, educating, and so on) is worth more, in the general scheme of things, than the lost consumer and producer surplus from lost sales of the taxed good, overall well-being is increased. That is, although the revenue raised comes from a loss in surplus in *this* market, the value of most of that lost surplus may return to producers and consumers in another way—perhaps with even more benefit—if the government uses the revenue wisely.

The only part of the lost surplus that cannot be used by the government is that represented by the deadweight loss triangle. This part of the lost surplus is lost to society as a whole, not just by a particular actor. A little inefficiency in one market may be a small price to pay, though, for the benefits of public purpose projects elsewhere. In the case of cigarettes and gasoline, to the extent that taxes reduce the quantity demanded, taxes might actually help *correct* situations of poor consumer choice or environmental externalities (a subject to be taken up at more length in Chapter 17).

Our previous discussion of price elasticity (Chapter 5), however, can be used to show that governments need to be careful about *which* goods they choose to tax. Comparing Figure 11.7 with Figure 11.8 reveals how a tax of the same amount per unit can cause different amounts of deadweight loss and revenue gain, depending on the elasticity of demand. In these figures the supply curves are identical, as is the initial equilibrium point. In Figure 11.8, demand is more elastic, so there is a larger drop in quantity demanded (to Q_2) than seen in Figure 11.7. Deadweight loss is larger, and the revenue gain is smaller, than in Figure 11.7. The more the buyers respond to the price change, the farther the market moves from its competitive equilibrium position, and the more inefficiency is created.

Imagine, for example, that a government imposed a very steep tax on butter but not on its close substitutes, margarine and oil. If people all immediately stopped buying butter and bought the other fats instead, butter lovers would lose some well-being because they would be deprived of a favorite food. And because no one was buying butter any more, the tax would be completely useless in raising revenue!

On the other hand, if you draw the same diagram but with a very inelastic demand curve, you will see that deadweight loss is quite small and tax revenues relatively large. Gasoline, as we have seen, is inelastically demanded, so gas taxes can raise substantial revenues with relatively little efficiency loss.

Governments should study the elasticity of demand (and of supply, as well) for a good when they are considering taxing it: The less elastic the demand, the less efficiency loss may be created, and the more revenue will be raised.

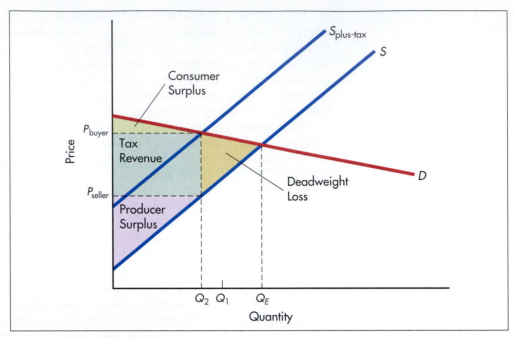

Figure 11.8 Tax with Elastic Demand
When demand for a good is very price-elastic, addition of a tax will cause buyers to cut way back on their purchases. Taxes on very elastically demanded goods will raise less revenue and generally cause more efficiency loss than taxes on less elastically demanded goods.

Unfortunately, the question of what goods to tax can be a tricky one, because the goal of making the economy run efficiently can sometimes collide with other interests. We have just seen that there is less efficiency loss when governments tax price-inelastically demanded goods. However, as we discussed in Chapter 5, some goods are inelastically demanded because they are necessary to life. A large tax on a life-saving drug might be justifiable on efficiency grounds but would probably be rejected on ethical grounds. It doesn't seem fair to raise funds at the expense of desperately ill people. Similarly, opponents of increased gasoline taxes argue that cheap energy is essential for the economic health of much of our society, creating, for example, a competitive advantage over Japan, Europe and other places where fossil fuels are heavily taxed.

3.5 | Policy Analysis: Rent Control

Some government regulations are explicitly designed for distributive purposes. They may transfer benefits from sellers to buyers, or vice versa, without raising revenue. Rent control is one example. In a rent control situation, a local government puts a price ceiling (as discussed in Chapter 4) on rents that landlords can charge for residential apartments. Usually, this is done because of the hardship that would be inflicted on a population that is low income, elderly, or both by steeply rising rents. Forcing low-income elderly people to move from the neighborhood they have lived in all their lives is often seen as cruel, especially if the landlords are already wealthy. Believing that the present rents are reward enough for the landlords' investment in their properties, cities sometimes enact laws that limit landlords' ability to raise rents and displace tenants.

If supply and demand for apartments are as pictured in Figure 11.9, with moderate elasticities, we can see the results of such a price ceiling. Renters pay, and landlords receive, $P_{ceiling}$. At this price, landlords are willing to supply Q_1 apartments. The rectangle

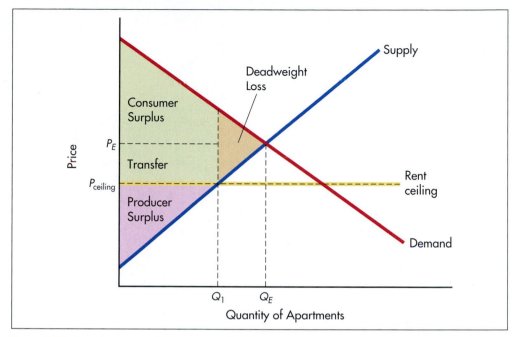

Figure 11.9 Rent Control with Moderately Elastic Supply

Rent control means that renters are required to pay no more than $P_{ceiling}$ in rent. With an elastic supply curve for apartments, producers will supply only Q_1 apartments to the market at the rent-controlled price. Relative to the competitive equilibrium, some renters gain. Their gains come at the expense of producers, potential renters who can't find apartments, and societal efficiency.

labeled "Transfer" now represents a transfer from landlords to renters: Compared to the competitive equilibrium sizes of producer and consumer surplus, this rectangle has been subtracted from producer surplus and added to consumer surplus.

This transfer is accompanied by a substantial deadweight loss (coming partly from consumer surplus and partly from producer surplus). There is a loss of residential housing because landlords have reduced the quantity they offer in the market compared to its competitive equilibrium level. In the case illustrated, some potential renters who would have gotten apartments in a competitive market will be shut out of the market by rent control.

How realistic is this, however? In most older city neighborhoods, which is where rent control is usually enacted, the stock of apartments is pretty much set. Landlords might consider converting existing apartments into offices or neglecting them until they fall apart and can be condemned and torn down. But if both of these options are forbidden by local zoning and health laws, it is not really possible to withdraw apartments from the market profitably. Landlords will probably not put as much into repair and renovation as they would with higher rents, but the tenants may be willing to accept lower quality if it means affordable rents. The supply curve for apartments then tends to be very inelastic, perhaps nearly vertical, as illustrated in Figure 11.10. In this case, the transfer from landlords to renters is large, and efficiency loss and apartment loss are nonexistent. In the case of a fixed quantity of apartments, rent control has purely distributional effects. If society perceives the transfer of benefit from landlords to renters to be a good thing, the policy may be a good one on equity grounds while involving little efficiency loss.

Of course, if the landlords are themselves low-income elderly people, or if the city that is considering rent control is one in which new apartments are just being built (and

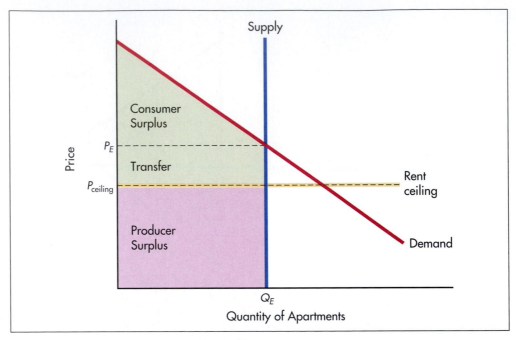

Figure 11.10 Rent Control with Perfectly Inelastic Supply

If the supply of apartments is perfectly inelastic, rent control will have purely distributional effects on landlords and renters. The quantity of apartments is not reduced, and there is no efficiency loss.

so supply is elastic), the analysis according to equity and efficiency effects could turn out differently. This example demonstrates, however, that policies that depart from unfettered market equilibrium are not always "inefficient" and "bad."

Discussion Questions

1. In most communities in temperate climates, water is very cheap. People get it from wells or city pipes at very low per-unit costs. Does the low price of water mean that water isn't "worth" much in terms of benefit to us? If the supply were severely restricted, how much would you really be willing to pay for that first glass of water? Draw a graph and explain how the notion of "consumer surplus" might help explain why some goods with high human or *use value* have low market or *monetary value*.

2. One reason why people sometimes work "off the books" (that is, illegally, for cash that goes unreported to any authorities) is to try to avoid the "wedges" between the amount of take-home cash the worker (seller/producer) gets and the amount the employer (buyer/consumer) pays. One of these wedges is the payroll tax. Suppose, for example, that it costs an employer/homeowner $20 per hour to hire someone to mow a lawn, through entirely legal channels, but that employee will take home only $17 after tax. Redraw Figure 11.7, with more specific labels pertaining to this example. Where, on this graph, can we see most clearly the incentive that some people will have to break the law and work "off the books"? (*Hint*: If everything is done legally, what happens to the worker who will work only for $18 or more and the employer/homeowner who will pay only $19 or less?) Does breaking the law increase or decrease efficiency? Do you think "off the books" work is a good idea overall?

4 | A Final Note

It is important to remember that perfect competition describes a *theoretical ideal case*— that is, a useful fiction—not the general nature of a real-world economy. In the real world, many buyers and sellers have some degree of control over the terms on which they trade. Producers rarely fit the traditional model image of the profit-maximizing firm facing a convex production problem. The idea that a competitive equilibrium represents a socially "best" outcome relies on assuming away issues such as transaction costs, issues of scale, externalities, bad information, public goods, and poverty and maldistribution, which are often very important in real economies. The model of perfect competition is important to learn in order to understand economic discussions, but it should always be considered "in context."

Review Questions

1. Describe how market power and competition are viewed differently by the "corporate climber," the "concerned citizen," and the traditional neoclassical economist.
2. What market conditions characterize perfect competition?
3. What are some additional assumptions of the model of perfect competition?
4. How is a perfectly competitive firm thought to maximize profits?
5. Are perfectly competitive markets seen as leading to efficiency? Why?
6. On a supply and demand graph, label the areas of producer and consumer surplus. Explain how these areas illustrate the concepts.
7. On a supply and demand graph referring to a perfectly competitive market, show how a restriction on the level of transactions leads to deadweight loss.
8. Use two graphs to explain how the deadweight loss from taxation and the amount of tax revenue raised are affected by the elasticity of demand.
9. Use a standard supply and demand graph to illustrate how a price ceiling transfers benefits from one group to another and can create deadweight loss.
10. Explain, in words and a graph, how the amount of inefficiency created by a price ceiling depends on the elasticity of supply.

Exercises

1. Suppose a perfectly competitive firm manufactures gizmos, with the following cost structure (including all opportunity costs):

Quantity of Gizmos	Total Cost ($)
0	75
1	150
2	250
3	425
4	675

a. Calculate the marginal cost schedule (the marginal cost for each successive unit of the good) for this firm in a table, and then graph the marginal cost curve. (Review material in Chapters 7 and 8 if necessary.)

   b. If the price of gizmos on the market is $175 each, how many gizmos should the firm produce to maximize profits? What is the level of the firm's revenues at its chosen output level? How much does it make in profit?

   c. Suppose more firms start producing gizmos, and the market price drops to $125. How many gizmos should this firm now produce to maximize profits? (*Note:* In the case of lumpy quantities such as these, interpret the $P = MC$ rule as "produce as long as price *is at least as great as* marginal cost.") What is this firm's new revenue level? How much does it make in profits?

   d. When the price is $125, will more firms want to enter the market? Will existing firms want to exit?

2. Match each item in Column A with an example in Column B.

   Column A

   a. a "corporate climber" view
   b. deadweight loss
   c. consumer surplus
   d. normal profit
   e. producer surplus
   f. a traditional neoclassical view
   g. a condition for perfect competition

   Column B

   i. getting $2000 for your painting when you would have accepted $50
   ii. when competitive firms make this, new firms won't be tempted to enter the market
   iii. the cost to society as a whole from a price floor
   iv. competition is something you try to "beat," to get the biggest market share
   v. paying less for a good that the maximum you are willing to pay
   vi. competition is good
   vii. firms can freely enter or exit the market

3. Marin Township has raised $50,000 through a sales tax on restaurant meals. The mayor argues that this has cost taxpayers $50,000, but an economist argues that the true economic cost to the community is greater than $50,000. What is the economist's reasoning? Does it help to know that dining in local restaurants has fallen off by 15% since the imposition of the tax? (You may want to review Figure 11.7 and earlier definitions of accounting costs versus economic cost and of opportunity cost.) Write a short paragraph, with a graphical illustration, explaining the economist's point of view.

4. Marin Township has spent $50,000 on a new bridge over the Muddy River. The mayor argues that this benefits the township by $50,000, but an economist argues that the true benefit to the community is greater than $50,000. What might be the economist's reasoning? Does it help to know that a recent survey of the 100 local commuters who use the highly convenient new bridge indicates that 10 of them would have been willing to be taxed $5000 each in order to get the new bridge built, 30 of them would have been willing to be taxed $1000 each, and 60 would have been willing to be taxed $100 each? (The price they actually pay for using the bridge, once it is built, is $0. *Hint:* Think about consumer surplus when the price charged is zero.) Write a short paragraph explaining the economist's point of view.

5. In late-17th-century England, only rather well-off people could afford to have windows in their houses. The government of King William III and Queen Mary II, therefore, decided to levy a property tax on each house, calculated as a certain dollar amount *per window*. Could this explain why houses of the time, after a while, tended to be rather dark? Why? Explain in a few sentences and a graph.

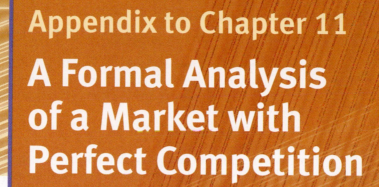

Appendix to Chapter 11

A Formal Analysis of a Market with Perfect Competition

Like the appendices to Chapters 7 and 8, this appendix shows how idealized market structures, as portrayed in 20th-century neoclassical economics, can be formally treated within a model of profit-maximizing firms that make static decisions based on solving convex problems. We will assume, for this appendix, that the firm is a hair dryer producer with the same cost structure described in the appendices to Chapters 7 and 8.

In Chapter 7, we assumed that the hair dryer producer was in a perfectly competitive market, facing a horizontal marginal revenue curve. As we left off the story there, the producer was making a positive economic profit of $39 by charging $20 apiece for selling 7 hair dryers. However, as described in the text of the present chapter, perfectly competitive firms should make zero economic profits. Other producers, seeing this firm making profits, should enter the industry, driving the price down.

Figure 11.11 shows the situation of a perfectly competitive firm after prices have been driven down to the lowest level that allows the firm to break even. At a price of

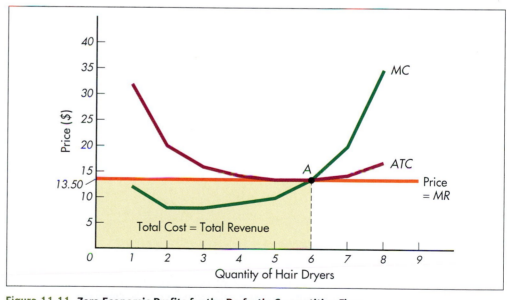

Figure 11.11 Zero Economic Profits for the Perfectly Competitive Firm
In the long run, the price in a perfectly competitive market is driven down to the point where total cost equals total revenue for each firm.

about $13.50, the firm will profit-maximize by setting $P = MC$ and producing 6 hair dryers.[2] At this output level, average total cost is at its minimum level: The price line, *ATC* curve, and *MC* curve all meet at point *A*. (We have suppressed the average variable cost curve for greater clarity.)

Revenues and costs are both about 6 × $13.50, or $81. The perfectly competitive firm makes zero economic profits.

If prices were driven down below about $13.50—perhaps because other firms have lower cost structures—this hair dryer producer would continue to produce for a while, as long as the price exceeded average variable costs, but would leave the industry as soon as it could dispose of the resources for which it pays fixed costs.

---

[2] We write "about $13.50" for simplicity. A table describing the cost structure for hair dryers appears in Chapter 7. Because of the fact that we are limiting production to integer numbers, we cannot describe, in numbers, *exactly* the point where the *ATC* curve, the *MC* curve, and the price line cross. At 6 hair dryers, according to that table, $MC = 14$, which is not exactly equal to $ATC = 13.50$. Technically, the optimal point should lie *between* 5 and 6 hair dryers.

Markets with Market Power

At the turn of the century, one of the ongoing big news stories concerned the lawsuits being brought against Microsoft Corporation—a company that made its founder, Bill Gates, the richest person on the planet. Did Microsoft have too much market power? Did it abuse its power? Should it be fined or broken up into smaller companies? Can economic analysis contribute to understanding these issues?

1 | The Traditional Models

Traditional neoclassical economics asks the question "How do the number of firms in a product market and the characteristics of the good being sold affect the profit-maximizing decisions of the firm?" There are four idealized types of market structure.

- Perfect competition: the case where there are many sellers, selling identical goods (see Chapter 11)

- Pure monopoly: the case where there is only one seller

- Monopolistic competition: the case where there are many sellers, but they sell slightly different things

- Oligopoly: the case where there are so few sellers that each needs to watch what the others are doing

> The four traditional idealized types of market structure are perfect competition, pure monopoly, monopolistic competition, and oligopoly.

We call these types idealized because they are *ideas* as opposed to realities (not because they are ideal in the sense of "best").[1]

The first three cases can be modeled elegantly using the basic neoclassical model. Because each actor is an entity unto itself, the market can be portrayed as working in a mechanically defined way, and theoretical conclusions are tidy and unambiguous.

---

[1] For example, in geometry the *idea* of a line includes the condition that it have no width. Real-world lines, on the other hand, always have width, no matter how small. But that does not necessarily mean that the idea of a line is not useful—as long as the differences between the ideal and the real are kept in mind.

In the last case, oligopoly, the simple mechanical approach breaks down, precisely because markets in this case are truly complex, evolving social *organizations*. Arguably, the case of oligopoly is the most important and prevalent in contemporary industrialized economies.

2 | Pure Monopoly: One Seller

The case diametrically opposed to perfect competition, the case of many sellers, is pure monopoly, the case of only one seller. Here, as for perfect competition, the traditional model of firm profit maximization leads to clear and definite predictions—but of a very different kind.

2.1 | The Conditions of Monopoly

The idealized market structure of monopoly is characterized by the following conditions:

1. There is only *one seller*.
2. The good being sold has *no close substitutes*. This means that buyers must buy from the monopolist or not at all.
3. *Barriers to entry* prevent other firms from starting to produce the good.

barriers to entry: economic, legal, or deliberate obstacles that keep new sellers from entering a market

Because the monopolist is the only seller in the market, it faces no competition from other firms. The condition of "no close substitutes" means that the good being sold must be substantially different from anything else, so the monopolist doesn't have to worry about losing buyers to markets for similar, even if not identical, goods. If the monopolist makes economic profits, other firms will, of course, want to enter the market. **Barriers to entry** are necessary to keep those other firms out.

Barriers to entry may be categorized as falling into three major types: economic barriers, legal barriers, and deliberate barriers.

Economic Barriers. Economic barriers derive primarily from the nature of the production technology. For example, the production technology may be characterized by high fixed costs, economies of scale, or network externalities.

High fixed costs prevent potential competitors from entering the industry on a small scale and expanding. Competitors must enter as very large-scale operations, which may be a difficult and risky thing to do. For example, the initial investment required to build facilities that can produce specialized military aircraft make it difficult for any potential entrant to challenge.

The size of the market relative to the minimum efficient scale of a firm is also important. For example, in discussing Figure 11.3 in the last chapter, we noted that firms did not reach low per-unit costs until they produced 50 units. But what if the total market quantity demanded of the good was less than 50 units? Any firm that wanted to produce for such a market would have to produce in the region of economies of scale. The more firms that tried to divide up such a market, the smaller each would have to be, and the higher their average costs. Only a monopolist, who captures the entire market, will be able to move further down along the long-run average cost curve, producing more efficiently. For example, pharmaceutical production tends to be characterized by economies of scale at low levels of output. As a result, medicines for very rare diseases that affect only a few hundred people each year tend to be manufactured by only one producer (at best). A monopoly that emerges because of economies of scale is called a **natural monopoly**.

natural monopoly: a monopoly that arises because the minimum efficient scale of the producing unit is large relative to the total market demand

Network externalities (see Chapter 8) can also lead to monopolization. The fact that nearly all PC users have come to use Windows operating systems, and software written for those systems, gives Microsoft a "first mover" advantage that a competitor would find extremely hard to challenge.

Legal Barriers. These include copyrights (which protect creative works), franchises and concessions (which directly prohibit entry), patents (which prevent other firms from using technological innovations), and trademarks (which protect brand names). Legal barriers provide the oldest and most secure foundations for monopoly. In times past, kings frequently granted monopoly rights as a reward for services rendered to them. In the United States, patent protection allows a firm exclusive use of an invention for an extended period of time, usually 17 to 20 years. If the invention produces a new and unique good, or facilitates production at much lower costs than competitors incur, a monopoly can result.

Deliberate Barriers. Deliberate barriers include physical, financial, and political intimidation of potential competitors, and many are illegal. For example, a monopolist may induce the supplier of some essential raw material not to supply potential competitors or may reach an agreement with a distributor that it will not distribute rival products. Such deals, designed to exclude competitors from access to necessary goods and services, are called **exclusionary practices**.

> **exclusionary practices:** a firm's getting its suppliers or distributors to agree not to provide goods or services to potential competitors

A powerful monopolist might also discourage potential competitors by engaging in **predatory pricing**. Whenever small competitors enter the market, the monopolist may temporarily lower its price to a level that does not cover costs, in order to drive the new entrants out of business. In international markets, selling output in another country at prices below the cost of production is called **dumping**.

> **predatory pricing:** a powerful seller's temporarily pricing its goods or services below cost, in order to drive weaker competitors out of business

A powerful monopolist may also threaten smaller potential competitors with unfounded (but very expensive) lawsuits, in attempts to intimidate or bankrupt them. In these cases, the size of the monopolist relative to potential competitors is clearly important: These strategies are possible only for relatively large, established firms with "deep pockets." Acts of violence are not unheard of as barriers to entry, most notably in monopolies run by organized crime.

> **dumping:** selling in foreign countries at prices that are below the firm's costs of production

2.2 | Examples of Monopoly

Examples of near-monopolies, if not pure monopolies, are fairly easy to find. Microsoft Corporation's dominance in PC operating systems, for example, and pharmaceutical companies that manufacture so-called "orphan drugs" for very small markets have already been mentioned. If a firm is the only supplier in a given geographical area, it is called a **local monopoly**. Wal-Mart Stores, a fast-growing American retail chain, has achieved a local monopoly in the distribution of many types of products in some small communities; in larger metropolitan areas, however, it usually competes with at least a few other suppliers in each of its lines of business. A firm does not necessarily have to be huge to have monopoly power—just large in relation to the relevant market. The only movie theater in a small, isolated town, for example, is also a local monopoly.

> **local monopoly:** a monopoly limited to a specific geographical area

In older textbooks, industries in transportation, communications, and public utilities were often cited as examples of natural monopolies. The U.S. Postal Service, for example, for a long time had a monopoly on delivery of letters and packages. Railroads, phone companies, and electric companies were traditionally operated either directly by the government or as **regulated monopolies**—that is, private companies run under government supervision. It would obviously be inefficient, it was argued, to have two mail carriers delivering to the same house, or two lines of railroad tracks, or multiple separate grids of electrical transmission wires.

> **regulated monopoly:** a monopoly run under government supervision

In recent years, however, competition, deregulation, and privatization have complicated this picture. Nowadays, the U.S. Postal Service has competition in many markets from FedEx, UPS, and other firms, and it isn't rare to see trucks with all three insignias delivering to the same business district or neighborhood on the same day. Market structure in communications and utilities has become more sophisticated; the aspects with large economies of scale (such as maintenance of the electrical grid) are

Economics in the Real World

The Issues in U.S. v. Microsoft

In the 1990s, Microsoft Corporation had undisputed dominance in the market for operating systems for PC computers. Over 90% of PCs used Microsoft Windows. Did Microsoft abuse this power? A lawsuit filed in 1998 by the U.S. Department of Justice and the attorneys general of 20 states and the District of Columbia charged that it did.

The government claimed that Microsoft engaged in both exclusionary and predatory anticompetitive practices and that these ultimately harmed consumers. Most notable were Microsoft's actions against Netscape, a Web browser that competed with its own Internet Explorer. Microsoft had reason to fear that Netscape could develop into a platform capable of supporting software that would not depend on Windows.

Microsoft's exclusionary practices included requiring computer manufacturers to install Internet Explorer if they installed Windows and involved striking deals with large Internet service providers that made it difficult for their subscribers to use any other browser. Predatory behavior included giving away Internet Explorer. Witnesses and internal memos introduced at the trial indicated that the explicit intent of this give-away policy was to squash Netscape. Although customers were made better off in the short run by receiving free software, the government argued that they were made worse off in the long run, because of a reduction in choice and in competition.

Microsoft argued that these policies were all adopted for legitimate, competitive reasons and that consumers benefited from its innovative, high-quality products.

In 1999 the U.S. District Court for the District of Columbia found that Microsoft had violated laws regarding monopoly practices and ordered that the company be split into two business, one for operating systems and another for applications. An appeals court, however, while upholding some judgments, reversed others and decided that the company need not be split. In 2001 the United States, Microsoft, and nine states reached a settlement that included some proposed changes in the company's practices. As of this writing, attempts by other states to get tougher remedies imposed have been unsuccessful. ◔

Richard J. Gilbert and Michael L. Katz, "An Economist's Guide to *U.S. vs. Microsoft*," *Journal of Economic Perspectives* 15 (2001), 25–44, and "United States' Motion for Entry of Final Judgment," U.S. Department of Justice, May 9, 2002, **http://www.usdoj.gov/atr/cases/ f11100/11120.htm**.

Outline the ways in which Microsoft allegedly behaved like a monopolist. Can you think of other examples in the news today?

separated from parts of the business where economies of scale are not so big (such as generation of electricity). The breakup of AT&T in the 1980s brought about competition in long-distance telephone services. What seems obvious in one historical period may not be so obvious later on.

2.3 | Profit Maximization for a Monopolist

In choosing what level of output to produce, a monopolistic firm will follow the general pattern of behavior of a profit-maximizing firm as described in Chapter 8, seeking the level at which its marginal cost is equal to its marginal revenue ($MC = MR$). But although its costs are determined in the same way as those of a perfectly competitive firm, its revenues are significantly different.

The price-taking firm has such a small market share that it can sell whatever it chooses at the going price. In contrast, because a monopolistic firm is the sole supplier of a given product, the demand curve for its output will be identical to the market demand curve for that product and thus will slope downward. The monopolistic firm can sell more only by inducing consumers as a group to buy more. That is, to sell more it must either mount an effective advertising campaign (to shift out the demand curve it faces) or offer its product at a lower price. Another way to look at the difference is to note that the monopolist can raise its price, losing some sales but obtaining more per unit for those remaining, whereas the price-taking firm will sell absolutely nothing if it raises its price above the existing market level.

price maker: a seller that can set the selling price, constrained only by demand conditions

In other words, a monopolist is a **price maker**, not a price taker. It can set both price and quantity, although the combinations of these that it can choose are constrained by market demand.

Consider how a producer would behave if, instead of receiving a flat amount for each unit of output sold, it were a monopolist and faced the full schedule of market demand. Table 12.1 shows how, in order to sell more of its output, this firm must drop its selling price. It can sell 1 unit if it sets the price at $44, for example. But if it wants to sell 2 units, it must drop the price to $40 each in order to find buyers. The first two columns of Table 12.1 thus describe the demand curve for this good.

The fourth column in Table 12.1 indicates how much *extra* revenue the monopolist gets for producing and selling an additional unit. For example, initial revenue for selling 1 unit is $44. When the monopolist wants to sell 2 units, however, it must sell *both* units at the lower price of $40, receiving total revenue of $80.[2] It thus gains $40 from selling the second unit but also loses the $4 that it would have gotten from selling the first unit alone. Marginal revenue from the second unit, then, is only $36 (= 40 − 4, or, what amounts to the same thing, = 80 − 44).

The remainder of Table 12.1 is calculated in the same fashion. Note that after this monopolist sells 6 units, total revenue starts to go *down* (from its peak at $144) and marginal revenue becomes negative. Recall, from Chapter 5, that the upper regions of demand curves (where quantities are low and prices are high) tend to be elastic, such that *de*creases in price *in*crease revenue. The lower regions tend to be inelastic, such that decreases in price *de*crease revenue. This is exactly what is illustrated, numerically, in Table 12.1.

The demand and marginal revenue curves in Figure 12.1 graph the second and fourth columns of Table 12.1 (price to buyers and marginal revenue to the firm) against the first column (quantity). The marginal revenue curve lies below the demand curve (after the first unit) and falls off more steeply, entering the negative part of the graph after 6 units. Whereas the perfectly competitive firm faces a horizontal *MR* curve, the *MR* curve for a monopolist is *downward-sloping*.

○ The marginal revenue curve for a monopolist is downward-sloping.

We graphically derived the shape of a marginal cost curve back in Chapter 8, and we show a possible one in Figure 12.1. (The cost curves are the same whether a producer is competitive or a monopolist; only the demand side of the market is different.)

The monopolist will maximize profits by producing the quantity at which $MR = MC$, which occurs at point *A* in Figure 12.1. This is an output level of about 5 units. The marginal cost of producing the fifth unit is, reading horizontally from the *MC* curve, about $12. The marginal revenue from the fifth unit is also, from the graph and table, $12.

The monopolist, however, will not charge its customers $12. Customers are willing to pay $28 each for the 5 units produced, as shown by point *B* on the demand curve in Figure 12.1 (and the Selling Price column in Table 12.1). The monopolist will produce at a marginal cost to itself of about $12 but will charge the customers $28 per unit to maximize profits.

What level of profits will the monopolist make over the long haul? Unlike in the competitive case, where economic profits are assumed to be driven to zero by the

---

[2] Unless it is a perfect price discriminator, as discussed later in this chapter.

Table 12.1 | Marginal Revenue for a Monopolist

Quantity of Output	Selling Price ($)	Total Revenue ($)	Marginal Revenue ($)
1	44	44	44
2	40	80	36
3	36	108	28
4	32	128	20
5	28	140	12
6	24	144	4
7	20	140	−4
8	16	128	−12
9	12	108	−20

entrance of new producers, monopolists *can* make sustained positive economic profits, as long as barriers to entry keep potential competitors out.

To determine the actual level of profits, you need to know more about the cost structure of the firm. This is investigated in the appendix to this chapter. If the monopolist's cost structure is such that it makes economic *losses*, presumably it will choose to exit the industry in the long run.

2.4 | Monopoly and Inefficiency

Monopoly power generally leads to inefficiencies in the form of deadweight loss, when compared to a competitive outcome. Because the monopolist produces at an output level at which price exceeds marginal cost, society could gain from increased output of

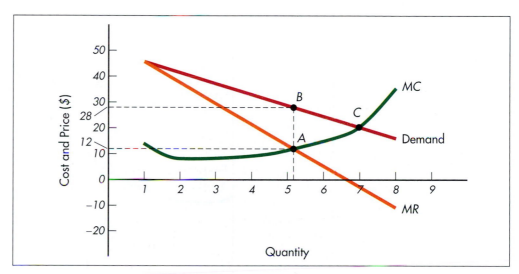

Figure 12.1 Monopoly Profit Maximization
A monopolist decides how much to produce by setting marginal cost equal to marginal revenue (point *A*). The price that buyers are willing to pay for this quantity is read off the demand curve (point *B*). The monopolist produces less, and charges more, than would firms in a competitive equilibrium (point *C*).

the product. The social cost of additional inputs shifted to this industry (marginal cost, assuming no externalities) would be less than the social benefit derived from the resulting additional output (measured by price, assuming no externalities).

For example, in the example above, buyers value the 6th unit at $24, whereas the resource cost of producing the 6th unit is less than $24 (as can be seen in Figure 12.1). The social benefit of producing the 6th unit is above the social marginal cost, and society would be better off if it were produced. The curving triangle *ABC* in Figure 12.1 is the deadweight loss from the monopolist's decision, compared to a competitive situation in which marginal willingness to pay and marginal cost would be equated (at point *C*).

We can also examine the efficiency and distributional effects by analyzing producer surplus and consumer surplus. In Figure 12.2 the competitive equilibrium (price-taking) situation is portrayed by thinking of the *MC* curve as the sum of the *MC* curves of numerous competitive firms. The resulting competitive price and quantity are P_E and Q_E. The contrasting monopoly price and quantity are P_M and Q_M. As we have already noted, the fact that the monopolist will supply a lower quantity and charge a higher price creates deadweight loss. It also causes a distributional shift away from the buyers of the good and toward the monopolist. The rectangle labeled "Transfer" would be part of consumer surplus in a competitive market, but in this market it is taken by the producer. Market power creates more benefit for the seller—which is why businesses like to get it—but at the expense of buyers of the good (lost consumer surplus) and of the efficiency of society as a whole (deadweight loss).

Often the story of the monopolist is extended to incorporate some notions of dynamics and innovation. The cost to society may be larger than just the static deadweight loss if the lack of competition makes the monopolist lazy. A secure monopolist has less incentive to please customers, manage its costs efficiently, and adopt new ideas than a firm whose survival is on the line.

The cost to society may also be larger than just the deadweight loss, depending on what the monopolists do with the positive economic profits they may be making. A

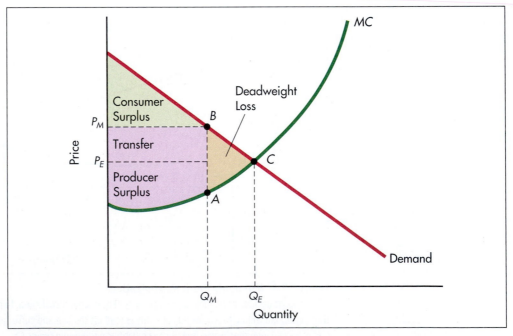

Figure 12.2 The Welfare Costs of Monopoly Power
A monopolist imposes deadweight loss on society and transfers surplus from consumers to itself, relative to a situation of perfect competition.

monopoly owner may, in fact, need to spend most or all of the positive economic profits just keeping up the barriers to entry. In a case where monopolies are generated by exclusive concessions or licenses given out by governments, for example, a monopolist may end up spending much or all of its economic profits lobbying and bribing government officials in order to maintain its exclusive right to produce a good. Expending economic resources simply to try to get transfers or favors, usually from governments, is called **rent-seeking behavior**. Rent-seeking behavior does not result in a productive use of resources, but only in the transfer of ownership of rights and resources among individual parties. Hence, from an overall societal perspective, resources used up in the process represent wasted resources.

rent-seeking behavior: behavior directed toward getting transfers or favors

2.5 | Can Monopoly Be Efficient?

On the other hand, in some situations the efficiency cost of monopoly may not be as bad as the foregoing analysis suggests. In some cases, monopoly may even be beneficial compared to a competitive market.

Natural Monopoly. We have already mentioned one case in which a single big firm may be socially preferable to many small ones: natural monopoly. Competitive firms would have per-unit costs that were unnecessarily high, but a monopolist can take advantage of economies of scale. Often natural monopolies are regulated. The government allows only one firm to produce the good but mandates that it produce at higher levels, and sell at lower prices, than the firm would choose on its own.

This can, however, lead to a dilemma when regulated firms are operating with substantial economies of scale. Often the marginal cost of production is very low. For example, on a passenger railroad the marginal cost of adding another car or another seat is very low once the rails, engines, and schedules are all in place. Efficiently setting the price of a ticket equal to the marginal cost of providing a ride, however, would mean that the monopolist's revenues would not cover its costs. The regulator can direct the monopolist toward optimally efficient pricing *or* self-sustaining revenues, but not both. Frequently in these cases, the government subsidizes the monopolist in order to encourage socially beneficial price setting and levels of production.

Intellectual Property. The problem of covering costs arises again in the case of research costs for the development of new technologies. Patents, copyrights, and other protections of intellectual property are not granted simply to enrich inventors. The rationale for these forms of government-granted monopoly power is to *encourage* research and innovation. Development of new computer technologies, medical technologies, and drugs can be very expensive. Firms argue that they need a period of exclusive, high profits in order to cover the costs of research and development. Without the ability to patent an innovation, it is argued, firms might find research unprofitable and so do less of it, to the detriment of all.

Of course, patents also have a social cost in that they restrict production of the good in question and raise its price. This cost can be extremely high, as in the case of human lives lost to the high pricing of AIDS drugs in Africa, especially in the early years of the epidemic. Other forms of government action have been suggested as ways of encouraging invention that would not carry the patent system's harmful effect of restricting production and use. These include direct funding of research, offering research prizes, and buying patents from companies for a one-time fee.

Pressure to Appear Competitive. In the idealized case of pure monopoly the monopolist is free to maximize profits with no concern for the consequences, but in the real world this is rarely the case. Even if monopolists do not have actual competitors, they may fear *potential* competitors or government action. They may be motivated to produce and price somewhat more as a competitive firm would, out of fear that too-high monopoly profits will attract too much attention.

Oftentimes the barriers protecting a monopoly can be bypassed by producing a similar, though not identical, product. Monopolies held by American railroads in the early 20th century, for example, were weakened not by competing railroads but by truck and airline competition that served to increase the elasticity of demand for railroad transportation. Textbooks written as recently as the 1970s sometimes asserted that there was no possibility of competition between telephone companies and postal systems, because there was no way of sending documents by telephone—an idea that seems quaintly old-fashioned in an era of fax machines and e-mail. Microsoft has argued that even though it currently enjoys a near-monopoly, it is "competitive" in a dynamic sense because new technologies could arise at any time to upset its dominance in the market for PC operating systems.

Also, firms might be cautious out of fear of governmental action. Since the 1930s, most industrial countries have developed government agencies charged with investigating cases of monopoly power. Governments may take over monopolies, regulate them, or break them up into smaller companies if their existence is found to be socially harmful (see Chapter 17). A first ruling in the Microsoft case mandated a breakup, although an appeals ruling focused instead on changing its business practices (see the Economics in the Real World feature on pages 282–283). Some monopolists may not fully exploit their power in order to be less visibly irksome—and hence less likely to be targeted for the sort of breakup that threatened Microsoft.

Perfect Price Discrimination.
Although we usually think of firms as charging the same price to all buyers, this need not be the case. An interesting—if rare—welfare result occurs in the case of what is called a "perfect price-discriminating monopolist."

price discrimination: a seller's charging different prices to different buyers, depending on their ability and willingness to pay

A **price-discriminating** seller is one that charges different prices to different buyers, depending on their ability and willingness to pay. How can a seller do this? One way is to keep the prices charged a secret. In the real world, car salespeople often carry out a version of price discrimination, holding closer to the list price and pressing more options on a buyer who comes in dressed in expensive clothing, while moving more rapidly into discounts for a less affluent-looking client. Another way is to offer discounts structured so that some people will pass them up. Why do stores sometimes offer bulk discounts or "two for the price of one" sales or offer discounts only if you come on particular "sale days" or go to the trouble of bringing in a coupon? They are also trying to separate out the price-unresponsive customers (who will buy anyway) from the price-responsive ones (who will buy only "on sale"). Airlines try to discriminate between business travelers (who need to travel) and vacation travelers (who are more price-sensitive) by offering discounts to travelers who are willing to stay over Saturday nights.

Consider the demand curve in Figure 12.3. Customer A doesn't care about getting a low price and would be willing to pay price P_A for the first few units (Q_A) of the good. The seller would like to be able to charge Customer A this high price and then drop the price a little for Customer B, who wouldn't buy any of the good at price P_A but is happy to buy at price P_B. And so on. In this case, consumer surplus is whittled away—each customer is paying close to the maximum that he or she is willing to pay. The seller is reaping the benefits—extra bits of revenue, represented by shaded rectangles on the graph, for each sale made above the price charged to the last buyer (P_D).

If a monopolist could vary the price continuously, we would have a case of "perfect" price discrimination, as shown in Figure 12.4. In this hypothetical case, the monopolist captures all of the surplus. Consumer surplus is completely eliminated, because the monopolist is able to tease out every penny of willingness to pay. From a social point of view, there would be a large transfer of benefit from buyers to the monopolist. But there would also be an elimination of the efficiency loss, compared to the case of a monopolist that is not perfectly price-discriminating. When a seller with market power can get every last penny out of customers in this way, it has no reason to restrict output and would produce until $P = MC$. Therefore, it would create no deadweight loss.

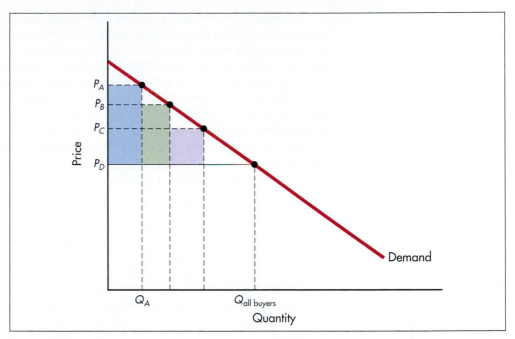

Figure 12.3 Price Discrimination
A price-discriminating seller can charge different prices to different people, thereby capturing what would otherwise be consumer surplus.

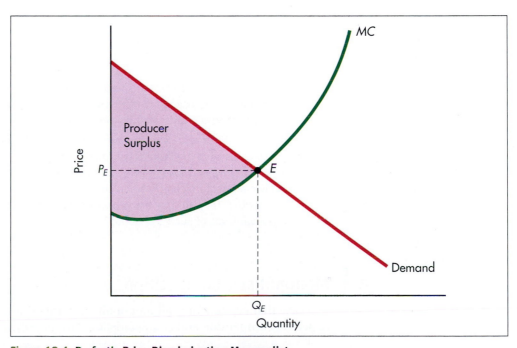

Figure 12.4 Perfectly Price-Discriminating Monopolist
With perfect price discrimination, a monopolist has no reason to restrict output and will therefore create no deadweight loss.

The equity consequences of price discrimination are interesting. In a case where the monopolist reaps large profits at consumers' expense, price discrimination seems unfair to consumers. However, it is sometimes the case that price discrimination may just allow a producer to break even financially. The only non-profit mental health clinic in town, for example, may offer its services on a "sliding scale," where the price charged to a client rises with his or her income. The care given to lower-income clients is thus subsidized by the higher prices paid by those with greater ability to pay. If it were forced to charge only a single price, the clinic might have to close or turn away its poorest clients.

We can summarize this discussion of monopolies and efficiency in a few points:

- When a monopolist could be broken up into many cost-efficient, more competitive firms, the competitive option would generally be socially beneficial.
- In cases of natural monopolies, where competitive firms could not be cost-efficient, the question is not one of "monopoly versus competition," but rather one of how best to structure and regulate a monopoly.
- When it comes to fostering innovation, a system of government-granted exclusive monopoly rights may bring about benefits. (However, alternative methods of encouraging research and development might bring about even higher benefits.)
- Monopolists may be motivated by fear of potential competition or of government action to behave in a more socially efficient manner than they would otherwise adopt.
- Perfectly price-discriminating monopolists do not restrict output, and therefore they cause no efficiency loss, although their actions may have negative distributional effects.

In the real world, however, cases of *pure* monopoly are somewhat hard to find. Most goods have *some* reasonable substitutes. If railroads are monopolized, people might turn to trucks or cars, for example. There are not a lot of anti-AIDS drugs at the time of this writing, but there are a few, produced by different firms. This brings us to a discussion of cases that exhibit neither perfect competition nor pure monopoly.

Discussion Questions

1. On many campuses, the official college or university bookstores used to have monopoly power in selling textbooks to students. Was this a case of local or global monopoly? Is it still the case at your institution? Why or why not?

2. Does it sometimes make sense to have just one company in charge of providing something? Some users of electronics get frustrated by the lack of compatibility among their gadgets and between their gadgets and their friends'. Might it be better to have just one company manufacture computers, planners, music players, cell phones and the like in such a way that they all work smoothly with each other? What would be the advantages and disadvantages of such a situation?

3 | Monopolistic Competition

The case that economists call monopolistic competition includes both characteristics of perfect competition and characteristics of monopoly.

3.1 | The Conditions of Monopolistic Competition

The idealized market structure of monopolistic competition is characterized by the following conditions:

1. There are *numerous small buyers and sellers*.

2. The sellers produce goods that are close substitutes but are not identical. *Product differentiation* means that each seller's product is somewhat different from that offered by the other sellers.

3. Producers of the good or service can *freely enter or exit* the industry.

4. Buyers and sellers have *perfect information*.

The conditions are all identical to those of perfect competition, except that products are differentiated instead of identical. In this case, buyers care which producer they buy from.

3.2 | Examples of Monopolistic Competition

How many different brands of blue jeans can you name? How many fast-food restaurants might you find in a large town or a city? Why might there be three different brands of gasoline offered at stations on the same busy intersection? Why can you find the same book at a newsstand, a bookstore, and online? These are all examples of differentiated products. McDonald's, Burger King, and Wendy's franchises all sell hamburgers, but they fix them a little differently, and each franchise is located in a different spot. Different gas stations may offer slightly different products, different levels of service, or different complementary products or services (for example, a mini-mart or a car wash). Even if the book you want to buy is the same physical book, you get a different consumption "package" of location, convenience, delivery costs, and the like, depending on whether you buy it at a local independent bookstore, a chain, Amazon.com, Barnesandnoble.com, or a publisher's outlet store.

While the parent corporations of the fast food restaurants shown here may be oligopolists (discussed on p. 291), individual franchises are often owned as small businesses that operate like monopolistic competitors, offering goods or services that are at least slightly differentiated from their local competitors. In such a setting the consumer faces a multitude of choices, and the sellers of differentiated goods are able to exercise some control over prices (though not as much as a monopolist). This particular strip of fast-food restaurants is located in Kingston, New York.

Situations of monopolistic competition—even if not in a pure form, with absolutely free entry and absolutely perfect information—seem to be ubiquitous in contemporary industrialized societies. In everyday life, we see many firms competing to sell us slightly different varieties of the same goods and services.

3.3 | Profit Maximization with Monopolistic Competition

Product differentiation means that each seller is a miniature monopoly, the only producer of its nonstandardized good. Some people claim that McDonald's hamburgers are far superior to Wendy's (or vice versa) and are willing to stay with McDonald's (or Wendy's) even if it raises its prices. You may be willing to pay a higher price to buy milk at a local convenience store, even though you know the price is lower at the big supermarket miles away. Whereas perfectly competitive sellers will lose *all* their customers if they raise their prices above what their products are being offered for elsewhere, a firm selling a differentiated product may not. Firms in a situation of monopolistic competition face a downward-sloping demand curve for their particular product.

The fact that these firms face a downward-sloping demand curve means that their profit maximization problem is the same as that of a monopolist, as illustrated in Figure 12.1. They will also face marginal revenue curves that lie below the demand curve. They will also choose an output level by setting $MR = MC$ at point A and will charge customers the price set by the demand curve, at point B.

Unlike what occurs in the case of monopoly, however, the demand for a firm's good is affected by the availability of close substitutes. If a Wendy's restaurant shuts down, demand at McDonald's, Burger King, and other restaurants and franchises nearby is likely to rise. If a new Burger King opens up, demand for food provided by many existing nearby restaurants may fall. Even though no other firm produces an *identical* good, close substitutes exist.

The fact that entry and exit are easy means that if any monopolistically competitive firm is making positive economic profits, new producers will be attracted to the market and will enter selling similar goods (for example, other hamburgers). As new firms enter, the demand for the specific product in question (for example, a *McDonald's* hamburger) will fall, as illustrated in Figure 12.5. This will cut into the existing firms' revenues and profits. How many new firms will enter, and how much will demand fall for any one firm? In the idealized model, this happens just up to the point where every firm is making zero economic profits. (See the appendix to this chapter for a graphical explanation.)

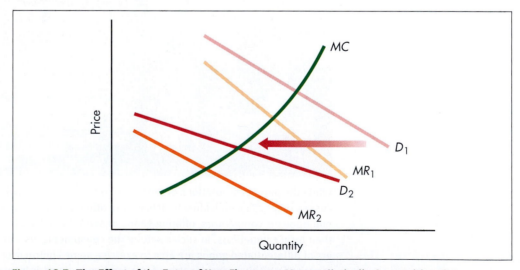

Figure 12.5 The Effect of the Entry of New Firms on a Monopolistically Competitive Firm
A condition of easy entry and exit means that new firms can enter, driving down the demand experienced by any one monopolistically competitive firm.

Like the monopolist, the monopolistically competitive firm faces a downward-sloping demand curve and so produces less, and prices its output higher, than a perfectly competitive firm. As for a perfectly competitive firm, on the other hand, free entry and exit mean that any positive economic profits to be gained from this pricing policy should be only temporary.

3.4 | Monopolistic Competition and Long-Run Efficiency

Compared to perfectly competitive firms, monopolistically competitive firms produce lower levels of output and charge higher prices. Like monopolies, they stop short of producing at levels where the social marginal benefit of production is just equal to the social marginal cost. It can also be shown (and *is* shown in the appendix to this chapter) that these firms have higher unit costs than would occur in a perfectly competitive market. In short, they operate inefficiently.

Monopolistically competitive firms may, like monopolists, also expend considerable resources trying to protect their miniature monopoly. They can't keep other firms from entering their general industry, but they can try to differentiate their product increasingly. Firms in this kind of market structure are observed to engage in a great deal of **nonprice competition**. That is, they compete with other producers by advertising heavily in order to make buyers want *their* particular product (for example, Gap jeans) and by using attractive signs and packaging, selecting better locations, varying their hours of operation, and so on.

In terms of social benefit, it would seem that resources would be better spent producing fewer varieties of goods and services, at lower costs, and with less advertising. Some economists, however, make an opposite argument based on the notion of consumer sovereignty. They argue that inefficiencies in production are just the price that must be paid to satisfy consumers' *desire* for variety (and, presumably, also for massive advertising and flashy packaging). It may be that the highest social benefit lies somewhere between dull, completely standardized products and the extreme proliferation of consumer goods we currently observe.

> **nonprice competition:** competition through activities other than setting prices, such as advertising and location

Discussion Questions

1. Think of a somewhat differentiated good or service that you can buy locally in any number of different places—for example, a gallon of gasoline or a cup of coffee. Do you observe differences in prices? What differences, do you think, might lead to these variations in prices? (Or could it be that the assumption of perfect information is violated? Does everybody know where the cheapest version can be found?) Can you identify examples of nonprice competition among the various sellers?

2. Do you think that the amount of variety in the goods and services you are offered as a consumer is excessive? Just about right? Too limited? Do some forms of nonprice competition have consequences for long-term well-being and sustainability?

4 | Oligopoly

Although the idealized case of perfect competition long dominated economic thinking, real-world markets are far more likely to take an oligopolistic form.

4.1 | The Conditions of Oligopoly

The idealized market structure of oligopoly is characterized by the following conditions:

1. The market is dominated by only a *few sellers,* at least some of which control enough of the market to be able to influence the market price.

2. *Entry is difficult.*

Products may be either standardized or differentiated. Various assumptions may be made about information.

The most important implication of the condition that there are few firms is that the actions of each firm have effects on the market that rival firms cannot ignore. This means, among other things, that the rivals may respond in ways that, in turn, require a response from the original firm(s). In short, oligopoly exists if each firm must include, among the factors it considers in deciding on its own actions, the possible reactions of rival firms.

Remember that in perfect competition the seller need not be concerned with the actions of others. All such a seller needs to know is the market price. In the case of monopoly, of course, there are no other sellers to worry about. In a case of monopolistic competition, with many sellers, the effect of the action of any one seller is spread out over many other sellers. In contrast, in an oligopolistic situation, each firm needs to be keenly aware of what each of the (few) other firms is doing.

4.2 | Examples of Oligopoly

Auto manufacturing is a classic example of oligopoly with few sellers. General Motors, Ford, and Chrysler were long the "big three" sellers of cars and light trucks in the United States. Even though competition from European and East Asian manufacturers has since somewhat diluted that tight oligopoly, GM's share of the U.S. market was still a substantial 28.5% in 2001.

concentration ratio: the share of production, sales, or revenues attributable to the largest firms in an industry

The **concentration ratio** is the share of total production attributable to the largest producers in an industry. For example, the share of the four largest manufacturing firms involved in the domestic production of a good is a traditional indicator of how oligopolistic an industry had become. According to the U.S. government's 1997 Economic Census, the concentration ratio for car and light-truck manufacturing was 88.3. For breakfast cereal manufacturing, it was 82.9, for household laundry equipment manufacturing 90.4, and for glass container manufacturing 91.1. Other concentration ratios are often calculated on the basis of the largest 8, 20, or 50 firms. However, because these measures count shares of domestic *production*, they are less meaningful as a measure of market power in industries with substantial international trade. When domestic producers compete against foreign producers, the share of *sales* may make more sense as a measure of market power (see the News in Context feature "GM, Ford, DaimlerChrysler Fall as Japan, Europe Gain").

For retail firms, sales are the basis on which concentration is measured in U.S. government statistics. For example, the top four hobby, toy, and game retailers had 70.3% of their market, and the top four discount department stores 87.9%, in the 1997 Economic Census. For financial firms, the measure used is revenues. In finance, nearly 54% of revenues from credit card issuing goes to the top four U.S. financial institutions, according to government statistics.

4.3 | Oligopoly and the Behavior of Firms

At this point, elegant models that give clear answers can no longer be found. The behavior of oligopolistic firms is truly *social*—interdependent with the behavior of other actors. Hence mechanical analogies do not apply, and simple marginal thinking is not adequate to the task. Instead of one theory for oligopolies, economists have many, any of which might be helpful but none of which is definitive. We briefly describe two of them here: first, the theory of strategic interaction and game theory and second, models of collusion, cartels, and price leadership.

Strategic Interaction and Game Theory. One theory is that oligopolistic firms will act strategically toward each other, plotting their moves as though they were generals planning a war or opponents in a game of chess. Oligopolistic sellers are often observed to engage in "competition" in the active, aggressive sense in which corporate climbers use this term. That is, oligopolistic firms choose prices, marketing strategies, and the like with an eye to "beating out" specific rivals and gaining greater market share at their expense. A classic example is the rivalry between Coke and Pepsi.

GM, Ford, DaimlerChrysler Sales Fall as Japan, Europe Gain

NEWS in context

DETROIT—As the dust clears on another month of U.S. car and truck sales, the story line is only too familiar. . . . In recent years, Detroit automakers' share of the U.S. auto market has been eroding at a steady rate while Japanese and European manufacturers have gained ground. . . . In April, the combined market share for domestic automakers fell to 62.4%, down a whopping 4.7 percentage points from last April, according to Autodata

Corp. . . . Analysts don't foresee Ford, GM, and Chrysler regaining the lost share or even holding their ground any time soon. . . . GM market analyst Paul Ballew insists that . . . the No. 1 automaker will be able to compete. . . . "We really have for the first time in a long time products that are very competitive and leveragable to meet [foreign] challenge head on," Ballew said.

Mark Truby and Joe Miller, "Domestic Automakers Drop 16%–18% in April," *Detroit News*, May 2, 2001, **http://detnews.com/2001/autos/0105/04/b01–219439.htm.**

duopoly: a market with only two sellers

payoff matrix: a table used in game theory to illustrate possible outcomes for each of two players, depending on the strategy that each chooses

price war: a situation in which a firm cuts prices in order to try to undercut its rivals, and the rivals react by cutting prices even more

Game theory, developed by mathematician John von Neumann (1903–1957) and economist Oskar Morgenstern (1902–1977), provides a framework for the formal analysis of some types of strategic behavior. For example, consider a market with two sellers, known as a **duopoly**. Suppose each is trying to decide whether to set a low or a high price for the good that they both sell. They need to pay attention to what the other one does, because if Firm 1 sets a high price, Firm 2 might set a low price and end up with all the customers (or vice versa). Using game theory, we can describe a **payoff matrix**, as shown in Table 12.2.

The numerical entries in the payoff matrix represent profit levels, in thousands of dollars. The combination (−2, 5) at the bottom left, for example, shows that if Firm 1 sets a high price while Firm 2 sets a low price, Firm 1 will make losses of $2000, while Firm 2—which now has all the customers—will make profits of $5000. (Test yourself: What does the upper right-hand cell represent?) Clearly, each firm would find it to its own advantage to be the low-price seller in the market. Recognition of this fact could lead to a **price war**, in which each firm progressively cuts its prices in order to try to be the low-price seller. Although a price war can, in some real-world cases, last until one party goes out of business, in Table 12.2 we have illustrated a case where the two firms might settle on a low-price situation, in which they both keep some customers but, with low revenues, profits are low at $2000 each. (This is shown in the cell at the upper left.) On the other hand, if both set a high price, they could both make sizable profits of $4000 each.

In this model, we assume that the firms are "noncooperative"—that they are archrivals and do not communicate or cooperate with each other. Noncooperative game theory suggests that a rational firm will choose the option that will leave it best off (or least damaged) regardless of what its rival does. Looking at the payoff matrix in Table 12.2, we can see that Firm 1 will choose to set a low price rather than a high price. If Firm 1 sets a low price and Firm 2 chooses "low," Firm 1 gets profits of 2. If Firm 1 sets a low price and Firm 2 chooses "high," Firm 1 gets profits of 5. Regardless of what Firm 2 does, then,

Table 12.2 | A Payoff Matrix

		Firm 2's Options	
		Low Price	**High Price**
Firm 1's Options	**Low Price**	2 / 2	−2 / 5
	High Price	5 / −2	4 / 4

Firm 1 gets better outcomes than the corresponding profits of -2 or $+4$ that it would get by setting a high price. A similar analysis for Firm 2 will show that it also will choose to set its prices *low*. The solution to the game is the (2, 2) cell.

Sometimes this setup is referred to as "the prisoner's dilemma" because of its well-known formulation in terms of prisoners who are held separately from each other and asked to confess to a crime they committed together. If neither confesses, they will both go free. However, if only one confesses (ratting on the other), the one who confesses will go free while the one who does not confess will go to jail for many years. If they both confess, they will both go to jail for one year. The best strategy, for a prisoner who doesn't know what his partner in crime will do, is to confess. That way, he is assured of not having to go to jail for more than one year. (What outcome would be *best* for both? What would be necessary for them to achieve it?)

Strategic thinking can also be applied to *non*price competition, which oligopolists also tend to use. For example, sellers may need to decide whether to spend a lot or a little on advertising, packaging, and booths at sales conventions. What they decide to do will depend on what their rivals decide to do. Nonprice competition is most likely when each firm is selling a somewhat differentiated product.

Another form of game theory imagines that the parties do not make their decisions simultaneously, as in our example, but one after the other. The theory of "sequential games" covers situations in which one firm moves first and then the second chooses its strategy. Each firm's expectations about the reaction of the other are key to describing the probable outcomes of such a game. More recently, formal game theory has also been applied to "cooperative" games in which, for example, actors may bargain toward a mutually beneficial outcome.

Collusion, Cartels, and Price Leadership.   Clearly, Firm 1 and Firm 2 in the above example (not to mention the prisoners) would do better if they got together and agreed on a joint strategy that gave them both their best outcomes. If the two firms could make a binding agreement to both keep their prices high, they could make profits of (4, 4) instead of ending up at the noncooperative solution of (2, 2). Firms that cooperate in this way are said to be **colluding**. They get together and form a monopoly (at least a local one) for pricing purposes, even though they keep their production activities separate.

Cartels, such as the OPEC oil cartel, are situations of explicit collusion. OPEC did not try to keep its collusion a secret but instead announced its formation and its high prices.

Tacit collusion takes place when sellers collude more subtly. Because cartels are by and large illegal in many industrialized countries, sellers may pass information around on the sly or without starting a formal organization. An industry association may collect information and post it on the Web so that all members will know what price the others are charging. Such flows of information make it easier to cooperate and to monitor compliance with tacit **price fixing**, where all firms implicitly agree to maintain a common price. One form of implicit collusion is **price leadership**, where everyone in the industry looks to one firm, raising their prices when it does and lowering them likewise. Such price leadership, many believe, characterized the U.S. steel and airlines industries for years. Price leadership tends to be more common when the firms all sell identical, standardized products.

As we noted in Chapter 4, however (regarding OPEC), collusion can be hard to sustain. Each seller has an incentive to undercut the set price privately, in order to sell a little more. Nevertheless, collusion has sometimes been persistent. Members may realize it is in their greater long-term interest to stick with the collusive price rather than to risk losing everything by starting a price war.

collusion: cooperation among potential rivals to gain market power as a group

tacit collusion: collusion that takes place without creation of a cartel

price fixing: a form of collusion in which a group of sellers implicitly agrees to maintain a common price

price leadership: a form of collusion in which many sellers follow the price changes instituted by one particular seller

4.4 | Is Oligopoly Rampant?

Oligopolistic industries tend to be inefficient, for the same reasons why monopoly often is. In fact, oligopoly may generally be even worse: Because production decisions remain separate, there is less possibility of even reaping advantages of economies of scale.

Although oligopoly has traditionally been defined in terms of few sellers and difficult entry, the key feature that distinguishes the *behavior* of sellers is not so much the number of them as the existence of interdependence among them. A market can, in fact, display oligopolistic characteristics even with easy entry and hence many possible sellers. When 4 firms control 80% of the market, for example, it has little effect on their behavior whether the remaining 20% of the market is divided up by 10 sellers or 1000.

Oligopolies can also be local. Not all industries have such high national concentration ratios as those we have cited. For example, the same data source indicates that the top four florist retailers shared 2.3% of the total national market, and the top four credit unions shared 8.4%. Even when industries are not so concentrated at the national level, however, firms may behave in somewhat oligopolistic ways more locally. If there are two florist shops in a town, for example, you can bet that each keeps track of what the other is charging, where it is advertising, and how it adjusts its prices on Valentine's Day and Mother's Day!

Market structures in which sellers need to take into account the actions of other sellers, and then respond effectively and creatively, are more prevalent in the real world than are the idealized market structures of perfect competition, pure monopoly, and monopolistic competition.

Microsoft may be a good real-world example of a recent near-monopoly, for example. But because computer users can still choose Apple or Linux operating systems (at the time of this writing), and because Microsoft can reasonably fear that the creation of a new technology could destroy its monopoly powers, it is not quite a pure monopoly. We mentioned McDonald's and Wendy's as monopolistic competitors, but you can be sure that they keep a watchful eye on each others' locations, pricing, and promotional strategies.

The need to take account of others' actions is important in traditional economics' narrowly defined (that is, "few sellers") idea of oligopoly. But it is also of broader importance, because rarely can *any* real-world company, of any size or in any industry, safely ignore the actions taken by others. Studies of economics, business, sociology, and politics share many common concerns when the prevalence of truly interdependent economic decision making is taken into account.

Discussion Questions

1. In Chapter 5 we described a hot dog stand being run by a non-profit Midnight Basketball program, selling hot dogs at $4.00 each. For the most part, we assumed that it was a price taker. But what if it and a *single* other supplier of hot dogs constituted a duopoly in the provision of food at the local street fair?
   a. What would it mean for these two sellers to act noncooperatively, in a "prisoner's dilemma" manner?
   b. What would it mean for these two sellers to collude?

2. Suppose that a seller in a duopoly needs to decide whether to spend a lot or a little on advertising. Assume the consumers are already reasonably well informed about the product, so the purpose of a lot of advertising is to draw customers away from the rival. How could the payoffs from this situation resemble those in Table 12.2? Draw a table illustrating this case (using the same *numbers* as in Table 12.2, but different labels), and describe the noncooperative solution. What if the government decided to ban advertising in this industry (as it has, in the past, banned advertising of cigarettes and alcohol in various media)? Would that help or hurt the companies' profits?

5 | Summary and a Final Note

The traditional four-way categorization of markets according to pure ideal forms, summarized in Table 12.3, can be helpful in thinking about how market structure can affect the incentives facing firms. However, it is important to remember that patterns in the real world need not be limited to such idealized structures. In particular, in very many

Table 12.3	Summary of Traditional Market Structures						
Market Structure	Number of Sellers in the Market	Type of Item(s) Sold	Market Power of an Individual Seller	Entry Barriers	Long-Run Economic Profit	Profit-Maximizing Condition for a Firm
perfect competition	many	identical	none	none	zero	$MC = P$
pure monopoly	one	unique	very high	very high	positive	$MC = MR$
monopolistic competition	many	differentiated	some	none	zero	$MC = MR$
oligopoly	few	varies	substantial	some	varies	varies

real-world markets, sellers need to keep track of what others in their industry are doing and to plan strategically, whether there are few sellers or many. Such interdependent activity requires analysis that is beyond the reach of simple models of marginal thinking. Moreover, as we think about market power, we need to recognize that global trends, which have become increasingly pronounced since the early 1970s, have made dramatic changes in market conditions, so that traditional categories may no longer cover all of the most important situations.

The traditional neoclassical discussion of markets tends to assume that, unless otherwise specified, markets were perfectly competitive. Within the neoclassical model, discussions of the allocative efficiency of "free" markets were often based on the benefits presumed to come from competition. When discussion turned to market power, economists focused largely on *firms* that may have the power to affect *prices* in the markets where they *sell* goods that they have *produced.*

Market power, however, is much more widespread. For example,

○ Governments, non-profit organizations, and individuals can have market power. In some states and counties, for example, governments have a monopoly on liquor sales. An individual selling a unique work of art has market power.

○ Nonprice terms and conditions of exchange such as delivery dates, quality standards, and length of contracts can be manipulated by economic actors with market power.

○ Market power can exist in nonproduct markets, such as markets for resale of goods, markets for resources, and financial markets.

○ Market power can occur on the *buyers'* side. That is, market power can be used to affect the prices *paid* by firms to their *suppliers* for *inputs,* including human labor. The cases of monopsony (one buyer) and oligopsony (few buyers)—will be discussed in Chapter 13 on labor markets.

The last of these topics seems especially likely to require more attention in the future, with renewed recognition that market power goes in two directions—to input as well as to product markets. Market power refers to much more than the ability of firms to set prices above marginal cost. While the traditional analysis of market power tends to stress its detrimental consequences in terms of lost efficiency—an issue of concern from the point of view of the consumer—the consequences of market power in terms of fairness and distributional effects for workers are often at least as important, if not more so, to human well-being. For example, if market power allows a powerful firm to squeeze wages below a living wage (whether these are the wages they are directly paying to their own employees, or the wages being paid by the firms that supply them with material inputs or services), this is potentially as damaging to human well-being as the market power that allows a firm to set prices above marginal cost.

These issues will be taken up in Chapter 16, when we will consider how the sheer size of organizations can be important in defining economic, financial, and political power. We will also see how the economic analysis of the effect of business firms on society needs to take into account the increasing globalization of commerce.

Discussion Questions

1. Recall Braeburn Publishing, the company selling poetry and humor books, that we studied in Chapter 5. How would you characterize the market structure that Braeburn is in? Do you think Braeburn probably engages in nonprice competition?

2. Have you ever worked for an organization that was concerned with its pricing and marketing strategies? Or has someone you know or someone in your family done so? Which market structure of the four we have discussed might best describe that industry? What sorts of strategies were employed by the organization?

Review Questions

1. List and briefly define the three idealized market structure types in addition to perfect competition.

2. What market conditions characterize pure monopoly?

3. Describe three types of barriers to entry, giving examples of each.

4. How does a pure monopolist maximize profits?

5. In what ways are monopolies inefficient?

6. Explain, with a graph, how monopoly market power generally leads to inefficiency.

7. List and describe four cases in which monopolies might be efficient.

8. Explain, with a graph, how a price-discriminating seller behaves.

9. What market conditions characterize monopolistic competition?

10. How is a monopolistically competitive firm imagined to maximize profits?

11. Are monopolistically competitive markets efficient? Explain.

12. What market conditions characterize oligopoly?

13. Describe two theories used to describe the behavior of oligopolists.

Exercises

1. In Chapter 5, we saw that where Braeburn Publishing priced its poetry book at $5, it sold 5 books, and where it priced the volume at $8, it sold 4 books. We saw that its revenues were higher with the higher price. Suppose that, from further test marketing, it determined that it faces the demand curve described by the following schedule.

Quantity of Output (demanded)	Selling Price ($)	Total Revenue ($)	Marginal Revenue ($)
1	17	?	?
2	14	?	?
3	11	?	?
4	8	?	?
5	5	?	?

a. Graph the demand curve for the poetry book, labeling carefully. (Compare your graph to Figure 5.1.)
b. Calculate total revenue and marginal revenue at each output level, and add a marginal revenue curve to your graph.
c. Can the $8 price be Braeburn's profit-maximizing choice? Why or why not?
d. Suppose that, thanks to computerized, on-demand publishing technology, Braeburn can produce any number of books at a constant cost of $5 each. (That is, average cost and marginal cost are both $5 for any quantity of books, and total costs are simply the number of books times $5.) Add a marginal cost curve to your graph. (It will *not* look like the "usual" *MC* curve shown in our illustrations—it will be horizontal.)
e. What are Braeburn's profit-maximizing price and output levels for the poetry book? State these, and label them on the graph.
f. What level of profits would Braeburn earn with the $8 price? (Recall that profits = total revenue − total cost.) What is the level of profits with the price you just found to maximize profit?

2. Suppose two oligopolistic retail chains are considering opening a new sales outlet in a particular town. The changes to each firm's profits, depending on the actions taken, are given in the following payoff matrix. If a chain doesn't open a new outlet, it gets no addition to profits. If one of the chains is the only one to open an outlet, it makes high additional profits (10 units). If they both open outlets, they have to split the available market, and they make only more moderate additional profits (3 units).

	Firm 2's Options	
	New Outlet	**No New Outlet**
New Outlet	3 / 3	0 / 10
No New Outlet	10 / 0	0 / 0

(Firm 1's Options on vertical axis)

a. If the firms are noncooperative and each firm makes the choice that will leave it best off regardless of the other's choice, what will the outcome be?
b. Is this like the "prisoner's dilemma," where the parties could both get a better outcome by communicating and cooperating?
b. Now suppose each firm is thinking of opening new outlets in a *number* of towns, and each town has a payoff matrix similar to this one. Would there be advantages to the two chains communicating and cooperating in this case? If they decide to collude, what form do you think their collusion might take?

3. Match each concept in Column A with an example in Column B.

Column A	Column B
a. a legal barrier to entry	**i.** lobbying to get a concession
b. predatory pricing	**ii.** patent rights
c. rent-seeking behavior	**iii.** electricity distribution
d. nonprice competition	**iv.** corn flakes in different-colored boxes
e. product differentiation	**v.** cutting prices below cost to drive out a rival
f. price fixing	**vi.** cooperating with a rival to charge the same price
g. natural monopoly	**vii.** advertising

Appendix to Chapter 12

Formal Analysis of Monopoly and Monopolistic Competition

A1 | The Assumptions

This appendix shows how monopoly and monopolistic competition market structures can be formally treated within a model of profit-maximizing firms that make static decisions based on solving convex problems.

We will assume, for this appendix, that the firm is a hair dryer producer with the same cost structure as that described in the appendices to Chapters 7 and 8.

A2 | Monopoly

Suppose that our hair dryer producer is a monopolist, with the marginal revenue schedule shown in Table 12.1 and Figure 12.1 and with the marginal cost curve of our hypothetical hair dryer producer from Chapter 7. (The marginal cost curve in Figure 12.1 was drawn, for convenience, to be identical to the one derived for hair dryers in Chapter 7.) As described in this chapter, the monopolist maximizes profits by setting $MR = MC$. It produces 5 units, at a marginal cost of about $12, and sells them for a price of $28.

Adding in the average total cost curve of the firm enables us to identify the area of economic profit, as shown in Figure 12.6. The firm's revenues include both shaded

Figure 12.6 Monopoly Profits
The monopolist sells its product at a per-unit price that is higher than its per-unit cost of production, thus reaping positive economic profits. Revenues are represented by the total shaded area. The part of revenues that goes to paying costs is represented by the dark shaded area. Thus the light area represents an excess of revenues over costs—the economic profit.

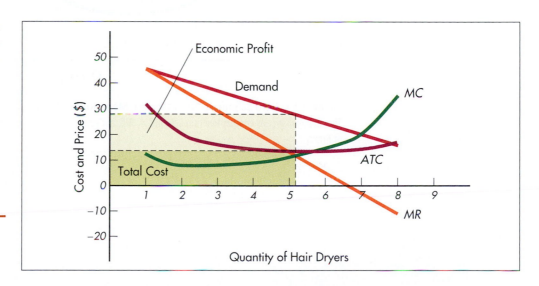

areas, whereas its costs are represented by the small rectangle whose northeast corner lies on the *ATC* curve. The monopolist makes positive economic profit equal to the area of the small rectangle whose southeast corner lies on the *ATC* curve.

A3 | Monopolistic Competition

The monopolistically competitive firm faces a downward-sloping demand curve. Yet, like a perfectly competitive firm, it also makes zero economic profits in the long run.

This case is illustrated in Figure 12.7. Like the monopolist, the monopolistically competitive firm will choose to produce the quantity corresponding to point *A*, where *MR* = *MC*. It will charge a price corresponding to point *B* on the demand curve. Point *B* is also on the *ATC* curve. Thus the rectangle with its northeast corner at point *B* represents both total revenue (price × quantity) and total cost (average total cost × quantity). The firm makes zero economic profits.

How does this come about? Look back at Figure 12.5. If the price were above the *ATC* curve, the firm would make positive economic profits, and (because there is free entry) new firms would enter the industry. This causes the demand curve for this firm's differentiated product to shift down. The demand curve is imagined to shift downward until it just touches the *ATC* curve, as shown in Figure 12.7.

There is no similar formal model for oligopoly, because interdependent behavior cannot be captured by simple mechanical modeling techniques.

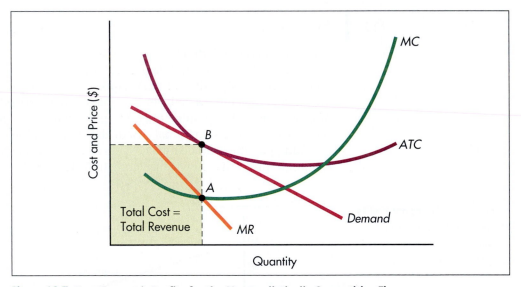

Figure 12.7 Zero Economic Profits for the Monopolistically Competitive Firm
The monopolistically competitive firm sets *MC* = *MR*, but economic profits are kept at zero by the free entry and exit of firms.

Markets for Labor

Chapter 13

Shaquille O'Neal, pro basketball player, earned $24 million in 2001, which comes out to nearly half a million dollars per week. The median earnings for aerospace engineers in 2001 were $1246 per week. For preschool teachers, the median weekly earnings were $480. Some jobs carry benefits such as health insurance and pensions, while others do not. What causes these differences?

1 | Thinking About Markets for Labor

In the last two chapters we have discussed mostly product markets. In this and the next chapter we look at factor markets—formal markets for inputs to production processes.

1.1 | Labor as an Input to Production

You probably do not think of yourself as an input to production. Yet from an economist's perspective, you are. Your labor and know-how, combined with materials, energy, and the services of capital goods, can produce valued goods and services. These may vary from the cleaning services you provide for your own upkeep to a stream of highly compensated services provided to a large corporation. Your education is part of your "human capital" formation, which will make you more productive in the future.

Because this chapter focuses on labor *markets*, we will examine here labor that is performed in exchange for a wage or salary. For the present discussion, we therefore exclude consideration of unpaid household labor, volunteer work, and self-employment, important as they are. We will examine some unique characteristics of labor markets and some of the factors that determine the levels of earnings for different kinds of jobs.

We will focus largely on the supply and demand for labor in specific markets—such as the market for star basketball players, or for aerospace engineers, or for preschool teachers. These all draw ultimately on the same total population of a society, but they are different enough from each other that they need to be considered separately. Most workers consider supplying their labor to only one, or at most a few, such markets, and most employers similarly engage workers for specific jobs.

There are also critical and difficult issues concerning labor demand and supply at the level of the economy as a whole; indeed, many forces resist the establishment of an equilibrium in which all those wishing to supply their labor are able to find jobs. Most such issues are beyond the scope of microeconomic analysis and will be left for studies in macroeconomics.

1.2 | Labor Productivity

The reason why markets for labor exist is that labor services play a role in production. In a general sense, then, the demand for labor—the employers' willingness to pay for hours or years of different types of labor services—is related to just *how productive* workers are. It only stands to reason that an employer who wants to run an efficient organization will want to hire and pay workers at least approximately in line with the contribution that the workers make to the organization.[1]

How much does a particular person's labor contribute to the production of any particular thing? This is a difficult question to answer. Because workers are living, breathing, complex human beings, "having" a year of a worker's time is quite different from "having" a new computer on a desk. Workers' contributions depend not only on their individual abilities but also on the social organization of work in their employer's enterprise. In the paragraphs that follow, we discuss a few main contributors to variations in labor productivity.

The skills of the workers. This is affected by (formal) general education and job-related training, by (informal) general and job-related experience, and by innate talents. The employer has to find ways to attract and/or train workers so as to achieve a desired combination of skills; the employer's ability to do so depends on its wages and training costs, along with subtler issues, such as the creation of a working environment that encourages more skilled workers to share their knowledge with those who have less skill.

The efficiency with which workers apply their skills. An important determinant here is management; a good manager can put each worker in the job that best suits his or her abilities, can see to it that work groups are organized in more rather than less efficient ways, and can try to organize an optimal interaction of workers with the technology available to them. The job of management is not simply that of mixing inputs in the optimal proportions. It also requires devising a strategy for mobilizing and combining human capabilities. Except in unusual circumstances, there is no single best way to manage. Moreover, different ways of managing workers lead to different levels of productivity and wages.

The level of effort with which workers work. The workers' level of effort on a job includes the pace at which they work, as well as how careful they are to do the job right. In almost every work setting, individuals have wide discretion as to how much energy they will devote to the job at hand. How the employee exercises this discretion depends on her or his intrinsic and extrinsic motivation. Because the employer's ability to use rewards and punishments is usually limited, morale is of great significance in determining the level of effort. This is likely to be strongly affected by management practices, but it may also depend on historical, cultural, personal, or other circumstances beyond the manager's control.

The quantity and the characteristics of the resources available to each worker. In the simplest terms, those who work with more, newer, and better physical plant and equipment, energy resources, and materials are more productive. Increasingly, there are many activities in manufacturing, transportation, communication, and information processing that simply cannot be performed at all without the appropriate capital

---

[1] This will be treated formally, in the last section of this chapter, for the case where productivity can be easily measured, historical and social context can be ignored, and a firm faces a "convex" profit maximization problem.

equipment. A lack of the appropriate quantity or quality of complementary factors of production can make even the most skilled and motivated worker unproductive.

For some jobs, such as light-assembly factory work for a manufacturing firm, the contribution to output of individual workers (or work groups) can be quite easily measured in terms of physical product over a time period. But what about the contribution of others in the same organization—for example, the CEO, an accountant, a salesperson, or the director of the company day care center? All, presumably, contribute to the success of the organization. But because productivity is a hard thing to measure, we need to look at many factors—including market forces of supply and demand, tendencies in human psychology, and social and historical context—to get insight into the functioning of labor markets.

Discussion Questions

1. Think of a job you have held. Describe how your productivity on the job was affected by (a) your skills, (b) the organization of the workplace (whether it encouraged efficiency), (c) your level of effort (and what it was about the job that encouraged this specific level of effort), and (d) the resources you had available to work with.

2. In any production process, when one factor limits what can be produced and other factors are in abundant supply, that one factor is called the *limiting factor*. Continue to reflect on the job you thought about in question 1. Which contributor to productivity would you identify as the "limiting factor" in that case? What change would have been most effective in bringing about increased productivity?

2 | Individual Decisions and Paid Labor Supply

Two forces govern the supply of factors of production: the total quantity available at any point in time and the willingness of their owners to actually supply them. Labor is fundamentally "owned" by the individual person who "rents" out his or her services when working for pay. In many cases, however, decisions about supplying paid labor are made not by individuals but jointly with other household members, as part of a general plan for family support and investments for the future. In this chapter we will discuss paid labor supply as though an individual person is making the decision.[2] Household decision making will be explored in Chapter 15.

In general, the willingness of an individual to supply a factor of production may be analyzed in terms of the return he or she can get, compared with the benefit to him or her of not supplying it or supplying it elsewhere. An individual who is weighing these decisions is assessing the opportunity cost of supply. This idea is applied broadly in the labor context; the "costs" and the "benefits" of supplying labor may be seen in terms of money but may also reflect almost any other gains or losses that are valued by the individual.

2.1 | The Opportunity Costs of Paid Employment

Most of the alternatives facing an able-bodied adult who is considering going out to work for a wage or salary fall under the following headings:

- *Household production:* The paid job may reduce the time that can be spent in productive but unpaid work at home raising children, caring for elderly or sick relatives, cooking, keeping house, gardening, and the like.

---

[2] We also do not address the question of people in institutions who have no choice about their use of time—even though the prison population of the United States has grown to include a significant fraction of potential workers.

O *Education:* As an alternative to seeking paid work immediately, individuals may decide to stay in school or return to school—either to prepare for better-paid future employment or simply to enjoy the process of education or the life of a student.

O *Self-employment:* People can work for themselves in household enterprises, making crafts, providing personal services (such as day care or yard work) to neighbors, writing or painting, or starting some other home-based business.[3]

O *Leisure:* Work cuts into the time available for playing music, fishing, camping, reading novels, playing or watching sports, hanging out with friends, playing computer games, traveling, and other pleasurable activities.

To the extent that you value any of these pursuits and reduce the hours you devote to them when you take a paid job, that job has a "cost." The cost is the lost opportunities for other activities.

In addition to the opportunity costs associated with your time, you may incur direct monetary costs to taking a paid job, such as the costs of work-related clothing and transportation. You may incur increased monetary expenditures for things that otherwise might have been home-produced (using your time resources), such as child care and meal preparation.

O The opportunity cost of engaging in paid work is the highest value of the time that might otherwise have been spent in alternative uses, such as household production, education, self-employment, and/or leisure.

2.2 | The Benefits of Paid Employment

On the other hand, paid jobs have many benefits. Most obviously, of course, is the fact that they are *paid.* In a contemporary industrialized economy, households need some

In modern societies, workplaces often provide camaraderie and a sense of identity. A wise employer realizes that employee productivity depends in part on employee morale. Thus, enjoying a co-worker's story, while taking time away from immediate tasks, may increase employee productivity in the long run.

---

[3] The income of self-employed proprietors tends to be a mix of returns to labor, returns to capital, and profits. In this chapter, we will not discuss the nature of their labor compensation, because we are focusing only on people who work *for wages or salaries.*

monetary income to survive and to participate in society. Even if paid work is unpleasant, boring, stressful, or even demeaning, wages and salaries are strong extrinsic motivators for encouraging individuals to supply their labor.

In addition, however, paid work itself has great significance in most people's lives. The nature of the work experience, for billions of people, is a decisive part of the quality of life: The work process determines whether a major part of life will be boring or interesting, lonely or companionable, comfortable or filled with bodily discomfort, tranquil or full of anxiety, stunting to personal growth or offering opportunities to develop mental or physical capacities. As we noted in Chapter 2, intrinsic motivations are important. Evidence from state lotteries in the last few decades, for example, illustrates this point. In a number of cases, winners of large lottery prizes have decided *not* to quit their jobs entirely, even when they could easily have done so. They usually cite their friendships on the job, and the sense of identity they have found in their work, as reasons for continuing at least some of their usual work activities.

Household production and self-employment can also supply many of the same intrinsic rewards, though often with less companionship and social interaction. Sometimes, a social perception that only work for wages or salaries is "real work" makes workers in such areas feel marginalized.

In industrialized countries there has been a striking trend since the early 20th century toward an increase in the (paid) **labor force participation rate** (defined as the percentage of the adult, noninstitutionalized population who are either working at a paid job or seeking paid work). In most countries this increase has been accounted for entirely by the increasing labor force participation of women. The increase in women's participation in the labor force has been partially offset by a small decline in men's participation; most of the change for men has resulted from decisions to stay in school longer and/or to retire earlier.

If we think about these social trends in "opportunity cost" terms, we can see that they involve changing perceptions of the costs and benefits of entering the paid labor market over the course of recent history. The cost of this choice has declined as improved technologies for the home and the increased availability of substitute services (such as child care and prepared meals) have reduced the number of hours of household work strictly necessary to maintain a family. The benefits have risen in societies where activism and changes in social norms and laws have opened a greater variety of paid occupations to women. The perceived benefits have also risen to the extent that increasingly consumption-oriented cultures have raised the value of money income (for making consumer purchases) relative to the perceived value of time for household production or leisure.

labor force participation rate: the percentage of the adult, noninstitutionalized population who are either working at a paid job or seeking paid work

2.3 | The Individual Paid Labor Supply Curve

For the moment, we will look at the decision of an individual to supply various amounts of hours over a week or year, assuming that the worker can find part-time, full-time, or overtime paid jobs that meet his or her desires. For now, we will also abstract from a worker's choices among different kinds of paid jobs, focusing only on the decision about how much time to put into paid work. As in all supply curve thought experiments, we abstract from all considerations *other than* the relation of price and quantity: In supply curve analysis, we abstract from intrinsic motivations and look simply at the effect of different wage levels on the individual's willingness to supply labor to the market.

In Figure 13.1 we show an upward-sloping supply curve like those presented for markets for apartments and oil in Chapter 4. The "wage," which we use as a shorthand term for the price paid for an hour of labor, is on the vertical axis. In practice, many blue-collar and service jobs pay an hourly *wage*, whereas professional and managerial jobs tend to pay weekly or monthly *salaries*. Jobs may also pay in the form of tips, bonuses, and/or stock options, and they may provide fringe benefits such as health insurance. For our simple supply-and-demand analysis, we include all these in the

Figure 13.1 Upward-Sloping Labor Supply Curve
In general, we think of supply curves as sloping upward as the reward for supplying the item increases.

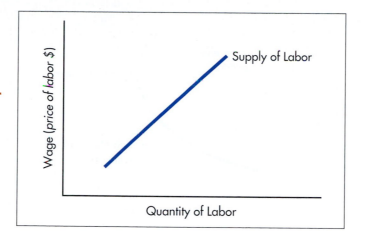

notion of "wage." The quantity of labor, which might be thought of as the number of hours the individual works in a week or a year, is on the horizontal axis.

Does this "usual" curve apply to labor? Following one line of reasoning, we can see that in many cases it does. From the perspective of an individual, the upward-sloping supply curve reflects the *substitution effect* of changes in prices: Individuals decide whether or not to substitute the attractions of working for a wage for the attractions of other activities. When offered a very low wage, an individual may be reluctant to join the labor market, because he or she may get more benefit from self-employment or other activities. The higher the market wage rate, the more attractive it is to engage in additional paid labor instead of unpaid household work, education, self-employment, or leisure.[4]

However, one of the important reasons why an individual works is to earn an income, which in turn is used to buy goods and services that he or she can then enjoy. As the wage gets higher and higher, will the person *always* want to work more and more? Probably not. Economists explain this in terms of the fact that leisure pursuits (and perhaps other unpaid activities) are usually "normal goods," in the sense explained in Chapter 5. As people get higher incomes, they may also want more time to enjoy the fruits of their labor! The rising wage also has an *income effect*: The higher the market wage, the more leisure (and other unpaid activities) people might want to "buy." Because "buying" leisure means reducing work hours, the paid labor supply curve will be *downward*-sloping if the income effect is dominant.

People may have a target level of income in mind, beyond which they feel less need for additional money. As we saw in Chapter 10, artisans in the era just before the Industrial Revolution were often said to have such income targets. Increases in wages above the traditional level led only to individuals celebrating longer weekends and offering fewer hours of work the next week. Today such extreme cases of income "targeting" are rare, but there still is a tendency for some people to reduce their willingness to work as their income rises. In such a case, the substitution effect may dominate at low wage levels, but the income effect dominates at high wage levels. The result is a **backward-bending individual paid labor supply curve**, as shown in Figure 13.2.

backward-bending individual paid labor supply curve: a pattern that arises because, beyond some level of wages, income effects may outweigh substitution effects in determining individuals' decisions about how much to work.

The presence of the income effect makes individual paid labor supply different from the usual supply of products by organizations. The income effect normally does not exist for organizations; a business or non-profit organization rarely has a target level of revenues. Usually, even if high revenues allow some employees to enjoy more leisure (for example, the founder might cut back on his or her work hours), the organization as a whole will expand its operations, perhaps by hiring more people.

[4] We are assuming that the potential worker can enjoy at least a minimal standard of living from activities other than market work when the wage is too low to make market work attractive. In situations of dire poverty, however, this may not be the case, and people may need to work two or three jobs at extremely low wages just to stay alive.

Figure 13.2 Backward-Bending Individual Labor Supply Curve
If beyond some level of income, people would rather do other things than additional paid work, the individual labor supply curve will bend backward.

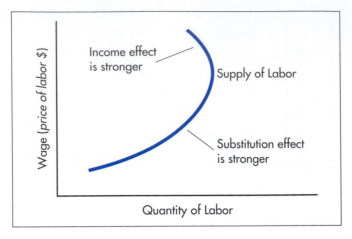

Discussion Questions

1. When you think of the years of life ahead of you, how do you see yourself dividing your time among paid employment and other possible activities? What would be your preferred hours of paid employment over the course of a week? Do you see yourself as always doing a paid job, at least part-time, or as taking some months or years off to do other things? How do these plans reflect your values and the constraints you face?

2. Think of the wage you make on your current job or one you have had recently. Would you, if you could, increase or decrease your hours of work per month if the wage doubled? If the wage increased by a factor of 10? By a factor of 100? (For example, a wage of $10 per hour would turn into $20, $100, or $1000 per hour.) Do your answers reflect a dominance of substitution effects or of income effects?

3 | Supply and Demand at the Market Level

To be able to think about labor markets in terms of supply-and-demand analysis, we need to consider how labor supply at the individual level will translate into labor supply at the market level. We also need to investigate the market demand for labor.

3.1 | Market Labor Supply

The supply of labor to a particular market, such as the national market for aerospace engineers or the market for restaurant waitpersons in Chicago, can be thought of as the horizontal sum of the supply curves of those individuals who could participate in the market.

Although the supply curves of individuals might be backward-bending, the supply curve for a particular market can generally be assumed to have the usual upward slope shown in Figure 13.1. This is because there are two ways in which employers can get a larger quantity of labor. The first is by getting workers already in the market to supply more hours, in which case income effects could become important. The second way, however, is to get more workers to enter the particular market, either by drawing them away from other jobs or by drawing them into the paid labor force from other activities. For most of these workers, we can assume that the substitution effect dominates, and so the supply curve will be upward-sloping.

Market labor supply is relatively wage elastic if a variation in the wage brings a large change in the quantity of labor supplied. This could occur if the (upward-sloping sections of) individual worker's supply curves are elastic. It also occurs when a rise in the wage easily draws more workers into the particular market being studied. Markets for types of labor that use general or more easily acquired skills, for example, tend to have relatively elastic supply curves. If the wage for local restaurant waitpersons rises, for example, people may leave jobs as salesclerks and delivery truck drivers in order to offer their services to restaurants. If the wages paid by restaurants fall, waitpersons may fairly readily look for jobs as salesclerks and drivers.

Market labor supply is relatively wage inelastic, on the other hand, if a variation in the wage brings little change in the quantity of labor supplied. At the extreme, the supply of labor might be "fixed" for some occupations, at least in the short run. For example, there are only so many aerospace engineers in the United States at any point in time. (What slope would the supply curve have?) Raising the wage might draw a few engineers out of retirement or self-employment, but it cannot instantly produce a large quantity of new, specialized engineers, because getting the skills necessary for this job requires many years of education. A drop in the wage, similarly, might not much decrease the quantity of labor supplied in the short run, because the engineers' specialized skills are not valued nearly as much in other markets. Changes in the quantity supplied will occur only over the long run, as high wages attract more students to train for the job, or low wages cause more engineers to become dissatisfied and retrain for something else.[5]

So far, we've discussed the responsiveness of quantity to price along a single supply curve. Market labor supply curves can also *shift*, in response to nonprice factors, just like the shifts in other supply curves that we studied in Chapter 4. For the economy as a whole, for example, labor supply curves tend to shift outward over time because of population growth. Changes in laws and norms and in household technology caused the supply curve to shift outward in many areas—very noticeably in fields such as medicine and law—when women joined men seeking employment in these markets.

Changes in one labor market may also have repercussions in other markets. For example, a rise in the wages of salesclerks (a movement *along* the supply curve for salesclerks) might decrease the supply of waitpersons (that is, *shift* the supply curve for waitpersons back), as people exit the waitperson market in order to take advantage of the higher wages now being offered for salesclerks.

3.2 | Market Labor Demand

For the most part, the demanders of labor—that is, the potential employers—are organizations, including businesses, nonprofits, and governments. A very small fraction of employers are households or individuals, who may directly employ people for tasks such as in-house child care and domestic service.

The demand curve for paid labor—whether for an individual organization or for a whole market—can generally be thought of as downward-sloping, like the demand curves we've examined in previous chapters. The demand for labor is largely a derived demand, based ultimately on the demand for an organization's produced goods and services.

The reason for the downward slope is as follows. When wages are high, employers have incentives to economize on the use of labor. They may cut back on their activities or try to substitute other inputs (such as another type of labor, or machinery, or computerization) for the type of labor whose wage is high. On the other hand, when wages are low, employers may be able to expand their productive activities or substitute relatively cheap labor for other inputs.

Labor demand will tend to be relatively wage elastic if there are good substitute inputs available and if the wage bill is a large proportion of total production costs (so that the employers are motivated to seek out substitutes). Labor demand will tend to be relatively inelastic if no good substitute inputs are available and the wage bill is a small proportion of total costs.

---

[5] The United States has also used immigration policies to increase the quantity of labor supplied in certain high-skilled areas experiencing labor shortages.

The labor demand curve may shift if demand for the good or service that it is used to produce changes, if technological developments change the production process, if the number of employers changes, or if the price or availability of other inputs changes. For example, when an organization experiences a fall in demand for its products, its labor demand curve will shift back as well.

3.3 | Market Adjustment

Starting from the same simplifying assumptions we made in Chapter 4—that a number of buyers and sellers come together in a spot, double-auction market and behave in a self-interested and rational way—we can examine how market forces might influence wage rates and the quantity of labor employed.

For example, let Figure 13.3 depict a stylized market for e-commerce website designers. In the late 1990s, e-commerce was booming, and demand for the services of such designers was high, as depicted by demand curve D_1. The short-run supply curve was fairly inelastic, because the job required a certain amount of specialized education and talent. Stories in the newspapers at the time touted the fat salaries being offered to talented, self-taught computer experts just out of high school and told of people being aggressively recruited by businesses, with large signing bonuses.

In 2000, however, many investors decided that e-commerce was not going to be the money maker they had expected, and financial capital for e-commerce dried up considerably. Many firms went out of business, and others laid off many of their employees. The market for website designers went from boom to bust. We can think of this as the demand curve shifting to D_2.

Comparing equilibrium E_1 to equilibrium E_2, we can see that the model predicts that the number of website designers will fall and that the wage will fall as well. In fact, many website designers became unemployed and had to search for other types of jobs, while signing bonuses and premium wage offers became a thing of the past. Students who had been training to enter the field found they had to make other plans.

It is debatable whether such a market can be described as a spot market, and whether it is ever in perfect equilibrium, but the supply-and-demand story can be a useful way of describing the observable consequences of market forces when they are strong, as in the case just described.

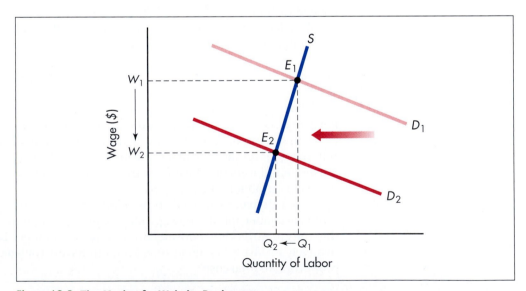

Figure 13.3 The Market for Website Designers
If market adjustment forces are strong, a drop in the demand for an particular skill will lead to a decline in the wage offered for that skill and to a reduction in employment in that occupation.

Discussion Questions

1. Suppose your college or university substantially raised the wages it offers to pay students who tend computer laboratories, monitoring the equipment and answering questions. What do you think would happen to the quantity of labor supplied? Why? Where would the extra labor hours come from? Do you think the supply of this kind of labor is elastic or inelastic? Why?

2. Opticians fit people who have poor eyesight with glasses or contact lenses, prescribed by an optometrist. Beginning in the 1990s, technological developments in laser eye surgery made surgery an increasingly popular way of correcting bad eyesight. What effect do you think this development had on the market for opticians? Draw a graph, carefully showing whether the shift is in demand or supply, and showing the resulting predicted changes in the quantity of labor demanded and in the wage.

4 | Explaining Variations in Wages

Among the things that people are especially eager to understand about the labor market are the differences among wages. Why do star basketball players make so much more than aerospace engineers, who currently make so much more than preschool teachers? In addition, within the same job definition it is possible to find workers receiving very different compensation, even though they seem to have equivalent qualifications and are hired out of the same job market. Are such patterns of wage differentials irresistibly determined by the logic of markets? If not, what other forces affect them?

Some economists, who are convinced that people behave in a rational, autonomous, self-interested way, that market forces are strong, and that markets tend to be competitive, stress productivity differences as nearly the sole source of wage variation over the long run. A high wage, in this view, is merely a sign that an individual is making a highly valued contribution. Examining economic behavior in social, historical, and institutional context, however, suggests that market forces and observable productivity differences are only part of the explanation of variation in wages.

4.1 | Human Capital

As we noted in Chapter 6, human capital consists of people's knowledge and skills. Variations in human capital can help explain variations in productivity and hence can help explain wage variation. Obviously, different kinds of jobs require different kinds of human capital, and work accomplished by someone with considerable skill may add more to production than the same hours of work contributed by someone with less skill.

Different levels of human capital often result from different levels of investment, in terms of education and training. The wages for skilled occupations, such as aerospace engineers (as compared, for example, to restaurant waitpersons), in part reflect the fact that aerospace engineers have normally taken formal training to acquire skills and credentials, whereas waitpersons largely use more common skills that virtually everyone possesses.

If we assume that nearly everyone (including engineers) possesses the qualifications for waitperson jobs and that relatively few people have the skills and knowledge necessary to be an aerospace engineer, it will be clear that the supply curves for the two professions are very different. Relative scarcity of supply (graphically, a supply curve that is farther to the left) is one factor that pushes up the wages of workers with more skills. An employer may be willing to pay a higher wage to get an engineer, to the extent that there are relatively few of them.

Human capital may also be accumulated through on-the-job training. For example, a more experienced waitperson can handle more tables with greater efficiency, and will hence tend to earn more than a new waitperson because of skills acquired on

general human capital: knowledge and skills that workers can take with them as they move from employer to employer. It may be formed before starting a job or through on-the-job training.

employer-specific human capital: knowledge and skills that have been gained on a particular job and are useful only as long as a worker remains with the same employer

the job. Human capital acquired on the job may be either general or employer-specific. **General human capital** consists of the knowledge and skills that workers can take with them if they leave one organization and go to work for another. **Employer-specific human capital** consists of knowledge and skills that are valued only by a particular employer. For example, many table-waiting and engineering skills may be general, but knowledge about a specific menu or a specific engineering project may be useless away from a particular employer.

How do employers judge a prospective worker's skills? On the employer's side, rational decisions require the ability to assess, before offering a wage, what skills the worker possesses and how much these skills will contribute to productivity. Because this assessment is often difficult to make, employers may use credentials, such as educational degrees or training certificates, as proxies for observed skills. A firm that is seeking to employ an aerospace engineer would look for someone with the appropriate degree.

In a subtler, but also common, example, firms may require credentials such as a college degree, or even a graduate degree, not because they are convinced that the undergraduate or graduate education has directly provided essential knowledge or skills but because the possession of the degree *signals* that the person is a certain kind of worker. A graduate must be someone who is capable of taking orders, absorbing unfamiliar information, meeting deadlines, and doing tasks (such as completing homework assignments and taking tests) that were not necessarily what he or she would have preferred to do with his or her time. Educational credentials such as these are used by employers as reassurance that the applicant possesses desirable characteristics such as self-discipline, patience, and the ability to work under pressure. The **signaling theory** of the value of education suggests that the value of a college education may be not so much in the way it creates human capital as in how it solves information problems for employers, revealing, or signaling, what type of worker a person already was before starting college.

signaling theory: a theory of the value of an education that suggests that an educational credential "signals" to an employer that a potential worker has desired character traits and work habits

4.2 | Market Power

Even with lots of training and practice, could everyone become a Shaquille O'Neal, making $24 million playing basketball? Clearly not. The story of competitive market equilibrium, as described above, assumes that in any labor market there are many buyers and sellers of undifferentiated labor services. In the real world, however, market power plays an important role in creating variations in wages.

Some people have particular talents. Part of Shaquille O'Neal's compensation is what economists would call **economic rents** accruing to his unique abilities and "star power." In a sense, having a very special talent or reputation is analogous to owning a highly prized piece of urban real estate: You can get high returns from it, while putting forth no greater effort than someone with lesser talents or a less prized piece of real estate. Economists often use the term *rent* to refer to returns received by something that is fixed in supply (that is, something perfectly inelastically supplied). We can think of this in terms of market power: For some really unique labor services (or unique plots of land), there is essentially only one seller. Shaquille O'Neal is the only producer of his "star power" talents and reputation. He offers a labor service that has no close substitutes.[6] He has market power. Part of what he earns is a return to his efforts; part is pure economic rent.

In the market for labor, *workers*, as the sellers, can be monopolists, monopolistic competitors, or oligopolists with market power in the *sale* of their services. This can

economic rents: returns to factors that are in fixed supply

---

[6] High rewards to "star power" exemplify what some economists call a "winner-take-all" market. In such markets, of which markets for athletes, actors, and top managers are prime examples, the rewards to being in first place are vastly superior to the rewards to being a few steps down, even if the actual difference in talents and skills between the competitors is negligible.

People with unique reputations do not have to compete for jobs in the same way that most do. Those with "star power" in the entertainment or sports industries, such as Los Angeles Laker's basketball player Shaquille O'Neal (shown on the right), are "selling" more than just their labor when they sign a contract. Due to their special ability to draw audiences, top celebrities can bargain with potential employers for the best deal often garnering salaries much higher than those possessed by actors, singers, or athletes nearly as talented.

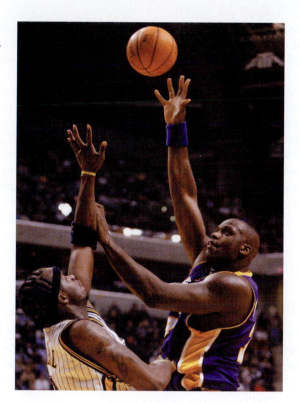

happen if they have unique or differentiated talents. It can also happen if a strong union federation represents all the workers in a particular occupation or region, so that employers have to bargain with *one* organization representing a number of sellers. Then employers may have to accept union demands as the price of remaining in business; the only limit is that if wages exceed a certain level, an employer may find it more profitable to close its local operation and reopen in a region where labor is cheaper.[7]

monopsony: the case of one buyer

When, on the other hand, there are many sellers of labor but only one *employer*, we call this a condition of **monopsony**. In the 1900s, for example, some manufacturing companies (including Hershey's for chocolate and Pullman for railway cars) set up "company towns" in which they were the sole major employer. Remote mining towns and logging camps are other examples. In such cases, employers have more discretion in setting wages than if workers could easily choose between working for them and working for other employers. The workers may have to accept the company's demands as the price of keeping their jobs. The limit on the employer's power is that if work becomes sufficiently unattractive or poorly paid, workers may decide to leave the area.[8]

bilateral monopoly: the situation in which there is only one buyer confronting only one seller

These examples—a single employer on the one hand and a single "star" or union federation on the other—represent the extremes of concentration of power in the labor market. If a single employer faces a single seller, the case can be described as a **bilateral monopoly**. In this case, the relevant market institutions are clearly characterized by bargaining, rather than by any kind of auction procedure. The outcome depends on the

---

[7] Note that what matters to the employer is not the absolute wage but the wage in relation to productivity. If wages in Country A are five times as high as in Country B, and Country A workers produce five times as much per hour as their Country B counterparts, then labor costs per unit of output are the same in both countries. If Country B productivity increases to, say, one-third that of Country A, then labor costs will be cheaper in Country B despite the much lower productivity.

[8] Some unethical company towns foreclosed this possibility by setting the wages and the prices at the company store in such a way that workers would be perpetually in debt to them and hence unable to leave.

strength, cleverness, rapport (or lack thereof), and perhaps political power of the parties and on the skills of professional mediators and litigators.

oligopsony: the case of few buyers

More common are cases of oligopoly and/or **oligopsony** (few buyers) in labor markets. In many labor markets the employers, employees, or both have some amount of market power, and their relative power is important in predicting outcomes. For example, in the U.S. music-recording industry, oligopsonistic record label *buyers* of musical works face uniquely talented but as yet unorganized *sellers* of musical work (see the accompanying News in Context feature.)

Market power in labor markets and in product markets can be related. If a business employer sells in a highly competitive product market, for example, it could be forced out of business if its workers organized into a union and demanded a higher wage. If the firm were making near zero profits to begin with, the extra costs would drive it into the red, assuming that the workers of its competitors remained unorganized. However, a business with some market power can make above-normal profits. In this case employees are more likely to be successful in their bargaining, because their demands are for a share of the extra producer surplus gained by the firm.

4.3 | Compensating Wage Differentials

Another theory put forth by economists to explain wage differentials is the idea that extra pay is required to attract workers into jobs that are especially unappealing, compared to other work that is available for people at the same skill level. What would make one job less or more appealing than another, apart from the wages? A short list would probably include

---

Recording Artists Sue, Aiming to Rock Industry

NEWS in Context

LOS ANGELES—A few female rock stars are taking legal aim at the monolithic music industry, just as lawmakers are beginning to scrutinize the industry's practices. And the common refrain is to rebalance the scales toward artists and consumers.

At the forefront of the movement are grunge rocker Courtney Love, alternative songwriter Aimee Mann, and the country-pop trio the Dixie Chicks. Emboldened by musicians' growing dissatisfaction with the industry, these artists have sued their record labels. . . .

The upcoming trials are expected to throw a spotlight on the practices of the music industry. About 90% of the music industry is controlled by the Big Five conglomerates—Universal Music Group, Sony Music Entertainment, Warner Music, BMG, and EMI Group—which all use the same contracts, distributors, promoters, and policies. . . .

Kathleen Sharp, *Boston Sunday Globe*, October 7, 2001.

Musicians must hand over 95% of their royalties to their labels, who charge them for producing their records, creating videos, and even promotion and packaging, said [music industry lawyer Don] Engle. Furthermore, say the Dixie Chicks, the labels often pad those charges. . . . In its defense, Sony cites a controversial clause contained in many record contracts: Basically, no matter how often a label overcharges or underpays the artist, and no matter for how much money, the artist can't walk out as long as the company repays the artist. . . .

Taken together, these lawsuits could force structural changes in the industry. . . . Industry lawyers compare the current litigation to the lawsuit of actress Olivia da Havilland, who challenged the movie studio system. . . . Her 1947 court case ultimately changed the law, weakened the studio system, and led to the rise of independent film producers.

Were you aware of the amount of concentration in the music industry? (The variety of labels under which music is released may be misleading. For example, Columbia Records, Epic Records, and a number of other labels are all a part of Sony Music Entertainment.) Do you think this situation is fair to recording artists?

○ *Working conditions.* These include physical discomfort or danger; stress; whether the job is interesting; how the worker is treated; degree of autonomy; flexibility of hours.

○ *Nonwage benefits.* Some firms provide nonwage benefits such as more vacation time, educational benefits for the worker's children, meals at company cafeterias, and housing.

○ *Opportunities for advancement* either within the firm or by moving to a new firm. Examples include opportunities to move into higher-echelon jobs and training or experience that other employers will value.

○ *Social contribution.* Many workers will ask not only whether the job is good for themselves but also whether it contributes to society and is consistent with their beliefs concerning ethics, vocation, and the like.

○ *Job security.* Because there are costs to being unemployed or searching for work, the likelihood that a job will continue is an important characteristic.

It is possible to find some real-world examples where people demand a higher wage to take on jobs with less appealing characteristics. For example, because most people prefer to work days, night-shift factory work generally pays slightly more than day-shift work even though the skills needed and the tasks accomplished are identical. There are also examples of people who accept a lower-than-necessary wage because it is attached to an especially appealing job. The example that professors always give is the job of being a professor: For those who like the intellectual life, this may be a very rewarding job, even though the pay is often below what professors believe they could earn elsewhere. In these cases, you can see the theory of **compensating wage differentials** at work.

On the other hand, you've probably noticed that many of the least attractive jobs in a society—such as garbage collection, agricultural field work, and boring and repetitive work in clothing manufacture or meat processing—are to be found at the lowest end of the pay scale. This is partly because they require relatively little in the way of formal qualifications. To the extent that this is true, the low wages they pay do not violate the theory of compensating wage differentials; this theory compares only jobs of equal skill. But even within the class of jobs that require few qualifications, some unpleasant jobs pay particularly badly, and one tends to find particular groups (usually minority and/or female, and nonunionized, and often immigrant) doing them.

For the theory of compensating differentials to operate in reality, it is necessary for workers to have very good information about job conditions and risks and to be able to move freely to alternative jobs for which they are qualified. It turns out that, especially when there is a significant level of unemployment, the effect of compensating differentials within jobs in the same skill class can be swamped by other factors such as bargaining power or discrimination.

compensating wage differentials: the theory that workers will be willing to accept lower wages for jobs with better characteristics and will demand higher wages for jobs with unappealing characteristics, all else equal

4.4 | Worker Motivation

A wage incentive may be enough to get workers to show up at a job for a specified number of hours. But is the wage alone enough to get workers actually to apply their effort and talents to the job?

For some jobs, employers pay piece rates—fixed amounts for the number of, say, shirts sewn, regardless of the amount of time involved, in a form of subcontracting for labor services. Workers paid on an hourly basis may be closely monitored to be sure they are producing the desired output. The monitoring might take the form of a supervisor looking over the shoulders of workers on a factory line or a computer program that counts keystrokes. Presumably, when such subcontractors or closely monitored employees do not produce up to standards, they will be fired and replacements found. In these cases, employers have pretty good information about worker productivity. They can transact on spot markets by contracting for specific lots of work with no promises made about future employment or by hiring day labor or temporary employees. Because they

Do "Warm Feelings" Substitute for Wages?

Sometimes you may hear economists arguing that occupations such as preschool teaching, nursing, and social work tend to pay less than many other jobs with similar levels of educational investment because the workers are willing to "take part of their pay" in the "warm feelings" they get from helping others. If an individual consciously and voluntarily takes such a low-paying job out of such motivations, when he or she could have chosen a higher-paying but less socially oriented job instead, we see the theory of compensating wage differentials at work.

However, it is equally obvious that many other people get particular enjoyment out of jobs that allow them, for example, to use their math skills (such as engineers) or to wield power (such as CEOs). Following the logic of the theory of compensating wage differentials, such workers should also be willing to "take part of their pay" in the enjoyment they get from these working conditions. Yet, in fact, engineering and upper-level management jobs tend to pay *more* than other jobs with similar levels of human capital investment.

Is this a contradiction?

To resolve this issue, you need to notice that the compensating wage differentials story is a theory about the location of the *supply curve*—about individuals' willingness to work in one job versus another. It is not a theory about the determination of the market wage, for which we would need to bring in consideration of the *demand* side of the market as well. In markets where we can imagine a demand curve intersecting a supply curve at a point far up and to the right, wages will tend to be high, irrespective of people's feelings about their jobs. To the extent that public spending, for example, emphasizes space exploration more than early childhood education, or to the extent that it funds advances in medical research more generously than hands-on care, the resulting difference in effective demand can help explain why caring professions are not well paid.

It's kind of a stretch, but by envisioning different priorities on the demand side, you could imagine a world in which some people would be richly rewarded for their caring skills and talents, while others would have to "take part of their pay" in the satisfaction they got from technical or managerial work! ◗

---

enter into no long-term contracts, they can easily adjust their volume of employment and their offers of compensation as supply and demand conditions change.

Monitoring, however, involves costs of its own—for example, paying the salaries of shirt inspectors and production line supervisors. In jobs characterized by high **monitoring costs**, employers will want to investigate other methods of encouraging employees to do good work.

Spot markets with piece rates or tight supervision may be inadequate for ensuring effort for other reasons, as well. In some cases, such as where the amount of work accomplished depends on the efforts of groups or is subject to factors beyond a worker's control, getting clear information about an individual's contribution may be impossible. In addition, the process of finding and hiring replacement workers involves transaction costs, which may be sizable. In jobs where a sizable amount of on-the-job training is necessary to do the job, employers need to find ways of encouraging worker loyalty so that the workers stay around long enough for investments in human capital to pay off.

The existence of monitoring costs, information problems, transaction costs, and training costs means that the model of spot markets is inadequate for analysis of many real-world labor markets. In most actual labor markets, explicit and implicit contracts, extrinsic and intrinsic motivations, and basic rules of psychology and social relations play important roles in ensuring worker motivation.

Economists have engaged in many statistical studies of wage variation and have developed a number of theories related to worker motivation that can help explain what

monitoring costs: the costs of inspecting and supervising work to make sure that the quantity and quality of work accomplished meet standards set by the employer

they observe. We will examine three. The theory of *efficiency wages* is in a sense a special case of theories about *employee morale,* whereas the theory of *dual labor markets* suggests that labor markets are segmented on the basis of approaches to worker motivation.

Efficiency Wages. Economists have theorized that employers may sometimes pay wages that are somewhat above the market-determined level as a way of motivating and retaining workers. **Efficiency wage theory** proposes that workers will work harder and "smarter" when they know that their present employer is paying them more than they could receive elsewhere.

In a perfectly competitive spot market, the workers, knowing they could get a job elsewhere at the same wage, would be fairly indifferent about whether their current employer wants to keep them on or not. They would have little motivation to work hard to keep from getting fired. If an employer pays more than the going wage, on the other hand, the employee has an incentive to try to hold on to this particular job. He or she may be motivated by the fear of losing the current "good" job and having to take one that pays less. The extra effort may also be motivated by a sense of gratitude, or identification with the firm, because we tend to like people who treat us well. Efficiency wages can be profit-maximizing: The cost to the firm of the extra wages may be more than made up for by the superior work effort and loyalty that they elicit.

efficiency wage theory: the theory that an employer can motivate workers to put forth more effort by paying them somewhat more than what they could get elsewhere

Employee Morale. Researchers have found that **employee morale**—the attitude of workers toward their work (and toward their employer)—can be very important in explaining productivity variations among workers who have the same skills and are using identical equipment. Morale is a subtle thing that can be analyzed in relation to many factors, including particular personalities, work organization and management, traditions within a firm or a culture, and relative pay. In some cases, employers try to increase good feelings through direct means, such as by hosting parties, giving nonmonetary honors to let employees know they are appreciated, or having "team-building" activities designed to increase cooperation among co-workers and identification with the organization.

employee morale: the attitude of workers toward their work and their employer

A key factor in morale is perceived equity: whether the workers feel that they are being treated fairly by management, especially as compared to expectations raised by history and by the wider culture. For example, people have expectations about the relative wages of different jobs. If the wage for one job goes up, there is strong psychological pressure for the wages of what are seen as related jobs (whether they are paid more, less, or the same) to rise enough to keep the wages in about the same relation.

Giving raises only to the nurses in a hospital (but not to the nursing assistants), or only to the nursing assistants (but not to the nurses), for example, may well diminish the morale of the excluded group, even if market conditions suggest that a raise is needed for only one group. **Wage contours** (wages that move together according to a traditional perception of "fair" rewards for related kinds of work) can persist for a long time, even while technology and other factors alter output prices and/or worker productivity. When this process causes wages to diverge too far from the value of labor's contribution, there will be pressure for wages to adjust. Because of the influence of norms, however, firms often try to make this adjustment in ways that look as though they are creating some *new* job categories (for example, "senior nursing assistants") rather than obviously changing the traditional wage relationships.

wage contours: historically determined patterns of relative wages among occupations. People often tend to think that deviating from established wage contours is "unfair."

Payment by **seniority**, or the length of time a worker has been at a particular organization, was historically used to increase morale—and especially to increase loyalty to the employing organization. When a job involves a great deal of on-the-job development of firm-specific human capital, it can be rational for the employer and employee to agree to a long-term relationship with a payment schedule that rises with time. If employees are underpaid relative to their contributions early in their employment, but with the promise of much more generous compensation later, they may be motivated to do good work, while costs to their employer stay reasonable on average. Such contracts may be explicit, as in the case of union-organized agreements.

seniority: the length of time a person has worked for a particular organization

Historically, contracts regarding seniority were often implicit. However, it is clear that if the employers can figure out other ways to motivate workers, they have an incentive to break such implicit contracts with their more senior (and thus more expensive) workers. During the massive business restructurings of the late 1990s, for example, many middle-aged workers found their expectations of long-term employment suddenly disappointed. New workers today are much less likely than workers of the 1950s to expect that they will stay with one organization and advance continuously though seniority.

Social norms not only vary from one culture (or subculture) to another but also can change over time. The pressure of international competitiveness that swept over the world especially during the 1980s had the effect of breaking down many norms: Expectations about job security were shattered in many parts of the world, and many wage contours shifted. However, such periods are generally regarded as exceptional; in more normal times, norms and expectations are slow to change. They continue to exert a force on wages and other aspects of employment that can alter outcomes sharply away from what is predicted by simpler forms of analysis.

Dual Labor Markets. Economists have on occasion identified **dual labor markets**. In these cases, the "primary" part of a workforce is motivated by high wages, opportunities for advancement, job security, and perhaps other favorable working conditions. Employment in the "secondary" workforce, on the other hand, is more closely driven by market conditions. These workers receive generally lower wages, enjoy no opportunities for advancement, and have no job security.

> **dual labor markets:** a situation in which "primary" workers enjoy high wages, opportunities for advancement, and job security, while "secondary" workers are hired with low wages, no opportunities for advancement, and no job security

Such labor market segmentation may take place across firms. A primary sector of large, established, oligopolistic firms (or entrenched government agencies), which use some of their surplus revenues to pay high wages, may exist side by side with a secondary sector of smaller organizations that are more subject to competitive pressures.

Dual labor markets may also exist within a single organization. For example, offices may employ regular workers with health and retirement benefits and, alongside them, hire temporary workers on short contracts with no benefits. In many colleges and universities, tenured faculty constitute the "primary" workforce. Then lecturers, adjuncts, and research associates who constitute a secondary workforce are hired as the need arises—and let go when the need falls. Such a structure allows an employer to keep a loyal core of employees *and* to avoid making new long-term commitments in times of—perhaps temporary—high demand. But for an individual worker, moving from the secondary to the primary labor force may be difficult indeed. Workers in the secondary sector have fewer opportunities to build up human capital and may quickly develop an "unstable"-looking work history.

4.5 | Discrimination

Not all social norms and customs that influence the labor market can be considered benign. **Labor market discrimination** exists when, among similarly qualified people, some are treated disadvantageously in employment on the basis of race, gender, age, sexual preference, or disability. Workers who belong to disfavored groups may be paid less for the same work or work of similar skill, may be denied promotions, or may simply be excluded from higher-paying and higher-status occupations.

> **labor market discrimination:** a condition that exists when, among similarly qualified people, some are treated disadvantageously in employment on the basis of race, gender, age, sexual preference, or disability

Historically, much labor market discrimination, particularly against African Americans and other minorities, was based on racist beliefs that certain groups were innately inferior. Some discrimination against women was similarly based on sexist notions of inferiority. However, gender discrimination was also historically rooted in social norms that reserved better-paying jobs for men (who were assumed to be supporting families), while making women (who were assumed to have husbands to rely on) solely responsible for providing unpaid household labor and family care.

Discriminatory attitudes may be held by employers, who discriminate on the basis of their own biases, expectations, and beliefs. They may also be held by customers or co-workers. This latter case poses a dilemma for employers, even if they themselves are not prejudiced. For example, suppose a law firm hires a skilled minority lawyer, but clients feel more confident being represented by European-American lawyers. The firm may find that the new lawyer attracts little business to the firm. A construction firm that hires a female forklift driver, or a preschool that hires a male teacher, may find that the morale of their other workers sinks, as the workers react badly to seeing someone of the "wrong" sex in "their" jobs. More insidiously, discriminatory attitudes can become self-fulfilling prophecies: Even though the minority lawyer, the female construction worker, and the male preschool teacher are all fully qualified in a technical sense, their contribution to the firm *will* be low, and perhaps even negative, if social norms create an environment in which their skills go unused or work group cooperation is jeopardized. Employers concerned with immediate productivity may hence fail to hire disfavored groups, even if they themselves do not harbor discriminatory beliefs about racial differences or gender roles. Such discrimination can be eliminated only by socially coordinated—and even courageous—action.

We can compare the wages of U.S. full-time, year-round workers in various groups, using government data for the year 2000. The median wage of African-American male workers was about 77% of the wage of their white male counterparts, and the median wage of African-American female workers was about 87% of that of white female workers. The median wage for women of all races was about 73% of that of men.[9]

However, given that some variations in wages may be due to factors outside the labor market itself, economists are careful about how much of this wage gap they attribute to discriminatory actions by employers. A wage difference is a sign of labor market *discrimination* only if the workers being compared have similar qualifications. Economists have estimated that differences in human capital formation explain about half of the gap between African Americans and whites. To use one measure of human capital, in the year 2000 about 26% of whites age 25 and over had a bachelor's or more advanced educational degree, and the corresponding figure for African Americans was only 17%.[10] African Americans are also more likely than whites to be high school dropouts. Getting to the bottom of earnings inequality by race would clearly require addressing problems of educational inequality, as well.

Differences in education are not nearly so pronounced for gender groups as they are for race. In fact, since about 1980, the number of women enrolled in college has exceeded the number of men. Yet differences in earnings are persistent. Figure 13.4 graphs median annual earnings for year-round, full-time workers according to their age, educational attainment, and sex. It illustrates two important points that we have discussed in this chapter. The first point is that earnings tend to rise with human capital investment. The median wage curves for college graduates are above the curves for high school graduates, within each sex. In the year 2000, the median wage for men with a bachelor's degree ($63,216) was nearly double that of men with only a high school diploma ($32,020), and women college graduates ($35,083) made 82% more than their high school counterparts ($19,269).

The second point, however, is that women make substantially less than men with similar education levels, at all ages. College-educated women age 45 or older in the year 2000 earned on average about the same or less than *high-school*-educated men in the same age groups.

---

[9] *Median* earnings are the earnings such that half the people in the group make more, and half less, than the stated level of earnings. Many more comparisons that could be made on the basis of other characteristics are beyond the scope of this text. Data are from the U.S. Bureau of the Census, *Historical Tables—People*, **www.census.gov**, Tables P-36, P-36a, P-36b, and P-40.

[10] U.S. Bureau of the Census, *Statistical Abstract of the United States 2001*, Table 217.

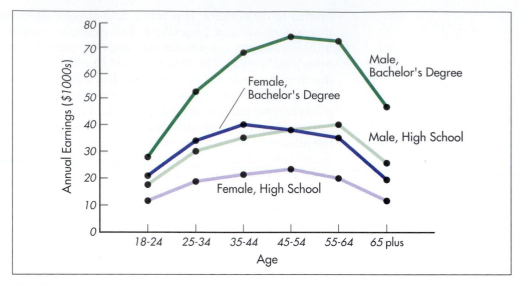

Figure 13.4 Median Annual Earnings by Gender and Educational Attainment, 2000

Earnings tend to rise with education levels for both sexes, but women's average earnings still lag behind those of men with the same levels of education.

(Source: U.S. Census Bureau, *Historical Tables—People*, www.census.gov, Table P-24.)

Part of the explanation for women's lower average earnings is that women in the year 2000 had less work experience than men, on average. Men as a group have tended to work more continuously on their jobs, whereas, given social norms about family responsibilities, many women have tended to be in the labor market less than full-time when their children were young. To the extent that time on the job can contribute to productivity, this could explain some of the difference. A careful statistical study has concluded that the difference in average work experience explains about one-quarter of the difference between men's and women's median wages.[11]

occupational segregation: the tendency of men and women to be employed in different occupations

Another important factor in explaining earnings differences by gender is **occupational segregation**—the tendency of men and women to be found in different kinds of jobs. For example, in the United States, jobs like bookkeeper, dental hygienist, child care worker, registered nurse, and teacher of young children are overwhelmingly held by women. Meanwhile, men notably dominate in occupations such as construction labor and the construction trades, metal working, truck driving, and engineering.

Occupational segregation can also be more subtle. For example, a lawsuit brought in 1992 against Lucky Stores, a supermarket chain, noted that the chain hired both men and women as "managers." Yet men held most of the jobs as produce and grocery managers, which were on the career track toward promotion to higher management levels. Women were given jobs managing deli and bakery sections, with less chance to move up.

Interestingly, the same job may be "gendered" differently in different countries. In the United States, where the majority of physicians are male, medicine is a highly lucrative and prestigious field. By contrast, in Russia, where the majority of physicians are women, both the monetary rewards and the prestige are far less.

Statistical studies suggest that about a third of the differences between men's and women's pay in the United States can be associated with differences in industry and

[11] Francine D. Blau and Lawrence M. Kahn, "Swimming Upstream: Trends in the Gender Wage Differential in the 1980's," *Journal of Labor Economics*, 15(1997), 1–42, as summarized in Table 7.2 of Francine Blau, Marianne A. Ferber, and Anne E. Winkler, *The Economics of Women, Men and Work*, 3d ed. (Englewood Cliffs, NJ: Prentice-Hall, 1998).

occupation. Various reasons have been offered to explain why the sorts of jobs women tend to work at pay less on average. One explanation is that because women were historically "crowded" into a narrow range of occupations, the supply curve in these job markets was artificially shifted outward, thus lowering the wage. Some have suggested that the average difficulty level of the job or the skill required might be less for "female" jobs. Others argue that differences in preferences between men and women workers could result in women trading high wages for other beneficial job characteristics (such as flexibility in hours). And still others argue that entrenched wage contours systematically devalue certain kinds of work (for example, work involving emotional empathy or work with children).

Even after accounting for differences in education, experience, *and* type of job, however, over a third of the difference between men's and women's earnings in the United States remains unexplained. That is, even comparing men and women with equal qualifications who hold the same jobs, differences in pay remain. In the United States, discrimination by sex and race in hiring and wages was made illegal by Title VII of the Civil Rights Act of 1964.[12] Enforcement, however, has proved difficult. Evidence suggests that bias, both blatant and subtle (see the accompanying News in Context feature), still plays a significant role.

Discussion Questions

1. "Economists assume that people just want to make as much money as possible." Is this statement correct or incorrect? Of the nonwage working conditions listed in the text, which ones are most important to you as you think about your future career?

2. Think about your current job or the last job you held. Would you say that it is in a "primary" or "secondary" labor market? To what extent do you think that the factors discussed above—human capital, market power, compensating wage differentials, worker motivation, and/or discrimination—explain the wage and working conditions you experience(d)?

5 | Labor in the Traditional Neoclassical Model

In the traditional neoclassical model, labor is demanded by profit-maximizing firms and supplied by utility-maximizing households. Given a number of assumptions, the traditional model describes how such actors would logically make decisions.

5.1 | Labor Supply

The utility theory model of behavior developed to explain consumption, and discussed in Chapter 10, can be extended to decisions about labor supply. As in that model, the potential labor market participant is assumed to have preferences that can be characterized by a "utility function." It is further assumed that the potential labor market participant is fully rational, has perfect information, and can freely vary his or her hours of paid work.

In the case of labor supply, however, the model defines the basic "budget line" according to the number of *hours* the individual has available to "spend" on activities, rather than according to the amount of money he or she has to spend on goods. Hours "spent" on paid labor result in wages, which in turn give opportunities for consumption. Hours "spent" on other activities yield utility either directly (as in the case of leisure) or indirectly through nonemployee production. (Generally, paid work is assumed to yield no direct utility.) According to this model, the potential labor market participant will

---

[12] This act also covered discrimination by "color," religion, and national origin. Later acts have addressed discrimination according to age and disability, and various states and localities have passed laws concerning employment treatment on the basis of sexual preference.

MIT Women Win a Fight Against Bias: In Rare Move, School Admits Discrimination

CAMBRIDGE, Massachusetts—The women professors at the Massachusetts Institute of Technology presumed that their numbers were low for the reason everyone had accepted as fact: Girls just don't like science. Then they took out their tape measures. Sneaking around the nation's most prestigious institute of science in 1994, 15 women went office to office comparing how much space MIT awarded women with what men of equal status got. It was less by about half. Salaries were less, too. As was the research money given to women. And the numbers of women on committees that made decisions about hiring and funding. There were no women department heads and never had been. . . .

The story of how these women got MIT to recognize and acknowledge bias offers a portrait of how discrimination works, often so subtly that many women themselves don't believe it exists. . . . It's not that women aren't entering academia; in 1995, 43% of faculty in tenure-track positions nationwide were women, according to the American Association of University Professors. The problem has been especially pronounced at elite universities. Because the numbers at the top were so small, a woman who suspected discrimination might as easily conclude that she was the victim of circumstances particular to her case.

That began to change in 1994, when MIT told Nancy Hopkins, a prominent DNA researcher, that it would discontinue a course she had designed that was now required for 1,000 students a year. She had worked for five years to develop the course; in the previous two years, a male professor had joined her in teaching it. The man, MIT informed her, was going to turn the course into a book and a CD-ROM—without her. Hopkins drafted a letter to MIT's President, Charles Vest, about how she felt women researchers were treated. . . . When Hopkins discussed it with a woman colleague, she asked to sign it, too. . . . [T]he discussion expanded to a third tenured woman. . . . They decided to poll every tenured woman in the School of Science . . . to see whether what they had experienced were individual problems or part of a pattern.

They were surprised to find out how fast they got their answers. Within a day, they had talked to all 15 tenured women (there were 197 tenured men) and agreed that something had to be done. . . .

Within a few months, the women presented a report to Robert Birgineau, dean of the School of Science. "The unequal treatment of women who come to MIT makes it more difficult for them to succeed, causes them to be accorded less recognition when they do, and contributes so substantially to a poor quality of life that these women can actually become negative role models for younger women," the women wrote. In short, they said, they were so miserable that any young woman looking . . . at them would think, "Why would I want that?" All 15 women crowded into his office to present the report.

. . . [Birgineau] did his own quick investigation to see if the numbers were correct. (They were.) And he made quick remediation. Immediately, he boosted women's salaries an average of 20 percent. . . ."

"It's not as if this was an institution that didn't want women," said Molly Potter, a cognitive scientist. "There's acceptance of them in general. But when it came to decisions about who gets what, who succeeds, who gets the creamy appointments, who gets the awards that can be distributed by recommendation or the will of the department head, it's the buddy system," Potter said. "The men were the buddies of the men."

. . . In addition to salary, space, and resource increases, Birgineau said he expects to have a 40% increase in the number of women with tenure next year, bringing the percentage to above 10 for the first time. . . . MIT is also looking at ways to allow women to incorporate child raising into scientific careers, with, for instance, a provision allowing them to stop teaching and then get back on the tenure track without penalty. Significantly, Birgineau said, five of the six women [who are] expected to get tenure this year have children. The report [of a School of Science committee] urges the establishment of . . . a similar effort to consider why minorities have not made progress in science." ◗

Kate Zernikein, *Boston Globe,* March 21, 1999.

Compare the facts of this case to the formal definition of "discrimination" presented in this section. Does this case fit the definition?

choose the level of labor market participation that maximizes his or her utility from activities and consumption.

5.2 | Labor Demand

Consider a firm that is seeking to hire a specific type of labor. What, logically, should guide the firm's decisions if it had perfect information about productivity and acted in a logical fashion? As always, in the traditional model, we assume that the firm is a unitary decision maker, that there are no externalities, that it faces a "convex" decision problem that can be addressed using marginal thinking, and that it is interested only in profit maximization. In addition, we assume that it hires labor in a spot, double-auction market. We assume that all other inputs are held fixed.

From the viewpoint of a profit-maximizing firm, an additional person-hour of labor will be desirable if it increases profits, but not otherwise. Hiring an additional person-hour does two—contradictory—things to the firm's profit position:

- ◖ Costs are raised by the amount of the additional wages paid.

- ◖ Revenue is increased by the value of the increase in output produced by the additional hour of work.

Clearly, as long as the firm gets *more* additional revenue than it has to pay out in additional wages, it should keep hiring workers. On the other hand, if it is getting *less* in additional revenue than it is paying out in additional wages, it should reduce the number of workers it hires. The profit-maximizing decision rule for the firm can thus be expressed as

$$MRP_L = MFC_L$$

marginal revenue product of labor (MRP_L): the amount that a unit of additional labor contributes to the revenues of the firm

marginal factor cost of labor (MFC_L): the amount that a unit of additional labor adds to the firm's costs

where MRP_L is the **marginal revenue product of labor**, or the amount that an additional unit of labor contributes to revenues, and MFC_L is the **marginal factor cost of labor**, or the amount the additional unit of labor adds to the firm's wage costs.

In other words, the firm should hire additional units of labor until the marginal benefits just equal the marginal costs. We saw very similar reasoning in Chapter 8, concerning a firm's decision about how much to produce—for exactly the same reasons. A formal derivation of this rule is described in the appendix to this chapter.

If the firm buys labor services in a competitive market, MFC_L will simply be the competitively determined market wage, and the rule will simplify to

$$MRP_L = \text{Wage}$$

If the firm is instead a monopsonist or oligopsonist, MFC_L will tend to be higher than the wage actually paid (because such an employer has to raise the wage for everyone when it hires more workers from along the worker-determined supply curve). Monopsonistic or oligopsonistic employers will tend to hire fewer workers than firms that compete in labor markets and will tend to pay the workers less than their marginal revenue product of labor. (This is analogous to how, in product markets, monopo*listic* producers tend to produce less than competitive producers and to charge more than the marginal cost for their products.)

The traditional neoclassical model offers an elegant solution for this streamlined case. It gives a formalized statement of the intuitive sense that workers should be rewarded in relation to their contribution to the organization. Of course, as we have seen, actual measurement of productivity is difficult, and worker motivation is a complex subject. We have also seen that market valuations can differ from social valuations because of externalities and distributional issues. Hence you should be careful about inferring that, in the real world, any observed wage accurately represents a contribution to well-being.

Discussion Questions

1. Assume that, after time for sleep and basic personal care, you have 14 hours a day that you can use for paid work or other activities. Suppose that you can freely vary the number of hours you supply to the labor market and that you will be paid one unit of "consumption goods" for each hour of paid work.

   a. Draw a budget line for consumption and other activities as follows. Label the vertical axis "Consumption Goods (units)" and mark the point that represents the maximum consumption level you could reach if you spent *all* of your 14 hours in paid work. Label the horizontal axis "Activities Other than Paid Labor (hours)," and mark the point that represents the maximum level of such activities you could engage in if you spent *none* of your 14 hours in paid work. Connect the two points with a straight line. (You might want to compare the resulting figure to Figure 10.1.)

   b. Suppose Lynn chooses a point up high and to the left on this line, while Hadi chooses a point far down and to the right. What does this imply about their preferences?

   c. Suppose that, instead of getting 1 unit of consumption goods per hour of work, you got 2 units. How would this change the budget line? (*Hint:* Would this change increase the time available for other activities?)

2. The traditional neoclassical model focuses on how people could make rational choices when faced with "convex" problems in a situation of full information. In Chapter 2, we discussed how habit and constraint can provide alternative explanations for observed behavior. Think of *one example each,* from your reading or personal experience, of a labor market supply behavior that strongly reflects (a) choice, (b) habit, and (c) constraint. Refer to the second section ("Motivation and Behavior") in Chapter 2 if necessary. Repeat for labor market demand behaviors.

Review Questions

1. What are four main contributors to variations in labor productivity?

2. What are four major alternatives, for an individual, to using time for market labor?

3. What are two major benefits, to an individual, of supplying market labor?

4. Explain how income effects and substitution effects can create a "backward-bending" labor supply curve for individuals.

5. Why are market labor supply curves thought of as upward-sloping?

6. What conditions would make a market labor supply curve relatively wage elastic?

7. Give examples of two changes that might cause a market labor supply curve to shift.

8. Why are market labor demand curves thought of as downward-sloping?

9. What conditions would make a market labor demand curve relatively wage elastic?

10. Describe, using a supply-and-demand graph, how a shift in one of the curves changes the equilibrium wage and quantity of labor.

11. Why do jobs with high human capital requirements tend to pay more than jobs that require fewer skills?

12. Explain how the different actors in labor markets can have market power.

13. Cite five job characteristics, other than wages, that people may care about.

14. How can monitoring lead to good information about employee productivity?

15. What are four approaches that employers might use to try to motivate their workers when monitoring or replacing workers is too expensive?

16. Explain how biased attitudes among co-workers and customers can make it hard to eliminate labor market discrimination.

17. What gaps have been observed between the median earnings of whites and blacks and between those of men and women? How do economists explain these gaps?

18. In the traditional model of labor supply, what does the "budget line" represent?

19. In the traditional model of labor demand, what is the profit-maximizing labor market decision rule for the firm? Why does this make sense?

Exercises

1. Reviewing Chapters 4 and 5 if necessary, illustrate on a labor market graph the following examples that were described in the text.
  a. A relatively elastic supply curve for waitpersons.
  b. A virtually "fixed" supply of aerospace engineers, in the short run
  c. The effect on the supply of lawyers of the reduction of barriers to women's participation in law
  d. The effect on the market for waitpersons of a rise in the wage of salesclerks

2. Draw labor market graphs illustrating the following examples that were mentioned in the text.
  a. A labor demand curve, when very good substitutes for labor in the production process exist
  b. The effect of a drop in demand for the organization's product
  c. The effect of a rise in the price of other inputs that have been used as substitutes for labor

3. Suppose that you observe that the wages for accountants in your town have gone up and that the number of accountants employed has also gone up. Which *one* of the following conditions could explain this? Illustrate your answer with a graph, and explain in a brief paragraph.
  a. Businesses are failing, reducing the need for accountants.
  b. Many accountants are leaving the field in order to train to become financial analysts instead.
  c. A rash of business scandals has increased the demand for auditing services performed by accountants.
  d. The local university has just graduated an unusually large group of accountants.

4. Professional groups may, like unions, create market power for their members by using their control over education, credentialing, and licensure to limit the quantity supplied of their services (much as the OPEC cartel limited the quantity supplied of oil). For many years the American Medical Association was often accused of creating such market power for doctors' labor services. Assuming (for our present purposes) that the AMA had *monopoly* power, what would this mean for doctors' wages? How would the number of doctors employed compare to those employed in the case of competition? (To gain insight, you may want to refer to Figure 12.1, which illustrates monopoly power in a product market.)

5. Match each concept in Column A with an example in Column B.

Column A	Column B
a. an alternative to wage employment	**i.** "Insurance adjustor" jobs are traditionally given to men, whereas "insurance representative" jobs go to women.
b. the income effect on individual labor supply	**ii.** Isabella cuts back her hours at her job after she gets a raise.
c. a cause of a shift in demand for professors	**iii.** Many professors reach retirement age.
d. a cause of a shift in the supply of professors	**iv.** Acme Corp. hires only college graduates for sales jobs but doesn't care about their majors.
e. using education as a "signal"	**v.** the salary of a supervisor
f. labor market monopoly	**vi.** Westinghouse is the only major employer in the county.
g. labor market monopsony	**vii.** Marshall is the only person who knows how to run his company's antiquated database.
h. compensating wage differential	
i. monitoring costs	**viii.** household production
j. wage contour	**ix.** Resident assistants get a rent-free apartment but little pay.
k. occupational segregation	**x.** "Insurance adjustors" traditionally make more than "insurance representatives."
	xi. a rising college-student-age population

6. The U.S. Department of Labor, Bureau of Labor Statistics, keeps track of the average wages and number of workers involved in various occupations over time and also makes projections about what jobs may show the most growth in the future. Using the bureau's website of data, **http://www.bls.gov**, try to look up information on an occupation that interests you. How does it pay, compared to other jobs? Is demand projected to rise in the future?

A Formal Model of a Firm's Hiring Decision in Perfect Competition

marginal physical product of labor (MPP_L): the amount that a unit of additional labor contributes to the physical product of a firm

Suppose a firm produces disposable razors. Holding all other inputs fixed, the relation between the number of workers hired and the number of razors that can be produced in a day is given in the first two columns of Table 13.1.[13] This curve is graphed in Figure 13.5. This is just a total product curve, similar to those we derived in Chapter 7.

From these first two columns, the **marginal physical product** of each additional worker (MPP_L) can be computed. For example, 1 worker can produce 5 razors, but adding an additional worker makes possible the production of 12 razors, so the *marginal physical product* of the second worker is 7 razors. Note that the marginal physical product of labor first rises and then falls—exhibiting initial increasing returns followed by diminishing returns, as we had posited in Chapter 7.

We will further assume that the firm sells the razors on a perfectly competitive product market. In this case, the price received per razor is constant and, we assume, is equal to $3. Hence the marginal *revenue* product of labor (MRP_L)—that is, the monetary value of the additional physical production—is just $3 \times MPP_L$. We assume that the firm buys labor on a perfectly competitive labor market, at a constant wage of $12. Hence the marginal factor cost of labor is constant at $12.

The MRP_L and MFC_L curves are graphed in Figure 13.6. The MRP_L curve has an initial hump, because the production function is characterized by initially increasing returns followed by steadily decreasing returns.

Table 13.1	Disposable Razor Production			
Number of Workers	Number of Razors Produced	Marginal Physical Product of Labor	Marginal Revenue Product of Labor ($)	Marginal Factor Cost of Labor ($)
1	5	5	15	12
2	12	7	21	12
3	18	6	18	12
4	23	5	15	12
5	**27**	**4**	**12**	**12**
6	30	3	9	12
7	32	2	6	12
8	33	1	3	12

[13] Wouldn't producing more razors also involve more of *other* variable inputs—such as materials and energy? The traditional neoclassical model abstracts from such complications, letting only *one* input be variable, which makes finding the *MRP* of the input easy. If labor, materials, and energy all varied at the same time, it would be more difficult to sort out the distinct contributions of the individual factors to revenues.

Figure 13.5 Production of Disposable Razors

With labor as the variable input, we can graph the total product curve for the production of razors.

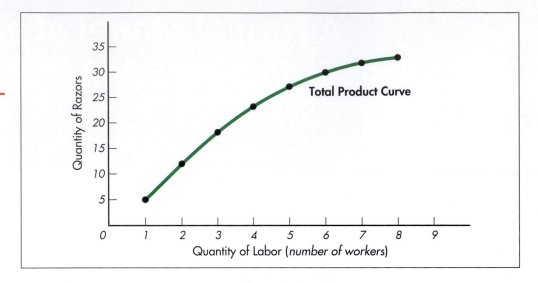

For all workers up to worker 5, hiring the additional worker adds more to revenues than to costs. The profit-maximizing firm should stop hiring workers when $MRP_L = MFC_L$, at an employment level of 5 workers.

You might note the similarities between this analysis, which is based on an examination of a factor market, and Chapter 7, which examined a firm's decision making by focusing on the product market. In fact, if you were given full information about a traditional model firm's technology and costs, you would see that the two decision processes would come to the same conclusion. Although we have just deduced the optimal *factor* market decision of the razor producer, you can see that we have also, in a backhanded way, derived the optimal *production* decision: At a product price of $3 per razor, the razor producer should produce 27 razors (the output level corresponding to the employment level of 5 workers—see Table 13.1). Product and factor market decisions are two sides of the same coin.

Figure 13.6 Marginal Revenue Product of Labor and Marginal Factor Cost of Labor

In the traditional model, the profit-maximizing firm will hire workers until the amount that the marginal worker adds to revenues (MRP_L) is just equal to the amount that workers must be paid (MFC_L).

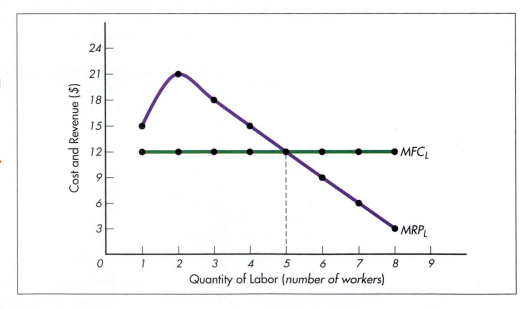

Markets for Other Resources

Chapter 14

Cisco Systems, in a move that surprised the business world, bought a start-up company called Cerent in August 1999 for an astounding price of $6.9 billion. Why was this a surprise? The value of the assets of Cerent, according to its accounting books, was only $100 million. Cisco paid this very high price because it wanted one of Cerent's *intangible* assets—a particular fiber-optic technology. By early 2002, the value of Cerent, as indicated by the value of its shares, had fallen to $2.7 billion. Had Cisco paid too much? What are some of the principles—and the difficulties—involved in making wise choices about buying and selling productive assets?

1 | Valuing Capital Stocks

Labor markets, discussed in the previous chapter, are institutions that allocate the labor services generated from human capital resources, according to the mode of exchange. As we noted in Chapter 6, however, human capital is only one type of economic resource. Natural capital and manufactured capital are two types of physical productive resources. Natural capital, such as iron ore or land, is provided by nature alone, whereas manufactured capital is the result of human activity applied to natural resources, a prime example being machinery. Social capital is the less tangible resource of shared knowledge, norms, trust, and social organization that facilitates economic activity. Financial capital consists of monetary resources, used to facilitate economic activity.

In many cases, the ownership claims to these resources are exchanged on markets—such as in markets for real estate, oil-drilling rights, computer equipment, the stock market, or the market for foreign currencies. In other cases, the owners of these resources "rent out" the services of their capital asset on a market, such as in the market for truck rentals or loans to home buyers. The present chapter explores some of the particulars of market exchange when resources and/or their services are involved.

What is a particular item of capital stock worth? The question of *valuation* is much more complicated for a capital stock than for an immediately consumable good because of the factor of *time*. If you buy and eat an apple today, you have the satisfaction now. In contrast, people want to own capital stocks because they expect them to be productive (or at least to hold their value) over some time period extending into the future. Because a number of different investments may be available—or may become available—and because we never know the future with certainty, estimating the value of any particular asset commonly involves a considerable amount of guesswork.

1.1 | The Value of Capital: A Simple Case with Certainty

To get the basic idea about valuation of a capital stock, we will begin with an example in which we (improbably) know all the relevant information with certainty. Suppose, for example, you run a small auto repair business and are considering whether to invest in an additional service bay for your garage. The service bay—a sheltered area with a car lift and tools—is an example of manufactured capital. Being a wise decision maker, you know that you should decide to invest in this asset only if the benefits to you of having the new bay exceed the costs of having it installed—and if this use of your limited resources of time and money will yield higher returns than alternative possible uses.

To make the case extremely simple, suppose you know with certainty all the factors relevant to your decision:

1. The service bay will be installed and paid for immediately and will last for 5 years. After 5 years, it will be totally worn out and worth nothing.[1]

2. In each of the 5 years to come, having the extra bay will add exactly $5000 to the net revenues of your business. (That is, your future revenues, less all the costs of running your business *except* those related to installation of the new service bay right now, will be increased $5000 per year.)

3. You will finance the bay, should you purchase it, out of equity. The best alternative use of your funds would be a bank account paying 5% interest per year.

What is the maximum amount, then, that should you be willing to pay to have the additional service bay installed? That is, what is the additional service bay worth to you?

The value of this service bay to you depends, first of all, on the stream of **returns to capital** that you expect to receive from it. This is the monetized value of what you expect to get back, in each time period, from making this investment. In your case, this stream of returns to capital is $5000 per year for 5 years.

Does this mean that the new service bay is worth $25,000 to you? (That is, 5 years × $5000)? Perhaps you should *make* the investment if the cost of installing the new bay is less than $25,000, because then your benefits (additional profits) will exceed your costs (of installing it), but should *not make* the investment if it costs more than $25,000. If you reason this way, you are on the right track.

There is, however, one complication: Even in a world of perfect certainty, a dollar next year is not worth the same as a dollar today. Using your own funds to buy the new service bay also involves an opportunity cost: You could have put your funds into a bank account instead. Because of this opportunity cost, the new service bay is worth somewhat less than the full $25,000 to you. (Alternatively, you might think about borrowing the money to buy the service bay and having to pay interest at an annual rate of 5%. In this case the cost of financing is even clearer.) The project of investing in the service bay will look less attractive the higher the rate of return that is possible on other investments. A project that looks attractive if the best alternative use of funds carries a 5% yield (or the cost of borrowing funds is a 5% interest rate), for example, may not look nearly so attractive if the comparison is to a 10% or 30% yield elsewhere (or cost of borrowing).

In the Math Review feature "The Present Value of Future Funds," we find that the correct number for valuing the flow of returns to capital associated with the service bay is the **present discounted value (PDV)**, which is calculated to be $21,647. This is the maximum amount you should be willing to pay, now, to make this investment in order to collect capital income in future periods. In a world of perfect information, perfect capital markets, and no externalities, we could say that this is the *value* to you of the new service bay.

returns to capital: the monetized value of what an investor expects to get back, in the future, from making an investment

present discounted value (PDV): the value *today* of *future* streams of funds

---

[1] This assumption is admittedly unrealistic. Its purpose is to keep the mathematics simple.

The Present Value of Future Funds

Math Review

Why isn't a dollar next year worth the same as a dollar today?

Suppose you have $1 today and invest it in a bank account at a 5% interest rate.[2] At the end of the year, you will have

$$\text{Value 1 year from now} = \$1 + (5\% \times \$1)$$
$$= \$1 + (0.05 \times \$1)$$
$$= \$1 + \$.05$$

Thus $1 now is "worth" $1.05 a year from now. Turning this around, we can also say that $1.05 a year from now is worth $1 today.

What, then, is the value of $1 a year from now, today? We can figure this out by doing a little algebra. We can write the formula we used above as

$$\text{Value one year from now} = \text{value now} + (\text{interest rate} \times \text{value now})$$
$$VALUE_1 = VALUE_0 + (i \times VALUE_0)$$
$$VALUE_1 = VALUE_0(1 + i)$$

where we have substituted symbols ($VALUE$ = dollar amount, 0 = now, 1 = 1 year from now, i = interest rate) and rearranged by factoring out $VALUE_0$. We can then divide through by $(1 + i)$ to get

$$\frac{VALUE_1}{(i + i)} = VALUE_0$$

Substituting in $1 for the value 1 year from now ($VALUE_1$) and 0.05 for the interest rate (i), we get

$$\frac{\$1}{(1 + 0.05)} = VALUE_0$$
$$\frac{\$1}{1.05} =$$
$$\$.9524 = VALUE_0$$

or a dollar a year from now is worth about $.95 today. In other words, if you had $.95 today, and invested it in the bank, you would have (about) $1 at the end of the year.

discount rate: the percentage by which future funds are discounted in order to be expressed in terms of present value

Sometimes, when the interest rate appears in the denominator like this, it is called the **discount rate**. It is the percentage by which future funds are *discounted* in order to be expressed in terms of value in the present. A value like $VALUE_0$ is called the present discounted value of the future funds.

Extending the exercise to another question, what would be the value of a dollar, invested now, 2 years from now? Let's call this $VALUE_2$. You would take the value of the dollar at the end of 1 year of investment, and then add another year's worth of interest to that:

$$VALUE_2 = VALUE_1(1+ i)$$

or, substituting in for $VALUE_1$,

$$VALUE_2 = [VALUE_0(1 + i)] (1+ i)$$

which implies

$$VALUE_2 = VALUE_0(1 + i)^2$$

---

[2] You may have noticed that banks sometimes report the rate they pay on accounts (or charge on loans) in two forms. One is usually called the interest rate or the continuously compounded interest rate or the instantaneous interest rate. The other is called the annual percentage yield (APY), the annual percentage rate (APR), or the effective annual rate and will be a slightly higher number. In these formulas, the "interest rate" (i) that we use is in fact the APR. We avoid using the "continuously compounded interest rate" in this textbook, because the mathematics for applying it are less intuitive. (The value after t years would be calculated as $VALUE_t = VALUE_0 e^{rt}$, where e is a mathematical constant and r is the continuously compounded rate.)

Now the second term is squared, because the initial amount gains interest for 2 years. Similarly, to calculate the value 3 years from now, we could take the term to the third power. We would similarly take this term to various powers when discounting. For example, we would calculate $VALUE_2/(1 + i)^2 = VALUE_0$ to find out how much an amount 2 years from now is worth now. Though tedious on a hand calculator, these calculations are easy to do on computer spreadsheets and are built into most spreadsheet software programs.

Returning to the example of the service bay given in the text, we will assume (for simplicity) that the first $5000 is received 1 year after the installation, the second after 2 years, etc. Hence the value of the capital income stream can be calculated according to Table 14.1 (rounding to two decimal places). The third year is left for you to calculate as an exercise, checking your calculations against the total.

Table 14.1 | Calculating Present Value

Year	Present Discounted Value of $5000
1	$= \$5000/(1 + 0.05) = \$4761.90$
2	$= \$5000/(1 + 0.05)^2 = \$4535.15$
3	$= \$5000/(1 + 0.05)^3 = ?$
4	$= \$5000/(1 + 0.05)^4 = \$4113.51$
5	$= \$5000/(1 + 0.05)^5 = \$3917.63$
Total present discounted value of returns to capital over 5 years =	**$21,647.38**

Note that because the expected return is in the numerator of all calculations, increases in expected returns will *increase* the present discounted value of the stream of returns. Because the interest rate appears in the denominator, increases in the interest rate will *decrease* the PDV.

You should make the investment if the present discounted value of the stream of returns to capital is greater than the cost of making the investment. Hence, you are more likely to make the investment

- ⊃ the greater the expected returns to capital
- ⊃ the lower the interest rate
- ⊃ the lower the price of capital

If the price of installation of the service bay is less than $21,647, then you will get more back, in present value terms, than you pay out, and you should therefore make the investment.

1.2 | Varying Returns, Varying Costs, and Risk

The above example is, admittedly, oversimplified compared to real-world decisions. Some possible complications, however, are easily handled within the framework already set out: varying returns, costs spread out over time, and what economists call "risk."

Varying Returns. The use of a capital asset may return more in some years than in others. This is easily accommodated in calculations such as those in Table 14.1 by replacing the "$5000" with a stream of varying numbers, as long as the numbers are known in advance. A more realistic stream of returns, for example, might show the service bay being highly productive when it is new and then yielding lower returns, as a consequence of wear and tear and technological obsolescence, as it gets older.

Costs Spread Out over Time. Suppose that you pay for the service bay in installments over 3 years and that at the end of 5 years you have to pay someone to demolish the service bay and haul it away. More complicated cost structures like this can be accommodated by straightforward extensions of the present discounted value formula.

Risk. If the outcomes of your investment are uncertain but you know exactly how likely it is that different outcomes will occur, your investment is characterized by what economists call **risk**. For example, suppose you know there is a 50% chance that your capital income will be $4500 per year and a 50% chance that it will be $5,500 per year. Using techniques derived from probability and statistics, an economist can incorporate "risk" into models of capital valuation fairly easily.

risk: as used by economists, a situation in which the exact outcome is unknown, but the chance of each possible outcome occurring is known

1.3 | A Tougher Complication: Uncertainty

Whereas "risk" can be easily incorporated into a present discounted value notion of the value of an asset, the far more common situation of real **uncertainty** cannot. Usually, we don't really know what probabilities to attach to various possible outcomes—or even what the possible outcomes are.

uncertainty: as used by economists, a situation where not only is the exact outcome unknown, but the range of outcomes and/or their probabilities of occurring are also unknown

In the real world, an auto repair shop owner's calculation of the returns he or she might expect would be far from an exact science. Will the demand for auto repairs boom or shrink over the next 5 years? What if auto mechanics form a union and demand higher wages? What will happen to interest rates over the next 5 years? What is the chance that the shop property will be bought out for suburban development or condemned because of soil contamination? What is the chance a new freeway will be built nearby, with an off ramp leading right to the shop? What will happen to the demand for services if another repair shop opens up down the block? What if new auto technologies make the tools purchased for the service bay obsolete before the end of the 5 years? In the case of Cisco's purchase of Cerent (mentioned earlier), Cisco made assumptions about what the future would be like in the highly unpredictable world of networking.

Clearly, with no way of knowing the future, present discounted value calculations can be no more than a useful tool. Many decision makers will run a **sensitivity analysis**, plugging a variety of different numbers into a calculation, in order to see under what *range* of assumptions (about revenues, the life of the investment, and interest rates) an investment might be a good idea. A project that still looks good under the most pessimistic assumptions is a surer bet than one that looks good only when the projections are very optimistic.

sensitivity analysis: the rerunning of a calculation with a variety of different numbers, in order to analyze the outcome of a decision under varying assumptions

In fact, however, you can never really know whether an investment *will be* profitable. All you can know, looking backward after time passes and the returns have been received (or not), is whether it *was* profitable.

1.4 | Market Value

The value you put on a particular asset will help determine the conditions of the market on which it trades. You have decided (in the simple case) that at a price of $21,647 or below, you will demand a new service bay in the current period. Presumably other auto repair shops engage in similar calculations on the basis of their own technologies, workplace organization, and expected revenues. You may also think about how low the price would need to be for you to consider adding *two* bays, or even more. All this information together can be thought of as creating the market demand for service bays. In this simple case, people's demand for newly manufactured capital assets depends fundamentally on the stream of returns to capital that they expect, the interest rate, and the price of capital goods.

In many cases, resale markets are at least as important as markets for new production. What if you invest in the service bay and then, partway through the 5-year period, decide to sell your business? Now your capital investment will be valued on a resale market. What should the service bay be worth to the new owner?

Under the assumptions of the simple case, with certainty, the value could be easily calculated. The more useful life the investment has left, the more valuable it will be. Economists have a special vocabulary to describe changes in the value of assets over time. If the value of an asset falls over time, we say it depreciates. As we discussed in Chapter 6, this is typically the case for manufactured capital because of wear and tear. Because your service bay has less useful life left after a few years of use, it will have depreciated by the time you decide to sell it—you will get less for the asset than what you paid for it. If the value of an asset rises over time, on the other hand, we say it **appreciates**. Bottles of fine wine, for example, often gain in market value as they age and the flavor of the wine matures.

appreciation: an increase in the value of an asset over time

However, changes related to the physical nature of an asset are not the only things that change its value. Many unexpected events might also happen between the initial purchase and the resale, changing the value of the investment. One such event could be a change in the returns to alternative investments. Potential buyers of your auto repair business will weigh the returns they will get from your business against the returns they would get from buying other assets instead—land, artwork, another business—or putting their money in the bank. An increase in returns to alternative investments will decrease the price that buyers are willing to pay for your asset. (You can see this in the formula for present discounted value: If the return on the next best investment rises to, say, 10%, then the present value of your asset will fall.)

Because *expectations* of returns are so important in determining asset values, **investor confidence**, or optimism or pessimism, is also very important in determining the price at which a capital asset sells. You may believe, for example, that your service bay will return $5000 in net revenues for 2 more years, but potential purchasers may be less optimistic. Perhaps their belief is that the demand for auto repair services is on a downward trend. Their degree of optimism or pessimism will determine whether the price you are offered is high or low.

investor confidence: investors' optimism or pessimism concerning future returns

Because attitudes of optimism and pessimism regarding economic events tend to be contagious, markets for both new and existing capital assets are often characterized by wide swings over time. Everybody in your community might be feeling discouraged about prospective sales during a period of economic slowdown, and you might find it hard to sell your business, even at a low price. Then, as economic activity picks up, people may get more optimistic—and even overly optimistic—as the social attitude turns positive. If people then overinvest, they may be disappointed by a lack of expected demand for their products, leading to another period of slowdown and pessimism.

General swings in economic activity are more the subject of macroeconomics than of microeconomics. However, the fact that economic activity takes place within complex social organizations, evolving unpredictably through time, is especially obvious in asset markets. In markets for capital assets, social behavior and beliefs, as well as uncertainty, play enormous roles in price determination.

Market value and value in terms of well-being, of course, are often not the same thing, as we have discussed frequently in this book. Only those purchasers with ability to pay affect the market demand—not people who are poor or future generations. Markets do not usually take into account environmental and other externalities. With externalities from petroleum depletion and carbon dioxide emissions fully taken into account, for example, the well-being value of your auto service bay would probably be *less* than its market value, whereas service centers for hybrid cars (or bicycles) could have *greater* social value than what we see reflected in current market transactions.

2 | Markets for Manufactured, Natural, and Social Capital

We have used an example of manufactured capital (an auto service bay) to introduce some basic concepts related to asset markets. Examining markets for particular kinds of resources, we can see that in some cases these concepts need elaboration and that in other cases their appropriateness can be questioned.

2.1 | Manufactured Capital in the Traditional Neoclassical Model

In the simple mechanical model, firms engage in production using two inputs: capital (generally assumed to be manufactured capital) and labor. In Chapter 13, we saw that under the assumptions of this model, and with the level of capital fixed, firms should hire labor until the marginal revenue product of labor equals the marginal factor cost of labor. In competitive markets, the marginal factor cost of labor is simply the wage rate. How, then, should the firm decide how much *capital* to use?

To keep consideration of a firm's use of manufactured capital simple, the model abstracts from the question of ownership. It assumes that units of the capital good can be rented for a fee. An auto service business, for example, might rent service bay space from a company that supplies such space, leasing it by the week or month. Using reasoning exactly analogous to the case for labor, the model concludes that the firm should hire capital services until

$$MRP_{MK} = MFC_{MK}$$

marginal revenue product of (manufactured) capital (MRP_{MK}): the amount that a unit of additional capital services contributes to the revenues of the firm

marginal factor cost of (manufactured) capital (MFC_{MK}): the amount that a unit of additional capital services adds to the firm's costs

where MRP_{MK} is the **marginal revenue product of (manufactured) capital**, or the amount that an additional unit of such capital services contributes to revenues, and MFC_{MK} is the **marginal factor cost of (manufactured) capital**, or the amount that the additional unit of such capital services adds to the firm's costs. In competitive resource markets, MFC_{MK} will just be equal to a competitively determined rental price of capital.

The traditional neoclassical model can be extended to more inputs as well. In each case, in perfectly competitive markets each factor is predicted to receive in compensation exactly the marginal value of what it adds to production.

2.2 | Should Natural Capital Be Treated Differently?

Natural capital stocks, as discussed in Chapter 6, include both renewable resources (such as forests) and nonrenewable resources (such as petroleum). To the extent that a resource is completely fixed in supply, as is land or the total amount of petroleum on Earth, its provision is not a matter of "production." The ownership of such an asset enables a person (or company or government) to collect economic rents. Two basic views regarding the valuation of natural resources can be identified.

The Economistic View. The economistic view treats natural resources in exactly the same way as the auto service bay discussed above. Natural resources—both renewable and nonrenewable—are seen as valuable only to the extent that they contribute to profit-

The National Park Service was created in 1916 to administer parks such as Yosemite (shown in this photo) "in such manner and by such means as to leave them unimpaired for the enjoyment of future generations." Recent federal administrations, however, have taken steps to privatize park jobs, turning them over to private, usually for-profit companies. Privatization, it is hoped, will lead to increased economic efficiency, as business-oriented park managers will emphasize "the bottom line." Some fear, though, that emphasizing short-term financial profit over long-term conservation will lead to the "disneyfication" of the parks and irreversible damage to ecosystems.

ability. Whatever expectations people have concerning future benefits and costs (even if they are ill-informed, from a scientific point of view) are taken as determining the appropriate return-to-capital stream. Future benefits and costs are discounted, using as a discount rate the yield on alternative investments. Market-determined prices are taken to represent "the" value of the resource, even if they don't reflect externalities and distributional inequities. As long as markets for resources are competitive, the economistic view claims, you can be assured that resources will be used at maximum efficiency.

The Ecological View. In the ecological view, the economy is seen as a system that operates *within* a complex variety of natural systems. Socioeconomic systems are seen as sustainable only if they operate within environmental constraints related to resource limits and the ability of the environment to absorb wastes. The precautionary principle (discussed in Chapter 6) suggests that when uncertainty is present, decisions that affect natural systems should err on the side of caution. Natural resources, in this view, are valued for the long-term survival of life on this planet. Sustainable production and consumption are achievable only with careful management of the resource base.

These two views are often at odds. For example, an animal species for which there is no use profitable to humans can be destroyed at zero cost, according to the economistic model. In the ecological view, on the other hand, extinction of species is a problem.

As another example, suppose an investment in nuclear power will create dangerous waste materials that will impose cleanup costs of $1 billion, but these costs won't arise for 500 years. At a 5% interest rate, the present discounted value of $1 billion 500 years from now is tiny—about 2.5¢! Making decisions about very long-term, environmentally sensitive projects using the same reasoning as applied to much shorter-term private investments means that costs and benefits to future generations have almost no weight in decision making.

Because the economistic point of view is based on market conditions that reflect how ability to pay is distributed throughout the world, it has also come under fire from people concerned with equity. Economist Larry Summers, then chief economist of the World Bank, for example, was widely taken to task for a 1991 memo that went out over his name. In the memo it was reasoned that toxic wastes should be dumped in low-wage countries, because the environmental costs, measurable in terms of wages lost due to poor health and death, would be lowest there.

Few thoughtful people hold to a strictly economistic view of natural resource markets anymore. Instead, discussion has turned to how good economic reasoning and such institutions as governments and markets can operate to preserve both current and future well-being, within a context of the natural systems that sustain life. Some economists, for example, have suggested that market institutions could be used to solve some of the problems of environmental externalities. The **Coase Theorem**, named after Ronald Coase, a Nobel laureate economist, states that if property rights are well defined, and there are no significant transactions costs, markets can efficiently allocate resources even in the presence of externalities. Externalities—costs and benefits that are "external" to the parties trading in a market—could be "internalized" by the clever assigning of property rights and could become themselves the subject of market behavior.

Consider, for example, what would happen if someone were given ownership rights to clean air. If you wanted to dirty the air, you would have to pay that party. In fact, the U.S. Clean Air Act amendments of 1990 did something like this by setting up a system of permits that allow factories to emit pollutants such as sulfur oxides and nitrogen oxides. The government controls the total amount of permits issued, but firms can then trade the permits among themselves.

Advocates of this program point out that this marketing of "rights to pollute" gives polluting firms incentives to cut emissions in the most cost-effective ways. Firms that cut their emissions drastically are rewarded, because they can then sell their permits to other firms whose technologies are harder to clean up.

On the other hand, the fact that larger problems (such as the appropriate level of overall pollution, effects on future generations and other species, and perhaps presently unknown complexities of the ecosystem) remain unaddressed means that "markets for pollution" cannot on their own solve the problem of economic and ecological sustainability. In addition, the transaction costs entailed in assigning property rights and setting up markets can be substantial, and the question of who is to receive the revenues from sale of permits (or whether they should be given away) remains unanswered. Government direct regulation (see Chapter 17) and activism by community and nonprofit groups and business leaders, are likely to remain important in the movement toward sustainability.

Coase Theorem: If property rights are well defined, and there are no significant transactions costs, then markets can efficiently allocate resources even in the presence of externalities.

2.3 | Social Capital and Markets

Social capital consists of socially held knowledge, ideas, and values, along with the social organization that shapes economic activities. At a society-wide level, and in many cultural contexts, social capital is not marketable. Nations do not, for example, sell rights to their languages or dominant cultural values. On a smaller scale, however, at the level of individual business organizations, markets for social capital are busy indeed.

How much is a particular business worth? Part of its value is what is often called its **liquidation value**—the market value of the tangible assets such as land, buildings, computers, machinery, pencils, and furniture (or auto service bays) that it owns. If it were dissolved as a business, these could all be sold off, so the value of the company to a buyer has to be at least equal to the liquidation value.

When a going concern is bought by another company, however, the price paid often far exceeds the liquidation value. A company may have valuable copyrights, trademarks, or special knowledge (such as the fiber-optic technology owned by Cerent), giving it

liquidation value: the value of the physical assets of a firm, should it be dissolved and its assets sold separately

intangible, privately owned intellectual property. It may have a well-known brand name or especially good relations with suppliers or customers, which also give it important advantages in the market. It may be known as a company that runs smoothly, attracts the best workers, follows honest accounting methods, and fosters innovation and high employee morale, all of which may lead to successful performance. (Conversely, it might be known as a managerial disaster—set on using obsolete knowledge, and full of internal strife, unethical behavior, dysfunctional lines of communication, and demoralized employees. In such a case, it will be worth only its liquidation value.)

goodwill: the accounting term for the premium that one company pays for another over and above the value of its physical assets. The premium for goodwill may represent advantages from specialized knowledge, effective organization, or other intangible assets.

Accountants call the premium that one company pays for another, over and above the value of its physical assets, the premium for **goodwill**. Clearly, the accountants' notion overlaps with the economists' notion of social capital—the knowledge and social organization that, above and beyond physical assets, makes economic activity go. Business analysts may refer to some of the same phenomena using words such as *synergy*.

Markets are thus capable of giving a positive value to social capital. On the other hand, some commentators have worried about whether *too much* emphasis on markets might actually *destroy* social capital. Generally, the target of this critique is not actual markets but rather the economistic way of thinking about the world. If you believe, for example, that everyone is out to act in her or his own individual self-interest and that markets have little to do with ethics, you are thinking economistically. Thinking economistically, you may be less likely to behave in a cooperative, trustworthy manner. Without cooperation and trust, social organization may break down.

It is also the case that social capital owned by individual businesses may be withheld from society at large, leading to considerable social loss. The example of patents on AIDS drugs held by pharmaceutical companies has already been mentioned. Social capital in the form of intellectual property is, in fact, currently very much in the market, but debates continue about whether this is a good thing.

Discussion Questions

1. Do you lean more toward the economistic or the ecological point of view in thinking about valuing natural resources? Why?

2. In the 1990s, following reports that corporations with strong "corporate identities," "vision," or "values" performed better than their peers, a number of consulting firms sprang up offering to help organizations develop identities, vision, and so forth. How is this an illustration of a market involving social capital?

3 | Markets for Financial Capital

In Chapter 6 we discussed two ways in which economic actors could get hold of monetary funds, which they might desire for purposes of facilitating production or consumption. Using the example of Gail, the farmer, we said she could get funds through *equity finance*—that is, by drawing on the wealth to which she has ownership rights. Or she could "rent" the services of money by taking out a loan and thus using *debt finance*.

In the real world, financial markets involve all sorts of actors, including nonfinancial businesses (which produce something other than financial services), financial businesses (such as banks and insurance companies, which specialize in financial services), households, nonprofits, and governments. The actors use financial markets to get funds for production and consumption, but they may also enter the market for entirely speculative purposes.

3.1 | When Businesses Need Financial Capital

Firms borrow money or sell stocks in order to finance business start-ups or expansions. For example, an entrepreneur may believe that she faces a growing demand for travel services; if she could rent a good office and hire some assistants, she could sell enough services to cover her operating costs and also to pay the interest and principal on the loan that she needed in order to get started. Financial markets that facilitate such investments are important to the efficiency of a market economy—particularly to its ability to respond rapidly to production or sales opportunities.

retained earnings: profits that a company keeps for its own uses

What happens when such formal financial markets are absent? One possibility is for firms to pay for capital goods out of their own accumulated profits, or **retained earnings**. An economy that finances growth only in this way cannot easily finance new firms and may be much slower to respond to new technological possibilities or changes in consumer demand.

Another alternative to formal financial markets is informal ones. In the latter, personal connections are the essential lubricant for the economy. Those who have more money than they need will seek opportunities to invest it in enterprises run by people they know. Entrepreneurs who don't know anyone with extra money are out of luck—they have no chance to borrow. This sort of situation is more like barter than like a market, because transactions can occur only when the individual with something to sell (or, in this case, with money to lend) happens to know an individual who wants to buy (or borrow) that very same thing. And, of course, the possibility of a deal depends not only on two such people knowing one another; there must also be some basis for trust, so that the lender feels secure about getting his or her money back. The insecurity of such informal arrangements generally results in lenders requiring a high return—or perhaps a large ownership position in the enterprise—to compensate them for the risk they are taking.

Informal connections flourish when formal financial markets are weak or limited. In some cases, members of an ethnic minority will lend only to each other, not to outsiders, relying on connections within their community to ensure repayment. In other cases, loans are made within criminal networks, where illegal but often effective means can be used to force repayment. In more favorable circumstances there are viable, formal financial markets through which businesses can obtain money in several different ways. The simplest of these to describe is firms borrowing from banks, promising to repay the money, plus interest, on a fixed schedule. Many corporations, however, use markets for bonds and stocks to raise funds.

3.2 | The Bond Market

bond: a financial instrument that, in return for the loan of funds, commits its seller to pay a fixed amount every year (called the **coupon amount**), as well as to repay the amount of principal (called the bond's **face value**) on a particular date in the future (called the **maturity date**)

When a large business sells a **bond**, it makes promises similar to those that a lender makes when taking out a loan. In this case, the bond buyer plays the role of the bank, providing money initially and receiving repayments over time. In return for lending the business a sum of money, the bondholder receives a promise that the company will pay him or her a fixed amount of money each year for a period of time and then, at the end of this time, will repay the principal of the loan. The fixed amount paid per year is called the **coupon amount**. The date that the principal will be repaid is called the **maturity date**. The amount of principal that will be repaid is called the **face value** of the bond.

So far it seems simple enough—a bond may specify, for example, that it will pay you $5 a year for 10 years and then pay you $100 at the end of 10 years. What makes bond markets more complicated, though, is that bonds are often sold and resold, changing hands many times before they mature. During the period to maturity, many factors affecting the value of the bond may change, and so the **bond price**—the price at which bondholders are willing to buy and sell existing bonds—may change.

bond yield to maturity: the amount a bond returns during a year, if held to maturity, expressed in percentage terms. The yield is determined by the coupon amount, the **bond price** (the price at which trades are made), and the time to maturity.

For example, suppose you bought the bond just described at its face value of $100, and you are sure that the bond will pay off as promised. The **bond yield to maturity**, or annual rate of return if you hold the bond until it matures, would obviously be 5% ($5 annually is 5% of the $100 bond price). But suppose that after a couple years you want to sell your bond (perhaps you need the cash), but meanwhile the market yield on similar bonds has risen to 10%. No one will be interested in buying your bond at a price of $100, because they would get only a 5% yield, whereas they can get 10% by investing elsewhere. To sell your bond, you will need to drop the price you demand until your bond looks as attractive as other investments—that is, until the $5 per year represents a 10% yield to maturity.[3]

Conversely, if the return on alternative investments has fallen, say to 2%, the $5 per year on your bond looks pretty good, and you will be able to sell it for *more than* $100.[4] As yields rise in the rest of the bond market, the price of an existing fixed-coupon bond will decrease, and vice versa.

○ As yields *rise* in the rest of the bond market, the price of an existing fixed-coupon bond will *fall*, and vice versa.

Another reason why bond prices may change over time is that the perceived riskiness of the investment may change. If the company you have loaned to cannot meet its loan obligations and goes bankrupt, you may get back only a fraction—or none—of your principal.[5] Hence, if rumors start to circulate that the company is in financial trouble, you may need to sell your bond at a steep discount to compensate the buyer for the newly perceived riskiness of the investment.[6]

3.3 | The Stock Market

stocks: financial instruments that, in return for a payment, give buyers a claim to ownership in the company that issues them

Large companies also raise money by selling **stocks**, which give the buyers ownership rights in the firm. This process is greatly facilitated if trades can take place through a stock market, rather than depending on face-to-face transactions between buyers and sellers. Virtually all of the largest companies do, in fact, sell their stocks in stock markets. Once the company sells them, they may then be traded and retraded many times on the market, at prices that may vary as people's expectations about the future profitability of the firm change over time. However, there are many companies that cannot qualify to "go public"; they cannot generate the necessary level of confidence, or are simply not large enough, to have their shares traded through any public stock market.

Although the buyer of a company's stock receives a share of ownership in the firm, he or she does not receive a guaranteed level of repayment. If a company does badly, its stockholders will receive no income; if the company goes bankrupt, its stockholders may lose the entire value of their investments. Not every business start-up or expansion is a success. An entrepreneur may misjudge the market, expanding in the wrong product lines or locations. Another company may find a way to produce the same outputs in a better, cheaper, or more desirable manner. A common business mistake is overexpansion in a growing market as a consequence of overestimating the rate of growth, ignoring the simultaneous growth of other, competing firms, or interpreting a temporary surge in demand as permanent. Moreover, a firm, particularly a new or small one, may simply lack the administrative and planning capacity to use its funds successfully. If the business fails entirely, banks, bondholders, and suppliers have first claim on the value of liquidated assets, according to U.S. law. Shareholders get money back only if there is something left after all these other parties have been paid.

---

[3] If the bond has 1 year left to maturity, for example, you can use the present discounted value formula introduced earlier to figure out what the new price should be, as follows. Its value 1 year from now is $105 (coupon + principal), and we can use the formula $\text{VALUE}_1/(1 + i) = \text{VALUE}_0$ to find the value now. If the interest rate on alternative investments is 10%, then $\$105/(1.10) \approx \$95.45$.

[4] Continuing from the previous footnote, if the interest rate is 2%, then $\$105/(1.02) \approx \$102.94$.

[5] In the United States, a Chapter 7 bankruptcy (so named for its location in U.S. legal codes) means that a firm that cannot pay its debts will be liquidated—the firm will be disbanded, and its assets will be sold off to pay creditors. (Individuals can also file under Chapter 7 for certain debts and can usually keep some assets, such as a house.) In a Chapter 11 bankruptcy, the firm stays in business but the debt is restructured into more manageable payments. A Chapter 13 bankruptcy is like a Chapter 11 bankruptcy, but for consumers: Debt is reorganized in such a way that the person can pay it off over time. Formal bankruptcy procedures protect the filer from the immediate demands of creditors, but they also damage the filer's access to future credit.

[6] Commentators on stock and bond markets do not make the economist's formal distinction between risk (where probabilities are known) and uncertainty (where they are not). *Riskiness*, as used in this section, also includes genuine uncertainty about the future.

dividends: payments in cash or extra shares paid out to shareholders

annual return on a share of stock: the sum of its dividends and any capital gains (or losses)

speculation: buying and selling assets with the expectation of profiting from appreciation or depreciation in asset values

growth stocks: stocks that are expected to return substantial capital gains

speculative bubble: the situation that occurs when mutually reinforcing investor optimism raises the value of a stock far above what could be justified by the actual assets and profitability of the firm

Why, then, does anyone buy stock? The hope is that the company will prosper and that the stockholder will benefit from this prosperity. This benefit can take two forms. One is that a portion of the company's profits will be distributed to stockholders in the form of **dividends**—payments in cash or extra shares to shareholders. The other is that the total value of the company, as perceived by other potential investors, will rise. When stock prices rise, the value of stockholdings increases, and the holders can sell their stocks and realize capital gains. The **annual return on a share of stock** can be found by summing the dividends it has paid plus any capital gains (or capital losses). For example, suppose you bought a share of stock for $100, and over the course of the year it paid a dividend of $1 per share (or 1%) and also rose in price to $106 (a 6% rise). The annual return, in percentage terms, would be 7%.

In any asset market, buying and selling with the expectation of making a profit by cashing in on appreciation or depreciation of the asset is called **speculation**. Commentators have noted the difference between "value investors," who buy shares of a company because they believe it will be able to produce and sell enough output, at a high enough price, to generate profits that can be distributed as dividends, and "speculators," who are primarily interested in watching the stock price go up. Speculators generally seek higher returns than value investors by investing in **growth stocks** and are therefore willing to take greater risks.

The most dramatic increases in the value of stocks are often based on large-scale speculation about future profitability. For example, stocks connected to the computer industry or the Internet enjoyed fabulous price increases in the late 1990s, with no obvious basis in the hard facts of the companies' performance. Measured by profits, sales, or employment, Microsoft was far from the largest company in the U.S. or world economy (in fact, it was number 400 on the list of the world's largest companies, ranked by sales, in 1997); but the value of its stock soared to the top of the charts, exceeding the value of the stock of traditional corporations with more than ten times Microsoft's sales and profits. Stock in Amazon.com, the leading online seller of books, rose by the late 1990s to the point where it was worth more than many established, well-known conventional retailers—even though it had consistently lost money and had never made a profit!

As long as *other people* believe a company is *going to be* profitable, shareholders can find a buyer for their shares in that company at a good—and even rising—price. The result can be what is called a **speculative bubble**, in which people's mutually reinforcing optimism causes stock values to rise far above any value that could be rationalized in terms of actual assets and profitability of the firm. When these expectations start to crumble—as they did, especially for e-commerce and technology stocks in the United States beginning in 2000—the bubble bursts, and stock prices fall. So-called "growth stocks" do not necessarily grow.

3.4 | Households and Governments as Borrowers

Households also borrow money. Unless they are planning to start a business, households most often borrow to finance consumption. Most household debt consists of borrowing to finance durable, long-lasting purchases such as homes and cars. A house or apartment will usually outlast its owner; a car is not quite so permanent, but with luck it will last for many years after it is purchased. In the absence of financial markets, households would have to save the substantial costs of these purchases in advance; a middle-income family might have to save for most of a lifetime before buying a house. In Japan, where it is usually possible to get a mortgage for only half the value of a home (rather than up to 97%, as in the United States), and where land values are very high, it is not uncommon for a family to save for two generations before the grandchildren of the original savers can purchase their own home.

Households borrow for other reasons as well. Borrowing to finance education can be seen as an investment in human capital, which will yield higher earnings over the rest of the student's lifetime. Borrowing for emergencies needs little explanation. Most

Reading Financial Market Reports

Newspapers and many websites report on the activity taking place in bond markets, stock markets (such as the New York Stock Exchange, the American Stock Exchange, and NASDAQ in the United States and Nikkei in Tokyo) and other markets where financial instruments are traded.

A typical entry for a corporate bond may look something like this:

	Yield	Close	Chg.
ATT 7½06	7.75	96.75	+.13

This is an entry for a bond issued by AT&T, the communications giant. It carries a coupon of $7\frac{1}{2}\%$ and matures in 2006. At the close of the yesterday's trading, the bond price was $96.75, a $.13 gain over the closing price from the day before. The yield to maturity is 7.75%. Financial media report similar entries for bonds issued by governments. (U.S. federal government bonds are also called Treasury notes or T-bills, depending on their maturities.)

A typical stock entry may look something like this:

	Tckr	Div	PE	Vol	Last	Chg.
McDnlds	MCD	.23	20	9781	23.30	−.87

This stock, in McDonald's Corporation (provider of fast food), can be identified by the ticker symbol MCD. Its current annual dividend rate (that is, the annual dollar amount of dividends per share) is $.23. This report says that yesterday a volume of 9781 shares changed hands. The last price at which a trade was made was $23.30 per share, a price that represents a loss of $.87 compared to the last price from the day before. The price/earnings ratio, which is calculated as the stock price divided by reported per-share earnings (that is, accounting profits) over the last year, is 20.

The media also commonly report activity in markets for other financial instruments, such as foreign currencies, mortgage funds, certificates of deposit, and mutual funds. They also report average results for large groups of funds, such as the Dow Jones Industrial Average ("Dow") and the Standard and Poor's 500 ("S&P") index, both of which track groups of stocks. ◖

dangerous is the ever-present temptation of borrowing to finance an unsustainably high level of consumption. This leads to future problems of indebtedness—those who borrow must sooner or later repay the loan, with interest. In extreme cases, borrowing can lead to personal bankruptcy.

Governments borrow money for reasons parallel to those of firms and households. Publicly owned enterprises have exactly the same uses for capital as private firms. Governments typically spend a lot of money on long-lived infrastructure, such as dams, bridges, roads, parks, and school buildings; financing such expenditures with bonds makes it possible to spread the payment over the lifetime of the goods in question. The alternative of requiring full payment in advance would impose huge tax burdens and would probably make even badly needed infrastructure investments quite unpopular. When the government in question is considered stable—as the U.S. federal government is—its bonds are considered to carry a very low risk of default, and hence they usually pay lower interest rates than more risky, corporate bonds.

If the infrastructure increases the wealth of the whole economy, the government can expect to raise more money in taxes; this kind of borrowing for infrastructure can therefore be seen as an investment. Other categories of public spending (on a national opera house or an elaborate embassy building for instance) do not enhance national

Consumer borrowing began in the United States in the mid–19th century with the use of install-ment plans to buy items such as sewing machines and furniture. In the early 20th century Ford Motor Company did not provide financing, and Model T cars, such as the one shown in this 1919 photo, cost the average wage earner nearly half a year's income. Auto financing by third-party companies soon developed, and by 1924 three-quarters of all automobiles were purchased using loans.

productive infrastructure, except perhaps quite indirectly. These types of spending should be viewed as consumption expenditures and should be judged not according to whether they will be able to "pay for themselves" but according to whether the public enjoyment of them is commensurate with their cost.

Governments also face emergencies that require borrowing; major wars are nearly always financed by high levels of debt, which is then gradually reduced in peacetime. And governments, like households, also face the temptation of living beyond their means, enjoying high levels of public spending on "consumption" as opposed to "investment," along with low levels of taxation. The eventual result is mounting public debt and a heavy burden of interest payments, which will necessitate unpopular taxes and/or spending cutbacks in the future.

Such irresponsibility in public finance is often associated with developing coun-tries, but it is not unknown in the industrial world. In the United States in the 1980s, some advisors claimed (following what was known as supply-side economics) that tax rates could be drastically reduced without any corresponding reduction in public spending or increase in debt. The consequences of a few years of following this mis-guided advice constrained the U.S. government throughout most of the 1990s; it cre-ated what was, for peacetime, a record-breaking level of public debt, which resulted in a later need for drastic cutbacks in public spending in order to reduce the deficit.

3.5 | The Supply of Financial Capital

With so many borrowers seeking money, who is there to supply it to them? The answer is, again, business firms and households, with special roles played by banks, pension funds, and other financial institutions. Governments can also be suppliers of capital in the financial markets, although in most cases their involvement is confined to rather limited special programs.

Businesses that borrow are generally new, struggling, or rapidly expanding companies. But many firms are already profitable, earning substantial amounts of profits each year; even after dividend payments to stockholders, major corporations typically have sizable retained earnings. These earnings are used above all to finance the firms' own investments in capital goods. If a corporation still has profits remaining after making its own investments, it may buy the stocks or bonds of other corporations—in effect, supplying capital to other companies. (If one company buys enough of a second company's stock, it may acquire control of the second company.) Businesses also keep large amounts of money in banks, which enables the banks to make loans to borrowers. Less frequently, a corporation may lend money directly to households. For example, automobile manufacturers sometimes set up subsidiaries to lend money to people who want to buy their cars.

While some households are borrowing money, others may be saving and thereby supplying funds that can be borrowed by others. A household may save money by depositing it in a bank, which then lends it to others. Or, increasingly commonly, middle-income and higher-income households may invest in stocks and bonds through mutual funds managed by financial companies. Households with some wealth may also buy stocks and bonds directly. Rates of household saving vary widely among industrial countries: Japan has a very high savings rate and the United States a very low one; most European countries are between these two extremes.

In addition to the visible, direct forms of savings, there are indirect ways in which many households save money. Payments into private pension funds and insurance policies are effectively savings: setting aside a portion of current income for use at retirement or in case of accident. (The money eventually received from pensions or insurance need not equal the amount paid in for any one household, but for the population as a whole, both pensions and insurance can be thought of as gigantic savings accounts.) Payments made into a pension fund by an employer may not appear to be part of a worker's wages, but from the employer's point of view these payments are part of the cost of labor, amounting to an indirect form of worker compensation.

institutional investors: economic organizations such as pension funds and insurance companies that invest funds that have been placed in their care

Households that have little or no money in savings accounts may still be paying insurance premiums and accumulating money in pension funds. As a result, **institutional investors** such as pension funds and insurance companies have become increasingly important sources of funds in financial markets. They own substantial fractions of the stocks and bonds in the United States and other countries. Because this trend seems to be gathering momentum rapidly, it is intriguing to ask whether institutional investors have different interests and objectives than individual investors. And if so, will this affect the management of companies whose stock is largely owned by institutional investors?

A public enterprise or government agency that has a surplus of funds can also supply capital in financial markets. In practice, however, it is much more common for governments to have deficits than surpluses. Public pension funds, such as the U.S. social security program, are the one major government institution that routinely supplies funds to capital markets. Frequently, public pension funds buy the bonds issued by other government agencies, thereby helping to finance government deficits.

3.6 | A Last Note on Financial Capital Markets

As we have noted, it is misleading to refer to financial capital as a factor of production. Financial capital is often used to buy manufactured capital goods, such as the buildings, vehicles, and equipment that are needed in production. In this sense, financial markets can be viewed as markets in the means of acquiring a factor of production.

We can think of financial markets as having supply and demand sides, even though they differ in a number of ways from the product markets that have traditionally been at the core of supply-and-demand analysis. One of the biggest differences, as we have seen, is that resale markets, where financial assets are traded and traded again, are very important. Whereas in product markets commonly one kind of actor sells (for example, a fruit wholesaler) and another kind of actor buys (for example, a retail grocer), active traders in financial markets may be on both sides of the market in the same day. Also, because expectations about the future play a key role in the valuation of capital assets, financial markets can be much more volatile, subject to swings—sometimes hour by hour—in investor pessimism and optimism.

Nonetheless, we can point to important supply-and-demand dynamics. For example, in a well-functioning market for loans, the going interest rate is determined by the willingness of lenders to supply funds and by the demand for loans from borrowers. When many people and institutions want to lend money and relatively few want to borrow, then lenders have to offer low interest rates to attract borrowers. When there are more borrowers and fewer lenders, then the borrowers have to pay high interest rates to obtain funds.

In stock and bond markets, the prices of the stocks and bonds will reflect market forces. For example, suppose that holders of stock in XYZ Corporation hear bad news about its future expected profitability. Many may rush to sell off their holdings as quickly as possible, before things get (they expect) worse. If this were the only shock to the market, we would see an increased volume of sales and a drop in price. If, however, potential buyers have also heard the news, they will be willing to buy XYZ stock only if the price is lowered enough to incorporate the effect of the bad news. The price of the stock will clearly fall, but because of the weakening of demand, the change in the volume of trade can't be determined in advance.[7]

The stock and bond markets are also highly interdependent. When the stock market takes a downturn, for example, it is common for a substantial number of investors to turn to (somewhat safer) bonds instead (as happened in the tumultuous 2002 market—see the accompanying News in Context feature). This causes the prices of stocks to decline even further, while driving up the price of bonds.

Financial markets are widely seen as important, if mysterious, forces in modern life. The ups and downs of the stock market are reported as part of the daily news and are interpreted (sometimes accurately, sometimes not) as signs of coming changes in the level of production and employment. Markets for stocks, bonds, loans, and foreign exchange all involve huge sums of money that are traded on a daily basis.

Like labor, financial capital is important both for its role in production and for its ability to generate income. However, financial capital is distributed unequally. Some economic actors have access to considerable funds of their own and, through their financial power, reputation, and connections, can relatively easily access additional funds through loans, bond sales, and/or sales of stock. Other actors have little wealth and little access to financial markets. The income from financial capital that accrues to persons—including the dividends, interest, and rents received by property owners—is also distributed unequally.

---

[7] Although it is easy to identify supply and demand *forces* in financial markets, it is harder, because of the role of expectations, to identify these in terms of static supply and demand *curves*. For example, a standard supply curve says that sellers will offer more of an item on the market when its price is high than when its price is low, all else equal. However, on a stock market, even though a rise in the price of a stock may cause some investors to cash in, it may make others *less* willing to sell because they believe the rise in price signals the beginning of a long climb, and therefore they want to *hold on to* the stock to reap capital gains.

Investors Dump Stock Funds for Shelter of Bonds

Investors poured a record $18 billion into bond funds in June [2002], yanking nearly $14 billion out of stock funds as they sought shelter from jarring stock-market losses, according to Lipper, Inc., a New York fund research firm. . . . In the latest bout of selling, growth funds were the most shunned category. Investors pulled $9.5 billion out of funds that buy technology and other growth stocks, out of a total $13.8 billion in stock fund exits. . . . The Dow Jones industrial average has plunged 12% this month and 19% since June 1, as investor angst over corporate accounting abuses and ethical lapses by CEOs came to a head. . . . ◑

Beth Healy, *Boston Globe*, July 23, 2002.

Discussion Questions

1. One aspect of financial markets that many people find confusing is how, when a bond price goes *down,* its yield goes *up.* Discuss this in a group, using examples and consulting your instructor if necessary, until you are sure you understand why this occurs.

2. One of the ethical lapses that so decreased the public's confidence in stock markets during the 2001–2002 period was "insider trading," which occurs when information that only a few privileged people inside a company have about its future profitability is used by some of them to make trades on the stock market that enhance their own personal wealth. Why is "inside information" so valuable, and its use so tempting? Why are stockholders who *don't* have inside information usually very angry when they discover that the managers of the company have engaged in such trades?

Review Questions

1. What are the four major categories of capital, besides human capital?

2. What factors go into determining the present discounted value of a future flow of returns to capital?

3. Which complications can be easily incorporated into a present discounted value method of valuing a capital asset?

4. Why is uncertainty a problem in valuing a capital asset?

5. What are three reasons why the market value of an asset might change over time?

6. What are two reasons why the market value of an asset might not be the same as its well-being value?

7. What is the rule for efficient use of capital services in the traditional neoclassical model?

8. Describe two differing views on the valuation of natural capital.

9. Can the marketing of "rights to pollute" help correct externalities? How? What are the limitations of this approach?

10. Can "social capital" be given a market valuation?

11. Which two formal markets do companies use to raise financial capital?

12. Describe what a bond is and how its annual yield is determined.

13. Describe what a stock is and how its annual return is determined.

14. How does a speculative bubble come about?

15. Why do households and governments borrow?

16. Who supplies financial capital?

Exercises

1. (If the Math Review feature "The Present Value of Future Funds" is assigned.) Perform a sensitivity analysis by calculating the present discounted value of the auto service bay, with the following changes in assumptions. (You may want to make a separate table like Table 14.1 for each case.)

   a. The stream of returns to capital is $5000 per year for 5 years, but the interest rate on the best alternative investment is 10%.

   b. The interest rate on the best alternative investment is 5%, but the stream of returns is $5000 per year only for the first 3 years. For the last 2 years, the return is $4000 per year.

   c. Suppose the price of the service bay (that is, the cost of installing it) is $19,000. Should the auto repair owner make the investment, under the original assumptions (in the text)? Under the assumptions in part (a)? Under the assumptions in (b)?

2. A bond with a face value of $100 pays a coupon amount of $6 per year and is risk-free.

   a. What will the bond price be if alternative risk-free investments pay a 6% interest rate?

   b. Will the bond price rise or fall if the yield on alternative risk-free investments rises to 8%? Explain.

3. A share of stock bought for $50 and held for a year earns a dividend of $1. In addition, over the course of the year the stock price rises to $54 per share. What is the annual return on the share of stock, in percentage terms?

4. Match each concept in Column A with an example in Column B.

   Column A

   1. something that can increase expected returns from an asset
   2. sensitivity analysis
   3. capital loss
   4. something that decreases the price of a bond
   5. business "goodwill"
   6. "rights to pollute"
   7. a factor in determining the return on a stock
   8. speculation
   9. a fixed amount paid every year

   Column B

   i. a rise in the interest rate on alternative investments
   ii. permits issued under the Clean Air Act of 1990
   iii. the value of good relations with suppliers
   iv. coupon amount
   v. rising investor optimism
   vi. checking the present discounted value at 3%, 5%, and 10% interest rates
   vii. the price of a stock drops by $2 a share
   viii. buying an asset with the intention of selling it after it appreciates
   ix. a dividend

Part Five

A Closer Look at Economic Organizations

The Core Sphere: Households and Communities

In a recent survey, when they were asked what is important "for you to consider your life as a success," 87% percent of the respondents answered that "having good friends" was "absolutely necessary." "Having a good relationship with your children" and "helping other people who are in need" were considered absolutely necessary by 94% and 87% of the respondents, respectively. In comparison, "having an interesting job" was considered absolutely necessary by a somewhat smaller percentage—only 79%. "Earning a lot of money" was considered absolutely necessary for a successful life by only 27% of the respondents.

1 | Households and Communities as Organizations

When it comes to determining actual well-being and happiness, the economic activities of the "core sphere" clearly loom large. As we discussed in Chapter 1, the core sphere of the economy consists of households, families, and community groups that organize economic activities at a small scale, usually in non-monetized ways. In this chapter we look more closely at this sphere of economic activity—its functions, its history, the challenges presented by the evolving interface between the core and other spheres, and what economists have to say about its organization.

1.1 | The Functions of the Core Sphere

The core economy is the central location of many important economic activities that sustain human life.

Child Bearing and Child Raising. Parents—even when assisted by family planning services, child care centers, public schools, extended family, and the like—still carry the primary responsibility for fertility decisions and for caring for and nurturing children. Bearing and rearing a child is the ultimate "human capital" activity—populating the society for the future. Younger children need feeding, dressing, bathing, holding, and responsive interaction with caring adults. Older children require less hands-on care but still need supervision and help in learning many physical, mental, and emotional skills.

Many economic activities vital to sustaining life and enhancing its quality are provided in the core sphere. For example, many elderly people, such as this woman being helped to a standing position by her daughter, could not live outside of institutions without the unpaid care of family and neighbors. About twice as many dependent elderly people live outside of nursing homes as in them.

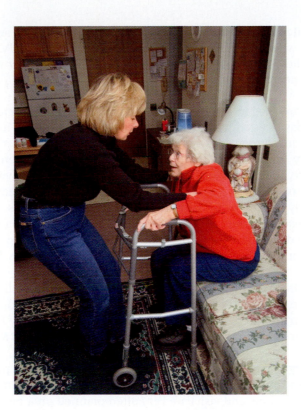

Much of the work of childrearing also involves the building up of "social capital"—helping children function in larger communities. Community supports such as playgroups and carpools can also assist in the productive activities of childrearing work.

Care of the Sick, Elderly, or Otherwise Needy. In countries like the United States, hospitals, nursing homes, mental health clinics, and other institutions exist for people who are acutely ill or incapacitated. However, families, friends, and neighbors remain the first source of support for people with dependency needs. People who are temporarily or mildly ill, recovering from surgery, or upset over life events are primarily cared for by friends and family. People with chronic mental or physical health problems may require considerable support services—such as monitoring and supervision, help with dressing or bathing, and transportation to doctors' appointments—from their families and other people in their communities, perhaps for decades.

The Final Stage of Production of Many Goods and Services. Pasta cannot be eaten until it is cooked. A vacuum cleaner provides no services until someone plugs it in and pushes it around. Grass seed does nothing until someone plants it. Household production activities such as cooking, cleaning, and house and yard maintenance convert many goods and services (often bought on markets) into forms suitable for final use.

The Organization of Savings and Investment. Households decide how much of their cash income to allocate to saving and investing, and how much to spend. They also decide how to allocate their saving—whether to invest in retirement funds, real estate, money market funds, or the like. Households also save through more structured (and less voluntary) channels such as pension plans, but the savings and investment decisions of individual households are of special interest to economists who study the core sphere. Family and friends also frequently use savings to make gifts or loans among themselves—for example, to finance someone's food and rent in times of need or to help someone acquire the funds to make a down payment on a house or to start a business.

The Allocation of Consumption Spending. Households are the final decision makers about whether to buy crackers or chips, a car or an SUV. This activity of households underlies the use of the terms *household* and *consumer* as synonymous in the traditional neoclassical model.

Decisions Regarding Investing in and Maintaining Human Capital. Decisions about such basics as education and diet are generally made by individuals and households. A major investment decision faced by all parents—often a subject of debate and even anxiety from the time a child is born—is how and whether to save for, or otherwise finance, their offsprings' education, beyond what is provided free by the government. Much of a child's health, knowledge, and habits on reaching adulthood have been strongly shaped by decisions made by his or her parents. Economists and sociologists have also examined the role of **neighborhood effects** on investments in education and on the development of work aspirations. Much of what people aspire to may be based on what they see around them in their community as possible.

neighborhood effects: the effects that the characteristics of particular local communities, beyond a person's family, have on economic outcomes

Decisions Regarding the Supply of Labor Services. As discussed in Chapter 13, decisions to work in the labor market, become self-employed, or engage in household production are often made not simply by individuals but by households, as part of a joint plan for family support. "Neighborhood effects" can play a role here, too.

The Organization of the Use of Leisure Time. Besides putting in work time in core sphere production, people enjoy "play" time with their family, friends, and neighbors as well. Vacations and visits are very often planned on a family basis, and recreation and relaxation are largely organized around core sphere networks of family and community.

1.2 | Getting Information on Core Sphere Activities

Because government economic statistics have tended to focus on monetized activities, it can be difficult to get good data on core sphere activities. We can get some sense of the structure of U.S. households and families by looking at U.S. government data from the 2000 census, although we have to interpret the data with care. The census defines a **household** as one or more people occupying a single housing unit, such as a house or apartment. A **family** is defined as two or more people in the same household who are related by birth, marriage, or adoption. People not living in households are classified as "living in group quarters"; they include residents of institutions such as prisons and nursing homes. In the 2000 census, 97.2% of the population was classified as living in households, and 68.1% of these households included families. Table 15.1 lists the percentages of the 105.5 million households identified by the census that fall into various classifications.

household: (U.S. census definition) one or more people occupying a single housing unit, such as a house or apartment

family: (U.S. census definition) two or more people in the same household who are related by birth, marriage, or adoption

Economics in the Real World

Valuing Core Sphere Activities

In Chapter 1 we noted that if we were we to put a monetary value on the production generated by this sphere in the United States, it would add up to about $3.9 trillion and account for about 30% of the total product.

There are also other ways of measuring its value. Instead of thinking about what the activities might earn if they were marketed, we might think of how the activities of various spheres contribute to well-being. You could imagine an economy existing without many of the important activities accomplished by businesses, governments, and nonprofits—an economy without commercial agriculture, for example, and without formal systems of law enforcement or higher-level education. It would limp along, but it would still exist. On the other hand, without the important activities of the core sphere, an economy or society couldn't exist at all. No one would survive past infancy!

Core sector activities tend to play a significant role in developing economies. While in industrialized countries gas and electricity are delivered by utility companies, in many poor countries women and children spend hours a day gathering fuel for cooking. This Guatemalan woman carries firewood back to her house aided by her sons. Since the firewood is for family use, and official systems of accounts tend to ignore activities outside markets, their work will likely not be registered as part of statistics on national "production."

The U.S. government has collected limited amounts of information about the need for family and community services and the satisfaction of these needs. For example, the census found that about 5 million people between the ages of 5 and 20 and about 44 million people aged 21 and up had disabilities. About 2.4 million grandparents are responsible for care of their grandchildren.

Other government statistics give some indication of how the needs of young children might be being met, by both nonmarket and market sources. In 2001, in 56.9% of married-couple families with children under the age of 6, both parents were engaged in paid employment. In 69.1% of families maintained by women (with no spouse present) with children under 6, the mother was in paid employment. In 88% of the families maintained by men (with no spouse present) with children under 6, the father was in paid employment.[1] Clearly, child-raising activities involve both parental and

Table 15.1 | Households in the Year 2000

	Percent of All Households
Families	
Married-couple family	51.7
Female householder, no husband present	12.2
Other families	4.2
Nonfamily households	
Householder living alone	25.8
Other nonfamily households	6.1
Total	100

Source: Authors' calculations based on U.S. Census, Table DP-1, *Profile of General Demographic Characteristics: 2000.*

---

[1] In 2001 in the United States, about 11 million families with children under 6 included married couples, about 3 million were maintained by women (no spouse present), and about 0.7 million were maintained by men (no spouse present).

nonparental care, where the latter may be provided within the core sphere or by organizations in the public purpose sphere or business sphere.

These figures give some limited insight into the activities of households. However, when we reflect on core sphere activities, it is not clear that the official definitions of families and households are the most relevant groupings. Many people find that the official definitions of marriage and family do not describe the important core economic relationships that define who they live with and how they provide for each other. About 30% of multiperson households in the United States in 2000 did not include married couples.[2] Moving to a global perspective, today nearly one-third of the world's households contain adult women but no able-bodied adult male, according to United Nations estimates. This occurs for a variety of reasons, including cases where mothers are unmarried, divorced, or widowed and cases where the father is absent as a consequence of war, long-term migration, economic necessity, or refugee status.

Many people also participate in core activities together even though they live in different housing units. This is especially true across generations and among cultural groups where extended kinship relations are particularly strong—perhaps including daily contact, transfers, and exchange among grandparents, cousins, and aunts and uncles spread out across a neighborhood or town.

time use survey: a survey designed to find out how much time people spend in various activities, including paid work, household production, and leisure

Statistics on household structure and paid employment measure only rather indirectly the need for core sphere economic activities and the degree to which these needs are satisfied. Such statistics do not tell us how much productive and other activity actually goes on within the sphere. Recognizing this lack, a number of industrialized countries have implemented household-based **time use surveys** in recent decades. These can be used to get a better grasp of how much production goes on within families and communities, by asking people how much time they spend in paid work, commuting, child care, elder care, volunteer work, house cleaning, yard work, watching TV, and the like. In the United States, the Bureau of Labor Statistics has implemented a national time use survey, and the first data were collected in 2003.

In 1995, the United Nations Development Program (UNDP) summarized the results of time use studies in 13 industrialized countries and 9 less industrialized, poorer countries. Globally, the report found that only slightly more than half of the total time spent on economically productive activities is included in conventional production measures such as gross domestic product (GDP), which look only at marketed activities. The report summarized:

> Of men's total work time in industrialized countries, roughly two-thirds is spent in paid . . . activities and one-third in unpaid . . . activities. For women, these shares are reversed. In developing countries, more than three-fourths of men's work is in [paid] activities [whereas women again devote two-thirds of their time to unpaid work]. So, men receive the lion's share of income and recognition for their economic contribution—while most of women's work remains unpaid, unrecognized and undervalued.[3]

Unpaid work in less industrialized countries often includes tasks such as growing food for household consumption, carrying water, gathering firewood, tending animals, and manufacturing and maintaining clothing and shelter.

---

[2] You could calculate this from Table 15.1 as follows: 25.8%, or about 27.2 million, of the 105.5 million households are householders living alone. About 54.5 million households include married couples (51.7% of 105.5 million). Thus about 78.3 million households (105.5 − 27.2) have multiple members. Of these, 23.8 million (78.3 − 54.5) do *not* include married couples, for a figure of 30.4% [(23.8/78.3) × 100].

[3] The passage quoted is from the UNDP, *Human Development Report* (New York: Oxford University Press, 1995), p. 98.

Discussion Questions

1. Which of the most important core sphere activities have you taken part in as a provider, recipient, or decision maker? Which do you expect to participate in, in the future?

2. Judging in terms of the census definitions, do you live in a household? In a family? Do the census classifications accurately describe the actual group(s) (if any) with whom you interact in core sphere activities?

2 | The Core Sphere in Historical Perspective

Just as markets and business organizations have evolved over time, so have economic relations within the core sphere.

2.1 | Pre-Industrial Economies

In subsistence economies, where people gather, grow, or hunt just enough food to survive, the core sphere *is* the economy: Everything that people need for their survival and flourishing is provided within family, kin, and village groups. Subsistence economies were the norm in early human development, and they still exist in some isolated, non-industrialized areas of the world today.

Even when agriculture began to yield surpluses, so that towns and cities, small-scale industries, and market exchange became more prevalent, the distinction between the core sphere of the economy and other spheres was not very sharp. Family farms and industries often involved everyone—men, women, and children—in one way or another. Whether gathering firewood, weaving cloth, or carrying eggs to the market, everyone was involved in provisioning the household. For examples of such family enterprises, you might think back to stories you have read about peasant life or life on the American frontier.

2.2 | "Outside" of the Economy?

It was only with the rise of industrialization, and the new pattern of people—especially men, "going out" to take wage work in factories—that the core sphere began to be distinguished from other forms of economic life.

cult of domesticity: the 19th-century notion that life in business and markets was suitable for men, whereas a more morally refined, "nonworking" life in the home was suitable for women

In 19th-century European and American culture, a new ideology arose, which historians call the **cult of domesticity**. Business activities, market life, and public policy, it came to be believed, were rough-and-tumble areas suitable for aggressive and competitive men. Women, on the other hand, were to be in charge of a protected sphere characterized by a higher moral order and more delicate, peaceful, and nurturing sensibilities: the family. The notion of childhood as a distinct stage of life, given over to attentive nurturance and education (rather than, as in earlier eras, to work in a family enterprise) gained ground. Thus the "traditional" family (a breadwinner husband, homemaker wife, and their dependent children) came to be a cultural norm. This belief system had several important consequences.

First, core sphere activities came to be regarded as "noneconomic." Economics in this period was often thought of as being about markets, instead of about provisioning for well-being. Because core activities are primarily nonmarketed, they were ignored. Also, as we have seen, the traditional model of "economic" behavior assumes that people act in rational, self-interested ways. Families were presumed to be based instead on emotional and altruistic behavior, so they were "noneconomic" in this way as well. Some aspects of this dichotomy are listed in Table 15.2.

Second, data gathering and analysis came to be shaped by these assumptions. Paid work in the market was called "work," but unpaid work within the household was not. Census takers in the 19th-century United States recorded housewives as being part of the "unproductive" or "dependent" segment of the population, along with children and the

Table 15.2	The 19th-Century "Cult of Domesticity"	
Business and Markets	**"The Family"**
economic	noneconomic
self-interested behavior	altruistic behavior
rationality	emotion
competition	nurturance
work	leisure
production	consumption

elderly.[4] Systems of national accounts (such as GDP) that were developed during this time excluded household and community production. Well into the 20th century, economists still ignored unpaid work by modeling the decision to participate in the paid labor market as simply a choice between "labor" (defined as paid work) and "leisure."

Third, the ideology strongly shaped opportunities for men and women according to their gender. Men were considered more suited for business and market life and had little opportunity to engage in childrearing or other family work. Women were considered more naturally suited to family life, were excluded from most paid occupations, and were considered the economic "dependents" of their fathers and husbands.

When women *did* work outside their homes, they tended to be in sex-segregated jobs that reflected extensions of their presumed special abilities with home and children. Women could, for example, do charitable and community-related work, such as visiting the poor or advocating civic betterment, on a volunteer basis. Primary school teaching, nursing, and social work were considered suitable paid professions for middle-class women. Some forms of paid industrial work, such as in textiles and sewing, that were similar to tasks formerly done in the home employed many working-class women. The expectation was usually that women would work in such professions and industrial jobs only until they married.

For men, pay rates tended (at least after heavy union pressure was exerted) to reflect a **"family wage"**—that is, a wage set high enough to support a man and his "dependents." Wages paid to women, on the other hand, tended to be low—they were sometimes referred to as just **pin money**—because it was assumed that women would be primarily supported by their fathers if they were single or by their husbands if they were married. The low wages may also have been supported by the presumption that women (at least of the middle and upper classes) were more altruistic and morally refined, and therefore less motivated by personal financial gain.

Of course, much of the "cult of domesticity" existed at the level of ideology only, not at the level of real day-to-day lives. Beliefs about innate delicacy were applied to native-born middle-class and upper-class U.S. white women, but this notion of delicacy was not applied to female slaves or to poor and/or immigrant women. They worked long hours in fields and factories, often under horrible conditions. Women of any class who lacked the support of a man as a consequence of abandonment or widowhood, or for other reasons, found economic life extremely difficult. Mothers who lacked access to a "family wage" often had no choice but to place their children with relatives or in orphanages run by community charitable or religious institutions, or to put them to work at a very young age.

During the early 20th century an awareness of the hardship inflicted on women who were left to support families by themselves inspired policies designed to keep families together. Starting with state "widows' pensions" in the United States, government funds would sometimes replace a missing husband's salary—though often at a very low rate—the idea being to allow mothers to stay home to care for their children. The sur-

"family wage": a wage high enough to support a wife and children, often associated with men's wages during the period of the cult of domesticity

pin money: a term used to refer to wages too low to provide a means of support, often associated with women's earnings during the period of the cult of domesticity

---

[4] Nancy Folbre, "The Unproductive Housewife: Her Evolution in Nineteenth Century Economic Thought," *Signs: Journal of Women in Culture and Society* 16, no. 1 (1991), 463–484.

vivor's benefit portion of the social security program designed in the 1930s, as well as the programs commonly known as welfare, were designed with this model of family life in mind. (In practice, however, the programs helped only *some* families stay together. For example, in some states "widow's pensions" were available only to *white* women.)

2.3 | Shifting the Boundaries

Much has changed since the 19th and early 20th centuries. Women have increasingly entered the paid labor market. In 2000, 60.2% percent of women, and 74.7% of men, over age 16 were in the paid labor force. Some women have achieved top-echelon jobs in business and traditionally "male" professions. And in 2001, for example, 29.3% of lawyers were female, up from only 4.9% in 1970.

Meanwhile, child care centers, family day care homes, nursing homes, home health aid services, prepared meals, commercial housecleaning services, and the like have developed to assist in many of the tasks that nearly always used to be done within households. Paid employment in the health care, education, social service, and personal and domestic care industries grew from 13.3% of total U.S. employment in 1900 to 22.6% in 1998.[5] Nearly 60% of all children under age 6 are in some form of nonparental care, regardless of their parents' work status. For children under age 1, the figure is 45%. [6]

The Personal Responsibility and Work Opportunity Reconciliation Act of 1996, popularly known as "welfare reform," brought about a major shift in U.S. welfare policy. Because sizable numbers of middle-class and working-class women were now in the paid labor force, it was decided that poor mothers should be required to do paid work. The old welfare program, Aid to Families with Dependent Children (AFDC), was replaced with a new one called Transitional Assistance to Needy Families (TANF). The new program provides families with financial benefits only if the mother complies with more rigorous employment requirements, and even then, it provides benefits for only a limited time.

It may seem that U.S. society has outgrown its ideology of the "cult of domesticity." But has it? Evidence suggests that at least some vestiges of this ideology are important in contemporary life. In Chapter 13, for example, we noted that labor market discrimination still occurs, partly because of the persistence of beliefs that certain kinds of jobs or job benefits should go only to people of a certain gender.

The idea that core sphere activities are not "work" also persists, even though the amount of work that is done in the household is still considerable. Studies of men's and women's work time suggest that many women, in particular, end up working "double-days"—working one shift for pay and another at home. (Surveys of men's time in household production in the United States have shown only a slight upward trend over time.)

As another example of the continued influence of the old ideology, the language of the Personal Responsibility and Work Opportunity Reconciliation Act reinforced the idea that "work" is something that goes on only *outside* households, whereas people giving unpaid care are "nonworking" and even "irresponsible." The act required increasing hours of paid work, with little recognition that this generally means reducing the amount of time spent caring for and supervising children (or investing in the kinds of education that could lead to long-term self-sufficiency). Furthermore, even today, official GDP statistics do not attempt to account for the value of work in the core sphere. Household work, it seems, still doesn't "count."

What about activities such as care for children and the elderly, now that they often take place within institutions run by for-profit businesses, nonprofits, or governments? Even when these activities are performed in more market-oriented spheres, you can still find signs of the "cult of domesticity." Jobs in child care, nursing home care, and home health provision, still dominated by women, are among the lowest paid in the U.S. economy. In

---

[5] U.S. government statistics, as reported in Nancy Folbre and Julie A. Nelson, "For Love or Money—Or Both?" *Journal of Economic Perspectives* 14, no. 4 (2000), 123–140.

[6] National Center for Education Statistics, *Child Care and Early Child Education Program Participation of Infants, Toddlers, and Preschoolers*, NCES 95–824 (Washington, DC: U.S. Department of Education, 1996).

1998 U.S. Department of Labor statistics, for example, the occupation of child care worker ranked 18th from the bottom in wages among the 774 occupations surveyed. Working in child care paid less than working in food service or as a parking lot attendant. One reason for these low wages is that the skills involved in caring work are often not recognized as real skills deserving of market rewards. Another may be the persistent belief that caring work should be motivated purely by unselfish, altruistic concern—meaning that employers are loath to pay "real" wages and that workers may be hesitant to unionize for fear of appearing "selfish." As a result, however, turnover rates of child care and health care employees are high. Even the most intrinsically motivated worker, after a while, gets tired of being poor.

2.4 | A Crisis in Care?

Of course, if any part of the economy is underprovisioned, relative to people's well-being needs, it will tend to falter. Although some U.S. nursing homes, day care centers, and hospitals provide excellent care, several recent surveys indicate that a distressing number do not. For example, a 1999 government report found that more than one-fourth of nursing homes actually cause harm to their residents.[7] A recent nationwide study of quality in randomly selected child care centers rated only 24% of preschool centers (usually serving children ages 3 to 5) as good to excellent. Most centers were rated minimal to mediocre, and some 40% of infant care centers were rated even lower, giving care of such inadequate quality that children's safety was potentially jeopardized.[8] A 2002 report found that nearly a quarter of reported errors causing death or injury to hospital patients were due to inadequate numbers of registered nurses on staff. Yet hospitals have tended to respond to nursing shortages not by raising wages substantially (as a market model would predict), but by increasing the workload of the remaining nurses—making it even more likely that they will quit.

Some social scientists have suggested that the United States is facing a crisis in care. Caring work that used to be provided by family, friends, and neighbors is being reduced or, when still done in those spheres, is accomplished under conditions of poverty, stress, and overwork. Meanwhile, caring services provided by businesses and governments are undersupported financially and are of uneven quality.

Why is this so? Insights both from economic theory and from a study of history and culture may help explain. From an economic point of view, we know that markets respond to "effective demand"—desires backed up by ability to pay. Yet the beneficiaries of caring services are often people who are too young, too old, too sick, or too poor to demand better quality by making their desires known on markets. For the same reasons, they are unlikely to be able to voice their needs directly through political processes.

Another economic reason may be that good care, particularly for young children who will grow to be society's future, has a "public good" aspect. We all benefit from children who grow up healthy and productive and can contribute to society, and we all suffer if children instead grow up stunted or disturbed, in need of expensive remedial care, or in jail. Yet public goods (see Chapter 1) tend to be underprovided by markets.

History and culture may offer yet another reason: Because caring services were provided "free" and invisibly within households and communities for so many years, societies may still tend to perceive them as deserving of only minimal financial support. Ways of thinking held over from the "cult of domesticity" may make it difficult for contemporary societies to recognize the pressing needs in this area and the tremendous societal effort that it will take to ensure adequate allocation of resources to this vital part of economic life. As economist Nancy Folbre has suggested, people need to recognize the "invisible heart" that undergirds economic functioning, rather than only the "invisible hand" of markets.[9]

---

[7] General Accounting Office, "Nursing Homes: Additional Steps Needed to Strengthen Enforcement of Federal Quality Standards," HEHS-99–46, March 18, 1999.

[8] Cost, Quality, and Child Outcomes Study Team, "Cost, Quality and Child Outcomes in Child Care Centers: Key Findings and Recommendations," *Young Children*, 50, no. 4 (1995), 40–44.

[9] Nancy Folbre, *The Invisible Heart: Economics and Family Values* (New York: New Press, 2001).

Bowling Alone?

What about the *non*household, nonfamily part of the core sphere—informal community activities among people who are less intimately attached? How have they evolved over time?

Robert Putnam's book *Bowling Alone: The Collapse and Revival of American Community* revived interest in this area among many researchers and commentators at the turn of the century.[10] This Harvard political scientist argued not only that the participation of people in the United States in formal and informal community groups had generally declined over much of the late 20th century but also that this had led to declines in social trust and reciprocity. Such shrinking of social capital, he suggested, was in turn a cause of problems, including declines in the safety of neighborhoods, the quality of government, and economic productivity.

Some of the evidence that Putnam pointed to concerned formal organizations, such as data on people's rates of participation in political parties, civic leagues, and churches. (We look at such organizations in Chapter 17.) He also examined evidence concerning people's family activities. One survey, for example, indicated that between 1976 and 1997, among families with children aged 8 to 17, the proportion who reported "just sitting and talking" together fell from 53% to 43%, and the proportion who reported vacationing together decreased from 53% to 38%.

Another class of activities he looked at was simple "schmoozing"—spending time with friends, having people over for dinner, playing cards, jamming with musical instruments, going to restaurants and bars, having picnics and parties, playing pick-up and team sports, and other informal sorts of social connection. Although schmoozing is generally highest among single and childless people, Putnam suggests that such activities declined for *all* age classes of people—even twenty-somethings—over the course of the late 20th century. Surveys that asked how often people entertained friends or went over to their friends' houses, for example, found declines of up to 45% between the mid-1970s and the late 1990s.

Putnam's provocative thesis revived research on social capital, its sources, and its effect on social and economic outcomes and spawned a renewed interest in the dynamics of community life. ◑

We don't usually think of "schmoozing" as an important economic activity. Can you see a possible link between such activity and things like neighborhood safety, good government, and economic productivity? Or does Putnam's argument seem strained to you?

Discussion Questions

1. Is it true, as the "cult of domesticity" claimed, that markets and business always follow rational and self-interested norms, whereas households are wholly devoted to emotion and altruism? Discuss this in the context of your own experience and in the context of earlier discussions in this book about goals, motivations, and economic organizations.

2. How do you and the people around you handle the economics of care? That is, how are children, the ill, and the elderly cared for in the family and community you live in now or grew up in? Do these processes seem to go smoothly, or do you see evidence of the problems mentioned in the text?

---

[10] New York: Touchstone, 2000.

3 | "Work/Family" Challenges

Another result of the "cult of domesticity" was that the structure of much paid employment and its treatment by government policies came to be shaped by the ideal of a breadwinner/homemaker family. Employers assumed that their employees possessed a home support system, invisibly taking care of the dependency needs of the employee and his children. Sometimes these positions have been referred to as "jobs with wives." Government rules and programs in areas of education, health, and income security likewise assumed that male workers would financially support a family, whereas women would engage in nonmarketed care. As more women have taken paid employment, however, the picture (inaccurate to begin with) has radically changed.

Economists and others have increasingly studied "work/family" or "work/life" issues and policies, examining how families, employers, and other economic actors and organizations have responded—or failed to respond—to the fact that many paid employees, both female and male, now have *both* paid work and home (and community) responsibilities.

3.1 | Employer Policies

In the era of "jobs with wives," employers were fairly free to demand uninterrupted, rigidly structured workweeks and even uninterrupted careers. They could demand mandatory overtime hours from production employees and assume that managers would be willing to uproot their families and move to new cities for a promotion. It was assumed that the paid job was the employee's top priority. These sorts of policies contributed to both job segregation by sex and the "glass ceiling" effect, whereby women could look up and see the top offices but were blocked from reaching them.

Some employers, however, have realized that such policies may cost them some of their best talent. Allowing their employees to arrange their hours more flexibly, work from home, work compressed hours, or work part-time may result in employees feeling much less stressed—and becoming more productive. Allowing employees to take leaves during times of heavy family responsibility—such as when bearing and caring for a new baby—and to return to their jobs without penalty, or to use their own sick leave to care for a sick family member, also enables employees to achieve a more satisfactory work/life balance.

Some employers have gone further, setting up programs such as on-site child care centers, offering assistance with finding or paying for child care or elder care, and helping find jobs for spouses. However, such work/family policies are far from universal. In 2000–2001, for example, over 70% percent of full-time paid workers did *not* have flexibility in setting their work hours, and only about 14% had employer-provided resource and referral services for help in locating child care.

3.2 | Government Policies

When a single company becomes "family-friendly," it may gain a more satisfied and productive workforce, but it may still find that it is at a disadvantage when competing against producers with lower employment costs. Public action—rules that cover *all* employers—may be needed to create a "level playing field" where companies that respond to the changing nature of family life are not penalized.

In the United States, the primary law related to work/family life is the Family and Medical Leave Act (FMLA). Passed in 1993, it requires businesses with 50 or more employees to provide up to 12 weeks of unpaid, job-protected leave per year to eligible employees who need leave to care for a newborn or a new adopted or foster child; to care for a child, spouse, or parent who has a serious health condition; or to treat their own serious health condition. Employees are eligible if they work for an employer covered by the law and have worked for that employer for at least a minimum number of hours during the year preceding the request for leave. Because of these restrictions, only about 47% of U.S. private-sphere employees are actually covered by the law. At least in part because the leaves are unpaid, eligible workers tend to take rather short leaves—an average of 10 days long. Workers who are not covered by FMLA may lose their jobs if they take time off for such reasons.

This contrasts with the situation in Canada and most European countries. Canadian parents, for example, can take up to 50 weeks of job-protected maternity and parental leave, with their wages partially replaced through the national employment insurance system. The Netherlands and Spain guarantee maternity leaves of 16 weeks at full pay. In Sweden, paid parental leave, which can be taken by either parent, can last as long as 18 months, and the policy includes incentives to promote use by fathers.

Many industrialized countries also offer more support to children directly, by providing or subsidizing professional early care and education. France, for example, has a system of free public preschools that enroll the majority of children aged $2\frac{1}{2}$ to 5. Sweden, in addition to providing generous parental leaves, has a large system of publicly subsidized early care and education. In the United States, by contrast, only very limited child care subsidies are available through the tax system for middle- and upper-income families and through programs targeted to the poor.

In many European countries, such policies of family support have been motivated not so much by an interest in enabling parents (particularly women) to take paid employment as by an interest in enabling paid *employees* to become *parents*. Fertility rates have dropped below the level necessary to maintain population size in most European countries (Russia, Spain, and Italy are outstanding examples), leading to fears that in the future, the ratio of the dependent elderly population to the working-age population will become impossibly large. Without young workers to actually produce goods and services, financial savings for retirement are worthless. Policies designed to distribute the cost of care are hence seen as vital for societal sustainability.

3.3 | Distributing the Costs of Care

Making time for core sphere activities and supplementing them with market or public programs are both expensive propositions. Many U.S. families cannot afford to take long unpaid leaves for child care, because they need the wages their jobs provide. Meanwhile, paid child care for a single 4-year-old averages $4000 to $6000 per year and can rise to $10,000 or more for the top centers. The average annual cost of full-time day care for a 4-year-old in an urban area is more than the average annual cost of public college tuition in nearly all states. Care for infants is even more expensive, and if a family

Nations differ in the amount of public support they provide for core sector activities. In the United States, qualified workers are entitled to up to 12 weeks of unpaid maternity or paternity leave. Mothers and fathers in Sweden can take 18 months of leave between them, while receiving payments equal to 80% of their normal salary from the social insurance system. For fathers, such as this young one in Medivi, Sweden, the law provides an incentive to take child care leave: One month must be used only by him, or else is lost.

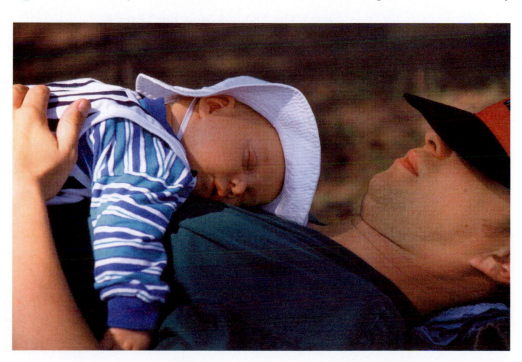

has more than one child in care, the costs multiply accordingly.[11] Care for the chronically ill and elderly raises similar dilemmas, although in the United States these areas have tended to receive higher levels of government subsidy.

Many issues concerning the changing boundaries between the core and marketed spheres of the economy inspire debate. Whose responsibility is the care of children, the sick, and the elderly? Is it just their immediate family's responsibility, or are there larger social interests? If parental and family leaves are paid, should the money come from employers or the government? How long should these leaves be? How should the costs of care, in terms of both money and time, be distributed between men and women?

These questions do not have easy answers. Both well-being and incentive effects need to be taken into account in thinking about changes. For example, it may seem helpful to families to mandate that employers offer—and pay for—extended parental leaves. Yet because such leaves are still more often taken by women than by men, such a policy could result in employers being reluctant to hire women of child-bearing age. Much work remains to be done in addressing the economics of care.

> ### Discussion Questions
>
> 1. How do you personally foresee handling caring situations that may come up in your future? If you do not have children now, but intend to have children in the future, how do you envision caring for them? What about caring for your elderly parents or for other relatives?
>
> 2. How do you think the costs of care *should* be distributed? Who should be responsible for the financial costs of caring for young, elderly, or sick people in a society? Who should do the actual hands-on work?

4 | Theories of Household Behavior

Economists have begun to develop theories about economic decision making within households. In general, these are theories about how married couples might behave. Other types of families, households, or community-based decision groups, such as multigeneration families, single-parent families, same-sex unions, and extended kinship groups, have not yet been the subjects of as much research.

4.1 | The "Glued Together" Family

The simplest model of families portrays them as acting as though they were individuals. Each family is envisioned to have a unified set of goals and to behave as though its choices proceeded from one rational mind—as though it were "glued together."[12] The household is also assumed to enjoy a single level of utility or well-being. Like the theory of "the firm," this theory of "the household" is the one that underlies the traditional neoclassical model.

This model is the one that justifies using the terms *family, household, individual, consumer,* and *worker* as synonymous. The family or household is considered to be a unitary economic actor, and its organizational aspects are ignored.

Although it may be a useful abstraction for some applications, the **"glued together" family model** is clearly unsatisfying on a number of fronts. For example, the utility theory of consumer behavior assumes that there is one decision maker, but obviously, in a multiadult household there are several candidates for this role. Empirical evidence confirms that people can have different interests and achieve different levels of well-being within a single household. And we all know, from living in households, that decision making is not always done in perfect harmony!

"glued together" family model: an image based on the assumption that families act as though they were single units, having a unified set of goals and attaining a single level of well-being

---

[11] Karen Shulman, "The High Cost of Child Care Puts Quality Care Out of Reach for Many Families" (Washington, DC: Children's Defense Fund, 2000), **http://www.childrensdefensefund.org/pdf/highcost.pdf**, accessed February 18, 2001.

[12] The use of the term *glued together* to describe this theory comes from the work of economist Amartya Sen.

4.2 | The Dictatorship Theory

Economist Gary Becker, writing in the mid-1970s, suggested that household decision making might be explained by the notion that each household contains an "altruist." In this case, one adult member is singled out as the decision maker. The "altruist," in Becker's theory, makes all the decisions for the household, transferring resources to other members from his or her own resources. Thus the household as a decision-making unit can just be identified with the household "head."[13]

dictatorship model (of households): the theory that household decisions are made by a single person (sometimes called the altruist)

Later commentators have chosen to call this a **dictatorship model** of behavior, rather than an altruistic model, and have noted its similarities to customary patriarchal notions of family structure that consider the husband to rule over his family. In other words, the crucial distinguishing characteristic of the "altruist" is not his degree of concern for other household members but, rather, his *power* to control the allocation of household resources.

Suppose, for example, that another adult member of the household—say, the wife of the "head"—cares even more about the welfare of the children (is even more "altruistic") than the household head. The wife's altruism will have no effect on the allocation of resources within the family, because only the "head" exercises control over family resources. This is true even if some or all of the household's resources result from the wife's own productive work. (Remember that until the late 1800s in the United States, a wife's earnings were controlled by her husband.)

Empirical studies have noted that, in fact, distribution within the household, and particularly between the genders, can be very unequal. It also, contrary to the "glued together" and dictatorship models, makes a difference who in the family is bringing in money.

4.3 | Specialization and Exchange

Another question addressed by Gary Becker and other "new home economists" of the 1970s was why married women were more likely to stay home, whereas their husbands nearly always went out to take paid jobs. Using the fairly new realization that female homemakers were engaged in "household production" rather than just "leisure," they reasoned that women traded the products of their work in the household, in which they were relatively efficient, for the financial support of their husbands from market work, in which the husbands were relatively efficient.

The theory is that there would be "gains from trade" from such specialization and exchange—exactly analogous to the story about English cloth and Portuguese wine described in Chapter 9. The traditional split of market and nonmarket work would be explained—and economically justified—simply by husbands and wives working where each had comparative advantage, these economists argued.

This theory has a few notable problems and limitations. First, there tended to be a circularity of reasoning in the assumptions about relative efficiencies. Women were assumed to be relatively inefficient in market work because their average earnings in market work were lower than men's—but the reason why their market earnings were low was, in turn, said to be their preoccupation with "household responsibilities." Second, the model assumes that "market work" and "household production" are areas that require completely different sets of skills and that people do not experience diminishing marginal utility in their activities. In fact, many people enjoy, and are skilled in, a variety of tasks and would be bored or otherwise stressed if limited to doing nothing but homemaking, or nothing but market work, for extended periods of time. Third, as in the story of "gains from trade" between countries, the theory neglects issues of power, vulnerability, and dynamics over time. Should such a marriage break up after a number of years, the wife, who has invested much in the marriage and little in her own marketable skills may be in a far more vulnerable financial position than the husband.

---

[13] The very term *head of the family* comes from an analogy with the human body, in which the head is considered to be the thinking part that rules the rest of the body.

"Missing Women"

In some theories, everyone in a family is presumed to acquire the same "utility," or the same standard of living. Yet according to economist Amartya Sen, 100 million women worldwide are "missing"—that is, they don't show up in population statistics even though, given the roughly equal chances of males and females being born, they should be there. Very unequal household allocation patterns seem to be the reason.

Women tend to live slightly longer than men in circumstances of relatively equal access to food and health care. In the United States and Europe, for example, there are about 105 women for every 100 men. Yet in a number of regions of the world, and especially in South Asia and China, the sex ratio goes markedly in the opposite direction. In India, for example, there are only about 93 women for every 100 men. Comparing actual sex ratios to a ratio that might reasonably be assumed to result from a state of equal access to resources, researchers have estimated that 44 million women are "missing" from China, 36.7 million from India, and smaller numbers from other countries, including Pakistan and Iran.

Why has this occurred? Although deliberate infanticide (killing girl babies) is not unknown in some areas, this does not seem to be the main reason. In the areas with very low numbers of women, the usual cause seems to be that much lower priority is put on the health and survival of females. Women may eat food with less nutritional value, waiting to eat until after the men have eaten. A sick boy may be taken to the doctor, a sick girl left to recover (or not) on her own.

4.4 | Bargaining

In 1980–1981, economists Marjorie McElroy, Mary Jean Horney, Marilyn Manser, and Murray Brown applied bargaining models that were originally developed for studying the actions of economic actors in other situations (such as employer–union bilateral monopolies) to married-couple households. In bargaining models, the relative power of the parties is of central concern. The more power you have, the better the outcome is likely to be for you.

bargaining theory: a theory about situations in which economic actors could benefit from coming to an agreement but may disagree about how to divide up the benefit they gain

In **bargaining theory**, two economic actors are imagined to meet in a situation where coming to an agreement will benefit both parties. However, the amount of surplus generated by cooperation needs to be divided between the two parties, and on this issue the parties might disagree. The situation is hence one of "cooperative conflict": The two parties both gain by cooperating but may be in conflict about the distribution of these gains between them.

What sorts of gains would need to be divided between a husband and wife? You might imagine that, in a subsistence economy, a couple would need to divide between them the food they jointly produced on their small plot of land. (See the Economics in the Real World feature above.) And you might imagine a couple in a more affluent economy debating how much of the family budget should go toward *his* spending priorities and how much toward *hers*—perhaps he wants a newer car but she would prefer a vacation trip, or she would like to build up their savings but he would like to make a loan to his brother, and so on.

fall-back position (or **threat point**): in bargaining theory, what each actor will get if the parties fail to make an agreement

Figure 15.1 illustrates a simple case for a couple consisting of Joe and Lynn. The axes measure utility, or satisfaction, for each actor. We label, on each axis, the level of utility each would have if they were *not* married. In bargaining theory, these are called the individuals' **fall-back positions** or **threat points**. The bowed-out line is a utility frontier (similar to a production possibilities frontier) showing the joint levels of satisfaction that the two can achieve together. At point C, for example, each reaches a level of utility that is higher than her or his threat point. The fact that each may reach a higher utility level married than alone might be seen as resulting from gains from trade, mutual

This lower priority, in turn, seems to be related to social customs that severely restrict the contribution a girl or woman can make to her family—or that even make a girl child an economic liability. The areas that have the lowest female survival within India, for example, tend to be areas where women are strictly limited to doing unpaid household work and where parents historically made payments (dowry) to the groom's family when their daughter was married. The areas with higher female survival in India tend to be areas in which women are more free to take paid employment and where parents historically got payments (bride wealth) from the groom's family when their daughter was married.

In China, a boy is expected to take care of his parents in their old age. A girl, on the other hand, is lost to her husband's family upon marriage and helps take care of *his* parents instead. With no broader-based program of old-age insurance available, parents with no sons fear destitution in their old age.

Discriminatory gender norms, then, and customs concerning the responsibility of care, it seems, make a very big difference in "who gets what."[14]

"What goes on inside households is not the government's business," some say. Yet, on the basis of this story, can you identify ways in which government policies about economic issues such as health care, retirement, and employment may affect who gets what within households—whether the effects are intended or not?

utility from having children, savings from sharing a common house and car, or the enjoyment of being together. The bowed-out shape may be thought of as reflecting diminishing marginal utility.

Bargaining theory gets interesting when we examine possible outcomes in terms of the utility of each actor and how these outcomes change as the threat points change. For example, in Figure 15.1, assuming that they will choose an efficient outcome, Joe and Lynn together might choose any point along the arc from *B* to *D*. They would not end up at point *A*, because in this case Lynn would be better off not being married and would prefer divorce, nor would they end up at point *E*, because then Joe would prefer

Figure 15.1 A Bargaining Model

In a two-person bargaining model, people must decide how to divide the benefits that will come from cooperating with each other. If Joe and Lynn don't cooperate, each gets only his or her own "threat point" or "fall-back" utility level. Any point that makes them both better off is a possible outcome of bargaining. If they choose efficiently, the bargaining outcome will be somewhere on the arc that connects points *B* and *D*.

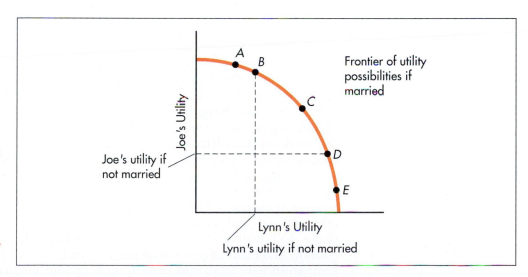

[14] This discussion is based on research by Amartya Sen and Jean Drèze, as summarized in Martha C. Nussbaum, *Women and Human Development* (Cambridge, England: Cambridge University Press, 2000), pp. 3–4.

Figure 15.2 **A Bargaining Model with a Reduced Threat Point**

If Lynn's fall-back position worsens, the outcome of bargaining may also become less favorable to her. An outcome like that of point *A*, which she would have rejected before as being worse than she could get on her own, may now look acceptable.

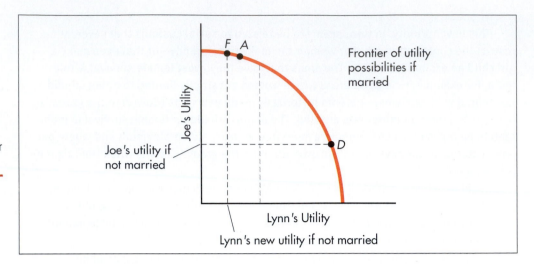

divorce. At a point like *B* or *D*, one of them would be just indifferent between staying married and not staying married.

What would happen if Lynn's threat point were to fall? For example, suppose that Lynn specializes in household labor, and so, over time, her earnings capacity outside of marriage falls. Or suppose that her spouse threatens her with violence if she leaves. In such cases, her utility associated with leaving the marriage falls. In Figure 15.2, Lynn's threat point is shown as lower, and the new area of possible outcomes is the arc from *F* to *D*. Point *A* is now a point that *could be* the outcome of marital bargaining. Her worse options *outside* the marriage mean that agreements *within* the marriage could turn for the worse, from Lynn's point of view. Of course, this is just fancy language for a common intuition: If people act self-interestedly, the person who can more credibly threaten to back out of an agreement is more likely to get terms in his or her favor.

Exactly which point on the frontier will be chosen? Economists have tended to concentrate on mathematical solutions to this question, but all solutions share the characteristic that lesser threat points lead to worse outcomes. More general studies of bargaining suggest that many factors (including customs, perceived fairness, and sheer arguing ability) can come into play in determining outcomes in the case of a dispute.

4.5 | Why All the Theories Are Inadequate

The "glued together" theory seems overly harmonious, with its absolute unity within a family. The bargaining model, on the other hand, may strike you as too crude and harsh—don't people create families because they care about each other, after all?

Meanwhile, the "families" in the theories discussed seem notably devoid of children, except as objects of the "altruist's" beneficence or objects bringing utility to their parents. The well-being of the children themselves does not enter into the models. Children's influence on decision making is also ignored. This is in stark contrast to a fact that marketers have learned and acted on through advertising strategies: Children have become increasingly important in influencing family consumption purchase decisions.

In reality, both common interests and conflicting interests are found within a family. None of the theories developed to date succeed in capturing the complexity of household economic life. Actors within households, including parents, children, and other relatives and nonrelatives, often behave partly out of habit and custom, partly under the influence of power and coercion, and partly—at least in households where customs of dictatorial power have been rejected—on the basis of democratic consent. Economists have more work to do to come up with adequate theories of households as economic organizations.

Discussion Questions

1. Think about the household in which you grew up. To what extent would any of the models just described—"glued together," dictatorship, specialization and exchange, and bargaining—describe how decisions were made in your family?

2. Discuss the strengths and weaknesses of the models of household behavior. Do any of them seem realistic? Do you think any of them offer better insights than others about household economic behavior?

Review Questions

1. What are eight main functions of the core sphere?

2. In what way are the data compiled by the U.S. Bureau of the Census limiting, in terms of the study of core sphere activities?

3. Identify two important stages in the history of the core sphere before contemporary times.

4. Describe the consequences of the "cult of domesticity" for how people thought about men's and women's work and wages.

5. What are some reasons for thinking that the "cult of domesticity" is over and past?

6. What evidence is there that the "cult of domesticity" is *not* entirely over and past?

7. Why do some economists point to a "crisis in care"?

8. How have some employers responded to the changes in family life?

9. How have some governments responded to the changes in family life?

10. What distributional concerns are raised by the question of the costs of care?

11. List and describe four models of household behavior.

12. What is missing from these models of household behavior?

Exercises

1. Referring to Chapter 9, describe how the "gains from trade" story can be applied to households. Replace "England" with "Husband," "Cloth" with "Market Earnings," "Portugal" with "Wife," and "Wine" with "Home Production."
   a. Using the same numbers as in Chapter 9 (that is, for example, assume that "Wife" can produce 200 units of "Household Production" or 100 units of "Market Earnings"), create a table like Table 9.1 and graphs like Figures 9.3 and 9.4.
   b. Write a paragraph explaining what your graphs and figures represent and how "gains from trade" arise.
   c. Create a table like Table 9.3, and explain what it means. Could you describe this as a bargaining situation? Why or why not?

2. Consider the case of Chris and Robin, as described in the figure on the following page. The frontier shows their utility levels if they decide to form a partnership.
   a. Which theory of household behavior does this illustrate?
   b. Identify, on the graph, the "threat point" of each person.
   c. What are the possible outcomes, assuming that Chris and Robin decide to get together?
   d. Whose threat point would have to be lowered to make point *E* a potential bargaining outcome? Explain why.
   e. Would point *F* be a possible outcome for this partnership? Explain.

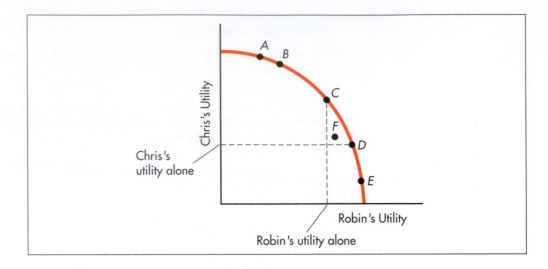

3. Find an article in a recent newspaper or news magazine that deals with some aspect of the economics of care. (For example, it could concern the quality of child care in your community, a debate about funding for health care, or a "family-friendly" business.) Does the article reflect a search for a solution to some of the problems mentioned in the text? Does the language used in the article reflect any "cult of domesticity" ideology? Write a paragraph relating the article to the issues discussed in this chapter.

4. Match a concept in Column A with an example in Column B.

Column A	Column B
a. neighborhood effects	**i.** cult of domesticity
b. family household	**ii.** concentration on homemaking may reduce potential market earnings
c. nonfamily household	
d. belief that mothers should stay home to take care of children	**iii.** a mother and her two children sharing a house
e. policy that mothers should not stay home to take care of children	**iv.** Family and Medical Leave Act
	v. a manager is expected to work both days and evenings, as needed
f. a problem with specialization	
g. policy that (some) parents can take 12 weeks off work to care for children	**vi.** Personal Responsibility and Work Opportunity Reconciliation Act
	vii. seeing that people in your community usually get a college education
h. "jobs with wives"	
i. "family-friendly" policies	**viii.** flexible work hours
	ix. an unmarried couple sharing an apartment

The Business Sphere: For-Profit Firms

Chapter 16

Economist Herbert Simon has raised a question about how appropriate it is to think of contemporary industrialized countries as having "market economies." Imagine that an alien from Mars were to take a photo of Earth using a special camera, he suggests. Photographed with this equipment, social structures that are organized along nonmarket lines (that is—to use our vocabulary from Chapter 2—they are organized by custom, consent, or administration) would show up as solid green areas. Market connections of exchange would show up as red lines running between them. The photo would be dominated, Simon suggests, by green areas. "Organizations," according to Simon, "would be the dominant feature of the landscape."[1]

1 | Businesses as Organizations

In the present chapter, we look inside one kind of "green area"—the business firm as a type of social organization. What do businesses do? What main forms do businesses take? How large can they get? What are some major issues in business history? What are the goals of businesses?

The business sphere is the major employer in the U.S. economy. In 2001, 115 million people were employees of businesses. Approximately another 17 million very small "nonemployer" businesses had no formal payroll employees and were generally operated by sole proprietors. Business activities run the gamut from professional services to warehousing, construction, retail trade, health care, and finance. Some firms, especially in such fields as transportation, accounting, finance, marketing services, and wholesale trade, sell all or nearly all their services to other firms. Others, such as those involved in retail trade and residential real estate, sell mostly to households. Some, such as weapons manufacturers, sell largely to governments. Many sell to a mix of clients.

1.1 | The Legal Organization and Ownership of Firms

Private for-profit enterprises in the United States and many other countries fall into four main legal forms: **proprietorships**, **partnerships**, **corporations**, and **cooperatives**.

[1] Herbert A. Simon, "Organizations and Markets," *Journal of Economic Perspectives* 5, no.2 (1991), 25–44.

proprietorship: a business owned by a single family or individual

Proprietorships. These are businesses owned by single individuals or families. Under the laws of most countries, they are the personal property of the proprietors, just as a home or car might be. Proprietorships tend to be small enterprises, often providing retail sales (such as farm produce or handmade crafts) or professional services (such as child care or auto repair). In some cases, the lines between personal and business property, between work and family life, and between production for the market and production for family use can become blurred. An important characteristic of this form is that legal ownership and immediate control over activities are usually not separated but, rather, are lodged together in a single individual or family.

partnership: a business owned by a group of two or more people

Partnerships. These are businesses owned by a group of two or more individuals. Such a business does not exist apart from the people who own it; if one of them leaves the partnership, or another individual joins, the entire partnership itself needs to be legally reconstituted. These firms also tend to be small, although the pooling of resources permits partnerships to be larger, on average, than proprietorships. Many law firms, for example, are run as partnerships.

Some partnerships have **limited liability**, which means that if the business fails, the owners' losses are limited to the amount of financial capital that they have invested in it. Other partnerships do not have limited liability. Without limited liability, people to whom the firm owes money can demand that the owners also liquidate their *personal* assets—such as stock holdings and bank accounts—to pay off debts of the business.

limited liability: a legal structure in which creditors of a business can demand from owners no more than the owners' investment in the business

corporation: a business firm that has been chartered by a state or the federal government and that has a status in law as a "person," with a legal existence separate from the individuals or organizations who own it

Corporations. These are legal entities separate from the people who own them: Individual owners can come and go, but the corporation remains. On the other hand, if the corporation goes bankrupt and is forced to dissolve, its debts and other obligations are dissolved with it. The limited liability ensured by the corporate form of organization means that in the event of its failure, the owners of a corporation cannot lose more than their investment. On the other hand, there is no legal limit to the profit they can make if the corporation is successful. This asymmetry, along with its other legal advantages, makes the corporation the preferred structure for major business activities in most countries.

Usually corporate ownership takes the form of holding shares of stock; individuals and financial institutions can buy or sell these shares without any effect on the legal status of the corporation itself. Corporations that issue stock are governed by shareholders according to the principle of one share, one vote. Generally, shareholders elect a board of directors, who in turn hire professional managers to run the day-to-day operations of the corporation.

cooperative: a business owned by a group of workers, suppliers, or consumers

Cooperatives. Cooperatives, in contrast to corporations, cannot issue stock and are governed by a different ownership principle. Each member of the cooperative, no matter what his or her position, has one and only one vote. This means, of course, that ownership in cooperatives cannot be accumulated. Usually the cooperative is run by hired managers, under the supervision of a board of directors elected by the membership.

In practice, cooperatives are owned by one of three groups: their workers, their suppliers, or their consumers. Individuals are usually required to invest some amount of money in order to join. Cooperatives tend to make decisions in the particular interest of their controlling group—for instance, by providing better working conditions (if a worker cooperative), negotiating higher prices (if a supplier cooperative), or charging lower prices (if a consumer cooperative). Credit unions are cooperatives, as are the Associated Press news organization and many agricultural marketing organizations such as Land O'Lakes (dairy) and Sunkist (oranges).

These forms of business organization, along with their main advantages and disadvantages, are summarized in Table 16.1.

The classification of firms by type of ownership in Table 16.1 is loosely related to our earlier classification of industries by market structure. In particular, in industries dominated

Table 16.1 | Forms of Private Business Organization

Type of Business	Key Features	Advantages and Disadvantages
Proprietorship	Individual or family ownership Unlimited liability	Easy to set up Can be integrated with family life Hard to attract outside resources
Partnership	Owned by named individuals Limited or unlimited liability	Can combine resources of several individuals Each change of ownership requires a new partnership
Corporation	Owned by stockholders (one share, one vote) Limited liability	Can raise funds by issuing stock Legal status of firm does not depend on identity of owners
Cooperative	Owned by workers, customers, or suppliers (one person, one vote) Limited liability	Can serve interests of groups who participate in firm Cannot issue stock; may have difficulty borrowing as well

by one or a few large companies, these companies are nearly always corporations. More competitive industries may include corporations, but they are also more likely to include proprietorships and partnerships than are the more concentrated (oligopolistic or monopolistic) industries. The legal and administrative costs of establishing and maintaining a corporate structure may outweigh the advantages of incorporation for a small farm, manufacturing enterprise, retail enterprise, or service provider. The larger the enterprise, the greater the benefits of incorporation for the owners and investors.

1.2 | Are Big or Small Businesses More Important?

Even though businesses all share the purpose of producing goods or services for sale, they vary dramatically in size and complexity. Are big businesses or small businesses more important in the U.S. economy? Finding the answer to this question is harder than you might think.

According to government statistics, there were 5.7 million business firms with payroll employees in 2001. Of these 5.7 million employers, the vast majority—89.0%—had fewer than 20 employees. Only 1.8% had 100 or more employees, and only 0.3% employed 500 or more people. Figure 16.1 illustrates these data.

In addition, the government keeps track of the many small businesses that do not have paid employees. Such small firms, such as real estate agencies and consulting firms, do not have a formal payroll but rather pay their (usually sole, or family) worker(s) directly from revenues. In 2001 there were nearly 17 million such "nonemployer" businesses—over twice the number of businesses with employees. It would seem, from this accounting, that small, and even *very* small, businesses are very important in the United States.

Statistics can often be examined from more than one angle, however. To analyze what the data just cited represent, consider that they come from tax data filed with the government. Imagine a big stack of tax returns: Each firm, of any size, files exactly one return. Now imagine that each return is a single sheet of paper. The foregoing analysis tells us that only a tiny slice of this stack of returns comes from firms that would be classified as "big."

But where do most people work? Although only 1.8% of employers had 100 or more employees, these few larger firms employ well over half—64%—of U.S. employees! Fifty percent of employees (over 57 million workers) work at firms with 500 or more employees. Only 18% of employees work in firms with fewer than 20 workers. This is illustrated in Figure 16.2.

Does this seem like a contradiction? It is not, because large employers, by definition, account for a large number of workers. The base (the size of the pie in the chart) for the first

Figure 16.1 Of the 5.7 Million Employers, What Share Had . . . ?

When the "pie" is made up of individual business employ*ers*, you can see that many firms hire few workers.

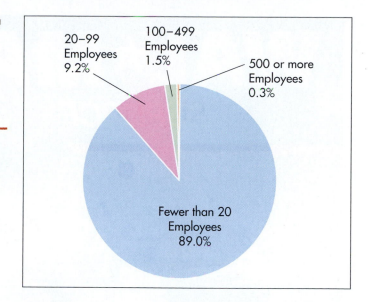

set of calculations is the tax returns of the 5.7 million employers. The corner grocery store files one tax return. So does Boeing Corporation. In the second set of calculations, however, the base (or pie) is the 115 million people who are paid employees. The two employees of the corner grocery obviously represent an extremely small share of these 115 million people. On the other hand, the roughly 200,000 people employed by Boeing in 2001 represent a larger slice of *this* pie. Similar tables could be constructed for the size of the payroll or the total revenues of firms. Here again, the large firms would play the major role.

We can see that the businesses in the U.S. economy are a mix of many small and fewer large enterprises, and that those large enterprises are very important players.

1.3 | How Large Are the Largest Firms?

Every year *Fortune*, the American business magazine, publishes a list of the world's 500 largest corporations. The companies that top the list are huge indeed. The world's biggest firm in 2003 was Wal-Mart Stores, with revenues of over $246 billion and more than 1.3 million employees. The five largest, ranked by revenues, were Wal-Mart, General Motors, Exxon Mobil, Royal Dutch/Shell Group, and BP (British Petroleum), all of which had revenues in excess of $175 billion. For comparison, Microsoft Corporation ranked 137th in revenues, with receipts of "only" about $28 billion. To get some sense of

Figure 16.2 Of the 115 Million Employees, What Share Worked for Employers Who Had . . . ?

When the "pie" is made up of business employ*ees*, you can see that almost half work for firms with many workers.

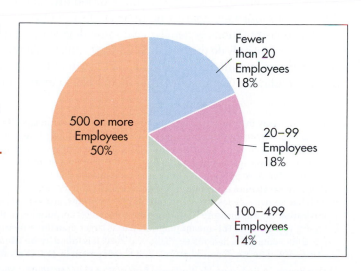

The largest corporation in the world, according to recent statistics, is Wal-Mart Stores. It sells 36% of all dog food, 32% of all disposable diapers, and 26% of all toothpaste sold in the United States. With the recent opening of Supercenters, such as this one in Hialeah Gardens, Florida, Wal-Mart has expanded beyond general merchandising into retail sales of groceries and, in some cases, services such as car maintenance and hair styling.

perspective on these very big numbers, note that the gross domestic product of Norway was about $143 billion, and that of Finland $136 billion, in 2002.[2]

Most of the companies in the Fortune Global 500 are based in the United States, Western Europe, or Japan. Canada, Australia, and South Korea have a number of companies on the list. Petroleum companies from countries such as Russia, Mexico, and India make the list, as do 11 state-owned companies from China. None of the Global 500 in 2003 was based in Africa.

Statistics such as these pose a challenge to any economic theory based on perfect competition. Firms with revenues larger than the GDP of entire European countries, with workers numbered in the hundreds of thousands, inevitably wield substantial economic and political power. An estimate based on data from 2001 suggested that these 500 corporations held nearly one-quarter of the world's productive assets.[3]

Large corporations generally have some degree of market power in all areas of their operations. Not only do they sell their products under oligopolistic conditions; they also buy their primary and intermediate inputs, and even obtain financing, in markets where they are major players. No one buys from them, sells to them, or negotiates with them without

---

[2] This is not to say that the large corporations are economically "bigger" than these European countries, although it is striking that the amount of money flowing through these companies is on a scale with some national GDPs. A country's GDP measures the total value of its monetized production, whereas the revenues of a company measure not only the monetary value of its own production but also the production of the other companies that have provided it with primary and intermediate inputs. A more appropriate measure, if we are to compare companies with countries, is value added, which is defined, for any particular firm, as the sum of what it has paid in salaries, what it takes in as pre-tax profits, and what it accounts for as depreciation and amortization. By this measure Wal-Mart is the 10th largest corporation in the world—and the 69th largest economy in the world. This means that Wal-Mart is larger than three-quarters of the nations of the world! The value-added data given here relates to the year 2000; it is found in the *World Investment Report* published by the United Nations Conference on Trade and Development in 2002 (New York).

[3] Brian Roach, "A Primer on Multinational Corporations" in *Leviathans: Multinational Corporations and the New Global History*, ed. Alfred Chandler and Bruce Mazlish (New York: Cambridge University Press, 2004).

being aware of their enormous size and economic power. Indeed, they are very often large enough to use direct political pressure to attain their economic objectives, both in their home countries and in other nations where they also buy, produce, and sell their products.

Discussion Questions

1. Do you have any personal experience with the inner workings of a business organized on a proprietorship, partnership, corporate, or cooperative basis? If so, who would you say made the decisions regarding the overarching policies of the business? Who made the day-to-day decisions? Whose interests do you think were given priority in these decisions—the interests of the owners, managers, workers, customers, or someone else? Were the various interests compatible with each other, or were there conflicts?

2. Did any of the statistics about the sizes of large firms surprise you? Some people regard big corporations negatively, because they believe that corporations abuse their immense power by manipulating people and governments. Others think of big firms positively, perhaps as future workplaces where they can advance their own careers. Do either, or both, of these views characterize your own perspective?

---

2 | The Goals of Firms

The traditional neoclassical model assumes that businesses are continually seeking to maximize their profits. This is often a plausible and powerful assumption, which explains many aspects of business behavior. At this point, however, we will pause to consider whether profit maximization is a sufficient description of what corporations actually do. While one popular line of thinking emphasizes profits and the interests of shareholders, another emphasizes the fact that firms are complex social organizations made up of many actors, who may have divergent interests.

2.1 | Shareholders and Profit?

A certain traditional line of thinking views corporations as simply instruments for carrying out business activities in the interests of their owners. The owners of a corporation—like the owner of a small proprietorship—are supposed to be able to set the policies of the corporation through the election of a board of directors. The shareholders also reap any residual gains, after all costs have been paid, in profits paid out as dividends or reinvested in the company to increase its value and hence the value of its stocks on the stock market. The corporation itself is considered merely a legal fiction—that is, a mere instrument for carrying out the will of shareholders (a term synonymous with *stockholders*).

The CEO and top officers of the corporation are assumed simply to carry out the policies set by the board of directors. Employees are seen as following the directions of the managers. In this image of the corporation, everyone works together to benefit the shareholders. As in the traditional neoclassical model, "firms maximize profits." This has also been called the **shareholder theory** of the corporation.

shareholder theory: the theory that corporations are merely legal instruments for carrying out the will of their shareholders

The image of the firm as profit maximizer plays an important role in the belief that "free market" economies are essentially self-regulating, with business interests automatically serving the common good (see Chapter 19). As conservative economist Milton Friedman put it, "Few trends could so thoroughly undermine the very foundations of our free society as the acceptance by corporate officials of a social responsibility other than to make as much money for their stockholders as possible."[4]

Shareholder theory also fits well with the idea of a *perfectly competitive* market structure. As we noted in Chapter 11, a perfectly competitive firm *has no choice* but to maximize profits—doing anything less would mean making less than normal profit. Owners would liquidate their investments in such a losing firm, and the firm would go out of business.

---

[4] Milton Friedman, *Capitalism and Freedom* (Chicago: University of Chicago Press, 1982), p. 133.

2.2 | Stakeholders and Diverse Interests?

This traditional view came under fire in the 1920s and 1930s, and again late in the 20th century, when people became concerned about the increasing influence of large and powerful corporations on the economy and society. Rather than thinking of corporations as legal fictions, an alternative view regards them as important societal institutions, subject to broader social criteria of legitimacy, responsibility, and accountability.

stakeholder theory: the theory that corporations are complex organizations that have responsibilities to many constituent "stakeholders," such as shareholders, managers, employees, customers, creditors, and the like

Beginning in the 1980s, this notion was expressed as the **stakeholder theory** of the corporation.[5] In contrast to *share*holder theory, *stake*holder theory sees the contemporary corporation as a complex social organization (see Chapter 2) with multiple constituencies. Shareholders have a stake in the success of a firm, but so do the firm's managers, employees, suppliers, customers, and creditors and the communities in which it is located. So, also, is the natural environment often affected by the actions of corporations.

In the stakeholder view, the firm has a responsibility to make reasonable profits for its shareholders. It will *not*, however, have a goal of *maximizing* profits, because it has other responsibilities as well. An often-quoted example of commitment to the stakeholder view is the credo of the Johnson & Johnson pharmaceutical company (see the accompanying Economics in the Real World feature). Many commentators attribute Johnson & Johnson's rapid response in 1982 to the cyanide tainting of its painkiller Tylenol on store shelves—voluntarily recalling enormous quantities of Tylenol from retail shelves, at considerable cost, and quickly developing tamper-proof packaging—to this company's broader-based view of its goals.

Stakeholder theory gained ground in legal cases in the late 20th century, in some instances spurred by the concerns of workers and managers about hostile takeovers that would have given shareholders capital gains but would have also destroyed the company as a going concern by selling off assets or shifting production elsewhere. By 2000, 32 states had "constituency statutes" that explicitly made boards of directors accountable to groups other than just shareholders. Rather than considering socially responsible behavior to be destructive of corporate interests, in 1994 the American Law Institute stated that "corporate decisions are not infrequently made on the basis of ethical considerations even when doing so would not enhance corporate profit or shareholder gain. Such behavior is not only appropriate, but desirable."[6]

Stakeholder theory is also consistent with the fact that many firms, and large corporations in particular, operate in ways that create, or take advantage of, various kinds of market power. Economic power gives corporations choices about many aspects of their operations. Instead of being driven to extreme cost cutting just to maintain "zero economic profits" by market competition, large corporations may instead operate with substantial "slack"—that is, with a surplus of revenues over the minimum costs necessary to run the business.

Division of this surplus then becomes an issue. The surplus could be distributed to shareholders as dividends or reinvested in the company with the goal of raising share prices, as a profit orientation would suggest. But the company's leaders could also use the surplus to start a company day care center, improve conditions or wages for workers, set up programs to reduce discrimination in managerial promotions, allow a more relaxed pace of work, take the lead in environmental cleanup, or make philanthropic donations to community organizations. Such policies tend to increase accounting costs and thus reduce measured profit, at least in the short run. However, it may be that they add to long-term profitability by providing the far-sighted company with the benefits of a loyal and productive workforce, peaceful relationships with a community, and long-term environmental sustainability.

Of course, as we will examine next, the surplus could also be used in less responsible ways, such as inflating the wealth of a few people at the expense of all other stakeholders.

---

[5] R. Edward Freeman, *Strategic Planning: A Stakeholder Approach* (Boston: Pitman, 1984).

[6] *Principles of Corporate Governance: Analysis and Recommendations*, excerpted in "Managerial Duties and Business Law" (publication 9-395-244, Harvard Business School, Cambridge, MA, July 1995).

The Founding Principles of Johnson & Johnson

OUR CREDO

We believe our first responsibility is to the doctors, nurses and patients,
to mothers and fathers and all others who use our products and services.
In meeting their needs everything we do must be of high quality.
We must constantly strive to reduce our costs
in order to maintain reasonable prices.
Customers' orders must be serviced promptly and accurately.
Our suppliers and distributors must have an opportunity
to make a fair profit.

We are responsible to our employees,
the men and women who work with us throughout the world.
Everyone must be considered as an individual.
We must respect their dignity and recognize their merit.
They must have a sense of security in their jobs.
Compensation must be fair and adequate,
and working conditions clean, orderly and safe.
We must be mindful of ways to help our employees fulfill
their family responsibilities.
Employees must feel free to make suggestions and complaints.
There must be equal opportunity for employment, development
and advancement for those qualified.
We must provide competent management,
and their actions must be just and ethical.

We are responsible to the communities in which we live and work
and to the world community as well.
We must be good citizens—support good works and charities
and bear our fair share of taxes.
We must encourage civic improvements and better health and education.
We must maintain in good order
the property we are privileged to use,
protecting the environment and natural resources.

Our final responsibility is to our stockholders.
Business must make a sound profit.
We must experiment with new ideas.
Research must be carried on, innovative programs developed
and mistakes paid for.
New equipment must be purchased, new facilities provided
and new products launched.
Reserves must be created to provide for adverse times.
When we operate according to these principles,
the stockholders should realize a fair return.

Source: Johnson & Johnson.

Describe the view of business presented in the credo of this health care products business, making use of the different terms used to describe motivations in Chapter 2: *extrinsic* or *intrinsic*; *self-interest, other-interest,* or *common good*; *habit, constraint,* or *choice*; and *high* or *low time discount rate*. (More than one term in each group may apply.)

2.3 | Principal–Agent Problems

There is another problem with the shareholder theory of the firm, besides the fact that it defines the goals and responsibilities of the corporation very narrowly. It assumes that CEOs, managers, and workers will all willingly work in the interest of the shareholders. This creates a problem of motivation. Why would the individuals work in the shareholders' interest if perhaps by doing something different they could get more of what they themselves want? How motivated will an employee really be, going to work every day at a place whose single-minded goal is making more money for "the boss"?

principal–agent theory: a set of ideas about how one economic actor, the "principal," can try to control the actions of another, the "agent," so that the principal's objectives will be achieved

Economists developed **principal–agent theory** as one way of dealing with this question. The "principal" is an economic actor that has an objective it cannot realize on its own. It therefore contracts for help, hiring "agents" that accept compensation in exchange for a promise to serve the principal. Unfortunately for the principal, the agent may not share the principal's objectives. In addition, the performance of the agent probably cannot be observed with certainty. Therefore, the principal must devise strategies to *motivate* the agent.

The stockholders of a corporation, for example, may be considered a "principal," and the elected board of directors their "agent." The stockholders may be primarily interested in getting higher share prices and dividends, but the board of directors can have somewhat divergent interests. For example, in a number of companies that came under fire for unethical conduct in 2001–2004, it was the case that the relatively few stockholders who held places on the board of directors used "inside information" about the poor financial state of the firm to sell their shares at favorable prices. Once the bad news became public knowledge, however, the many "outside" stockholders—the "principals" in whose interests the "agent" board had presumably been acting—were left holding worthless stock.

Principal–agent theory tells us that this problem of motivations arises at many points in the chain of relationships that make up a modern firm. As Table 16.2 shows, the entire bureaucracy of a corporation may be seen as a sequence of principal–agent relationships. The stockholders are principals to the board, which in turn is principal to the top managers, who are principals to lower-level managers, who are principals to workers. Creditors, such as banks and bondholders, are principals with respect to the firm, because they want the firm to pay them back but cannot be sure whether it is actually being managed with that objective in mind.

As developed by economists, principal–agent theory focuses on the strategies available to principals. For example, they can attempt to design contracts in such a way as to create the desired incentives, including gain-sharing arrangements that provide a financial incentive for agents to identify with the goal of firm profitability. At the upper echelons of management, devices such as bonuses and partial payment in company stock options rather than money were designed to serve this purpose, and often they constitute half or more of an executive's compensation. As one moves down the ladder, gain sharing becomes more moderate, but even rank-and-file workers may be offered bonuses tied to performance, employee stock ownership plans (ESOPs), spe-

Table 16.2 | Common Principal–Agent Relationships

Principal	Agent
Lending institutions	Borrowing institutions
Stockholders	Board of directors
Board of directors	Top management
Top management	Lower management
Managers	Workers

Audacious Climb to Success Ended in a Dizzying Plunge

NEWS in context

Not long ago, the Enron Corporation's name was part of the lexicon of corporate and political power. The company's contacts and influence in the White House and Congress bred envy among competitors. Enron was a driving force behind a radical shift in the nation's energy policy, and its fortune seemed guaranteed for years.

But in a matter of weeks, [the name] Enron [was] transformed into shorthand for a corporate scandal . . . that has engulfed company executives and Wall Street accountants, raised questions for politicians and regulators in Washington, and cost employees and other shareholders tens of billions of dollars as the company tumbled into bankruptcy protection.

. . . Competitors and analysts said the ultimate cause of Enron's brutal collapse was a culture of greed and arrogance that bred excessive secrecy. As some of the company's secrets began to be revealed [in fall 2001]—stunning Wall Street with tales of mysterious partnerships that had been used to pretty up Enron's books—the stage was set for disaster.

"The woods were filled with smart people at Enron, but there were really no wise people, or people who could say 'this is enough,' " said John Olson, a veteran energy industry analyst with the investment firm Sanders Morris Harris. "Given an adrenaline-driven culture, given an obsession with 15% a year or better earnings growth, you had this situation develop where Enron was set to metastasize."

The trading of natural gas and electricity used to be tightly regulated. . . . But after oil prices collapsed in the mid-1980s, many users of natural gas switched to cheaper fuel oil, and Enron, led by Mr. Lay [chairman], helped convince federal regulators that pipelines would falter unless they were freed to shop for customers and for the best deals from producers. . . . Flying high after being unshackled from regulation, Enron crashed quickly [in fall 2001] after a series of revelations about its bookkeeping practices—in particular, concealing huge chunks of debt by transferring them into still-murky partnerships.

By reducing the debt on its books, the company looked healthier and its profits looked more robust, even as the results of its trading operations and energy sales were flagging.

Out of a job or still working, many Enron employees—and many retirees—have seen their retirement savings plans, which were overinvested in Enron stock, plummet in value as the stock price has plunged to near nothing.

Lara Leibman, 31, of Houston, who lost her job in governmental affairs at Enron after four and a half years, said today she was wavering between sorrow and anger.

Ms. Leibman said she was particularly troubled by recent disclosures about the destruction of records by the firm's accountants, and retention bonuses of up to $5 million paid to high-ranking executives shortly before the company went bankrupt.

Kurt Eichenwald, *New York Times*, January 13, 2002, **http://www.nytimes.com/2002/01/13/business/13ENRO.html?pagewanted=print**, accessed February 17, 2002. Copyright ©(2002) by The New York Times Co. Reprinted with permission.

Compare the principles followed by the leaders of Enron to those espoused by Johnson & Johnson (see the Economics in the Real World feature on its credo). Can one set of principles be used to describe "corporate behavior" in general?

cial company benefits, or similar inducements. This theory was much touted among economists in the late 1990s, and these programs, in fact, became very popular during this period. As long as the stock market boomed, people were satisfied.

By 2001, however, drawbacks to the strategy of giving managers and workers interests in the stock value of the firm began to become apparent. Rather than giving top executives the proper incentives to run a firm for *long-term* profitability, stock options, as then structured, meant that unscrupulous executives could make windfall wealth from actions taken to promote *short-term* profitability—or even the short-term *appearance* of profitability. After inflating the value of the stock, the top executives could cash in their stock options and retire rich, before the long-term negative consequences of an action or the accounting tricks that gave the illusion of profitability became apparent.

The CEO of Enron Corporation, for example, made $78 million in stock sales from 2000 to 2002, while his company went bankrupt and faced legal scrutiny for shady accounting practices. The CEO of Global Crossing made $273 million in stock sales from 2000 to 2002, before his company went bankrupt and faced investigations from Congress and other authorities. Adelphia, AOL Time Warner, WorldCom, and Tyco were among other companies where exceedingly high compensation for top executives accompanied large losses or bankruptcy. Meanwhile, rank-and-file workers at many such companies found that their retirement funds, invested in company stock, became nearly worthless (see the accompanying News in Context feature). Clearly, something more than spreading around interests in stock value will be necessary to solve the problems of corporate governance, responsibility, and performance.

2.4 | Conflict, Cooperation, and Motivation in Social Organizations

Principal–agent theory assumes that at every level of an organization people act from self-interested, largely financial motivations. The actions of unscrupulous CEOs in the 1990s suggests that this is in some cases a reasonable assumption. However, as discussed in Chapters 2 and 13, people are also often motivated by interests beyond simply financial ones, including pride, loyalty to employers or co-workers, and/or a desire to contribute to society. Once again, it is clear that social capital, in the form of trust and cooperativeness in a common venture, is vital to the running of private enterprises for both personal and social well-being.

For the rest of this section, we will concentrate on the relationship between managers and workers, although some of the concepts apply to other levels of corporate bureaucracy as well. Economist Harvey Leibenstein, writing in the 1960s, coined the term **X-inefficiency** for the situation in which more labor time is being used in a given production process than is actually necessary, usually as a consequence of "slack" in less than perfectly competitive markets. Employers and managers recognize that one of their greatest challenges is to reduce X-inefficiency (whether or not they know this term) by making people *want* to work efficiently.

X-inefficiency: the situation where more labor time is being used in a production process than is actually necessary

Two main theories of management have been discussed by economists: the conflict theory and the cooperation theory. The *conflict theory* identifies the problem as follows. On the one hand, managers generally want workers to work harder and produce more. On the other hand, workers want more control over the conditions and pace of work, and this frequently implies that they want to produce less than management thinks they should. Conflict theory focuses on ways of eliciting work effort through coercion. Workers are motivated via threats of demotion, job loss, and so on.

Yet coercion is only one of the options available to management in its attempts to motivate workers. As we noted in Chapter 13 when we discussed efficiency wage theory and morale, management can motivate workers by cultivating their loyalty and appreciation. People feel better and work harder when they know that they are respected and that their work is meaningful and makes a contribution (however small) to a worthy project. A cooperative style elicits voluntary cooperation with management goals.

The *cooperation theory* of management, which appears to be especially appropriate for highly mechanized, integrated, and continuous-flow processes, stresses the ways in which productivity depends more on the effective interaction of many different people than on the motivation and effort of single individuals. Under some circumstances threats may be effective in maintaining a reasonably high level of individual effort, but they do not work so well in eliciting the imagination and creativity that support teamwork in complex activities. For the cooperative model of management to work, workers must feel they have a stake in the long-run success of the firm.

Where labor relations are already conflict-ridden or antagonistic, threats are management's strongest motivators. In this case productivity suffers when workers' power rises relative to that of management—for example, when they gain more workplace rights or when the general level of unemployment goes down. But in firms that have adopted a cooperative management model, the opposite is true.

The difference between the two management models becomes particularly important when companies face new or intensified competitive pressure. In the quarter-century after

World War II, American corporations faced unusually little international competition. Wartime destruction in Europe and Asia meant that the United States had few economic rivals; leading American companies thus enjoyed a high degree of slack. By the 1970s, however, reconstruction in Europe and Japan had led to renewed global competition, and many American companies began losing markets to lower-cost foreign producers.

How did U.S. business respond to renewed competition? In theory, it would be possible to rely on either model of management. The cooperation model would suggest that firms maintain their existing workforce and wage levels, while retraining workers for new skills, seeking ways to produce higher-quality goods and services, and making the company's operations more efficient and more responsive to market demand. Some economists have referred to this option as taking the "high road" to competitiveness. Most large U.S. companies, unfortunately, took the "low road" based on the conflict model of management: firing many workers, cutting wages, subcontracting work to smaller, low-cost firms, and demanding longer hours and a faster pace of work from those employees who kept their jobs.

In terms of our earlier discussion, each strategy could be seen as emphasizing one aspect of the goal of maintaining profits. To maintain profits, revenues have to be kept high and costs low. The high-road, cooperative management strategy emphasizes developing high revenues, whereas the low-road, conflict-oriented management strategy emphasizes cutting costs.

Not surprisingly, the bias of most economists who study industrial relations is on the side of the revenue-emphasizing approach. This option appears to contribute more to the economic growth and development of the entire economy than the cost-cutting alternative, and it promises greater social equality and cohesion. Nonetheless, it is not possible simply to command an emphasis on revenues in each and every situation. In the end, the path taken by firms will depend on a wide variety of factors, ranging from financial and labor market institutions and the position of the country within the world economy to the educational and social progress of the population. In a sense, the gradual shift of employers in the direction of a more humane utilization of their workers' capacities is at the core of economic development.

Discussion Questions

1. Do you think corporations should be *socially responsible*? What does that term mean to you? What theory and evidence can you use to support your view?

2. Can you think of any specific "principal–agent" problems that have arisen in your own life, outside of work? (For example, are there things your parents or teachers want you to do, or things you want your children to do, that put you in a principal–agent situation?) To what extent could the situation be resolved by structuring incentives? To what extent might the principal have to rely on other factors, such as norms of honesty and loyalty, to make sure that a desired action is undertaken?

3 | The Evolution of Big Business

As we discussed in Chapter 3, the original Industrial Revolution was about increasing the productivity of labor through technology and capital inputs and the reorganization of workers. Some people use the term *second industrial revolution* to describe a process beginning in the late 19th century, in which discoveries in science and engineering were used to rationalize a vastly increased flow-through of materials and energy, making possible the creation of new industrial forms—giant corporations. The trend toward increasingly large firms has continued to the present; we have seen that nearly 50% of U.S. employees work at firms with 500 or more employees and that some of these firms can be huge. Why has the modern economic landscape become so dominated by firms of great size?

One reason is that combining many activities into a single large organization may be *more efficient* than having small, autonomous organizations do them. As suggested by Herbert Simon's analogy at the beginning of this chapter, one way of understanding the existence of a firm is to see it as a small island of relatively cooperative organization within a surrounding sea of market competition. Within a firm, individuals tend to be organized not by market transactions but by administration, custom, or consent—around the (at least partially) shared goal of advancing the firm's interest. Thus a large firm can be seen as a way of transforming a great number of relationships from arm's-length market exchange to more complex and intertwined forms.

3.1 | Technology and Economies of Scale

Economies of scale arise when, as discussed in Chapter 7, large enterprises are able to operate at a lower cost per unit of output. When economists talk about economies of scale, they have in mind cost savings that arise from producing some single good or service in larger "batches," using larger quantities of all inputs.

The possibility of a new type of business enterprise was spurred, in the second industrial revolution, by the development of technological breakthroughs in communication and transportation, such as telegraphs, railroads, and steamships, which made it possible to keep productive inputs flowing into any given plant, and products flowing out, at a scale and speed never before imagined. The new methods of transportation made possible the rapid physical movement of vast quantities of material; the new communications technologies made it possible to coordinate these flows, even when they involved suppliers, workers, and distributors operating in places that were widely distant from one another.

One implication was a dramatic size advantage: Corporations large enough to make the investments necessary to utilize the new technologies could produce at a lower cost per unit of output than could their smaller competitors. The minimum efficient scale (see Chapter 7) became very large in many industries. In some industries the minimum efficient scale became so large that a small number of plants could meet the existing national, or even global, demand. An outstanding 19th-century example was the petroleum industry's becoming dominated by the Standard Oil Trust, which concentrated close to a quarter of the world's kerosene production in three refineries in the United States. Up until the early 1880s, a similar feat of concentration was achieved in Europe by the Nobel Brothers Petroleum Production Company, based in Azerbaijan.[7]

During the late 1880s and 1890s, new technologies involving a fairly large minimum efficient scale were discovered and introduced in a variety of other industries, such as chemicals, steel, and aluminum. Each of these industries became dominated by a small number of firms that had the organizational capability to coordinate a massive volume of throughput. In many cases the first company to build a plant of minimum efficient scale and to recruit the essential management team remained the leader in its field for decades or longer. As we have already discussed for the more contemporary case of Microsoft Corporation, such companies had achieved "first-mover" advantage.

Any challenger to an established "first mover" in an industry had to make massive investments to compete in plant size, distribution system, and managerial capacity. The first movers had a head start not only in these functional capacities but also in systems of purchasing, research, and finance, not to mention massive advertising campaigns that ensured brand-name recognition. These advantages all created formidable barriers to entry, making it very difficult for new firms to enter these markets.

horizontal integration: the expansion of a firm achieved through growth or merger while it continues to make the same or similar products

Economies of scale can thus be a reason for firms either to expand into making more of the same or similar products or to merge with other companies that make the same or similar products. Economists call this **horizontal integration**.

---

[7] The Nobel Prizes in physics, physiology, chemistry, literature, and peace were funded by Alfred Nobel's interest in this oil company, as well as by his wealth acquired from the development of dynamite and other explosives.

3.2 | Diverse Products: Economies of Scope

Sometimes firms find that they can reduce their average costs by producing a number of *different* products. In a city with cold winters and warm summers, for example, it can make sense for a bike shop to expand to sell skis as well. Rather than paying for under-utilized retail space during the off-season for bikes, the shop can diversify into two product lines and stay busy all year.

economies of scope: cost savings achieved when a firm increases the range of products it makes

Economists call the case where firms can achieve cost savings by selling a range of products **economies of scope**. Such economies may arise from an underutilized capacity, such as in the example of the bike/ski shop. In other cases, a certain physical plant and technology can be flexibly varied to produce distinct lines of goods. For example, a factory may be able to produce a variety of consumer electronic goods. Economies of scope may also arise in the use of distribution or marketing networks. A company with a well-known website, for example, might capitalize on it by expanding into providing a greater variety of information and services.

3.3 | Avoiding Transaction Costs

transaction cost economies: savings on the costs associated with market transactions, which may lead to organizing production within a single enterprise

Transaction cost economies are size advantages that occur when the transfer of goods and services can be carried out more efficiently among operating units within a single firm than is possible through the open market. That is, some operations may cost less when done within the "green areas" than when done over the "red lines."

There are many situations in which organization of a production process through the market—with its associated problems of uncertainty due to shifts in supply, demand, and prices, and the associated transaction costs of gathering information, negotiating contracts, and then enforcing them—is simply too clumsy and expensive for coordinating a complex process.

Take the production of an automobile, for instance. Automobiles are assembled from many parts, such as engines, transmissions, frames, and so on, and these are in turn assembled from many subparts, all the way down to the individual bolt or weld or pin. In theory, every one of these components could be produced separately by independent firms consisting of single individuals or small groups of individuals, and then sold to other small firms that would perform later stages of assembly, until the major components themselves were bought by the firm that put the finished automobile together.

In this imaginary world, the forces of supply and demand would determine the exact specification of each part and its price: The bits and pieces of the car would be manufactured and shipped in response to market demand, just as final products are. If the design changed at any level of the process, each level below would experience the new set of demands as a change in its market and would respond accordingly. At the level of final assembly, on the other hand, the relative costs of different designs would be conveyed by the prices that would have to be paid to suppliers—prices set in a free market. In such a world we would see no Ford, no VW, no Toyota—just small companies that purchase large prefabricated components, perform a few operations on them, and (perhaps) attach a nameplate.

vertical integration: expansion of a firm achieved by adding new products to its output, where the new products are related to the old but represent different stages of production

This is not the world we live in. Goods such as automobiles are produced by large, **vertically integrated** manufacturers. Although they contract out some parts of the production process, most of their components are specified, produced, and shipped in-house without any role whatever for the market. (Vertical integration is the combining of different stages of the production process, from the extraction of raw materials to final sale.)

Transaction costs are often related to issues of trust and social capital. Highly complicated market transactions and transactions in which either the buyer or the seller is in a position to take advantage of the other can be very costly to monitor and enforce. Consider the auto company again. It must have a steady supply of engines whose design and construction will be tailored to the finished product. Engines are extremely complex pieces of equipment; if it buys them from an outsider, how can the automobile firm know that its supplier is not cutting corners? And once it has made an agreement, it is potentially at the mercy of its supplier: Getting the cars off the assembly line requires a continuous flow of engines. How can the firm be sure it will not be subject to delays or demands for renegotiation when "new" circumstances arise? One solution is to avoid going through the market altogether by producing the engines within the same company that does the assembly. That is to say, it is easier to check up on people if you are their boss.

The fundamental insight of the transaction cost approach is that the market is only one route available to business firms; they can also acquire the capacity to supply themselves. Which route they take will depend in part on the extent of the transaction costs in each situation. Where the costs are low, firms will be likely to go with the market; where the costs of market supply and coordination are too high, activities will be conducted within the firm. As we will see later in this chapter, supply relations are becoming a major issue in the evolving structures of corporations and the global markets in which they operate.

3.4 | Conglomerates

conglomerates: combinations of unrelated businesses

Beginning in the 1960s, firms increasingly began to merge with, acquire, or otherwise combine with other businesses in largely unrelated industries. Combinations of unrelated businesses are called **conglomerates**. General Electric, for example, is a company that has grown over the years; it now includes subsidiaries involved in the production of goods and services as diverse as aircraft engines, home appliances, nuclear reactors, plastics, and financial services.

In some cases these combinations reflect economies of scope. A conglomerate, for example, may be able to centralize research and development to the extent of creating what are in effect miniature research universities, whose scientists can benefit from the synergies of collegiality. When it is possible to shift production from one product line to another, the conglomerate structure provides a way of riding out temporary fluctuations in demand.

But other explanations have also been offered. Businesses may find it advantageous to form conglomerates because of treatment in tax laws—for example, when the losses of one subsidiary can be written off against the profits of another. In a situation of imperfect capital markets, the conglomerate possesses an especially important financial advantage: When capital to support the development of a new product is not available commercially, profits from one division of a conglomerate can subsidize development in another. Conglomerates may arise from the desire of top managers to rule a larger empire or from the emergence of what has become a new form of business: the buying and selling of corporations. Over the longer term, however, many conglomerates have proved to be unstable, collapsing after a time, at least partly because of the difficulties of managing a collection of unrelated activities.

Attempts to estimate the power of conglomerates must rely on different kinds of measures from the calculation of economic concentration (see Chapter 12) used to measure the market power of older, more focused firms. It would be foolish to take a conglomerate's share in any one market as representative of its real power in that market. However small this share, the enterprise is backed by financial reserves derived from its other operations. Obviously, a huge conglomerate with only a tenth of the market in one of its many activities is far stronger than a firm with the same share of that one market and nothing else.

Discussion Questions

1. What distinguishes economies of scale from economies of scope and transaction cost economies? Can you think of an additional example of each?

2. What recent mergers have you seen talked about in the news media? Would you characterize these as vertical mergers, horizontal mergers, or the formation of conglomerates?

4 | Is Bigger Always Better?

The giant corporation is central to the business sphere today, but it is not yet universal. Small firms can still be found in many areas, such as retail trade and services and some parts of agriculture and manufacturing. As the power of big business continues to grow, will small firms survive? Or will every facet of the market economy come to be dominated by a few hundred huge corporations? In this section we examine the reasons why small businesses are likely to survive, in spite of—or in some cases, because of—the strength of big business.

4.1 | Small Firms and Efficiency

There are industries in which little or no economic efficiency is added by increasing the scale of production. Economies of scale are of little significance in most personal services, repair services, and food service operations. Also, after some point of expansion in any business, *dis*economies of scale may set in as a consequence of problems that arise in managing a large organization. The maximum efficient scale for firms may vary by industry. In industries with few economies related to bigness, or with particular problems with effective management, firms will not grow forever. Firms may be small and independent, or may be independent but affiliated with a larger organization.

franchise: a legal agreement between an independent enterprise and a larger corporation in which the enterprise agrees to abide by standards set by the larger corporation and to compensate it for use of its brand name and other services

In the case of **franchise** operations, some of the benefits that come from "big" brand-name recognition are combined with the benefits of small-scale ownership and management. The franchise grantor (for example, McDonald's Corporation) gives small franchise operators (that is, local investors) permission to use its brand name and offers support in areas like supplies and marketing. In return, the local operator pays a fee and agrees to a number of contract terms. Although the decision-making power of the franchise operator may be very limited by the terms of the contract, the franchise is legally an independent enterprise, and after payment of expenses including the franchise fee, any profits—or losses—belong to its owner/operator. Many of the consumer-oriented businesses you see all over U.S. cities and towns—Dunkin' Donuts shops, McDonald's restaurants, Jazzercise fitness centers, AAMCO transmission repair centers, Exxon Mobil gas stations, to name a few—are franchise operations. These businesses are often oligopolistic at the national or international level but are more like monopolistic competitors at the local level, to use the vocabulary of Chapter 12.

Even within manufacturing there is a wide range in technical economies of scale. In contrast to petroleum refining, in which there are overwhelming advantages to being large, there is relatively little advantage to large-scale production in clothing assembly, for example. Brand names are increasingly important, but even the most famous lines of clothing are actually produced in small enterprises under extremely competitive conditions. Clothing assembly is often done in small shops or may even be subcontracted out to people (often women, and often immigrants from or residents of poorer countries) who do the work in their own homes.

The advantages of recognized brand names are likewise less important in some areas than in others. In the case of most services and in much of retail trade, health, and education, consumers may make judgments as much on the basis of personal knowledge of the supplier as on recognition of a brand name. Customers may also react negatively to the standards of uniformity imposed on corporate-owned and franchised products, preferring the more original and idiosyncratic products of truly independent firms. This enables successful small-scale enterprises to develop a local reputation and to thrive—in part *because* they are not affiliated with a larger firm.

Even in the most market-dominated economies, major corporations have established themselves in bottled beverages (Coke and Pepsi), in fast food (McDonald's and its other franchised competitors), and in some mid-priced restaurants (Red Lobster,

Small businesses remain a part of the American scene. Ken Ballanger, shown in this photo, owns Native American Products in Minneapolis, Minnesota. The sale of items like these three-dimensional beaded pieces by an Ojibwe artist keeps his business profitable. People often prefer to buy certain goods and services, such as unique artwork or expensive meals, from small companies whose goods are not mass-produced and uniform.

Olive Garden, Applebee's, and the like), but have had less success in setting up chains of expensive restaurants. Why should low-priced restaurants become an oligopoly, but not more expensive ones? In the former, customers may want immediate information about the type and quality of food; in the latter, they may be more willing to pay for a unique cuisine or ambience that cannot be mass-produced but is known through local reputation.

4.2 | How Big Firms Depend on Small Ones

In addition to areas where the conditions are not right for big business to enter, there are also cases where big business relies on the continued existence of smaller firms. One form of this dependence of the big on the small is sometimes referred to as an "oligopoly with a competitive fringe." The least-cost production methods in capital-intensive industries may require large fixed costs. If a company can maintain a high level of output, these fixed costs can be spread over many units of production, but if output is reduced when sales fluctuate, then unit costs rise rapidly. One strategy for maintaining steady sales is to capture the stable core of market demand, while leaving smaller firms to produce for the fluctuating remainder of the market; these firms will be less profitable, because they must swallow the losses that result from the occasional reductions in buyer demand.

This point is vividly illustrated in the history of the du Pont family enterprises. The du Ponts became one of the biggest American manufacturers of chemicals and many related products. In the words of a 1903 letter to one of the young du Pont cousins from an associate (who was working with him on the reorganization of a major part of the explosives industry in the United States):

If we could by any measure buy out all competition and have an absolute monopoly in the field, it would not pay us. The essence of manufacture is steady and full product. The demand of the country for [gun]powder is variable. If we owned all therefore when slack times came we would have to curtail product to the extent of diminished demands. If on the other hand we control[led] only 60% of it all and made the 60% cheaper than others, when slack times came we could still keep our capital employed to the full and our product to the maximum by taking from the other 40% what was needed for this purpose.[8]

This advice was followed, and it could be used to describe a good deal of the continuing activities, and the success, of the Du Pont Corporation.

dual-sector theory: the theory that economies may include primary sectors containing firms with market power side by side with competitive secondary sectors

Some economists have pointed to dualism as an important characteristic of developed market economies. The theory of **dual sectors** describes markets as divided into primary and secondary sectors. The primary sector is composed of (often large) firms that have succeeded in achieving enough shelter from competition to generate substantial surplus revenues. The secondary sector consists of (usually small) firms that cannot shelter themselves from the market but, rather, are forced to compete on terms that leave them with little if any capacity to generate surplus.

Other ways in which big firms depend on small ones will be discussed in the next section, when we address issues of globalization.

4.3 | Too Many Mergers?

Not all of the variation we see in firm size is related to economic efficiencies. Firms may grow beyond the size at which they are most efficient—or the size at which they can be reasonably managed at all.

Corporate CEOs, in particular, may pursue goals that do more for their own egos than for their firm's profitability. For example, expanding the business too fast or building unneeded large new facilities may satisfy the CEO's desire to manage a very big company or to create a tangible monument to his leadership (and we do mean "his"—of the 1000 CEOs of the largest U.S. companies in 2002, only 11 were women). Such practices can be gratifying to the man at the top, even when slower growth and a more cautious approach to new construction would lead to a more efficient, profitable, and sustainable enterprise. Firms may be expanded beyond maximum efficient size, simply because sheer size makes a corporation, and its leader, more visible. Chief executives of larger companies can also gain power in other ways, particularly in the political realm, as they make campaign contributions to, and advise, government leaders.

In the 1990s the U.S. experienced a wave of merger activity among larger corporations. Big oil companies Exxon and Mobil merged to become Exxon Mobil; U.S. automaker Chrysler merged with German automaker Daimler-Benz to become Daimler-Chrysler. These mergers, as well as other notable ones within the fields of banking, telecommunications, and entertainment, were horizontal. Other mergers crossed fields, making conglomerates. The merger of America Online with Time Warner created a mega-corporation involved in the Internet, mass media, and entertainment.

Early in the present century it became clear that a number of previous mergers did not have a sound economic rationale behind them. Tyco International Ltd. had become a mega-conglomerate, producing electronics, security and fire protection systems, medical equipment, and fiber-optic cable. During the 2001–2002 period, however, the value of Tyco stock plunged by $80 billion, and analysts suggested that the various parts of the conglomerate were worth more separately than together. Likewise, the AOL Time Warner merger, announced with great fanfare in January 2001, was in severe straits by

---

[8] A. J. Moxham to T. C. du Pont, 1903, cited in *Scale and Scope: The Dynamics of Industrial Capitalism,* Alfred D. Chandler, Jr. (Cambridge, MA: Harvard University Press, 1990).

July 2002. The difference in products and in corporate cultures at the two original firms made working together difficult, and stock values fell 70% in the course of a year.[9]

Discussion Questions

1. Some food service businesses, such as McDonald's and Dunkin' Donuts, are franchises. Others, such as Olive Garden and Red Lobster locations, are wholly owned by their parent corporation. And some—Applebee's is an example—may be either franchises or company-owned. Suppose you were in a position to start a nationwide chain of restaurants spread out over many different states and cities. Can you think of some advantages of granting ownership to franchise operators? Can you think of some advantages of managing all the restaurants directly?

2. Many consumer services that used to be provided by small "mom and pop" businesses, where both ownership and control were strictly local, are now largely provided by corporations, either directly or through franchise operations. Do you think this change is largely positive or largely negative? What are some of the well-being costs? What are some of the well-being benefits? Be sure to consider the interests of people as owners, workers, and citizens, as well as consumers.

---

5 | Globalization and the Information Revolution

By the last decades of the 20th century, some observers were suggesting that we have moved into yet another phase, a "third industrial revolution," in which new information technologies are leading to yet more changes in industrial structure, including businesses and markets that are increasingly global, along with ever more complex relationships among size, market power, and competition.

globalization: an increase in many kinds of global or transnational interactions and effects, including companies that span the globe; transactions in global retail markets and markets for capital, labor, and other inputs; and the trans-boundary flow of ideas, cultural influences, and environmental impacts

Globalization is an increase in many kinds of global or transnational interactions and effects. These include companies that span the globe; transactions in global retail markets and markets for capital, labor, and other inputs; and the flow of ideas, cultural influences, and environmental impacts across national boundaries.

Because we are still in the midst (or perhaps in the very early stages) of this latest set of changes, it is not yet fully understood. A key to understanding the 21st-century world of globalization is the ongoing contest between forces fostering competition and forces working against it. As has been the case throughout the 250-year span of the three industrial revolutions, sometimes one side seems to be winning, sometimes the other. Anti-competitive forces sometimes appear at the top of the economic pyramid, among owners of large productive resources who would like to be able to maximize their profits without having to meet competitors' lower prices. They may also arise from lower down, among workers and managers who recognize that the impetus of competition can push firms to seek ways to reduce their employees' compensation and to exact greater effort from them. As we will see below, a new trend in the current era is that in some areas of the globalized economy, the forces of economic power appear to be allied with competition, against the wishes of workers.

5.1 | Multinational Corporations

multinational corporation: a corporation that owns and operates subsidiaries in more than one country

In the early period of the growth of big corporations, problems in long-distance communication made it difficult to manage companies that were widely dispersed geographically. By the mid-1980s, however, **multinational corporations** were prominent features of the business sphere of economic activity. These are corporations that own and operate subsidiaries in more than one—and often in many—countries.

---

[9] See Daniel Eisenberg, "And Then There Were Two," *Time*, July 29, 2002. (*Time* is, of course, a division of AOL Time Warner.)

Today the world's largest corporations are generally multinationals. General Motors, for example, has operations in 64 countries.

Businesses may create or acquire foreign subsidiaries as a way of entering new markets or of tapping into cheaper resources. Sometimes there are accounting or tax advantages to having goods that are transported across national boundaries recorded as within-firm transactions, rather than as market transactions. For example, firms may manipulate **transfer prices**—prices that subsidiaries within the firm charge to each other—in such a way that most of a multinational's profits appear to be earned in countries with low tax rates and little profit appears on the books of divisions in countries with high tax rates. Businesses can also attain monopoly power by controlling the production of a particular good or service across many countries. Large multinational corporations can wield considerable political as well as economic power.

transfer prices: the prices that subsidiaries of a multinational corporation use when making transactions with each other

5.2 | Global Markets

Firms may also become "global" even if they do not actually grow by expanding their numbers of overseas subsidiaries. Many have come to sell their products, or to buy more of their inputs, on international markets. Computerized marketing and inventory systems have facilitated this expansion of markets.

The giant retailer Wal-Mart, for example, has been a leader both in using new information technologies to keep track of inventories and in looking to global markets for the wholesale goods that it purchases. In 1995 Wal-Mart said that imports accounted for no more than 6% of its products. More recently, although the company has refused to provide a breakdown on the national origins of what it sells, various analysts have suggested that as much as 50% to 60% of the merchandise in the company's U.S. stores is imported. Some even believe that this number might be as high as 85%.

5.3 | Subcontracting and Offshoring

In addition to buying goods from companies located around the globe, many businesses have actually moved their own production lines—or large parts of them—from high-wage countries to lower-wage countries. A firm is said to **subcontract** (or **outsource**) when it hires another firm to produce particular products or services for it, in accordance with the firm's exact specifications. Subcontracting differs from simply buying inputs from an independent firm on an open market, because the production is customized to the particular buyer and produced under contract.

subcontracting (or **outsourcing**): hiring another firm to provide services or goods made to one's own firm's specifications

Subcontracting began as a phenomenon that went on *within* countries. The use of elaborate networks of smaller suppliers was especially important to the success of Japanese manufacturers from about 1950 to 1990. One important reason for subcontracting is to keep labor costs down. Large Japanese firms traditionally paid generous wages and guaranteed lifetime employment to most of their male employees. Often the dominant firm in a network can force its subcontractors to compete with each other and lower their prices. Indirectly, therefore, it can force the subcontractors to offer much less attractive wages and working conditions than the dominant firm's workers enjoy. In the 1990s, during Japan's long economic slump, many big companies shifted more work to their subcontractors, thereby lowering their average labor costs without changing the terms of employment for their own workers.

Similar uses of low-wage suppliers and subcontractors can now be seen in corporations in many countries. A unionized American corporation may fear that if it hires its own custodians to clean its buildings, it will have to pay them union wages. But if it hires an outside, nonunionized custodial service—and demands that custodial service companies compete to offer the lowest possible price—then the corporation can reduce the cost of having its buildings cleaned without changing the union wages paid to its regular employees.

With the increasing ease of communicating between countries, American, Japanese, and European firms have come increasingly to put their own brand names on products manufactured abroad in lower-wage countries, doing little or no actual production in the high-wage home country. When entire production divisions—and the jobs they entail—are shifted abroad, the process is called **offshoring**.

offshoring: the shifting of production units to foreign locations

Initially, it was assembly-line work that was offshored. The best-known brand of American footwear, Nike, has no production facilities in the United States; all of its athletic shoes are manufactured in low-wage, developing countries. If you check your tags, you will probably find that most of your clothes were stitched overseas. More recently, white-collar work in computer programming, data entry, and even telephone customer service has been offshored by U.S. firms to educated, English-speaking workers in India.

5.4 | Global Competition and Well-Being

Globalization has added new dimensions to discussions of competition, market power, and well-being. "Perfect competition," in the traditional economists' view, is desirable because it is expected to promote efficiency. The traditional models of market power, discussed in Chapter 12, focused on how market power can enable *sellers* of goods and services to raise their prices above marginal cost, causing economic inefficiency and occasioning welfare losses to consumers. As we briefly discussed in Chapter 13, *buyers* of goods and services can also have market power, enabling them to pay lower prices for inputs, and, in particular, to pay workers less than their marginal revenue product. What is clear when we look at many contemporary markets, however, is that active—even aggressive—competition is increasingly being combined with oligopolistic market power in complex ways and that efficiency is only one of the many goals we need to take into account if we are to understand the complex effects of this trend.

The activities of Wal-Mart, for example, have attracted much attention both because of the firm's unprecedented scale of operations and because of the way the "Wal-Mart model" has affected numerous countries and markets. This general-merchandise retailer's tremendous growth has been fueled by a strategy of offering absolutely the "best deal possible" to the consumer. Wal-Mart is able to offer customers lower prices than competing retailers by keeping both its costs and its profit margin low. Profits come from selling in large volume. The widespread benefits of lower prices are not felt only in the United States; Wal-Mart is already the largest retailer in both Mexico and Canada, and it is aiming for major expansion in China.

Economies of scale and innovations in technology and marketing explain a part of Wal-Mart's ability to keep costs low. The company has been an innovator in the use of "third industrial revolution" information technologies, from wireless bar code scanning and electronic data exchange to tracking trends in demand for its products and in the supply of its inputs. And it is not only inside Wal-Mart's own stores that consumers benefit from lower prices. The Wal-Mart business model has pressed competitors and suppliers alike to strive for greater efficiency. In fact, some analysts believe that total U.S. productivity growth in recent decades received a significant boost from Wal-Mart's contributions to efficiency—both in its own operations and among other firms emulating, competing with, or selling to Wal-Mart.[10]

The general-merchandise retail market could hardly be called "perfectly competitive" in the traditional sense: Oligopoly would seem to be indicated by the fact that Wal-Mart has achieved about a 30% market share in the United States. Indeed, the normal economic categories used in analyzing firms are difficult to apply here. Wal-Mart's low prices and high volume essentially *set* the "market price" for retail goods in many local communities, and thus Wal-Mart is not a "price-taker" as portrayed in the perfectly competitive model. Yet it passes on cost savings to consumers rather than using its market power to raise prices or increase its profit margins, as predicted by models of

---

[10] "U.S. Productivity Growth, 1995-2000," Washington DC: McKinsey Global Institute, October 2001.

Subcontracting and offshoring are especially prevalent in the apparel and footwear industries. Nike athletic shoes and equipment, for example, are not produced by the company itself but by subcontracting factories in more than 50 countries. Most workers, as in this Nike production line in Vietnam, are young women. In the late 1990s, advocacy groups exposed the use of child labor in Nike production lines; Nike admitted the problem in 2001, and promised to better monitor its subcontractors. Some suggest, though, that additional independent monitoring is necessary.

monopoly or oligopoly. Traditional theories of monopoly and oligopoly predict that a firm with the ability to set prices will inevitably hurt consumers by charging more. That is clearly not the case with Wal-Mart. Instead, the negative impacts most commonly cited with respect to this remarkable firm generally involve its effects on its competitors, its suppliers, and its workers.

Many economic news reports have told of other retail firms going out of business because they could not lower their costs enough to meet Wal-Mart's prices. Using only an efficiency criterion, this may seem to be a good thing, if less efficient retailers are being replaced by a more efficient one. Greater efficiency, however, is not the only explanation for Wal-Mart's low costs. Another way that Wal-Mart keeps costs low is by aggressively pressuring its suppliers to lower prices, by searching the globe to find the least-cost producers of the goods it buys, and by carefully watching its own labor costs. It is not a "price-taker" in the markets in which it buys but, instead, actively haggles with potential suppliers for continual cost and quality improvements. Because it buys in such large volume—it has been estimated that Wal-Mart bought 10% of all imports from China in 2002—suppliers often have little choice but to agree. The result is, in many cases, increasing use of subcontracting and offshoring by the manufacturers that supply Wal-Mart with goods.

Producers in low-wage countries such as Honduras and Bangladesh often find themselves competing for Wal-Mart-related business with producers in even lower-wage countries such as Vietnam and China. Standards governing health and safety, work hours, breaks, ventilation, crowding, and the like are also generally lower in such countries, leading to working conditions that many people would judge to be inhumane.[11] Meanwhile, the

---

[11] Nancy Cleeland, Evelyn Iritani and Tyler Marshall, "Scouring the Globe to Give Shoppers an $8.63 Polo Shirt," *Los Angeles Times*, November 24, 2003.

opening of a Wal-Mart store in a community in the United States does not usually mean the creation of more employment. Because consumers have only so much money to spend, Wal-Mart's hiring is often roughly balanced by the loss of jobs at other retail stores that have to close down. The new jobs at Wal-Mart are often lower-paid than those of its defeated competitors. One reason why Wal-Mart has been able to maintain lower compensation is that it has effectively resisted attempts by its workers to unionize.[12]

Wal-Mart is not alone in looking for the cheapest inputs: Many producers in wealthy countries seek to buy raw materials and manufactured inputs at the lowest cost in a wide variety of mostly poor countries. Looking only at efficiency issues, it may seem that these companies are simply following the principle of comparative advantage (Chapter 9). Consumers win when they are able to buy goods very cheaply. Manufacturing workers in poor countries gain if the work opportunities provided are better than the alternatives available to them. On the other hand, when the input being bargained over is human labor, more than just a line on a cost tabulation is at stake. Living wages and working conditions consistent with human dignity are part of any definition of human well-being, whether the worker lives in a poor country or a wealthy one.

The Wal-Mart model of competition has been described by Robert Reich, U.S. secretary of labor under President Clinton, as creating a situation in which people have "split brains." The split is between our working selves and our consuming selves. When we act as consumers, he says, "the half of our brain that wants the best deal prevails."[13] However, the workers—not only those at Wal-Mart, but also the employees of competing firms or suppliers whose wages have been forced down—end up with less money to spend. Can the lower prices make up for the lower wages and, in some cases, degraded working conditions? Because people's overall well-being depends on both their well-being as consumers and their well-being as workers, new trends in corporate concentration and global competition merit careful analysis.

Discussion Questions

1. Do you think that corporations always experience a conflict between social responsibility and profitability? How does the global nature of much of contemporary commerce affect the constraints that firms face in trying to meet their various responsibilities?

2. In what sense is a company such as Wal-Mart an oligopoly or oligopsony, or engaged in monopolistic competition? To what extent is it a "competitive" firm?

Review Questions

1. Describe the four legal forms of business organization.

2. Which countries host the world's largest corporations, and how big are these companies?

3. How is the "stakeholder theory" of the corporation different from the "shareholder theory" of the corporation?

4. What is principal–agent theory?

5. Describe two main models of management.

6. Describe the three kinds of "economies" that may make bigger operations more efficient.

7. List some reasons why some businesses may stay small.

8. Describe three ways in which businesses can become "globalized."

---

[12] Wendy Zellner, "How Wal-Mart Keeps Unions at Bay," *Business Week*, October 28, 2002.

[13] Abigail Goldman and Nancy Cleeland, "The Wal-Mart Effect: An Empire Built on Bargains Remakes the Working World," *Los Angeles Times*, November 23, 2003, home edition, pt. A, p. 1. The Times Mirror Company.

Exercises

1. Most large corporations and cooperatives now have their own Web pages. There are also many financial Web pages that offer investment advice concerning corporations whose shares are traded on the stock market and Web pages associated with financial publications (such as *Fortune* magazine) that also give information on individual companies. This information may include types of products made, the number of employees, the countries the organization operates in, its current share price, the value of its assets, whether it franchises, and so on. Using Web sources (carefully documented), write a one-page essay describing a for-profit business of your choice. (To start, you might go to **www.google.com** and type in the name of a business that has been in the news or that you are otherwise familiar with or have an interest in.)

2. Match each concept in Column A with a definition or example in Column B.

   Column A

   a. cooperative
   b. horizontal integration
   c. vertical integration
   d. transaction cost economies
   e. stakeholders
   f. conglomerate
   g. franchise
   h. conflict theory of management
   i. gain-sharing arrangement
   j. "second industrial revolution"

   Column B

   i. eliminating the cost of looking for a supplier and writing a contract
   ii. the rise of corporations
   iii. a restaurant that pays for the right to use a brand name
   iv. workers are motivated by threats
   v. a credit union
   vi. stock options for CEOs
   vii. the merger of an ice cream restaurant with a dairy farm
   viii. people in the community where a corporation is located
   ix. the merger of a restaurant with a sewage-processing facility
   x. the merger of two restaurants

3. Using a newspaper, a newsmagazine, or a World Wide Web source, find a business news story dealing with an issue addressed in this chapter (for example, merger, bankruptcy, debates about the interests of shareholders or other constituents, fraud, conflict versus cooperation approaches to management, subcontracting, or franchising). Cut out or print the article, and write a short paragraph describing in ordinary language what the article is saying. Also note any parts of the article that you don't understand.

4. Answer the following questions, with reference to Figures 16.1 and 16.2.
   a. What percentage of employers had between 20 and 99 employees?
   b. What percentage of workers worked for employers with between 20 and 99 employees?
   c. *How many* employers had 20 or more employees?
   d. *How many* workers were in firms with 20 or more employees?

5. Traditional models of market power, as discussed in Chapter 12, focus on firms that sell identical or differentiated goods, but always within one market. How does the existence of conglomerates and multinational corporations complicate this discussion of market power? How can operating in various industries or in various countries give a corporation additional advantages?

The Public Purpose Sphere: Governments and Nonprofits

Chapter 17

During your lifetime, chances are you have attended one or more schools, received mail through the postal service, and visited a park or museum. You may also have taken a standardized exam, attended a religious service, and visited a licensed physician. In all of these activities, and many others, you have been interacting with the public purpose sphere. We are all intimately familiar with some activities of the public purpose sphere, though we may not have studied about it in economic terms.

In the year 2000, the U.S. federal government employed 2.9 million civilian workers, including hundreds of thousands of workers in the postal service alone. In addition, the federal government employed 1.4 million people in military service. The 50 state governments employed, together, more than the federal government: 4.9 million workers, over 3 million of whom were involved in higher education. The 11 million people employed by local governments included 4 million public school teachers. The 1997 Economic Census found that 8.9 million people in the United States were employed by tax-exempt service enterprises, over two-thirds in non-profit health care.

1 | Public Purpose Organizations and Their Functions

As we discussed in Chapter 1, public purpose organizations are established for some public purpose beyond individual or family self-interest and do not operate with the goal of making a profit. This group includes formal domestic non-profit organizations; local, state, and national governments; and international non-profit or quasi-governmental organizations. It thus includes all organizations *other than* informal (unincorporated) groups of neighbors, family, friends (discussed in Chapter 15), on the one hand, and for-profit businesses (discussed in Chapter 16), on the other.

Public purpose organizations form to provide social coordination beyond that which can be accomplished *within* other organizations such as families, informal community groups, or individual businesses or *among* such actors by way of custom or unregulated market exchange. In this chapter, we take a closer look at these organizations' functions, types, and history and at theories about how they behave.

We can break down the economic functions of public purpose organizations into two general categories: *regulation*, where the public purpose organization sets rules or standards for the actions of other economic entities, and *direct provision*, where a public purpose organization itself takes on economic activities.

1.1 | The Regulatory Function

regulation: the setting of standards or enactment of laws to govern behavior

One very basic function of public purpose organizations is to **regulate** economic activities—that is, to set the standards and "rules of the game" by which other economic actors will "play." In Chapter 9, for example, we noted that property rights are fundamental to economic systems; in Chapter 3 we noted how enforceable contracts and good flows of information are important in facilitating market exchange; in Chapter 15 we noted how obligations about who is responsible for care of children and the elderly shape activities in the core sphere. Public purpose organizations that promote, legislate, or enforce property rights, rules about contracts or disclosure of information, laws, or norms of obligation; promulgate standards; and/or perform other coordinating functions thus create the legal and social infrastructure for economic activity.

Many people think of regulation entirely in terms of government regulation, and it is true that the government sets many rules and standards with which other economic actors are legally obligated to comply. However, many non-profit groups participate in regulating economic activity, particularly in the area of standard setting.

For example, you have probably taken a standardized exam such as the AP, SAT I or II, GRE, GMAT, or TOEFL. These are all developed and administered by the Educational Testing Service, which is a large private non-profit organization. Although we might not commonly think of such privately provided standards as "regulation," the standards implicit in these exams do, in fact, influence what is taught by institutions, if they wish their students to be well prepared for taking the exams. The impact of such nongovernmental standards, then, may not be much different from the effect of standards formally adopted and enforced by a government authority, such as a school board.

open-access resources: resources for which it would be difficult to exclude anyone from benefiting. Their use by one person may diminish the amount or quality available to another, at least beyond some point.

One situation where regulation is often necessary is the case of **open-access resources**. These are resources that, like public goods (see Chapter 1), are "nonexcludable"—that is, it would be difficult to exclude anyone from benefiting from them. Thus, as in the case of public goods, it can be difficult to provide them adequately through market institutions.[1] Generally, ownership rights for them are not defined. Recently the term *open access* has been used in regard to open-access computer resources, such as the Internet and the Linux operating system.

Open-access resources are like public goods in being nonexcludable but differ from public goods in that they may be "diminishable." Resources are diminishable when their use by one person reduces the amount or quality of the resource available to another, at least beyond some point. Examples of diminishable open-access resources include the fish in oceans and seas, which provide food for anyone who can catch them; the water in a lake or river, which can absorb and neutralize pollutants; the trees and plants in large natural forests, which serve a wide variety of human needs; and the atmosphere, which both provides things necessary for life and absorbs pollutants.[2]

---

[1] Recall the discussion in Chapter 1: Because of the property of nonexcludability, a private supplier of public goods cannot limit access to people who pay. This creates a temptation to "free-ride"—to enjoy the benefits while leaving it up to other people to pay the costs. Public goods are likely to be provided at an inefficiently low level when they are privately supplied with no way to require payment from users.

[2] You may note that we have used the example of atmospheric quality in discussing both open-access resources and public goods. To clarify, the atmosphere is an open-access resource that may be diminishable (for example, become dirty) through overuse by individuals. On the other hand, having *clean* air is a public good, because the benefit I get from enjoying clean air is not diminished by your enjoyment of the same.

It may be impossible to exclude users from open-access resources either because of logistical problems (such as a high cost of monitoring access) or because of pre-existing legal and social arrangements. For example, questions of ownership or management of fisheries and forests may never have been raised, reflecting a time in the past when open-access resources were more like public goods in that they appeared to be non-diminishable. When there were only a few users, there always seemed to be more than enough left for the next person to share.

As such resources approach the point of overexploitation, traditional assumptions of limitless abundance no longer apply, and it becomes vital to manage them more carefully. Because the individual user bears only a small fraction of the costs incurred by reducing the quantity or quality of the resource, open-access resources tend to be over-exploited unless they are managed by some form of coordinated administration for the public good. This is an important function of public purpose organizations.

In a democratic society, necessary regulating organizations may originate "sponta-neously" with custom and informal community organizations, as we will see in this chapter when we look at the history of public purpose organizations in the United States. However, even regulatory functions that start at the grassroots level often become more institutionalized over time.

Of course, not all public purpose regulatory organizations are democratic. Historically and cross-culturally, there are also many examples of laws and standards put into place to serve the interests of a powerful elite. These may be backed up by the force of the army and police, against the will of those being governed.

Public purpose organizations often provide the legal, social, and informational infrastructure that both supports other actors and constrains their economic activity.

1.2 | The Direct Provision Function

Public purpose organizations produce many goods and services, including national defense, physical infrastructure such as highways and port facilities, and such services as education and, in many countries, health care. Many of these things—including a good transportation infrastructure and the benefits of living among healthy and edu-cated peers (as distinct from the excludable good of access to health care for oneself)—are public goods that are both nondiminishable and nonexcludable and that can be provided only by explicit social coordination. It is beyond the ability of individual fami-lies, communities, or businesses to provide clean air or to ensure that no one in the neighborhood is carrying the polio virus, because the contribution of any individual actor is very small relative to the problem at hand. As we have noted earlier, families or markets alone do not work well in providing public goods. Only by their joining together and spreading the costs through direct social coordination can an adequate level of production or resource maintenance be achieved. Some forms of physical infra-structure, such as water distribution systems, may also be "natural monopolies" (see Chapter 12) that may either be run as regulated private enterprises or be directly operated by governments.

Even when goods do not fit the exact definition of a "public good" or a "natural monopoly," there may be other reasons for having them publicly provided by govern-ments or non-profit organizations. Health care and education provide many private, as well as public, benefits. Notions of fundamental human needs and rights, and concerns about the quality of services provided by for-profit firms, have led many people to believe that even the "private good" elements of these benefits are better provided through noncommercial organizations.

Historically and cross-culturally, public purpose organizations have also played a large role in distribution. Organized religious groups and municipalities have often taken the lead in trying to meet the minimum dependency needs of individuals and families who have been unable to provide for themselves. In past centuries, and in con-

Economics in the Real World

Can a Market Be an "Open-Access Resource"?

You can't prevent someone from trying to sell a product in a free market. In this sense, a market is an open-access "resource," from which no one can be excluded. A problem with open-access resources, however, is that they may be overused. Is it possible that overuse of a market "resource" might make everyone worse off?

A 2002 news story from Peru offers one example of how this might be the case. Afraid of weather changes that might be caused by El Niño, all the country's potato farmers sowed their crops early, at about the same time. Consequently, all the potatoes ripened at the same time, flooding the market. The result of this and of increases in crop yields was a substantial boost to supply and, of course, a plummeting of the price of potatoes. This in turn created a severe crisis for the country's 3 million potato farmers, many of whom had already been scraping by on per capita incomes of less than $1.25 per day.

Interestingly, historians have determined that during the time of the ancient Inca empire, which existed in Peru before the arrival of the Spanish in the 1500s, agriculture was under tight administrative control, with the timing of all sowings and harvestings dictated by central authorities. Perhaps today a historical cycle is coming full turn. In 2002, the Agriculture Minister of Peru gathered together farmers, potato traders, and government officials. The goal of the newly created potato board was, according to its president, "to make the potato profitable by increasing communication among different regions to better schedule crops."

Based on "Peru Reaps Problems with Over-Abundant Potatoes," by Tania Mellado, Reuters, *Boston Globe,* August 28, 2002.

Some people believe that attempts by governments to coordinate markets often end up creating unnecessary regulatory burdens for businesses. Yet when markets are coordinated by boards of private producers or buyers, instead of by governments, the specter of collusion (see Chapter 12) rears its ugly head. What institutions do you think could most fairly and efficiently coordinate markets that might otherwise (as in this example from Peru) be chaotic?

temporary less industrialized countries, this often took the form of local direct charity, orphanages, and "work houses." In contemporary industrialized and democratic countries, these responsibilities have generally been shifted to the state and/or national level through systems of taxation, transfer, and social service.

Of course, distributional concerns are not always directed only toward the poor. In oligarchies or among affluent subpopulations, some public purpose organizations may be primarily concerned with providing goods and services desired by elite groups; examples include the preservation of government policies that privilege these groups, as well as exclusive social clubs and cultural events.

Discussion Questions

1. Your college or university probably has some open-access resources, such as computer labs or reserve readings, that every student has the right to access but that not all students can access at the same time (without severely downgrading the quality of the service). Think of some examples for your university, and discuss the techniques used to regulate these resources.

2. Before studying more about *non-profit organizations,* take a moment to think about what sorts of organizations come to mind when you hear that term. What activities do you see them doing, and how do you see them getting funding?

Many goods and services essential to economic vitality are provided by institutions and agencies within the public purpose sector. This fifth grade teacher in greater Boston, Massachusetts, is an employee of the local public school system. In the United States, about 90% of students from pre-kindergarten through high school are enrolled in public schools. Most of the remainder are in private schools, usually religious-affiliated non-profit institutions, while less than 2% are educated at home.

2 | Types of Public Purpose Organizations

In our earlier discussions of public purpose organizations, we said that they included government and non-profit organizations. Now that we are exploring them in more detail, we will add a third, overlapping category: international non-profit or quasi-government organizations.

2.1 | Government Organizations

Most nations include many different scales and types of governments. Your town or city government is organized at a relatively small scale, although it carries out a great variety of projects. Municipalities in the United States are usually in charge of providing public schools, police and fire protection, local roads and parks, and other goods and services designed to improve the quality of life of city residents.

Figure 17.1 shows employment according to broad areas of activities for all state and local governments in the United States in 2001. In the United States, the federal

Figure 17.1 U.S. State and Local Government Activities, by Employment

Over half of U.S. employees of state and local governments work in education.

(Source: Authors' calculations based on data for March 2001 from the U.S. Census, http://www.census.gov/govs/apes/01stlus.txt.)

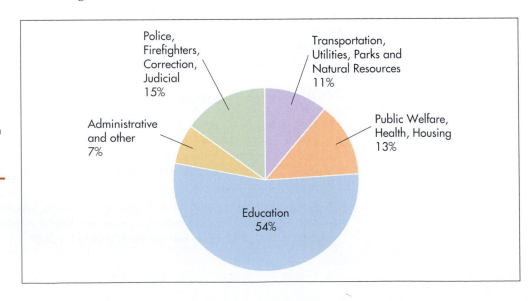

Police, Firefighters, Correction, Judicial
15%

Transportation, Utilities, Parks and Natural Resources
11%

Administrative and other
7%

Public Welfare, Health, Housing
13%

Education
54%

Figure 17.2 U.S. Federal Government Activities, by Employment

Over half of U.S. federal government employees work in national defense.

(Source of data: Authors' calculations based on data for March 2001 from the U.S. Census, http://www.census.gov/ govs/apes/ 01fedfun.txt, and the Department of Defense, http://web1.whs.osd.mil/mmid/m05/ hst0301.pdf.)

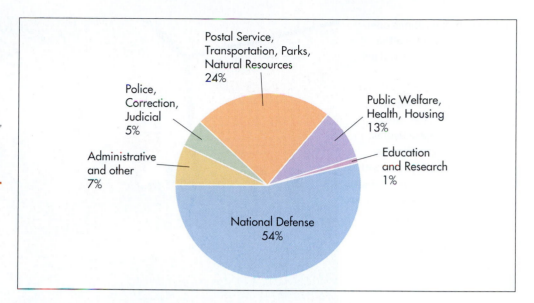

government is the primary level of government entrusted with national defense and international diplomacy. It also plays many roles in other economic activities across the board, including (but not limited to) regulation of commerce, administration of systems of taxes and transfers, regulation of interstate transportation, guaranteeing of loans to university students, and funding of basic research. It generally administers social welfare programs in cooperation with the states.

Government organizations include legislative, executive, and judicial bodies. Governmental regulatory directives are backed up by force of law, and ultimately by the system of courts, with penalties for noncompliance, including fines and imprisonment. For example, state medical boards in the United States grant medical licenses that allow physicians to practice. Anyone found practicing medicine without a license from the state can be fined or thrown in jail. It is also state governments that grant businesses the charters that turn them into corporations, with associated legal benefits such as limited liability (see Chapter 16). Government agencies that provide direct services operate under the authority of the official bodies. For example, if you attend a state university, chances are that its chancellor is appointed by the governor and that its budget undergoes annual review and approval by the state legislature.

Governments, of course, collect a good deal of their operating revenue from taxes on individuals, families, and businesses. However, governments also count on user fees (for example, postage, tuition, and tolls) and donations (for example, alumni donations to state universities).

2.2 | Domestic Non-Profit Organizations

Non-profit organizations are not parts of governments, nor do they operate with the purpose of generating profits for their owners.[3] Like businesses, they are often incorporated by state charters and governed by boards of directors. Unlike businesses, however, any financial surplus they generate is required, by law, to be channeled back into the

---

[3] The class of formal (usually incorporated) organizations that neither are a part of an official government nor are run with a goal of profit has been identified by many different terms. The organizations in this class may be described as nonprofit or not-for-profit or tax-exempt, to distinguish them from for-profit private businesses. They are also commonly described as nongovernmental organizations (NGOs) to distinguish them from official public organizations. Sometimes the class is called the independent sector, the third sector, or civil society to distinguish it from both governments and the business sphere. You may also hear references to "the charitable sector" or "the voluntary sector," although these are appropriate descriptors of only some nonprofits. We will generally use the term *nonprofit*, and our typology puts both nonprofits and governments together into what we call the public purpose sphere.

Non-profit organizations operating within a country often participate in international networks as well. The International Federation of Red Cross and Red Crescent (IFRC) societies coordinates cross-national charitable activities. Here, officials of the Iranian Red Crescent society meet with representatives of international groups to organize assistance for the victims of a January 2004 earthquake in Barn, a city in southern Iran.

organization. The organization's goal is described in a mission statement in its articles of incorporation.[4]

Your local animal shelter is probably a non-profit organization whose stated mission is to prevent cruelty to animals. Charities that raise funds to help impoverished or refugee communities in poorer parts of the world are nonprofits. These examples may seem obvious to you, but the type and function of other nonprofits may be less obvious.

For example, the National Board of Medical Examiners is a U.S. non-profit organization that provides the exams that physicians take in order to obtain their licenses. Its stated mission includes "protection of the health of the public." You might be surprised to learn that the New York Stock Exchange (NYSE) is also a non-profit organization. In Chapter 3 we described how it originated when a group of brokers organized themselves. This organization was later incorporated as a non-profit institution whose members are the companies and individuals who "own" a seat on the exchange. Its current mission statement begins with the words "To add value to the capital-raising and asset-management process by providing the highest-quality and most cost-effective self-regulated marketplace for the trading of financial instruments. . . ."

Non-profit organizations can be divided into four main types: public benefit service and action, member-serving, religious, and funding intermediaries.[5]

1. *Public benefit service and action.* The missions of these nonprofits include supplying health care, providing education, improving neighborhoods, promoting the arts, ensuring civil rights, and advocating for better social policies. While organizations like animal shelters and international charities are in this group, the largest of such organizations tend to be hospitals and educational institutions.

2. *Member-serving.* The missions of these nonprofits are to provide benefits to their own members. For example, trade associations (such as the American Association of Manufacturers), professional organizations (such as the American Medical Association), labor unions, political parties, farmers' cooperatives, and social clubs are nonprofits of this type.

---

[4] Because of the tradition of separation of church and state in the United States, religious congregations are exempted from some of the legal requirements imposed on other types of nonprofits.

[5] Lester M. Salamon, *America's Nonprofit Sector: A Primer*, 2d ed. (New York: Foundation Center, 1999), pp. 23–24, 38.

3. *Religious.* Churches, synagogues, mosques, and related organizations (such as religious conventions and religious orders) are religious nonprofits.

4. *Funding intermediaries.* These include charitable foundations (such as the Ford, Rockefeller, and Gates Foundations, as well as numerous smaller foundations), funding federations (such as the United Way), and non-profit professional fundraisers.

Figure 17.3 shows the relative importance of each of these types of nonprofits within the United States, according to the numbers of people they employ (for pay). In addition to hiring paid employees, nonprofits often benefit from services donated by volunteer workers. For example, it has been estimated that every year the public benefit service nonprofits mobilize volunteer labor that amounts to the equivalent of almost 5 million full-time people.

Within the United States, nonprofits are sometimes referred to by the number of the section of the federal tax code under which they have incorporated. All nonprofits are "tax exempt"—that is, they do not need to pay federal taxes on their income. In addition, donations to organizations that are "501(c)(3)" are "tax deductible"—that is, the donor can subtract the amount of the donation from his or her income before calculating the amount he or she owes in federal income tax. Public benefit service organizations, religious organizations, and related intermediaries are generally 501(c)(3) unless they are heavily involved in political campaigning and lobbying for specific pieces of legislation. Public benefit action organizations that engage in such political activity are "501(c)(4)." Member-serving organizations fall under other sections of the tax code. Only the 501(c)(3) organizations (and a few closely related organizations organized under different parts of the code) benefit from tax deductibility.

Focusing on taxes and donations, however, may reinforce the stereotype that nonprofits run primarily on donations. This is not the case. Since the 1970s there has been a strong trend for nonprofits, particularly those that provide services such as education, health care, housing, or job development, to depend for a growing portion of their revenues on fees and government funds. For example, non-profit universities typically charge students tuition, and bills at non-profit hospitals are paid partly from charges to patients (or the patients' insurance companies) and partly from reimbursements from government programs such as Medicare and Medicaid. In 1996, monetary private donations provided only about 19% of the revenues of nonreligious, service-providing 501(c)(3) organizations large enough to show up in the statistics. Government programs provided 32%, fees charged provided 39%, and other sources (such as investment income) provided the remaining 10% of revenues.[6]

Figure 17.3 U.S. Non-Profit Organization Types, by Employment

Most employees of nonprofits work in public benefit service and action organizations such as hospitals, schools, advocacy groups, and charities.

(Source: Lester M. Salamon, *America's Nonprofit Sector: A Primer*, 2d ed. [New York: Foundation Center, 1999], p. 23.)

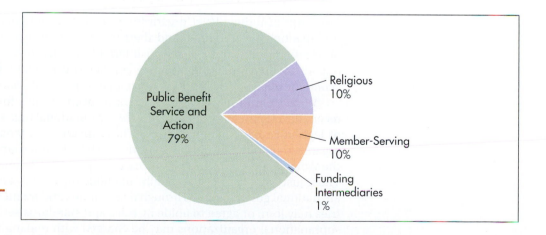

Public Benefit Service and Action 79%

Religious 10%

Member-Serving 10%

Funding Intermediaries 1%

[6] Elizabeth T. Boris, "Myths About the Nonprofit Sector," a brief in the series *Charting Civil Society,* Center on Nonprofits and Philanthropy (Washington, DC: The Urban Institute, July 1, 1998).

Economics in the Real World

Two New York Nonprofits with a Focus on Government

The mission of Legal Services for Children, Inc., is to advocate on behalf of economically disadvantaged children in New York City. Many of these are disabled children who require special education services to which they have a legal right but that are not being provided by their school districts. The organization also helps immigrant children and other children in need to receive mental health counseling and other government benefits. It educates parents about the civil rights of their disabled children and teaches them how to advocate effectively on these children's behalf.

Environmental Advocates is unique in the state in possessing the staff and the expertise to read regularly all of the hundreds of initiatives introduced in the New York State Legislature. This organization has a membership of 130 other nongovernmental organizations, which rely on it to keep them up to date on national and state policies, laws, and trends that have environmental implications. ○

Do you know of organizations such as these in your community?

Note that the interplay of governments and nonprofits in providing and regulating services can be quite complex. As we have seen, for example, physicians are regulated by a process in which *states* give medical licenses on the basis of exams that have been written and administered by *non-profit* organizations. Regarding services, a great many *non-profit* hospital services are paid for by *government* programs. Treating government and nonprofits as independent spheres could be misleading. At the same time, there are some nonprofits that are seen as gadflies by governments: They focus on making sure that government agencies actually act in the public interest.

An important historical role of nonprofits has been to lead the way in major reform movements, such as women's rights; the abolition of slavery and, later, equal rights for African Americans; environmental protection; workplace safety; civil rights for prisoners and the disabled; child welfare; and the humane treatment of animals. In each of these cases, individuals grouped together to create movements that finally resulted in substantial changes in behavior—and laws that reinforced such behavioral change. In each of these areas there are many people who believe that the job is not yet finished; nonprofits are still needed to raise the public consciousness and to keep up the pressure for social and policy change.

2.3 | International Organizations

Going up yet another level, organizations including national governments, national and multinational corporations and their trade associations, and national public benefit nonprofits can combine to form international organizations. The purpose of these organizations is often to minimize conflict and regulate commerce, finance, and/or economic and social development on an international scale.

Whereas international charities have been around for a very long time, a more recent development is the formation of supranational organizations with some amount of legislative or regulatory power. These include supranational quasi-governmental organizations such as the United Nations (UN), the International Monetary Fund (IMF), the World Bank, the World Trade Organization (WTO), and the European Union (EU). Those just named are all essentially "membership organizations" in which the members are national governments. Through negotiations and treaties, the governments of countries may join, or agree to abide by rules and standards set by, such organizations. The supranational organizations may be charged with making rules and policies (many of economic significance) and/or with administering policies previously agreed on by the member governments.

Yet other international agencies with regulatory power are *non*governmental in form. Why are bank ATM cards all over the world the same thickness? Why do many manufacturers around the world use the same symbols on dangerous cargoes, or on automobile controls? Setting such standards is the goal of the International Organization for Standardization (ISO), an international nongovernmental organization. Its members are national standards-setting institutes, including both governmental and nongovernmental organizations. If you have ever lived in a country where, for example, there are no standards for the shape or size of wall outlets—so that every electrical appliance has to be wired specifically for the location where it will be plugged in—you will appreciate how national and global standards can make life easier and more efficient.

Because international agreements can have repercussions for domestic economies, they add a new layer of complexity to economic analysis. It can become unclear not only which "public" is being served in these organizations, but even who is governing whom. We will examine this issue further below, when we look at the regulation of international trade.

Discussion Questions

1. Did any of the information in this section surprise you? Which facts, and why?

2. Recall that in the traditional neoclassical model, the only actors are "firms" and "households." How sophisticated do you think an economy could really become if it had no public purpose organizations?

3 | The Public Purpose Sphere in Historical Perspective

The founders of democratic government in the United States, reacting against oppressive British regulation and taxation, envisioned a very limited role for centralized government. In 16th-century England, even the kind of clothing a person could wear was regulated by Parliament according to the person's status as belonging to a particular class: that of knight and ladies, squires, yeomen, merchants, artisans, or laborers. The American republic was supposed to be free of such constraints.

On the other hand, Alexis de Tocqueville, a French political scientist and writer who traveled the United States in the 1830s, noted Americans' penchant for creating community organizations at the local level to deal with issues of common concern. Not infrequently these beginnings in community activism have expanded into lobbying for action at a state level—and finally for establishment of policies at a federal (or international) level. Over time, and in the face of the increasing complexities of industrialization, urbanization, and even globalization of economic activity, centralized government has come to play a much larger role in the United States than was originally intended.

Varying and complex patterns of government and non-profit organizations have emerged across different countries, while the debate about the appropriate scope of the public purpose sphere continues unabated. In this brief historical review we will look only at four examples of areas of public purpose activity: social welfare, regulation of monopolies and trade practices, regulation of financial markets, and environmental protection. As usual, we will focus primarily on the United States.[7]

3.1 | Social Welfare

How should a society protect the welfare of its members? What should it do when people are not, by their own efforts, able to avoid unsafe living or working conditions? What

---

[7] Other areas could certainly be studied as well—for example, labor market policies, education, health care provision, and scientific research.

These young "breaker boys," pictured in a 1911 Lewis Wickes Hine photo, labored for the Pennsylvania Coal Company. Working 14 to 16 hours a day in choking coal dust, they separated coal from slate and rock pieces. Hine's photos of young workers in mills, mines, and factories helped galvanize a public reform movement leading to the regulation of child labor in the United States in the early 20th century. Employment of children for long hours and in such dangerous conditions may no longer go on in the United States, but it continues in various places around the world into the present.

should it do when people can't find work? How should it assist indigent people who are too young or too old or too infirm to work?

During the very early years of industrialization, such problems were left to religious charities and local municipalities—or were not addressed at all. With the increasing concentration of people in urban areas, however, issues of communicable diseases, food and water quality, and working conditions became increasingly pressing, and disparities between the rich and poor were harder to ignore.

State and local laws dating from America's colonial times set a few standards for honest weights and measures and other issues related to trade in certain foods. However, as urbanization increased, so did health problems related to adulterated and unsanitary products. By the late 1800s, activism by labor groups, women's associations, and muckraking journalists succeeded in raising public awareness of these dangers. Various states and localities, as well as trade associations of food manufacturers, began to set and enforce more standards. Federal legislation came about in 1906 with passage of the Meat Inspection Act and the Food and Drug Act. Besides making many unsanitary practices illegal, these acts were welcomed by some food and drug manufacturers because they made it easier to do business: It was simpler to follow one set of national standards than to try to meet rules that varied from place to place.

Progressive Era: a period in U.S. history from the late 1800s to the early 1920s, during which many government programs concerned with social welfare and economic regulation were initiated

Regulation of food safety was just one of the innovations of the **Progressive Era** in the United States—a time that historians identify as lasting from the late 1800s to the early 1920s. Prominent during this time were social movements for women's rights, labor rights (see below), trust busting (see below), and resource conservation (see below). Many of these movements resulted in new government economic programs, as people struggled to come to grips with industrialization and large-scale business enterprise.

The abysmal conditions endured by workers in factories and mines in the period of early industrialization created unrest, encouraged the formation of labor unions, and drew the attention of humanitarian reformers concerned about the health and well-being of laborers. In England in the early 1800s, for example, children often worked long hours beside their parents. In the mines they often began working at the age of 5—and usually died by the time they reached their mid-20s. Under pressure from religious groups, England's first "Factory Act" was passed by Parliament in 1833, prohibiting the hiring of children under age 9 in textile factories and limiting the work of 9- to 13-year-olds to

8 hours per day. State and local regulation began in the United States at about the same time and expanded during the Progressive Era, but it wasn't until the enactment of the Fair Labor Standards Act in 1938 that labor, including child labor, was regulated at a national level in the United States.

The 1930s also saw the beginnings of many federal social welfare programs under President Franklin D. Roosevelt's "New Deal." With the national economy in a deep depression and the unemployment rate peaking at over 25%, the federal government stepped in to create jobs and relieve poverty. The social security system, with its programs of old-age assistance, widows' benefits, unemployment compensation, and disability insurance, came into being. Other forms of aid spread at the level of states; an example is workers' compensation, paid to workers injured on the job. Labor unions also obtained increased rights and protection during this period. The programs were limited in scope, however, and failed to provide a safety net for many groups.

The next wave of federal government involvement in social programs came about with the "War on Poverty" program, part of President Lyndon Johnson's "Great Society" plan, in the mid-1960s. Growing awareness of the existence of poverty amidst plenty, the civil rights movement, and urban riots inspired greater federal involvement in employment and training, social service and housing aid for the disadvantaged, and the financing of health care for the elderly and the poor. While government spending grew, so did the service provision portion of the non-profit sphere, because the federal government, in particular, rarely delivers services directly but operates instead through other organizations.

social insurance programs: programs designed to transfer income to recipients if and when certain events (such as retirement or disability) occur

means-tested programs: programs designed to transfer income to those most in need

Economists often distinguish between two major types of government transfer programs related to income security. **Social insurance programs**, such as social security and unemployment compensation, are designed to help workers and their families should a worker get too old to work or suffer a disability or a period of unemployment. **Means-tested programs** are intended to help people with low resources. In the latter, in contrast to most of the social insurance programs, recipients do not need to have established a substantial history of market work in order to qualify for benefits. Also unlike the social insurance programs, recipients must demonstrate that their other means of support (income and resources) are very low.

Since the 1970s, spending on social insurance programs has grown considerably, while federal spending on means-tested programs has declined (when adjusted for inflation). In 2000, of the $489 billion paid out in cash transfers by all levels of government, 83% went to social security retirement and disability payments. Only 5% went to what we normally think of as "welfare" (that is, payments under the Transitional Assistance to Needy Families and general assistance programs).

Cutbacks in government social welfare spending during the administrations of President Ronald Reagan and (the first) President George Bush were often justified by the idea that these would create more opportunity for private, non-profit charitable initiatives. By that time, however, such organizations were already heavily reliant on government financing.

Many federal government agencies that exist today, such as the Occupational Safety and Health Administration (OSHA), the Consumer Products Safety Commission (CPSC), the Food and Drug Administration (FDA), and the Department of Health and Human Services (HHS), have their roots in a long history of citizen activism beginning at the state and local level and may also reflect the interests of related labor and trade associations.

3.2 | Regulation of Monopolies and Trade Practices

In the 1800s, U.S. railroads were natural monopolies in the areas they served. Users of their services—particularly farmers, who relied on them to ship their grain—were at their mercy, having to pay whatever price they might set. The railroad companies also engaged in stock manipulations and wielded influence in politics. All this led to activist movements demanding regulation of the railroad industry for the protection of the rest of society.

Interstate Commerce Act: the first U.S. federal act regulating monopolies and business practices, passed in 1887 in response to practices in the railroad industry

Early state laws that attempted to regulate the industry were ineffectual, but in 1887 the U.S. Congress passed the **Interstate Commerce Act**, marking the first federal regulation of monopolies and business practices. This act created the Interstate Commerce Commission, charged with preventing monopoly and discriminatory pricing.

And railroads weren't the only industry in which monopoly power was bringing forth accusations of unfairness. Standard Oil, during this same period, for example, was moving toward taking over 90% of U.S. oil refinery capacity, both by growing and by acquiring other firms.

Hence a number of additional laws regulating monopoly and trade practices were passed during the Progressive Era. The Sherman Antitrust Act (1890) outlawed price fixing and forbade monopolization, more generally.[8] (In 1911, Standard Oil was broken up into several smaller companies.) The Clayton Antitrust Act (1914) prohibited certain practices that created barriers to entry and outlawed mergers that threatened competition. The Federal Trade Commission (FTC) was established in 1914 to investigate and act on violations of the law.

The idea behind these rules was to create a fair, competitive basis for business activity. It was well known that monopolies could act unfairly toward consumers by charging prices far above the cost of production and that they could drive out potential competitors through the use of unfair business practices. Economists can point out, as well, the efficiency losses to society in general arising from monopoly power (see Chapter 12). Along with the Antitrust Division in the U.S. Department of Justice, the FTC is to this day charged with maintaining fair competition in the U.S. economy. The antitrust case brought against Microsoft (see Chapter 12) was the biggest case of the 1990s.

Violations of domestic antitrust law can result in damages being paid to the parties harmed, companies being broken up, or criminal wrongdoers being fined or sent to jail. However, the strictness with which laws have been interpreted and the enthusiasm with which they have been enforced have varied, depending on who was sitting on the courts that interpret the laws and on the political administrations in charge of the enforcing agencies.

The FTC and the Antitrust Division of the Department of Justice are charged with enforcing rules about fair business practices domestically. But what about rules for *international* trade?

After World War II, a number of governments signed a General Agreement on Tariffs and Trade (GATT), with the goal of encouraging free trade among member countries by reducing tariffs and providing a way to resolve trade disputes. For example, it sometimes happens that one country will accuse another of "dumping" (selling its goods below cost), or of unfairly subsidizing production of its exports, or of establishing spurious regulations and standards designed merely to prevent importation of another country's products. GATT was intended to be a forum in which countries could iron out such disputes, coming to agreements that would result in a mutual lowering of barriers to international trade.

World Trade Organization (WTO): an organization, created by a group of national governments in 1995, that regulates international trade

In 1995, GATT was superseded by a more formal body, the **World Trade Organization (WTO).** Currently with 144 member countries, the WTO is, among other things, a forum for international trade negotiations, a place where disputes are discussed, and an agency for monitoring national trade policies. Countries that participate in the WTO can be disciplined by the organization if their trade practices are found to violate the agreements (see the accompanying News in Context feature).

As in the case of regulating domestic trade, nongovernmental organizations in the international arena can work alongside a governmental forum. For example, whether a restriction on trade is considered reasonable or unreasonable must be decided by reference to some set of international standards. A government may, for example, want to ban importation of certain products because of concerns about consumer safety, the use of child or slave labor in production, or a failure to meet desirable environmental

---

[8] At that time, very large companies such as Standard Oil were called trusts.

U.S. Tariffs on Steel Are Illegal, World Trade Organization Says

WASHINGTON—The World Trade Organization ruled on Monday that steel tariffs imposed by [the U.S.] last year were illegal, clearing the way for the European Union to impose more than $2 billion of sanctions on imports from the United States unless Washington quickly drops the duties.

[T]he W.T.O. panel ruled that the American tariffs went beyond the rules allowing countries to protect themselves against sudden surges of imports. . . .

Some members of Congress quickly urged [President] Bush to ignore the W.T.O. ruling. Rep. Sherrod Brown . . . referred to the W.T.O. as a "secret" court and said the president should let the tariffs run their . . . course.

But Senator Charles E. Grassley . . . urged Mr. Bush not to undercut the organization's authority, even if he does not like its decisions. "Complying with our W.T.O. obligations is an important sign of American leadership," said Senator Grassley. . . .

Adapted from an article by Elizabeth Becker, *New York Times*, November 10, 2003.

How many supranational quasi-government organizations can you identify in this news story? Do you think international organizations should be able to decide what it is legal and illegal for countries to do? Does it make a difference to your answer what sort of policy you have in mind—say, an international environmental standard (like the Kyoto Protocol) versus levying tariffs on imports to protect a domestic industry from international competition? (*Note:* A few weeks after this WTO ruling, the U.S. administration announced that the tariffs on steel would be rescinded.)

standards. In these cases, organizations such as the International Organization for Standardization (ISO), with its standards for safety and environmental protection, can be very influential. If the internationally adopted standard is weaker than the standard imposed by the national government, the national government may be found to be in violation of the international trade agreements and may face sanctions.

The sheer volume of standards-setting activity required in contemporary markets, where the creation of new products is a major source of profits, makes it hard for public purpose organizations—whether government or non-profit—to act as effective monitors of business. On any single day in 2001, six ISO standards were completed. It is estimated that 200 new standards-setting organizations were formed just between 1995 and 2001. The number may be even higher, but a firm count is hard to come by because there is no readily accessible registry of these bodies. Only a handful of public interest nonprofits make concerted efforts to participate in standards setting. Those with an interest often do not have the financial wherewithal to attend the numerous meetings around the world where standards are being developed. As a result, the overwhelming majority of the participants in standards-setting processes are business association representatives and industry attorneys and lobbyists.

3.3 | Regulation of Financial Markets

As we have seen, flows of financial capital through bank deposits and loans, or through the issuance and trading of stocks and bonds, are important to economic activity. A rather high degree of trust is required, however, for one economic actor to (temporarily) give over his or her funds for the use of someone else.

In the 1800s, banks were primarily chartered and regulated at the state level. In 1907 a particularly severe spate of bank failures and bank panics (in which depositors all wished to withdraw their funds at once) made many people critical of this system. Pressure for more fairness and stability in banking led to the establishment in 1913 of the Federal Reserve as a "lender of last resort" to banks in trouble. The policies, however, did not prevent a severe reoccurrence of bank failures in 1930–1933, helping to trigger the Great Depression. Another massive failure of savings and loan associations in the

1980s, following a deregulation that created unusual opportunities for fraud, cost the government billions of dollars in guarantees on deposits. Although it is too complicated to address in a brief history, effective regulation of the finance industry remains a topic of considerable concern today.

During the Progressive Era, states began to try to regulate the sales of securities (such as stocks and bonds), motivated by a desire to curtail dishonest practices such as the sale of worthless shares in fictitious gold mines. In 1933 Congress created the Securities and Exchange Commission (SEC) to regulate the exchange of securities at a national level. Whereas some of the state laws included attempts to make judgments about the merits of particular investments, the federal law followed what has been called the "sunlight theory of regulation." That is, sellers of securities are required to make a full disclosure of all material facts, via a registration statement and a prospectus. It is then left up to the buyer to determine whether the investment is a wise one. In the **Securities Act of 1933**, which created the commission, Congress stated that the legislation was designed not only to protect investors from fraud but also to "promote efficiency, competition, and capital formation."

Of course, the disclosure of information about any enterprise is meaningful only if it conforms to adequate standards of honest reporting; an enterprise shouldn't be able to claim that it is profitable unless it can produce numbers to prove its claim. During the scandals of 2001–2002 involving Enron, WorldCom, and other large corporations that engaged in misleading accounting practices to create the appearance of profits, standards of reporting came under much scrutiny. Here we see yet another example of government and nonprofit regulatory interaction: The SEC accepts what are called generally accepted accounting principles (GAAP) as the authoritative standard for financial reporting. These principles are actually written, however, by the nonprofit Financial Accounting Standards Board.[9]

Meanwhile, massive swings in capital flows from country to country during the late 20th century, particularly during the Asian financial crisis of 1997–1998, began to spur renewed calls for controls on international capital flows and speculative trade in foreign currencies. One proposal, for example, was enactment of a "Tobin Tax," so called because it was originally suggested by Nobel laureate economist James Tobin. Its proponents argue that a small tax on currency trades would discourage speculative trades, while still allowing for productive trading. The revenues, some suggest, could be put into an international fund to combat poverty and disease. Several governments, including the government of Canada, have passed legislation agreeing to implement a Tobin Tax if enough other countries agree to participate.

3.4 | Environmental Protection

Public purpose organization activity related to preservation of the environment has evolved in the United States from a number of disparate concerns. In the early years of the 20th century, the "conservation movement" increased public appreciation of the natural environment. Many in it were inspired by writers such as naturalist John Muir (1838–1914), who also was the first president of the non-profit Sierra Club. U.S. President Theodore Roosevelt made conservation a high priority, doubling the number of national parks during his term in office (1901–1909).

By the 1950s, the air and water pollution generated by industrial plants had become increasingly noticeable. Regulation at the local level was often very difficult, because flows of water and air cross political jurisdictions—for example, most of the smoke generated in one state or county might blow into the next. The first federal agencies formed to protect water and air quality were established in the 1950s and 1960s as part of the U.S. Public Health Service.

Securities Act of 1933: the first federal act to regulate trade in securities (such as stocks and bonds). It created the Securities and Exchange Commission (SEC).

▷ "Everybody needs beauty as well as bread, places to play in and pray in, where nature may heal and give strength to body and soul alike."
—John Muir, *The Yosemite* (1912)

---

[9] The stated mission of the Financial Accounting Standards Board is "to establish and improve standards of financial accounting and reporting for the guidance and education of the public, including issuers, auditors and users of financial information" (**http://www.fasb.org/facts/index.shtml**).

Public concern increased to the level of a national environmental movement in the 1960s. The publication of biologist Rachel Carson's *Silent Spring* in 1962 was an important factor in bringing about increased public awareness of environmental degradation and species extinction due to pesticides and other pollutants.

Since the formation of the U.S. Environmental Protection Agency (EPA) in 1970, improvements have been made in many areas. Some especially dangerous pesticides have been banned for specific uses in the United States (although many continue to be manufactured here and exported to Third World countries with weaker regulations), and progress has been made in cleaning up air and water in many areas of the United States. By the turn of the century other concerns, such as global warming, the loss of genetic diversity in agriculture, the continuing extinction of animal species, and the availability of fresh water, were receiving increased attention. International activities had also increased.

Global warming (see the News in Context feature in Chapter 6) is an environmental problem whose solution will require social coordination on a global scale. In November 2001, all of the world's industrialized nations except the United States agreed to adopt the Kyoto Protocol on Greenhouse Gas Emissions, which aims to reduce the emissions of greenhouse gases that cause climate change (such as carbon dioxide) to 5% to 7% below 1990 levels. Although polls showed that most Americans perceived global warming to be a serious problem, the U.S. federal government was unwilling at that time to address climate change as an issue warranting concern and action (see the accompanying Economics in the Real World feature).

How can governments go about reducing the carbon dioxide emissions that have led to global warming? Directly mandating maximum levels of emissions by regulation is one option, of course. We have also already discussed the more market-oriented option of selling "rights to pollute" (see Chapter 14). Yet another means is to create "environmental taxes," such as a special tax on activities according to how much carbon dioxide (or other pollutants) they produce. Economists, at first glance, usually tend to assert that taxes lead to efficiency losses, because the taxes are imagined to be imposed on otherwise well-functioning competitive markets with no externalities (see Chapter 11). Yet in the presence of externalities, the story changes.

Economist Arthur Pigou (1877–1959) pointed out that in the presence of externalities, markets function more efficiently if governments tax activities that cause negative externalities and subsidize those that generate positive externalities. By making the price of engaging in a polluting activity more closely resemble its social cost, environmental taxes give people and firms a financial incentive to change their behavior in socially beneficial ways. Revenues raised by such **Pigovian taxes**, their advocates also point out, may allow other taxes to be reduced, such as those on individual and corporate incomes.

As of 2002, environmental taxes—and, in particular, taxes on activities that lead to emissions of greenhouse gases—had been adopted by several countries in Europe and some U.S. states and localities. However, except for a tax on ozone-depleting chemicals, environmental taxes had not played much of a role in U.S. federal environmental policy.

Pigovian taxes: (named after economist Arthur Pigou, who suggested them) taxes on activities that generate negative externalities. To the extent that they make prices paid more closely resemble social costs, they can increase economic efficiency.

3.5 | Is Government Too Big?

In recent decades, a number of people have argued that the size of the public purpose sphere (particularly government) should be reduced and that the business sphere should grow to fill the gap. Instead of providing services such as education, health care, corrections, environmental protection, and security directly, they have argued, the government should encourage or pay businesses to provide them. The rationale behind this point of view is that businesses will be motivated, through the profit incentive, to act more efficiently.

However, such efforts encounter a major problem: Efficient business operations depend in many ways on precise definitions of goals and on measurement in dollar terms of inputs and products. And it is often difficult, or even impossible, to define clearly the value of such things as good health and good health care; the value of what goes into an education and what comes out of it; the value of a good prison system;

Public Purpose Organizations and the Kyoto Protocol

Although the U.S. federal government declined to adopt the Kyoto Protocol on Greenhouse Gas Emissions, many other U.S. public purpose organizations did not wait to take action.

State governments. By June 2002, the six New England states (and five provinces in eastern Canada) had agreed to reduce greenhouse gas emissions, New York State was working on a plan for action, and California legislators had mandated improvements in the fuel efficiency of cars. Close to 40 states had adopted rules that allowed utility customers not only to generate energy at home (using such technologies as wind power and solar arrays) but also to sell any extra energy back into the electric power distribution system. Clean-energy funds to help in the development of energy from nonfossil fuel sources had been established by 15 states, and 13 states were requiring that a certain proportion of their power supplies come from renewable sources.

City governments. By June 2002, 119 city governments had developed plans to reduce their greenhouse gas emissions up to 20%. Chicago had declared a requirement that renewable sources provide 20% of its energy needs. Voters in San Francisco had passed a referendum requiring that city rooftops be used for solar energy collection. Seattle and Boulder had passed formal measures adopting the Kyoto Protocol. In some cases, the city governments were assisted in their efforts by NGOs such as the International Council for Local Environmental Initiatives.

Religious groups. Faith-based groups in over 20 states had organized interfaith campaigns on climate change, working to educate and organize their congregations on the issue. Religious groups in 8 of these 20 states had also established an Interfaith Power and Light Initiative to improve energy efficiency and move toward switching to

what constitutes a healthful environment and how this is to be valued; and the value of security, including national defense.

The profit incentive *may* inspire businesses to produce superior service in these areas. However, when the quality of the service is difficult to evaluate, a business may be tempted to achieve those profits simply by cutting costs—and may, in the process, drive quality below an acceptable level. Staff members of for-profit prisons, for example, have complained about being required to supervise more inmates than they feel is consistent with acceptable levels of security.

In addition to questions about direct provision, many have argued that government regulation has become unduly burdensome on businesses. Some business leaders claim that they are overly constrained by regulations on everything—from safety regulations for their workers, to quality regulations for their products, to accounting regulations for their financial reports. Extensive regulation can be particularly daunting for people who run small businesses, who may feel anxious about their lack of professional expertise on business law and resent the time it takes to do additional paperwork.[10] Even a regulation originally enacted for a very good public purpose may, through inertia or because it serves a special interest, remain in force long after the need for it is past.

The question, however, is not *whether* public purpose organizations should be active in providing services and regulating economic activity—as we have seen, some forms of coordination, whether through trade associations, local government, national government, or international regulatory organizations, are a necessary part of making economies (including their market institutions) work.

---

[10] For this reason, some federal regulations are written in such a way as not to include small businesses (for example, businesses with 50 or fewer employees).

clean energy. In some cases, the religious institutions were assisted in their efforts by nongovernmental organizations such as the Regeneration Project.

Educational institutions. Several universities had adopted the Kyoto Protocol and were in the process of analyzing their impact on carbon emissions and designing strategies for reductions. Wesleyan University, Connecticut College, Colorado University, and a consortia of schools in Pennsylvania and New Jersey had committed themselves to purchasing some of their power from renewable sources.

Many individuals and organizations in the core and business spheres, of course, have taken action as well. For example, a number of corporations (including Du Pont, 3M, IBM, Johnson & Johnson, BP Amoco, and Royal Dutch Shell) have agreed to reduce their greenhouse gas emissions to 15% below 1990 levels by 2010. Yet even here the actions of non-profit service and advocacy groups were important in raising public awareness on the issue of global warming. Organizations such as the Sierra Club distributed information on global warming and encouraged citizens to change their consumption habits and to lobby their representatives in government. Groups such as the Coalition for Environmentally Responsible Economies (CERES) reminded businesses that a world altered by global warming is not in their long-term interest and convinced a number (including Sunoco, Ford Motor Company, General Motors, and other large corporations) to endorse a statement of pro-environment principles. ◔

Based on Michael Northrop, "Addressing Global Warming: A Way Forward," Rockefeller Brothers Fund, **http://www.cleanenergyfunds.org/CaseStudies/Northrop_Climate_Change.pdf**, and on materials from other non-profit organizations.

---

self-regulation: an individual organization setting up and abiding by standards on its own, without the need for outside oversight or enforcement

The question is *how* to make economies work best. Governments have an advantage over nongovernmental organizations in that they can collect taxes to support programs and can make use of their police powers to enforce laws and regulations. In a world in which everyone simply acted in an honest and common-good-promoting way, living up to their promises, and behaving charitably toward those in need, the need for governmental agencies and regulations would be far reduced. If every individual and every organization were **self-regulating**, the need for government regulation would shrink. As we saw, however, in looking at the history of public purpose activity, most expansions in the size and reach of government were reactions to distinct events in which private provision and self-regulation proved themselves inadequate for preventing human suffering and/or maintaining trust in economic institutions.

There was a trend in the late 20th century for the federal government to move away from directly providing services and peel back regulations, but in some cases this has been reversed. After September 11, 2001, for example, having discovered private provision of airport security to be unacceptably weak, the federal government took over the job. A direct focus on the mission of providing security, it was decided after much debate, would be more likely to yield favorable results than a business orientation with its concern about profit.

Similarly, after the Enron, WorldCom, and other corporate debacles of 2001–2002, there was increased concern about whether the Securities and Exchange Commission was doing *enough* to protect investors and employees. There was also an increased interest in business ethics, and questions were raised about what changes in social norms regarding the responsibilities of business leaders might help prevent future disasters.

Boston Beer Pulls Ad After Complaints

NEWS in context

. . . [T]he Boston Beer Co. agreed yesterday to temporarily pull a TV ad for its Sam Adams Light beer that a law-enforcement group said encourages underage drinking. The National Liquor Law Enforcement Association said it first asked Boston Beer to pull the ad in May. . . . [T]he group is asking the Federal Trade Commission to investigate because, it said, the beer industry is unable to comply with its own standards and because Boston Beer took so long to heed its request.

In a TV spot titled "Noise" . . . young people hide their beer when a police officer responds to complaints about a loud party. If the young people were of drinking age, there would be no need to hide the beer. . . .

. . . The National Liquor Law Enforcement Association . . . persuaded the American Medical Association, Mothers Against Drunk Driving, and other advocacy groups to write letters of protest to Boston Beer. . . . In [the view of Aidan Moore of the National Liquor Law Enforcement Association,] the ad violated the guidelines of the Beer Institute, an industry trade group.

The guidelines state, "Beer advertising and marketing material should not depict situations where beer is being consumed excessively, in an irresponsible way, or in any way illegally." Moore said his group sought the Beer Institute's help in getting "Noise" off the air. But Beer Institute general counsel Arthur DeCelle said that enforcing the code is "not our job. The code is not going to work if we become the judge."

Chris Reidy, *Boston Globe*, August 31, 2002.

How many non-profit organizations can you identify in this news story? What do you think would be the best resolution to this case? Should the government (the FTC) step in? What sorts of actions by other parties might avoid the need for government involvement? (Do you think that avoiding government involvement is desirable?)

Discussion Questions

1. "Governments should get out of the way so that markets can work efficiently and create wealth." "Government regulation and oversight are essential for keeping markets competitive." Discuss.

2. Review the histories of public purpose action just described. Where did nonprofits take action? Governments? When was the action that was taken direct provision, and when was it regulation? When did nonprofits advocate for more government regulation or provision?

4 | Theories of Organizational Behavior

Governments and nonprofits are often associated with bureaucracies and an administrative mode of organization, but this is only one aspect of organization in the public purpose sphere of the economy. The achievement of public consent, for example, is the reason why legislative bodies exist. Exchange plays a role, as public purpose organizations hire workers and purchase materials, generally through the same labor and product markets used by the other economic spheres. Custom, habit, and protocol structure political (and religious) ceremonies, hiring preferences, and work routines that take place within the public purpose economy.

Recognizing that governments and nonprofits are complex social organizations brings us back to the same questions we have addressed in regard to the business and core spheres of the economy: Whose interests are served? How do the varied and perhaps conflicting interests and motivations of the individuals and subgroups that make up the organization result in action by the organization? We can identify two extreme theories—pure public service, and pure "capture" by special interest—as well as a more sophisticated way of thinking that draws on notions of civic responsibility.

4.1 | The Theory of Pure Public Service

Sometimes it is assumed that the government acts as though it were a single "benevolent dictator," much like the "altruist" in the dictatorial model of the family. It is assumed that the government, perceiving a societal need, will simply act to meet it, even in the absence of participation or advocacy by citizens or interest groups.

Or, much like the "shareholder theory" of the firm and the "glued together" model of the family, the **theory of pure public service** may suggest that all the people involved in government or other non-profit organizations simply carry out the purpose with which they are charged. Similarly, a charity can be assumed to spend all its income on good works, and a group with, say, "nature preservation" in its title can be counted on to work to preserve nature. Likewise, according to this view, if "the American people" want a sustainable economy, the U.S. government can be trusted to work to provide it. This assumes that no one needs to monitor the organization or its employees to be sure that the mission of the organization is actually carried out.

This view assumes that all of the individuals who make up public purpose organizations are motivated by concern for the common good. This motivation is suggested, for example, by use of the venerable term *public servant* to refer to government employees. The pure theory of public service also implicitly assumes that the entities are well organized enough to be able to carry out their mission efficiently.

Many people are, in fact, motivated by concern for the common good, and such motivations can be encouraged and nourished by a culture that stresses civic duty. History suggests, however, that it is naive to subscribe to a theory of organizational behavior in which it is assumed that an understanding of *one* kind of motivation can cover *all* situations.

public service (theory of pure): the idea that public purpose organizations act purely in the interest of the common good, with no need for monitoring or citizen involvement

4.2 | The Theory of Pure Special-Interest "Capture"

At the other extreme is the theory that any organization, no matter what its stated purpose, will eventually be "captured" by powerful special interests and turned to their own self-interested uses: the **theory of pure special-interest capture**. For example, it is often argued that government regulation of the railroad and trucking industries in the United States, though originally intended to protect consumers and nontransportation businesses, eventually came to serve the interests of the railroad and trucking industries and their workers. Similar complaints have been raised more recently—for example, about the relationship of the National Marine Fisheries Service, a government agency charged with maintaining sustainable fisheries, to the interests of the fishing industry. In addition, one can see ebbs and flows in the rigor with which government agencies enforce antitrust policy, antidiscrimination policy, and environmental standards, depending on the interests and loyalties of the administration currently in power.

Many analysts have pointed out that the system of campaign finance in the United States, combined with the importance for campaigns of expensive media advertisements, tends to make politicians reliant on constituents with "deep pockets." The employees of the regulatory agencies themselves may also put their own interests first—for example, by resisting the repeal of an outdated regulation, or resisting attempts to make the work process more efficient, because they feel these changes would threaten their jobs.

As another example, although most charitable organizations are reputable, there are always a few that spring up to play on people's sympathies, while passing on little if any of the funds raised to people in need. In this case, the leader and perhaps the employees of the organization are often the real beneficiaries.

"capture" (theory of pure special-interest): the idea that public purpose organizations are always taken over by powerful special interests and used for their own self-interested ends

International organizations may also be "captured" by special interests. For example, the amount of pesticide residue permitted on imported fruits and vegetables is set by a United Nations body called the Codex Alimentarius. Some health experts feel that that organization has been "captured" by the growers and sellers and hence sets its standards too low, permitting unsafe residual levels of pesticides and other chemicals.

Of course, "watchdog" groups, such as groups that gather and publish information about agencies or charities, can be set up, as can rating systems to rank the agencies or charities according to how well they perform their stated purpose.[11] But then the question "Who will watch the watchdog?" arises. If everyone is really only self-interested, then the watchdog agency itself is liable to be "captured" by the groups it is supposedly watching. A "watchdog" group might be expected to realize that it can make more money by taking bribes in return for giving a group a better rating than it deserves, than by offering objective information.

In a worst-case scenario all parties use their advantages—in terms of money, influence, employment, or information—in their own self-interest.[12] In fact, you can find many examples, both historical and contemporary, of organizations rife with corruption, bribery, favoritism, sloth, and patronage. We would be in terrible shape, however, if this were the inevitable pattern!

4.3 | The Theory of Civic Responsibility

civic responsibility (theory of): the idea that public-oriented values and active citizen participation are possible and in fact are vital for the healthy functioning of public purpose organizations

A more adequate theory of public purpose organizational behavior, the **theory of civic responsibility**, recognizes that people are interested in outcomes both for themselves and for others and that they are intrinsically as well as extrinsically motivated.

Research on social capital suggests that belief systems, norms, and traditions play a substantial role in how well public purpose organizations function. When there is a tradition of having an honest, efficient government and of demanding that leaders model these values in their own behavior, governmental agencies and public-spirited organizations can work quite well. People usually do, in fact, like to do things that they believe are socially useful, and—when adequately paid and supported—will therefore often carry out tasks not in their own immediate self-interest.

Along with a culture of public-oriented values, structural features of organizations can also be important. Systems of checks and balances, audits, and reporting requirements can spread out power and increase transparency within an organization, thus also encouraging honest and goal-directed behavior. These structural features cannot usually do the job on their own, however. When corruption and dishonesty are the norm, when greed is elevated to a virtue, and/or when leaders are "on the take," dishonest people can usually find ways to work around or otherwise cheat on merely formal requirements.

Democratic societies implicitly rely on both personal and civic norms of responsibility to see that public purposes are carried out. They rely on *personal* responsibility, because it would be impossible to police each and every worker, manager, politician, and leader to make sure that he or she is honest. The majority of individuals have to behave with integrity for a democratic system to work.

Democracies rely on *civic* responsibility as well, precisely because *not all* individuals can be trusted to act honestly or in the public interest. It is only by keeping informed, actively monitoring the state of public institutions, and demanding accountability from

---

[11] Many non-profit advocacy organizations have just such a purpose. For example, the Marine Fish Conservation Network is a coalition of groups that "watchdogs" the National Marine Fisheries Service, and the Institute for Agriculture and Trade has a project monitoring the WTO on behalf of civil society groups.

[12] The theory that the activities of politicians and other agents of government can be explained by theories of self-interested, rational behavior has also sometimes been called, perhaps confusingly, public choice theory.

representatives, leaders, and organizations that citizens can ensure that public purpose organizations do their job.

Public purpose organizations in a democracy are not like clockwork mechanisms that can simply be put in place and trusted to do their jobs: A tradition of active, democratic citizen action is an ongoing necessity. Such a tradition might be thought of as the ultimate public good.

Discussion Questions

1. Recall some direct dealings that you personally have had with public purpose organizations (even if these dealings consisted only of getting a driver's license from a local motor vehicle registry, being treated at a public clinic, or taking a class at the local "Y"). Which (if any) of the three theories of organizational behavior just described seems to explain the behavior you experienced?

2. Consider a recent piece of legislation that has been in the news, and discuss whether you think it primarily reflects pure public service, "capture," or responsibility.

Review Questions

1. What are the two main functions of public purpose organizations?
2. What are the three main types of public purpose organizations?
3. What are some of the main activities of state and local governments?
4. What are some of the main activities of the U.S. federal government?
5. What are the four main types of domestic non-profit organizations?
6. Describe some of the major characteristics of U.S. policies regarding social welfare in the following time periods: (a) before the late 1800s, (b) the late 1800s to the early 1920s, (c) the 1930s, (d) the 1960s, and (e) since the 1970s.
7. How did federal regulation of U.S. businesses first come about? What laws followed?
8. How did international trade coordination first come about? What institutions followed?
9. What important events occurred in the banking industry in the early years of the 1900s and in the 1980s?
10. What act created federal regulation of trading in stocks and bonds, and what did it specify?
11. Describe some important events in the history of environmental protection.
12. What are some arguments for (a) making government smaller? and (b) government having a large role in the economy?
13. What are three theories about the behavior of organizations in the public purpose sphere?

Exercises

1. Distinguish between the terms in the following pairs, and give an example of each.
   a. An open-access resource and a public good
   b. Regulation and direct provision
   c. Tax exempt and tax deductible
2. Indicate whether each of the following statements is true or false.
   a. Only the government can regulate economic activity.
   b. Over 20% of U.S. federal employees are involved in education and research.

c. Non-profit organizations are primarily charities supported by private donations.

d. The U.S. social security system was created during a time of economic prosperity.

e. The federal government decided to regulate markets in stocks and bonds in order to discourage competition and the use of these instruments for capital formation.

f. Federal initiatives to preserve natural resources began in the early years of the 20th century.

3. The text mentions some institutions involved in regulating two areas, medical practice and beer advertising. Choose a business product or service, or an area of special interest to you—perhaps a favorite food you consume (other than beer) or a profession you are considering entering (other than that of physician). Do a search on the Internet, and see how many government agencies, non-profit domestic organizations, and/or international organizations you can find that are active in providing or regulating economic activities in this area. (You may want to use search words such as *trade association, agency, regulation, nonprofit,* and *nongovernmental.*) Record the number of organizations you find, and make a list of at least three such organizations, including, if possible, the mission statement of each. As far as you can tell, do the various organizations seem to work together toward a common purpose, or do some of them act in opposition to, or as watchdogs of, each other?

4. Match each concept in Column A with a definition or example in Column B.

Column A	Column B
a. an open-access resource	i. Sherman Antitrust Act
b. regulations designed by a non-profit organization	ii. a proposed tax on currency trades
c. a funding intermediary	iii. a non-profit hospital
d. 501(c)(3)	iv. the Ford Foundation
e. a supranational quasi-governmental organization	v. the idea that investors should be fully informed about securities
f. a Progressive Era policy	vi. a tax on an activity that generates externalities
g. a New Deal policy	vii. International Monetary Fund
h. "sunlight theory"	viii. an ocean fishery
i. Tobin tax	ix. the social security system
j. Pigovian tax	x. standards for business accounting practices

5. Internet Exercise: Using **http://www.census.gov/**, find *for your state* the statistics related to levels of government employment for 1999 or a more recent year. How many people in your state are employed by the federal, state, and local governments? Briefly describe the kinds of jobs they do.

Part Six

Economic Outcomes and Economic Ideology

Chapter 18

The Variety of Economic Systems

On August 22, 1991, Mikhail Sergeyevich Gorbachev resigned as the general secretary of the Soviet Communist Party and dissolved its Central Committee. On December 25, 1991, Gorbachev announced on television that he was stepping down as Soviet president. The Soviet Union, a world superpower that had operated since 1917 under a regime of economic central planning, was dissolved. One writer, commenting on the demise of the major challenge to capitalistic economic systems, declared the "end of history." Yet in spite of such dramatic upheavals, it would be a mistake to think that countries of the world now all answer the basic economic questions—"what," "how," and "for whom"—in the same way.

1 | Comparing Economic Systems

comparative economic systems: the branch of economic study concerned with differences in economic institutions across societies

The analysis of differences in economic institutions across different countries and societies is the focus of the study of **comparative economic systems**. Now that we have developed some basic tools of economic analysis, it is useful to recognize the ways in which societies can and do differ with respect to their basic economic institutions.

Chapter 1 raised some fundamental questions about well-being. In creating and distributing the goods and services that contribute to well-being, every society must in some way solve what economists regard as the three "basic economic questions": *What* should be produced, and *what* should be maintained? *How* should production and maintenance be accomplished? *For whom* should economic activity be undertaken?

In this chapter we will investigate how different economies around the world put different emphases on the various modes of economic organization and patterns of ownership in addressing the basic economic questions. We will also examine what we know about well-being outcomes as they relate to these processes and other factors.

1.1 | Modes of Organization: An Elaboration

We noted in Chapter 2 that we can identify four major modes of economic organization. We can now elaborate on them a bit more, exploring how they function at local, national, or international levels.

Customary organization uses traditions and habits to answer the basic economic questions. At a large-scale level, this form of organization is prominent in parts of rural Africa, Asia, and Latin America, where much production and consumption is still accomplished today as it was hundreds of years ago. Oftentimes, such customs have developed over centuries as ways of effectively organizing economic activities for surviving and flourishing within specific ecological and social settings. For example, religious planting and harvesting celebrations may mark the most opportune times for these activities. They may also, however, sometimes constrain improvements in well-being, as occurs when traditional strictures prevent adoption of techniques that would increase productivity or when they limit social roles, such as the activities of women. In industrialized societies, customary organization plays less of a role, although we can still sometimes see it at work. For example, traditions about which jobs are "appropriate" for men and which for women still sometimes guide people's choices of occupations and employers' decisions about hiring.

Consensual organization occurs when people come to democratic, explicitly negotiated agreements about what, how, and for whom. Although no national economy has ever been organized completely along consensual lines, smaller societies, such as collective *kibbutzim* organized in Israel and some religious communities in the United States, have—at least for a time—succeeded in organizing their economic activity according to a consensual system. Consent is also an important organizing principle *within* organizations such as families, workgroups, cooperatives, and other relatively nonhierarchical non-profit organizations and business firms. In democracies, consent also plays an important role in shaping government economic policy, although the process is less direct and is strongly influenced by powerful corporate and bureaucratic interests.

Administrative organization involves the delegation of decision-making authority to some person or agency, often a bureaucracy.

Administrative organization is present in every society. Governments carry out many administrative activities (see Chapter 17), and a government's exercise of authority to direct economic activity is especially noticeable in times of war or national crisis. Administration is also the main mode of organization within hierarchically organized business firms and is the purpose of many non-profit standards-setting agencies and associations. Almost every organization of any size involves some sort of administrative structure.

command economies (or planned economies): national economies characterized by administrative direction of economic activity via a central bureaucracy

At a large-scale level, this mode of organization was applied to the entire economic system in the **command economies** of the Soviet Union and Eastern Europe before the overthrow of their communist parties, and in Cuba, China, and a few other Asian nations. In these countries the direction of investments in industries and agriculture, and decisions about what to produce, where people would live and work, what their incomes would be, and what prices would be charged were largely made by centralized administrative government agencies. Also called **planned economies**, these economies concentrated a great deal of power—and huge responsibility for compiling and processing information—in bureaucratic institutions. They were also characterized by authoritarian, nondemocratic political regimes.

market economies: national economies in which decentralized exchange plays a substantial organizing role

Exchange as a mode of organization exists when people trade one thing for another, often through established market institutions. At a national scale, economies wherein exchange plays a substantial role are often referred to as **market economies** (although, as we noted in Chapter 16, major components of such economies are governed by custom, consent, and/or administration).

Market exchange is an inherently decentralized process in that individual participants in any given market generally make decisions about buying and selling subject to their economic circumstances, rather than to the will or directive of some higher authority. Market systems are compatible with widely varying political systems; they have prevailed historically in countries with well-established democracies (such as the United States, the United Kingdom, and Sweden), as well as in countries with repressive dictatorships (such as Spain in the 1950s and 1960s, Chile in the 1970s and 1980s, Indonesia from 1967 to 1998, and South Korea for most of the years since World War II). Since the breakup of the Soviet Union in 1991, most of the former command economies have moved in the direction of increasing reliance on market institutions, although some have moved further in this direction than others.

1.2 | Patterns of Ownership

We can also look at economic systems from a somewhat different angle, comparing them in terms of patterns of ownership. As we saw in Chapter 9, ownership rights are important in determining the shape of economic activity.

In nearly all societies, individuals or families retain ownership of a certain amount of personal property for their own use. That is to say, individuals or families have possession and control of certain goods that are intended for consumption or small-scale production purposes; they may determine when and how these goods are to be consumed or used (within the bounds of legality) and whether and under what terms they are prepared to transfer the goods to someone else. Typically, people have de facto or legal ownership of their own clothing, cooking equipment, bicycles or cars, and the like. They also (except in conditions of slavery) have legal possession of their own labor, even if their choices of how to put it to use are limited. What distinguishes fundamentally different types of economic systems is the pattern of ownership of larger-scale productive assets—natural capital (including land, mineral resources, water and energy resources, etc.), equipment, factories, intellectual property, and financial capital.

As we discussed in Chapter 9, ownership can be a complicated thing. For example, sometimes people have use rights to an asset but do not have the right to transfer it (that is, to sell it or give it away). Owners rarely enjoy unlimited rights. The use of a productive asset must not violate the laws or the conventional practices of the land: You must drive a vehicle on the designated side of the road, you must keep a restaurant kitchen clean, and so on. In transferring assets, you may have to meet certain exchange regulations and possibly pay a sales, gift, or inheritance tax. And the income received from putting an asset into production may well be taxed or have to be shared in certain ways.

Yet, when we consider the important question of how productive assets are owned, we can still identify four major types of systems: individual ownership, corporate ownership, cooperative ownership, and state ownership.

individual ownership: ownership of productive assets by individuals and families

With **individual ownership**, productive assets are owned by individuals and families, in much the same way as they own property for personal use. Individual ownership of an enterprise may take several different forms, including ownership by a single individual, ownership by members of a family, and ownership by partners (usually a small group of friends and/or relations). Where ownership involves more than one individual, the ownership claims may be divided up in any way; in other words, family members or partners may own different proportions of the asset.

corporate ownership: ownership by shareholders of corporations, who are primarily individuals and nongovernmental institutions

In **corporate ownership**, assets are owned by shareholders (often a large number of unrelated individuals and/or institutions), who hold ownership rights in proportion to the number of shares of the enterprise's stock that they own.[1] Corporations, as we have seen, are legal entities whose existence does not depend on who their owners happen to be at any given time; shares can be traded freely on stock markets. The shareholders of an enterprise may include its own managers and workers, and institutional shareholders may include government agencies as well as private organizations. (However, if the corporation is *primarily* state-owned, we would classify that with *government* ownership, discussed below.)

cooperative ownership: ownership by a collective

In **cooperative ownership**, assets are owned collectively by a group. In many parts of the less industrialized world, for example, resources such as grazing land and water from local lakes and rivers are cooperatively owned. That is, rights to an asset are held jointly by a group of people (such as farmers living in the area), and any individual who wants to use the asset must join with the others in a system of local group control, sharing rights and duties related to the asset. Cooperative ownership also exists in industri-

---

[1] In practice, corporate enterprises frequently offer different kinds of shares with differing rights attached; for the purpose of the present discussion, we will assume that all shares confer the same ownership rights.

alized societies—for example, when a cooperative business enterprise is owned by its workers, its consumers, or its suppliers. Cooperative enterprises are most common in Italy, where they employ more than 2% of the labor force.

government ownership: ownership by an agency of the government

In **government ownership**, assets are owned (exclusively or predominantly) by an agency of government—in principle, on behalf of the people represented by that government. Government enterprises may be owned outright by government agencies, or they may be corporations in which such agencies hold all or a majority of the shares. Government enterprises vary in many respects: in the level of government (national, regional, local, or municipal) by which they are owned and to which they are accountable; in their degree of autonomy from the government officials involved; and in the way in which the income accruing to them is distributed (to managers, employees, state treasuries, or the general public). Most industrialized countries include a mixture of state ownership and other ownership patterns.

Not all assets are owned according to one of these four ownership systems. Open-access resources (see Chapter 17), such as fish in the ocean and the capacity of Earth's atmosphere to absorb wastes, do not come under any one country's legal jurisdiction. Whether these can become effectively managed through international cooperation is currently a pressing issue.

Discussion Questions

1. What do you think of when you hear the terms *capitalism* and *socialism*?

2. What do you already know, coming into this class, about the history of countries such as Sweden, India, Russia, China, and Japan? Have you ever studied their economic systems? Do you think it is worthwhile to study such systems and their histories, or not? Why?

---

2 | Varieties of Capitalism and Socialism

capitalism: a system characterized by predominantly private ownership (either individual or corporate) of productive assets

socialism: a system characterized by predominantly shared, public ownership (either cooperative or state) of productive assets

In a very simple method of classification, sometimes you will see actual economies classified as exhibiting either **capitalism**, if they rely primarily on private ownership (either individual or corporate) of productive assets, or **socialism**, if they rely primarily on public ownership (either cooperative or state). Less industrialized countries might be classified according to which of these two system predominates in their commercialized and industrialized sectors, or they might be called traditional (or premodern or feudal) if they have a largely agrarian economy characterized by individual and/or cooperative ownership.

in the Real World

Common-Property Resources

common-property resources: resources that are owned collectively by a defined group

When groups of farmers or ranchers, for example, collectively own grazing land or water from lakes and rivers, such an asset is called a **common-property resource**.

Economists have debated the efficiency of such local systems of common ownership. In the absence of clear individual or corporate property rights or formal administration, economists have sometimes assumed that a resource must therefore be an "open-access resource" and will tend to be overexploited. Sometimes other problems also occur, such as farmers having difficulty getting credit because they cannot offer their use rights in the common property as collateral for a loan in the same way that they would be able to use their rights to an individually owned asset.

However, other researchers point to cases in which local common-property systems made up of particular individuals or families organized by tradition or consent, and often backed up by social or other sanctions, have been remarkably effective in managing local common-property resources. The lack of individual, corporate, or state ownership does *not* necessarily imply that *no one* is in control. ◁

corporate capitalism: a national system in which a great deal of the ownership of productive assets is through corporations, which are in turn primarily owned by private (non-governmental) shareholders

state socialism: a national system characterized by a great deal of state ownership of productive assets

However, such categorization views ownership issues in a very simplistic way and does not look at all at organizational issues. In contemporary economies, corporate ownership tends to predominate over individual ownership, in terms of employment and the value of productive assets. A system in which private (that is, nongovernmental) corporate owner-ship and direction of investment dominates is called **corporate capitalism**. Among the world's economies, the United States is the most prominent example of reliance on private corporate ownership of productive assets; other industrialized nations, as we will see, tend to have corporate capitalism but with a larger role for governmental institutions.

Likewise, there is a type of shared ownership, in which state ownership tends to predominate over cooperative ownership. Economies that have a great deal of state ownership are referred to as **state socialism**.

Although contemporary economic systems in major countries tend to be either *cor-porate* capitalist or *state* socialist, these terms are often abbreviated to just *capitalist* and *socialist*. For the rest of this section we will adopt this convention.[2]

When we bring in modes of organization as well, we can see that the simple capital-ist/socialist classification hides a great deal of variation among countries. We can iden-tify four distinct subgroups of actual economies by mode of organization, as listed in Table 18.1. We will discuss each in turn.

2.1 | Classifying Capitalist Systems

Capitalist systems may be distinguished according to the extent to which state adminis-tration, planning, and social welfare programs—including government agencies at all levels—play a role in the economy. In Chapter 17 we discussed how governments (as part of the public purpose economy) can both regulate economic activity and directly provide goods and services.

Because of the variety of ways in which government agencies may play a role in capi-talist economies, it is impossible to develop any simple indicator of the extent of the state's involvement. We may nonetheless distinguish between two prototypical kinds of capital-ism. Under **laissez-faire capitalism** the role of the state is supposed to be relatively small; at least in theory, it is confined to maintaining a legal–institutional environment conducive to corporate ownership and market exchange. By contrast, **administrative capitalism** involves a more substantial amount of state activity alongside market-organized activity.

It should be apparent that the differences between these two variants of capitalism are matters of degree. A continuous spectrum runs from the completely unregulated to the heavily administrative form of capitalism, and where one divides the spectrum is somewhat arbitrary.

laissez-faire capitalism: a national system characterized by private cor-porate ownership and a great reliance on exchange as a mode of organiza-tion (with relatively little organization by public administration)

administrative capitalism: a national system characterized by private corporate ownership and a substantial reliance on public admin-istration (as well as exchange) as a mode of organization

Among major countries in the contemporary world, the United States and the United Kingdom are in practice closest to the laissez-faire end of the capitalist spec-trum; Japan, Sweden, and France are closer to the administrative end. Canada, Australia, and New Zealand have tended to be nearer the middle of the spectrum.

Table 18.1 | Types of Contemporary Economic Systems (with examples)

Ownership ▶ Organization ▼	Capitalist	Socialist
Administrative	Administrative Capitalism: Japan, France, Sweden	Administrative Socialism: North Korea, Cuba
Exchange	Laissez-Faire Capitalism: United States, United Kingdom (toward this end of the spectrum)	Market Socialism: China, Vietnam

[2] Could other systems, such as individual-ownership-based ("proprietary") capitalism or socialist systems based on cooperation and consent, survive in the contemporary world? This interesting question is beyond the scope of this text, except for a brief discussion in the next chapter.

In both the United States and the United Kingdom, the government is less active in terms of owning or regulating business than in France or Japan. Japan's economy is run by a close partnership of government and business. Nearly 30% of French industry is government-owned, including many high-technology firms and leading exporters.

Social welfare programs are also considerably less extensive and less generous in the United States than in the other countries (see Chapter 17). Sweden (like most of the rest of Northern and Western Europe) has very extensive welfare programs (unemployment compensation, health care, social security, and the like), many policies designed to improve workers' labor market prospects (such as extensive employee retraining and relocation measures), and various income support programs that strongly influence the economy.

Yet the Japanese, French, and Swedish economies are all called "capitalist" because their economies are dominated by large corporate enterprises owned by private stockholders and run by private businesspeople.

The contemporary United States, however, is far from the kind of laissez-faire system that it was in the first half of the 19th century. The U.S. federal government undertakes major transfers of income to the elderly (in the form of pensions and health insurance); it runs a massive military structure with close ties to private business (the "military–industrial complex"); and, as we saw in Chapter 17, it propounds and enforces numerous regulations affecting, among other things, working conditions, consumer safety, and the environment.

Getting quantitative comparisons of the size of government across different countries is difficult. Although it is relatively easy, among countries with similar statistical accounting standards, to get information on the government's role in the economy as concerns total taxing and spending, it is much harder to find information in other areas. The existence of different ways of keeping statistics means that numbers on employment and on enterprise ownership are frequently not comparable, and measuring the role of government as an administrative regulator of economic activity is difficult indeed. Table 18.2 presents one measure of the size of government across the countries we have just discussed. The share of government consumption expenditures in GDP (at all levels of government) is highest in Sweden and France, as we might expect, and lowest in the United States, with the United Kingdom and Canada in between. The relatively low percentage of GDP in Japan that goes to government expenditures does not reflect the large role the government plays in influencing and supporting business activity.

2.2 | Classifying Socialist Systems

We defined capitalism and socialism strictly in terms of their forms of ownership, without mentioning modes of organization. Yet isn't it also true that capitalist systems use the market, whereas socialist systems are based on administration? The answer is yes and no.

In corporate capitalist systems, markets do indeed play a very large role in economic organization, because the heavy-handed use of administrative directives would be incompatible with the property rights held by the (private) enterprise owners.

In state socialist systems, administrative directives can serve as the means by which state agencies exercise their property rights in state enterprises. But administrative

Table 18.2 | One Measure of the Size of Government

	General Government Final Consumption Expenditure (% of GDP)
Sweden	26
France	23
Canada	19
United Kingdom	19
Japan	16
United States	14

Source: World Bank, *World Development Indicators, 2002.* (Japan and U.S. data are from 1999; data for other countries are from 2000.)

market socialism: a national system in which state ownership predominates but much activity is organized by exchange

administrative socialism: a national system in which state ownership predominates and activity is primarily organized by public administration (command)

allocation need not be dominant. It is also possible, in socialist systems, for relatively autonomous state enterprises to operate within economies in which market methods of resource allocation are the norm. This kind of socialist system can be called **market socialism**—as distinct from the alternative based on administrative allocation (or, as it is often called, "command"), which may be labeled **administrative socialism**.

At its peak (from the 1950s through the 1970s), administrative socialism characterized economic systems in countries containing about one-third of the world's population, but the collapse of this system in the Soviet Union and its satellites and its modification in China and elsewhere have meant that few countries follow it today. North Korea and Cuba are contemporary examples of countries characterized by administrative socialism.

China has pursued market socialism since 1978. Although the central government continues to control and support many large state enterprises, the government has encouraged the growth of a variety of productive enterprises and activities beyond its direct control. Farms formerly were communally managed, but with market socialism, farmers have been allowed to lease land individually from the state. After delivering a fixed amount of their produce to the government, they may sell the rest on markets. State firms have also been allowed to sell some of their output on markets, and new firms owned collectively and controlled by local or municipal government agencies (the "township and village enterprises") have become increasingly important. Market socialism was also characteristic of some countries of Eastern Europe, such as Yugoslavia and Hungary, until the late 1980s.

Discussion Questions

1. Choose a country that you are somewhat familiar with and that is not one we have just discussed. What do you know about its economic system? How would you classify it?

2. "Capitalist systems depend on markets, socialist systems on systems of command." Is this statement true or false? Why?

---

3 | Comparative Systems in Historical Perspective

In looking at historical experience, it is important to keep in mind that the two countries most often cited as archetypical market economies—England for reasons of historical primacy and the United States because of its economic dominance during much of the 20th century—in fact followed atypical development paths significantly different from those of all the other industrialized countries. In this section we look briefly at the history of a few industrialized countries with which the United States commonly compares itself, as well as of a few countries and regions with very different experiences.

3.1 | The Anglo-American Experience of Laissez-Faire Capitalism

The era of modern economic industrial expansion began in England in the 1700s. At that time England was already the most developed country in the wealthiest corner of the globe. It had an elaborate financial and commercial system, a unified national government, a large internal market, and a well-established trading and naval presence in the world. By 1700 the English economy was already highly market-oriented, and 40% of the population lived in urban areas. Specialization and the systematic application of scientific methods to agriculture and industry increased rapidly during the next century, and standards of public health and literacy improved significantly. The economic benefits of the Industrial Revolution of the late 1700s were enhanced by the development of colonies as sources of raw materials and markets for manufactures, while regulations and tariffs discouraged the importation of manufactured goods. The ensuing era of economic growth rested on more than a century of uniquely favorable circumstances, some of which are clearly not reproducible.

Early in the 1800s, sustained industrial expansion also began in the United States, shortly after the country shed its status as an English colony. The United States also took off from a wealthy base, but the high standard of living in America was often overlooked because the elites here did not live at the level of European nobility. In fact, at the time of the American Revolution, the colonies enjoyed roughly the same average material standard of living as the colonial power, England. The new nation briefly fell behind, but growth began again after the War of 1812, and the United States quickly overtook English living standards. By the mid–19th century, the United States was exporting technology to Europe in some industries and was inspiring German railroad builders.

The rapid urbanization and industrialization of the early years of growth in relatively laissez-faire capitalist economies were destabilizing for much of the population. By the early 19th century, increasing misery and social disorder led in England to the enactment of legislation providing aid to the poor and the unemployed. For example, the British "Factory Acts," adopted early in the 19th century and vigorously enforced by the middle of the century, restricted the length of the working day and prohibited the employment of women and children in onerous forms of labor. The United States was slower to adopt such legislation, but in the early 20th century, it too developed significant government-run social programs. Increasing government activity was the overall trend up through the 1960s.

In the late 20th century, the pendulum swung back in the opposite direction, toward laissez-faire. Starting in the 1970s, the worldwide economy experienced significantly less prosperous economic conditions. Although economic growth did not come to a halt, the willingness and the ability of governments to maintain their welfare-state programs diminished, and political leaders who were less sympathetic to administrative forms of capitalism gained power. As a consequence, the scope of social programs was cut back in many countries, and programs of **privatization** of government-owned enterprises and **deregulation** of private industries were undertaken.

The debate about the merits of different economic systems continues today. Early in the present century, for example, crises in energy provision in California in 2000–2001 and the financial instability of airline companies in 2002 led some analysts to question whether deregulation of these industries had been a wise idea.

3.2 | Capitalism and Social Democracy in Western Europe

The countries that began to modernize in the mid– to late 19th century (such as France, Germany, and Sweden) developed from the beginning a form of capitalism considerably more regulated than the early Anglo-American model. In these countries the state played a substantially greater role than it had in England and the United States at a comparable stage of development, not only in adopting social policies to protect the people most vulnerable to the changing economy but also in promoting industrial growth.

In virtually all the industrializing countries of Europe and North America, except for England and the United States, state agencies actively helped private business to make use of new technologies and to adopt more efficient practices. Following World War II, a new economic, social, and political configuration often called "welfare state capitalism" emerged in much of Western Europe. This new form of administrative capitalism resulted from the gradual expansion of economic and social rights in countries with open political systems (such as the Scandinavian countries) or from the dictates of military occupation authorities designed to weaken previously powerful pro-Fascist elites in defeated countries (notably Germany, Austria, and Italy). The scope of the welfare state in these countries varies a great deal: It is very substantial in countries with strong labor movements and long periods of rule by social democratic parties.

Modern Sweden provides an example of capitalist development in which the government has played an active role. There is very little direct government involvement in the affairs of Swedish business enterprises. However, the Swedish government assists in providing for people's welfare in numerous ways, from birth to death. High-quality health care is virtually free, as are child care, higher education, and a wide array of other

privatization: the conversion of enterprises from public to private ownership (encouraged in many countries in the late 20th century)

deregulation: the reduction of governmental administrative oversight of private enterprises (encouraged in many countries in the late 20th century)

While France is a capitalist country, a significant portion of its major industries are publicly owned to some degree. To exactly what degree companies should be publicly owned, however, is a matter of dispute. Employees of France Telecomm, Air France, and the French post office and public utilities (EDF and GDF) gathered on October 3, 2002, to protest government plans to privatize parts of public companies. Fearing loss of jobs and social benefits, trade unions called a 24-hour strike.

social services. The elderly are generously covered by social insurance. Families receive paid parental leaves for pregnancy, birth, and the early months of raising a new child, with incentives for fathers as well as mothers to share in child care.

Most of these services are provided by categorical programs with universal entitlement, rather than on the needs-tested basis (available only to those who are sufficiently poor) that is common in the United States. In Sweden, for example, anyone who has a child receives the same cash benefit regardless of income level, whereas in the United States, only the very poorest single mothers receive welfare payments to support their families—and even this benefit has become politically unpopular and has been severely constrained. The Swedish approach is expensive, but it has low administrative costs, enjoys widespread popular support, and avoids the kind of government intrusion into the details of individual citizens' lives that is a major feature of any needs-tested system.

Enterprises are subject to strict health and environmental regulation in Sweden. Despite high wages, unemployment was comparatively low throughout most of the second half of the 20th century. This was due in part to the government's "active labor market policies," including nationwide job postings and referral centers, worker retraining programs, and relocation assistance.

High-productivity industries were subsidized and low-productivity industries were penalized by Sweden's unique wage bargaining system, which was in effect until the early 1980s. A large union federation, representing virtually all of the country's workers, met with a comparable nationwide employers' association to set wages on a centralized basis. The unions pressed, quite successfully, for a "solidarity wage policy," moving toward equality of wages for all workers regardless of their industry or individual productivity. Wages were never entirely equal, but inequality between workers was far less than in most capitalist economies. If skilled metalworkers were paid the same amount as restaurant waiters, metalworking industries would be profitable (they would be competing against other countries where metalworking wages were higher), whereas restaurants would be unprofitable. This is not just a theoretical possibility. In fact, Sweden excels in some metalworking industries but has surprisingly few—and very expensive—restaurants.

However, in the 1980s, centralized wage bargaining and the solidarity wage policy began to break down, in part because profitable industries insisted on separate bargaining in order to pay more so that they could attract more labor and expand their operations. The Swedish system was built up under the long rule of the Social Democratic party, which, with the support of the country's strong labor movement, has been in power for most of the time since the 1930s. In recent years the conservative opposition and the pressure of the international economic slowdown has led to waves of cutbacks in the Swedish welfare state, and the remarkable harmony of Swedish business–labor relations has sometimes given way to discord.

Yet the Swedish system of administrative capitalism and social democracy remains quite different from that of the United States and that of the United Kingdom, and it appears likely that it will continue to represent a distinct model of capitalism more oriented toward distributional equity and social justice. The 1990s move toward smaller governments, Swedish-style, included a reduction in the guaranteed nationwide sick pay from 90% of wages beginning on the first day of an illness to 75% of wages beginning on the third day! The example of Sweden shows that widely differing roads have led to capitalist economic development, many of which bear little resemblance to the simple prescriptions of laissez faire.

3.3 | Industry and Government in Japan and the Newly Industrializing Economies

The Japanese economy grew rapidly for several generations after World War II, turning the country into a developed industrial nation with the world's second-largest economy (measured by GDP). Japan's ability to achieve this growth can be attributed in part to the tradition of close coordination between government and business. Ironically, the effects of U.S. occupation after Japan's wartime defeat also made a substantial contribution to its later growth.

The Japanese state began to play a crucial role during the industrialization drive of the second half of the 19th century. After establishing much of the industrial sector with public funds, the state sold off enterprises at bargain prices to private owners and subsequently nurtured these enterprises with favorable economic policies. The militarists who gained political power in the 1930s took for granted the need for coordination with the private sector; the army leadership won acceptance of its Five-Year Plan for heavy industry in 1936. After the war, the symbiotic relationship between the Japanese government and the business community continued, with agencies such as the Ministry of International Trade and Industry (MITI) helping Japanese corporations identify and move into promising, rapidly growing industries.

Almost immediately after Japan's surrender in 1945, U.S. occupation authorities began to reorganize the economy, initially with the objective of weakening the old elite who had supported the war. Production of weapons and military equipment was prohibited; some of the biggest business corporations and holding companies were broken up in order to promote competition; a sweeping land reform distributed assets to much of the rural population, boosting their incomes; and rapid unionization was allowed, so that more than half of all Japanese employees belonged to unions by 1948.

Thus the Japanese economy experienced major shocks in the late 1940s. Japanese business was forced to be more competitive and to abandon military production in favor of new civilian industries; household incomes and consumption were raised by land reform in the countryside and by unionization in the cities. As the cold war began, the United States quickly abandoned any punitive intentions toward Japan and instead concentrated on building up the Japanese economy as a bulwark against communism in Asia.

The strength of the labor movement, in the context of rapid economic expansion, soon led to one of the best-known characteristics of the Japanese economic system: the guarantee of lifetime employment for workers in large enterprises. This arrangement has supported an unusual degree of worker loyalty and commitment; among other advantages, lifetime job security means that workers can participate in reorganization efforts without fear of losing their jobs. Relatively small pay differentials within Japanese companies meant that the rewards derived from productivity increases were widely spread.

Workers in large Japanese enterprises enjoyed an array of benefits, including housing credits or company housing, medical insurance with company clinics or hospitals, internal retail and service shops, low-interest loans, and cultural and recreational facilities. Department chiefs often became involved in the personal problems of workers—for example, offering mediation of marital disputes. The broad scope of enterprise activities has roots in Japanese culture and flourished in a rapidly growing, unionized economy.

There were always limits to the Japanese "miracle," however. Small businesses were never able to match the benefits or lifetime employment guarantees of large industry; the resulting dualism in the labor market has been analyzed at length by Japanese economists. Large enterprises often subcontracted substantial parts of their production processes to small firms; this led to lower average labor costs and transferred the burdens of market fluctuations to the small companies and their employees. Nor did the "miracle" last. Economic activity slowed down dramatically in the 1990s, plagued by problems in banking and financial institutions. Regulations on banks were fairly loose in Japan, and its banks had run up bad loans worth hundreds of billions of dollars.

newly industrializing countries (NICs): countries of East Asia that followed Japan's pattern of export-led industrial growth (primarily South Korea, Taiwan, Singapore, and Hong Kong)

Many features of the Japanese model of regulated capitalism were also adopted in some of the **newly industrializing countries (NICs)** of East Asia—for example, South Korea, Taiwan, Singapore, and Hong Kong—which demonstrated rapid export-oriented economic growth after World War II. In these countries, predominant (but not exclusive) private ownership was combined with a significant degree of government influence over industrial structure, the direction and character of new investment, the banking system, and foreign trade. These successful modernizers routinely used tariffs and other trade barriers to protect home markets while local producers worked to reach the levels of sophistication and scale sufficient for them to succeed under world competitive conditions.

These countries also encountered economic problems and slowdowns in growth in the late 1990s. Speculative movements of financial capital set off the regionwide Asian financial crisis of 1997–1998, leading to economic distress in even relatively well-off Asian countries and spawning disastrous increases in poverty and unemployment in poorer countries. The depth of the crisis was partly due to inadequate standards of auditing and accountability, particularly in banking. Nonetheless, most countries would be delighted to reach the level of commercial and industrial development of contemporary Japan and the NICs. Their route to development may not be one that other countries can follow—but neither did they follow the English or American path, let alone a textbook prescription of laissez-faire economics.

3.4 | Russia and the Transition Economies

The Soviet Union was the traditional exemplar of administrative socialism. According to economic historian Alec Nove, Soviet economic planning at its peak spelled out production targets for almost 50,000 commodities, a task that involved a staggering and virtually unmanageable level of detail. Separate production decisions had to be made for the millions of distinguishable commodities in the Soviet Union (differing sizes and styles of shoes are just one example). The economy was steered very much toward heavy industry and military production—allowing the Soviet Union to become a world power—while neglecting consumer goods and agriculture.

The resulting high levels of inefficiency contributed, along with growing political and ethnic unrest, to the dissolution of the Soviet Union in 1991 and the collapse of the economic structure of command in 1992. In that year, the Russian government abolished price controls on most goods and began the rapid privatization of state-owned enterprises. Hopes were initially high that this "shock therapy" would allow for a prompt transition to a (presumably) more efficient market economy.

The reality, however, was quite different. Without the social, legal, and financial infrastructure necessary to support a market system, the economy collapsed and production plummeted. In 1994, measured national income was only a little over half what it had been 5 years earlier, and measures of human distress rose. Many of the newly privatized firms came to be controlled by "insiders," and "Russian Mafia" activity with its concomitant violence also ensued.

While China is a socialist country, it has become increasingly open to some market activities. Wal-Mart established a retail outlet in China in 1996, and opened this Sam's Club store in Beijing in July 2003. China also exports many goods into international markets, in 2002 selling $12 billion worth of products to Wal-Mart Stores Inc. alone.

transition economies: economies that gave up administrative state socialism during the late 20th century and are (presumed to be) on a path toward more market-oriented economic systems

The countries of the former Soviet Union and the countries in Eastern Europe and Asia that used to be under its influence are now often called **transition economies**. Some are negotiating a path to a more market-reliant system with relative success; others are still suffering from lower levels of production and lower living standards than they had under communist rule.

3.5 | China: From Administrative to Market Socialism

China is the largest country that still claims to be socialist. Under the leadership of Mao Zedung, China had built up an administrative socialist economy during the first 25 years after the triumph of the communist revolutionary forces in 1949. The Chinese model of administrative socialism differed in some important respects from the Soviet model. It put a greater emphasis on agriculture, delegated substantial powers to regional and local organizations, and periodically resorted to nonmaterial incentives on a wide scale. However, after Mao's death and the rise to power of Deng Xiaoping in the late 1970s, Chinese economic decision makers shifted course to a much more market-oriented form of socialism.

The Chinese model developed after 1978 was characterized by market socialism. Trade and exchange between Chinese centrally controlled state enterprises and other firms now follow market channels. From the mid-1970s to the mid-1990s, the central state sector did not shrink in absolute size, but it became an ever-smaller proportion of a rapidly growing overall economy. Most of the dynamism of China's economy stems from enterprises outside of the central state sector. China has succeeded in attracting many kinds of advanced technologies and new productive investments from the capitalist nations both in the West and in nearby Asian countries, often through joint ventures between foreign and Chinese enterprises.

There has been much corruption and personal appropriation of the fruits of such ventures, which has resulted not so much in slowing economic growth as in distributing its benefits quite unequally. An even more dangerous potential problem is related to the environmental unsustainability of the Chinese economic expansion. The depletion and/or degradation of natural resources (soil, water, air, and forests) that typically accompanies industrialization creates special concern for the future viability of the economy in the dual context of high population density and late industrialization (since early industrializers have already stretched the limits of global environmental tolerance for some by-products of human activity).

3.6 | Economies in Less Industrialized Countries

As we have seen, the approach to organizing an economic system is not always chosen by the residents of the country in question. The influence that the United States exerted on the economic organization of its former enemies after World War II is an example. During the cold war period of U.S./Soviet tension, the "choice" between capitalism and socialism as a declared economic system was for many countries more a matter of bowing to military force or forming a strategic alliance than of choosing a system by its merits. Nor can a resulting economy necessarily be called a "system" in any organized sense, as we saw in the case of the disorder that characterized the privatization of the Russian economy. These factors—foreign influence and/or disorder—are particularly relevant when we look at many of the less industrialized countries of the world.

Many countries of Asia, Latin America, and Africa were once colonies of European nations. In the colonial system, the colonies were dominated by the military and economic force of their colonizers. They supplied raw material resources such as minerals (gold, copper, and tin), textile fibers (cotton), and agricultural products (sugar and coffee) to the industries of Europe. The European colonizers, through either state enterprises or regulated private corporations, ran the mines, organized agricultural production along plantation lines, and developed railroads and roads laid out in such a way as to get the desired resources to ports where they could be shipped. The export-oriented sector usually existed side by side with a subsistence-oriented sector run along small-scale, traditional lines.

High tariffs and other barriers discouraged colonized countries from developing industries themselves. In British-run India, for example, cotton fiber was exported, while cloth made on British looms was imported to India at high cost. One of the symbols of the movement for independence from British rule was domestically spun clothing, representing resistance to the constraints that had been imposed on domestic manufacturing. Even after political independence, however, the legacies of colonial infrastructure and continuing barriers to the sale of their manufactured exports have put these countries at a distinct disadvantage, relative to the starting points enjoyed by such countries as the United Kingdom and the United States.[3]

In some less industrialized countries, the state has played a very large role, whereas at the other extreme, some have hardly any systematic governance at all. In some countries, rather than acting in the long-run economic interest of much of the population, the state has been responsive only to the demands of traditional vested interests (for example, the established producers of agricultural or mineral products) or to the demands of a new but narrow business elite. The result has sometimes been an incoherent development of the state apparatus and a proliferation of rules and regulations that throttle rather than stimulate development.

Such a pattern of unproductive state activity—illustrated by the experience at various times of such countries as Argentina, India, and Egypt—can lead to an undesirable form of regulated capitalism. Its prevalence in many parts of the world serves as a warning that government involvement in the economy is no panacea. A substantial government role may well be a necessary condition for economic progress in modern times, but it is surely not sufficient.

Other countries, such as, recently, Angola and the Sudan, have been troubled by border wars, civil wars, and rapidly changing political regimes. Sometimes such conflicts have been funded or otherwise encouraged and aided by richer countries for their own political or economic ends. In such cases, meaningful discussion of economic "systems" is almost impossible.

In the latter part of the 20th century, another new pattern emerged in which another resource plentiful in many poorer countries—inexpensive labor—was tapped for certain labor-intensive manufacturing processes. Clothing manufacture and elec-

---

[3] Exceptions are, perhaps, the oil-exporting countries of the Middle East, because rising global demand for their particular raw resource has in many cases created considerable wealth without much industrialization.

Patterns of colonization, trade, and investment have played important roles in the development of industry (or lack thereof) in many Asian, Latin American, and African countries. Cotton, for example, is an important crop in India. During the colonial period, India exported raw cotton to England. Later, the Indian government encouraged the development of domestic industries, like this contemporary cotton mill in Bombay. The state was often deeply involved, but in 1991 the government instituted changes that weakened industry regulations and attracted more foreign investment.

tronics assembly, for example, largely disappeared from the richest countries. (Check the tags in your own clothing if you want to confirm this.) Some corporations first moved their operations from the rich countries to the NICs and then, more recently, as wages in the NICs rose, moved on to cheaper countries still. Such industries often provide better terms of employment (wages and conditions) than can be found elsewhere in the poor country, yet these terms of employment are still far inferior to standards in rich countries.

Discussion Questions

1. "Strong state regulation, history shows, helps create a strong economy." What historical evidence is there to support this statement? What historical evidence contradicts it?

2. "Capitalist, market-based systems have historically sprung up when governments stop interfering in the economy." What historical evidence is there to support this statement?

4 | Comparing Economic Performance

By what criteria should economies be compared? What are meaningful ways to describe how economies meet, or do not meet, well-being goals? Although the question of final goals, raised in Chapter 1, introduces many complexities and difficulties into measurement, some measures related to intermediate goals offer meaningful standards of comparison.

In comparing economic performance across countries, we must remember that economic outcomes depend not only on economic ownership and organization but also on the global distribution of resources. Some countries have tremendous mineral and energy resources, whereas others are endowed with little. Countries in temperate zones tend to have advantages over tropical zones in many kinds of agriculture. Tropical countries also tend to have more severe health problems as a consequence of such diseases as cholera and malaria. Mountainous countries have more problems in agriculture and transport than flatter countries. All of these factors, added to the legacies of history and to the forms of ownership and organization, explain why assessing comparative economic success is a complex undertaking.

4.1 | Average Incomes

Gross domestic product (GDP) is limited as a measure of economic production because it leaves out most core sphere activities. However, it has the advantage that data on it are gathered by nearly every country of the world and published in *World Development Indicators* by the World Bank. We will look at GDP per capita (that is, the average level per person) as a rough indicator of average incomes in various countries.

Figure 18.1 charts GDP per capita for a selected list of high-income countries (the United States, the United Kingdom, and Japan), medium-income countries (Russia and Brazil), and low-income countries (China, Indonesia, India, Vietnam, and Nigeria). The numbers are given in U.S. dollars, figured on a "purchasing power parity" (PPP) basis that takes both international exchange rates and price level differences into account. U.S. GDP per capita is the highest, at $34,142; Nigeria's is the lowest in this group, at $896.

To give you a more vivid indication of what these numbers mean in terms of lifestyle in comparison to your own, we also include in the figure the number of personal computers per 50,000 people. The United States is highest of this group, at 29,260; India was (in 2000) the lowest, at 225. (Given the explosive growth of computer-related industry in India in the last few years, it is likely that this number will have changed significantly by the time you are reading this.)

To get an idea of what this means in global terms, it is important to note where the bulk of the world's population lives. Figure 18.2 shows the proportion of the world's population that lives in each of the selected countries. Overall, only 15% of the world's population lives in countries that the World Bank classifies as "high-income."

4.2 | Health and Literacy

We can get a little closer to a "capabilities" standard of looking at outcomes (see Chapter 10) by examining the sorts of outcomes that various societies provide in terms of health and education. For example, data are gathered internationally on child mortality—that is, on the number of children, per 1000 live births, who will die before reaching the age of 5. Figure 18.3 charts these data for the selected countries.

As you might expect, there is a general pattern of child mortality rates rising as income levels fall. Richer countries can afford to provide better health care and nutrition. However, as a consequence of circumstances, distributional patterns, and policies within countries, this relationship is not unvarying. Whereas in most of the high-income countries 7 or fewer people per 1000 births can be expected to die in early childhood, in the United States the number is higher (9 per 1000 births). Greater inequality in the United States and the unusually privatized nature of health care provision are often thought to contribute to this difference. Vietnam, a market socialist coun-

Figure 18.1 GDP per Capita and Computers per 50,000 People in Selected Countries in 2000

Among these countries in the year 2000, U.S. GDP per capita was the highest, at $34,142, and Nigeria's was the lowest, at $896. The number of personal computers per 50,000 people was 29,260 in the United States and 225 in India.

(Source: The World Bank, *World Development Indicators, 2002*.)

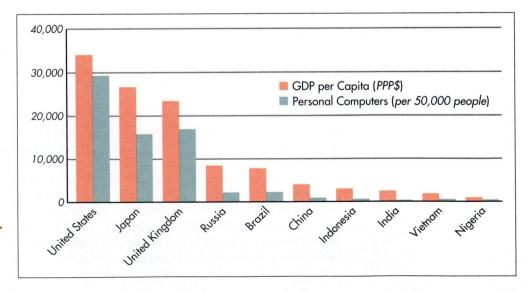

Figure 18.2 Percent of Global Population in Selected Countries in 2000

Only a small proportion of the world's population lives in high-income countries.

(Source: World Bank, *World Development Indicators, 2002*.)

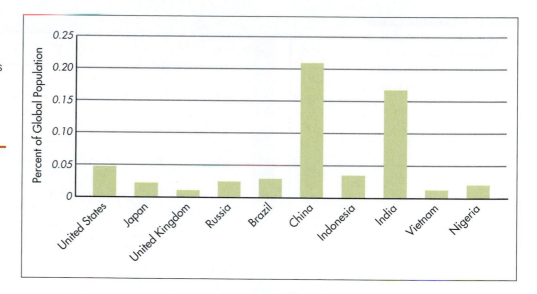

try, on the other hand, has unusually low child mortality for a low-income country, because resources have been specifically directed to this problem.

One could also compare life expectancies, illiteracy rates, and levels of education achieved to get comparisons that are meaningful in a "capabilities" approach. For example, whereas the high-income countries have very low rates of illiteracy, in China 16% of the population age 15 and over cannot read, and in Nigeria the figure is 36%.

4.3 | Sustainability

In Chapter 1, we also mentioned ecological balance and sustainability as goals of economics. Through much of history, "advancement" and "development" were thought of in terms of *industrialization*. As problems of the "global commons" become more pressing, however, it is necessary to take note of the effects of industrial pollution on the environment.

Figure 18.3 Child Mortality Rates for Selected Countries in 2000

Although it is generally the case that more poverty leads to more child mortality, some countries have mortality rates that are higher or lower than would be predicted on the basis of GDP per capita.

(Source: World Bank, *World Development Indicators, 2002*.)

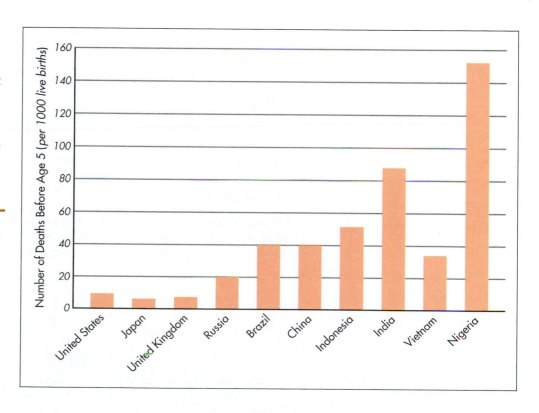

Figure 18.4 Industrial Carbon Dioxide Emissions in Selected Countries in 1998

The industrialized countries lead the world in emissions of greenhouse gases when these are expressed on a per-person basis.

(Source: World Bank, *World Development Indicators, 2002.*)

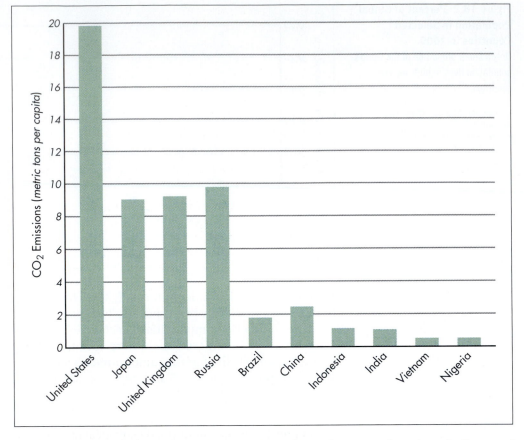

The amount of CO_2 (carbon dioxide) released into the atmosphere is an indicator of the use of fossil fuels; it is also an indicator of a country's contribution to problems of global climate change. Figure 18.4 shows the per capita industrial emissions of CO_2 in selected countries.

The United States leads the world in per capita industrial CO_2 emissions, with about 20 metric tons per person. Emissions per capita in Europe and Japan are only a fraction as high—even though outcomes in terms of health and education are close, and in some cases superior, to those in the United States. Russia's high level of emissions is the legacy of Soviet emphasis on heavy industry. China, with heavy dependence on coal as an energy source, has a fairly high level of emissions for a low-income country (2.5 metric tons per person).

The growing importance of issues of sustainability require a rethinking of the criteria by which economic performance has been traditionally judged. Is more GDP always better? Are more industrialization and more consumption always better, or should some types (and levels) of production and consumption be encouraged and others discouraged?

Discussion Questions

1. Which of the measures of economic performance suggested in this section do you think are best for analyzing the attainment of economic goals? Why? Can you think of additional measures that could be helpful in evaluating economic outcomes?

2. Comparing the figures in this section, do you think it is always true that higher GDP per capita leads to better measures on the other indicators? What do you think might explain variations?

Review Questions

1. Describe the four basic modes of organization, giving examples of each.
2. Describe the four major types of ownership, giving examples of each.
3. Define capitalism and socialism and the *specific* kinds of ownership structures that are most common in contemporary economic systems.
4. Describe two major types of (corporate) capitalist systems, and give examples of countries in which they occur.
5. Describe two major types of (state) socialist systems, and give examples of countries in which they occur.
6. Describe some key factors in the development of economic systems in each of the following countries and groups of countries: the United Kingdom and the United States; the European "welfare states"; Japan and the NICs; Russia and Eastern Europe; China; the less industrialized countries.
7. Describe how several countries vary in average income, health (and literacy), and contributions to environmental sustainability.

Exercises

1. Distinguish among individual, corporate, cooperative, and state ownership, and give examples in contemporary economies (at the local, national, or global level) of each.
2. Find a news article, editorial, political brochure, or other publication that contains a debate about economic systems. Analyze it in terms of the categories discussed in this chapter. In what way are terms such as *capitalism, markets, socialism,* and *big government* being used?
3. Choose a country not described in this chapter. Use library or Internet resources (as guided by your instructor) to access summaries of information about this country's economy. Does it fit into one of the classes of economic systems described in this chapter? Do any particular endowments of natural resources or historical events help to explain the evolution of the economy in this country? How does the country compare to those discussed in the text in terms of outcomes such as GDP per capita and in measures of health, literacy, and ecological balance and sustainability?
4. Match each concept in Column A with a definition or example in Column B.

Column A	Column B
a. a country with a market socialist economy	**i.** Russia
b. a country that is toward the laissez-faire capitalist end of the spectrum	**ii.** child mortality rate
	iii. Soviet Union (until 1991)
c. a command economy	**iv.** fish in a cooperatively managed village pond
d. a common-property resource	**v.** China
e. a newly industrializing country (NIC)	**vi.** clothing and cooking equipment
f. a transition economy	**vii.** United Kingdom
g. a measure of health	**viii.** South Korea
h. property typically individually owned	

Market Systems and Normative Claims

An old joke says that if you put five economists in a room, they will give you six opinions. Some economists argue that "free market" economic systems always work best. Some argue against market systems. Others argue that yes, market systems have advantages in addressing certain economic questions, but other modes of economic organization have other advantages. Yet these different views are not just economists' "opinions" in the same sense that you might form a quick opinion about the quality of a movie you've just seen. Economists base their diverse conclusions on different theories, interpretations of history, and/or empirical evidence—as well as on varying criteria for making judgments. In this chapter, we examine the arguments and evidence that economists use to support their claims.

1 | Why Discuss Normative Claims?

Economics, as a social science, is about learning how economies function, so that well-being can be maintained and increased for current and future generations. In the last chapter, we saw how various actual national economies have developed historically, with different patterns of ownership and modes of organization. Normative questions, you may recall from Chapter 1, have to do with the ways things *should* be. Is there some particular form of economic organization that all societies *should* adopt?

1.1 | Debating the Merits of Systems

During the 20th century, there was much debate about the merits of capitalism versus socialism. With the dissolution of command economies in the former Soviet block, and China's move toward more use of markets, many commentators proclaimed victory for capitalist forms of ownership and/or market modes of organization. The administrative form of socialism has, indisputably, been on the wane.

As we have seen in previous chapters, however, actual contemporary economies, whether with primarily private or primarily state ownership, generally include quite a mix of ownership and organization forms. The value of markets for organizing decentralized activity has been recognized in many countries. On the other hand, the problems of coordination, standard setting, provision of public goods, and the like mean that the role of administrative organization cannot be overlooked. Likewise, it would be naive to ignore the economic and political influence wielded by large corporations. The relevant question for economies thus seems to be not so much *whether* to have private or public ownership, or *whether* to have markets or administration, but *how* best to combine these to meet economic goals.

You may, however, have heard normative claims about economic systems that were delivered in far more absolutist terms. During the late 20th century, and continuing today, many influential leaders and policymakers have propounded a radically "free market," laissez-faire ideology. Also sometimes called a "neoliberal" position (or, in terms of international relations, a "free trade" position), it says that societies *should* be organized with almost exclusive reliance on markets and private ownership.

The role of governments, free market ideologues assert, should be limited to reinforcing property rights, and little more. Private enterprise should be allowed to function as free from government "interference" (in the form of regulation, taxes, subsidies, or transfers) as possible. These "market fundamentalists" argue that even regulations and social welfare transfers that seem to be serving a public purpose really do more harm than good. They maintain that cutting these back would allow the economy to function more efficiently, eventually leading to growing prosperity for all.

Of course, not everyone who advocates the repeal of some *particular* regulation (or the reform of a particular tax or transfer program) is a "free market ideologue." In specific cases there may be good reasons for increasing the role of markets and decreasing the role of government. What we mean by "free market ideology" is the belief that the prescription "more markets, less government" should be applied *across the board*, with no regard for the specifics of a case. That is, its policy prescriptions arise from a particular prior belief about how economies work, rather than from a careful analysis of a situation in its broader historical, environmental, and social context.

1.2 | Theory and Ideology

Although promoters of free market ideology draw on a variety of arguments to support their case, one important set of arguments about "how economies work" comes out of the 20th-century academic discipline of economics. In earlier times economists had held more diverse views, but beginning in the 1930s, **neoclassical economics** increasingly dominated teaching and research in the field in the United States and elsewhere.[1]

neoclassical economics: the school of economics that takes the traditional model as its starting point, emphasizing competitive markets and equilibrium

You have seen the core assumptions of the pure neoclassical model in this textbook, in the discussions of what we have called the traditional neoclassical model. That is, neoclassical analysis begins with an image of the economy as fundamentally made up of exchange relations among unitary "firms" and "households." Actors are assumed to be self-interested, optimizing, and autonomous. Marginal thinking is assumed to apply. Exchanges are envisioned as being made on frictionless double-auction spot markets ("frictionless" in that there is no need to take into account transaction costs, information problems, or underlying institutions). Unless specified otherwise, markets are assumed to be competitive.

Many—and probably the vast majority—of contemporary neoclassical economists believe that the simple model needs modification in one way or another, in order to be useful for real-world analysis. However, what makes an economist "neoclassical" is his or her belief that this simple story is the *best starting point* for understanding economic functioning, even if it will be modified and elaborated on later. It would be a mistake to think that all neoclassically trained economists are free-marketeers. Yet the core theory of neoclassical economics provides the intellectual justification for the free market position.

---

[1] The theoretical developments that led to "marginal thinking" were accomplished in the late 1870s by Stanley Jevons (1835–1882), Léon Walras (1834–1910), and Carl Menger (1841–1921). These were consolidated into "neoclassical" thinking by other U.S. and European economists, including Alfred Marshall (1842–1924), in the 1890s and early 20th century. It was not until the 1930s, however, that the school began to dominate the field. Paul Samuelson's (1915–) *Economics: An Introductory Analysis* (1948) set the standard for introductory economics teaching in many educational systems for the rest of the century.

The next section of this chapter spells out how this theory can be used to justify the "markets are best" position. Under certain crucial assumptions, questions of well-being can be boiled down to questions about efficiency, and, in turn, it can be demonstrated that perfectly competitive markets best solve the efficiency questions. In the later sections of the chapter, we return to a contextual view.

Discussion Questions

1. Have you seen "free market" thinking influencing any contemporary debates on economic policy? Which ones? Who is taking this point of view? What counterarguments have you heard offered?

2. In Chapter 3 we discussed the institutional requirements of markets, and in Chapter 17 the functions of public purpose institutions. In light of these discussions, would you say that government activities "interfere" in economic life? Could an economy function without collective institutions?

2 | The Theory Behind the "Free Market" Argument

To understand the intellectual underpinnings of the free market argument, you must first understand the idealized world against which real-world economies are judged. You must also understand the standard by which the "best" economy will be chosen.

2.1 | The Setup: The Idealized World

Imagine a world of only utility-maximizing "households" (thought of as individuals) and profit-maximizing "firms," as in the traditional model.

Further, imagine a world in which human dependency needs are irrelevant—every decision maker is an autonomous individual (presumably a healthy, prime-age adult), ready and able to fulfill his or her desires through market transactions. Imagine that everyone is perfectly rational and that each person acts to maximize his or her own level of utility. Imagine that each individual in this world is endowed with a certain set of resources. We won't worry about whether any actor has a shortfall in resources—our imaginary actors have only mental desires and preferences, not bodily survival needs. We also won't worry about future generations or other species: Their well-being in this idealized world is important only to the extent that it is reflected in the preferences of present-day economic actors.

All individuals in this society are free to exchange their resources (such as their labor services or the services of capital goods they own) for an income and, from that income, to spend on their most preferred collection of consumption goods and services. Imagine that consumption and leisure are the only things on which their utility depends.

Production is, in this economy, accomplished exclusively by firms. Firms maximize their profits subject to the existing technology, any input limitations they may face, and market conditions for their inputs and outputs.

Imagine that the markets in which these individuals and firms make exchanges are all perfectly competitive. That is, in each market there are numerous small buyers and sellers, only units of an identical good are traded, and there are no barriers to entry. In addition, everyone has perfect information (as discussed in Chapter 11). Technology is characterized by diminishing returns, so firms will stay relatively small and numerous, and firms' decision making is accomplished by applying marginal thinking to circumstances characterized by convexity (see Chapter 8). There are no transaction costs—that is, all exchanges take place without friction of any kind, in an atmosphere of complete trust and transparency (because there is, remember, perfect information).

The assumption that well-functioning, perfectly competitive markets exist for everything relevant to utility also has other implications. In particular, it means that there are no externalities: There are no positive or negative nonmarket impacts of economic activities on the well-being of uninvolved third parties. (If negative externalities, such as pollution impacts, ever existed, they have been thoroughly "internalized" through Coasian property right designations—see Chapter 14.) It also means that there are no public goods. To the extent that the passage of time is important in this economy, there must also exist a complete set of futures markets, allowing current market participants to make agreements now for later delivery.

2.2 | The Normative Standard: Pareto Efficiency

How will we decide what constitutes a "good" or "best" economy? One approach might be to compare economies with different distributions of resources; for example, we might think about the experience of living in an economy in which some people are very poor and some are very rich, as contrasted with a more egalitarian society. Or we might compare economies that have different mixes of customary, consent, market, and administrative modes of organization. Presumably, our standard for designing our own "best economy"—or for preferring some existing systems over others—should have something to do with people's well-being.

As discussed in Chapter 10, the "new utility theory" view of well-being of the mid-to-late 20th century ruled out any comparison of levels of well-being across different people. Well-being was identified with utility, and utility in turn was thought of as the amount of happiness people derived from their free choices. Neither questions of poverty that had been important to older generations of economists, nor questions of capabilities as developed in more recent years, were part of the picture. With well-being associated with personal happiness alone, who is to say that a beggar in the gutter isn't "happier" enjoying a sunset than a rich (but sad) person surrounded by wealth in her mansion? So the reasoning went.

If the standard for a "good" economy cannot be defined as the alleviation of poverty or the enhancement of capabilities, then what could it be? Neoclassical economists chose a standard called **Pareto efficiency**, after its inventor, early-20th-century Italian social scientist Vilfredo Pareto.[2] A Pareto efficient situation exists when there is no opportunity to make changes in such as way as to make at least one person better off without making anyone else worse off. (Or, stated another way, a situation is Pareto *in*efficient if there *is* a way to make at least one person better off without making anyone else worse off.)

Pareto efficiency: the situation where there is no opportunity to make changes in such a way as to make at least one person better off without making anyone else worse off

Note that when we use the Pareto efficiency criterion, there is no need for us to compare different people's utility levels. All we need to know is whether each individual considers himself or herself to be better off or worse off, in various situations.

Pareto efficiency is a somewhat difficult and subtle concept. A common mistake in thinking about Pareto efficiency is to think that it should enable us to choose one kind of situation as unambiguously "best." This is not correct. Suppose, for example, we want to compare three very simple scenarios, from a hypothetical economy populated by two people, Roberto and Meng. You may think of the scenarios as differing, for example, according to how much is produced, and whether the goods and services produced are more in line with the preferences of one actor or the other.

Table 19.1 gives the utility levels that Roberto and Meng would reach in Scenarios A, B, and C. For example, in Scenario A, producing more of a good that Roberto likes or needs, and little of what Meng likes or needs, Roberto reaches utility of 200 while Meng reaches utility of 5. If we assume that people do not get utility from other people's happiness (as is assumed in the ideal world we are discussing), we can evaluate these scenarios as shown in Table 19.2.

Scenario A is *not* Pareto efficient, because there *does* exist a change that would make "one person better off without making someone else worse off." In this case, a

---

[2] You may see this referred to as *Pareto optimality*. But because this term misleadingly seems to suggest that there is one "optimal" or "best" outcome, we prefer to use *Pareto efficiency*.

Table 19.1	Utility Levels in Three Scenarios	
Scenario	Roberto's Utility	Meng's Utility
A	200	5
B	199	100
C	201	6

change from A to C would make both better off. Both of the other two cases *are* Pareto efficient, because no such opportunities for unambiguous improvement exist. You can see that Pareto efficiency is more a rationale for *eliminating* certain options than a standard for *selecting* a particular one.

The Pareto efficiency standard, in fact, says nothing about distributional issues. *Both* Scenario B and Scenario C in our example are Pareto efficient, even though Meng is much worse off in C than in B, whereas Roberto is only a tiny bit better off in C than in B. We can't say that B is better than C using the Pareto standard, because if we said that B was better, we would be implicitly claiming that an additional 94 utils to Meng is more important than the loss of 2 utils to Roberto. This is exactly the kind of judgment across different people that "new utility theory" rules out.[3]

Another way to think about this standard is to note that a situation is Pareto *in*efficient if there exists some change to which all parties would unanimously agree. For example, a movement from A to C would get both Roberto and Meng's approval, so A is Pareto *in*efficient. Starting at B, however, or at C, there are no changes they would both vote for. (Remember, we have assumed that Roberto doesn't care even a little about Meng's utility.)

The Pareto efficiency criterion, although it is extremely narrow in its reach, is not completely vacuous as a standard of judging the goodness of an economy. It ranks more efficient situations as better than less efficient ones. This standard of judgment has been implicit in a number of discussions we have had in this text. For example, in the

Table 19.2	Determining Pareto Efficiency	
Scenario	Pareto Efficient?	Explanation
A	No	Changing to C would make "at least one person better off without making anyone else worse off." (Both would be better off.)
B	Yes	Changing to A or C would make one person (Meng) worse off.
C	Yes	Changing to A or B would make one person (Roberto in the case of B) or both persons (in the case of A) worse off.

---

[3] Another common misconception about the Pareto criterion is that it means that neoclassical economists believe that there is something "best" about the existing distribution of utility, well-being, or income. This misunderstanding arises because the Pareto criterion does *not* justify changes between scenarios on the basis of distributional criteria. If an economy happens to start off in Scenario C, for example, the Pareto criterion does not justify a switch from C to B. Not justifying *a change* from C to B, however, is not the same thing as saying that C *is better than* B. If the economy happened to start off in B instead, the Pareto criterion *also* wouldn't justify a change in the opposite direction—from B *to* C! Confusing? This is a subtle point. The Pareto criterion, as a theoretical construct, does not say any particular distribution is "best"—and yet its *silence* on distributional issues can make it useful in defending the status quo, for those whose politics lean in this direction.

production possibilities frontier introduced in Chapter 1, we said that points on the frontier were to be preferred to points in the interior. This is because a movement from an interior point to a point on the frontier can make it possible for everyone in the economy to have more (or, alternatively, for all but one person in the economy to have the same amount and for the one remaining person to get *all* the additional goods—also a move in the direction of Pareto efficiency.)

2.3 | The Result: "Markets Are Best"

Combining the above-described idealized world with a sole normative standard of Pareto efficiency, pure neoclassical theory arrives at a very clear conclusion: *A perfectly competitive free market economy will be Pareto efficient.*

first fundamental theorem of welfare economics (neoclassical theory): A perfectly competitive free market economy will be Pareto efficient.

This conclusion, sometimes called the "**first fundamental theorem of welfare economics**," can indeed be logically proved with great precision by using a mathematically formulated, and extended and generalized, version of the traditional model.

As we saw in our discussions of the traditional model, in perfect competition goods will be sold at precisely their marginal cost of production ($P = MC$), and resources will receive in compensation the exact value of their marginal product ($MRP_L =$ competitive market wage, $MRP_{MK} =$ competitive rental price of capital). Consumers will get exactly the same marginal utility from the last unit of each good consumed ($MU_x/P_x = MU_y/P_y$).

general equilibrium (neoclassical theory): a situation in which the relevant information flows unimpeded and instantaneously throughout an entire economy, so that all prices and quantities are simultaneously determined

Whereas we have looked at only one market at a time in this textbook, mathematical economists extended this model to the case of **general equilibrium**—where all markets are interconnected, and the prices and quantities in all markets are simultaneously determined. The mathematical proofs they generated showed that, given all of the assumptions previously discussed, no resources would be involuntarily unemployed, and every resource would be put to *exactly* its most valuable use.[4] Firms would minimize costs, households would maximize utility, and the "right" mix of goods would be produced. Once a perfectly competitive general equilibrium was attained, no further Pareto efficient changes would be possible.

This conclusion formally states and "proves" Adam Smith's original insight about the "invisible hand." Smith's essential insight was that independent, decentralized, voluntary individual decisions can give rise not to chaos but to spontaneous social order. "As if by an invisible hand," markets lead people to make individual decisions that jointly result in an overall allocation of resources that is orderly and efficient. The economy, in this idealized world, is a perfect "self-regulating" system.

These Pareto-optimal efficiency properties of a hypothetical perfectly competitive general equilibrium represent the intellectual foundation for the view that "free market economics" is the best way for a society to maximize its overall welfare.

2.4 | The Policy Prescription: Don't "Interfere"

Continuing with this line of reasoning leads to the conclusion that government should play an extremely limited role in the economy. According to the "fundamental theorem," perfectly free markets lead to an efficient outcome, so diluting them by adding organization by administration (or custom or consent) could only make things worse. In free market thinking, the government's role is only to ensure that contracts and property rights are enforced, thus creating the legal and political environment within which the market economy can function. Only that role is consistent with a model of market

---

[4] The normative part of the definition of *most valuable* is so large that it deserves repeated emphasis. In the model we have been describing, "value" is the same as price. Price, as we have seen, depends on the intersection of supply and effective demand—that is, demand that is backed up by the ability to pay. The determination of the "most valuable" use for any resource is therefore a determination made through a voting system in which each dollar counts as one vote: Those with little money have little voice in determining how such a system will prioritize its "values."

"perfection." (Other nonmarket institutions, such as families, community groups, and the internal organization of firms, are ignored entirely.)

Government taxes, subsidies, price floors or ceilings, tariffs, or other policies are considered bad, because they "interfere" with free market outcomes. We saw this in Chapter 11, where we discussed the effect of taxation on producer and consumer surplus. We saw that by preventing the achievement of competitive equilibrium, taxation created deadweight loss. Likewise, free market thinkers evaluate price floors and ceilings, such as minimum wages and rent controls, primarily in terms of the inefficiency they might generate.

The noninterference prescription has been extended to many other areas as well. Social welfare transfers of any kind tend to be seen primarily as a form of harmful, incentive-distorting interference with market outcomes, rather than as ways of addressing inevitable human dependency needs.

On the issue of "free trade" versus "protectionism" (discussed in Chapter 9), free market thinkers find much to praise in the "gains from trade" story because of how it demonstrates increases in efficiency. The assumptions of diminishing returns, no barriers to entry, perfect information, perfect competition, and perfect capital markets remove most of the issues that might be used to defend protectionist policies. For example, concerns about "infant industries" can be dismissed by noting that if an industry were going to be successful eventually, it would not *need* government help. The industry could simply get funding on the (assumed) perfect capital markets. Issues about unemployment caused by trade, similarly, need not be treated seriously because of the assumption that labor markets will automatically move to an unemployment-free equilibrium. Issues about national vulnerability such as food security or energy self-sufficiency become moot when it is assumed that no actors have market power.

Similarly, free market thinkers do not take labor market discrimination very seriously. Lower pay for traditionally female jobs is not considered a problem because, by the assumptions of the model, workers are simply paid the value of their marginal product. Hence women's traditional work, they reason, must simply be of less marginal value. Exclusion of qualified women or minorities from jobs is assumed to be something that will disappear over time. Why? An employer who refuses to hire the most productive worker, free market thinkers reason, will make less profit than his or her nonprejudiced competitors. In a world of perfect competition and zero economic profit, such discriminating employers will be driven out of business. According to this theory, even racism and sexism, however deeply rooted in history, custom, and belief systems, would simply be swept aside by market forces.

Free market ideology contributed to the prescription of a "shock therapy" approach to the Russian transition in the 1990s—a rapid withdrawal of government from the economy, accompanied by a faith that efficient markets would appear to fill the gap.

In all these cases, the bottom line is that there should be no conscious, collective effort to remedy economic and social problems. The market, it is believed, will take care of things best on its own.

2.5 | Variations in Neoclassical Thinking

The model of perfect competition was first seriously challenged from *within* the neoclassical school in 1933, when economists Joan Robinson and Edward H. Chamberlain published books, independently of each other, on the theory of monopolistic competition. As we saw in Chapter 12, the model of monopolistic competition can be expressed using a style of thinking and diagrams very similar to those applied in the traditional model of perfect competition.

Generations of economists followed suit, finding ways to vary the model of perfect competition to adjust for discrepancies they perceived between the model and the real world. By the later part of the 20th century, the model had been modified and extended many times, to include such things as externalities, public goods, transaction costs, imperfect information, broader notions of rationality and behavior, preferences that change over time, problems in writing contracts, and the fact that there are some valuable goods and services for which markets don't exist. In 2001, for example, economists George Akerlof, Joseph Stiglitz, and Michael Spence were honored by the Nobel Committee for their previous work on behavioral economics and imperfect information.

In many cases, these extensions have justified a larger role for government in the economy. Some of the economists who have introduced these innovations have continued to identify themselves as neoclassical, whereas others call themselves **new institutionalist** or use other designations. You have seen some of this analysis reflected in earlier chapters in this book.[5]

new institutionalist economics: the school of economics that shares many assumptions with neoclassical economics but looks at how economic institutions may develop to address problems such as those arising from transaction costs and imperfect information

These late-20th-century (and continuing) developments still have shared many of the core assumptions and methods of the perfectly competitive, mechanical way of thinking. For example, models that include market power have been referred to as models of "*im*perfect competition," implicitly assuming market "perfection" as the relevant standard. Models that include externalities or public goods have been referred to as models of "market *failure,*" implicitly assuming that market functioning is somehow prior to other modes of economic organization. The mathematical style of the traditional model has continued to set the standard for research methods in neoclassical economics and closely related research programs.

Often, the newer models have been developed piecemeal. For example, when a researcher explores broader notions of rationality, he still assumes that markets are perfectly competitive. On the other hand, when a researcher looks at issues of market power, she assumes perfect rationality. As long as pure neoclassical theory continues to hold center stage, any divergence from the core model of a perfectly competitive general equilibrium has to be individually explained and justified.

The Pareto efficiency standard also has still tended to hold sway. Much attention has been paid to how markets with "imperfections" could be made to act more like perfectly competitive markets. Although many neoclassical economists are and have been, as private citizens, deeply concerned about issues of poverty and inequality, the neoclassical model does not provide them much in the way of tools for directly addressing these questions. Within neoclassical economics, "badness" in economic outcomes is still analyzed primarily in terms of inefficiency and deadweight loss.

Once "imperfections" were recognized, however, imagining the achievement of even so limited a goal as Pareto efficiency became much more difficult, even in theory. The **second-best theorem**, formulated by economists R. G. Lipsey and Kelvin Lancaster in 1956, demonstrated that if one of the conditions for full, first-best Pareto efficiency cannot be satisfied, then the *second-best* outcome can usually be reached only by departing from all of the other conditions. If, for example, there exists a problem in just one market, then in order to achieve the next highest utility, it may be necessary to impose a whole system of taxes and subsidies. Once there is even one "imperfection," in other words, the whole idea of seeking efficiency through nonintervention no longer holds.

second-best theorem: the theorem that states that if first-best Pareto efficiency (based on nonintervention) cannot be achieved, then achieving the second-best outcome may require intervention in many markets

Still, many economists in the late 20th century—and on to our own day—have continued to focus narrowly on mechanically modeled "households" and "firms," on markets as the only mode of organization, and on efficiency as the only goal. This has often made it seem unnecessary to pay attention to such issues as poverty, unpaid work in households, social behavior within firms, the relation of consumption to well-being, and environmental sustainability.

The later careers of Chamberlain and Robinson illustrate, in fact, the split between the narrow, efficiency-based approach to economics and a broader, contextual approach. Chamberlain went on to refine his theory of monopolistic competition many times along its original lines. Robinson, however, later criticized her own work on

---

[5] You can find further discussions in the economics literature under the terms *transaction cost economics, the economics of information, bounded rationality, endogenous preferences, new institutionalist economics,* and *missing markets.*

monopolistic competition, preferring to call attention to pressing problems of unemployment, poverty, and injustice.[6]

2.6 | Precision Versus Accuracy, Once Again

As an intellectual exercise, the models and theorems underlying the free market view (and its variants) are interesting—at least to many economists. The fact that the theorems can be formally and precisely proved using highly complex mathematics may make them seem "scientific." Mathematical economists sometimes feel that they are uncovering "laws" of economic functioning that are analogous to theorems and proofs in the field of pure mathematics or to "laws" of nature discovered in the field of (mechanical) physics. Indeed, the position of many free market thinkers that they are not making normative judgments but are simply explaining "how the economy works" is based on an analogy with physics. The core neoclassical model tells them the "laws" by which economies work, they say; the only job remaining is to explain these laws to policymakers and the public.

○ The free market, general equilibrium model is *precise*. Is it *accurate*?

However, the belief that the "laws" of perfectly competitive market equilibrium, and a Pareto efficiency normative standard, are the most relevant concepts for understanding contemporary economies is not a result that proceeds directly from an impartial scientific analysis. It is a matter of belief, open to discussion. Even though the free market model is undeniably *precise*, you are free to make your own evaluation of its *accuracy*. (Recall the discussion of the difference between these in Chapter 4.)

As you may guess, there is growing criticism of the free market view. For many, the assumptions described earlier in this chapter are not sufficiently related to what we see around us to be a good guide for thinking and policy; nor is the normative standard of Pareto efficiency sufficient for understanding and promoting well-being.

Discussion Questions

1. Which of the following statements are (or is) correct, and which are (or is) incorrect?
   a. A Pareto efficient situation is one where everybody is well-off.
   b. You can evaluate whether a situation is Pareto efficient without knowing what alternatives are possible.
   c. For any economy, there is only one Pareto efficient outcome.
   d. An economy in which one person gets everything, and a thousand other people get nothing, could be Pareto efficient.

2. Discuss the questions:
   a. Are the assumptions of neoclassical economics sufficiently related to what we see around us to be a good guide for thinking and policy?
   b. Is the normative standard of Pareto efficiency sufficient for thinking about well-being?

---

3 | Contextual Economics: Into the Future

The "contextual" approach to economics uses the insights that can be gained from the neoclassical model as they apply to *some* economic organizations, at *some* times. It does not, however, adopt the economistic thinking that characterizes the pure neoclassical view and undergirds free market ideology. It does not confuse the assumptions of the model with the full nature of reality.

Now that you have almost finished your study of the basics of microeconomics, it is time to reflect a little about how economics has developed and where it is going. We give a very brief overview of some schools of thought, and then we raise two issues that are

---

[6] Many people expected Joan Robinson to be the first woman to win the Nobel Prize in economics in 1975, but it was not awarded to her. Observers debated whether the prize committee was biased against her gender or offended by her politics.

likely to be crucial in thinking about economics in the future: intergenerational equity and the relationship of individuals to society.

3.1 | Varieties of Economic Thought

Not all economists have been free marketeers, of course. The neoclassical school of economics, built around the traditional model, has been the most likely to produce economists who support free market policies, and this school of thought has been dominant in academic institutions in the English-speaking world (and elsewhere) in recent decades. Yet, as we have noted, even many neoclassical economists have tended to emphasize market "imperfections" and practical solutions, rather than staying focused on the competitive ideal. Other groups of economists diverge from pure neoclassical theory, not by making modifications and elaborations to it, but by adopting very different starting points.

institutionalist economics: the school of economics that emphasizes the complex and evolving nature of organizations and the strong influence of habit on individual behavior

In the decades before the ascent of neoclassical thinking, for example, **institutionalist economics** was very influential in the United States.[7] Institutionalist economists start from a less individualistic view of economic actors than the neoclassical school, and they emphasize the complex and changing nature of economic and social organizations and the strong influence of habit on individual behavior. Founded by John R. Commons (1862–1945) and others, institutionalist economics often also takes a meliorating view of social policy, examining how policies could help solve problems such as poverty and unemployment. This kind of analysis was influential in shaping many of the regulatory and social welfare policies of the Progressive Era and the New Deal in the United States (see Chapter 17). Groups of institutionalist economists have remained at work since then in the United States, Europe, and elsewhere, sometimes calling themselves "evolutionary" economists. Another group, adherents to the school of **social (or socio-) economics**, have tended to focus their analysis on the requirements for humane community life, exploring the ethical dimensions of economic life.

social (or socio-) economics: the school of economics that emphasizes the requirements for humane community life, focusing on ethical dimensions

Marxist (or radical) economics: the school of economics that emphasizes the power that comes with the ownership and control of capital

Radical and Marxist (named after Karl Marx, 1818–1883) economists have been especially attuned to struggles over power, property, and class—and particularly to the advantages in these struggles that are gained by people with ownership of capital. Their prescriptions for change have often called for radical shifts in the ownership and control of economic resources.[8] Some of the leaders and theoreticians of **Marxist (or radical) economics** had in mind an image of consensual, cooperative socialism in which citizens would jointly own assets and democratically direct economic activity, starting with their local workplaces. When ownership "by the people" was put into practice in the various communist and socialist economies of the last half of the 20th century, however, systems of centralized command usually resulted. In recent years, a number of radical and Marxist economists have been thinking about ways in which the efficiency advantages of market allocation might be combined with systems of organizing ownership and control that are more democratic and egalitarian than those of corporate capitalism.

post-Keynesian economics: the school of economics that emphasizes the dynamic nature of the macroeconomy and the importance of uncertainty in explaining economic behavior

Post-Keynesian economists, a group that takes as its starting point insights of the influential economist John Maynard Keynes (1883–1946), reject the neoclassical emphasis on equilibrium and instead emphasize the dynamic nature of economies and the importance of uncertainty about the future in explaining economic behavior. Most of the theories of this **post-Keynesian economics** are more relevant for macro- than for microeconomics.

Austrian economics: the school of economics that emphasizes the development of markets over time, information, and entrepreneurship, along with marginal thinking, markets, and prices

Austrian economics is named after the homeland of its founders, beginning with Carl Menger (1841–1921). Like neoclassical economists, Austrian economists tend to emphasize marginal thinking, markets, and prices. However, they break from neoclassical

---

[7] Sometimes this school is referred to as "old institutionalist" economics to distinguish it from the more neoclassically oriented "new institutionalist" school.

[8] Some left-leaning economists have also called themselves "political economists," though this is a potentially confusing term because *all* of economics used to be called political economy. Groups across the entire political spectrum occasionally claim this name for themselves.

theory in giving more attention to the development of markets over time, the importance of information, and the role of the entrepreneur. They also tend to differ from most contemporary neoclassical economists in their energetic advocacy of an extreme laissez-faire position.

In recent decades, other varieties of economics have also evolved, sometimes with their own theoretical starting points, and sometimes overlapping with other schools. **Ecological economics** emphasizes issues of environmental sustainability. **Feminist economics** emphasizes issues of gender equity in paid employment and pays increased attention to the economics of households and of caring labor. Such groups tend to find some useful viewpoints and analytical methods, *and* some things to be critical of, within the other existing schools of economics.

In many cases, the increased attention that these groups devote to real-world problems means that their analysis is necessarily less precise than that used in the pure neoclassical model. Taking into account history, culture, norms, power issues, and human interdependence does not always lead to tidy, mathematically or graphically elegant conclusions.

You will probably recognize that the contextual economics you have learned in this book draws, to a greater or lesser extent, on *all* of the schools of thought mentioned in this chapter. Many economists, in fact, would identify themselves with more than one school. If you continue to study economics, you may learn more about some of these schools, their methods of analysis, and their debates. Or you may decide to focus on a specific set of real-world problems and explore the extent to which each of these schools (or new ones that may yet develop!) help you understand problems and their solutions.

ecological economics: economics that emphasizes the dependence of economies on the natural world and the long-term environmental effects of economic activity

feminist economics: economics that emphasizes nonsexist approaches to policies, topics, and methods

3.2 | A Point to Ponder: Intergenerational Equity

Although the use of the Pareto efficiency standard enables "market fundamentalists" to sidestep issues of distribution, in the real world these issues are crucially important to human well-being.

Concerns about fairness are not limited to the distribution of income and wealth across the existing members of a society. There is also the very important question of distributional equity across different generations. Here the basic problem is that the (as

Trusting the market to make important economic decisions leads to outcomes that reflect the preferences of current market participants. To some extent, current decision makers do consider the well-being of future generations; very likely, this harmonica-teaching grandfather cares about the well-being of these little girls. Yet there is reason to believe that current decisions, based on current private returns and discount rates, will not lead to intergenerational equity. How would decisions differ if we followed the saying, "We do not inherit the earth from our ancestors; we borrow it from our children"?

yet unborn) individuals who will inhabit a society in the future own no resources in the present; they cannot enter markets and act in their own behalf. Market outcomes necessarily reflect only the interests of current market participants.

To some extent, the interests of the future will be represented via the private bequests of the current generation, willing their possessions to their descendants. Also, some capital assets that are created in order to yield current profits will continue being productive in the future. However, not everyone has the ability either to build up capital assets or to leave them to descendants. The current distribution of assets largely determines who can and who cannot make decisions affecting people of the future.

If we assume that most people care that their children and grandchildren should be given economic opportunities at least as good as their own, then we can understand this issue as fitting into our earlier discussion of public goods. The overall well-being of as yet unborn individuals is a public good from the perspective of individuals living in the present, to the extent that the well-being of future generations will depend on the overall resources and opportunities bequeathed by today's society to tomorrow's. This "social bequest" depends not so much on the actions of any particular individual as on the actions of everyone else. Each individual will therefore tend to underbequeath, hoping to free-ride on the contributions of others to future well-being. Only a deliberate commitment to the future, determined collectively and enforced by society as a whole, will be able to solve this "future public good" problem and ensure socially optimal provision for the future.

Why should we be concerned about the welfare of future generations? Over the past several centuries, the long-term trend has been toward steadily rising real incomes. If we were confident that this trend would continue indefinitely, we could simply assume that future generations will be better able to provide for themselves than we are at present and could leave concern for the future to the people who will inhabit it. However, it is hard to be confident today that the upward trend of incomes will continue. There are credible threats of major, long-lasting environmental damages that could result from current economic activity.

If our unsustainable use of fossil fuels, fisheries, and forest resources in this generation, for example, might lead to the environmental impoverishment of our great-grandchildren, then the question of intergenerational equity becomes a serious concern for public policy today. The same is true if there is degradation of social capital. As public goods, these are not issues that will be taken care of by market forces alone.

3.3 | A Point to Ponder: Individuals and Society

The defense of free markets is based on the premise that each individual is the best judge of his or her own welfare. In choosing between alternative possibilities—with respect to the supply of labor or the purchase of commodities—the individual makes the "right" choice for herself or himself, and that choice is therefore also assumed to be best for society as a whole. From a philosophical point of view, this is a radically *individualistic* assumption.[9] As we saw in Chapter 10, it underlies the doctrine of "consumer sovereignty."

From a radically individualistic perspective, society is nothing more than the aggregate of individuals composing it. This conception of society leads to a number of normative claims. For example, it is said that people have an inviolable right to keep what they have earned and to spend it as they please; no higher authority, therefore, should judge or alter a social outcome determined by freely contracting individuals. No interference with the free operation of markets can be justified by appeal to some nonindividualistic ethical objective. Instead, such interference must be grounded in an effort to make markets function more competitively or to simulate the operation of markets when they are absent or fail.

---

[9] Sometimes it is also known as the classical liberal position. *Liberal* here, however, means liberal in the sense of 17th- and 18th-century philosophers such as John Locke and Thomas Jefferson, not in the sense of contemporary political affiliations.

While markets appeal to the "private consumer," many important decisions need to be made by people in their "public citizen" capacity. If our "citizen" voices are to be heard, non-market political and social institutions require regular, active support and maintenance, just as the Lincoln Memorial pictured here receives physical maintenance.

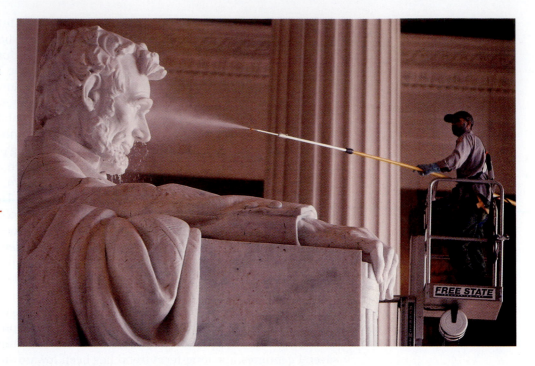

individualistic ethic: the normative judgment that only the preferences and choices of individuals carry ethical weight and that society is merely an aggregate of individuals

There is much that is attractive in the **individualistic ethic**. Much human progress can be attributed to the spread of the premise that the individual, as an autonomous human being, should have the freedom to choose to make voluntary contractual exchanges on the basis of her own sovereign preferences, within the constraints of her own resources. Yet there are still important situations where there is good reason not to rely simply on the judgment of individuals making free choices.

First of all, nearly everyone would probably agree that individual choices that have the effect of depriving a person of his autonomy should not be respected. Thus people are not allowed to sell themselves or their children into servitude, or to sell their vote in an election, no matter how much a person might value the proceeds of such a sale. From here it is a short step to ruling out free markets in addictive drugs or other activities likely to undermine a person's capacity for independent judgment, on the grounds that choices in such markets made freely (and perhaps desperately) in the present will deprive the individual of autonomy in the future—or may be based on an earlier loss of autonomy, such as the acquisition of an addiction or simply of bad, but hard to overcome, habits.

There is somewhat more debate around the proposition that "constitutive" as well as addictive goods and services should not be freely traded on markets, on the grounds that people should not be tempted to trade away the very qualities that constitute them as human beings—in particular, qualities that derive an important part of their meaning from the fact that they are not subject to purchase or sale. Under this rubric one could make a strong case for banning markets in babies, or in brides, or in surrogate motherhood, or in human organs. Voluntary contractual exchanges in such situations affront socially and culturally determined notions of what it means to be a child, a wife, a mother, or an intact physical person, so that the violation of such social and cultural norms—even by freely consenting transactors—has the effect of demeaning every individual in the society. There is thus a kind of social negative externality involved; these transactions made by individuals have an impact on the sense of human-ness, and thus on the welfare, of a vast number of nontransacting parties. However, there are inescapable debates about how far this category should be extended; the same arguments could be used to support parochial requirements for conformity to social norms that many would find oppressive.

A further problem with the individualistic ethic is its assumption that people's preferences reflect their well-being interests and are stable and consistent. People's true well-being depends, however, at least as much on having a "good" set of preferences as on the fulfillment of currently articulated preferences. Both subjective satisfaction and objective well-being may sometimes be better served by overcoming our current desires than by fulfilling them; what people are willing to pay for now is not the same as what will actually and ultimately satisfy them. Many people who are addicted to smoking wish that they could stop. That is, they wish that they did not prefer cigarettes, even while voluntarily buying them.

Most people's preferences over many significant choices are, in addition, not very stable and not really independent of context. People's preferences do very often depend on the particular context in which they find themselves and on the particular role in which they are functioning at the time. In our society they are liable to be strongly influenced by suggestions emanating from sources that have an interest in inculcating unhealthful eating habits and materialistic wishes that, when achieved, do not necessarily lead to enduring happiness or well-being. Moreover, most people are internally divided over courses of action; they experience inner conflict over many important decisions. Which way you decide is likely to depend on particular and arbitrary circumstances—what you have recently read or heard, whom you have talked to, what advertisements you are exposed to, and so on.

A particularly important conflict tends to arise within individuals, between one's preferences as a (private) consumer and one's preferences as a (public) citizen. As a consumer I tend to make decisions based on straightforward self-interest (or the interest of my immediate family); I am concerned to discover and act upon what is best for me or for us. As a citizen, however, I take a broader view and reflect on what is good for the society as a whole. Here I tend to bring in moral and aesthetic considerations: My preferences reflect what kind of person I think I should be and what kind of society I think we should all live in.

As an example of this conflict, consider the choice of whether to develop a city park into a new and comfortable residential area or to preserve and upgrade it as a site for public recreation. As a private consumer, I might well leap at the chance to purchase a new and better house for my family if the area is developed for private residential housing. On the other hand, as a citizen and city dweller, I am concerned about the quality of city life and would like to see green areas protected from urban development. If this kind of decision is left up to the atomistically expressed preferences of individuals in the marketplace, then it is highly likely that the site will be developed for private housing; anyone who holds back for the sake of the public good will simply be made a fool of by others who are less conscientious. Only if there is some other kind of mechanism for formulating and assessing the collective preference of all city residents *as citizens* will it be possible to follow what may well be a greater overall preference for preserving the site for public recreation.

Note that the issue here is not simply one of externalities. It is true that a problem of externalities is involved: The individual preferences of affected nontransacting parties (other city residents) fail to get reflected in market transactions between transacting parties (the housing developer and prospective house buyers). But there is another, more important point: The hidden interest of many citizens in a public recreational site may not even become a conscious preference for individuals unless there is an arena for collective discussion, deliberation, and articulation of such issues. In other words, the goals that people determine for themselves as a community cannot be arrived at as an aggregation of individual preferences. Markets tend to privilege the "private consumer" part of one's identity; nonmarket institutions are needed to enable the "public citizen" part of one's identity to express itself.

The issues raised here are not meant as a rejection of the belief that people's individual preferences and choices should be respected. However, the fact that most of the important decisions that people make are context- and role-dependent should remind us that true social welfare requires much more than a response to each individual's current preferences. It requires a social environment that encourages and enables people to reflect on what they are doing and to discuss and deliberate matters with other people. It requires that there be ample opportunities for collective social decision making as well as individual private decision making. In sum, market organization alone is far too limited a mechanism to ensure social well-being. It is a very useful mode of organization in many ways, but it is only one part of the larger complex of institutions needed to enable people—as individuals *and* as members of a society—to promote their overall well-being.

Discussion Questions

1. People come in a variety of sizes, races, genders, and ages, in various physical conditions, and with varying amounts of income and wealth. Are some sorts of people, do you think, more likely than others to notice issues of well-being, dependency needs, and distribution? Who, and why? (Do you think this might have had an effect on the development of 20th-century economics?)

2. You may have noticed that Chapter 18 did not include either laissez-faire *proprietary* capitalism or *consensual cooperative* socialism as categories of contemporary economic systems. That is because actual contemporary examples of these as national systems do not exist. ("Self-managed" firms did exist in Yugoslavia under communism, but these cannot accurately be described as worker-owned because ownership was shared with the state.) Yet free market advocates often talk about corporate capitalist systems in language more appropriate for a system of small business entrepreneur–proprietors. Meanwhile, some left-leaning thinkers promote a consensual cooperative socialist ideal. Do you think one or both of these views is or are hopelessly romantic and idealistic? Or could one or the other of them instead be visionary—an ideal to strive for in the future?

4 | Last Words

In this textbook, you have learned about microeconomics "in context"—about how economic activities, whether paid or unpaid, and whether in the core, business, or public purpose spheres, can contribute to well-being.

We saw how systems of markets can often help promote well-being. Markets help communicate important information about desires and scarcity among buyers and sellers. The extrinsic motivations that arise from rewards in terms of wages, rents, interest, and profits help give people the incentive to put the resources they own to productive use. Markets help coordinate economic activity without the need for a centralized bureaucracy. Decentralization also allows people more freedom of choice, compared to systems based on customary or administrative modes of organization.

We also saw how markets can sometimes fail to add to well-being. Markets do not directly address human dependency needs. They do not, in themselves, correct for gross inequalities in the distribution of resources, which leave some people desperately poor. Markets may become places for the exercise of power in undemocratic ways that undermine well-being. Markets do not by themselves take into account the issues raised by the presence of externalities, outcomes that affect parties not directly involved in a market transaction. Markets are unable to provide an appropriate level of public goods, because the difficulty in excluding anyone from enjoying them allows people to "free-ride." Markets do not, in themselves, make the hard decisions necessary to ensure ecological sustainability of the economic system.

Overall, we hope that after studying contextual microeconomics, you will be able to discuss intelligently issues related to the organization of society's economic functioning, including the strengths and weaknesses of markets as a form of social organization. Every individual in an economic system plays a role in the ongoing creation of some or all of the contexts we have discussed. It is up to individuals to work through the organizations they are involved in—family and community groups, businesses, non-profit organizations, and governments—to ensure that all economic organizations advance the goal of well-being.

Review Questions

1. What are some key assumptions about the economic world as imagined in the free market view?
2. What normative standard is adopted in the free market view?
3. How did free market thinkers "prove" that "markets are best"?
4. Give some examples of arenas where, according to the free market view, government action is unnecessary or harmful.
5. Give some examples of variations on the free market model.
6. Give some examples of alternative approaches to economics.
7. Why is intergenerational equity an issue?
8. Why is it inadequate to think of people only in an individualistic way?
9. What, in the contextual economics view, are the strong and the weak points of markets as a mode of organization?

Exercises

1. Determine which, if any, of the following three scenarios is Pareto efficient, and explain why or why not.

Scenario	Jean's Utility	Olga's Utility
A	90	200
B	100	100
C	200	100

2. Illustrate your answer to the previous question on a production possibility frontier, with Jean's utility measured on the vertical axis and Olga's utility measured on the horizontal axis. (You may also consult the bargaining graphs in Chapter 15.) Recall that situations that are *not* Pareto efficient will not lie on the frontier.
3. Explain briefly, in a paragraph, the assumptions and logic behind the free market conclusion that "markets are best."
4. Write a short (two double-spaced pages) essay comparing contextual economics with pure neoclassical theory.
5. Match each concept in Column A with a definition or example in Column B.

Column A	Column B
a. an assumption of the free market view	**i.** power and ownership of capital
b. a Pareto efficient outcome	**ii.** taking into account imperfect information
c. a variation on the free market view	**iii.** everything people care about is traded on markets
d. a focus of radical economics	**iv.** ethics
e. a focus of social economics	**v.** the only standard of what is good for a person is that person's own preferences
f. the individualistic ethic	**vi.** the ideal of a perfectly competitive market equilibrium

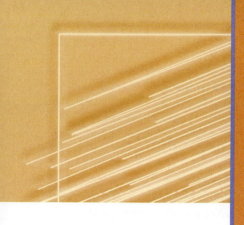

Glossary

ability-to-pay principle: the idea that the more resources you have, the more you should be required to contribute to public projects (9)

absolute advantage: the ability to produce some good or service at a lower absolute cost than other producers (9-appendix)

absolute deprivation: lack of the minimal necessities for sustaining life (10)

abundance: resources are abundant to the extent that they exist in plentiful supply for meeting various goals (1)

accounting costs: the costs of a project, figured in terms of monetary outflows alone (7)

accurate: describes something that is correct (even if only in a general way) (4)

administration (organization by): a means of organizing an economic unit that gives decision-making authority to some person or agency (2)

administrative capitalism: a national system characterized by private corporate ownership and a substantial reliance on public administration (as well as exchange) as a mode of organization (18)

administrative socialism: a national system in which state ownership predominates and activity is primarily organized by public administration (command) (18)

allocative efficiency: the allocation of resources to their most (market-) valued uses (11)

altruistic motivation: motive for action that reflects concern only with the well-being of others (2)

annual return on a share of stock: the sum of its dividends and any capital gains (or losses) (14)

appreciation: an increase in the value of an asset over time (14)

aspirational group: a group to which we would like to belong (10)

attributes (or characteristics): the specific qualities of a good or service that are of interest to the consumer (10)

auction market: a market where an item is sold to the highest bidder (3)

Austrian economics: the school of economics that emphasizes the development of markets over time, information, and entrepreneurship, along with marginal thinking, markets, and prices (19)

average cost (average total cost): cost per unit of output, computed as total cost divided by the quantity of output produced (7)

backward-bending individual paid labor supply curve: a pattern that arises because, beyond some level of wages, income effects may outweigh substitution effects in determining individuals' decisions about how much to work (13)

bargaining: an activity in which a single buyer and a single seller negotiate the terms of their exchange (3)

bargaining theory: a theory about situations in which economic actors could benefit from coming to an agreement but may disagree about how to divide up the benefit they gain (15)

barriers to entry: economic, legal, or deliberate obstacles that keep new sellers from entering a market (12)

barter: exchange of goods, services, or assets directly for other goods, services, or assets, without the use of money (9)

basic Neoclassical model: see *traditional microeconomic model*

bilateral monopoly: the situation in which there is only one buyer confronting only one seller (13)

bond: a financial instrument that, in return for the loan of funds, commits its seller to pay a fixed amount every year (called the coupon amount), as well as to repay the amount of principal (called the bond's face value) on a particular date in the future (called the maturity date) (14)

bond price: the price at which a bond is traded (14)

bond yield to maturity: the amount a bond returns during a year, if held to maturity, expressed in percentage terms. The yield is determined by the coupon amount, the bond price (the price at which trades are made), and the time to maturity (14)

bounded rationality: the identification of some arbitrarily defined subset of information to consider when making decisions (2)

break-even price: the price at which a profit-maximizing firm makes zero economic profits

budget line: a line showing the possible combinations of two goods that a consumer can purchase (10)

business sphere: firms that produce goods and services for profitable sale (1)

capability approach: the economic approach that assesses institutions and policies in terms of the opportunities they create for people to live valuable lives (10)

capacity constraint: a case in which some fixed input (or inputs) limits the amount that can be produced in a given period of time (7)

capital constraint (in production): a situation in which an inability to obtain financing imposes limits on production decisions (8)

capital stock: a quantity of any resource that is valued for its potential economic contributions (6)

capitalism: a system characterized by predominantly private ownership (either individual or corporate) of productive assets (18)

"capture" (theory of pure special interest): the idea that public purpose organizations are always taken over by powerful special interests and used for their own self-interested ends (17)

cartel: a group of producers who mutually agree to limit their production in order to sustain a price floor (4)

ceteris paribus: a Latin phrase meaning "other things equal" or "all else constant" (7)

change in demand: a shift of the demand curve in response to some determinant other than price (4)

change in quantity demanded: movement along a demand curve in response to a price change (4)

change in quantity supplied: movement along a supply curve in response to a price change (4)

change in supply: a shift of the supply curve in response to some determinant other than price (4)

choice behavior: behavior selected by a person from a range of alternatives, generally involving the person's conscious deliberation (2)

circular flow diagram: a graphical representation of the traditional view that an economy consists of households and firms engaging in exchange (2)

civic responsibility (theory of): the idea that public-oriented values and active citizen participation are possible and in fact are vital for the healthy functioning of public purpose organizations (17)

Coase Theorem: If property rights are well defined, and there are no significant transactions costs, then markets can efficiently allocate resources even in the presence of externalities (14)

collusion: cooperation among potential rivals to gain market power as a group (12)

command economies (planned economies): national economies characterized by administrative direction of economic activity via a central bureaucracy (18)

common property resources: resources that are owned collectively by a defined group (18)

comparative advantage: the ability to produce some good or service at a lower opportunity cost than other producers (9)

comparative advantage (principle of): gains from trade occur when producers specialize in making goods for which their opportunity costs are relatively low (9)

comparative economic systems: the branch of economic study concerned with differences in economic institutions across societies (18)

compensating wage differentials: the theory that workers will be willing to accept lower wages for jobs with better characteristics and will demand higher wages for jobs with unappealing characteristics, all else equal (13)

competitive equilibrium: equilibrium in a market where all buyers and sellers are price takers, unable individually to influence the price they pay or charge (11)

complementary good: a good that is used along with another good (4)

concentration ratio: the share of production, sales, or revenues attributable to the largest firms in an industry (12)

conglomerates: combinations of unrelated businesses (16)

consent (organization by): agreement among a group of people reached through discussion or negotiation (2)

constant marginal costs: the case where the cost of producing an additional unit of output stays the same as more output is produced (7)

constant marginal returns: the case where the use of an additional unit of a variable input produces the same quantity of output as did the previous unit of the input (7)

constant returns to scale: these occur when the long-run average cost of production stays the same as the size of the enterprise increases (7)

constrained behavior: behavior of a person subject to limits set by others, who usually have some power over the person (2)

consumer sovereignty: the idea that consumers' needs and wants determine the shape of all economic activities (10)

consumer surplus: the excess (summed over all the buyers in a market) of the amounts that buyers would be willing to pay for a good or service, over the amounts that they actually pay (11)

consumerist values: the belief that meaning and satisfaction in life are to be found through the purchase and use of consumer goods (10)

consumption: the final use of a good or service (1)

convexity: a mathematical term used to describe the special assumptions necessary for marginal thinking to lead to maximization of net benefits. With convexity, net benefits can be maximized by taking incremental steps along a smooth path (8)

cooperative ownership: ownership by a collective (18)

cooperative: a business owned by a group of workers, suppliers, or consumers (16)

core sphere: households, families, and communities (1)

corporate capitalism: a national system in which a great deal of the ownership of productive assets is through corporations, which are in turn primarily owned by private (nongovernmental) shareholders (18)

corporate ownership: ownership by shareholders of corporations, who are primarily individuals and nongovernmental institutions (18)

corporation: a business firm that has been chartered by a state or the federal government and that has a status in law as a "person," with a legal existence separate from the individuals or organizations who own it (16)

cost/benefit analysis: a procedure, often used by governments, for attempting to determine the net benefits of proposed projects (8)

coupon amount: the fixed amount paid every year by the seller of a bond to the owner of that bond (14)

cult of domesticity: the 19th-century notion that life in business and markets was suitable for men, whereas a more morally refined, "nonworking" life in the home was suitable for women (15)

custom: body of traditions, habits, and expectations about what it is proper and necessary for people to do in given circumstances (2)

deadweight loss: the loss in efficiency (measured in terms of producer and consumer surplus) that is said to arise if market transactions take place at other than the competitive market equilibrium level (11)

debt finance: money obtained by borrowing and used to cover some costs of an enterprise (6)

decreasing marginal costs: the case where the cost of producing an additional unit of output falls as more output is produced (7)

demand curve: a curve indicating the quantities that buyers are ready to purchase at various prices (4)

dependency needs: the need to have others provide one with care, shelter, food, and the like when one is unable to provide these for oneself (9)

depreciation: decreases in the value of a stock of capital due to wear-and-tear or obsolescence (6)

deregulation: the reduction of governmental administrative oversight of private enterprises (encouraged in many countries in the late 20th century) (18)

derived demand: demand for an input that is based on demand for the output it will help to produce (4)

dictatorship model (of households): the theory that household decisions are made by a single person (sometimes called the altruist) (15)

diminishing marginal returns: the case where the use of an additional unit of a variable input produces a lesser quantity of output than did the previous unit of the input (7)

diminishing marginal utility: the tendency of additional units of consumption to add less to utility than did previous units of consumption (10)

discount rate: the percentage by which future funds are discounted in order to be expressed in terms of present value (14)

discrete decisions: decisions that involve "jumps" between different distinct choices (8)

diseconomies of scale: these occur when the long-run average cost of production rises as the size of the enterprise increases (7)

disembodied technology: technology in the form of shared understandings and procedures (6)

disequilibrium: a situation of either shortage or surplus (4)

distribution: the sharing of products and resources among people (1)

dividends: payments in cash or extra shares paid out to shareholders (14)

double-auction: an auction in which both the buyers and sellers state prices at which they are willing to make transactions (3)

dual labor markets: a situation in which "primary" workers enjoy high wages, opportunities for advancement, and job security, while "secondary" workers are hired with low wages, no opportunities for advancement, and no job security (13)

dual-sector theory: the theory that economies may include primary sectors containing firms with market power side by side with competitive secondary sectors (16)

dumping: selling in foreign countries at prices that are below the firm's costs of production (12)

duopoly: a market with only two sellers (12)

Dutch auction: an auction in which the opening price is set high and then drops until someone buys (3)

dynamic analysis: analysis that takes into account the passage of time (8)

dynamic model: a model that takes into account the passage of time required for changes to occur (4)

ecological economics: economics that emphasizes the dependence of economies on the natural world and the long-term environmental effects of economic activity (19)

economic actor (economic agent): an individual, group, or organization that is involved in the economic activities of resource maintenance or the production, distribution, or consumption of goods and services (1)

economic costs: the costs of a project, including opportunity costs (7)

economic organization: an entity that it is made up of individual economic actors and sub-organizations, which may have common or conflicting interests (2)

economic profit: revenue less economic costs (8)

economic rents: returns to factors that are in fixed supply (13)

economics: the study of the way people organize themselves to sustain life and enhance its quality (1)

economies of scale: these occur when the long-run average cost of production falls as the size of the enterprise increases (7)

economies of scope: cost savings achieved when a firm increases the range of products it makes (16)

economistic thinking: thinking that confuses the assumptions of the traditional model with reality (1)

effective demand: the desire for a product that can be translated into purchasing behavior because it is backed up by enough money to pay the going price (4)

efficiency wage theory: the theory that an employer can motivate workers to put forth more effort by paying them somewhat more than what they could get elsewhere (13)

efficiency: the use of resources in a way that does not involve any waste. Inputs are used in such a way that they yield the highest possible value of output, or a given output is produced using the lowest possible value of inputs (1)

elasticity: a measure of the responsiveness of economic actors to changes in conditions (5)

embodied technology: technology incorporated into forms of manufactured capital (6)

empirical investigation: the observation and recording of the specific phenomena of concern (4)

employee morale: the attitude of workers toward their work and their employer (13)

employer-specific human capital: knowledge and skills that have been gained on a particular job and are useful only as long as a worker remains with the same employer (13)

equilibrium: a situation in which the quantity supplied is equal to the quantity demanded (4)

equity finance: an economic actor's use of its own funds to finance investments that will support future production (6)

exchange: the trading of one thing for another (1)

exclusionary practices: a firm's getting its suppliers or distributors to agree not to provide goods or services to potential competitors (12)

explicit contract: a formal, often written agreement that states the terms of an exchange and may be enforceable through a legal system (3)

external benefits: the benefits of a project that accrue to persons, or entities such as the environment, that are not among the economic actors directly responsible for the activity (8)

external costs: the costs of a project that are borne by persons, or entities such as the environment, that are not among the economic actors directly responsible for the activity (7)

externalities: see external benefits, external costs, positive externalities, negative externalities

extrinsic motivation: impetus to perform an activity that arises from reasons "outside" the person and the activity, such as doing something to obtain a reward in terms of money, status, or power or to avoid punishment (2)

face value (of a bond): the amount that the seller of a bond promises to pay to the bond's owner on the maturity date (14)

factor markets: markets for labor, natural resources, and manufactured capital goods (3)

fall-back position: see *threat point*

false economies: cost savings that are illusory because long-term and/or social costs have not been taken into account (7)

family (U.S. census definition)**:** two or more people in the same household who are related by birth, marriage, or adoption (15)

"family wage": a wage high enough to support a wife and children, often associated with men's wages during the period of the cult of domesticity (15)

feminist economics: economics that emphasizes nonsexist approaches to policies, topics, and methods (19)

final goal: a goal that requires no further justification; it is an end in itself (1)

final goods: goods that are ready for use by people (7)

financial capital: funds of purchasing power available to facilitate economic activity (6)

financial markets: markets for debt and equity finance (3)

first fundamental theorem of welfare economics (neoclassical theory): A perfectly competitive free market economy will be Pareto efficient (19)

fixed cost: the cost associated with using fixed inputs, which is the same no matter what quantity of output is produced (7)

fixed input: an input to production that is fixed in quantity, no matter what the level of production (7)

fixed manufactured capital: manufactured goods that yield a flow of productive services over an extended period of time (6)

flow: something whose quantity can be measured over a period of time (6)

franchise: a legal agreement between an independent enterprise and a larger corporation in which the enterprise agrees to abide by standards set by the larger corporation and to compensate it for use of its brand name and other services (16)

free riders: people who would like to enjoy the benefit of a public good without paying for it (1)

free trade: exchange in international markets not regulated or restricted by government actions (9)

futures market: a market in which it is possible to negotiate in the present for the purchase of something that will be delivered in the future (3)

general equilibrium (neoclassical theory): a situation in which the relevant information flows unimpeded and instantaneously throughout an entire economy, so that all prices and quantities are simultaneously determined (19)

general human capital: knowledge and skills that workers can take with them as they move from employer to employer. It may be formed before starting a job or through on-the-job training (13)

Gini ratio: a measure of inequality, based on the Lorenz curve, that goes from 0 (perfect equality) up to 1 (complete inequality) (9)

globalization: an increase in many kinds of global or transnational interactions and effects, including companies that span the globe; transactions in global retail markets and markets for capital, labor, and other inputs; and the trans-boundary flows of ideas, cultural influences, and environmental impacts (16)

"glued together" family model: an image based on the assumption that families act as though they were single units, having a unified set of goals and attaining a single level of well-being (15)

goodwill: the accounting term for the premium that one company pays for another over and above the value of its physical assets. The premium for goodwill may represent advantages from specialized knowledge, effective organization, or other intangible assets (14)

government ownership: ownership by an agency of the government (18)

growth stocks: stocks that are expected to return substantial capital gains (14)

guilds: medieval European organizations of artisans or merchants (3)

habitual behavior: repetitive behavior that involves minimal thought and is often based on social custom (2)

high time discount rate: the economist's phrase for describing a strong preference for present benefits over those that might be enjoyed in the future (2)

historical investigation: study of past events (4)

horizontal integration: the expansion of a firm achieved through growth or merger while it continues to make the same or similar products (16)

household (U.S. census definition): one or more people occupying a single housing unit, such as a house or apartment (15)

human capital: people's capacity for labor and their individual knowledge and skills (6)

implicit contract: an informal agreement about the terms of exchange, based on verbal discussions and on common norms, traditions, and expectations (3)

import substitution policies: policies undertaken by governments seeking to reduce reliance on imports and encourage domestic industry. These often include the use of industry subsidies as well as protectionist policies (9)

inadequacy: a situation in which there is not enough of a good or service, provided at prices people can afford, to meet minimal requirements for human well-being (4)

incentive: a reward or punishment that motivates action (2)

income effect of a price change: the tendency of a price increase to reduce the quantity demanded of normal goods (and increase the quantity demanded of any inferior goods) (5)

income elasticity of demand: a measure of the responsiveness of quantity demanded to changes in income (5)

increasing marginal costs: the case where the cost of producing an additional unit of output rises as more output is produced (7)

increasing marginal returns: the case where the use of an additional unit of a variable input produces a greater quantity of output than did the previous unit of the input (7)

indifference curve: a curve consisting of points representing combinations of various quantities of two goods, such that every such combination gives the consumer the same level of utility (10-appendix)

individual demand: the demand from one individual buyer (4)

individual economic actor: an entity that is largely self-contained and acts as a unit (2)

individual ownership: ownership of productive assets by individuals and families (18)

individual supply: the supply from one individual seller (4)

individualist ethic: the normative judgment that only the preferences and choices of individuals carry ethical weight and that society is merely an aggregate of individuals (19)

infant industry: an industry which is relatively new to its region or country (9)

inferior goods: goods for which demand falls when ability to pay rises, and rises when ability to pay falls (5)

informal sphere: businesses operating outside of government oversight and regulation. In less industrialized countries, it may constitute the majority of economic activity (1)

in-kind transfers: transfers of goods or services (9)

input substitution: increasing the use of some inputs, and decreasing that of others, while producing the same good or service (7)

inputs: resources that go into production (7)

institutional investors: economic organizations such as pension funds and insurance companies that invest funds that have been placed in their care (14)

institutionalist economics: the school of economics that emphasizes the complex and evolving nature of organizations and the strong influence of habit on individual behavior (19)

institutions: ways of structuring social interactions, including both formally constituted establishments and the generally recognized patterns of organization embodied in customs, habits, and laws (3)

instrumental behavior: see *purposeful behavior*

intangible capital: sources of productivity and well-being that cannot be seen or touched (6)

interest: the charge for borrowing money (6)

intermediate goal: a goal that is desirable because its achievement will bring you closer to your final goal(s) (1)

intermediate goods markets: markets for unfinished products (3)

intermediate goods: goods that will undergo further processing (7)

internal benefits: the benefits of a project from the perspective of the economic actor making the decisions (8)

internal costs: the costs of a project, from the perspective of the economic actor(s) making the decisions (7)

Interstate Commerce Act: the first U.S. federal act regulating monopolies and business practices, passed in 1887 in response to practices in the railroad industry (17)

intrinsic motivation: impetus to perform an activity that arises from reasons "inside" the person, such as doing something for enjoyment or adherence to one's ethical values or sense of identity (2)

inventories: stocks of raw materials or manufactured goods being held until they can be used (6)

investment: actions taken to increase the quantity or quality of a resource now, in order to make benefits possible in the future (6)

investor confidence: investors' optimism or pessimism concerning future returns (14)

"just price" doctrine: the mandate of the medieval Catholic church that prices charged should always be fair (3)

labor force participation rate: the percentage of the adult, noninstitutionalized population who are either working at a paid job or seeking paid work (13)

labor market discrimination: a condition that exists when, among similarly qualified people, some are treated disadvantageously in employment on the basis of race, gender, age, sexual preference, or disability (13)

labor markets: markets where people offer their labor services to employers (3)

labor productivity: the level of output that can be produced per worker (6)

labor: the flow of time, effort, skill, and knowledge that humans directly provide as inputs into productive activities (6)

laissez-faire capitalism: a national system characterized by private corporate ownership and a great reliance on exchange as a mode of organization (with relatively little organization by public administration) (18)

laissez-faire economy: an economy with little government regulation (3)

limited liability: a legal structure in which creditors of a business can demand from owners no more than the owners' investment in the business (16)

limiting factor: the fixed input that creates a capacity constraint (7)

liquidation value: the value of the physical assets of a firm, should it be dissolved and its assets sold separately (14)

living standard (or lifestyle) goals: goals related to satisfying basic needs and getting pleasure through the use of goods and services (10)

loan: money borrowed for temporary use, on the condition that it be repaid with interest (6)

local monopoly: a monopoly limited to a specific geographical area (12)

long run: (in terms of production processes) a time period in which all inputs to production can be varied in quantity (7)

long-run average cost: the cost of production, per unit of output, when all inputs can be varied in quantity (7)

long-run elasticity: a measure of the response to a price change after economic actors have time to make adjustments (5)

long-term contracts: contracts whose terms extend over a long period of time (3)

Lorenz curve: a line used to portray an income distribution, drawn on a graph with percentiles of households on the horizontal axis and the cumulative percentage of income on the vertical axis (9)

low time discount rate: the economist's phrase for describing a strong concern with future benefits, even if getting them is costly in the present (2)

macroeconomics: the sub-field of general economics that focuses on the economy as a whole (1)

manufactured capital: all physical assets that have been made by people (6)

marginal benefit: the benefit that accrues from producing the last unit of output (8)

marginal cost: the cost associated with producing the last unit of output (7)

marginal factor cost of (manufactured) capital (MFC$_{MK}$): the amount that a unit of additional capital services adds to the firm's costs (14)

marginal factor cost of labor (MFC$_L$): the amount that a unit of additional labor adds to the firm's costs (13)

marginal physical product of labor (MPP_L): the amount that a unit of additional labor contributes to the physical product of a the firm (13)

marginal rate of substitution: how much of one good the consumer is willing to give up to get more of another (10-appendix)

marginal return: the additional quantity of output gained by using an additional unit of a variable input (with all other inputs held fixed) (7)

marginal revenue product of (manufactured) capital (MRP_{MK}): the amount that a unit of additional capital services contributes to the revenues of the firm (14)

marginal revenue product of labor (MRP_L): the amount that a unit of additional labor contributes to the revenues of the firm (13)

marginal revenue: the revenue received from the last unit sold (8)

market (first meaning): a physical place where there is a reasonable expectation of finding both buyers and sellers for the same product or service (3)

(second meaning): an institution that brings buyers and sellers into communication with each other, structuring and coordinating their actions (3)

"the market": a phrase that people often use to mean an abstract situation of pure exchange or a global system of exchange relationships (3)

market demand: the demand from all buyers in the market (4)

market adjustment (theory of): the theory that market forces will tend to make shortages and surpluses disappear (4)

market economies: national economies in which decentralized exchange plays a substantial organizing role (18)

market failure: when markets yield inefficient or inappropriate outcomes (2)

market incentives: market signals that motivate economic actors to change their behavior (perhaps in the direction of greater economic efficiency) (4)

market power: the ability to control, or at least affect, the terms and conditions of the exchanges in which one participates (11)

market socialism: a national system in which state ownership predominates but much activity is organized by exchange (18)

market supply: the supply from all sellers in the market (4)

market value: the price for an item that would be freely determined by interactions of buyers and sellers in a (perhaps hypothetical) auction-type market (3)

markets: social organizations set up to facilitate exchange (2)

mark-up (or cost-plus) pricing: a method of setting prices in which the seller adds a fixed percentage amount to his or her cost of supplying the item (3)

Marxist (or radical) economics: the school of economics that emphasizes the power that comes with the ownership and control of capital (19)

maturity date: the date on which the principal of a bond is repaid, and coupon payments cease (14)

maximum efficient scale: the largest size an enterprise can be and still benefit from low long-run average costs (7)

means-tested programs: programs designed to transfer income to those most in need (17)

melioration: starting from the present level of achievement and continuously attempting to do better (2)

membership group: a group to which we belong (10)

microeconomics: the sub-field of general economics that focuses on activities that take place within and among the major economic organizations of a society (1)

minimum efficient scale: the smallest size an enterprise can be and still benefit from low long-run average costs (7)

model: an analytical tool that highlights some aspects of reality while ignoring others (1)

money: a medium of exchange—something that people trust has value and so will accept in exchange for goods or services. It is desirable that money also be a durable store of value and have minimal handling and storage costs (3)

monitoring costs: the costs of inspecting and supervising work to make sure that the quantity and quality of work accomplished meet standards set by the employer (13)

monopoly: the case where there is only seller. In a monopolized market, there are no close substitutes for the item being sold and barriers prevent additional potential sellers from entering. (12)

monopolistic competition: the case of many sellers, each selling a somewhat differentiated product. As in competitive markets, there is free entry and exit and perfect information (12)

monopsony: the case of one buyer (13)

moral hazard: a situation that encourages actors to change their behavior in undesirable ways in order to take advantage of a policy (9)

motivation according to interest in the common good: motive for action with the goal of improving social well-being, including one's own well-being (2)

multinational corporation: a corporation that owns and operates subsidiaries in more than one country (16)

natural capital: physical assets provided by nature (6)

natural monopoly: a monopoly that arises because the minimum efficient scale of the producing unit is large relative to the total market demand (12)

needs: what people require for healthy, flourishing lives (10)

negative externalities: harmful side effects, or unintended consequences, of economic activity that affect persons, or entities (such as the environment) that are not among the economic actors directly responsible for the activity (1)

negative (or inverse) relationship: the relationship between two variables if an increase in one is associated with a decrease in the other (7)

neighborhood effects: the effects that the characteristics of particular local communities, beyond a person's family, have on economic outcomes (15)

neoclassical economics: the school of economics that takes the traditional model as its starting point, emphasizing competitive markets and equilibrium (19)

net benefits: total benefits less total cost (8)

network externality (in production): a property that a particular technology exhibits when it is advantageous to adopt that technology because other economic actors have adopted it (8)

new institutionalist economics: the school of economics that shares many assumptions with neoclassical economics but looks at how economic institutions may develop to address problems such as those arising from transaction costs and imperfect information (19)

newly industrializing countries (NICs): countries of East Asia that followed Japan's pattern of export-led industrial growth (primarily South Korea, Taiwan, Singapore, and Hong Kong) (18)

nonconvexity: a mathematical term used to describe a number of situations in which marginal thinking is an inadequate guide to maximization of net benefits (8)

nonprice competition: competition through activities other than setting prices, such as advertising and location (12)

nonprice determinants of demand: everything affecting the quantity for which there is effective demand, except the price for which the product is being sold (4)

nonprice determinants of supply: everything affecting the quantity supplied, except the price for which the product can be sold (4)

nonrenewable resource: a resource that can only diminish over time (6)

normal goods: goods for which demand rises when ability to pay rises, and falls when ability to pay falls (5)

normal profit: see *zero economic profit*

normative questions: questions about how things should be (1)

occupational segregation: the tendency of men and women to be employed in different occupations (13)

offshoring: the shifting of production units to foreign locations (16)

oligopoly: the case of few sellers. Entry into an oligopolistic market is difficult. (12)

oligopsony: the case of few buyers (13)

open-access resources: resources for which it would be difficult to exclude anyone from benefiting. Their use by one person may diminish the amount or quality available to another, at least beyond some point (17)

open auction: an auction in which the opening price is set low and then buyers bid it up (3)

opportunity cost: the value of the next-best alternative, foregone when a choice is made (1)

optimize: to choose, out of all available options, that option which best achieves what is desired (2)

outputs: the results of production (7)

outsourcing: see *subcontracting*

Pareto efficiency: the situation where there is no opportunity to make changes in such a way as to make at least one person better off without making anyone else worse off (19)

partnership: a business owned by a group of two or more people (16)

path dependence: a condition that exists when economic developments depend on particularities of past developments—that is, when "history matters" (8)

payoff matrix: a table used in game theory to illustrate possible outcomes for each of two players, depending on the strategy that each chooses (12)

perfect capital markets: idealized markets for loans or equity shares, in which all profitable ventures can find funding (8)

perfect competition: the case where there are many buyers and sellers, all units of the good or service are identical, and there is free entry and exit and perfect information (11)

perfect information: the assumption that economic actors know with certainty everything that is important to their decision making (2)

perfect rationality: the assumption that actors can optimize, arriving at the decision that maximizes profit or utility (2)

perfectly elastic demand curve: a demand curve that is horizontal, which means that quantity demanded is extremely sensitive to price (5)

perfectly inelastic demand curve: a demand curve that is vertical, which means that quantity demanded does not respond at all to price (5)

physical capital: assets that are tangible (that is, can be seen and touched) (6)

physical infrastructure: equipment, buildings, physical communication lines, roads, and other tangible structures that provide the foundation for economic activity (3)

Pigovian taxes: (named after economist Arthur Pigou, who suggested them) taxes on activities that generate negative externalities. To the extent that they make prices paid more closely resemble social costs, they can increase economic efficiency (17)

pin money: a term used to refer to wages too low to provide a means of support, often associated with women's earnings during the period of the cult of domesticity (15)

positive (or **direct**) **relationship:** the relationship between two variables when an increase in one is associated with an increase in the other (7)

positive economic profit (above-normal profit): the amount by which revenues exceed opportunity costs (11)

positive externalities: beneficial side effects, or unintended consequences, of economic activity that accrue largely to persons or entities that are not among the economic actors directly involved in the activity (1)

positive questions: questions about how things are (1)

posted prices: prices set by a seller (3)

post-Keynesian economics: the school of economics that emphasizes the dynamic nature of the macroeconomy and the importance of uncertainty in explaining economic behavior (19)

precautionary principle: the principle that we should err on the side of caution when dealing with natural systems (6)

precise: describes something that is exact (though it may be unrealistic) (4)

predatory pricing: a powerful seller's temporarily pricing its goods or services below cost, in order to drive weaker competitors out of business (12)

present discounted value (PDV): the value today of future streams of funds (14)

price ceiling: a law or agreement that puts an upper limit on prices (4)

price discrimination: a seller's charging different prices to different buyers, depending on their ability and willingness to pay (12)

price-elastic demand: a relationship between price and quantity characterized by relatively strong responses of buyers to price changes. In this case, revenues to the seller change inversely with the price (5)

price elasticity of supply: a measure of the responsiveness of quantity supplied to changes in price (5)

price floor: a law or agreement that puts a lower limit on prices (4)

price inelastic demand: a relationship between price and quantity characterized by relatively weak responses of buyers to price changes. In this case revenues to the seller change directly with the price (5)

price leadership: a form of collusion in which many sellers follow the price changes instituted by one particular seller (12)

price war: a situation in which a firm cuts prices in order to try to undercut its rivals, and the rivals react by cutting prices even more (12)

price-fixing: a form of collusion in which a group of sellers implicitly agrees to maintain a common price (12)

price maker: a seller that can set the selling price, constrained only by demand conditions (12)

price taker: a seller that faces perfectly elastic demand for its good (5)

principal: the original amount of money borrowed (6)

principal-agent theory: a set of ideas about how one economic actor, the "principal," can try to control the actions of another, the "agent," so that the principal's objectives will be achieved (16)

private property: ownership of assets by nongovernment economic actors (3)

privatization: the conversion of enterprises from public to private ownership (encouraged in many countries in the late 20th century) (18)

producer surplus: the excess (summed over all the sellers in a market) of the amounts sellers actually receive, over the amounts that would make them just willing to supply the good or service (11)

product markets: markets for newly produced goods and services (3)

production: the conversion of resources into goods and services (1)

production function: an equation or graph that represents a mathematical relationship between types and quantities of inputs and the quantity of output (7)

production possibilities frontier (PPF): a curve showing the maximum amounts of two outputs that society could produce from given resources, over a given time period (1)

Progressive Era: a period in U.S. history from the late 1800s to the early 1920s, during which many government programs concerned with social welfare and economic regulation were initiated (17)

proprietorship: a business owned by a single family or individual (16)

protectionist policies: the use of tariffs and quotas to protect domestic industries from foreign competition (9)

public goods: goods for which [1] use by one person does not diminish usefulness to others, and [2] it would be difficult to exclude anyone from benefiting (1)

public purpose sphere: governments and other local, national, and international organizations established for some public purpose beyond individual or family self-interest and not operating with the goal of making a profit (1)

public service (theory of pure): the idea that public purpose organizations act purely in the interest of the common good, with no need for monitoring or citizen involvement (17)

purposeful (instrumental) behavior: actions taken with the expectation that these acts will lead to desired goals (2)

quotas: restrictions put on the quantities of a good that can be imported (9)

rational choices: thoughtful choices that would normally be expected to move people toward their goals (2)

rationing function of markets and prices: to determine who gets what (4)

real income: the purchasing power of income, with prices taken into account (10)

reference group: a group to which we compare ourselves (10)

reference point: a situation to which we have adapted. We have a tendency to notice changes in satisfaction relative to this point, rather than our absolute level of satisfaction (10)

regulated monopoly: a monopoly run under government supervision (12)

regulation: the setting of standards or enactment of laws to govern behavior (17)

relative deprivation: the feeling of lack that comes from comparing oneself with someone who has more (10)

renewable resource: a resource that regenerates itself through short-term processes (6)

rent-seeking behavior: behavior directed toward getting transfers or favors (12)

resale markets: markets for items that have been previously owned (3)

resource maintenance: the management of natural, manufactured, human, and social resources in such a way that their productivity is sustained (1)

retail markets: markets where goods and services are sold to consumers (3)

retained earnings: profits that a company keeps for its own uses (14)

returns to capital: the monetized value of what an investor expects to get back, in the future, from making an investment (14)

revenue: the amount received from sales of produced goods and services (8)

risk: as used by economists, a situation in which the exact outcome is unknown, but the chance of each possible outcome occurring is known (14)

satisfice: to choose a level of outcome that would be satisfactory and then seek an option that at least reaches that standard (2)

scarcity: resources are scarce to the extent that they are not sufficient to allow all goals to be accomplished at once (1)

sealed-bid auction: an auction in which bids are given privately to the auctioneer (3)

second-best theorem: the theorem that states that if first-best Pareto efficiency (based on nonintervention) cannot be achieved, then achieving the second-best outcome may require intervention in many markets (19)

Securities Act of 1933: the first federal act to regulate trade in securities (such as stocks and bonds). It created the Securities and Exchange Commission (SEC) (17)

self-interested motivation: motive for action based on the goal of improving one's own well-being (2)

self-regulation: an individual organization setting up and abiding by standards on its own, without the need for outside oversight or enforcement (17)

seniority: the length of time a person has worked for a particular organization (13)

sensitivity analysis: the rerunning of a calculation with a variety of different numbers, in order to analyze the outcome of a decision under varying assumptions (14)

shareholder theory: the theory that corporations are merely legal instruments for carrying out the will of their shareholders (16)

short run: (in terms of production processes) a time period in which at least one input to production cannot be varied in quantity (7)

shortage: a situation in which the quantity that buyers wish to buy at the stated price is greater than the quantity that sellers are willing to sell at that price (4)

short-run elasticity: a measure of the relatively immediate responsiveness to a price change (5)

signaling function of markets and prices: to carry information throughout the economy (4)

signaling theory: a theory of the value of an education that suggests that an educational credential "signals" to an employer that a potential worker has desired character traits and work habits (13)

social (socio-) economics: the school of economics that emphasizes the requirements for humane community life, focusing on ethical dimensions (19)

social capital: the stock of trust, mutual understanding, shared values, and socially held knowledge that facilitates the social coordination of economic activity (6)

social costs of production: the costs of a project, both those borne by the economic actors involved and those borne by others, figured in terms of opportunity costs (7)

social insurance programs: programs designed to transfer income to recipients if and when certain events (such as retirement or disability) occur (17)

social organization: structured ways of coordinating human activities (6)

socialism: a system characterized by predominantly shared, public ownership (either cooperative or state) of productive assets (18)

speculation: buying and selling assets with the expectation of profiting from appreciation or depreciation in asset values (14)

speculative bubble: the situation that occurs when mutually reinforcing investor optimism raises the value of a stock far above what could be justified by the actual assets and profitability of the firm (14)

spot markets: markets for immediate delivery (3)

stakeholder theory: the theory that corporations are complex organizations that have responsibilities to many constituent "stakeholders," such as shareholders, managers, employees, customers, creditors, and the like (16)

state socialism: a national system characterized by a great deal of state ownership of productive assets (18)

static analysis: analysis that does not take into account the passage of time (8)

static model: a model that ignores time, implicitly assuming that all adjustments occur instantaneously (4)

stock (economic definition): something whose quantity can be measured at a point in time (6)

(finance definition): a financial instrument that, in return for a payment, gives its buyer a claim to ownership in the company that issues it (14)

stock-flow diagram: a diagram that illustrates how stocks can be changed, over time, by flows (6)

subcontracting (outsourcing): hiring another firm to provide services or goods made to one's own firm's specification (16)

substitutability: the possibility of using one resource instead of another (6)

substitute good: a good that can be used in place of another good (4)

substitution effect of a price change: the tendency of a price increase for a particular good to reduce the quantity demanded of that good, as buyers turn to cheaper substitutes (5)

sunk cost: an expenditure that was made in the past and is now irreversible (8)

supply curve: a curve indicating the quantities that sellers are willing to supply at various prices (4)

surplus: a situation in which the quantity that sellers wish to sell at the stated price is greater than the quantity that buyers will buy at that price (4)

sustainable socioeconomic system: a system in which the overall quality and quantity of the resource base required for sustaining life and well-being do not erode (6)

switching costs: the transaction costs associated with a change in production technology (8)

tacit collusion: collusion that takes place without creation of a cartel (12)

tariffs: taxes put on imports (9)

technically efficient: the quality of a production process if no other process exists that can produce the same output with smaller quantities of some input(s) and no more of other inputs (7)

technological progress: the development of new methods of converting inputs to outputs (1)

technology: methods for combining resources to produce outputs (6)

theoretical investigation: analysis based in abstract thought (4)

threat point (or fall-back position): in bargaining theory, what each actor will get if the parties fail to make an agreement (15)

time series data: observations of how a numerical variable changes over time (4)

time use survey: a survey designed to find out how much time people spend in various activities, including paid work, household production, and leisure (15)

total cost: fixed cost plus variable cost (7)

total cost curve: a curve showing the total cost associated with producing various levels of output (7)

total product curve: a curve showing the total amount of output that can be produced when the quantity of one input is varied (other inputs held fixed) (7)

traditional microeconomic model (or basic Neoclassical model): a simple, mechanical model that portrays the economy as a collection of profit-maximizing firms and utility-maximizing households interacting through markets (1)

transaction cost economies: savings on the costs associated with market transactions, which may lead to organizing production within a single enterprise (16)

transaction costs: the costs of arranging economic activities (1)

transfer prices: the prices that subsidiaries of a multinational corporation use when making transactions with each other (16)

transfer: the giving of something, with nothing specific expected in return (1)

transition economies: economies that gave up administrative state socialism during the late 20th century and are (presumed to be) on a path toward more market-oriented economic systems (18)

uncertainty: as used by economists, a situation where not only is the exact outcome unknown, but the range of outcomes and/or their probabilities of occurring are also unknown (14)

underground markets: markets where illegal goods and services are sold or legal goods and services are sold in an illegal way (3)

use right: the right of an owner to use or control a designated property, but not necessarily the right to sell it or give it away (9)

utility function (or total utility curve): a curve showing the relation of utility levels to consumption levels (10)

utility: pleasure or satisfaction from goods, services, or events (10)

utils: imaginary units in which utility is measured (10)

variable cost: the cost associated with using variable inputs, which rises with the quantity of output (7)

variable input: an input to production the quantity of which can be quickly changed, resulting in changes in the level of production (7)

vertical integration: expansion of a firm achieved by adding new products to its output, where the new products are related to the old but represent different stages of production (16)

wage contours: historically determined patterns of relative wages among occupations. People often tend to think that deviating from established wage contours is "unfair" (13)

wants: what people simply desire (10)

waste products: outputs that are not used either for consumption or in a further production process (7)

wealth: whatever confers the ability to produce and procure valued goods and services (1)

well-being: a shorthand term for the broad goal of promoting the sustenance and flourishing of life (1)

wholesale markets: intermediate markets between producers and retailers (3)

World Trade Organization (WTO): an organization, created by a group of national governments in 1995, that regulates international trade (17)

X-inefficiency: exists where more labor time is being used in a production process than is actually necessary (16)

zero economic profit (normal profit): the amount (zero) that is left over when revenues just meet the opportunity costs of supplying all resources, including an entrepreneur's capital and time (11)

Index

The letter n *following a page number denotes a footnote.*

Credits

Text and Figure Credits

Chapter 1: p. 16, source of feature box material, "The State of the World's Children 1996," United Nations Children's Emergency Fund (UNICEF).

Chapter 4: p. 82, source of feature box material, "All the Spin Came First, and Then the Agitation," *The New York Times*, October 23, 2001. Copyright © 2001 by The New York Times Co. Reprinted with permission.

Chapter 6: p. 129, source of feature box material, "Panel Tells Bush Global Warming is Getting Worse," *The New York Times*, June 7, 200l. Copyright © 2001 by The New York Times Co. Reprinted with permission.

Chapter 7: p. 163, source of feature box material, "Hospital Network Could Be Split Up" by Liz Kowalczyk, *Boston Globe* (Staff Produced Copy Only), January 16, 2002, p. E1. Copyright 2002 by Globe Newspaper Co.(MA). Reproduced with permission of Globe Newspaper Co. (MA) in the format Textbook via Copyright Clearance Center.

Chapter 8: p. 187, source of feature box material, "Clio and the Economics of Qwerty" by Paul A. David, *American Economic Review* 75 (2), May, 1985. Used by permission of the American Economic Association; p. 186, source of discussion question, "Ask Marilyn," *Parade Magazine*, p. 10, March 31, 2002.

Chapter 9: p. 218, source of feature box material, "Dozens of Rich Americans Join in Fight to Retain the Estate Tax: Buffet, Soros and Gates's Father Call It Only Fair," *The New York Times*, February 14, 2001. Copyright © 2001 by The New York Times Co. Reprinted with permission; p. 219, source of feature box material, "Dying for a Tax Cut," *Wall Street Journal*, April 16, 2002. Wall Street Journal Eastern Edition by Editorial. Copyright 2002 by Dow Jones & Co., Inc. Reproduced with permission of Dow Jones & Co., Inc. in the format Textbook via Copyright Clearance.

Chapter 10: pp. 248-249, source of Figures 10.5 and 10.6 are graphs from "Population, Environment and Development 2001" from **www.un.org**.

Chapter 13: p. 314, source of feature box material, "Recording Artists Sue, Aiming to Rock Industry" by Kathleen Sharp, *Boston Globe*, October 7, 2001. Copyright 2001 by Globe Newspaper Co. (MA). Reproduced with permission of Globe Newspaper Co. (MA) in the format Textbook via Copyright Clearance Center; p. 322, source of feature box material, "MIT Women Win a Fight Against Bias: In Rare Move, School Admits Discrimination" by Kate Zernikein, *Boston Globe*, March 21, 1999. Copyright 1999 by Globe Newspaper Co. (MA). Reproduced with permission of Globe Newspaper Co. (MA) in the format Textbook via Copyright Clearance Center.

Chapter 16: p. 379, source of feature box material, "Audacious Climb to Success Ended in Dizzying Plunge," *The New York Times*, January 13, 2002. Copyright © 2002 by The New York Times Co. Reprinted with permission.

Chapter 17: p. 401, source of Figure 17.3 is a graph from *American's Non-Profit Sector: A Primer*, 2/e by Lester M. Salaman, © 1999, p. 23; p. 412, source of feature box material, "Boston Beer Pulls Ad After Complaints" by Chris Reidy, *Boston Globe*, August 31, 2002. Copyright 2002 by Globe Newspaper Co. (MA). Reproduced with permission of Globe Newspaper Co. (MA) in the format Textbook via Copyright Clearance Center.

Photo Credits

Chapter 1: p. 6, © Ryan McVay/Taxi/Getty Images; p. 10, © Robert Giroux/Getty Images; p.19: © Tom & Dee Ann McCarthy/Corbis

Chapter 2: p. 41, © Pablo Corral/Corbis; p. 42, © Spencer Grant/PhotoEdit

Chapter 3: p. 51 (*left*), © Tony Savino/The Image Works; p. 51 (*right*), © Jason Laure/The Image Works; p. 56, © HIP-Archive/Topham/The Image Works

Chapter 4: p. 80, © W. Geiersperger/Corbis

Chapter 5: p. 114, © Oliver Benn/Stone/Getty Images

Chapter 6: p. 125, © A. Ramey/PhotoEdit; p. 128, © Marcel Mochet/AFP/Getty Images; p. 141, © Toby Melville/Reuters